California
Real Estate Finance

FOURTH EDITION

J. W. Pugh

Assistant Vice President and Branch Manager, Retired, Crocker National Bank
Instructor, Retired, American River College and Anthony Schools

William H. Hippaka

Professor of Real Estate, College of Business Administration
San Diego State University

PRENTICE-HALL, INC., Englewood Cliffs, New Jersey 07632

Pugh, J. W.
  California real estate finance.

  Bibliography: p.
  Includes index.
  1. Mortgage loans—California. 2. Real estate business—California.
I. Hippaka, William H.
II. Title.
HG2040.5.U6C36   1983   333.7′2′09794   83-13762
ISBN 0-13-111955-9

Editorial/production supervision and interior design: Susan Adkins
Manufacturing buyer: Ed O'Dougherty

Prentice-Hall Series in Real Estate

Printed in the United States of America

10 9 8 7 6 5 4 3 2 1

ISBN 0-13-111955-9

Prentice-Hall International, Inc., *London*
Prentice-Hall of Australia Pty. Limited, *Sydney*
Editora Prentice-Hall do Brasil, Ltda., *Rio de Janeiro*
Prentice-Hall Canada Inc., *Toronto*
Prentice-Hall of India Private Limited, *New Delhi*
Prentice-Hall of Japan, Inc., *Tokyo*
Prentice-Hall of Southeast Asia Pte. Ltd., *Singapore*
Whitehall Books Limited, *Wellington, New Zealand*

Contents

iii

5

Savings and Loan Associations and Real Estate Loans   67

6

Life Insurance Companies as Real Estate Lenders and Owners   83

7

Banks as a Source of Real Estate Financing   89

8

Basic Legal Concepts of Real Estate Financing   97

9

Operative Legal Aspects of Real Estate Financing   121

10

Loan Applications, Processing, and Closing   156

11

The Mathematics of Finance 169

12

Appraisal for Real Estate Financing Purposes 185

13

Government Real Estate Finance Programs 195

14

Secondary Mortgage Market, Investors, and Organizations 254

15

Construction and Off-Site Improvements Financing 264

16

Income Tax Aspects of Real Estate Financing and Ownership 277

17

Financing Shopping Centers and Office, Special-Purpose, Industrial, and Apartment Buildings 289

Appendix: Compendium of Laws Dealing with Equal Access to Residential Accommodations and Credit 315

Glossary 330

Answers 335

Index 336

PREFACE

The years 1978 through 1981 have seen greater, more bizarre, changes in the financing of real estate than occurred during the first seventy-eight years of the twentieth century. Change—massive, sudden, often incomprehensible—has been an almost daily phenomenon. Knowledge of mortgage loan sources; loan standards; expected national, regional, and local economic conditions and trends; and the legal aspects of real estate financing contracts has been buffeted about by the winds of legal, economic, and financial change until the world of real estate finance has been turned upside down and inside out.

During this short, turbulent period, the usual sources, procedures, analytical standards, cost, and risks of financing real estate have all changed. Major effects upon the provider and the user of real estate funds have been

1. Greater risk of substantial financial loss for both the provider and user of funds.
2. Greater cost of obtaining needed financing to the user.
3. The relatively short-lived duration of financial arrangements (fixed interest, twenty- to thirty-year repayment amortized mortgage loans became as rare as the bower bird of New Guinea).

It is said that history repeats itself and that those who do not know the mistakes of the past are doomed to repeat them. This is certainly true in the world of real estate finance.

Contractual arrangements for residential purchase money loans are now more like they were during the first twenty years of this century than at any time between 1934 and 1977. Residential purchase money financing arrangements during the 1920s had the characteristics of

1. Term loans of five to ten years' duration.
2. Second mortgages to cover the "equity gap" created by the difference between the purchase price of such properties and the low (50 to 60 percent of market value) first mortgage purchase money loans from institutional

lenders such as savings and loan associations and commercial banks.
3. The inability of many borrowers to accumulate the funds to pay off the two term purchase money mortgages when the debts came due five to ten years after such loans were made.

As a result, the Great Depression of the 1930s, which produced both reduced market values (reducing substantially or eliminating altogether debtor equity in the collateral property) and limited opportunities to refinance mortgage debt as it became due, caused a massive wave of foreclosures of housing mortgages. Studies of the collapse of the structure of purchase money mortgage housing finance during the Great Depression have placed a substantial part of the blame (outside the severe general economic collapse itself) upon

1. Short-term nonamortized mortgages.
2. The frequent use of second mortgages to bridge the gap between low loan-to-value ratio of institutional first purchase money mortgages (creating two such debts for many residential buyers), which they could not pay off when due.
3. Appraisals at the time such loans were made that were overoptimistic about the long-run market value of the collateral property.

A response to the huge wave of foreclosures of residential purchase money mortgages in some states in the early 1930s were the mortgage foreclosure moratorium laws, designed to prevent foreclosure of mortgages on such collateral property. A legal solution to the problems of the distressed real estate debtor today is the recently revised federal bankruptcy statute, which, when used effectively by a delinquent debtor, prevents a secured real estate lender from conducting a foreclosure sale of the property.

Real estate financing is again undergoing major change in the 1980s. This change has a number of significant characteristics.

1. Rapidly changing general economic conditions in the form of periodic economic recessions, accompanied by relatively high annual rates of inflation (often double-digit 11 to 16 percent price increases). These combine to produce the incredible, financially painful, condition known as *stagflation*.

2. Federal government statutory changes in the powers, duties, and functions of savings and loan associations and commercial banks under the statute known as the Financial Institutions Deregulation Act of 1980. This makes savings and loan associations more like commercial banks, with checking accounts, the authority to make non–real estate loans, and the elimination of the savings and loan associations' advantage in making higher interest rates to depositors (compared with what commercial banks can pay), which they previously enjoyed under Federal Reserve Bank Regulation Q.

3. Increased use of the federal bankruptcy law by delinquent real estate debtors to prevent secured lenders from foreclosing on collateral property. This is forcing some real estate lenders such as a number of real estate investment trusts, weak savings and loan associations, and commercial banks, into bankruptcy themselves.

4. A much reduced constant volume of debt financing available to real estate borrowers from traditional institutional sources of mortgage credit, such as savings and loan associations, life insurance companies, mutual savings banks, and commercial banks.

5. The virtual disappearance of real estate investment trusts from the construction lending scene after their construction loan debacle of the mid-1970s.

6. Much greater reliance upon equity capital instead of mortgage debt funds to finance nonresidential investment real estate.

7. The struggle of savings and loan associations and mutual savings banks to adjust to the rapidly changing cost of funds to them (the cost of funds usually going higher for the institutions). They do this by making more purchase money mortgage loans when the rate of interest paid by the borrower can be changed upward periodically during the life of the loan in relation to an index of the cost of money to the lender.

8. Interest rates on fixed interest, long-term institutional residential purchase money loans that were unaffordable by 95 percent of California households. The interest rate often ranges from 13 to 20 percent per annum.

9. More than 80 percent of the sales of existing houses in California being financed without an institutional lender making a new first mortgage loan to the buyer. Such sales are financed mainly by the buyer assuming an existing institutional first mortgage loan, making a cash down payment, and the seller taking back a rather large second purchase money short-term trust deed. This type of sale price financing often has the effect of reducing the effective rate of interest paid by the buyer on all debt funds to between 10 and 13 percent. This is more easily affordable than the 16 to 20 percent interest rate that would have to be paid on any fixed interest rate, long-term loan from an institutional lender, if such a new loan was available, and often it was not.

10. Federal Housing Administration–insured and United States Veterans Administration–guaranteed loans were almost as expensive for buyers as conventional institutional loans. These loans often have interest rates in the 13 to 17.5 percent range; hence the use of these government-assisted purchase money loans has been declining.

11. The California Veterans Administration's program for purchase money loans direct to the buyer of property from time to time runs out of loanable funds, and the interest rate charged to those veterans able to obtain such loans increases as the cost of interest in selling California state bonds increases.

12. Large well-managed savings and loan associations and mutual savings banks lost money in 1981 for the first time in many years. Such losses for California state-chartered savings and loan associations were caused primarily by (a) reduced loan volume; (b) unstable, much higher cost of funds to them than their mortgage loan portfolios yielded; (c) inability to eliminate a large number of old longterm, fixed rate, low-interest mortgages because the California Supreme Court (in the case of *Wellenkamp* v. *Bank of America*, 148 Cal. Reptr. 379, 1978) nullified the enforceability of the due-on-sale clause in the purchase money mortgage or trust deed.

13. The Federal National Mortgage Association lost money for the first time in years due to the much higher cost of investment funds to it and the relatively lower yields on its existing portfolio of mortgages.

14. The new preeminence of the individual as an essential source of purchase money financing relative to the volume of new mortgage funds available from typical institutional lenders making purchase money loans.

15. A bevy of new exotic arrangements for purchase money mortgage loan financing, such as variable rate mortgages (VRMs); graduated payment mortgages (GPMs); shared appreciation mortgages (SAMs); and reverse annuity mortgages (RAMs). RAMs are not a purchase money loan, but are a way for the elderly to use the equity in their house by receiving annuity-type payments.

The role of institutional lenders in financing most of the purchase price of houses has been minimized during the last three years. The result is the absence, in the financing and closing of sales, of the knowledgeable, relatively impartial personnel of these institutions. These are the people who used to appraise financed properties to determine present and future market values; who used valid, realistic credit qualification standards and procedures to qualify prospective buyers as financially acceptable borrowers; who used standard financing contracts and documents that were basically fair to both seller and buyer; and who, after such loans were made, effectively supervised the collection of payments due from the debtor.

In the absence of these personnel and services, the real estate finance professional must now be more research-minded than ever before. If operations are not based upon thorough research into economic and real estate trends in an area, coupled with an unbiased realistic analysis of the prospective debtor's ability to meet his or her obligations, any success in the field will be merely by chance.

To render the highest quality service, the real estate professional must always recognize the great common interest in this activity and therefore conduct operations so that the public, the lender, and the debtor are fully served.

Recent major economic, financial, and legal changes in the world of real estate finance have substantially changed the essentials of successful real estate financing. Welcome to this new world.

ACKNOWLEDGMENTS, WITH GREAT APPRECIATION FOR THEIR HELP

Robert Bonano, Statewide City Mortgage Company

Marvin Butler, Crocker National Bank

B.C. Cook, Wells Fargo Bank

Leonard Dye, Sacramento Savings and Loan Association

Escrow Officers of the Title Insurance and Trust Company in Sacramento

Ann Hamilton, Sacramento Office of HUD's Federal Housing Administration

John Knutson, Bank of America National Trust and Savings Association

Brooks Lowe, Masson-McDuffy

E. Vincent Mahoney, Lumbleau Real Estate School

Tim Phillpotts, Avco Thrift

Sacramento Office of the California State Banking Department

San Francisco Office of the Comptroller of the Currency

Wayne Stoops, Wayne Stoops Real Estate Investments

1

Introduction to Real Estate Finance

IMPORTANCE OF REAL ESTATE FINANCE

Real estate finance is the lifeblood of the real estate industry. The extension of credit in proper amounts and on suitable terms is essential even to merely satisfactory levels of real estate sales, transactions, and development. A large amount of money is necessary to buy or develop real estate. This fact alone creates a compelling necessity for the borrowing of large sums of money in order to carry on real estate activity. Although salesmanship, law, appraisal, and property management are certainly significant in the world of real estate, it is real estate finance that determines to a great extent what will or will not be done. A common example of the controlling influence of finance over real estate operations occurs in the sales field. In numerous cases the sale of a home or other property depends upon whether a major portion of the sales price can be borrowed by the buyer. If he or she cannot borrow from 70 to 80 percent or even more than 90 percent of the selling price of the property, there will simply be no sales transaction; most buyers in the real estate market are either financially unable to pay the entire price immediately or, for reasons such as maximizing yield and tax aspects of the investment, they are not interested in purchasing real estate unless most of the purchase price can be borrowed.

REAL ESTATE FINANCE DEFINED

What is meant by the term *real estate finance?* From the institutional standpoint, real estate finance is the raising and accumulation of money under the management of an organization whose primary purpose is to lend to purchasers and users of real estate sums which are large enough to be of practical benefit to the borrower. In financing real estate transactions, the lender will make sure that the sums lent are not excessive in terms of either the borrower's ability to repay or the market value of the

real property used by the borrower as security for loan repayment. If these prudent qualifications for the extension of credit to real estate borrowers are not observed, lending operations may well be merely a prelude to the loss of ownership of real estate through foreclosure. Incautious loans may also be the basis for financial loss due to inability to collect the principal of the loan from the debtor, or to sell the property under a lien for an amount equal to or exceeding the amount of debt left to be repaid at the time of the debtor's default.

SOURCES OF FUNDS

The real estate finance industry is composed of lending institutions, such as commercial banks, savings and loan associations, insurance companies, and mutual savings banks; noninstitutional lenders, such as mortgage companies, real estate investment trusts, and finance corporations established as business enterprises for the primary purpose of making loans to qualified real estate borrowers; private individuals; pension funds; credit associations; mortgage loan brokers; government organizations, such as California Veterans Administration, California Housing Finance Agency, Farmers Home Loan Administration, Small Business Administration; syndicates; real property security dealers; real estate brokers; trust departments of banks; bonds, such as those typically underwritten by investment banking firms; personal property brokers; and joint venture arrangements.

LENDING ACTIVITIES OF INDIVIDUALS

The real estate finance function—that is, the accumulation of funds for the purpose of making loans to borrowers who need credit to purchase or improve real property—is also performed by individuals. The individual engages in financing real estate when he or she sells property owned to a buyer who pays only a portion of the selling price and obligates himself or herself to pay the remainder of the sales price over a period of time. Individuals also invest accumulated capital in secured real estate loans. In doing so they are acting in an institutional fashion, in that they have accumulated capital in amounts sufficiently large to be in demand by real estate borrowers.

So far we have considered a basically functional definition of real estate finance. In conjunction with this definition we must consider organizations that engage in activities connected with real estate lending and the technical requirements for making loans. The field is very broad in terms of the organizations and activities included in it. A major portion of the study of real estate finance concentrates on determining the sources of lendable funds, understanding the operation of individual lenders, and comprehending the quantity and cost aspects of credit, which involves understanding the organization and operation of the money markets.

GOVERNMENT AGENCIES IN REAL ESTATE FINANCE

Federal government agencies such as the Federal Housing Administration and the Veterans Administration are significant in real estate finance; they facilitate the creation of certain types of loans (construction, home improvement, and purchase money mortgages) made to home purchasers and residential investors. The importance of these mortgage loan insurance and guarantee agencies is primarily their risk assumption activities, credit extension programs, credit requirements, property standards, and appraisal policies and methods. The Federal Housing Administration and the Veterans Administration insure and guarantee loans mainly on the *primary* real estate mortgage loan level, where loans are made by private lenders to borrowers. The federal government also has an array of agencies that operate in the *secondary* mortgage market, which exists among institutional lenders such as savings and loan associations, commercial banks, life insurance companies, and mutual savings banks that typically desire to sell existing mortgages they hold to long-term investors. While privately owned financial institutions can be buyers of mortgages and thus make up the other side of this secondary market, since 1935 the federal government has created special agencies to perform this investment function. Federal agencies presently carrying on secondary mortgage market purchase and investment activity are the Federal National Mortgage Association, the Government National Mortgage Association, and the Federal Home Loan Mortgage Corporation. These federal secondary mortgage market investment agencies derive the capital for their mortgage purchase and investment activities from the United States

Treasury, from interest and profits obtained from mortgage investments, and from the sale of equity and debt securities in the security markets. On the state government level, activities in real estate finance are carried on by agencies such as the California State Department of Veterans Affairs, which administers the California Veterans Farm and Home Purchase Plan (popularly known as Cal-Vet Loans), and by the Housing Finance Agency, which is empowered to raise capital for direct loans for residential property from the State of California and which sells bonds for this purpose. During the last decade there has been increasing federal and state government involvement in financing real estate through direct loans, loan guarantees, and insurance, especially in the residential category.

LEGAL ASPECTS OF REAL ESTATE FINANCE

Collectible debts and liens on real property were mentioned earlier as a fundamental part of real estate lending. This aspect of real estate finance involves the legal documents of secured lending, such as mortgages, promissory notes, trust deeds, and land contracts. Complex legal questions often arise out of such transactions, requiring the services of a lawyer skilled in real estate matters. The individual who arranges real estate loans must be acquainted with the basic legal aspects of the transaction if he or she is to be successful in his or her chosen occupation. On the other hand, persons facilitating the establishment of a real estate loan should not engage in the practice of law and should have the expert advice of legal counsel whenever it is needed.

REAL ESTATE AS LOAN SECURITY

If real property is to provide security for a real estate loan, one of the basic requirements is that the title to the property pledged as security is sufficiently clear of adverse claims to constitute a marketable title. For a secured real estate loan to provide the lender security in addition to the borrower's capacity and willingness to repay the debt, the collateral property must be readily salable through the foreclosure process. A marketable title to a specific parcel of real estate is free enough from defects to be readily acceptable by most buyers in the market. This means that virtually every loan made with the advantage of hypothecating real property as additional security involves the determination of the legal quality of a land title. No acceptable loan is made, therefore, unless a title insurance policy is issued for the lender's protection or a lawyer's opinion is obtained as to the marketability of the title to the property. By having the legal quality of a land title checked before accepting the land as security for a loan, the lender is taking a precaution to prevent his or her interest in the property from being defeated by mechanics' liens, tax liens, assessment liens, state welfare liens, easements, homestead rights, community property rights, claims of heirs of former owners, and a host of other interests possibly adverse to the owner and lender. The quality of land titles is one very important area where real estate finance practice is controlled almost completely by the law.

Why are we so concerned about the legal aspects of land titles? Because real estate loans today are primarily secured loans. The term *secured loan* means that real property is subject to a lien (preferred claim) of the lender that establishes the lender's prerogative to force sale of the property if the debtor fails to meet his or her obligations established by the loan contract. In California the lien a creditor will have on real property is usually a first trust deed, with mortgages used only occasionally for this purpose. The trust deed is used often instead of the mortgage primarily because of the ease and speed with which the foreclosure process can be accomplished by the trust deed trustee's sale procedure. Thus, the secured lender is obviously in a much better position to have the loan repaid than is the unsecured lender, since he or she can proceed against the property to collect the debt as well as hold the borrower personally liable on the debt.

LENDING CUSTOMS AND PRACTICES

The customs and traditions of lenders and lending institutions are essentially local in character, possibly varying from city to city and from state to state. The important differences in lending methods throughout California constitute essential knowledge for the lending officer and the real estate professional.

STATE REGULATION OF REAL ESTATE LENDING

Firms as well as individuals engaging in real estate lending are subject to complex and extensive regulations established by the federal government and the state of California. The regulations governing institutions differ from those imposed on individuals, who either make real estate loans or arrange for them in the capacity of a mortgage loan broker. The California Department of Real Estate is charged specifically with supervising and regulating real estate loan brokers and real estate brokers as they conduct real estate loan activities.

Both the federal and the state governments are now especially concerned with eliminating discrimination in real estate lending on the basis of race, creed, color, national origin, religion, or sex. Recently, the California and federal governments have taken legislative and ad-

ministrative action to curtail the practice commonly known as redlining—refusing to make loans on properties located in what the lender has determined is a blighted or increasingly undesirable neighborhood, without giving due consideration to the credit worthiness of the individual loan applicant. The intent of anti-redlining programs is to increase the amount of real estate credit available for purchase money and construction loans in such neighborhoods, thereby retarding the trend of physical deterioration and declining market values that has historically been a prominent feature of inner cities.

State usury statutes limit the amount of interest that certain lenders can charge on real estate loans.

REAL ESTATE AND THE NATIONAL ECONOMY

It is extremely desirable that individuals working in real estate realize and fully appreciate the place in our national economy of real estate and the financing of real estate development and ownership. Such knowledge will make obvious the necessity for constant personal research into economic trends and financial markets. In the process, individuals interested in real estate finance will increase their appreciation of our economic system and its advantages, as well as their understanding of its problems.

The economic system that predominates in the United States is known as capitalism. This system emphasizes ownership of all types of property by private parties, with the individual maintaining virtually complete control over the use and disposition of the property. In our capitalist economy the government traditionally plays a relatively minor part in the ownership of property and in decision making which affects the productive processes carried on in the nation.

Because of the nature of our economy, real estate financing through financial institutions is essentially a privately operated and owned activity. It is true that the government does exercise significant control over actual lending operations by chartering and regulating certain financial institutions or systems composed of many individual corporations. However, the relationship between the regulated and the regulators is, to some extent, mutually cooperative. The essential common interest existing among regulatory agencies and banking or savings and loan institutions is safety of capital and facilitation of private economic activity by providing adequate amounts of capital at reasonable cost.

Real estate finance is very closely related to the field of general finance; therefore, an understanding of the various aspects of the field of finance is necessary. It is unquestionable that the economy of the United States is a credit economy. Except for inexpensive personal purchases, purchases or investments are usually made possible by the buyer or investor borrowing a considerable percentage of the sale price of an item or of the amount to be invested.

Banks are the most significant general source of credit available to individuals, institutions, and business establishments. Historically, they have participated materially in real estate lending on improved property. They have made both insured and uninsured loans. Despite considerable participation in this type of lending, their major loan activities involve personal and commercial loans. Emphasis upon these loans is logical, since banks are normally established to serve such borrowers.

Savings and loan associations (the present-day version of the early building societies and building and loan associations) were established for the purpose of making loans on residential real estate, often to provide credit to a group of individuals so that they could buy or build homes for themselves. There are now two classes of savings and loan associations: state-chartered stock companies and federally chartered mutual corporations. The applicable regulations, powers of firms to lend, and regulatory bodies supervising the savings and loan associations are largely governed by whether the federal or the state government chartered the organization.

Real estate finance is important to our national economy. Historically, when real estate has prospered the entire economy has been operating at a high level, and a substantial decline of real estate activity has typically been accompanied by a national recession or depression. A large portion of our national wealth is represented by ownership of real estate. A substantial portion of all private debt consists of obligations created by real estate borrowing. If an adequate amount of credit is not available to finance real estate activity, the volume of sales and construction declines, reducing the gross national product. If a suitable amount of public and private new construction does not take place every year, the level of economic accomplishment in this country declines significantly.

Although investments in securities constitute a significant outlet for investment capital, real estate is still an important medium. This importance has been maintained despite increasing competition from public and private securities available through securities association member firms and exchanges. Because of this increasingly effective competition for investment funds, the efficiency and safety aspects of real estate investment have to be constantly improved. The method of making real estate investment decisions must include scientific approaches unnecessary a century ago, when for most Americans real estate was virtually the sole outlet for investment capital.

Examining some statistical information to emphasize relevant relationships will reinforce our appreciation of the present and future importance of real estate to our nation. In 1890, when the population of the United States was 63,000,000, only 21,000,000 people lived in urban areas. In 1980 the United States had a total population of 226,504,825. During this period the geographical center of population changed from Cincinnati, Ohio, to DeSoto, Missouri—45 miles southwest of St. Louis, Missouri. This shift is important because it dramatically illustrates the continuing westward population movement in the United States, which has necessitated monumental efforts to provide residential, commercial, industrial, and public facilities. Most of this construction has been made possible only through the extension of real estate credit. To house this urban population the value of residential nonfarm construction increased from $1,220,000,000 in 1915 to $16,571,000,000 in 1957, and rose to $63,100,000,000 in 1980. While indicating the size of the investment in urban housing over the past sixty years, these facts also illustrate the phenomenon of a slowly increasing annual value of investment in nonfarm housing after the middle of the twentieth century.

As these great increases occurred, bank deposits increased from $5,859,000,000 in 1896 to $1,043,300,000,000 in 1978. While this substantial increase in bank deposits was taking place, the number of annual bank failures decreased from 1,352 in 1930 to 2 in 1960 and 2 in 1975. The improved safety of banks is due to improvement in bank management practices and to certain bank reform measures. Since 1947, banks have been increasingly active in real estate lending. Evidence of their greater participation in such lending is the increase in dollar value of real estate loans made by banks, from $9,393,000,000 in 1947 to $214,000,000,000 in 1978.

During the period under examination the savings and loan industry has experienced tremendous growth, which can be measured by the increase in assets from $571,000,000 in 1900 to $523,600,000,000 in 1978. The number of mortgage loans in force in 1950 was 13,749,000; it increased to 379,509,000 by 1977.

There is no question of the great importance of real estate activity and financing of real estate sales to our economy and the people of the nation. In our modern urban society, developments in real estate finance will inevitably have far-reaching effects upon the entire population.

HISTORY OF REAL ESTATE LENDING

It is important for anyone who finances real estate to be aware of the history of this activity in order to recognize any currently developing difficulties in real estate lending operations and to avoid repeating common mistakes committed in the past. The history of this field involves a study of value theory, credit requirements, the law of real property, business and real estate cycles, technological development, city growth patterns, foreign relations, and the psychology of the public. The brief description presented here will develop a basic historical background in these areas.

The development of general lending practices in a capitalistic economy is of vague origin. In England, where land was the repository of most wealth for centuries, and where experience had indicated that borrowers did not always live up to their word and pay their debts on time, land became a most acceptable security for promises to pay. There were some technical difficulties in perfecting the mortgage as a legal and enforceable claim against a debtor's real property. These difficulties involved the state and the basic conflict that has always existed between debtor and creditor—namely, that the creditor wants to lend money so as to produce the highest income consistent with safety of principal, whereas the debtor wants to pay as little as possible for loans made to him or her and to have some other way of ultimately escaping his or her obligation if it becomes too difficult to pay in accordance with its terms. The state still has a substantial interest in the rights and obligations of creditors and debtors and in the general effect that certain lending practices have upon society and the economy in general. The interest and participation of the state in mortgage lending have steadily increased during the twentieth century. Not only has there been the usual interest of the several states in mortgage lending practices within their boundaries, but there has also been a substantial increase in federal government regulation and participation in this field through various agencies. This constantly changing situation has caused the traditional practices necessary to effect a secured real estate loan to become, in many transactions, the simplest aspect of real estate lending. Thus we have proceeded from the single concept of a debtor deeding his or her real property to a lender as security for the repayment of a debt (which conveyance will be nullified by a reconveyance from the creditor to the debtor upon the debtor's paying the debt on the terms of the debt contract) to the present era of a multitude of federally supported or insured lending programs complemented by state lending programs and extensive regulation of lending. One thing that has not changed over the centuries since the concept of the loan secured by a mortgage is land as the supremely acceptable collateral for loans.

The statement that land is the best generally acceptable collateral for a loan implies that the property, upon default by the debtor, can be disposed of by the creditor for pecuniary benefit. This means that at the time of the sale according to the lien on the property, the real property must have some value. To be satisfactory as security

for the loan, the value of the land should at least equal the amount of the debt. Property, accepted as security for a loan, that does not retain a dollar value at least equivalent to the amount of the unpaid debt does not really fulfill the desired function of constituting security for a loan. Thus for centuries, but especially at the present time, valuing property for loan purposes is a major problem for the lender. There was no real analysis of value theory as applied to real property until after the disastrous real estate debacle of the early 1930s. This great deflation of real estate values in terms of prices obtained in the marketplace was accompanied by the greatest economic depression in the history of the United States. One may argue that this momentous economic disaster was beyond human comprehension and prediction, and to some extent this may be true. But the problem of the 1930s, with regard to valuing real property as security for real estate loans, was that because of excessive valuation estimates in the 1920s, loans had been made which were excessive in terms of market value upon foreclosure in the 1930s.

The American Institute of Real Estate Appraisers and the Federal Housing Administration are two organizations that have taken an intense interest in real estate value theory and appraisal practices for more than thirty years. One of the main objectives of these organizations is to refine real estate value concepts and practices to the point where what may be termed a scientific approach is taken to placing a value upon a particular parcel of land. There is no question whatsoever that comprehension of value theory and ethical real estate appraisal practice is essential to sound real estate lending programs.

REASONS FOR PAST LENDING FAILURES

Many past real estate lending failures involving borrowers unable to repay their loans can be traced to lack of a credit analysis of the debtor or his or her business. More recently, such difficulties have been traced to inadequate information about the debtor's managerial abilities and source of income. In too many instances lenders have completely disregarded prudent lending practices by lending to recent bankrupts or to people whose present financial obligations are so large in relation to their income that the possibility of their meeting the existing or proposed obligations is almost nonexistent. Such loans are typically made by lenders who practice very questionable lending ethics. In the early 1970s the Federal Housing Administration conducted two subsidized mortgage loan insurance programs designed to provide housing for low income families: Section 235 for individual buyer-borrowers and Section 236 for loans made to rental apartment property owner-borrowers. Loans insured under the 235 program too often allowed borrowers with incomes inadequate to meet the expense of making mortgage payments, paying taxes, and maintaining the property to buy houses so decrepit as to be unlivable. Such buyer-borrowers had no motivation to live in old houses with leaking roofs and inoperative furnaces—and could not meet their housing financial obligations anyway. So they abandoned the houses and defaulted on their mortgage payments. The resulting foreclosures meant that the FHA ultimately owned large numbers of houses whose market value was only a small fraction of the amount of the unpaid mortgage. The losses sustained by the FHA in the virtual collapse of the 235 subsidized mortgage loan program have run into hundreds of millions of dollars. The obvious causes of the failure of this program were borrowers who could not or would not make the payments of principal and interest called for by the mortgage contract, and the total inadequacy of the collateral real property in terms of the relationship of its market value to the size of the secured debt.

During the early 1970s various lenders such as real estate investment trusts made construction loans on office buildings, shopping centers, and large rental apartments and condominium projects. These loans were often made before the borrower-developer had obtained a take-out loan commitment with which to pay off the construction loan upon completion of the improvements. If the newly completed project could not be sold to a buyer with financial resources to pay off the construction loan, or if the construction loan debtor could not obtain a long-term loan to retire the construction loan, default and foreclosure would likely occur—and often did. The lack of long-term financing adequate to pay off the construction loans was due in part to the worst recession in the United States (in 1974–75) since the Great Depression of the 1930s. This recession occurred at a time of strong inflationary pressures that generated a large demand for credit, causing a mortgage credit shortage, resulting in mortgage interest rates above 10 percent. Business profitability decreased (and demand for office space slumped), and families' financial ability or inclination to borrow expensive mortgage money for the purpose of buying housing was severely limited. Real estate lenders and developers allowed many housing market areas to become oversupplied with housing offered for sale—especially with condominiums. As a result of the operation of the law of supply and demand, there was insufficient effective demand in such market areas for the newly built housing, and much of it was sold in auction situations at prices that were less than the cost of construction. The losses resulting have amounted to many millions of dollars. If improved real estate that is obviously intended to produce rental income (apartment houses, office buildings, and shopping centers) is to have value, it must produce enough net income so that when this income is capitalized with a suitable capitalization rate, there is a recognized value

of the property based upon the existence of an income stream. During the early 1970s some real estate developers and lenders thought that the cost of constructing such income-producing buildings was the value of them. After losing many millions of dollars, they have learned that the cost of new improvements of the income producing type is *not* the equivalent value; such properties have value only to the extent that they can successfully compete for tenants in the marketplace and produce net income year after year. Demands by officials of lending institutions and regulatory agencies have prompted a reexamination of real estate appraisal techniques, economic feasibility determination, and credit evaluation practices. This has led to more realistic investigations of both the prospective debtor and the collateral property as sources of repayment of the contemplated mortgage debt.

BUSINESS AND REAL ESTATE CYCLES

Individuals participating in real estate lending should be aware of past national, regional, and local business cycles and real estate cycles. Under no circumstances should the person responsible for recommending, negotiating, or making a real estate loan make the dangerous mistake of believing that these cycles have been eliminated. It is true that since the Great Depression so-called stabilizers or supports have been developed. To some extent such safeguards as insured deposits in financial institutions, insurance of real estate debt, unemployment compensation, social security, and workmen's compensation have reduced the extent of variations in both cycles. However, on a local or regional level the fluctuations can still be substantial and cause great distress—especially if imprudent property valuation and individual credit analysis practices have been employed.

THE CHANGING ENVIRONMENT OF REAL ESTATE

Related to business and real estate cycles are city growth patterns, technological developments, and United States foreign relations. The relative importance of these factors to each other and to development and support of real property values will vary from situation to situation. Real estate finance personnel should develop the technique of predicting phases of real estate activity and the future of a community and of the various neighborhoods found in most urban areas. Technological developments in an industry can revolutionize production processes and thereby favor communities whose industries fully use new processes over locations where manufacturers are less progressive. Technology applied to construction has had a significant effect upon urban development in areas previously considered uninhabitable. Such technology has made it possible to develop land for residential and other uses in areas where lack of water and extreme heat had made the sustenance of human life impractical. Modern developments in insulation and air conditioning, for example, have contributed directly to the great commercial, industrial, and residential expansion that has taken place in the Southwest since 1950. Of course there had to be an economic base for these communities or they could not have come into existence or continued to grow. A number of the new or expanding urban areas of the Southwest are based upon the demands of the national defense establishment. What this vast establishment needs in terms of research work, maintenance of operational bases, and actual production of the hardware of defense depends rather directly upon the foreign policy of this country. In turn, United States foreign policy depends in no small part upon the aims of other nations and the actions they take to achieve their objectives. For the Southwest a continued significant tension in international relations is necessary to provide the financial support for the many communities in this area significantly dependent upon defense activities.

PUBLIC ATTITUDES

Mass psychology as it influences decisions by the heads of family units is an important factor that can and usually will affect the state of the local, regional, and national economy. Many Americans lack any real knowledge of economics and the operation of our economic system. Therefore, they often make economic decisions on an emotional basis. Such people are also ignorant of economic trends and therefore are unable to forecast economic conditions for even a short period of time. In the past the result of this situation has been that periods of economic upturn are blown up into boom conditions, followed by the resultant bust. During periods of economic recession or depression, pessimism about the economic future due to lack of economic sophistication extends these difficult times for longer periods than necessary. The individual deciding whether to lend money on real estate must be aware of this economic ignorance and realize fully the part that mass psychology plays in changing or perpetuating conditions in the business and real estate cycles.

CHANGING REAL ESTATE LENDING PRACTICE

From 1900 to the present, how have the lessons of history changed real estate lending? To examine this subject properly we will have to break it down into specific topics. The experience of history has effected changes with regard to (1) the power of institutions to lend on real estate; (2) the extent of the state's participation in or regulation of real estate lending; (3) loan payment methods; (4) debt as a percentage of estimated value of

property; and (5) specialized situations where government enters the real estate financing field for the purpose of carrying out authorized programs designed to benefit groups considered to be in special circumstances justifying such extraordinary treatment. The corrective steps taken in these various areas are based upon the typical real estate finance disaster. This unhappy event usually involves a period of high-level economic activity culminating in a real estate boom accompanied by wild speculation. With few controls on loans and lending practices, the only restriction upon estimates of property value, prices paid for real estate, and amount of money loaned is the judgment of the individual, which has not been very effective in preventing the development of boom-and-bust cycles. A basic difficulty has been the inability to prevent a high level of economic activity from developing into a volatile boom. In times of increasing economic activity people in general and officers of lending institutions in particular have too often assumed that the relatively high level of production, prices, and profits is a normal state of affairs that will continue for an indefinite period. Toward the end of a real estate boom certain weaknesses appear in the economic aspects of real estate development and in the market. Accompanying these weaknesses is the decreasing liquidity of lending institutions. As these conditions slowly develop, conditions in general deteriorate toward a comparatively sudden economic collapse. This precipitous economic downturn can be commenced by the failure of well-known financial institutions, by a sharp increase in defaults within a short period of time, or by speculative excesses in the stock and real estate markets. One or more of these failures may start the pebble rolling downhill from the precipice of excessive business activity, and as the vibrations are transmitted throughout the rest of the community on the way down, mass hysteria and fear precipitate an economic avalanche.

In the past, financial institutions participating extensively in lending often lent themselves into positions where their liquidity was drastically reduced. As fear and doubt spread throughout the state, region, or country, withdrawals of deposits from banks and savings and loan associations proceeded apace. In the typical real estate finance crisis of the past, the financial institutions were in a position to demand payment from their debtors virtually at their convenience. Under these circumstances the borrower did not know specifically when his or her debt would have to be paid. The debtors usually were not able to respond to these demands with payment of the debt due. The result was foreclosure of mortgages and trust deeds on property, which inceased the amount of property for sale, and consequent depression of the market price of real estate. Another depressant connected with this situation was the negative psychological aspect of the foreclosure sale. Such sales advertised to the countryside that real estate in that place and at that time was a failure in that it could not pay its way.

In the past such financial nosedives either have been allowed to run their course like a high fever or have been stemmed early, either by a restoration of public confidence or by the ability of financial institutions to pay all demands made on them by depositors and thus prevent general panic. Whether curtailed in initial stages or allowed to turn into a major crisis of the economy, such real estate gyrations injured too many people. The debtors usually lost their property through foreclosure, and the lenders on real estate were not repaid their loans in full because the property foreclosed upon was sold at a distress sale in a depressed market for a price less than the unpaid balance of the loan. This historical pattern of boom and bust in real estate was examined in great detail during the 1930s to discover what caused the zoom upward to the eerie heights and the express-elevator descent to the depths of the financial basement.

Many areas of real estate finance operations were examined and corrections made. Lending institutions were more closely regulated in their appraisal practices and in the percentage of estimated property value for which a loan could be made. More rigorous regulations often governed the liquid reserves that would have to be maintained and the percentage of total assets that could be used to make real estate loans. Appraisal practices were substantially revamped by the professional appraisers' association and by newly created federal agencies established to assist in raising the depressed level of real estate. Federal Housing Administration appraisal methodology served as a model for appraisals performed by financial institutions throughout the country. Secondary mortgage market outlets were provided for real estate loans so that institutions initiating loans could sell them to organizations such as the Federal National Mortgage Association and thus expand their lending capacity and increase their general financial strength by their resultant increased liquidity. Along with more highly disciplined appraisal procedures, loan credit approval was stricter in requiring both more information about prospective borrowers and demonstration of greater capacity to service their debt obligation. In addition to these steps a very important concept of mortgage insurance was developed under the auspices of the Federal Housing Administration, which initiated a loan insurance program financed basically by a premium paid by the borrowers whose loans were insured by FHA. Over the years this program has provided, through the collection of insurance premiums, a fund to insure the repayment of defaulted loans covered by inadequate security. Added to this insurance program was the amortizing loan concept. Before the general implementation of this method of repaying loans secured by liens on real property, real estate lending was based upon

so-called straight loans. These loans were made for a relatively short duration of one to ten years. Upon their expiration (assuming no distress or unwillingness on the part of the financial institution), they were often renewed for a fee, with the result that for an indeterminate period of time the debtor never had to face involuntarily the task of paying the principal of the debt. Under this initiating and servicing procedure, loans that were excessive in terms of the long-term market value of the security and the financial ability of the debtor to repay were made with no practical possibility of the principal debt being reduced. This type of loan usually continued until a sudden call for payment caused default and sale at distress prices that did not result in full payment of the debt due. Under the amortizing loan, the debtor makes regular payments consisting of debt retirement and interest (usually monthly in the case of residential loans), with the result that over the life of the loan the principal amount due is constantly reduced. This continual reduction of the total amount of the debt obviously increases the safety of the loan from the standpoint of the lender, because the owner's equity in the property is constantly increasing. Thus, even if serious mistakes have been made regarding the long-term value of the property hypothecated for security purposes or the ability of the borrower to repay, these mistakes can be compensated for by the constant reduction of the debt due the lender. Included in many amortizing loans is the obligation of the debtor to pay, in addition to principal and interest due, sums large enough to pay, when due, insurance premiums on property improvements and property taxes levied against the property. In these comprehensive amortizing loans with impound accounts for insurance premiums and taxes, the debtor is put on a mandatory pay-as-you-go basis with regard to apportioning his or her income to service the real estate loan. The lender, then, under the amortizing loan, influences family budgeting in residential loans to the extent that the family must apportion a certain amount of its monthly income for this obligation. Generally speaking, the amortizing loan has been a success in that it has very likely substantially reduced the number of defaults on residential loans.

CURRENT REAL ESTATE LOAN PROBLEMS

Despite the great changes in real estate lending theory and practice, difficulties can and do arise in this field. Present-day troubles may usually be traced to unemployment or to a reduction in income of the family breadwinner, which makes meeting real estate loan obligations difficult or impossible. Lack of control over financial commitments assumed after qualifying for a real estate loan is another problem in that a debtor's originally sound financial position can be eroded or virtually destroyed by his or her imprudently incurring other obligations.

One problem that exists to some extent in all real estate finance businesses is failure to follow regulations designed to assure maximum probability of receiving required repayment of real estate loans. Deliberate overvaluation of real property for loan purposes, overstatement of effective yearly income, and unjustified minimization of existing financial obligations at the time application is made for a loan are fraudulent methods that have occasionally been employed to qualify property and borrowers for loans. These very harmful, dishonest practices are not to be engaged in and are unqualifiedly condemned.

Problems that exist in real estate finance are to some extent created by the changing aspects and makeup of society. Age-group distribution of the population, level of formal education, size of families, skilled and unskilled employment, and apparent willingness to pay debts when due are all constantly changing factors that affect collectibility of real estate loans.

The general real estate finance failures of the 1930s in this country set the stage for significant analysis of the real estate market and development of improved lending procedures. The initial impetus for private investigation and research is continuing and increasing in strength. The person in real estate sales or finance must keep up with real estate market research and general analysis of the economy, which means that a considerable amount of time must be spent studying economic, financial, governmental, and sociological material. This vast quantity of material must be examined so that the lender can properly discharge responsibilities to the borrower and the community in general. Specifically, the obligation of the lender is to make sound, collectible, reasonably profitable loans. He or she should enable the borrower to borrow money at reasonable cost under terms and conditions resulting in a loan that is a servant, not a master. His or her responsibility to the community is to provide credit in reasonable necessary amounts, at a fair price, and without engaging in irresponsible loans that excessively expand construction or sales for a short period of time only to result in a long-term glut of space in the market, which is detrimental to all members of the community. Without a continuing, alert, and conscientious research program these responsibilities cannot be adequately discharged.

PRIVATE MORTGAGE LOAN INSURANCE

In recent years mortgage loan insurance has been provided by private corporate sources (typified by Mortgage Guaranty Insurance Corporation—MGIC), whose basic idea is the same as that of the Federal Housing Administration program. With regard to cost, size of loan insured, time necessary to complete issuance of insurance for lender's benefit, and other particulars, there are some differences between the FHA and the private loan insurance programs. The amount of private loan insurance in force has been increasing by substantial amounts from year to year since its inception.

PERSONAL QUALITIES NECESSARY TO SUCCESS

Comprehension of real estate finance is absolutely essential to maximize success and financial reward for the individual selling real estate. To be truly successful in his or her chosen occupation, the real estate salesperson must have certain essential personal qualities in addition to mastery of the subject matter of real estate finance. He or she must have tact, industry, a cooperative spirit, high standards of ethics and honesty, intelligence, and a desire to be of real service to the public. If the salesperson possesses and employs these qualities, profit from his or her labors will usually follow.

KNOWLEDGE OF REAL ESTATE FINANCE

In the practical world of financing specific real estate transactions, one body of knowledge is absolutely essential for the successful real estate financier: current knowledge of loan terms, conditions applying to loans, and minimum credit standards established by lenders. Along with specific information relating to the lending activities of certain institutions, the mechanics of decision making by such lenders must be understood. This involves knowing what official or officials of a lending institution make the ultimate decision as to whether a loan will be granted. In addition to having this vast body of information pertaining to private lending organizations, the real estate professional must understand the functions and methods of operation of state and federal agencies that either make or insure loans.

All this information about the sources of funds, agencies insuring real estate loans, and specific requirements for individual loans is relatively useless unless one has the ability to analyze realistically the financial situation of a prospective borrower. Such analysis must be done correctly to avoid trying to obtain financing for prospective borrowers who will never be approved for a loan or who should not obtain one because of the great likelihood of their defaulting on the obligation. The required analysis cannot be done unless one understands the appropriate mathematical techniques and has the ability to apply them to relevant loan data.

To be effective in arranging suitable loans, one must

understand at least the legal structure of contracts, negotiable instruments, and real property liens. When executing the requisite legal documents (being careful not to engage in the unauthorized practice of law) such as contracts of sale, land contracts, and liens, one must develop a "philosophy of detail." This means that an individual active in real estate lending should have on hand, prior to completing the instruments of real estate sales and finance, all the many items of informational detail necessary to create complete, unambiguous documents.

REAL ESTATE LENDING—A SERVICE

As we have emphasized before, real estate lending includes many service aspects. The shortsighted viewpoint—that the chance to earn a commission justifies the establishment of any kind of loan, suitable or unsuitable for borrower and lender—is no longer acceptable. To be of maximum service to the borrower it is necessary to have complete knowledge of his or her financial circumstances, the requirements of the lender, and the money market and its operation. This information should facilitate prediction of the cost of a loan and the quantity of funds available for loan purposes. This type of accurate prediction will in turn facilitate the decision making relative to the timing of borrowing and the size of loans that should be obtained.

SPECIFIC SUBJECTS TO BE COVERED

The basic subjects covered in the subsequent chapters of this book are the mortgage money market and its relationship to the economy; sources of real estate loan funds; the mathematics of real estate finance and financial statement analysis; legal aspects of real estate finance; loan applications; closing loans; appraising property for financing purposes; Federal Housing Administration; United States Veterans Administration; California Veterans Administration loans; construction financing; existing residence financing; income tax aspects of real estate finance; lease and leasehold financing; shopping center and office building financing; industrial buildings and apartment house loans; junior financing; financial arrangements for special purpose properties; equity participation financing by institutional lenders; the all-inclusive trust deed—also called the wraparound mortgage; and alternatives to mortgage financing. Serious study of these subjects is necessary for education and preparation for effective real estate sales and lending activity. However, this is just a beginning of the true understanding of real estate finance. Research, *constant research,* in the many areas of real estate finance will always be essential to the achievement of truly professional service in the field.

QUESTIONS

1. Institutional real estate lenders consist of
    a. savings and loan associations
    b. life insurance companies
    c. commmercial banks
    d. mutual savings banks
    e. all of the above
2. "Other" noninstitutional governmental sources of real estate loans include
    a. real estate investment trusts
    b. syndicates
    c. bonds
    d. Farmers Home Loan Administration
    e. all of the above
3. Reasons for past real estate lending failures include
    a. inadequate appraisal of the collateral property to establish its future value
    b. incomplete analysis of the borrower's credit worthiness
    c. unexpected economic recessions
    d. operation of the law of supply and demand in a given real estate market
    e. all of the above
4. To be successful in the field of arranging financing for home buyers, one must
    a. be reasonably knowledgeable about the legal aspects of interest in real property and financing contracts
    b. know what the commercial bank prime interest rate is
    c. know what the Federal Housing Administration's maximum purchase money loan interest rate is
    d. be able to distinguish a term loan from other types of loans
    e. all of the above

BIBLIOGRAPHY

BEATON, WILLIAM R., *Real Estate Finance,* Englewood Cliffs, NJ: Prentice-Hall, 1982, Chapter 1.

CASE, FREDERICK E., and JOHN M. CLAPP, *Real Estate Financing,* New York: John Wiley, 1978, Chapter 1.

HINES, MARY ALICE, *Real Estate Finance,* Englewood Cliffs, NJ: Prentice-Hall, 1978, Chapter 1.

2

The Federal Reserve System and the National Economy

Any study of economics, real estate, or finance must include the role of the Federal Reserve Bank in the economy of our nation. By regulating the amount of money in circulation, the Bank exerts powerful control over our economy. The Federal Reserve Act, which established the Federal Reserve Bank system, was a Christmas present from President Woodrow Wilson on December 23, 1913. Originally the Act had three major purposes.

ORIGINAL MAJOR PURPOSES

First, the Act was intended to provide the country with an elastic currency. Second, it was to provide facilities for the discounting of commercial paper or, in essence, the sale of commercial notes held by banks to a central holding agency. Third, it was to improve supervision of banks and provide an agency that would make an annual inspection of all member banks of the Federal Reserve system and determine whether they were in a relatively liquid condition.

ORIGINAL SECONDARY PURPOSES

In addition to these major purposes were some secondary ones. The first of these secondary purposes was to help counteract inflationary and deflationary movements within the national economy. Second, the Act was to share and aid in creating conditions favorable to high employment, stable values, national growth, and a rising level of consumption. Strangely, after 1935 these items, originally secondary, became the primary and major purposes of the Federal Reserve Bank system.

CONDITIONS PRIOR TO THE FEDERAL RESERVE ACT

To understand the Federal Reserve system we should have some conception of the conditions that existed before the establishment of the Federal Reserve system.

Before the passage of the Federal Reserve Act, banks in outlying areas carried their cash reserves in large city banks or in central reserve city banks. Even in those days it was not customary for the banks to maintain high cash deposits within their own vaults; instead they shipped them, through such media as Pacific Express, Southern Pacific, or by common registered mail, to large banks in large cities where the money received was deposited to the credit of the shipping bank.

National banks in the large central cities were required to carry all their reserves in cash so that if there should be a sudden demand, cash would be available for shipment to the correspondent or depositing bank. As in all banks, the income of the central reserve city bank comes from the loaning of money received as deposits. During the period when a farmer was receiving money for his or her crops, money would flow from the farmer to the rural bank, from the rural bank to the central reserve bank, and from the central reserve bank, after its reserves were deducted, to borrowers in the city.

During periods of normal money flow, there was little problem, and those who had received loans were allowed to carry those loans until maturity; however, during the preparation of the soil for crops, when the farmer's expenses were high, a large demand was placed on the rural bank by the farmer. The rural bank, in turn, would make its demand on the central city bank, and because the central city bank had loaned the funds to some borrower, it would have to make demand upon the borrower in order to make payment of the demand of the rural bank. Such situations gave rise to the short-term demand note, which could be called at any time as the need arose for the funds which had been loaned.

This demand, of course, could come at a time when it would be difficult for the borrower to make payment, forcing him or her to sell some of his or her inventory at a loss or certainly at less profit than anticipated, or to discount accounts receivable in order to pay the loan. It

11

might also cause the central city bank to refuse renewal of matured loans or to sell securities, an action that could, if the demand were widespread enough, depress the market. Finally, it might cause the large city banks to stop making commercial loans, which are relatively short-term loans made for business purposes. The refusal of the large city bank to make such loans could, in turn, affect business in the city and could cause a period of "tight money." Of course, after the harvest was completed and funds deposited in rural banks, the cycle would start again as the funds were shipped to the city bank. Funds would be immediately available for loans, and the central banks would be making an effort to put these funds to work.

In view of conditions such as these the Federal Reserve Act was passed in the hope that the surge of money into the banks and the later withdrawal of funds, which caused peaks and valleys in the deposit picture, would level out. The decision of Congress to write a Federal Reserve Act was encouraged by the success of the Bank of England, which was established in 1680, and the Bank of France, which was established by Napoleon I during his reign.

STRUCTURE OF THE FEDERAL RESERVE SYSTEM

The Act that Woodrow Wilson signed on December 23, 1913, provided the United States of America with a regional system of twelve Federal Reserve Banks coordinated through a Board of Governors in Washington, D.C. Figure 2-1 represents the organization of the Federal Reserve system. Each Federal Reserve Bank is administered by a Board of Directors composed of nine directors divided into three equal groups known as Class A, Class B, and Class C directors.

Class A and Class B directors are elected by member banks of the Federal Reserve. In each class, one director represents the large, one the medium-sized, and one the small banks in his or her own Federal Reserve District.

Class A directors may be bankers. Class B directors must be active in agricultural, commercial, or industrial pursuits in their districts. Class C directors are appointed by the Board of Governors of the Federal Reserve system and may not be officers, directors, employees, or stockholders of any bank. The Board of Governors designates one of the Class C directors as chairman of the Board of Directors to act as the Federal Reserve Bank's reserve agent. A second director is designated as deputy chairman.

The chief executive of each Federal Reserve Bank district is the president of the District Bank, who is appointed for a five-year term by the Board of Directors with the approval of the Federal Reserve Board of Governors.

As indicated, all Federal Reserve districts and all Boards of Directors are under the direct supervision of the Board of Governors of the Federal Reserve system. The Federal Reserve Board of Governors consists of seven members, each appointed by the President of the United States with the approval of the Senate. The appointment is for a fourteen-year term, with one term expiring every two years. If one of the governors should resign from the Federal Reserve Board before his or her fourteen-year term expires, the President appoints somebody to complete that unexpired term. The nominee is also subject to approval by the Senate. The Board members are chosen by the President to represent the agricultural, commercial, industrial, and financial interests of the country. No two board members may come from the same Federal Reserve district. This is, in effect, a federal agency and a bankers' bank. The President also designates who is to be chairman of the Board of Governors.

The Federal Reserve Board of Governors is probably the most powerful group of men in our government. It is not expected to change in makeup when a new President is elected nor when a different political party comes into power. In fact, the fourteen-year term was designed so that no President could control the Board. The President can suggest policy, but the Board does not have to comply with the suggestion, as President Lyndon Johnson found out.

The Federal Reserve Bank is not subject to review by the General Accounting Office, the Congress, the Treasurer of the United States, or the Comptroller of the Currency.

TODAY'S MAJOR FUNCTION OF THE FEDERAL RESERVE SYSTEM

The principal function of the Federal Reserve Bank is to regulate the flow of money and credit. (See Figure 2-2.) Other important functions today include essential services such as handling Federal Reserve member banks' reserve accounts; effecting telegraphic transfer of funds; making par collection of checks through different districts; acting as fiscal agents for the United States government and as custodian and depository for the Treasury and other government agencies; furnishing currency for circulation; shipping currency and coin to member banks as they are needed by them; furnishing a bank audit and examination of state banks that are also member banks of the Federal Reserve system; and collecting information and making economic surveys to facilitate decisions that affect the control and flow of money.

FIGURE 2-1   Organization of the Federal Reserve system

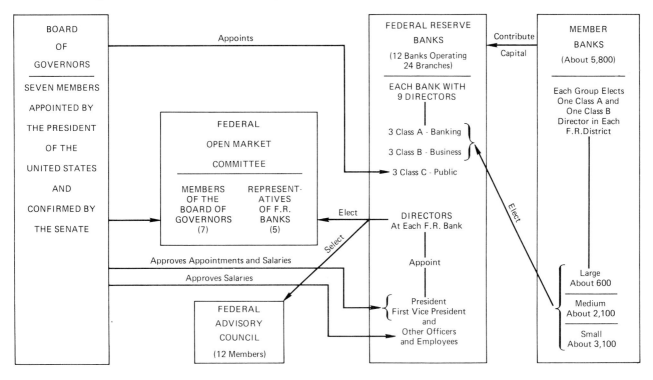

FIGURE 2-2   The Federal Reserve system—relation to instruments of credit policy

Source of Figures 2-1 and 2-2: Board of Governors, *Federal Reserve System, Purposes and Functions*. Washington, DC: Federal Reserve Board.

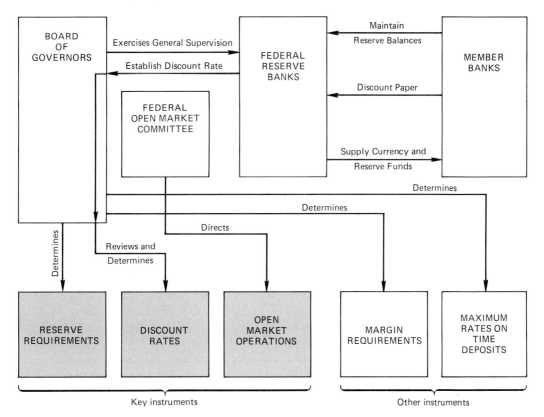

MONEY AND CREDIT AND THEIR EFFECTS

Because the Federal Reserve Bank regulates and controls the flow of money and credit, we should first understand what is meant by the term *money* as it is used by the Federal Reserve Bank, and how it is related to credit. We should also consider how changes in credit and monetary conditions affect people's lives. Third, we should investigate the means by which the Federal Reserve Bank regulates credit and money.

What is money? We can better understand its definition if we consider what money will do for us. It has three main functions. First, money is a means of payment or a medium of exchange. Second, it is a storage of purchasing power. Third, it is a standard of value. In view of these functions, let us see what items would qualify as money. We think first, of course, of the paper money and coins in our pockets, since they do fulfill the functions described.

What about money on deposit in checking accounts? It serves the same purposes as currency and can be converted to it easily. Factually, checks are considered a medium of exchange and are accepted almost as freely as currency and coin. Therefore, funds on deposit in a checking or commercial account would be considered money.

Now let us consider savings accounts and time deposits that are, according to the terms of the deposit, subject to prior notice of conversion or subject to a maturity date (time deposits). We have here a storage of purchasing power that still acts as a medium of standard value; however, it is not acceptable as a means of payment nor can it be readily converted into cash. Therefore, it cannot be considered as money whose flow is regulated by the Federal Reserve Bank. However, both savings and loan associations and banks were authorized in January 1981 to create a new type of account on which interest could be paid. It was designated as a negotiable order of withdrawal (NOW) account. Since these accounts allow a person to issue what amounts to a check, they must be considered as money. Money, as defined above, and time deposits can originate from bank loans and bank investments, and it is the Federal Reserve Bank's chief task to influence this flow of credit and money by affecting its general availability and cost to borrowers.

We may now consider the second point: How do changes in credit and monetary conditions affect the lives of people? We might say that the more credit and money people have the better off they are; however, it is not the number of dollars a person has that is important, but what they buy. Different people determine whether they have sufficient money in different ways. The manufacturer, for example, is interested in borrowing enough money at a reasonable cost to buy raw materials, pay his or her employees, pay other costs necessary for a profitable operation, and maintain a strong credit position through prompt payment of loans and accounts payable. The consumer, however, wants to have enough money, on credit charges and repayment terms he or she can meet from his or her income, to buy what is needed or what is thought to be needed. Whether merchant, farmer, banker, or consumer, each is interested in the purchasing power of the dollar. In a dynamic and growing economy, a sufficient amount of money and credit is that which will help maintain high and steadily rising levels of production, employment, and consumption, and foster a stable value of the dollar. When credit becomes scarce and expensive, stores, manufacturers, farmers, and others may curtail their operations and lay off employees, which leads, of course, to smaller payrolls and, in turn, to smaller purchases. Merchants then reduce their orders to the manufacturers, who in turn find it necessary to lay off employees. When credit is abundant and cheap, however, the reverse of these situations develops, and we have a potential inflationary boom. This means that when employment is high, people are buying at an increased pace, manufacturing increases, and prices rise because of the greater demand caused by the availability of money. In this way, therefore, money and credit can influence people's lives and, in turn, the economy of an area.

MEANS OF CONTROLLING THE FLOW OF MONEY AND CREDIT

How can the Federal Reserve influence credit and money? First, all money used by people reaches it directly or indirectly through a bank. You may receive your pay in cash; however, your employer obtained this money from a bank to pay you. You may receive change from a grocery store when you pay your grocery bill; however, the grocer receives the change originally from a bank. You may cash your check in a grocery store, but the person cashing it for you receives that money from a bank, possibly through a bank loan for the specific purpose of cashing payroll checks. Therefore, we can say that the flow of money depends upon the ability of the bank to meet monetary and credit requirements placed upon it by trade, industry, agriculture, and other economic sectors of life. The Federal Reserve Bank's controlling this ability enables it to control the monetary and credit flow.

The Federal Reserve Bank can exercise its control in five different ways. First, it can control the amount of reserves required by member banks. Second, it can set the discount rate for its member banks. Third, it can enter the United States Government bond market in either a selling or a purchasing capacity, either to limit or to increase the amount of cash available to the public. Fourth, it exercises certain regulatory controls over member banks on amounts of loans that can be made against securities as collateral, on the amount of down payment required for the purchase of automobiles and other consumer goods, and on the amount of down payment required and length of time allowed on a real estate loan. Fifth, it maintains control of interest paid by member banks through regulation Q, which is to be phased out in the near future.

Reserve Requirements of Member Banks

The Monetary Control Act of 1980 (Public Law 96-221), enacted on March 31, 1980, is designed to improve the effectiveness of monetary policy by applying new reserve requirements set by the Federal Reserve Board to all depository institutions. Among its other key provisions, the Act (1) authorizes the Federal Reserve to collect reports from all depository institutions (for the first time the Federal Reserve was given the right to set reserve requirements for organizations other than banks); (2) extends access to Federal Reserve discount and borrowing privileges and other services to nonmember depository institutions; (3) requires the Federal Reserve to set a schedule of fees for Federal Reserve services; and (4) provides for the gradual phasing out of deposit interest rate ceilings, coupled with broader powers for thrift institutions.

What institutions come under the provisions of the Monetary Control Act? Uniform reserve requirements are required for member and nonmember banks, savings banks, savings and loan associations, credit unions, and industrial banks that have transaction accounts such as (1) demand accounts; (2) deposits or accounts subject to check, draft, negotiable order of withdrawal, share draft, or other similar items, and savings deposits; (3) savings accounts against which automatic withdrawals may be made; (4) deposits or accounts in which payments may be made to third parties by means of an automated teller machine (ATS accounts); (5) deposits or accounts under which the depositor is allowed to make more than three withdrawals per month to transfer funds to another account or for credit to a third party. The same reserve requirements also extend to U.S. agencies and branches of foreign banks. As of May 1981, all such institutions are affected.

The Monetary Control Act has had an effect in areas one would not expect, such as brokerage houses, finance companies, and even some mortgage companies. By forcing these institutions to set up reserves, the amount of money available for loans was reduced and the cost of using these funds increased.

The Board has also established a 3 percent reserve requirement on net Eurodollars borrowed from related foreign offices; gross borrowing from unrelated foreign depository institutions; loans to United States residents made by overseas branches of domestic depository institutions; and sales of assets by depository institutions in the United States to their overseas offices.

By raising or lowering the reserve requirement the Federal Reserve Bank can decrease or increase the amount of money that is available for loans. Refer to Table 2-1 to see how $100 in deposits can become $500 with a 20 percent reserve requirement or $1,000 if the reserve requirement is only 10 percent.

Discount Rate

The second means of controlling credit and thus the flow of money is the discount rate that the Federal Reserve Bank charges member banks. It is important to remember that the Federal Reserve Bank is a bankers' bank and did business with banks only until 1980, at which time Federal Reserve Banks were authorized to make overnight loans to any nonmember institution that has reservable transaction accounts or nonpersonal time deposits. The nonmember institutions are given access to the discount window only when the institution is unable to gain immediate access to its special industry leaders. The institution has to show the Federal Reserve why such access is not available. This would apply to savings and loan associations, mutual savings banks, credit unions, and nonmember banks. A surcharge will be added to the current discount rate for such borrowings by nonmember institutions.

Occasionally the required reserves of a member bank may fall below the minimum, and it then becomes necessary for the bank to obtain funds from some source to bolster the reserves it is supposed to maintain in the Federal Reserve Bank. There are several ways these funds might be obtained, such as selling bonds from its bond portfolio, borrowing from other banks or from Federal funds (excess reserves of other banks on deposit in the Federal Reserve Bank), or borrowing directly from the Federal Reserve Bank.

When a bank borrows from the Federal Reserve Bank, the Federal Reserve charges interest for the privilege of borrowing, just as a regular bank charges the individual borrower interest for the privilege of using money. If this practice becomes habitual, the Federal Reserve Bank can impose a service charge over and above the amount of the discount.

It is this interest or discount rate that the Federal Reserve can control, increasing or decreasing it as conditions may warrant. As a rule this type of borrowing is short-term, and the member banks do not like to use it any more than necessary; however, the discount rate does

TABLE 2-1 Control of money and credit by reserve requirements of Federal Reserve Board

TRANSACTIONS	AMOUNT DEPOSIT IN CHECKING A/C	AMOUNT OF LOAN	AMOUNT OF RESERVE AT 20%
Bank 1	$100.00	$80.00	$20.00
2	80.00	64.00	16.00
3	64.00	51.20	12.80
4	51.20	40.96	10.24
5	40.96	32.77	8.19
6	32.77	26.22	6.55
7	26.22	20.98	5.24
8	20.98	16.78	4.20
9	16.78	13.42	3.36
10	13.42	10.74	2.68
Total for 10 banks	$446.33	$357.07	$89.26
Additional banks	53.67	42.93	10.74
Grand total for all banks	$500.00	$400.00	$100.00

TRANSACTIONS	AMOUNT DEPOSITED IN CHECKING A/C	AMOUNT OF LOAN	AMOUNT OF RESERVES AT 10%
Bank 1	$100.00	$90.00	$10.00
2	90.00	81.00	9.00
3	81.00	72.90	8.10
4	72.90	65.61	7.29
5	65.61	59.05	6.56
6	59.05	53.15	5.90
7	53.15	47.83	5.32
8	47.83	43.05	4.78
9	43.05	38.74	4.31
10	38.74	34.87	3.87
11	34.87	31.38	3.49
12	31.38	28.24	3.14
13	28.24	25.42	2.82
14	25.42	22.88	2.54
15	22.88	20.59	2.29
Total for 15 banks	794.12	$714.71	$79.41
Additional banks	205.88	185.29	20.59
Grand total for all banks	$1,000.00	$900.00	$100.00

have an effect upon the member banks and their policies. An increase in the discount rate is an indication to the member bank that the Federal Reserve feels that the economy is threatening to become inflationary and that the Bank is acting to minimize this undesirable condition. Since the individual banks are reluctant to borrow from the Federal Reserve Bank, they become more careful of the funds they are loaning. When the discount rate is high the individual banks will not make marginal loans, and even people with good credit will often find it difficult to obtain the loan they desire. The bank, in turn, to compensate for a potential increased cost, will increase interest rates to its customers, who will then think twice about borrowing. In this way, the Federal Reserve system curtails expansion of credit and consequently the flow of money.

Whenever a member bank borrows from the Federal Reserve Bank, it is in one of two ways. The bank can take one of its customer's notes that is eligible for acceptance by the Federal Reserve Bank and rediscount it with the Federal Reserve Bank. It can also give its own note to the Federal Reserve Bank and offer notes from its own portfolio as security. In either case the Federal Reserve Bank credits the member bank's account and thus covers that bank's shortage in the reserve account. For a note to qualify as eligible security it must be secured by obligation of the United States or it must be a commercial note of limited maturity that was borrowed to meet the demands of commerce, industry, or agriculture. This list, however, does not include loans made for investment or speculative purposes. It is interesting to note that the Federal Reserve Bank is not obligated to extend credit to member banks. If it feels that the need is sufficient and the use of the funds proper, then the Federal Reserve Bank may make a loan to the member bank; however, the Federal Reserve Bank keeps itself informed of the activities of its member banks, and if it feels that a member bank is conducting its business improperly, such as by making loans of a speculative nature, then the Federal Reserve Bank can refuse the credit request of the member bank.

In the past the entire credit market has reflected the amount of borrowing member banks are doing from the Federal Reserve. When member banks are not borrowing from the Federal Reserve Bank, then bank credit is liberal and the flow of credit and currency increases; at this point the credit market is said to be "easy." When member banks find it necessary to borrow from the Federal Reserve Bank, then they discourage additional loans and credit is said to be "tight."

Open Market Operations

The Federal Reserve Bank can also influence the flow of credit and money by entering the United States Government bond market. If the Federal Reserve Bank feels there is a money shortage, it can supplement this shortage by buying United States Government bonds on the open market in the following way.

The Federal Reserve Bank goes to the twenty-one brokers through which it buys and sells and indicates its desire to buy, for example, $10 million in short-term government obligations that will mature within five years. There is a good market for government obligations, Treasury bills, Treasury notes, Treasury bonds, as evidenced by an active market. An indication of this activity is the fact that on December 18, 1981, the total U.S. government debt was $1,015.404 billion, compared with $265 billion on June 15, 1964. Of this debt, one-half matures within one year and four-fifths within five years. An active market is needed in order to be able to buy or sell quickly. The brokers then go to the various holders of the issues the Federal Reserve Bank desires and advise them that they have a buyer for their bonds. The brokers purchase the bonds, notes, or bills and then sell them to the Federal Reserve Bank. In return, the Federal Reserve Bank gives the brokers a check drawn upon the Federal Reserve Bank. The brokers deposit this check in their bank. The check is deposited in the reserve account of the depositing bank at the Federal Reserve Bank. The deposit of the bank at the Federal Reserve Bank is thus increased beyond that which is necessary for the reserve for bond purchases or additional loans. In either event, the Federal Reserve Bank's purchase of government obligations has placed into circulation $10 million which the member bank has available to loan. As the section on reserve requirements illustrated, this $10 million will increase manyfold if the total is loaned out as permitted by the reserve requirements.

Conversely, if the Federal Reserve Bank feels that

money is too free and needs to be tightened somewhat, it can sell government obligations on the open market. In selling it will remove money from circulation, and the money removed will be reflected in the reserve account of a member bank. This decrease will require the member bank to immediately find additional funds to place in the reserve in order to meet the requirement, which can be done by calling loans, by borrowing from the Federal Reserve Bank, or by selling some of the bank's bond portfolio. This constriction moves quickly from one bank to another and in a short time will affect the borrowing power of the entire district.

It takes a longer time for the open market activity of the Federal Reserve Bank to be felt, compared with the reserve requirements or discount changes, and for the money and credit to show the effect of such activity; however, it certainly does influence the flow of credit and money, because by decreasing or increasing the member banks' indebtedness, the Federal Reserve Bank tends to encourage or discourage the expansion of deposits of member banks. This action, of course, has a direct effect on the credit market.

Regulation

A fourth way in which the Federal Reserve Bank is able to influence flow of credit and money is through regulations directed at specific industries. As of December 31, 1981, the Federal Reserve Bank was still using Regulations U and V, which are directed against the purchase of listed stocks on the New York Stock Exchange, American Stock Exchange, and Pacific Coast Stock Exchange. (There are other exchanges on which stocks might be listed, but these are the three major ones.)

Regulation U is directed against the individual purchasing stocks, and Regulation V against the stockbroker. With these regulations the Federal Reserve determines the amount of margin that a purchaser is allowed. Margin is the amount of loan that can be used in connection with purchase of stocks, using listed stocks as security for the loan. If the Federal Reserve Bank feels that the stock market is becoming unstable, it can lower the amount that can be borrowed.

Since January 3, 1974, it has been possible for investors to borrow the larger of the two following standards: 50 percent of the current market value of the security, or 100 percent of the lowest market value of the security in the preceding thirty-six months, but not more than 75 percent of the current market value of the stock used as collateral to purchase additional stock. (From June 8, 1968, to May 5, 1970, it was possible to borrow only 20 percent of the current market value of the security.)

By putting restrictions on this particular industry it is possible for the Federal Reserve Bank to influence the amount of speculative buying. In turn, it also influences the amount of borrowing that is done by the purchasers of the stock and consequently influences the flow of credit and money.

The Federal Reserve has used two other regulations. Regulation W was directed against manufacturers of refrigerators, televisions, radios, automobiles, and other hard goods. This regulation was placed into effect during World War II to reduce the demand for these items. It controlled the amount of down payment necessary for the individual to make a purchase and the length of time that could be used for the payment of the debt. People who were accustomed to purchasing hard goods on the basis of 100 percent financing were unable to compete in the open market for the purchase of items which, during World War II, were in very small supply.

Regulation X, adopted during the Korean conflict, was directed against the real estate industry. It was another effort on the part of the Federal Reserve to reduce the demand for an item that was in short supply. Reducing the demand was an attempt to maintain the price structure so that there would be no inflation during this period in the purchase of real estate. Regulation X designated the amount of minimum down payment and the maximum term for which a real estate loan could be written. It also forbade secondary financing or second trust deeds or any type of junior lien. The regulation in itself was not dissimilar to present-day Federal Reserve regulations on real estate except that a higher down payment was required. Regulations W and X have been inactive since the end of World War II and mid-1953, respectively; however, periodically requests appear in the newspapers that they be reactivated, not so much now to slow down purchase of these items, but to overcome some of the undesirable practices used by salespeople and dealers.

The Unruh Act has done much to counteract some of these undesirable sales practices. This act affects instalment buying in California and requires, among other things, that the amount of interest charged be shown on the contract and that the exact payment be shown before the purchaser signs the contract. Other ramifications of the Unruh Act are more appropriate to a text on consumer financing. It is mentioned here to show that other methods have been taken to eliminate undesirable practices and that any reactivation of Regulation X or Regulation W would again be an attempt to influence the flow of credit and money.

The fifth control against credit, known as Regulation Q, was originally intended not as a credit control but as a means of controlling competition among banks in the payment of interest on time deposits. It actually functioned in this manner until the United States Government found it necessary to borrow more and more money. To attract investors to United States Treasury bills and notes, the government increased its interest rates until it exceeded the amount of interest the banks and savings and loan associations were allowed to pay to their customers through Regulation Q. In 1969 and again in 1973–74 the rate of return on ninety-day Treasury bills reached an amount in excess of 8 percent; the rate continued to rise almost steadily until it reached 9.8 percent on August 23, 1974. Money became tight again from 1978 through 1981, and the return on ninety-day Treasury bills climbed to 15.1 percent on December 19, 1980; by December 18, 1981, the return was 11.35 percent, but this was still more than the 5 percent return allowed from banks on any of the dates mentioned above. This caused treasurers of states, counties, cities, and districts to withdraw their funds from banks and savings and loan associations and invest them in United States obligations. Because of the yield on short-term obligations, the long-term United States bonds were being discounted so that they would yield approximately the same rate of return. In the first six months of 1969, the banks and savings and loan associations lost over $13 billion in time deposits to United States Government obligations. No fault could be found with the treasurers for obtaining the maximum return for their people. In fact, they would not have been performing their duty had they done otherwise; however, such a large reduction in deposits certainly affected the amount of credit that banks and savings and loan associations were able to extend.

There was another result of the high rates of interest that the federal government paid. For the first six months the major withdrawals were made by treasurers in control of public funds. After that, individuals became interested in these high-yield investments that, since they were United States Government obligations, were as safe as the local bank. The banks and savings and loan associations suffered additional heavy losses of time deposits. A person needed only $1,000 to be able to buy a Treasury bill or note, and the public took advantage of the opportunity. This continued until March 1970, when a minimum sale of $10,000 was established by the Federal Reserve Bank. This slowed the loss of deposits, but not before a great deal of the funds which could have been used for credit had been assimilated by the United States Government.

Hard pressed for loanable funds, the banks used great ingenuity to find funds that could be used for credit. The first source was the Eurodollar, a deposit in United States dollars in a bank outside the United States, including the foreign branches of United States banks. In the summer of 1969 there were $40 billion deposited in foreign banks, up from almost nothing ten years before. The Eurodollar market has become the depository of almost everyone who can get United States dollars and place them overseas. It is a source of huge amounts of dollars for anyone willing to pay the price of about 10 percent a year. It has been used to a great degree by American commercial banks, American corporations operating overseas, importers and exporters, foreign corporations, and government agencies. In 1969 the Eurodollar relieved the very tight credit when several large United States banks borrowed in excess of $7 billion to replace lost domestic deposits. The Federal Reserve Bank felt that this was defeating its planned credit restrictions and therefore placed a curb on the use of Eurodollars by requiring a 10 percent reserve against all Eurodollar borrowings. This reserve requirement, plus the high interest rate required in payment for the use of Eurodollars, made it impractical for American banks to use Eurodollars.

The second attempt to bring loanable deposits into a bank was made by the use of One Bank Holding Companies. The Federal Reserve through its Regulation Q was regulating the payment of interest on time deposits, but it had no regulatory powers over the holding company. The One Bank Holding Companies decided to issue capital bonds for periods of 90, 180, and 360 days. They would be issued in $100 denominations (to appeal to the small investor) as well as in larger denominations. They would be sold at par to yield 7.5 percent interest. The funds realized from the sale of these bonds would then be placed in the bank and used as a basis for credit.

Once again the Federal Reserve Bank found its control being bypassed and decided to place regulations on the funds received by banks from this type of operation; it established an extra 10 percent reserve requirement. Again the source of funds found through the banks' ingenuity became too expensive to use.

In January 1969 the Federal Reserve Bank allowed an increase in the payment of interest under Regulation Q. It appeared that the banks and savings and loan associations would be able to regain some of their deposits; however, the federal government had $6.9 billion of United States bonds maturing in February and March of 1969. They were originally issued to yield 1.5 percent interest and 3.5 percent interest, respectively. The government indicated that these bonds would be funded (paid) by issuing United States Treasury notes to yield from 8 to 8.5 percent. Deficit spending continued, requiring additional borrowing.

These, then, are the ways in which the Federal Reserve Bank tries to influence the flow of credit and money. Of course, outside items also affect the credit flow. These include the bargaining strength and policies of management, labor, agriculture, and other sectors of our economy; government policy regarding expenditures, debts, and taxes; the course of foreign trade; foreign investment; and the prospect of peace or war. Although these are influential factors in our economy, the Federal Reserve, through the five methods we have discussed, also has a decided influence on the economic picture in the United States.

The revised Federal Reserve Act has now been in operation long enough to reveal some of its shortcomings and advantages. The Federal Reserve Bank has found that it is able to bring to a halt an upward-spiraling inflationary economy. The problem seems to be that after causing a halt it has not been able to maintain a stable plateau, and therefore a recession has followed each halt in an upward swing.

As the economy dropped off, the Federal Reserve would first decrease the discount rate, then it would decrease the reserve requirements and take the necessary steps to make additional funds available for credit through the banks. However, once people have felt a slight panic regarding economic conditions, it is difficult to reinstill a feeling of good will. As a result, although money and credit are available, it takes some time to restore confidence so that people will go into the competitive market and spend their money and credit in order to bolster the sagging economy.

You can lead a horse to water but you cannot force it to drink; a similar problem faces the Federal Reserve when it is trying to make credit available. People cannot be forced to use credit. They will do so only when their confidence has been restored; usually, as in the latter part of April 1958, there is an immediate spiral upward, a heavy rash of purchasing, and additional demand for properties and goods that are in short supply. These events lead to additional price increases and additional labor and material costs. This trend continued until May 1960.

The brakes that were applied to such an upward spiral in 1960 led to the recession of 1960–61, the mildest in history, and 1962 saw the quickest recovery, which failed to live up to expectations. This produced a plateau that gave way to methodical growth in 1963 and into 1964. The income tax cut of 1964 lent impetus to the growth so that the economy in 1964 was very strong, and growth continued until November 1969. There was another strong expansion period from November 1970 until November 1973. There have been some interesting cycles of recession and inflation since 1947. The *San Francisco Federal Reserve Bank Monthly Review* of September 1960 showed that there were five periods from 1949 to 1959 during which the number of housing starts rose each month for at least six months, and in three periods there were booms: 1949–50, 1953–55, and 1958–59. Since 1959 there have been three other periods of strong building. The years 1963–64 and 1968–69 were about as strong as 1958–59, while 1971–72 saw more starts than 1949—almost 2.5 million starts for single family units. The real estate boom in each of these periods carried over into the whole economy, resulting in a substantial increase in the level of activity.

The 1949–50 boom had several causes. First, during 1948 there had been a recession; since loans were not being made, money accumulated in bank vaults. The Federal Reserve relaxed its controls in an effort to have the banks encourage borrowers to partake of the loans which were available and thus get the economy moving again. Second, a strong demand for new housing existed, caused by the increase of family units as men who had married during World War II returned to civilian life. At this time new families were being formed at record rates. Also, during World War II many people made and saved money. They wanted better housing than they had, and they could now afford it. In its legislation of 1948, Congress paved the way for this particular boom by liberalizing the FHA and VA loans. With United States bonds yielding only 2.25 percent, the 4.5 and 4 percent of the FHA and VA loans, respectively, were inviting to banks, which proceeded to place their money in this kind of investment. Prices began to increase, and the Federal Reserve Bank imposed its restrictions to bring the boom to a close.

The boom of late 1953 through 1955 was brought about by similar conditions. Recession in early 1953 brought on relaxed Federal Reserve Bank controls. Interest on United States bonds dropped to 2.5 percent, and the Federal Housing Administration again relaxed its requirements and brought on a new demand for new housing; however, there were differences. In the boom of 1949–50 the increase in construction was in both single- and multiple-dwelling units, with financing in all three general classes: FHA, VA, and conventional. The boom of 1953–55 was the result of construction of single-family units almost without exception. There were three reasons for this difference. First, almost all families living in multiple units had found other living facilities. Second, the increase in new families had materially declined. Third, many renters and owners who had wanted better homes in the past had been excluded because of lack of down payments or of incomes sufficient to keep up the monthly payments. With a smaller down payment

and the extension to a thirty-year maturity, this market was tapped.

The 1958–59 boom had a similar economic background: a decline in credit demand in 1957 with subsequent relaxing of Federal Reserve Bank restrictions and an increase in Federal Housing Administration permissive interest to 5.25 percent plus 0.5 percent for Mutual Mortgage Insurance (MMI). This made these loans more acceptable than the rate of 3.7 to 4.15 percent on United States obligations. Vying for the investment dollar, which was becoming more and more scarce, were two government agencies: the United States Treasury, whose bond interest had risen from 2.25 to 3.8 percent, and the Federal Housing Administration, whose allowable interest rate had risen from 4.5 to 5.75 percent; however, over 60 percent of the loans in this period were made on a conventional loan basis. The funds being tapped were savings deposits accumulated during 1958–59. The demands that caused the boom were similar to those for the period of 1953–55, but they were not as strong or as pressing; however, the strongest demand at this time was caused by those who wanted to upgrade their housing standards.

It might be of interest to check the required monthly payments for amortization of $1,000 at 14 percent, as shown in Table 2-2. You will see that the difference between five year and ten year amortization of $1,000 at 14 percent is $7.74 per month; in other words, the monthly payment required for ten years is $7.74 less than is required to amortize in five years. The monthly difference between amortization for thirty and for forty years is only $0.14.

Another point of interest on five-year amortization is that thirty days' interest on $1,000 is $11.67, which leaves $11.60 for principal payment, thus returning the funds to the bank so they can be loaned out again. With an $11.67 interest payment on the forty-year loan, only $0.04 is returned on the principal. The bank or lending agency must therefore wait a long time before its loan-to-deposit ratio is reduced to the point where it can loan additional funds.

With FHA loans available on a thirty-year basis and down payments at a very low 3 percent for the first $25,000, where is the next demand for housing going to

TABLE 2-2   Monthly payments for amortization of $1,000 at 14 percent

	NUMBER OF YEARS						
	5	10	15	20	25	30	40
Monthly payments	$23.37	$15.53	$13.32	$12.44	$12.04	$11.85	$11.71
Difference		7.74	2.21	.88	.48	.19	.14
Payment to principal	11.60	3.86	1.65	.77	.37	.18	.04
Payment to interest	11.67	11.67	11.67	11.67	11.67	11.67	11.67

come from? Down payments are about as low as possible, and extension of amortization time to forty years, as some have suggested, would reduce monthly payments only $9.80 on a $70,000 loan. This amount is not enough to qualify a whole new segment of people for FHA loans.

This is another reason funds for housing have been in short supply in 1979–81. When the maximum maturity was ten years, 49.8 percent of the monthly payment was returned funds that could be loaned again; whereas with a thirty-year maturity, only 1.5 percent of the first month's payment is available to be loaned. This means that on a ten-year $70,000 loan, $812 would be available for another loan; whereas on a thirty-year amortization, only $12.60 would be available.

CONSUMER CREDIT PROTECTION ACT OF 1968

Regulation Z, Definition and Scope

Public Law 90-321 was enacted by Congress in 1968. Title I of the law is known as the Truth in Lending Act and Title V as the general provision of the act. *The law applies to all persons who, as a part of their business, regularly provide, extend, offer to extend, arrange, or offer to arrange for the granting of consumer credit.*

To implement the Act, the Federal Reserve Bank was asked to draw a regulation that would be the vehicle by which all people interested in use of consumer credit would be given pertinent information concerning the cost of the credit, expressed in dollar amounts of the financing charge, and as an "Annual Percentage Rate" on the unpaid balance of the amount to be financed. Other credit information must also be disclosed so that the customer can readily make comparisons of various terms available to him or her. In this way the use of uninformed credit will be avoided. The regulation was also to control advertising for consumer credit. Terms not usually available were not to be advertised. The regulation would set up conditions whereby certain credit transactions could be cancelled if the transaction involved a lien on the creditor's residence. This is the job the Federal Reserve Bank had before it when it drafted Regulation Z, which became effective July 1, 1969.

Penalties, liabilities, and enforcement. Section 112 of the Act establishes criminal liability for willfully and knowingly failing to comply with the Act. The penalties for failure to provide a disclosure statement are set as twice the amount of the finance charges with a minimum of $100 and a maximum of $1,000. Court costs and attorney's fees would be added. Willfully and knowingly failing to follow the law or the Regulation could result in a fine of $5,000 and one year's imprisonment if convicted. Clearly, Regulation Z has teeth; federal agencies have been set up to enforce it.

There are nine such agencies, each covering a certain type of business:

1. National banks—Comptroller of the Currency
2. State member banks—Federal Reserve Bank of that area
3. Nonmember insured banks—Federal Deposit Insurance Corporation for that area
4. Savings institutions insured by Federal Savings and Loan Insurance Corporation, and members of the Federal Home Loan Bank system—Federal Home Loan Bank Board's supervisory agent for the district
5. Federal credit unions—regional office of the Bureau of Federal Credit Unions
6. Creditors subject to Civil Aeronautics Board—Director, Bureau of Enforcement, Civil Aeronautics Board
7. Creditors subject to Interstate Commerce Commission—Office of Proceedings, Interstate Commerce Commission
8. Creditors subject to Packers and Stockyards Act—nearest Packers and Stockyards Administration area supervisor
9. Retail department stores, consumer finance companies, and all other creditors—Federal Trade Commission

Definitions

Since Regulation Z considers all consumer credit, including real estate loans, to be covered, we must consider its effect on real estate transactions and loans. To understand the effect of the Act, it will be necessary to review definitions of certain words and terms.

Amount financed. This is the amount that the customer will actually have available to use from the amount of the loan that has been made to him or her. Prepaid interest would be deducted from the amount of the loan. If a certain deposit balance is required before the loan can be made, to be retained by the lending agency for the life of the loan, this amount must also be deducted from the loan because the customer will not be allowed the benefit of its use. Any other charges that are individually itemized and deducted from the amount of the loan must be deducted to determine the *amount financed.*

Annual percentage rate. This term is often abbreviated APR. This is the finance charge expressed as an annual percentage rate to the nearest quarter of 1 percent. The charge is computed on the unpaid balance for the actual time the amount is in use.

Consumer credit. Consumer credit is credit extended or offered to a *natural person.* It is money, service, or property used primarily for personal, family, household, or agricultural purposes. Consumer credit is subject to either a finance charge or the possibility of a finance charge by agreement, and may be paid in more than four payments.

Credit.   Credit is the right of a customer to defer payment of a debt, to incur a debt and defer its payment, or to purchase property or services and defer payment for them.

Creditor.   A creditor is a person who in the ordinary course of business *regularly* extends or arranges for the extension of consumer credit, or offers to make such arrangements.

Customer.   A customer is a natural person to whom consumer credit is offered or to whom it will be extended or is extended. It is the maker, co-maker, endorser, guarantor, or surety who may be obligated to repay the extension of the consumer credit.

Disclosure statement.   The disclosure statement is the printed statement that must be given to all credit customers, showing all aspects of the credit transaction. The amount financed, prepaid finance charge, and payment are indicated by boldface type larger than the normal type, and the finance charge and annual percentage rate must be indicated by boldface type larger than any other type on the page. The disclosure statement must also reveal the security, if any, and the penalties for prepayment or late payment.

Dwelling.   A dwelling is a residential-type building and is real property. It contains one or more living units. It may also be a condominium unit, wherever situated.

Finance charge.   The finance charge is the cost of the credit to the customer. This will include charges other than interest or prepaid interest. In a real estate transaction the finance charge will include the following, whether paid for by the customer, deducted from the loan, or paid by a third party, as in the case of points: loan fees, commitment fee, tax service, contractor's bond, disbursement control, FHA mortgage insurance, reconveyance fee, escrow fee, finder's fee, investigation fees (credit reports, termite inspection, and so forth), and prepaid interest.

Organization.   When the word *organization* is used it may mean a corporation; trust estate; partnership; cooperative; association; government; or government subdivision, agency, or instrumentality.

Person.   When reference is made to a person it may be a natural person or an organization.

Principal residence.   This is an important definition because any transaction which may result in a lien against a natural person's principal residence is subject to rescission (discussed later), unless it is for the original purchase. The principal residence is that one in which the natural person lives most of the time. If he or she lives in an apartment that he or she owns and that may be one of several units, that is his or her principal residence and is subject to the Regulation. If he or she lives in a living unit attached to, above, or below a commercial building, that commercial building is the principal residence. A summer home used by a natural person less than seven months of the year is not a principal residence. If a natural person rents his or her home instead of owning it and buys a lot upon which he or she someday hopes to build a principal residence (there is no time limit to when it is to be built), that lot then becomes his or her principal residence for the purposes of Regulation Z.

Real property.   Any property considered real property under the laws of the state in which it is located is considered real property by the Regulation.

Residence.   A residence is any real property in which the customer resides or *expects to reside.* The term includes a parcel of land on which the customer resides or expects to reside.

Right of rescission.   All customers making a purchase that might result in a security interest, either consensual or involuntary, in their principal residence are to be given a written notice that they have three business days in which to revoke the contractual agreement. This written notice is their notice of right of rescission.

Security interest and security.   A security interest is any interest in property that guarantees payment or performance of a debt. A security interest includes, but is not limited to, interests under the Uniform Commercial Code, real property mortgages, trust deeds, and other consensual or acknowledged liens whether recorded or not, mechanics' and material liens, and any lien on property that is the result of the operation of law, and any interest in a lease when it is used to guarantee payment or performance of a debt.

Scope of the Regulation

Credit to a person (remember, a person includes organizations), a government, or a government agency for business or commercial purposes is exempt from Regulation Z. Credit extended for *other than real property in the amount of $25,000 or more,* or where there is a written agreement to loan $25,000 or more, is exempt. *All real property transactions* and agricultural loans are affected by Regulation Z, regardless of the amount of the credit. It is not the intent of the Truth in Lending law to impose restrictions on fees and charges that might be assessed. It is the intent that the lender can do almost anything he or she wants *but* must tell the customer exactly what he or she is doing in connection with the transaction. It is the intent that more meaningful disclosures will be made of the credit terms, and that all annual percentage rates will be computed in the same way so that it will be easy for the customer to make comparisons and avoid the uninformed use of credit.

The Effect of Regulation Z on the "Purchase" of Real Estate

Regulation Z caused one major change in the financing of the *purchase* of real property. It is now necessary for the creditor to give to the borrower a disclosure statement and to take back his or her acknowledgment of receipt before the customer signs the note and deed of trust. The figures on the disclosure statement are to be explained before the borrower signs the acknowledgment. There is one figure that appears on all disclosure statements except the statement given in connection with the purchase of real property. The figure that is missing from the statement in connection with the *purchase* of real property is the total amount of payment that will be made over the life of the note. This figure includes the total of interest and principal. It does not include amounts that are collected for impounds.

The Effect of Regulation Z on Refinancing Real Property

Regulation Z has its biggest effect in the area of refinancing a customer's principal residence. The Regulation says that in the case of refinancing a customer's principal residence, the creditor must give a notice of right of rescission. The federal law is explicit about the wording of the notice of right to rescind. (See Figure 2-3 for an example.) In effect this statement says that the customer has three business days from the consummation of the contract to rescind the agreement. It also states that the customer cannot be held liable for any expenses incurred by the creditor during the three-day period. It also states that in case of work being done on the residence, the contractor, material provider, or laborer has ten days in which to remove the work done, or material delivered, or both, or the work, material, or improvements become the property of the customer, without obligation.

What does this mean? First, that a creditor cannot

safely start any of the paperwork until three business days after midnight of the day in which the contract is consummated. The third business day goes until midnight of that day. If the creditor normally is open on Saturdays, then Saturday is a business day. If the creditor is not open on Admission Day or another legal holiday, then it is not considered a business day, even though all other businesses may be open for business. Second, since all expenses are refundable in case of rescission, the creditor will not do any of the preliminary work until he or she knows that there will be no rescission. This will slow the processing of loans and will increase the paperwork needed.

There is one more important condition that the right of rescission brings out: Everyone whose name is on the title of the property must sign and acknowledge the right of rescission statement. Any or all of these may rescind a transaction; it does not have to be unanimous. If the wife feels that she does not want to refinance, she can rescind the transaction by delivering in writing (by mail, telegram, messenger, or in person) her intent to rescind the transaction. The notice must be given within the three business days of her notice of the transaction or consummation. If the husband takes home the papers for signatures but signs them himself in front of the creditor before leaving, his three days start from midnight of that day; however, if he forgets to show the papers to his wife for a week, her period for rescission starts from her actual signing. Therefore, it is desirable for all parties to the contract to be present at one time and all signatures obtained at that time.

The Act says that the customer will have three business days from the *consummation of the contract* in which to rescind the transaction. When is the contract consummated? Some feel that the contract is consummated when the application is signed by both parties or all parties to the application. This might be true, but at this point there is only a signature of the customer, not of the creditor, and the application says that if the credit of the customer is satisfactory, if the property is of adequate value, and if property title can be delivered, the creditor will consider making a loan. That does not sound like much of a contract, does it?

Some feel that the contract is consummated when the note and deed of trust, or mortgage, is signed. Certainly there is a valid contract under these circumstances; however, some feel that there should be a contract executed before the expense of a title search, an appraisal, or the preparation of the legal documents is expended. A form is therefore used that states in effect that the customer and the creditor have reached an agreement and that one agrees to borrow and the other agrees to loan a specific amount based on certain security. It also agrees that the

FIGURE 2-3   Notice of right to rescind

(Identification of Transaction)

Notice To Customer Required By Federal Law:

You have entered into a transaction on_____which may
(Date)
result in a lien, mortgage, or other security interest on your home. You have a legal
right under federal law to cancel this transaction, if you desire to do so, without any
penalty or obligation within three business days from the above date or any later date
on which all material disclosures required under the Truth in Lending Act have been
given to you. If you so cancel the transaction, any lien, mortgage, or other security
interest on your home arising from this transaction is automatically void. You are
also entitled to receive a refund of any downpayment or other consideration if you
cancel. If you decide to cancel this transaction, you may do so by notifying

_____
(Name of Creditor)

at _____
(Address of Creditor's Place of Business)

by mail or telegram sent not later than midnight of_____. You
(Date)
may also use any other form of written notice identifying the transaction if it is
delivered to the above address not later than that time. This notice may be used for
that purpose by dating and signing below.

I hereby cancel this transaction.

_____   _____
(Date)   (Customer's signature)

EFFECT OF RESCISSION. When a customer exercises his right to rescind under paragraph (a)
of this section, he is not liable for any finance or other charge, and any security interest becomes
void upon such a rescission. Within 10 days after receipt of a notice of rescission, the creditor shall
return to the customer any money or property given as earnest money, downpayment, or otherwise,
and shall take any action necessary or appropriate to reflect the termination of any security
interest created under the transaction. If the creditor has delivered any property to the customer,
the customer may retain possession of it. Upon the performance of the creditor's obligations under
this section, the customer shall tender the property to the creditor, except that if return of the
property in kind would be impracticable or inequitable, the customer shall tender its reasonable
value. Tender shall be made at the location of the property or at the residence of the customer, at the
option of the customer. If the creditor does not take possession of the property within 10 days after
tender by the customer, ownership of the property vests in the customer without obligation on his
part to pay for it.

---

consummation date is the date of the signing, that the rescission date is three business days after the date of signing, and that the confirmation date can be the day after the rescission date. Lack of receipt of a notice of rescission does not necessarily mean that there has not been and will not be a rescission of the transaction. Therefore, confirmation of the transaction is desirable; it is received by written notice but it must be signed and dated after the rescission date. It is important that the confirmation be delivered to the creditor as soon as possible after the confirmation date, since the disclosure statement has been prepared to disclose certain items based on

certain dates. If these dates are not accurate in accordance with the facts, then a new disclosure statement must be prepared. See Tables 2-3 and 2-4 for a typical work sheet and disclosure statement given later in this chapter.

The definition of a disclosure statement given above listed the items included in the finance charge. It is necessary to list all charges which are made; however, the following are *not* included in the finance charge: recording charges, secretary of state fees, title insurance, property surveys, preparation of documents, notary fees, appraisal fees, impounds for future payment of taxes on insurance, and taxes due on security.

TABLE 2-3   Real estate loan APR work sheet

a. *Single advance loans with equal payments*

Amount of loan	$ 52,000.00
Minus prepaid finance charge	− 4,124.61
Amount financed	$ 47,875.39
Monthly payments	$ 616.20
Times number of months	× 360
Total payments	$221,832.00
Minus amount of loan	−52,000.00
Total interest	$169,832.00
Plus prepaid finance charges	+ 4,124.61
Finance charge	$173,956.61

$173,956.61 × 100 ÷ $47,875.39 =   363.35
(Finance charge)   (Amount financed)
From Federal Reserve Bank's APR table   15¼%

b. *Single advance loan with buy down* $ 12,841.92
interest rate for 24 months at 12% or
535.08 × 24

336 months at 14% or 616.20 × 336	207,043.20
Add prepaid finance charge	+ 4,124.61
	$224,009.73
Less loan amount	−52,000.00
Finance charge	$172,009.73

$172,009.73 × 100 ÷ $47,875.39 =   359.28
(Finance charge)   (Amount financed)
From Federal Reserve Bank's APR table   15¼%

c. *Single advance loan with 59 equal payments and a balloon. Payments based on 30-year term.*

Amount of loan	$ 52,000.00
Less prepaid finance charges	− 4,124.61
Amount financed	$ 47,875.00
59 Equal monthly payments at $616.20	36,355.80
Balloon payments of $50,726 plus interest for 30 days at 14%	51,317.80
Total payments	87,673.60
Less amount of loan	−52,000.00
Total interest	35,673.60
Plus repaid finance charge	+ 4,124.61
Finance charge	$ 39,798.21

39,798.21 × 100 ÷ 47,875.00 ≠   83.13
(Finance charge)   (Amount financed)
5 days' interest on $52,000 at 14% =
$101.11

The Effect of Regulation Z on Home Improvements

One of the areas the Consumer Credit Protection Act is to regulate is that of home improvements. The Act is designed to protect the consumer from the suede-shoe salespeople who use high-pressure tactics in selling aluminum siding, patio cover, fire alarm systems, water softener systems, and other additions to the present home.

In improvements such as these, a lien is given against the property. The lien may be consensual as in the case of an agreement not to encumber, or a trust deed or mortgage, or the lien may be involuntary as in the case of material or labor liens. If the lien is against the customer's principal residence, then the customer has the right of rescission and the right to cancel the transaction within three business days of the consummation of the sale or order. Of course, this also means the customer cannot be charged for any work done before the expiration of the three days. It also means that any work that is done must be undone if the right of rescission is exercised.

This portion of the Act leads to some interesting problems. For example, suppose that a mortuary located in a very hot climate suddenly has an air conditioner failure. The mortician calls the air conditioner repair shop and tells them that he needs immediate help. A repairperson goes to the mortuary and finds that a new unit is needed. He advises the mortician, who says to install the unit immediately. The repairperson asks that the mortician sign a purchase order and then advises him that the unit will be installed after the expiration of three business days. The mortician informs the repairperson that he intends to pay cash, so there is no reason to wait the three days. The repairperson replies that there are potential labor and material liens and therefore he must wait for the three days to pass. To this the mortician states that the property is a commercial property and the rights of rescission only apply to residences. The repairperson replies that the mortician lives in an apartment over the mortuary, and since he lives there all the time the property is designated as his principal residence and is subject to the rights of rescission. About this time the mortician is growing desperate. He points out that to continue without an air conditioner will endanger the property, his family, himself. The repairperson then informs the mortician that he has the right to waive his rights of rescission, but that the waiver must be in his own handwriting and must be worded by him. There can be no preprinted forms for this purpose.

Work could also be started if the workers and material supplier will waive their rights to file labor and material liens against the property. If one worker or material supplier agrees to waive lien rights, all workers and material suppliers must waive their lien rights in order for the right of rescission to be waived.

This would indicate that all repairs to a principal residence, such as replacing a water heater, installing an icemaker refrigerator, installing a 220-volt line for an electric range or clothes dryer, mending a roof, or any other repair that might involve a labor or material lien or a consensual lien, would be subject to the rights of rescission.

TABLE 2-4 Disclosure statement

ORGANIZATION The National Bank of Blueaire

ADDRESS Blueaire, California
As creditor pursuant to the Consumer Credit Protection Act, and in connection with the below described proposed loan advises

CUSTOMER John J. and Jane D. Lavender

ADDRESS 1516 Gran Blanco Way
Blueaire, California

1. Amount of credit	$ 50,675.39
Net loan balance refinance	$
Insurance credit life	$
Credit life and disability	$
Fees/charges Property	$
ITEMIZED Column B of Item 2	$
IN Column B of Item 3	$ 1,324.61
	$
Amount of loan (total of above)	$ 52,000.00
Prepaid finance charges (Item 3)	$ 4,124.61
Less required deposit balance	$
Total prepaid finance charges and required deposit balance	$ 4,124.61
AMOUNT FINANCED	**$ 47,875.39**

2. *Certain fees. Charges not included in finance charges*

	A ESTI- MATE[a]	B INCLUDED IN THE AMOUNT OF THE LOAN	C PAID SEPARATELY BY CUSTOMER OR OTHER
Records	X	$	$ 9.00
Secretary of State			
Title insurance	X		396.20
Property survey			
Preparation of papers			
Notary fees			2.00
Appraisal fees			150.00
Credit reports			10.00
Impounds for insurance			
Future tax payment			
Taxes due on property			
Taxes due on security			
Total (Column B included in Item 1)		$	$567.20

3. *Certain fees and charges included in finance charges*

	A ESTI- MATE	B INCLUDED IN THE LOAN AMOUNT	C PAID SEPARATELY BY CUSTOMER OR OTHER
Loan fee		$1,040.00	
Commitment fee			
Tax service		15.00	
Contractor's bond			
Disbursement control			
FHA mortgage insurance			
Reconvertance fee			
Escrow fee		168.50	
Finders fee			2,800.00
Termite inspection		101.11	
5 days' interest at 14% to 10-01-81			
Totals (Column B included in Item 1)		$1,324.61	2,800.00
Prepaid finance charge (Total of columns B and C)			$4,124.61

26

TABLE 2-4   **Disclosure Statement**

4. **ANNUAL PERCENTAGE RATE 15¼% *(5a)* 15¼% *(5b)* 14¼% *(5c)***

5.

a. Amounts included in finance charge

Interest (simple) at **14%** per annum on loan balance	$169,832.00
Prepaid finance charges as itemized in Item 3	$ 4,124.61
FINANCE CHARGE	**$173,956.61**

b. Interest (simple) based on **2-year** 12% buy down and **28-year** regular payment at **14%**.

	$167,885.12
Prepaid finance charges as itemized in Item 3	$ 4,124.61
FINANCE CHARGES	**$172,009.73**

c. Interest (simple) based on **5-year** note with **30-year** amortization payment and a balloon payment of **$51,317.80**. Interest rate **14%**

	$ 35,673.60
Prepaid finance charges as itemized in Item 3	$ 4,124.61
FINANCE CHARGES	**$ 39,798.21**

6.

a. **TOTAL OF PAYMENTS** including interest and principal over the term of the loan	**$221,832.00**
b. **TOTAL OF PAYMENTS** including interest and principal over term of loan for buy down	**$219,885.12**
c. **TOTAL OF PAYMENTS** including interest and principal over term of loan with balloon	**$ 87,673.60**

ªAmounts not known are estimated as shown in Column A.

Summary

It is not the intent of the Act to limit the amount of interest charged by a creditor; however, it is the intent to force creditors to disclose all aspects of a credit transaction with the disclosure being in writing and given to the customer before the consummation of the transaction.

The disclosure statement will have the words "Amount Financed," "Prepaid Finance Charge," "Finance Charge," "Total of Payment," and "Annual Percentage Rate" in larger and blacker type than any other print on the statement.

All credit transactions over $25,000, except those pertaining to real estate or agriculture, are exempt from the Act.

Credit given for the *purchase* of real estate must be disclosed to the customer in all aspects except for "Total of Payment." This transaction is not rescindable. When the credit is for refinancing, "Total of Payment" must be shown also, and such a transaction may be rescinded if it concerns the principal residence.

When credit is given that might result in a lien against a customer's principal residence, that transaction is subject to rescission, and the customer must be notified of this condition. Any person whose name is on the property title can enforce the rescission within three days after the completion of the transaction. Rescission rights can be waived, but the waiver must be in the customer's own handwriting and words. Rescission rights can be avoided by the workers and material suppliers waiving their lien rights on a home improvement transaction; however, all material suppliers and workers concerned with the transaction must waive their lien rights. Notice of rescission must be in writing. The customer can sign and date the notice that federal law requires be given him or her and either mail it to the address of the creditor shown on the notice, or deliver the notice to the creditor at the address shown, in person or by messenger. Notice of rescission may be accomplished also by sending a telegram to the creditor at the address shown, and giving a brief description of the transaction. Notice can be accomplished also by writing a letter to the creditor at the address shown and mailing the letter, or delivering the letter in person or by messenger. Notice of rescission cannot be accomplished by telephone; it must be in writing.

There is one other peculiar aspect of the Regulation. A lot bought for the purpose of constructing the principal residence of a family is considered to be the principal residence even though there is no house on the lot. When the lot is used as security for the construction loan, it is in effect a refinancing; however, the Regulation states that such a transaction is not to be considered as a rescindable transaction.

Example

Tables 2-3 and 2-4 have provisions for three types of loans: (a) 360 month maturity with 14 percent interest and equal monthly payments; (b) buy down interest for 24 months at 12 percent and 336 months with interest at

14 percent maturity of 30 years with equal monthly payments; (c) 59 months equal payments based on 30 year maturity with 14 percent interest and a balloon payment at maturity of $51,317.80. The process for completing the form for the (a) type will be discussed. By referring to one form, you should be able to see how the other types are computed.

Mr. and Mrs. Lavender want to refinance their principal residence in order to obtain approximately $48,000 to be used for another investment. They decide to go to their bank, the National Bank of Blueaire, and request a loan. The first form that is completed is an application for a real estate loan. The application is divided into two sections—a description of the property and a review of the Lavenders' assets, liabilities, income, and personal information such as where they work, how long they have held their jobs, number of dependents, amount of life insurance, and their ages. From the application a work sheet is started (see Table 2-3). The amount of the loan applied for is $52,000. The application shows that this amount will be paid back in 30 years by making payments of $616.20 each month if the interest rate is 14 percent. Since 30 years converts to 360 months, $616.20 times 360 will give the total amount that will be paid by the customer over the life of the contract—$221,832. This is one of the items that must be disclosed and can be transferred to the disclosure statement; see Table 2-4, "Total of Payments." It is necessary now to work from the disclosure statement in order to transfer certain figures to the work sheet. Some of these will be estimates and some will be known. Some of the expenses will be deducted from the amount of the loan. This is why the loan was suggested to be in the amount of $52,000 when the Lavenders wanted only $48,000. You will notice from Table 2-4 that under Section 2 there are certain fees to be paid by the customer and not deducted from the loan. You will also note that two of the figures are estimated. If these charges had been deducted from the loan, they would have been shown in Column B instead of C and would have been deducted in Section 1 immediately above the $1,324.61. This would have reduced the net loan proceeds by an additional $567.39. The amount of the loan would still be $52,000. The charges shown to this point do not affect the annual percentage rate. In Section 3 of the disclosure statement are the items that will bear directly on the annual percentage rate. The first item is the loan fee. Since this is known to be 2 percent of the loan, the amount of $1,040 is shown. The tax service is known to be $15, and this amount is entered. There will be an escrow fee in the amount of $168.50 charged by the title company. It is estimated that the deed of trust would be recorded by September 25, 1980. The first regular payment would be made on November 1, 1980; therefore, it will be necessary to collect 5 days' interest on $52,000 at 14 percent, or $101.11 as shown on the

work sheet and transferred to the disclosure statement. The National Bank of Blueaire charges a finders fee of 5.385 points. The Lavenders choose to pay this rather than have it deducted from the loan, so it is entered as $2,800 in Column C. Although this is paid separately, Regulation Z considers it a part of the prepaid finance charges. This amount is carried to Section 1 and entered immediately under "Amount of Loan." If a deposit balance of a certain amount is required at all times during the life of the loan, this amount is entered and added to the prepaid finance charges, and that figure is subtracted from the amount of the loan. In this case, the amount is $52,000, from which prepaid finance charges of $4,124.61 are deducted, leaving a balance of $47,875.39. This is another of the figures that must be disclosed. Now refer to the work sheet, Table 2-3. The amount of the loan is $52,000, and the prepaid finance charges of $4,124.61 shown on the disclosure statement are deducted from the loan amount. This gives the amount financed, or the amount that the customer will have available for his or her use. There will be 360 monthly payments of $616.20, or a total payment of $221,832—see line 6 of the work sheet. By subtracting the amount of the loan from this figure, the amount of total interest for the 30 years is obtained. The amount is $169,832. This figure will be transcribed to the disclosure statement in Section 5. The prepaid finance charges are then added to the total interest figure to obtain the total finance charge. Reference to Figure 2-4 shows the figure to be $173,956.61. This figure is also transcribed to the disclosure statement and is one of the items that must be shown in large black letters (see Section 5 of the disclosure statement). To find the annual percentage rate it is first necessary to find the cost per $100 for the life of the loan. This is done by multiplying the finance charge by $100 and dividing the result by the amount financed. Referring to the work sheet, the cost per $100 is found to be $363.35. In the annual percentage rate tables supplied by the Federal Reserve Bank, a portion of which is shown in Table 2-5, the figure closest to $363.35 is located opposite the 360 shown in the number-of-payments column. In the table the figure is circled. It is 362.40. Going up this column, we find the annual percentage rate to be 15.25 percent. The Act requires that the percentage rate be to the nearest one-quarter of 1 percent. The disclosure statement can now be completed by showing the annual percentage rate as 15.25 percent.

All aspects of the transaction have been disclosed to the customers, Mr. and Mrs. Lavender, and they can decide whether they want to accept the transaction. If they so desire, the note and deed of trust are prepared and signed by the Lavenders. This constitutes consummation, but since the transaction is for refinancing a principal residence, it is rescindable and the customers must be advised in the exact wording of Figure 2-3. The

TABLE 2-5 Federal Reserve Bank's annual percentage rate table for monthly payment plans

NUMBER OF PAYMENTS	ANNUAL PERCENTAGE RATE							
	14.00%	14.25%	14.50%	14.75%	15.00%	15.25%	15.50%	15.75%
301	262.20	267.97	273.77	279.58	285.41	291.26	297.13	303.02
302	263.27	269.07	274.88	280.72	286.58	292.45	298.34	304.25
303	264.34	270.16	276.00	281.76	287.74	293.64	299.55	305.49
304	265.42	271.26	277.12	283.00	288.91	294.83	300.77	306.72
305	266.49	272.36	278.24	284.15	290.07	296.02	301.98	307.96
356	322.13	329.17	336.23	343.31	350.41	357.52	364.65	371.80
357	323.23	330.13	337.38	344.48	351.60	358.74	365.89	373.06
358	324.34	331.43	338.53	345.66	352.80	359.96	367.14	374.33
359	325.45	332.56	339.69	346.83	354.00	361.18	368.38	375.59
360	326.55	333.69	340.84	348.01	355.20	(362.40)	369.63	376.86

Effect of Rescission printed at the bottom of Figure 2-3 may be printed on the reverse side of the notice of the rights of rescission. Shortly after the expiration of the three-day waiting period, the creditor will probably have the customer sign a statement indicating he or she does not intend to rescind the transaction, and the loan will be completed; however, if the customer delivers the notice of rescission within the three-day period, the transaction will be cancelled and no charges can be made to the customer for expenses incurred by the creditor.

A whole chapter has been devoted to the Federal Reserve Bank because, if you are going to be able to understand interest rates and make an educated guess concerning their rise and fall, you must have an understanding of the Federal Reserve Bank in order to interpret its actions. In conjunction with understanding the Federal Reserve Bank's actions, watch the interest rate on ninety-day United States Treasury bills. The rate fluctuations reflect the actions of the Federal Reserve Bank to increase or decrease money and credit supply. It is an excellent and accurate indicator.

QUESTIONS

1. The Federal Reserve Bank, as authorized by the Federal Reserve Act of December 23, 1913, controls
   a. member banks
   b. insurance companies
   c. private lenders
   d. mortgage bankers

2. The major function of the Federal Reserve Bank in 1982 is to
   a. provide insurance for bank depositors
   b. regulate the various stock and commodity exchanges
   c. regulate the flow of money and credit in an effort to control inflation
   d. provide financing for the Federal Home Loan Mortgage Corporation

3. Purchase of United States Government bonds by the Federal Reserve Bank would
   a. increase the amount of money banks would have to loan
   b. only be done during a period of inflation
   c. result in a recession
   d. none of the above

4. If a bank's reserves fall below the legal limit, the bank must deposit enough money in its reserve account to clear the deficiency. It may get the funds by
   a. selling bonds from its bond portfolio
   b. borrowing from other banks
   c. borrowing from the Federal Reserve Bank
   d. all of the above

5. There are seven members of the Federal Reserve Bank Board of Governors. They are nominated by
   a. the President of the United States and ratified by the Senate
   b. Congress and approved by the President
   c. the presidents of the district Federal Reserve Banks and approved by the President
   d. none of the above

6. Each Federal Reserve Bank Board member is appointed for a term of fourteen years, with
   a. each member's term expiring at the same time
   b. each member resigning when a new President is elected
   c. a new Board member being appointed for a full term on the death or resignation of one of the present Board
   d. one term expiring every two years

7. The actions of the Federal Reserve Bank Board can influence
   a. the New York Stock Exchange
   b. the interest rates charged by lenders
   c. the money supply
   d. all of the above

8. The Federal Reserve Bank cannot make loans to which of the following:
   a. savings and loan associations
   b. state-chartered banks
   c. national banks
   d. individuals

9. The district Federal Reserve Bank has a board of directors. How many different classes of directors for each district are there?
   a. one
   b. two
   c. three
   d. four

10. How do individuals become directors?
    a. They are elected by member banks.
    b. They are appointed by the president of the district bank.
    c. They are appointed by the Federal Reserve Board of Governors.
    d. Some are appointed by the Federal Reserve Bank Board of Governors and some are elected by the member banks.

BIBLIOGRAPHY

Board of Governors of the Federal Reserve Bank, "Federal Reserve Bulletin", Published Monthly.

Board of Governors of the Federal Reserve Bank, "Annual Report of the Board of Governors of the Federal Reserve Bank."

Federal Reserve Bank, "The Federal Reserve System—Purposes Functions, 1974."

Federal Reserve Bank, "The Federal Reserve Act as Amended".

3

The Mortgage Money Market and Its Relation to the Economy

This chapter is concerned primarily with the structure, functions, and operations of the mortgage money market and with its relationship to the availability and cost of real estate loans. While it is difficult to predict accurately the long-term cost and availability of credit for real estate loans, such prediction must nevertheless be done by institutional lenders and persons participating in borrowing decisions. Failure to study the mortgage money market and to make reasonably accurate predictions of price and supply trends can have adverse results when attempts are made to borrow in order to finance real estate. The unsatisfactory results can be failure to obtain a loan at all due to the absence of lendable funds, payment of a comparatively high interest rate, or ability to obtain a loan only for a relatively short term.

To deal with this subject competently, we must first understand its vital concerns.

MONEY MARKET

The money (or credit) market consists of the lending and borrowing that take place between those in need of funds and those with money to lend. Today this market is not located in one place, as is, for example, the New York Stock Exchange. Since modern communications facilitate the arrangement of loans, it exists virtually on a national basis. If there is one major money market in the United States, however, it is in New York City, because major banks, industrial corporations, and the very important Federal Reserve Bank of New York are located there. The loan transactions of these parties are significant enough to have a decided effect upon monetary supply, demand, and price.

CAPITAL MARKET

The capital market may be thought of as an institution, such as a stock exchange, where new issues of securities are offered to the public at a price and where transactions

regarding these securities are carried on for interested parties through intermediaries.

MORTGAGE MONEY MARKET

The mortgage money market is composed of parties with funds to lend on real estate and of borrowers or borrowers' representatives who negotiate for the use of such funds. This business may be conducted by borrowers who, after obtaining a loan, will in turn lend the borrowed funds, or by debtors who will use the credit obtained for their own purposes.

BUSINESS CYCLE

The operations of the money market will be affected by the business cycle, that phenomenon common to an economic system such as ours. This cycle can be described as a sequence of changes in the amount or level of business activity, and is commonly considered to have four phases: (1) depression, (2) revival, (3) prosperity, and (4) recession. Each phase has particular characteristics that will affect the money market.

REAL ESTATE CYCLE

The real estate cycle is a means of describing changes in the level of real estate activity alone. The same general terms used to describe the identifiable phases of the business cycle can be applied to this more specialized concept. A relatively high degree of similarity exists between the actions of these two cycles, because to some extent the same economic forces operate to produce each cycle, and thus whatever assists or depresses one cycle will very likely have a similar effect upon the other. The business cycle at the prosperity phase, for example, is characterized by a high level of profitable economic activity, and the real estate cycle at such time is identifiable by a high level of sales transactions, construction, and borrowing activity.

Since 1946 the typical patterns of business and real estate cycles have been more moderate than the economic crash of 1929 and the prolonged Depression of the 1930s. Business and real estate cycles still exist as an economic fact of life, and therefore anyone dealing with the financing of real estate in a successful manner must always be aware of these phenomena. Because of the federal government's commitment to full employment and a relatively high level of economic activity under the Employment Act of 1946, after this year, the general business cycle was smoothed out in a comparative sense. Its continued existence, however, is proven by the recessions in years such as 1954, 1958, 1960, 1970, 1974–75, mid-1980, with a short revival phase in the latter part of 1981, followed by a deep recession that continued well into 1982. There have also been economic booms such as the one that began in 1971, roared on through 1972, subsided in 1973, and was followed by the major recession of 1974–75.

The deep recession of 1981–82 was very serious compared with what happened to major segments of the country's economy in previous recessions. During this economic downturn, several major elements of the American economy such as housing construction and sales, automobile manufacturing, the aerospace industry, the thrift industry (savings and loan associations and mutual savings banks), and timber cutting and lumber production, were simultaneously reduced to prolonged depressed levels of lower economic activity. The depressed levels of economic activity and profitability of concerns making up these economic keystones of the American economy started in 1980 and continued through 1981 and well on into 1982. The immense adverse economic impact of the depressed state of these significant basic vital industries in the United States created economic crises in various regions of the country. The original homes of the automobile industry—the states of Michigan, Ohio, Indiana, Illinois, and Wisconsin—suffered massive economic losses because of much lower rates of car production accompanied by the inability of the manufacturers to conduct profitable production and sales activities. What can correctly be called a depression in the automobile industry resulted in massive layoffs of personnel on car assembly lines as well as severely curtailing employment in parts manufacturing firms. As basic employment in "automobile towns" fell drastically, the entire economy of this region of the country went into a recession because large layoffs in this basic industry reduced secondary employment in the local economies and generally reduced household income. The depressed state of the automobile industry affected the economic base of certain sections of California with the closing of car assembly plants in Los Angeles and the San Francisco Bay Area. Markedly reduced residential construction volume in the United States has reduced employment and production volume in the timber and lumber industry of the Pacific Northwest to near historic lows. As if this alone was not enough of a blow to the basic economy of this area, new orders for airplanes for Boeing in Seattle, Washington, have all but disappeared as airline after airline suffering millions of dollars in annual losses canceled orders for new planes that they could not pay for. New housing unit production in the United States went from 2,020,300 units in 1978 to 1,745,100 units in 1979, to 1,292,200 in 1980, to an annual rate of 918,000 in September 1981. This falling rate of new housing production produced a domino effect in the employment of all sorts of other industries such as roofing, electrical wiring, appliances, plumbing, plastics, fabrics, windows, cement, bricks, paint, and insulation.

There have been four severe economic downturns during the past 50 to 60 years, namely, the crash of 1929, the long continuing Great Depression of the 1930s, the deep recession of 1974–75, and the deeper recession of 1981–82. The last two recessions have been accompanied by higher than usual interest rates, stifling economic recovery in such industries as automobiles, and real estate and housing.

One of the most difficult aspects of the latest recession is that it has occurred when interest rates such as the Federal Reserve Bank discount rate (ranging from 12 to 14 percent in 1981–82), the commercial bank prime rate (ranging from 16.5 to 20.5 percent in 1981–82), and the real estate residential purchase money mortgage loan rate (16.5 to 18.5 percent) were at nearly historic highs for the twentieth century. These high interest rates existed for various reasons: The Federal Reserve Bank tried to reduce the annual inflation rate through a policy of credit restraint; commercial banks charged higher interest rates to compensate for higher interest costs to them in order to retain existing accounts and attract new ones, thus adding an "inflation factor" of more interest to account for the expected continuance of inflation; and real estate mortgage lenders increased interest rates on mortgage loans to compensate for the higher cost of money to them, expected future inflation, and the somewhat higher risk in making such secured real estate loans. The severity and duration of the 1981–82 recession and the great damage it has done to major industries in this country distinguish it from any recession since the Great Depression of the 1930s. It is expected, therefore, to result in major changes in the structure and function of the financial institutions of the country such as commercial banks, savings and loan associations, and mutual savings banks. These changes will occur as the federal and state governments, executives of these real estate lenders, and insurance agencies such as the Federal Savings and Loan Insurance Corporation and the Federal Deposit Insurance Corporation adapt statutes, regulations, and practices to the new, more difficult, economic situation.

The local real estate cycle is often of greater importance to real estate lenders than the general business cycle. The greater significance of local real estate activity and market conditions is due to the direct relationship between the level of real estate activity governed by the real estate cycle and the amount of money borrowed for real estate purchases and construction. Therefore, the real estate finance professional must be familiar with the status of the national economy generally and knowledgeable about the state of the local real estate cycle specifically.

SUPPLY AND DEMAND FOR LOANABLE FUNDS

The level of business activity in general and of real estate in particular affects the supply and demand for lendable funds. Past experience generally indicates that, as a rule, when business activity increases it adds to the income of people and they tend to save more, thus increasing the total dollar amount of savings. (An exception to this rule occurred in the years 1978, 1979, and part of 1980, when the annual rate of savings as a percentage of disposable personal income was below 6.0 percent at levels of 5.2, 5.2, and 5.6 percent, respectively.) The major explanations for the decrease in the percentages of disposable personal income saved during this period were

1. A relatively high rate of inflation, making goods and services more expensive. As a result, people felt "poorer."
2. "Bracket creep" in the federal income tax schedules of taxpayers; for instance, if they received a pay increase to compensate for an annual 10 percent increase in the consumer price index, this increased compensation would place them in a higher tax bracket, causing them to have to pay more federal income taxes and to have reduced purchasing power of the dollar due to inflation. Thus they had less real income.
3. Annual rates of inflation of 10 percent and more created an "inflationary psychology" in the United States, which translated into the "buy-it-now-and-borrow-to-do-it" ethic because the car, appliance, or house you want will cost more next year.
4. Some people found themselves in an economic condition called "stagflation," wherein they experienced reductions in income due to losing jobs or working less while prices went up. Thus, they just did not have as much money to save as they did before.

When the business cycle is in the recovery or boom phase, there is usually an initial surge in the percent of disposable personal income saved. This percent declines as prices increase, and a general aura of well-being seems to stimulate a tendency to spend money rather than to save it.

Toward the end of 1981 and through 1982 a greater percentage of disposable personal income was being saved because (1) the public's "inflationary psychology" lessened, (2) more people became fearful of their economic future as the recession deepened, (3) the federal government enacted changes in the federal income tax law which reduced personal income tax rates over a period of three years, and (4) special savings plans were introduced that exempted deposits and interest in certain savings accounts and plans from federal income taxation. So as the year 1982 commenced, certain segments of the population had more money to save and were motivated to do so by the lessened inflation rate, reduced income tax liability, and the relatively high yields on certificates of deposit and other types of accounts.

A recent negative development in terms of increasing the supply of funds for real estate loans through the mortgage money market due to increases in the percentage of disposable income saved from the year 1978 is the development of mutual investment funds called *money market funds*. These funds are investment vehicles similar in purpose and operation to real estate investment trusts. However, money market funds use the funds people invest with them to invest in high interest–yielding debt securities such as those issued by state and local government entities. The money under their control is usually not available for loans or investments in real estate. The main attraction of money market fund investments to individuals is the very high yields achieved. Another attraction is that, after the investor receives the interest, much of it is not subject to state or federal income taxes. These funds obtain money from the current wages and salaries of investors as well as from depositors in savings and loan associations, mutual savings banks, and commercial banks who withdraw money from lower yielding accounts. The result, since 1974, has been an increasing disintermediation problem for financial institutions that finance real estate and a massive decrease in the supply of money available to finance real estate activities. The magnitude of this diversion of money from institutional lenders that finance real estate is indicated by the growth of the assets of money market funds—in 1974 $2 billion, in 1977 $4 billion, in 1978 $11 billion, in 1981 $200 billion. There is no indication that the ability of money market funds to attract funds controlled by individuals will diminish very soon.

As a result of this intense, very effective competition from money market funds and other investments (such as United States Treasury bills), regulating authorities for savings and loan associations and commercial banks authorized new certificate-type accounts that afforded depositors higher yields on the money deposited. This slowed the shift of money—to some extent—out of these institutional real estate lenders, but it also raised the cost of funds to the institutions to an average of 12 percent by 1982. To obtain a reasonable profit on operations when making mortgage loans, these real estate lenders usually need an interest rate margin of 1.5 to 2 percent over the cost of money to them.

The result of this situation is obvious—a prime conventional purchase money mortgage interest rate minimum of 14.5 to 16 percent. When such an annual interest rate was coupled with large increases in the market price of housing, such as occurred between 1975 to 1980, the median price of "just a house on a lot" in Southern California rose to $100,000 by 1981–82. This situation resulted in a conventional long-term purchase money loan at 80 percent of value, 16 percent per annum, for thirty years, with 360 monthly payments of $1,075.81. If a traditional monthly borrower income standard is applied to this monthly mortgage loan obligation (the debtor should not pay more than 25 percent of assured monthly income for housing expense), a minimally financially qualified buyer-borrower must have a monthly income of at least $4,303.24 or an annual income of $51,638.88. With the median annual household income at about half the required $51,638.88, hardly 10 percent of the households in the United States were really financially qualified to obtain the required standard conventional institutional loan. Thus there was a substantial reduction in demand for purchase money real estate loans, resulting in typical institutional lenders having a reduced volume of loans and in fewer would-be buyers of housing able to afford the needed loans. Thus the volume of real estate sales at these interest rates declined.

It should be noted that during 1978–82 in major urban areas of California, 70 to 80 percent or more of purchase money loans by traditional institutional real estate lenders to finance home purchases were not the familiar type of loan at 80 percent of value, 20- or 39-year fixed interest rate. Rather, they were variable rate loans (VRMs), wherein the interest rate went up or down according to an agreed index. The lender, with suitable notification, could charge more or less interest during the repayment period of the secured real estate loan. This VRM loan interest arrangement added uncertainty to the cost of purchase money financing from the usual institutional lenders and added impetus to the use of "creative alternative" financing arrangements that did not directly involve financial institutions making new purchase money loans in sales situations.

Major results of this dilemma of supply and cost of institutional real estate mortgage money have been

1. A much less active residential real estate market in both construction and sales volume

2. Less profitable savings and loan and commercial bank operations

3. Increased use of innovative purchase money loan financing arrangements, wherein the buyers of used houses assume existing, relatively low-interest, institutional mortgage loans. (This was made possible since 1978 by the California Supreme Court's *Wellenkamp* decision, which nullified enforceability of due-on-sale clauses in such loans made by California-chartered savings and loans and commercial banks. Federally chartered savings and loan associations and commercial banks contend that the decision does not apply to them because of their federal charters and the jurisdiction of the federal government over them.) In these arrangements, the seller finances much of the difference between the sale price and the balance of the assumed loan by taking back a large second trust deed

4. Reduction of the interest rate paid by home buyers through such devices as (a) mortgages funded by government bond issues, wherein the interest paid to the bond holders is not taxable as income by either state or federal governments. Thus the cost of money is lower (often resulting in a mortgage loan interest reduction of 3 to 5 percent to the borrower); (b) "buying down" interest rates by residential developers paying lenders money "up front" to maintain an acceptable yield to the lender on the loan made, thereby providing buyers with a lower than market interest rate; and (c) the seller of a house accepting a lower than market level interest rate on the relatively large second mortgage loan taken back from the buyer to finance most of the sale price of the property sold.

So, as the decade of the 1980s commences, a major change in sources of mortgage money for home purchasers and others has occurred, namely, traditional institutional suppliers of real estate money in California—savings and loan associations and commercial banks—are no longer the dominant suppliers of the needed funds. Other sources and other methods predominate. The major change has been to make individuals and other noninstitutional suppliers of mortgage money more vital than ever in the supplying of the funds needed to finance real estate sales and other types of activities. This dramatic change in the source of vital funds to complete financing plans for sales and development will likely continue until interest rates on real estate loans are reduced to 11 percent or less.

NATIONAL INCOME, SAVINGS, AND INVESTMENTS

The gross national product (GNP) is a measure of the goods and services produced by the nation during any one calendar year. This measure of national economic activity (in current dollars) has increased from $363.1 billion in 1954 to $618.5 billion in 1964, to $2,626.1 billion in 1980, to approximately $2,947 billion in 1981. The GNP, measured in 1972 dollars, amounted to $1,500 billion in 1981. In 1954 personal savings amounted to

$18.9 billion, $35.4 billion in 1964, $84 billion in 1975, $68 billion in 1976, $67 billion in 1977, $77 billion in 1978, $86.2 billion in 1979, $101.3 billion in 1980, and about $100 billion in 1981. As a percentage of disposable personal income saved for the various years, the percentage is low—definitely less than 6 percent or barely at that level. During these years there was typically a strong upward trend in real estate mortgage loan interest rates. From 1970 through 1976, the percent of disposable personal income saved was typically close to or above 6 percent of this income, sometimes getting up to the level of about 8 percent. During the seven years from 1970 through 1976, real estate mortgage interest rates tended to increase, but not by as much as they did from 1977 through 1981–82. While factors other than the reduced rates of disposable income saved also affected these interest rates, causing them to increase markedly, the reduction in the rate of increase in the pool of funds available to financial intermediaries for the making of mortgage loans was undoubtedly also a significant factor in causing interest rates to increase. Total private investment, in current dollars, increased from $144.2 billion in 1970 to $229.8 billion in 1973, falling to $228.7 billion in 1974, declining further to $206.1 billion in 1975, increasing to $257.9 billion in 1976 as the deep recession ended, and amounting to $395.3 billion in 1980 and about $450 billion in 1981. These data from the United States Department of Commerce illustrate the proportion of savings and investment to the gross national product as well as the changes in growth that have occurred. Obviously, any reduction in the amount of personal savings or in the proportionate relationship to gross national product may well increase the cost of real estate credit while at the same time limit its availability. During 1977–81, the inadequacy of the supply of real estate mortgage money, due in part to the reduced percentage of disposable income saved, was made worse by newcomers to the investment community such as money market funds, which drew off a substantial amount of funds from real estate intermediaries.

POLICIES OF FEDERAL GOVERNMENT AGENCIES AFFECTING REAL ESTATE CREDIT

The Federal Reserve system is the federal agency that controls the flow and supply of credit in the United States. Consequently, its activities affect the cost of real estate credit. One of the Federal Reserve's primary concerns during 1979–82 was to combat the inflationary surge in the United States. The Board of Governors of the Federal Reserve tries to counteract inflationary and deflationary movements within the national economy and also to create conditions favorable to high levels of employment,

stable values, national growth, and a rising level of consumption. The Board believes that double-digit inflation rates work against these aims. Therefore, during this period of time it continued to pursue a tight money policy by (1) increasing the discount rate to 14 percent in 1981, and later to 12 percent in 1982; (2) increasing member bank reserve requirements in 1980; (3) using "moral suasion" (indicating to banks seeking to borrow at the discount window that they were not welcome): and (4) limiting the growth of the money supply through open-market committee operations. As the cost of money increases for commercial borrowers and the supply relative to demand is reduced, similar changes usually occur in the mortgage money market.

Whenever residential purchase money mortgages are expensive to borrowers and in short supply, Congress may take action to increase the supply of such funds and reduce interest rates on them. Such a phenomenon is a classic example of one segment of the federal government counteracting the effect of actions taken by another. The result is a nullification of one agency's actions and a vague definition of effective financial policy. These types of direct policy and action cross-purposes have occasionally occurred since the mid-1940s and will likely be repeated in the future.

SUPPLY OF MORTGAGE FUNDS IN WESTERN STATES

Historically, the West has always lacked capital and therefore has had to obtain it from the financial centers of the East. Although this shortage has been less critical in certain years as far as mortgage credit is concerned, California usually finds itself in the situation of an inadequate supply of reasonably priced real estate loan funds. There have been four periods of serious shortage recently: during the mid-1950s, 1966–70, 1974, and 1980–82. An adequate supply of real estate credit has historically been available in California, but at a somewhat higher interest rate than in Eastern states. For most of the twentieth century, California real estate borrowers have paid a premium in interest for real estate loans, sometimes as much as 20 to 35 percent more than borrowers in Midwestern, Northeastern, and Southern states. During the period of nationwide high interest rates commencing in 1979 and continuing into the decade of the 1980s, California rates tended to be about the same as those in Eastern states.

For more than forty years California has had a usury statute limit of a 10 percent interest rate, basically applicable to all secured real estate lenders in the state except savings and loan associations and commercial banks. This meant that savings and loan associations and commercial banks could make real estate loans at any interest rate obtainable from borrowers, but that no other lenders could make such loans at more than 10 percent per annum even if they were responding to important factors affecting interest rates, such as the cost of loanable funds to them, future inflationary expectations, or the interest rates that could be obtained on loans in other states. This restriction affected such lenders as life insurance companies, real estate investment trusts, individuals, mortgage companies, mortgage loan brokers, pension funds, credit unions, syndicates, real estate brokers, and commercial bank trust departments. Therefore, during shortages of mortgage loan funds when interest rates would exceed 10 percent nationally, major sources of real estate credit were denied access to financing real estate in California. In November 1979, this usury statute was repealed by a voter ballot initiative known as Proposition 2. It became effective November 7, 1979. Technically, Proposition 2 amended Article XV, Section 1, of the California Constitution and California Civil Code, sections 1916–1 and those following. Proposition 2 removed the old 10 percent per annum maximum interest rate from real estate loans made by important lenders such as those given above. One of the more significant sources of real estate credit not subject to the usury law after the passage of Proposition 2 was the real estate broker, who could now make loans or arrange them on behalf of an individual to finance real estate.

After the passage of Proposition 2, the 10 percent per annum usury statute maximum was still applicable to individuals who wanted to loan money directly on real estate in bad faith, that is, with malicious intent to exceed the 10 percent per annum interest rate maximum. Such a loan is still illegal. Now, after the passage of Proposition 2, if the seller of property finances part of the sale price using a land contract, trust deed, or mortgage and if the transaction is a good faith transaction or if it is arranged through a real estate broker, any reasonable annual rate of interest may be legally charged, even if it is in excess of 10 percent per annum.

Proposition 2 greatly increased the potential supply of mortgage credit in California after 1979, although the borrowers may well have had to pay more than 10 percent per annum interest to borrow funds. While this is, in a historic sense, quite interesting, the alternative would have been no secured real estate loans available at all to most potential borrowers. When there is no mortgage money available to most borrowers, there is inevitably, little construction, refinancing, or sales activity.

In 1980 the federal government, by enacting the Depository Institution Deregulation and Monetary Control Act of 1980 (effective April 1, 1980), nullified certain provisions of the usury sections of California law that were inconsistent with this new federal statute. The effect of this 1980 Congressional action was to nullify after March 31, 1980 any state law limiting the rate or amount of interest, discount points, finance charges, or other charges that may be charged, taken, received, or reserved on a "federally related loan," that is, on a loan made by a federally chartered, regulated, or insured lender and secured by a first lien on (1) residential real property, (2) stock in a residential cooperative housing corporation when the loan is used to finance the acquisition of such stock, or (3) a residential manufactured unit. This federal statute nullifying state usury statute interest limitations expires on March 31, 1985 unless Congress renews it.

California's Proposition 2 and the federal government's Depository Institution Deregulation and Monetary Control Act of 1980 have virtually eliminated usury statute maximum interest rate limitations on most real estate loans made in California, at least until March 31, 1985

THE OUTLINE OF THE MORTGAGE MONEY MARKET

The essence of the mortgage money market is that funds are typically made available through financial intermediaries who obtain the money from depositors-investors through depository accounts, pension funds, insurance policies, or corporate-type securities, or mortgages on a future loan or existing loan basis. The accumulated funds are then made available to borrowers—or equity capital users—through the following institutional and noninstitutional intermediary sources of funds.

FINANCIAL INSTITUTION INTERMEDIARIES

Savings and loan associations (ultimate sale to FHLMC or FNMA)

Mutual savings banks (ultimate sale to FNMA)

Life insurance companies (could sell to FNMA)

Commercial banks (could sell to FNMA)

NONINSTITUTIONAL SOURCES

Pension funds

Mortgage companies (could sell to FNMA)

Mortgage loan brokers

Government (direct loans by Cal-Vet, Farmers Home Loan Administration, Federal Housing Administration, Veterans Administration, Small Business Administration, California Housing Finance Agency)

Credit unions

Individuals

General business corporations

Syndicates (limited partnerships, general partnerships, corporations)

Finance companies (such as Household, Beneficial, Dial)

Real peoperty securities dealers (licensed real estate brokers, often mortgage loan brokers)

Commercial bank trust departments

Real estate investment trusts

Bonds (state and local government bonds, private bonds)

Personal property brokers

It should be noted that during the 1980–82 period of real estate mortgage credit, which was accompanied by high interest rates (see Figure 3-1), secondary mortgage market investors, the Federal National Mortgage Association (FNMA) and Federal Home Loan Mortgage Company (FHLMC) in particular, have been very significant as ultimate sources of real estate credit. They are, in effect, buying residential mortgages after or before they exist. These investors usually dictate the standards for loans (amount, acceptable collateral property, credit-worthiness of borrower, down payments, and repayment terms) made by locally based lenders such as savings and loan associations, commercial banks, and mortgage companies. Since many primary (local) institutional-type real estate lenders only make residential property loans that can be readily sold in the secondary market to investors such as the Federal National Mortgage Association and the Federal Home Loan Mortgage Company, the minimum property valuation and debtor credit standards for buying such loans have become *the* standards for obtaining credit to buy residential properties in local market areas.

MAKING THE MORTGAGE MONEY MARKET WORK FOR YOU

A borrower, or anyone advising a borrower, wants to borrow the largest sums of money when the availability of funds is highest and the cost is lowest. Accomplishment of this feat will be facilitated by (1) knowing the present state of the national business cycle; (2) being aware of any particular problems or policies that may reduce the supply of mortgage credit or increase its cost; (3) knowing the present phase of the local real estate cycle; and (4) formulating a knowledgeable opinion of the total national demand for credit and of the demand for real estate credit in the local area. By gathering the economic information concerning all those areas that influence the mortgage money market, one can formulate a learned opinion on the present state and immediate future of that market, which will be of assistance to any prospective borrower. The fundamental principle of the mortgage money market is that it is subject to sudden extreme fluctuations in the cost of borrowing and the availability of funds. Wise real estate mortgage lenders and borrowers will watch and predict trends so that they can maximize their lending or borrowing activities during periods when the condition of the mortgage money market is most favorable to them.

FIGURE 3-1

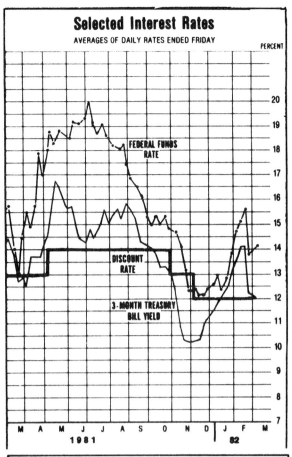

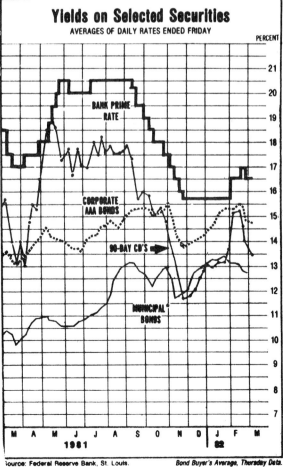

Source: Federal Reserve Bank, St. Louis.   Bond Buyer's Average, Thursday Data.

QUESTIONS

1. The mortgage money market is composed of
   a. lenders
   b. borrowers
   c. governmental organizations
   d. financial intermediaries
   e. all of the above

2. The annual supply of real estate mortgage money depends upon
   a. how many savings and loan associations there are
   b. whether or not the U.S. Treasury Department is still selling bonds to individuals
   c. the general level of national business activity
   d. whether or not new inventions of national significance have been developed
   e. none of the above

3. Real estate mortgage borrowers can make the mortgage money market work for them by
   a. reading the financial page of the local newspaper daily
   b. knowing who the members of the Federal Reserve Bank's Board of Governors are
   c. knowing what the next six months' weather forecast is
   d. being aware of the present state of the national business cycle
   e. all of the above

4. The size of the supply and the cost to real estate borrowers of mortgage money in any given year is dependent upon
   a. the percentage of the labor force that is unemployed
   b. the annual rate of inflation in this country
   c. the level of interest rates on debt-type securities offered by governmental and other investment entities that receive personal funds for investment
   d. the annual volume of life insurance company policy sales
   e. all of the above

BIBLIOGRAPHY

BEATON, WILLIAM R., *Real Estate Finance*, Englewood Cliffs, NJ: Prentice-Hall, 1982, Chapter 2.

CASE, FREDERICK E., and JOHN M. CLAPP, *Real Estate Financing*, New York: John Wiley, 1978, Chapter 3.

HINES, MARY ALICE, *Real Estate Finance*, Englewood Cliffs, NJ: Prentice-Hall, 1978, Chapter 3.

HOAGLAND, HENRY E., LEO D. STONE, and WILLIAM B. BRUEGGEMAN, *Real Estate Finance* (6th ed.), Homewood, IL: Richard D. Irwin, 1977, Chapter 14.

4

Creative Finance and Noninstitutional Lenders

By 1978 the Federal Reserve Bank had placed such heavy restrictions on the growth of money and credit that banks and conventional lenders found themselves without adequate funds to make all of the loans requested. This resulted in ever-increasing interest rates, and, in some cases, the rejection of all real estate loan applications. In order for real property to be sold, it became necessary to find some way to find financing that would provide monthly payments the buyer could afford. The following are some of the programs that were developed over the years.

One of the biggest problems for the first-time home buyer is the down payment. There are several sources that might be explored.

Cash Value Life Insurance

Many times there is a life insurance policy that has a cash value, if not on the life of the buyer, then on some member of the family who would be willing to obtain a low-interest loan for the benefit of the buyer.

Equity Loan

The buyer often has property, real or personal, in which he or she has equity. A loan can be arranged against this equity. When buyers are trying to sell their present home and buy a new home, a bridge or equity loan can be arranged against the equity on the current home. Loans against personal property such as automobiles, boats, trailers, stocks or bonds, and furniture can be arranged.

Loans from Relatives

Sometimes it is possible to borrow the down payment from a relative with no payment due until the property is sold. Such loans are interest free in many cases. Parents and grandparents are anxious to see their children and grandchildren established and gladly help them if they can afford it.

Cosigners

Most buyers of a first home are financially weak and a relative or a friend may help with the down payment and cosign the note and trust deed.

Swing or Bridge Loan

These are temporary loans that usually carry a higher interest rate than normal loans. They can sometimes be made unsecured against future earnings as well as against equities.

METHODS OF CREATIVE FINANCE

Another problem facing home buyers is choosing the best possible method of creative financing. Following is a list of some of the most common methods.

Assumption of seller's existing loan
Assumption by the buyer and giving of a junior lien by the seller
Wraparound (all-inclusive) trust deed or mortgage
Multiple junior liens
Real estate installment sale contract, also known as a real estate land contract
Builder participation (buying down rate, sales subsidy)
Shared appreciation trust deed or mortgage (SAM) or appreciation participation mortgage (APM)
Equity participation deed of trust or mortgage
Subordinated fee loan or streamlined trust deed on mortgage
Renegotiable rate trust deed or mortgage (RRM), also known as rollover trust deed or mortgage
Variable rate mortgage or trust deed (VRM)
Flexi loan
Adjustable rate loan or adjustable rate mortgage (ARM)
Graduated payment mortgage or trust deed (GPM)
Partnership, coowner, ticket

39

Piggyback loans, hard money junior liens, or tandem loans

Swing or bridge loans

Time sharing

Sell the improvements and lease the land

Lease-purchase agreement

Exchange

Cash rebate

Graduated payment adjustable interest mortgage (GPAIM) or graduated payment adjustable mortgage loan (GPAML)

Price level adjustment mortgage (PLAM)

Growing equity mortgage (GEM)

Builder approach to creative finance

METHODS OF FINANCING PURCHASE

Assumption of Seller's Existing Loan

There are some loans that cannot be assumed. All HUD-FHA and Veterans loans can be assumed at the present time. In 1978 the Supreme Court ruled in the case of *Wellenkamp* v. *Bank of America* that the due-on-sale clause could not be enforced by an institutional lender unless its position was placed in jeopardy by the assumption. The ruling does not affect individuals holding trust deeds with due-on-sale clauses. On June 2, 1981, the California Court of Appeals ruled in the case of *Panko and Sinclair* v. *Pan American Federal Savings and Loan Association* that federally chartered savings and loan associations fell under the *Wellenkamp* v. *Bank of America* decision and could not enforce the due-on-sale clause unless the loan was placed in jeopardy.[1]

---

[1]On June 28, 1982, the United States Supreme Court handed down its decision on *Fidelity Federal Savings and Loan* v. *De La Cuesta*. This decision makes it possible for all federal savings and loan associations to enforce the due-on-sale clause in their trust deeds.

This will lead to many state-chartered savings and loan associations switching to federal charters, unless the California State Legislature passes a bill making the Wellenkamp decision null and void.

Also, on October 15, 1982, President Reagan signed the Garn–St. Germain Depository Institutions Act. This Act allows lenders that make conventional loans with due-on-sale clauses in their papers after October 15, 1982, to enforce the due-on-sale clause, unless there are state regulations restricting the enforcement of the due-on-sale clause. If no such restriction exists, then the due-on-sale clause can be enforced on all conventional loans made prior to October 15, 1982 as well. However, unless those states banning the enforcement of the due-on-sale clause do not act within three years to extend the restriction, the lenders will be free to enforce their due-on-sale clauses.

The Federal Home Loan Bank has, under its regulations, allowed federal savings and loan associations to enforce their due-on-sale clauses on all of their conventional loans. The *De La Cuesta* decision has reenforced its position.

The National banks' regulators might possibly be able to make similar regulations.

Assumption by the Buyer and Giving of a Junior Lien by the Seller

For example, a home sells for $100,000. Twenty-five years remain on a thirty-year loan of $48,000 at 9 percent, on which monthly interest and principal payments are $386.23. The current balance is $46,032. The buyer makes a down payment of $19,968, and the seller takes back a note for $34,000, which is secured by a short-term junior lien payable over a period of ten years and having monthly payments of $358.02 including interest at 12 percent. At maturity, there will be a balloon payment of $29,852. This will make a monthly payment, including the assumed loan, of $744.25, including interest and principal. If the sale had been made as a straight real estate loan, the rate would have been approximately 14 percent on $80,000, given an interest and principal payment of $908 per month for thirty years. In the example given above, the seller could have taken a note with the same payment without the balloon payment for a period of twenty-five years, and both notes would have matured at the same time.

The amounts, payments, terms, and interest rate are different in each potential sale and depend on the agreement that the seller and buyer reach.

ADVANTAGES

a.   Allows buyers to buy a home they might not have been able to buy under normal loan requirements.

b.   Allows a lower interest rate than the prevailing rate.

DISADVANTAGES

a.   Seller must be in a position to take over first loan in case of default.

b.   Unless the trust deed provides for notice of default, the seller may never know of a default before the first trust deed is foreclosed.

c.   The seller must be in position to pay off note and trust deed if the lending agency will not allow the takeover of the first lien.

Wraparound (All-Inclusive) Trust Deed or Mortgage

Use the example above and assume a $20,000 down payment. The seller takes back a junior lien for $80,000 at 11 percent for twenty-five years but could take it beyond the maturity of the first lien if the seller is willing. Let us assume a junior lien for twenty-five years in this case. The buyer would then make payments of $761.60 per month for twenty-five years to the seller. The seller would then make the payment of $386.23 on the first trust deed and use the balance—$375.37—on his or her lien of $33,968.

ADVANTAGES

a. Seller gets a loan at a lower than market rate, which makes a lower payment. Thus the buyer can afford a more expensive home.

b. Seller gets a higher return on his or her money since 11 percent is received on the whole loan and only 9 percent is paid on the first.

Interest income on $80,000 at 11 percent = $8,800.00
Interest expenses $46,032 at 9 percent = $4,142.88
Net income = $4,657.12
$4,657.12 ÷ $33,968 = 13.7 percent net return

c. Could lead to a higher price for seller because of built-in financing.

d. Seller retains existing terms of original first trust deed in case of foreclosure.

e. Buyer receives title to the property.

f. Usually a lower down payment is acceptable.

DISADVANTAGES

a. Down payment might not provide funds to pay real estate broker, expenses, and the needs of the seller.

b. A large discount would be required in case the seller needed to dispose of the junior lien to meet a requirement for cash flow.

Multiple Junior Liens

Before we complete our discussion of assumptions, we should look at the possibility of the seller taking back a second junior lien and a third junior lien. This might be considered when the down payment is quite small and is not enough to cover the seller's needs—realtor's fee, closing fees, and funds for deposit or payment on a new residence. As an example, consider a home selling for $95,000 with a loan of $20,000 at 6 percent. (It is an old loan.) The buyer only has $5,000 for a down payment but wants to assume the low-interest loan at 6 percent. The seller wants to buy a mobile home. Taxes, license, and initial space rental will cost more than $45,000. The buyer is making a $5,000 down payment, so there will be $70,000 left to be financed. The buyer could give two junior liens against the property. The first junior lien would be for the larger amount and would be recorded first. The amount would be enough to provide $45,000 plus a discount from 10 to 30 percent, for a total of approximately $49,500. This would leave a third junior lien of $20,500.

This method can be very costly to the seller and is the same as discounting the sales price by $4,500. Part of this might be recovered by adding it to the sales price. When no cash is needed by the seller and when the seller carries the total difference between the sales price and down payment, the broker, in order to close the sale, might split the cash available ($5,000 in our example) to satisfy his or her fee. Or the broker could take back a note for his or her fee, either in part or in full, and payable at a later date.

Real Estate Installment Sale (RE Land Contract)

This is a contract for the sale of property under which the buyer receives possession of the property but not the fee title. The title is to be delivered at some later date after certain conditions have been met. The real estate installment sale is used when the buyer can make only a small down payment and when the seller wants to dispose of the property quickly. It is also used when property is such that the buyer and/or the property will not qualify for a conventional or government-insured loan.

Under the *Tucker* v. *Lassen Savings and Loan* decision, the California Supreme Court ruled on October 10, 1974, that the sale of a property under a real estate conditional sales contract does not necessarily trigger the due-on-sale clause of a deed of trust, since (1) no title has passed; (2) the original borrower is still liable for the payments; and (3) the original borrower wants to see that his or her original investment and equity are protected. There is some belief that in case of default, possession can be obtained under a real estate conditional sales contract more quickly than under a trust deed. Caution is needed here, since some courts have ruled the foreclosure suit to a "quiet title" of a real estate sales contract must be treated as a mortgage, including the lengthy redemption period.

Builder Participation (Buying Down Rate, Sales Subsidy)

This is a program in which the builder pays for a part of the monthly payment for at least one year. The purpose of this is to reduce the effective interest rate to the borrower for at least that period. Amounts of at least $100 per month for at least one year, but not over $200 per month for two years, will be considered in the analysis of the borrower by the HUD-FHA. The builder must place the funds in escrow or in a trust account at the time the loan closes. The account may be an interest-bearing account if he or she so desires. The agreement calls for a cancellation of the program if the buyer sells the property before the agreement expires or if the buyer should refinance or default on the loan. The full participation does not belong to the original mortgagor (trustor) unless that person(s) retains the original loan and owns the property for the full period of the participation. The agreement between the builder and the buyer also states that the escrow provisions are a private contractual matter between the builder and the buyer. If the participation ar-

TABLE 4-1   Builder participation—$100 a month for two years (HUD-FHA loans)

	WITHOUT PARTICIPATION	WITH PARTICIPATION	COMPUTING LOAN
sales price	$59,500	$59,500	*With Participation*
closing costs	500	500	$24,250 = $25,000 × 0.97
acquisition costs	$60,000	$60,000	$30,970 = $32,600 × 0.95
builder participation	none	2,400	$55,220 round to $55,200
to be financed	$60,000	$57,600	*Without Participation*
maximum loan	57,500	55,200	$24,250 = $25,000 × 0.97
cash investment	$ 2,500	$ 4,800	$33,250 = $35,000 × 0.95
acquisition cost	60,000	60,000	$57,500

rangement is set up in this manner, it will be acceptable to HUD-FHA; however, it will require a larger down payment in order to qualify. See the example given in Table 4-1.

The Federal National Mortgage Association (FNMA, nicknamed Fanny Mae) will not buy the HUD-FHA or conventional buydown loans. It has its own program in which it holds the funds in trust itself. Of course, there are no restrictions as to amounts of time under conventional loans. Some builders are paying up to $540 a month for two years. This would amount to $12,960. This money has to come from either a reduction of the builder's profit or an increase in the cost of the home.

Some builders are participating in financing the sale of their new homes by taking a junior lien for up to 15 percent of the purchase price. This reduces the amount of down payment and thus eases the burden of the high interest rate. The lien can be paid off anytime without penalty. The notes can be drawn to suit the parties. Sometimes the note does not require principal payment for two years. After two years, some notes will require monthly payments. Some may be written so that they will have to be paid off. This requires refinancing in most cases. It is expected that by the time the note matures, interest rates will be down and the value of the property up, so that the obligations can be combined into one affordable, single note.

Shared Appreciation Trust Deed/Mortgage (SAM) or Appreciation Participation Mortgage (APM)

This is a loan that gives the borrower a below market rate of interest. In exchange, the lender is given an interest in the appreciated value of the home either when it is sold or on a predetermined date—usually seven to ten years from the date of the note, whichever comes first. The lender usually gives a reduction of from 3 to 4 percent in the interest rate in exchange for a 30 to 40 percent participation in the equity built.

Let us assume, as an example, the current interest rate is 14 percent and appreciation participation is 40 percent.

A home qualifies for a loan of $48,000. The payment required to pay off the loan, including interest, in thirty years would be $568.80 per month. A SAM loan, if written at 10 percent, would require a payment of $421.44, a difference of $147.36. This note would have the payments of a thirty-year loan but would mature on sale of the home or in an agreed time of seven to ten years, but not more than ten years. SAM loans are being written for forty years by some lenders; so let us look at the difference the additional ten years of payments would make. The monthly payment would be $407.52 instead of $421.44, a difference of only $13.92. At the end of ten years, the balance on the thirty-year payment loan would be $43,824; whereas the balance on the forty-year payment loan would be $46,560. If the property has appreciated at an average rate of 5 percent per year over the ten-year period, the home that originally cost $60,000 would have a value of $97,750. If the home had not been sold and if the owner wanted to remain in the home, he or she would have to pay the lender 40 percent of the appreciated value.

$$\$97,750 - \$60,000 = \$37,750 \times 0.40 = \$15,100$$

For the lender, this would probably mean a need for refinancing the existing balance plus $15,100, or $58,924. The new note rounded to $58,900 would be at the then current interest rate, and for thirty years. The payments would be $615.43 per month, assuming an interest rate of 13 percent. This would be an increase in interest and principal payment of $193.99 per month.

DISADVANTAGES

a. There is a sizable increase in the payment if the owners want to keep the property. It is possible that they will not be able to afford the additional payment if their income has not kept pace with inflation. They will have to sell.

b. The lender may have some say in the sales price in order to get the highest amount of appreciation. This could lead to a hardship on the borrower if the property did not sell quickly. In case of a disagreement, an appraisal by an uninterested party has to be made, adding to expenses and time.

c. The lender must treat his or her gain as normal income. The IRS has ruled that the lender's gain is actually deferred income.

d. The interest rate, maturity date, payment schedule, and percentage of participation are set by agreement between the borrower and the lender. The lender is well versed in such procedures, although the borrowers are usually inexperienced individuals buying their first home. They usually end up taking the program presented by the lender.

e. Out-of-pocket expenses for improvements made by the borrower can be deducted from the lender's share of appreciation but not the appreciation created by the improvements.

f. The borrower might feel that the cost upon settlement of the shared appreciation was too great and sue the lender under state unconscionability laws that protect borrowers from loan agreements that heavily favor lenders. This could tie up the settlement for a couple of years.

ADVANTAGES

a. SAMs make it possible for borrowers to qualify for a home that would have been out of their reach under the current interest rate.

b. Some lenders write the SAM agreement so that at the end of the seven or ten years an appraisal by an independent appraiser is made. The lender will accept a buy out of his or her shared appreciation, and allow the loan to run to its maturity (twenty years in the case of a ten-year buy out, twenty-three years in the case of a seven-year buy out agreement) at the nominal interest rate.

c. The appreciation paid by the borrowers is considered contingent interest by the IRS and as such is a deduction, but only up to the amount of the borrower's taxable income. Any excess cannot be carried over to the next year.

The discussion above is based on continued appreciation. Should there be a turnaround in our economy and should there be no appreciation at the time of the sale or maturity of the SAM agreement, there would be no appreciation to divide. In case of a loss the lender would not share that with the borrowers, although the lender would suffer a loss due to a reduced interest rate.

Equity Participation Deed of Trust or Mortgage

For several years insurance companies have been using equity participation in order to increase the yield on their loans when they were not satisfied with the current rate of interest. This program is, in effect, a joint venture. In exchange for a lower interest rate the borrower gives a proportion of his or her project to the lender. Because of the high interest rates on loans, others such as savings and loan associations, individuals, pension funds, and institutional investors are becoming interested in equity participation. This is a program that is workable only

when there is to be an income from the project or speculative profit from the sale. As an example, a lender receives an application for a loan of $1,000,000 from a builder who is going to build a commercial building. The total cost is to be $1,250,000. The builder has leases on all the units, which will return a gross income of $200,000. The current rate of interest is 14 percent. The lending institution says it will loan the borrower-builder $1,000,000 in exchange for a 25 percent interest in all new profits for the duration of the loan and draws the note for 10.5 percent interest. In case of a sale, the lender will receive 25 percent of the profits from the sale. Assuming an annual expense of $137,250, including interest and principal payment, there would be $62,750 profit for the year. Of this amount, the lending institution would receive 25 percent, or $15,687.50, in addition to the interest it receives on the $1,000,000 loan at 10.5 percent, or $105,000, or a yield of 12.1 percent. The builder holds the property for three years and sells it for $1,750,000, a profit of $500,000. The selling expenses were $112,500, giving a net profit of $387,500, of which the lender gets 25 percent, or $96,875. This equals $32,291.67 annually. This, added to the interest on the loan and the annual profit, would show a yield of approximately 21.8 percent on the loan for the three years.

Another way the lender can participate in the equity would be to buy the land and lease it back to the builder and take a note and deed of trust or mortgage on the lease improvements. This would be a long-term lease and would continue if and when the lease improvements were sold.

Using the example above, the lender would buy the land for $250,000 and lease it back to yield 10 percent, or $25,000, a year. The note and deed of trust or mortgage are drawn at an interest rate agreed to by the lender and the borrower, say 12 percent. The yield under these circumstances would be 14.5 percent.

Subordinated Fee Loan or Streamlined Trust Deed or Mortgage

This is the result of a loan which has the characteristics of a fee mortgage-trust deed and a leasehold mortgage or trust deed, but it is really neither, for the landowner ground lessor subordinates his or her fee to the leasehold mortgage, and the landowner joins in the mortgage, thus assuring the lender that in the event of foreclosure the lender will have the security of the landowner's rights to the land.

The subordinated fee loan can be used when land costs and interest rates are high. Developers like a leasehold under these conditions, as it gives them the opportunity to maintain a high leverage. The landowner likes to retain the land as a hedge against inflation, and the developer likes to lease the land since it gives him or her a land rent expense that is deductible. The lender likes it because he or she has as security not only the leasehold improvements but also the fee.

The ground lease can be an extensive document and should be drawn by an attorney. It should follow the requirements of the leasehold mortgages, such as

a.   The owner of the land must not mortgage his or her fee unless the mortgage is subordinate to the lease.

b.   The lessee must be allowed to sublet, assign, or mortgage his or her rights without restriction.

c.   In case of a casualty loss, the insurance must go to the lessee so he or she can restore the building.

d.   The mortgagee must receive a notice of any default under the lease in time so the default can be cured.

e.   The lease terms are not to be changed without the approval of the mortgagee.

f.   In case of condemnation of the leasehold improvements, the lessor cannot share in the condemnation award.

g.   The mortgagor must be able to take over the lease in case of default.

h.   The term of the lease must be for at least the length of the mortgage, preferably at least six months longer.

i.   The ground lease should specify that the landowner is to join in the mortgage.

j.   The ground lease should be subordinate to the mortgage.

k.   The lease provides for the recognition of the fee owner and the mortgagee as the landlords, and rent is paid to them by the tenants of the building.

Renegotiable Rate Trust Deed or Mortgage (RRM), Also Known as Rollover Trust Deed or Mortgage

The cost of money to the lending institutions has become so great that they have had to increase their interest rates to borrowers. The $10,000 six-month money market certificate in 1981 reached a yield of 16 percent to the depositor, and a thirty-month certificate with various minimum requirements by different institutions, some as low as $100, yielded as high as 12 percent.

It requires at least 2 percent over the cost of money for a lending institution to break even on the loans it makes, so it is easy to see that the old 6 to 9 percent loans are loss loans as far as cost of money is concerned. The RRM is an effort to make it possible for new loans to be written in such a way that the lending institutions can keep up, in some degree, with the cost of money.

The RRM is written for a term of three, four, or five years, and it can be automatically renewed at maturity with an adjustment, up or down, in the interest rate. The note is written with a twenty-five- or thirty-year monthly payment schedule, so that the note would be paid in full in twenty-five or thirty years. At the end of the three, four, or five years the interest rate would be adjusted up or down at the rate of 0.5 percent per year, with a max-

imum of 5 percent increase. In order for the note to mature in the original time frame, the monthly payment on the balance owing at the time of adjustment is increased. The basis for the adjustment would be the cost of money from the Federal Saving & Loan Bank Board. This rate is published monthly.

The RRM is not like the variable rate mortgage in that the lender is not required to give the borrower a choice between the fixed payment term loan and the RRM. He or she can offer only the RRM although the fixed payment term loan might be made. Some lenders offer the borrower a RRM at an interest rate 0.25 percent below the current rate for fixed payment loans; others write the note for the current rate.

Suppose a client borrows $60,000 at 11 percent on a three-year RRM. The monthly payment would be $571.20 with a thirty-year maturity. Three years later the cost of money has gone up to 15 percent, at which time the RRM would be adjusted to 12.5 percent on the remaining balance of $59,100. This would require an adjustment in the monthly payment to $637.69. At the end of another three years, the cost of money is still 15 percent, and the RRM interest would go to 14 percent on the then remaining balance of $58,450. The monthly payment would be increased to $707.25.

The difference can be more traumatic in the case of a five-year RRM. Using the example above, the first five years would require a payment of $571.20. At the end of five years, the balance owing would be $58,320, and the new interest rate would be 13.5 percent. The new monthly payment would be $680.01.

The borrower may look for different financing at any time he or she cannot afford the increased payment, and the lender cannot charge a penalty for prepayment. The borrower may also ask the lender to rewrite the note for the outstanding balance on a new five-year RRM. The lender can do this, but the borrower must pay for the cost of the new loan.

Variable Rate Mortgage or Trust Deed (VRM)

In 1974 some of the state-chartered savings and loan associations exercised the right, which they had had for many years, to increase the interest rate on their loans to offset their cost of money. The cost of money had increased during 1974–75 and again in 1979–81 as well as the ever-rising average cost of single-family dwellings. As the money shortage continued, more and more savings and loan associations started writing variable interest rate loans (VRMs). Some lenders offered VRMs at 0.025 percent less than the fixed rate loans but required that loans over a certain amount be written with the variable interest rate. Several California banks are now using the

VRMs, and the Bank of America started using them in 1976.

The VRM program ties the loan interest rate to the Federal Home Loan Bank's cost of money index, which is issued twice a year. If the cost of money index increases or decreases less than 0.10 percent, there will be no increase or decrease in the note's interest rate. There may be an increase or decrease if the change is greater than 0.10 percent. The maximum change that can be assessed in any six-month period is 0.25 percent, with the total change over the life of the loan limited to 2.5 percent in any direction. The monthly payments increase or decrease as the interest rate fluctuates, since the maturity of the note remains the same.

As an example, consider a loan that was made on May 1, 1975, at the rate of 7.75 percent. The following has happened since then, to up to November 1, 1980. Since the spread has occurred over a period of five years, it is safe to assume that there was more than a 0.10 percent change in ten of the six-month review periods. This means the interest could have been increased 0.25 percent each six months and that the interest rate on December 1, 1980 was 10.25 percent, or an increase might have occurred in the last six-month period, in which case the interest rate would be 8 percent. (See Table below.)

The first decline in the Federal Home Loan Bank's cost of money since 1975 occurred in June 1980, when it dropped from 9.530 to 9.486 percent, a change of 0.044 percent. That was not enough to cause a change in a VRM rate, since it did not drop 0.100 percent.

Flexi Loan

The flexi loan was another attempt to reduce monthly payments to a point where individuals would be able to afford to enter the housing market. The flexi loan first came into being in late 1975, and was first known as the flexible payment loan. It was used by some savings and loan associations as early as 1975. The Federal Home Mortgage Company (FHMC, nicknamed Freddie Mac) buys flexi loans from savings and loan associations.

The flexi loan provides for payment of only interest, insurance, and taxes during the first five years of the loan, with the principal amount to be amortized over the remaining twenty-five years. Under the flexi loan, a person can qualify for a loan from $1,000 to $1,500 more than under a fixed payment loan. It is felt that by the end of the five-year period, the buyer's income would have increased enough to make the higher payment. The equity would have also increased, due to inflation.

For example, assume a borrower has a home loan of $50,000 with interest at 14 percent. During the first five years the borrower will pay $583.33 interest monthly. Taxes and insurance would be added to this amount, but not a principal payment. At the end of five years, the payment would increase to $602 per month and would remain at this amount until maturity in twenty-five years. The payments under a level payment loan for thirty years would be $592.50 each month, a difference for the first five years of only $9.17. The total payments under the flexi loan would be $215,599.80, whereas under the level payment loan the total would be 213,300.00. The small difference in the payments, monthly and total, is one reason the flexi loan has not been too well accepted.

Adjustable Rate Loan or Mortgage (ARM)

The Federal Home Loan Bank authorized federal savings and loan associations to make adjustable rate mortgages after June 1, 1981. This type of loan differs from the variable rate mortgage in that there is no limit to the increase that can be made in the interest rate during the life of the loan, and the change can be made as often as every thirty days. There is no common nationally recognized rate index named as a guide to interest rate raises. Because of this, there could be great confusion from one organization to another, with no uniformity in rates. It could certainly result in maximum increases during the life of the loan.

The adjustable rate mortgage provides for no increase in monthly payments at the time of the increase in the interest rate; however, it is possible that a home buyer who starts with a $650 payment will be guaranteed that payment for one to five years, even though the interest rate index governing his or her loan rises or falls within the agreed time frame. At the end of that period, the payment is adjusted up or down to provide for the rate change.

There have been a few savings and loan associations that indicate they are going to take advantage of the ARM plan. Most are indicating that the maximum rate increase or decrease they will have in their plan will be 7.5 percent. They also indicate that any increase or decrease will not be more often than at three- or six-month intervals. The savings and loan associations indicate that they

INTEREST ADJUSTMENT DATE	CURRENT RATE (%)	COST OF MONEY (%)	INITIAL SPREAD (%)	SPREAD DIFFERENCE (%)
5/1/75	7.75	6.445	1.305	
11/1/80	14.00	9.486	4.514	3.209

will continue to offer level payment loans but at an interest rate from 1 to 3 percent higher than the ARMs. Most agree the loans will have a maturity of thirty years.

The main problem with ARMs is much the same as that with VRMs—a sudden jump in the interest rate could price a person out of his or her home. The ARM is even more hazardous since there is no limit to the amount the interest rate can be increased in one jump. The Comptroller of the Currency, in March 1981, authorized national banks to offer the ARM.[2] However, neither state-chartered banks nor the state-chartered savings and loan associations were authorized to make adjustable rate mortgages as of July 8, 1981. Legislation permitting ARMs has also been introduced in the California legislature but has had problems since the bill calls for no increase in monthly payments when the interest rate is increased. This would create a negative amortization and, in an extreme case, the borrowers could end up owing more at the loan's maturity than they did when the loan was obtained. Another controversial point is that the bill calls for annual adjustments. Realtors lobbied for the same Act for state-chartered institutions now available for federally chartered organizations. This Act was passed in the fall of 1981.

The agency that will bring order out of the ARM confusion is the Federal National Mortgage Association. Remember, it was able to bring uniformity to various types of loan application, note, and trust deed forms when it announced that the FNMA would not buy a loan unless the loan documents were forms it approved. Thus, if a lender expects to sell ARMs to the FNMA, it must follow guidelines set by FNMA. FNMA has accepted ARMs since August 1981 if they are set up in one of eight programs.

Five of these programs provide ceilings of one kind or another. Three offer payment limits of increases in monthly payments of 7.5 percent per year for mortgages tied to an index of one- to three-year Treasury securities and 7.5 percent every six months when indexed to six-month Treasury bills. These programs allow considerable latitude, but over a period of time the number of programs will probably be reduced to one or two.

Five other indexes that are acceptable by FNMA are Treasury securities of six-month and one-, two-, three-, and five-year maturity. FNMA also accepts indexes tied to the Federal Home Loan Bank Board's index of new loans on existing housing because the Federal Home

Mortgage Corporation accepts them. However, FNMA does not like this index, as it does not reflect the cost of money as quickly as the others. The shorter the index term, the quicker the mortgage payments can change. However, the changes in indexes with longer terms tend to be greater.

If inflation causes the index to rise more than 7.5 percent, the borrower can either have the payments increased or have negative amortization in states where it is permitted. However, if negative amortization occurs, the payments must be adjusted upward every five years so the monthly payments amortize the loan. In this way there will be no large balloon payment at the loan's maturity. Under no circumstances will negative amortization be allowed to grow beyond 125 percent of the original loan amount.

The Bank of America announced its ARM plan on June 20, 1981. At that time it stated that the plan would be available on loans up to $250,000. On that date the loans would be written for 16.5 percent, whereas conventional loans would be written for 18 percent for a maximum fixed rate loan of $200,000. The ARMs are indexed to the six-month Treasury bill rate, which is to remain unchanged during the first year of the loan. After that, the interest rate may be adjusted up or down by no more than 2 percent and no more than 1 percent every six months thereafter. If the interest rate continues to rise on Treasury bills, it is possible that by the end of the second year the interest could climb 4 points to 20.5 percent. This means that payments on a $75,000 loan could increase from $1,038.87 per month to $1,284.04 per month. Computed on the original balance, the first month's interest would be $1,031.25 or a payment to principal of $7.62; whereas at 20.5 percent the payment to principal would be only $2.79 in spite of an increase of $245.17 in the monthly payment. Negative amortization amounts to $242.38 if the balance is $75,000 and if the payment isn't increased, and would increase to $246.52 the next month, and so forth.

The Bank of America's program calls for an adjustment for each 0.1 percent based on the monthly average of the weekly auction rate on six-month Treasury bills. The rate the bank charges must be reduced if the index declines; however, the Treasury bills have increased an average of 0.5 percent per year from 1970 to 1980. Also, there is no prepayment penalty under this program.

Graduated Payment Mortgage or Trust Deed (GPM)

For a complete understanding of the GPM, refer to Housing and Urban Development and Federal Housing Administration Loans, Chapter 13, section 245(a) and 245(b). Some savings and loan associations are using a combination of shared appreciation mortgages (SAMs)

---

[2]The Comptroller of the Currency, who issues regulations concerning the operation of national banks, signed adjustable rate mortgage regulations in the late spring of 1981. The regulations allow an interest adjustment of 1 percent each six months with no limit to the amount over the life of the loan. The regulations also provide for the use of any one of three indexes: the six-month Treasury bill rate; the return on Treasury securities adjusted to a constant maturity of three years; or the Federal Home Loan Bank Board's average real estate loan rate on homes that have been occupied previously.

for a period of seven years with a $33^{1}/_{3}$ percent reduction of the current interest rate in exchange for a 30 to 50 percent share of the profit when the house is sold. They guarantee that they will refinance at the end of seven years with a GPM loan at the then market rate of interest.

Partnership; Co-owner; Ticket Mortgage Home Ownership; Coinvestment Program of the State Home and Community Development Department

The partnership loan for the purchase of a real estate parcel is becoming increasingly popular. Under this program two or more individuals, not necessarily related, buy the property and take title as tenants in common. They may or may not both live in the home. They share in the monthly payments and the upkeep, and, if the property is sold, they share in the profits. Since the title is held by tenants in common, either can sell his or her share at any time and retain the profit from the equity.

There are some builders who are building especially for the partnership market. The homes have two master bedrooms and baths separated by the common area—kitchen and living room. These are being sold to individuals and couples who may be total strangers.

In the case of home partnership loans it is very important for a lawyer to draw an agreement between the buyers covering all problems that might arise. Some things that should be covered are

1. Who paid for what?
2. What are the responsibilities of each buyer?
3. Who owns what?
4. Who is to pay what?
5. What happens if one decides to sell his or her equity?
6. What happens in the case of the default by one co-mortgagor?
7. What happens if incompatibility develops?
8. Is there to be a time limit to the partnership?

A partnership can develop in another way. Suppose a family has a home in which they have an equity of $20,000. Through tax and insurance increases the payments have increased to the point that they can no longer afford the home, but they do not want to sell and move. They sell a portion of their equity, usually 50 percent, to an individual or individuals for, in this case, $10,000 and relief from a portion of the monthly payments. The buyer, in effect, becomes a silent partner with a tenant in common ownership. The buyer benefits from a share of the interest, tax deductions, and future participation in the profit when the property is sold. The seller continues to live in and maintains the property. Once again, there should be an agreement between the parties drawn by a good lawyer.

The State of California has entered the partnership financing program. In 1980 the state legislature committed $1 million to such a program. In 1981 the program was allocated $8.2 million for a demonstration program. Under the program the State Department of Housing and Community Development (HCD) will pay up to 49 percent of the purchase price but will not reduce the down payment below 3 percent. The funds are being routed through local governments. As an example, a young couple finds a home they want to buy. The price is $70,000. They have $5,000 for a down payment. A savings and loan association will make a loan of $56,000. The state would make up the remaining $9,000 required for the down payment and would receive 13 percent of the sales price when sold. This would mean that if, at the end of five years, the home was sold for $90,000, the state would receive $11,700 ($90,000 × 0.13) and the family $78,300 ($90,000 × 0.87), from which the balance of the $56,000 loan would have to be paid. In order for a family to qualify, its income cannot exceed the median of the county adjusted for family size. It is possible the program can be used in connection with HUD-FHA Section 235 loans.

Piggyback Loans, Hard Money Junior Liens, or Tandem Loans

Some institutions are allowing a buyer to make a down payment of 20 percent of the purchase price or appraisal value, whichever is less, and will take a purchase money junior lien for the balance down to the existing assumable first lien. As an example, assume a home is valued at $70,000. There is a first lien of $40,000. The buyer pays 20 percent down ($14,000), and the lending institution makes a purchase money second (junior) lien for $16,000. The note and deed of trust or mortgage would be drawn in such a way that the junior lien could be sold at a later date if the lender so desired.

Swing or Bridge Loans

Swing loans are short-term loans at high rates of interest that are taken in anticipation of a drop in the long-term interest rate. They usually have a maturity of from one to five years. They may be secured by equities in other real property owned, stocks, bonds, life insurance, or the financial statement of the borrower. In some cases they may be secured by the real property being purchased.

Time Sharing

Time sharing is a program under which a specific week or period is sold to buyers of the property. Occupancy of the property is granted to the buyers every year at that particular time. This has been a successful way of selling property, particularly in resort areas or areas of historical importance.

In some areas whole subdivisions have been established as time-sharing units. In others, where certain units have not sold because of cost, they have been sold under time sharing; and, in some instances, the sale of the time parts have exceeded the price of the unit if the total fee had been sold to one individual. The cost of the week or weeks use is determined by the season in which the week or weeks fall. For instance, in a ski area, the period from January 1 to April 15 is a prime period. The Presidents' birthdays in February are also prime time. Thus the costs during these times are high. Then the period from the last of April through June 7 is less expensive because of school attendance. During summer vacation the week ownership cost goes up again until school reconvenes in September. Then the price drops about 50 percent until the Thanksgiving holidays, when the cost for a week increases. After the Thanksgiving holidays, the cost falls drastically until Christmas and New Year's week, when it reaches an all-time high. Under this program one home in Tahoe sold under fifty-two weeks of time sharing for $389,025. Actually, only fifty weeks were sold because a week in May and a week in November were reserved for annual maintenance. The cost of a week's ownership in this home ranged from $13,500 to $2,475. The owners of this particular time-sharing property have a monthly maintenance charge of $26 for each week of ownership which is paid quarterly for a total of $312 maintenance cost per year for each week of ownership.

The sellers of this particular time-sharing home cite the following advantages for buyers:

1. You buy future vacations at today's prices.
2. You will always have a vacation reservation as long as you own your time slot.
3. You have all the benefits of pride of ownership. This includes a deed, title insurance, equity appreciation, interest on the loan, if any, and proration of the taxes.
4. The property is maintenance free.
5. The home is completely furnished, so all you have to do is arrive for your week.
6. There is an organization that will allow the exchange of one unit's time for another in another location. For instance an owner of a week might exchange his or her week at Tahoe with the owner of a time-sharing week in Florida.

There can be problems also, as follows:

1. Be sure management is adequate and professional.
2. Be sure to see the development. Don't buy under pressure.
3. Be sure you get a title and not a long-term lease that will allow the lessor to take full title after the lease expires.

Sell the Improvements and Lease the Land

Such a program would allow a buyer to qualify for a home that he or she would not be able to buy under a fee simple, since the payment would be smaller. This is an ideal way for individuals who buy houses on speculation to sell. It assures them of a continuing income from the lease rent, and if they want to carry the purchase money note and deed of trust, they have an opportunity to increase the yield on their investment. Such a program for a home sale could be written either as a long-term lease without provisions for the purchase of the land being leased by the owner of the leaseheld improvements, or with provisions for a future purchase of the land after some definite time has elapsed.

As an example, consider a home that is for sale for $70,000. A lender makes a loan of $56,000 at 14 percent with monthly payments of $663.60 for thirty years. The buyers cannot pay the $14,000 down payment, but they could pay $10,500 down and have monthly payments of $497.70 for thirty years on a leaseheld improvement loan of $42,000 for thirty years. Under this type of loan, a lease on the land is worked out between the seller and the buyers, and the lender only loans on the leaseheld improvements. The lease could be set up in many ways. One would be to have smaller payments for two years, then larger payments for two years, and a third increase that would remain over the balance of the lease term starting with the fifth year. The privilege of having smaller payments at first could be in exchange for a share of the appreciation in the land value for the first ten years of the lease, should the buyer decide to purchase the land and hold the property in fee simple. Also incorporated in the lease could be the provision that the money paid on the lease as rent be deducted from the total amount accrued toward the value of the land.

Now assume the rent for the first two years is 4 percent of the land value; for the next two years, 6 percent; and for the balance of the lease, 8 percent. Assume that the lease calls for an 8 percent appreciation each year through ten years. The land is valued at $17,500; the improvements at $52,500. Under these conditions, the rent for the first two years would be $58.33 per month; for the next two years, $87.50 per month; and from then on to the end of the lease or the purchase of the lease by the buyer, $116.67 per month. Now assume the buyer decides to buy the lease after six years. At that time the total rent paid would be $6,300. The value of the lot at 8 percent annual appreciation would be $27,770.30. In order to buy the total fee the seller would receive $21,470.30 ($27,770.30 − $6,300).

As previously stated, the terms of the lease could be drawn in any way that is satisfactory to both parties;

however, a good attorney should draw the lease in order to protect all parties.

Lease-Purchase Agreement

Under this program a lease and a sales contract are completed at the same time. The sales contract has a closing sometime in the future, when it is felt the interest rates will be lower. At that time the buyer agrees to buy the property. The buyer makes a down payment and makes monthly rental payments under the lease. The payments are large enough to at least pay any monthly payments that fall due on any outstanding note and deed of trust or mortgage. The rent may be larger than the outstanding loan payment, and part of the rent may be credited toward the purchase price.

Exchange

This is an old form of acquiring and disposing of property that has been used in the past to defer payment of capital gains tax. With the shortage of real estate loan money and the resulting high interest rates, exchange has become a means of acquiring property. Exchange is a transfer of owner equity in one property for the equity in another property owned by a second party. In almost all exchanges, some money changes hands because no two equities are exactly the same. A two-way exchange is a relatively simple procedure, but when a three- or four-way exchange is proposed, an attorney and accountant should be consulted about procedures. A realtor who specializes in exchanges can help put together an exchange.

Cash Rebate

Although it is not a creative financing program, the cash rebate idea is becoming a good sales tool where there is a high inventory of houses. The cash rebates made by automobile manufacturers in 1980 and 1981 gave home builders in the East the idea of trying the rebate principle on their inventories in 1981. This rebate system is slowly spreading to the West.

A loan is arranged on the appraisal value of the home. After closing, the builder gives a cash rebate, either a flat amount or a percentage of the sales price. The rebate belongs to the buyers to do with as they see fit. They may decide to use the money to buy new furniture, or they may put it in an account to help with the monthly payments.

This program differs from the builder's participation in that the money can be used in any way, whereas under the builder's participation the funds must go into an escrow account and can be used only for reducing the monthly payments.

Graduated Payment Adjustable Interest Mortgage (GPAIM) or Graduated Payment Adjustable Mortgage Loan (GPAML)

The Federal Home Loan Bank Board authorized all federally chartered savings and loan associations to combine the benefits of the graduated payment mortgage with the characteristics of the adjustable interest mortgage in July 1981. This allows a loan to be made with small monthly payments during the first year and with increasingly larger payments each year for a period up to ten years. At the end of this time, the payments reach an amount that will amortize the loan over the balance of the thirty-year period. However, it allows the lender to control the interest rate. The GPAIM has no limitations on the amount of change, up or down, allowed, or on the number of times the changes in the interest rate may be made in a year. As time goes by, however, competition will set limits on the maximum interest rate, the criteria for changes in the rate, and the frequency of the changes.

Price Level Adjustment Mortgage (PLAM)

The PLAM is different from the usual creative financing instrument in that the interest on the mortgage is not adjusted but the principal is adjusted periodically. The nominal interest rate is the real net rate adjusted for inflation. This could indicate a rate as low as 4 percent. The monthly loan payment is based on this real interest rate. At the end of each year the loan amount is adjusted by an inflation factor. In this way the principal balance is increased so that it bears the same purchasing power as the original principal less the payments to that principal amount.

The PLAM will yield the lowest initial payment. The monthly payments will increase at the same rate the general inflation index increases. The borrower, as in so many creative finance programs, is contracting an obligation that, should the inflation increase more rapidly than his or her income, he or she may be unable to meet the increasing monthly payments.

Growing Equity Mortgage (GEM)

The growing equity mortgage is a guaranteed thirty-year term loan but one that can be paid off rapidly. The interest rate is fixed at 1 to 3 percentage points under the current rate at the time the loan is made. However, the payments are flexible. The amount of the interest is based on the United States Commerce Department's index that measures disposable income after taxes. If that index increases 5 percent, the borrower's annual payment would be increased by 75 percent of the disposable money increase, resulting in an increase of $3^3/_4$ percent. In other words, if the annual payment is $12,000, the payment for the following year would be $12,450. However, none of this money would go to interest. All of the difference in the additional payment would be applied to the principal. This would increase the return of loanable funds to the lender which could be loaned at the current rate of interest. This program allows the loan to be paid off before the stated maturity. It is more fair to the borrower since the increase in payment is not be tied to some government interest base, but to the increase in spendable income after taxes. Although loanable funds return faster, the interest income does not increase as the cost of money increases.

Builder Approach to Creative Finance

Many builders found themselves with a large inventory of unsold homes in 1981. Out of this situation grew various programs to create sales and reduce inventories, reducing, in turn, the heavy interest burden on interim loans. The buy-down program was discussed previously under Builder Participation. In 1981, there were two programs introduced by builders that created sales. One was the rebate program. This was taken from the auto industry. One builder who had a large inventory of houses in the $150,000 bracket offered a $10,000 rebate to anyone buying one of his homes. This could be used in any way the buyer wanted, from part of the down payment, to an around-the-world cruise, to a special trust fund set up to pay the buyer $240 a month for five years.

The second program that was very successful for the builder was for the buyer to pay 30 percent down and receive an interest-free loan, which would amortize in five years from equal monthly payments. There were variations of this program that called for smaller down payments and small interest on the balance ranging from 1 to 6 percent, depending on the down payment and the length of the loan (not to exceed ten years).

Caution

There is need for a word of caution at this point concerning creative finance. Almost all creative finance is based on smaller payments now in order for the buyer to be able to qualify. It is also based on an anticipation of increased earnings for the buyer in the future at which time an increase in payments will, hopefully, fit into his or her budget. Some of the programs call for balloon payments in two, five, or ten years or sometime in between. It is hoped that, at the time the balloon payment is due, the equity value will have increased to a point where refinancing will be possible at a lower interest rate. However, it is possible that the buyer could lose the property and everything he or she put into it if his or her income did not increase or if the property cannot be sold or refinanced. It is possible that the buyer can sue the realtor, the salesperson, or the seller because there was not a full disclosure made concerning the amount of increase in payments or the amount of the balloon payment before he or she bought the property.

In order for all parties to be protected, the sales agreement should be drawn by an attorney and accepted by the buyer, the seller, and the realtor.

The Federal Reserve Bank Board was so concerned about all of this that on October 19, 1981, it proposed that individuals who had been exempt from the truth-in-lending consumer protection regulations should be subject to the regulations. This would have required real estate brokers who help arrange more than five seller-financed transactions a year to make a complete disclosure of the transactions. This would require use of the same forms as those used by banks and savings and loan associations. In this way the buyer and the seller would be told the amount of the financing charges over the life of the contract, the annual percentage rate, the amount of the balloon payment and when it would come due if there was to be a balloon payment, and the total cost of the property including interest over the term of the loan.

Interested parties were given forty-five days to express their desires in connection with the proposed regulation. The real estate industry was expected to oppose the regulation but in December 1981 the feeling was the regulation would become effective in early 1982. However, there was so much opposition, written and verbal, to this proposed regulation that it was withdrawn on February 10, 1982.

NONINSTITUTIONAL LENDERS; MORTGAGE COMPANIES AND BANKERS

Although state and national banks, state and national savings and loan associations, and insurance companies are responsible for the majority of real estate loans made by institutional lenders in California, other sources of real estate finance influence the purchase of real estate in California by making funds available to the borrower.

The most important of this group is probably the mortgage company. In most instances there are mortgage bankers, subject to rules and regulations of the Department of Real Estate of California and also to the Business and Professions Code of California.

Section 10131 of the California Real Estate Law states in part that a real estate broker within the meaning of the Real Estate Law is a person who for compensation or an expectation of compensation

(1) solicits borrowers or lenders for loans for clients or negotiates loans or collects payments or performs services for borrowers or lenders or note owners in connection with loans secured directly or collaterally by liens on real property and (2) sells or offers to sell, buys or offers to buy, or exchanges or offers to exchange a real property sales contract or promissory notes secured directly or collaterally by lien or real property and performs services for the holders thereof.

Because a mortgage company is in the business of providing funds for a borrower and negotiates with companies to purchase such a loan, and because the mortgage company expects remuneration for this service, such an organization falls within the definitions of a real estate broker and consequently is subject to the limitations imposed upon individuals or companies by the Real Estate Law.

Under these provisions a mortgage company must have a real estate broker's license. The company as such is usually a corporation chartered by the state of California through the Office of the Corporations Commissioner, who has authorized the issuance of stock from which the capital for the operation of the company is obtained.

After the corporate charter has been approved, stock is sold, and with these funds the mortgage company is ready to start business. In many instances a mortgage company is nothing more or less than a correspondent of life insurance companies, mutual savings banks, or pension funds. The mortgage company obtains the type of loans for which the various organizations are looking and then sells the loans to them. In some instances the mortgage company, acting as a correspondent, will not actually make the loan but will use the forms of the insurance company, mutual savings bank, trust fund, or pension fund in documenting the loan and disbursing the funds directly from the life insurance company or other institution to the borrower. Unless some unusual agreement has been made, after the loan has been sold to the take-out company, the servicing remains with the mortgage company, which has a servicing department for this purpose. Fees for servicing are the source of some of the revenue of the mortgage company.

When a mortgage company is acting as correspondent it receives a finder's fee for the loans it obtains for the lending institution. Because of its brokerage license a mortgage company may increase its income through other sources of revenue such as property rentals and property management. It is not unusual to find a mortgage company also acting as a real estate broker, and in some instances as an insurance agency. In its lending operations a mortgage company enjoys a minimum of supervision and has a wide latitude of powers. Because a mortgage company's loans find their way into other portfolios, the loans made by the mortgage company must be of the type its clients need. Because most mortgage companies are correspondents of life insurance companies, and since life insurance companies are interested in insured as well as conventional loans, the loans made by the mortgage company and intended for the life insurance company's portfolio must meet the standards of the life insurance company.

Some life insurance companies may want only conventional loans, in which case the loan limitations would be those imposed by the state in which the life insurance company is chartered or by the state of California, whichever has the stricter regulations.

Other life insurance companies may be interested only in FHA or VA loans, in which case the mortgage company must make loans for those companies, portfolios that comply with the FHA and VA regulations. However, most mortgage companies have a backlog of funds available for loans that do not fully comply with the more restrictive agencies. These funds may come from individuals who desire to invest in first and second trust deeds. Consequently, if the mortgage company knows an individual who will purchase a certain loan that is offered to him or her, the mortgage company will probably make the loan, take it into its portfolio, and subsequently sell it to a preferred private individual who has asked the mortgage company to be on the lookout for trust deeds in which the individual can invest.

At times a mortgage company may find itself short of ready cash for the purchase of additional desirable loans. In such a case it is not unusual for the mortgage company to go to a commercial bank and obtain a short-term loan, if necessary pledging as security some of its existing trust deeds and notes with the understanding that as soon as a certain block of loans has been sold to a client, the bank will be paid in full.

Since the mortgage company is required to have a real estate broker's license, it is subject to periodic examinations by the representatives of the Real Estate Commission to see that it is complying with the state laws of that division.

We have primarily discussed mortgage companies that make loans and immediately resell them to organizations the mortgage companies are representing. However, another type of mortgage company uses funds it has accumulated through the sale of stock to make loans that it takes into its own portfolio with the idea that such loans will provide good revenue. In these cases the company is usually free of the lending limitations placed against institutional lenders such as banks, life insurance companies, and savings and loan associations. These mortgage companies establish their own lending policies and servicing procedures.

Mortgage companies in California have also served

as a source of construction loans, such loans being made from their own funds or, in some instances, from funds of organizations they represent. Loans that result from construction financing may be either retained by the organization or sold if it can find an interested purchaser and if it will make more money by selling the loan than by retaining it.

Mortgage companies are mostly temporary lenders dealing in loans that are readily assimilated through the secondary market of real estate finance. In working with this market a company may have a definite commitment for a certain number of loans from an organization. It may have a firm commitment on a certain parcel of land owned by a certain individual before the loan is made. Under certain circumstances the mortgage company will make a series of loans and then find a purchaser for the loans after they have been made and entered on the mortgage company's books.

Since World War II, with the growth of the need for real estate financing, there has been a continuous increase in the popularity of the mortgage company. Through these organizations insurance companies in various parts of the United States have placed real estate loans on parcels of land far removed from the insurance companies' normal areas of operation.

After life insurance companies, probably the second most important sources of funds to the mortgage companies in California are the mutual savings banks of Oregon and Washington and of Northeastern states such as Pennsylvania, New Hampshire, and New York.

The Federal National Mortgage Association has become another important purchaser of mortgage companies' loans. The mortgage companies purchase future rights to sell blocks of loans to FNMA, as described in Chapter 14. Since the advent of tandem financing, the mortgage company has played an important role in financing new homes under that plan.

MORTGAGE BROKERS

A mortgage broker, like a mortgage company or mortgage bank, must have a real estate broker's license; however, unlike a mortgage company or mortgage bank, the mortgage broker does not need a large office with a large staff. A mortgage broker can, and sometimes does, work out of his or her briefcase.

A mortgage broker is an individual who has contact with several agencies that are looking for real estate loans and who acts as an intermediary between this group of agencies and an individual desiring a loan. The mortgage broker does not make the loan, but acts for the organization he or she is representing by preparing the application (and sometimes the appraisal) and presenting it to

the lending agency for approval. If the loan is approved, the lending agency prepares all the documents and the mortgage broker obtains the necessary signatures and returns them to the lending agency for closing.

The mortgage broker is paid a finder's fee, which is sometimes passed on to the borrower, for his or her service in bringing together the borrowing individual and the lending institution. The mortgage broker can build such a good reputation that borrowers will be referred to him or her by people for whom he or she has obtained loans in the past. Institutions that are unable to make a desired loan to a borrower, but that know of a mortgage broker's ability and honesty, will sometimes refer clients to him or her.

Because of many complaints concerning hidden charges and commissions that some mortgage brokers were extracting from borrowers who were desperate for loans, the California state legislature passed in 1955 and subsequently amended, the Real Property Loan Brokerage Law. Although this law pertained to real estate transactions, it was made a part of the Civil Code rather than of the Business and Professional Code. Later it became apparent that real property loan brokerage laws were not adequate to correct the abuses of the bulk trust deed market and the practices of those who came to be known as the "10 percenters." AB 1344 removed the old mortgage loan brokerage provisions from the Civil Code, reinstated them in the real estate law, and made some changes and adjustments. It also established a new classification for real estate brokers engaged in the sale of real property securities, designated such individuals as real property security dealers, and established control over such dealers.

In 1963 the legislature took another long look at this particular problem and, in view of the two years' experience with the regulation, added more provisions and strengthened the act, particularly in the areas of conservatorship, liquidation proceedings, and the treatment of out-of-state subdivision properties merchandised under the securities section of the law. The only transaction exempt from this 1963 regulation is the negotiation into which a real estate broker or mortgage broker enters to obtain a loan in connection with a property sale or exchange that the broker or licensee is negotiating; or the sale or exchange by him or her of a note made or taken in connection with such a sale or exchange. However, the regulation covers all other transactions in which the broker is attempting to find real estate financing for an individual who may have come to him or her voluntarily or who may have been solicited by him or her for such an application and for which service the mortgage broker expects to receive a fee. It can also apply where the broker expects to perform a service such as collecting payment or attempting to sell an existing loan for a client. For this service a mortgage broker may not accept funds in advance from a prospective purchaser or lender with the intention of purchasing sales contracts or deeds of trust as they become available.

Funds may be accepted by the broker only for a specific transaction and for specific loans for which the broker has a bona fide authorization to buy or sell. Any broker who collects funds payable according to the terms of the sales contract or note must disburse such funds within sixty days of their receipt unless he or she holds a written agreement with the purchaser or lender allowing him or her to hold the funds for a longer period.

To make collections on notes secured by deeds of trust on real property sales contracts, a broker must possess a written authorization from the borrower to make such a collection. It is illegal for a mortgage broker to advertise that a note or contract of sale secured by a lien on real estate yields a rate of interest higher than that specified in the body of the note. However, he or she may advertise the rate specified in the body of the note and indicate the discount at which the balance of the note is being offered for sale.

The 1963 legislative act also places upon the mortgage broker the responsibility of seeing that a deed of trust upon which he or she has negotiated a loan is recorded and that the deed of trust shall name as beneficiary the lender or the lender's nominee. This recording must be made in the county in which the property is located, before any funds are disbursed, except when the lender has authorized in writing the prior release of the funds. If such authorization has been given, the deed of trust must be recorded or delivered to the lender or beneficiary with the recommendation of the mortgage broker that the deed of trust be recorded within ten days following the release of the money. When the mortgage broker arranges for the sale of a note and deed of trust, it is his or her responsibility to see that the assignment of the note and deed of trust is recorded naming the purchaser of the note or the purchaser's assignee. In no case can the assignee be the mortgage broker or the mortgage broker's nominee. The assignment of the note and deed of trust must be recorded in the county in which the real property is located within ten working days after the mortgage broker or the seller receives funds from the buyer of the note and deed of trust or after the close of escrow. If the mortgage broker does not record the document, it is his or her responsibility to see that the document is delivered to the buyer with a written recommendation that such recording be done immediately.

The 1963 act also limited the commissions and charges the broker can make. The maximum amount of expenses, charges, and interest to be paid by a borrower with respect to any loan for appraisal fees, escrow fees, title charges, notary fees, recording fees, and credit investigation fees may not exceed 5 percent of the principal amount of the loan or $195, whichever is greater, but in no event may it exceed $350, provided that in no event may the maximum amount exceed the actual costs and expenses paid, incurred, or reasonably earned.

The maximum charges for bonuses, brokerage, or commissions contracted for or to be received by a broker for negotiating, procuring, or arranging or making a loan may not exceed the following amounts: (1) in the case of a loan secured directly or collaterally in whole or in part by a first deed of trust, 5 percent of the principal amount of the loan where the term of the loan is less than three years, and 10 percent where the term is three years or more; (2) in the case of a loan secured directly or collaterally by a trust deed other than a first trust deed, 5 percent of the principal amount of the loan where the term of the loan is less than two years, 10 percent where the term is at least two years but less than three years, and 15 percent where the term is three years or more; (3) with respect to a further advance on a note, the charges may not exceed the charges for an original loan in the same amount as the further advance and made for a term equal to the remaining term of the note on which the further advance is being made, including any extension thereof.

The loan itself, if it is on an instalment basis and is written for less than three years, may not have a balloon payment. If the collateral securing a junior trust deed loan is an owner-occupied dwelling, a balloon payment is not permissible if the loan payment term is six years or less. In both the three-year and six-year term loans the balloon payment restriction does not apply if the junior lien is a purchase money loan.

A mortgage broker procuring loans in the above category must prepare for the borrower, before the consummation of the loan, a broker's loan statement in a form approved by the Real Estate Commission. Such a form will carry the following information: (1) the name and address of the individual or organization obtaining the loan for the borrower; (2) the street address or legal description of the property being offered as security; (3) a statement of all liens against the property existing at the present time; (4) a description of the loan that is to be secured (including the principal amount of the note, the rate of interest per year, the term of the note, the number of instalments, the amount of each instalment [which includes interest and principal], the approximate balance on the note that will be due at maturity if the note is of the balloon payment type, and the terms of prepayment privileges and penalties, if any); (5) the deductions that will be made from the principal sum of the note;[3] and (6) the estimated balance that would be available to the borrower after all the deductions had been cleared. The broker should list those services he or she anticipates doing for the borrower to justify the fee that he or she will receive. The broker then makes a representation that he or she is not the lender of the funds described in the loan statement and that the loan is being made in compliance with all California real estate law. The broker then signs the statement and includes his or her license number and business address. After the form has been completed in full the borrower acknowledges receipt of his or her copy of the form by signing the statement. The broker retains a copy and delivers a copy to the borrower.

The reason for such a statement is to give the borrower a reasonably exact picture of the transaction as it is to occur. This allows him or her to decide whether to accept the loan that is being prepared; he or she knows, with reasonable certainty, the amount of money that will be available to use after completion of the loan. In the past some individuals borrowed what they considered to be sufficient money for their purposes; however, after all charges had been deducted from the loan, they found that they did not have sufficient funds to satisfy their needs. Therefore, this statement was developed.

The one exception to the requirement for a broker's loan statement is in the case of the real estate licensee who is the representative of a bank, insurance company, industrial loan company, or savings and loan association, and who does not charge more than 2 percent commission for his or her services.

Since the mortgage broker also holds a real estate broker's license, it is possible for him or her to participate in the sale of real estate if so desired. Of course, this is a natural source of business to the mortgage broker and a means by which he or she can develop additional applications for his or her loan business.

REAL PROPERTY SECURITIES DEALER

Sections 10-237 through 10-239.35 of the Business and Professions Code define the transactions that can be handled only by real property securities dealers, in order to control bulk sales of trust deeds and real property sales contracts as well as investment plans proposed for dealing in such documents. To qualify as a real property securities dealer the applicant must have a real estate broker's license. A written application for endorsement as a real property securities dealer is sent to the real estate commissioner together with an application fee of $50 and a corporate surety bond in the amount of $5,000. In place of the corporate surety bond the individual may submit a receipt showing that he or she has placed with the treasurer of the state of California a cash bond in the amount of $5,000 or that he or she has deposited with the state treasurer United States or state bonds with a face value of $6,000.

To qualify as a real property securities dealer, the broker must be engaged in the business of selling real property securities, such as deeds of trust and real estate contracts, to the public, or of offering to accept money from the public for continual reinvestment in real property or for placement in an account or program from which the dealer implies, guarantees, or indicates that a return will be received from a specific sales contract or promissory note secured by a real property lien that is not specifically stated in the contractual payment of that note and deed of trust or sales contract.

Selling to the public does not include selling to corporations; to pension, retirement, or similar trust funds; to institutional lending agencies; to real estate brokers; to attorneys; or to general building contractors.

Section 10-237.1 broadly defines real property securities as deeds of trust sold under an instalment program in which the dealer guarantees the deed of trust in one of several ways or makes advances to or on behalf of the investor. Also included in the definition is the sale of one or more of a series of promotional notes or sales contracts. "Promotional" in this case designates a note secured by a deed of trust on unimproved real estate, or a note on an improved property that was executed after the construction of the improvements but before the first sale or was used as a means of financing the purchase of the property as improved but that is subordinated to another trust deed. An example of such a note and deed of trust would be one used as a portion of the purchase money on a house in a new subdivision.

Before real property securities dealers may participate in the sale of such securities, they must receive permission to do so from the real estate commissioner. These permits may authorize dealers to sell existing securities that they or their representative holds, or they may authorize the applicant to acquire and sell securities under a proposed plan or program. If the permit is to acquire and sell under a plan or proposed plan, the plan must be submitted to the real estate commissioner in detail before the permit can be issued. If the commissioner determines

---

[3]These will include the maximum cost and expenses estimated by the broker—items such as escrow fees, notary fees, recording fees, appraisal fees, title fees, credit report fees, and other expenses that might be incurred. All of these should be totaled so that the total cost can be quickly determined by the borrower. Other deductions would be the bonuses, commissions, or brokerage that will be paid to the individual negotiating or arranging for the financing. The estimated disbursements to be paid at the order of the borrower for items such as fire insurance premiums, payment of prior liens including reconveyance fees, assumption fees, and any other insurance costs other than fire insurance should also be included. The borrower could then instruct that other items be deducted and paid from the loan proceeds.

that the plan is fair and equitable to all concerned, a permit will be issued. For each plan a separate permit must be obtained before the securities are acquired by the real property securities dealer.

As a means of controlling the real property securities dealer, an annual financial statement must be submitted to the real estate commissioner. This statement is an audited report that must list the total number of sales, the dollar volume, and other information the auditor feels is desirable for the real estate commissioner's information. If such an audit is not obtained, it is within the power of the real estate commissioner's office to authorize such an audit to determine that the real property securities dealer is operating properly.

The real property securities dealer is allowed to advertise in connection with his or her operation, but the advertisement must be submitted to the commissioner ten days before its use so that the real estate commissioner can approve the information used in the advertisement. If the commissioner decides that the advertising is not fair, he or she has the power to deny its use; and should such a denial occur, the dealer may not, under any circumstances, use the information. If any information is reported to the dealer as being false or misleading, this information may not be used in future ads.

When a dealer sells a security (a note secured by a deed of trust) to a purchaser, he or she must supply the purchaser with a real property security statement. The form of this statement must be approved by the real estate commissioner. The disclosure statement should contain (1) the name and address of the firm; (2) information concerning the property owner;[4] (3) information concerning the property that is securing the obligation;[5] (4) terms and amounts of prior assessments or taxes that might exist against the property; (5) information concerning prior deeds of trust recorded against the property, the principal balance, and status of their payments;[6] (6)

the terms and conditions of the note or contract that is being offered for sale. This last item should include the present balance, original amount, date of the note or contract, interest rate, maturity date, amount of monthly payments, and status of the payments. If they are not current, an explanation should be given along with a statement whether a request for notice of default will be recorded. Terms and conditions of subordination agreements, if any, should be shown. If it is indicated that a balance will be due at maturity of the note, this amount should be shown.

The dealer then signs an affidavit that he or she is complying with the California real estate law, that he or she is acting either as principal or agent, and that the information in the statement of disclosure is true and correct. After the dealer signs the contract, the purchaser signs a statement that he or she has received a copy of the statement of disclosure, has read it, and has approved the purchase of the note or contract. A copy of this statement must be kept in the dealer's office for at least four years.

The mortgage broker, the mortgage banker, and the real property securities dealer are sources of secondary financing. Particularly in the case of the securities dealer and the mortgage banker, their own funds are sometimes invested in notes and trust deeds and then the notes and trust deeds are sold to other organizations or to individuals.

The mortgage broker is a representative rather than an investor, who represents organizations that would not be making real estate loans in the broker's district were he or she not finding the loans for them to make.

BANK TRUST DEPARTMENTS

Most larger banks are authorized to do a trust business. In the pursuit of such business the trust department receives funds for which it must find sources for investment. Unlike the banking departments of commercial banks and savings banks, the trust department is not limited to specific percentages of value in its investments but is required to invest all funds in a prudent manner, whether in stocks, bonds, or real estate.

A prudent stock investment would have to be more or less of the blue chip variety. It could not be a speculative issue, because if the bank were to suffer a loss for the client's account, it would be faced with a suit for the replacement of the funds. This, in turn, would lead to the loss not only of this particular account but of other

---

[4]This would include the name and address of the fee owner, whether the property is purchased under real property sales contract; and credit information relative to the maker or obligor, including employment information such as his or her employer, years employed, monthly salary, and other assets. It is also desirable to show the monthly payments the individual is now making.

[5]This would include the street address or legal description of the property; whether it is improved; type of improvements; information concerning sewers, curbs, gutters, streets, water mains, and other improvements. If any improvements have not been paid for, or if there are assessments against the property, the balance of the assessments should be shown. If the security is a note, the date of the last sale of the property, the purchase price, and the down payment should be indicated. If there has been an appraisal of the property, the appraised value, the date of the appraisal, and the name of the appraiser should be given. The dealer should also give his or her opinion of the current fair market value of the property. If no appraisal has been made, the purchaser should sign a statement that he or she does not want or require an appraisal to be made.

[6]From this it would be possible to determine the total amount that would be held as an obligation against the property. Deducting this from the fair market value, it would be possible to determine the equity the owner has in the property at the present time; that amount should be shown.

accounts as well. A prudent investment is one that, although not having a probability of large gains, will provide a continued return.

The trust departments of banks are allowed to invest in real estate loans; of course, the requirement of prudence applies to the transaction. Since the bank does not want to place itself in a position in which it would suffer a loss for the client, the trust department will continue to be conservative in its real estate loan policies. In most instances the trust department will follow fairly closely the requirements set forth by the governing body of the bank involved, to be protected under the prudent investment ruling, often called the prudent man investment policy.

PENSION FUNDS

There is increasing awareness of the need for pension funds for all workers. The state of California, which has a pension fund, has recently established a real estate division for investment in real estate trust deeds. It is also exploring various other methods of operation, including the use of mortgage bankers. In many instances the pension programs are represented through mortgage brokers or mortgage bankers. Pension funds have become an increasing source of secondary real estate financing for the mortgage banker to depend on.

Early in 1950 mortgage bankers first recognized that pension funds would be useful to them and started trying to interest the trustees of the various pension funds in investing in real estate trust deeds.

In 1956 the corporate pension funds amounted to $16.6 billion; only $230 million of this amount was invested in real estate trust deeds or mortgages. By 1982 there was approximately $600 billion, and the investment in real estate trust deeds had increased to only $7 billion. Only 1.5 percent of the total assets were in trust deeds or mortgages. It is estimated that by 1995 the total assets of pension funds will be at least $3 trillion.

In 1981 the Government National Mortgage Association started courting the various pension funds, suggesting that they consider investing, not in mortgages, but in securities guaranteed by GNMA and secured by notes and deeds of trust. These could be delivered in denominations of $5,000 and $10,000. In this way the pension fund trustees would not have to set up departments for accounting since payments would be made to and accounted for by GNMA. It was hoped that this would open a completely new source for large amounts of money for investment in real estate.

California has followed the national pattern of investment and growth of pension funds. This source of funds continues to be a prime area for secondary financing in the real estate market, and additional growth is likely.

REAL ESTATE SYNDICATES

A real estate syndicate is an organization, either formal or informal, usually a group of friends, who have joined together for the purpose of buying a specific parcel of real estate or of providing funds for the purchase or making of trust deeds. A real estate syndicate may also be established for the purpose of buying various parcels of property that might be acceptable to the syndicate as the occasion arises.

When a syndicate is established for the purpose of purchasing a specific parcel of land, the individuals in the syndicate must each contribute sufficient funds so that either the property can be paid off in full or sufficient money can be obtained for down payment on the property with the arrangement for the balance of the funds being financed through normal channels such as banks or insurance companies.

When a syndicate is formed for the purchase or making of trust deeds, a group of people contribute varying amounts to the syndicate. In turn, they receive a share of the profits in proportion to the amount of money that they have invested.

A real estate syndicate may be a general partnership or a limited partnership. It is possible for partners to be individuals, corporations, or combinations of these. The real estate syndicate itself is not a corporation, as there are tax benefits for the partnership concept since a partnership is only taxed on the money distributed whereas a corporation pays corporate taxes and the owners pay a tax on funds distributed. At least one of the partners must be a general partner who is responsible for the operation of the syndicate. The general partner, however, may be a corporation. There are two basic types of real estate syndicates—private and public. If the syndicate is to be classified as private, there can be no more than fifteen limited partners. A public syndicate is limited to thirty-five limited partners; however, there is no limit on the amount each limited partner is allowed to invest.

In California, although a syndicate may be established as a general partnership, if it has many of the attributes of a corporation and functions as a corporation, the state may say that the organization is using the partnership to evade being taxed as a corporation. Unless the state issues a license empowering it to act as a partnership, it will be taxed as a corporation. Such an occurrence will also cause the syndicate to be taxed by the Internal Revenue Service as a corporation. For example, suppose a syndicate has a general manager, a loan committee, and a group that directs the functions of the syndicate. These are attributes of a corporation; however, the syndicate will probably fight, if necessary, to prove that it is a partnership, is acting as a partnership, and should be taxed as a partnership rather than as a corporation.

Although syndicates can be organized for the purchase or making of first trust deeds, they are usually interested in the purchase or making of second trust deeds or junior liens. If a person has his or her property cleared to the extent that a loan can be made against it and a first trust deed obtained, that individual will expect to receive the consideration of the low interest rate and extended term that accompany a first trust deed. However, if there is already a first trust deed on the property and the individual needs to borrow additional funds, naturally he or she should expect to have to pay a higher interest rate to obtain the funds and should also expect to have to pay a second trust deed note in a shorter period of time. If a person is offering a first trust deed for sale, he or she certainly will not agree to the sizable discount that a holder of a second trust deed would expect to pay. As a result, the first trust deed market does not offer the profit for the syndicate organized for the making of trust deed loans that is available in the second trust deed or the junior lien trust deed market. Naturally, such syndicates are mainly interested in making or buying second trust deeds. In many instances the anticipated yield on a second trust deed is increased because the property is sold and refinanced or just refinanced and the second trust deed paid off before its due date. It is not uncommon to find yields up to 35 percent on a 7 percent trust deed that has been discounted 30 to 40 percent and paid off in advance of its due date.

The major disadvantages of the small syndicate is that it is usually not large enough to hire competent full-time management. Consequently, it must rely on members of the syndicate to manage the debts and notes receivable. Like all other loans, the loans that a syndicate takes into its portfolio must be followed up in case there is a delinquency. If provision is not made for such follow-up, the syndicate may find itself holding a piece of paper that it will have to foreclose to protect itself. If it does find it necessary to foreclose, another disadvantage is that the syndicate is usually not large enough to provide the capital to place the foreclosed property into an earnings position, or to stand the loss of the earnings of the funds that have been placed into the foreclosed property. Consequently, if the property does not sell immediately after foreclosure, the syndicate finds that it is losing earnings and is further restricted in its operations.

Another disadvantage of a syndicate is that the members of the syndicate are seldom professional real estate people; indeed, most have had no prior experience in real estate. Unless steps are taken to form an investment

committee, the syndicate has a difficult time determining what investments to make. For the most part, however, it appears that a syndicate can be formed and a good income obtained through its operation if proper precautions are taken.

There are few laws governing syndicates. It is not necessary for any member of the syndicate to be a real estate broker provided that the syndicate does not sell more than eight trust deeds in a year; otherwise it must either have a broker's license or sell the trust deeds through a mortgage broker and pay his or her commission. A syndicate can sell seven or less trust deeds in one year without any restrictions. If the syndicate makes a loan, it may not charge fees or interest rates that would cause the total rate of return to exceed 10 percent or to be 5 points over the current Federal Reserve Bank's discount rate at the time the note is signed, whichever is larger. Anything above this would be usurious.

REAL ESTATE INVESTMENT TRUSTS (REITs)

In 1960, because of a tax interpretation, a new real estate financing entity became popular. It is a modern version of the Massachusetts trust, which was popular in the early nineteenth century but lost favor when the trust was taxed as a corporation on all net income. Looking for a source of investment in which the income would not be so heavily taxed, investors turned to stock investment companies because the earnings of such companies were not taxed if they were distributed to the investors, and only those earnings that were retained were subject to income tax.

In 1960, a court ruling equalized the stock investment company and the real estate investment trust. This ruling allowed the investment trust to distribute income from investments to the investors with only the income retained being taxed.

A real estate investment trust can be either an unincorporated trust run by a board of trustees or an incorporated organization managed by a board of directors. It is the board's obligation to raise capital, both equity and debt; to set investment policy; and to approve the recommendations of an outside advisor. The REIT must, by tax law, not be involved in the trade or business of real estate. Were it not for the 1960 ruling, the REIT would be taxed as a corporation.

There are several advantages to the real estate investment trust that are shared with the stock investment companies: (1) Because of the size of the trust and stock companies, they can obtain the best legal advice. (2) They are regulated by state agencies (the corporations commissioner, in California) and by federal agencies (if the trust or company does business across state lines or sells shares across state lines). (3) Through the use of real estate investment trusts and stock investment companies, the small investor is able to pool his or her resources with others and take advantage of large investment opportunities. (4) They offer the small investor the additional security of participation in a variety of investments. (5) There is the prospect of an annual income and a capital gain through the increase in value of property owned by the REIT. (6) The investment can be liquidated quickly through the sale of the ownership shares. Some REITs are even listed on stock exchanges. (7) There is outside professional management. (8) There is central management and limited liability. (9) The REIT may continue for many years.

To qualify as a real estate trust under rules set forth in Sections 856–858 of the Internal Revenue Code, and to be able to pass through gains and income without paying tax, REITs must comply with two separate types of rules—those relating to their organization and operation and those relating to their income and assets.

RULES CONCERNING OPERATIONS AND STRUCTURE

1. It must be managed by a board of directors if it is a corporate entity or by a board of trustees if it is a trust. The trustees or directors, as the case may be, can be individuals or corporations.
2. There must be at least 100 or more persons owning beneficial interest shares. These persons may be individuals, partnerships, corporations, estates, and trusts.
3. There must be shares of beneficial interest issued to the owners of the REIT. These shares must be issued in such a manner that they are transferable.
4. Not more than 50 percent of the stock in the REIT can be held by as few as five or fewer individuals, as defined under item 2 above, otherwise the tax benefits under the REIT would be voided.
5. The REIT must not hold any property primarily for sale to customers in the normal course of business.

RULES CONCERNING INCOME AND ASSETS

1. At least 95 percent of the REIT's gross income must come from interest, dividends and gains from the sale of stock, rents, and gain from sale of real property, including mortgages.
2. Less than 30 percent of the gross income may come from the sale of real estate held under four years and from stock held for under six months.
3. At least 75 percent of a REIT gross income must come from mortgage interest, gain from the sale of real property (this would include sale of notes and trust deeds or mortgages), rents, and dividends and gains from shares of other qualified REITs.
4. At least 95 percent of the taxable income must be distributed to the shareholders each year.

5. The REIT must have at least 75 percent of its assets in real estate, including notes, trust deeds or mortgages, cash, and government securities.

If any one or more of these rules are not followed, the REIT becomes subject to income taxes as if it were a regular business corporation. The 5 percent of the taxable income retained by the REIT is subject to income tax; however, the total taxable income before distribution to the shareholders may be reduced by setting up the proper reserves for losses thus retaining additional cash above the 5 percent retained. The REIT may also retain the cash flow created by depreciation deductions.

A public real estate syndicate may notify the general public that interests are for sale; however it must file with the Securities and Exchange Commission and with the National Association of Security Dealers in every state in which interests in the real estate syndicate are to be offered. If interstate sales of interest are not expected, filing needs to be done only with the state authorities. A prospectus has to be given to the prospective investor. It has to tell in detail what is proposed for the real estate syndicate and give the history of past performance.

In the case of the private real estate syndicate, the investors must be known to and qualified by the syndicate concerning their investment capacity and whether this type of investment will fit into their investment program. A prospectus is also required for a private syndicate, but it is made available to the investors only if they request it. The past performance can be in the form of a brief history. Most private real estate syndicates are made up of close acquaintances.

The California Real Estate Investment Trust, a good example of such an association, is the realization of a dream of the directors of the California State Employees' Credit Union No. 2. They felt that many state employees would be interested in making investments in a trust that would be dedicated to the investment of trust funds in real estate as set forth in the regulations governing real estate investment trusts. Today there are more than 2,000 shareholders with investments over $12 million.

CALIFORNIA HOUSING FINANCE ACT

On January 27, 1975, the governor of California signed Assembly Bill 1, which provided for the sale of state revenue bonds, the appropriation of funds to be used by the California Housing and Finance Agency to make loans for the financing of housing developments, and the submission of the bond issue to the people of California in November 1976. The amount of the bond issue was $450 million.

The Act went into operation on September 21, 1975. It empowered the Housing and Finance Agency (HFA) to lend money (1) through specified intermediaries and intermediary operations including the creation of secondary mortgage markets, (2) directly to the ultimate borrower, or (3) to qualified mortgage lenders, for the purpose of financing the construction, rehabilitation, or acquisition of housing for persons and families of low or moderate income.

The Agency received $10,750,000 for initial expenses in setting up accounting and loan procedures. The proposed revenue bond issue of $450 million was rejected by the voters in November 1976. The HFA is still operating on the initial grant from the legislature and expects to receive additional funds from general obligation bonds approved by the legislature. Such bonds do not need to be approved by the voters.

The Agency is too new for its future operation to be certain; however, at present it seems interested in making loans to sponsors of housing that will qualify under Section 8 of the Housing and Urban Development Department. It does not intend to enter the secondary market under the present regime. It will eventually enter the direct loan market for the construction and purchase of single-family homes. The Agency may participate in the Farmers Home Loan program. The Agency will establish an internal servicing department for following the direct loans that it makes. Early in 1977 the HFA obligated the funds then on hand to builders for the purchase of new FHA and VA loans to individuals of lower incomes.

REAL ESTATE BONDS

In the 1920s real estate bonds were a source of financing for large properties requiring large loans. A real estate bond is not actually a note, but one of a series of notes secured by a deed of trust. These notes usually vary in amount from $500 to $1,000 each; in some instances $100 bonds have been issued. Because it costs as much to print a $100 bond as it does to print a $1,000 bond, the cost of such printing is less if fewer bonds are involved; therefore, the higher denominations are more acceptable for the persons trying to obtain financing on the property.

In 1930, because bonds had been used extensively for the financing of real property, many people lost considerable money on the defaults that occurred, and the real estate bond lost its popularity as a source of financing. Although this popularity has not yet been fully recovered, the real estate bond is again finding acceptance and is being used when large sums of money are needed. Churches seem to be using this means of financing extensively; see Figure 4-1 for one such offering.

Real estate bonds usually provide for a certain number of bonds to fall due at specifically timed intervals and provide for interest to be paid either quarterly or semiannually on the total indebtedness. Bonds usually contain a provision that the mortgagor has the right to pay off the bonds in advance if he or she so desires. This gives the mortgagor the advantage of being able to reduce the bonded indebtedness whenever he or she desires or to reduce it through refunding, which means that a new issue of bonds is made to pay off the prior bond issue. A mortgagor might want to take advantage of refunding when there has been a sizable drop in the interest rate that would allow him or her to save considerable money over the total bond issue.

An individual investing in a real estate bond should be as interested in the organization proposing the bond issue, in its earning capacity, and in the real property offered as security, as a lender is when he or she analyzes the potential earning capacity of, the character of, and the property offered as security by, an individual, since all the same risks are involved. As stated previously, a real estate bond is one of a series of notes secured by one piece of property. The parties to such a transaction are three in the case of a deed of trust: the trustee, the issuing corporation, and the bondholder. The bond describes on its face the collateral used to secure it, including the legal description of record, the buildings in existence or that will be constructed, and all other tangible assets. It is possible to default on a bond, by failure to pay interest as it comes due, to pay any bond as it matures, or to perform any other act supposed to be performed by the company and indicated in the bond. Default may also occur if the borrowing corporation becomes bankrupt or does not pay a judgment against it within sixty days if that judgment totals more than 5 percent of the original bond issue, or if a court action results in a decree that the corporation ignores. In case of such default, the required percentage of bondholders request the trustee to file notice with the borrowing corporation that all the bonds are immediately due and payable. If they are not paid, the trustee is empowered to take possession of the property, to liquidate it, and to distribute to the bondholders whatever income he may realize. In so doing the trustee will, of course, incur expenses, and he is entitled to deduct these expenses from the proceeds before distribution is made.

FEDERAL HOME LOAN MORTGAGE CORPORATION

The Emergency Home Finance Act of 1970 authorized the Federal Home Loan Bank Board to set up its own secondary market. The Federal Home Loan Mortgage

FIGURE 4-1   An example of mortgage bond financing. *Courtesy Dempsey-Tegeler & Co., Inc.*

Architect's drawing of majestic new sanctuary of The First Methodist Church, Palo Alto.

$700,000.00

First Mortgage Serial Bonds of

THE FIRST METHODIST CHURCH

Palo Alto, California

Corporation, a result of that authority, purchases mortgages and trust deeds from savings and loan associations. Congress allocates funds to the Federal Home Loan Board which in turn makes them available to the FHLMC. The Federal Home Loan Mortgage Corporation may buy FHA, VA, or conventional loans. This procedure was intended to make savings and loan associations more interested in making FHA and VA loans.

The Federal Home Loan Mortgage Corporation has been buying at a price of $97 on each $100 of loan principal. There is no fee in connection with immediate delivery (ninety-day) commitments. The fee for twelve-month commitments is 1 percent, and for eighteen months 1.5 percent.

Mortgage brokers were unhappy to see the FHLMC enter the secondary finance field, because it made more money available to savings and loans, thus reducing demand for their service and reducing the need for outsiders to service loans sold.

The advent of the Federal Home Loan Mortgage Corporation into the secondary mortgage market provided FNMA and GNMA with competition that, on occasion,

FIGURE 4-1 (continued)

BONDS WILL PROVIDE FUNDS TO BUILD NEW SANCTUARY

The construction of a beautiful new sanctuary is the first step in the master plan of improvements for The First Methodist Church of Palo Alto. Funds from the sale of these bonds, plus pledges of 966 families of the congregation, will finance the program.

The new sanctuary, which combines the best of traditional church architecture with contemporary concepts, will have a seating capacity of 1,100. This is almost double the capacity of the present sanctuary. In addition there will be a small chapel for 150. There will also be rooms on the lower floor for youth gatherings,

church school classes, for music requirements, for fellowship and hospitality.

A picturesque court will separate the new sanctuary from the present educational building. Later, this building will be expanded to include offices for the Ministers and staff, and kitchen facilities will be enlarged.

It is a soundly conceived plan of expansion and improvement . . . a plan that meets the needs of the Church today and well into the future.

BONDS SECURED BY PROPERTY VALUED AT $1,850,000

These bonds are the direct obligation of The First Methodist Church of Palo Alto, a California Corporation. The property mortgaged consists of five valuable parcels of real estate together with all buildings and improvements. Conservatively this property is

valued at $1,850,000. The average annual income of the Church for the past three years is more than 11 times the average yearly interest requirement of this Issue.

BONDS GIVE YOU EXCELLENT INCOME EVERY SIX MONTHS

Your money will be earning from 5¼% to 6% (depending on maturity), and interest will be paid to you semiannually (March 1 and September 1) until your bonds mature or are redeemed. The rate of

interest is exceptionally high for an investment of this quality. As a matter of fact, it is higher than the yield from savings accounts. And, your principal is soundly secured besides.

YOU CAN INVEST AS LITTLE AS $500 FOR ONE BOND

You do not have to be a big investor to participate. You can buy just one bond for $500, if you choose. Also you can choose the maturity that best suits you

(see table on back page). If you have money to invest, these sound First Mortgage Bonds deserve your careful consideration.

PRESENT FACILITIES OF

THE FIRST METHODIST

CHURCH OF PALO ALTO

Sanctuary which will be replaced by beautiful new structure illustrated on front.

can become confusing because of the different attitudes in purchasing.

PRIVATE INDIVIDUALS

Throughout California a great number of individuals make a business of investing in first and second trust deeds. These individuals are not restricted by any rules or regulations on the ratio of the loan to the value of the property. They are not restricted by any agency as to the term

that the loan may run, and they may charge any interest rate not considered usurious under the laws of California.

Individuals are usually unable to compete with institutional lenders for prime real estate loans. However, they can obtain a higher interest rate than institutional lenders because of the higher degree of risk involved in the loans that they make.

Most banks, real estate agents, and savings and loan associations know of individuals who are in the real estate financing business. When they receive application for a loan that they know will not be accepted by their organ-

FIGURE 4-1 (continued)

Original Church Building — 1894.

Church Has Grown Steadily in Size and Service

The First Methodist Church of Palo Alto, California, was organized January 14, 1894 with just 24 members, and was incorporated February 20, 1895. The first sanctuary was built in 1895. It was replaced by the present sanctuary in 1914.

The present senior minister, Dr. R. Marvin Stuart, was appointed in 1942, at which time the membership was approximately 700. Today the membership is 3000, with a projected growth of 4200 by 1980. The church has always played a prominent role in the religious and cultural life of the Palo Alto-Menlo Park area.

The church's objective, as stated in a bulletin to its members, is to "build today for tomorrow that we may fulfill our obligations as a strong and growing church, that we may better serve those who look to us for leadership." The construction of a new sanctuary and other facilities will enable The First Methodist Church to attain this objective. By buying bonds that make this new construction possible, you not only have a good investment, but you also have the satisfaction of knowing that you are enabling a fine church to become an even greater strength in its community.

Educational building. Later will be expanded and modernized.

Elementary school building, part of First Methodist Church property.

ization, they often refer the applicant to such an individual, who, they feel, might be interested in the application. Such individuals often advertise in the newspapers that they are in the business of making real estate loans. If the individual has considerable funds available he or she may work through a mortgage broker or a mortgage banker, in which case he or she will be expected to pay the usual fee for services rendered. Although there is no legal requirement as to the amount or the length of time for which an individual may make a real estate loan, loans made by individuals are usually relatively short-term and for relatively small amounts.

FARMERS HOME ADMINISTRATION

Program 502. The Farmers Home Administration, an agency under the United States Department of Agriculture, administers a program known as 502 for financing homes for individuals who qualify under its low-income definition. There was a ceiling, for all areas, of $15,600 maximum income in order to qualify until January 1, 1982, when it was decided that the maximum would be determined by area. At that time the study of the areas had not been completed so a formula was set up until area maximums could be determined. Low in-

FIGURE 4-1   (continued)

Palo Alto — City of Charm, Culture and Progress

Situated in the northern part of Santa Clara County, California, Palo Alto is adjacent to the beautiful campus of Stanford University and the rolling foothills of the Coast Range mountains. The city was founded in 1889 and incorporated in 1894. Palo Alto means Tall Tree — a name given by the early Spanish explorers to the historic redwood tree at the northwest entrance to the city.

Palo Alto is a city of beautiful homes, a city carefully planned to enhance its charm. Its beauty, ideal climate and unexcelled religious, cultural and educational advantages, have attracted men and women of the arts, sciences and professions, many of whom are world famous.

Palo Alto is also noted as a center for the following manufacturing industries: electronic instruments and research, radio and communications systems, plastics, household and garden equipment, metal and wood products, printing and publishing, film processing, and medical instruments and research. The city has become a gathering ground for a well-educated and technically trained labor force.

Palo Alto is on the mainline of the Southern Pacific railroad, two major highways, and is only a few minutes from the great ports of San Francisco and the International Airport. Present population is approximately 53,000.

MATURITIES AND RATES OF INTEREST

September 1, 1963	. . . . $25,000.00 . . . . 5¼%	
September 1, 1964	. . . . $30,000.00 . . . . 5¼%	
September 1, 1965	. . . . $30,000.00 . . . . 5¼%	
September 1, 1966	. . . . $35,000.00 . . . . 5½%	
September 1, 1967*	. . . . $35,000.00 . . . . 5½%	
September 1, 1968	. . . . $40,000.00 . . . . 5½%	
September 1, 1969	. . . . $40,000.00 . . . . 5¾%	
September 1, 1970	. . . . $40,000.00 . . . . 5¾%	
September 1, 1971*	. . . . $40,000.00 . . . . 5¾%	
September 1, 1972	. . . . $45,000.00 . . . . 5¾%	
September 1, 1973	. . . . $45,000.00 . . . . 5¾%	
September 1, 1974*	. . . . $45,000.00 . . . . 6%	
September 1, 1974	. . . $250,000.00 . . . . 6%	

Maturities indicated by an asterisk have bonds in the denomination of $500.00. All other maturities have bonds in the denomination of $1,000.00. The above bonds are to bear interest from the date to maturity at the rate set out opposite each maturity.

Dated September 1, 1961   Principal Payable Annually
September 1, 1963 through
September 1, 1974

Principal payable September 1st; interest payable semi-annually March 1st and September 1st at the office of the Boatmen's National Bank of St. Louis, Missouri, Corporate Trustee and Paying Agent.

Bonds are in coupon form in $500.00 and $1000.00 denominations.

Any or all bonds of this issue may be prepaid and redeemed at the option of the Maker, on any semi-annual interest paying date, at par and accrued interest, upon giving of twenty (20) days previous written notice to the Corporate Trustee. J. F. Tegeler, St. Louis, Missouri, Individual Trustee.

INSURANCE AND LEGALITY

The Indenture of Trust provides for the maintenance of insurance against fire and perils covered by extended coverage insurance in an amount at least equal to the amount of bonds outstanding from time to time.

All legal papers and proceedings have been prepared or approved by our attorneys, Messrs. Bryan, Cave, McPheeters & McRoberts, St. Louis, Missouri.

---

come was determined to be 80 percent of an area's median income. Those who find themselves in the low-income bracket—$11,500 to $18,000—qualify for interest rate assistance. The rate they will pay could be as low as 1 percent; whereas those in the moderate-income level—$18,000 to $23,500—will pay 13.25 percent on their loans.

There is an indication that the Reagan administration will reduce the amount of money available to the Farmers Home Administration in 1983. The indication is that the program to provide low-interest mortgages to low-income Americans will be reduced from $2.3 billion in 1982 to $900 million in 1983 (this is for the fiscal year starting October 1). This would provide for approximately 27,100 new loans in 1983, compared with roughly 68,000 in 1982. The program for those with moderate income is to be completely discontinued in 1983; the 1982 budget for this program was $430 million.

Program 515. Program 515 is the same as Program 502 except that it provides for subsidies for those whose adjusted gross income is under $8,500. The Farmers Home Administration requires that 25 percent of the gross income be paid as a home payment, and it will subsidize the balance of the loan payment.

From time to time the Farmers Home Administration

sells blocks of loans, either through the pass-through method to GNMA, or to other interested investors. This unusual procedure has been initiated on occasion to develop additional funds for loans. The funds used by the Farmers Home Administration are allocated to it by the United States Treasury. Applications for loans are made directly to the Farmers Home Administration.

PERSONAL PROPERTY BROKERS

Another source of real estate loans is the personal property broker, for example, Avco Financial Services and Ford Consumer Credit Company. The personal property broker is under the supervision of the state commissioner of corporations. Each organization sets its lending policies and procedures. Some companies collect interest on the unpaid balance each month, while others use the gross rate (add-on) method. Interest rates vary from company to company; the average APR is 18 to 21 percent. Variable interest is not allowed. The ratio of loan to value also varies from company to company; the average is 80 percent of the present market value less the present amount of the first lien, if one exists.

The length of time for which a loan may be written varies with the amount of the loan. A loan against real estate must be for at least $5,000. The maximum term for a $5,000 to $6,000 loan is 102 months. The maximum term for a loan from $6,000 to $10,000 is eighty-four months and fifteen days, and for a loan of $10,000 or over the term varies from sixty months to 120 months. The Personal Property Brokers Act does not permit loan fees, points, or prepayment penalties on loans up to $10,000. Since, however, most personal property brokers are also industrial property brokers, real estate loans up to $10,000 are made under the Industrial Property Brokers Act. Loans secured by real estate over $10,000 must also have a security agreement on the borrower's furniture and/or car, and are made under the Personal Property Brokers Act under which points may be charged on loans secured by a trust deed if the amount is over $10,000.

The personal property broker may make loans secured by either first or second trust deeds. Most of the loans are secured by second trust deeds because of the higher interest rates and the shorter term that the loan can run. The loans are usually made against the equity in property for one or more of the following purposes:

1. Cash for a seller to use to buy a new home. Such a loan is usually paid off after his or her old home is sold.
2. Consolidation of existing debt load to reduce monthly payments.
3. Additional funds to complete a down payment on a new home or for other consumer purchase.
4. Additional cash for home improvements.
5. Cash to buy a desirable lot for a future second home or cabin.
6. Cash to make necessary improvements to present home before placing it on the market.

Purchase money loans are sometimes made when it is difficult to obtain a loan from sources that usually make the loans secured by first trust deeds. For example, a person might obtain a purchase money loan when buying an apartment house with more than four units when the amount of the loan is not enough to justify a loan from an insurance company or a savings and loan association, yet it is too large for a bank loan.

Credit Unions

Credit unions consist of a group of people who have pooled their savings so that others of that group may borrow money at a reduced rate. Those who provide the money may receive a higher interest payment than that paid by other savings accounts. Originally they were interested in relatively short-term loans for personal use, such as buying a TV, furniture, or a car. As the credit unions grew, they expanded into longer-term loans for land acquisition; home improvement; and even purchase of a principal home, a rental, or even a vacation home.

Credit unions may be fraternal or union-oriented, community developed, or established by individuals in the same business or occupation. In July 1981 there were 22,000 federally and state-chartered credit unions with a total membership of about 44 million. In order to borrow from a credit union, it is necessary to be a member of that credit union.

Although most credit unions were not making real estate loans in 1982, they had the legal right to make them with a term of thirty years. The rate would be slightly under the current rate. They can also make loans on mobile homes for a term of fifteen years. The interest rate is set by the directors of the credit union. In 1982 the average rate was 12 percent. The maximum amount for the real estate loan and the mobile home loan is based on the individual credit union's capital base. For instance, the Superior California School Employees Credit Union has a limit of $40,000 total of all kinds of loans to one individual.

Home improvement loans can be made for a period of eight years, and personal, unsecured loans for a period of three years. Credit unions are also a source of loans on second trust deeds for improvements to a member's property. The amount is based on the equity in the property.

The National Credit Union Administration authorized an increase in the regulated interest rate to 21 percent. Also, credit unions were authorized to accept deposits to

Individual Retirement Accounts (IRA's) as of January 1, 1982. This should bring additional savings into credit unions, so that they may become more interested in real estate loans.

All accounts are insured for up to $100,000.

QUESTIONS

1. A bridge loan is
   a. a loan for the construction of a bridge
   b. an advance earned playing professional bridge
   c. a short-term loan to bridge the time while waiting for long-term financing
   d. none of the above

2. The graduated payment mortgage (GPM)
   a. is the same as the adjustable mortgage rate loan
   b. provides for negative amortization during the first years of its life
   c. is the same as a variable rate mortgage
   d. requires the same down payment as a level payment loan

3. The wraparound trust deed is the same as
   a. the all-inclusive trust deed
   b. the flexi loan
   c. the piggyback loan
   d. none of the above

4. Time sharing is
   a. the same as a partnership loan
   b. similar to an equity participation loan
   c. a junior lien
   d. a sales tool

5. The lease purchase sale allows
   a. the buyer to purchase only the improvements and lease the land with the right to buy the land at a future date
   b. the buyer to buy only the improvements and lease the land with no possibility of ever buying the land
   c. the buyer to purchase only the improvements with the requirements to buy the land at some definite predetermined date
   d. all of the above

6. Equity participation is
   a. the same as shared appreciation
   b. in effect the same as a partnership purchase
   c. in effect a joint venture
   d. none of the above

7. Builder approach to creative finance is
   a. an amortized loan with a high down payment, short term, and no interest
   b. to buy down the interest rate
   c. to sell the property through time sharing
   d. all of the above

8. A flexi loan is a loan that is
   a. written for the usual term with interest to be reviewed every five years
   b. written for the usual term with low monthly payments to interest and principal during the first five years and large enough monthly payments to amortize the balance due in the remaining twenty-five years
   c. written for monthly payments over a thirty-year term but reviewed for interest rates every five years, at which time the loan can be renewed or called
   d. provides for interest only to be paid monthly for five years and the balance to be amortized over twenty-five years with monthly payments to interest and principal

9. An adjustable rate mortgage is the same as a variable rate mortgage except
   a. there are no restrictions on the number of times the interest rate can be adjusted in one year
   b. the base to justify the interest rate adjustment is not specifically identified for all lenders
   c. there is no limit to the amount of increase or decrease of the interest rate
   d. all of the above

10. The *Wellenkamp* v. *Bank of America* ruling affected
    a. renting of apartments to families with children
    b. assumptions
    c. renting to no one under fifty-five years of age
    d. renting to the elderly with pets

11. A mortgage company (bank)
    a. makes several real estate loans and then sells them in a block to an investor
    b. negotiates with investors to make a loan to an individual
    c. does not require a large office and staff
    d. does not service loans it sells

12. A mortgage broker is an individual or an organization that
    a. has contact with several agencies or individuals who are looking for real estate loans
    b. acts as an intermediary between agencies or individuals and those looking for a real estate loan
    c. does not make the loan, but acts for the lender by preparing all papers in connection with the application, even the appraisal in some cases
    d. all of the above

13. In the real estate loans they may make, bank trust departments are limited to
    a. loans a prudent man would make
    b. a loan-to-value ratio of 50 percent
    c. none
    d. smaller amounts than the parent bank would make
14. A prudent man investment has been interpreted as one that
    a. would have the probability of large gains
    b. would be speculative
    c. would not be speculative, but provide a continued return on the investment
    d. would have a high return but a poor payment history
15. Pension funds have
    a. been very active in the real estate loan field
    b. too many regulations for them to become active in real estate loans
    c. become more active in the real estate loan field recently but have funds to use for additional loans
    d. none of the above
16. Pension funds found their way into more activity in the real estate loan field through
    a. participation certificates issued by organizations such as GNMA
    b. electing new trustees for the fund
    c. accepting a smaller return on investments
    d. all of the above
17. Real estate syndicates must have at least
    a. fifty members
    b. twenty-five members
    c. five members
    d. two members
18. A real estate syndicate may be all of the following except
    a. a general partnership
    b. a limited partnership
    c. a corporation
    d. a group of individuals acting without any legal agreement
19. A real estate investment trust must have at least

    a. 50 members
    b. 75 members
    c. 100 members
    d. 125 members
20. A real estate investment trust can be
    a. a general partnership
    b. a limited partnership with at least one general partner
    c. a corporation
    d. any of the above
21. Which of the following is incorrect? Individuals are
    a. not subject to usury laws
    b. not restricted to the types of loans they can make
    c. allowed to make real estate loans that will mature in more than ten years
    d. able to make loans on a single payment note basis
22. Personal property brokers under the supervision of the state commissioner of corporations can make real estate loans
    a. for $10,000 to $15,000
    b. secured by either first or second trust deeds and personal property security agreements
    c. amortized over a period of fifteen years but, in most cases, due and payable in three years
    d. all of the above
23. Most personal property brokers are also industrial property brokers. As industrial property brokers they are interested in
    a. real estate loans from $5,000 to $10,000
    b. loans with loan-to-value ratio of 60 percent
    c. maturities that do not exceed eighty-four months
    d. all of the above
24. Real estate bonds are
    a. slowly finding their way back to acceptability
    b. secured by second liens on real estate
    c. drawn so that interest is paid annually
    d. none of the above

5

Savings and Loan Associations and Real Estate Loans

The savings and loan association industry is big business. On June 30, 1980, the savings and loan associations of the United States had real estate loans on their books totaling $479,780 million. The organizations responsible for the second largest number of real estate loans were the commercial banks, with a total of $251,198 million. The third largest category in this field was the insurance companies, with a total of $122,471 million. The fourth largest maker of real estate loans was the mutual savings banks. Although they are found in only seventeen states, mostly in the northeastern United States, a total of $99,151 million was on their books. About 7 percent of these loans were on property located in California, although there are no mutual savings banks in California.

DEFINITION

A savings and loan association is a locally owned and privately managed savings and home-financing institution. Its two functions are to accept savings deposits from individuals, partnerships, organizations, corporations, and other sources; and to invest these savings advantageously in real estate loans. Originally the real estate loans primarily covered housing and home financing. A savings and loan association is able to pay a higher dividend on savings deposits because of its specialization in real estate loans. For the most part the real estate loans are long-term, so that interest returns can be fairly well computed in advance, expenses closely estimated, and a high percentage of deposits loaned.

ORGANIZATION

California savings and loan associations may be mutual organizations or corporations. A mutual association has no capital stock; the holders of savings accounts are the owners of the association. After expenses have been computed and reserves established, the earnings are distributed as dividends to the depositors. A corporately or-

ganized savings and loan association issues organizational common stock that is nonwithdrawable but can be transferred from one individual to another. This stock is usually sold at a cost higher than the par value and the surplus placed in an account for paid-in surplus. The capital and surplus accounts thus raised are, in effect, protection for the depositors and others who do business with the company; they also act as a cushion for the Federal Savings and Loan Insurance Corporation, should a sizable loss occur. The holders of the common stock become the owners of the association; should it become necessary to liquidate, their stock may be charged with the losses to the total amount of their investment if the ordinary reserves and undivided profits are insufficient to cover the losses. Usually no dividends may be paid on the common stock until such time as adequate reserves have been established in the eyes of the examining body, and dividends paid on the savings deposits.

As of December 31, 1981, there were 127 state-chartered savings and loan associations in California; there were 87 on December 31, 1975. In 1981, there were 70 federally chartered savings and loan associations, compared with 78 in 1975. Due to mergers, the number of branches has increased and the total number of offices is now over 1,100. Many savings and loan associations also have minibranches and satellite offices operating out of mobile offices (motor homes going to different communities on different days at different hours).

Savings and loan associations can operate under a state or federal charter. If under a state charter, they are subject to the rules and regulations of the state savings and loan commissioner. If they are a federal association, they operate under the rules and regulations of the Federal Home Loan Bank. It is possible for a state-chartered organization to become a member of the Federal Home Loan Bank system, in which case it must abide by the rules and regulations of the Federal Home Loan Bank as well as by those of the savings and loan commissioner. In case of conflict, the Federal Home Loan Bank rules will prevail.

Under the regulations of the Federal Home Loan Bank all savings and loan associations must maintain certain liquidity. They must have 7 percent of their total assets in either government bonds or cash. They must also maintain 2 percent of the total unpaid balance of the home mortgage loans in stock of the Federal Home Loan Bank. The balance of the deposits may be invested in mortgage loans, which, on an amortized basis, provide a monthly inflow of cash that again finds its way into cash, bonds, or mortgage loans.[1]

1932: THE FEDERAL HOME LOAN BANK

The Federal Home Loan Bank was established by law in 1932. Twelve separate districts were established that followed very closely the pattern of the Federal Reserve Bank districts. The primary purpose of the Federal Home Loan Bank was to provide a credit reserve system for the savings and loan associations through which they would be able to borrow for a short or long term from the district home loan bank. It was hoped that this system would provide a means of stabilizing local economies in which savings and loan associations were influential.

The district bank would work in the following way. If a run started in a basically stable community, the

Federal Home Loan Bank could make a loan to the savings and loan associations in that community to bolster their deposits until the adverse influence was withdrawn. These loans would be secured by assignments of deeds of trust or by mortgages and would be assigned to the Federal Home Loan Bank. The bank would also be able to provide funds to a savings and loan association that had loaned up to its maximum and that desired to give a favorable report on a loan application. An association would be able to borrow sufficient funds from the Federal Home Loan Bank to make such a loan in anticipation of additional future deposits.

The Federal Home Loan Bank Act allowed both federally and state-chartered associations to become members. However, before associations could become members, they had to meet the qualifications established by the Bank.

In 1970, Congress passed the Emergency Home Financing Act of 1970. The provisions of the Act allowed the Federal Home Loan Bank to establish the Federal Home Loan Mortgage Corporation (FHLMC), which became known as Freddie Mac. Freddie Mac's job was to become part of the secondary mortgage market by buying and selling FHA, VA, and conventional loans made by approved lenders. It was also allowed to participate in loans.

Additional information will be found in the chapter on the Federal National Mortgage Association and the Federal Home Loan Mortgage Corporation.

1934: THE FEDERAL SAVINGS AND LOAN INSURANCE CORPORATION

In 1934 a very important step was taken: The Federal Savings and Loan Insurance Corporation was formed. This insurance corporation was created by the National Housing Act to restore confidence in the savings and loan industry, just as the Federal Deposit Insurance Corporation was formed to restore confidence in banks, by insuring all depositors of savings and loan associations qualified to carry such insurance.

The Federal Savings and Loan Insurance Corporation is an agency of the United States Government. To pay for the insurance that it provides, member savings and loan associations pay a premium based on a certain percentage of the deposits on their books. The Corporation insures withdrawable savings and credited earnings up to $100,000 for each depositor in an insured institution. All federal savings and loan associations must be insured under this program, and all state-chartered savings and loan associations are eligible for the program.

When an examination of a savings and loan association by the Federal Savings and Loan Insurance Cor-

---

[1]The first loan made by a savings and loan association in the United States was made by the Oxford Provident Building Association on April 11, 1831. It might be interesting to follow the results of that first loan. The loan was put up for bids. A man by the name of Comly Rich felt he could build a home for $375, and he wanted very much to be the first to borrow money from the Oxford Provident Building Association. He therefore made the following bid: In exchange for a loan of $375 he would pay a premium of $10 and a monthly interest of 6 percent. On this bid he was granted the first loan to be made by a savings and loan association in the United States. It is also interesting to note that, although they called it a premium at that time, the $10 actually constituted 2.7 points charge for making the loan. Do you suppose this was the beginning of today's real estate point system?

With the $375 Comly Rich built a home that had a stone foundation one foot thick and measured fifteen feet by eleven feet. The house had three rooms and three stories. The living room was on the ground floor, the bedroom was on the second floor, and there was a garret room above the bedroom. This building was still standing 100 years later, when it was being rented for $10 a month. Although the convenience of the house left something to be desired, the construction was solid. In 1960 the Philadelphia Historical Commission designated the house a historical landmark.

There is one other interesting bit of history connected with Comly Rich. In April 1836, just five years after he obtained his loan from the Oxford Provident Building Association, it became necessary for the association to foreclose due to nonpayment of his monthly payments. Although there was a loan committee review of the appraisal of the proposed property, even as today, and although there was a requirement of fire insurance, it is evident that Comly Rich's capacity for payment had been misjudged, even as other individuals' capacities are misjudged today.

poration shows that association to be in financial difficulties, the Federal Savings and Loan Insurance Corporation will usually try either to arrange a merger with a sound savings and loan association, or to arrange for a reorganization of the association in difficulty. If this fails and it is necessary to liquidate the association, payment of each insured account in such an insured institution that is surrendered and transferred to the Federal Savings and Loan Insurance Corporation shall be made by the Corporation as soon as possible either (1) by cash, or (2) by making available to each insured member a transferred account in a new insured institution in the same community or in another insured institution in an amount equal to the insured account of such an insured depositor.

In 1933 came a step forward for the state-chartered savings and loan associations. This step was the direct reduction plan, which changed the method by which loan payments were credited. Under this plan, as each payment was made, a reduction was made in the principal after the interest had been credited. Before this, payments had been credited to an account which, when it equalled the principal amount of the loan, was used to cancel out the loan.

With the recovery of the economy and the changes that had been made in the regulations of the operation of savings and loan associations, the associations again began to come into their own, and although the recovery started around 1938 and progressed slowly, growth was continuous and became rapid. With the development of suburban areas and the subsequent demand for construction money, it became natural for savings and loan associations to establish branches in areas convenient for the customers. Therefore, from 1949 to date, a number of branches were established throughout the United States, occupying separate quarters but following procedures and dictates of a central office.

SPECIALISTS IN REAL ESTATE LOANS

Savings and loan associations are specialists in the business of lending on real estate. Their loan portfolios consist mainly of real estate loans. They can therefore operate on higher loan-to-value and loan-to-deposit ratios. The majority of their loans are on single-family dwellings, and since this is the area with which they are most familiar, it is also the area in which they are most proficient. As they move into types of loans in which they have less experience, the risk increases. Savings and loan associations in the Central Valley of California experienced sizable construction loan losses when money became tight in 1966 and demand lessened, and many fore-closures against large contractors became necessary. Savings and loan associations have always made construction loans; in most loan portfolios about 30 percent of the loans are for the construction of residential property and 67 percent of the loans are for the purpose of purchasing or refinancing existing property; however, financing of construction loans has always posed a risk and requires specialists when a large operation is contemplated.

There has been some discussion for several years as to whether savings and loan associations should be allowed to enter the consumer loan field, an area of operation that has been completely foreign to the savings and loan associations. The Housing Act of 1968, signed by President Lyndon Johnson in August 1968, permitted federally chartered savings and loan associations to make loans up to $5,000 for equipping a home. This has been increased to $10,000 for equipping a home or for home repairs and modernization. The term is for twenty years with a five-year call date and with monthly payments. This development has been interpreted as allowing the federal savings and loan associations to enter the consumer loan field to finance such items as air conditioners, refrigerators, dishwashers, garbage disposals, and stoves. There is some question whether items such as carpets, furniture, and television sets could be included. No association will be allowed to make loans of this type totaling more than 5 percent of its total assets. Since only a small portion of the loan portfolio is to be in consumer-type loans, it is felt that there will be no need for additional reserves for losses. As this is a new field to savings and loan associations, it will be necessary for specialists in this field to be hired.

On October 1, 1982, all savings and loan associations in California were given permission to enter the consumer loan field. The total of such loans can not exceed 5 percent of the association's total assets in 1983, $7^1/_2$ percent in 1984, and 10 percent in 1985 and forward. All types of consumer loans are permitted from personal loans to automobile loans. The prudent man loan restriction as to term and amount is used. By 1984 competition and regulation will replace the prudent man restriction.

Consumer lending involves short-term loans in which the exposure to loss can be high. If the savings and loan associations go into this type of financing they will lose some of the benefits they presently have. They will have to establish a larger reserve for losses and a larger cash reserve and reduce the ratio of loans to deposits. To be successful in this operation, they will again have to bring in specialists from outside their field. There will have to be a consumer loan specialist among those who examine the assets of the savings and loan associations to see that they are acting in the best interests of the depositors.

INTEREST RATES

Because of the higher interest rates paid for savings funds, the savings and loan associations characteristically have charged higher rates for their mortgage money than other institutional lenders. As funds accumulated and the need arose to put money to work, the savings and loan associations developed new ways of putting the money into the field until they reached a point where they now offer the most complete real estate lending service available among institutional lenders.

It is possible for savings and loan associations to lend on everything from bare land to subdivision improvements to the completed house on a lot. There are two types of savings and loan associations in California: those under federal charter, governed by the Home Loan Bank Board, and state-chartered savings and loan associations, under the supervision of the savings and loan commissioner of California. Some state savings and loan associations that have qualified as members of the Federal Home Loan Bank system also operate under the Board's regulations.

LOANS ALLOWED

Permissive legislation allows savings and loan associations to make real estate loans of all types, but whether a savings and loan association actually makes all kinds of loans depends on the economic conditions of the area, the demand for money, and the availability of money.

STATE-CHARTERED SAVINGS AND LOAN ASSOCIATIONS

Shares and Certificates of Deposit

A California state-chartered savings and loan association may make a loan against its shares (deposits) or certificates of deposit. There is no limit on the term for this type of loan. The association may lend up to 100 percent of the balance in the individual's account or 100 percent of the value of the certificate of deposit. Such a flat note requires no payment on principal until maturity. This means that an individual having a savings deposit of $1,000 could borrow $1,000 for an indefinite period, or until such time as the deposit is withdrawn. At the time of the withdrawal the note would have to be paid in full.

Bonds as Collateral

A savings and loan association may loan against state, county, municipal, or federal bonds for an unlimited time, assuming the bonds do not mature before the notes' due date. It may loan up to 90 percent of the face value or market value, whichever is smaller, with no payment required on the principal until maturity. It is suggested that where there is no amortization of the principal, interest should be collected monthly. This type of loan must be followed closely to see that the amount of the loan never exceeds 90 percent of the market value of the bonds.

Existing Loans as Collateral

If an individual has a first trust deed on a piece of property that would qualify for a loan by a savings and loan association, the association may make a loan whose term is determined only by the note secured by the deed of trust. The term cannot exceed the maturity date of the note being given as security. The amount of the loan may not exceed the smaller of the following: 90 percent of the balance owing at the time of the loan or 90 percent of the loan that could be made if the savings and loan association were making a new loan. This qualification is placed in the State Savings and Loan Act to take care of the notes secured by the trust deed that are larger than the amount for which the savings and loan association would normally appraise the property.

Assume that a client has a trust deed for $10,000. Under the 90 percent clause there would be a possible loan of $9,000. However, an appraisal reveals to the savings and loan association that the property is worth only $9,000. With this appraisal the savings and loan association normally would make a loan of $8,100 (if it qualified for a 90 percent loan, or $7,200 in the case of an 80 percent loan). Under the qualification stated above, the savings and loan association can make a loan of 90 percent of the $8,100, or $7,290, secured by an assignment of the note and deed of trust. The note to the savings and loan association must be paid in full by the time of the maturity of the assigned note and trust deed.

Loans on Single-Family Owner-Occupied Dwellings

The maximum term for a loan on a single-family dwelling occupied by the owner is thirty years. The maximum amount possible is 90 percent of appraised value or sales price, whichever is smaller. Note that this is a high percentage-to-value loan and that it carries a heavy restriction. Under no circumstances can there be a second trust deed. The dwelling must be owner-occupied. All bonds or assessments against the property must be paid. As with all savings and loan association loans, interest must be paid monthly; however, if the house is completed, there need be no principal payment for the first three months. After that period principal and interest will be collected. If the loan is for construction there need be no principal payment for twenty-four months; however, interest must be paid each month. After the twenty-fourth month, monthly payments to principal and interest begin.

The maximum amount of such a loan is $107,000. A loan of 95 percent of value or sales price, whichever is the lesser amount, may be made if the top 20 percent is insured by a private insurance company such as Mortgage Guarantee Insurance Company (MGIC, known as "Magic") or Tico Mortgage Insurance Company. The maximum loan under these conditions is $108,300. This type of financing is also available for condominiums, co-ops, and cluster-type housing. The maximum term is thirty years.

Because of the very high loan-to-value ratio of such a loan, an additional restriction has been placed upon it regarding the total amount the association may carry in its portfolio. Under no circumstances shall the total of the 90 percent loans exceed 5 percent of the total assets of the savings and loan association.

Loans on One or More Residential Units

Savings and loan associations may make loans on one or more residential units, including single-family homes, duplexes, quadruplexes, and five-unit (and over) apartments. The restrictions are not as severe as on the 90 percent loan-to-value loans. There can be junior financing. The owner does not have to occupy the building, but the loan-to-value ratio is only 80 percent. There is no maximum amount of loan; the maximum is controlled by the 80 percent of loan to value. If the loan is for construction, the first principal payment may be delayed for twenty-four months. The first principal payment may be delayed for three months if the loan is for the purchase of an existing structure. The first principal payment may be delayed for six months if the loan is made for the purpose of facilitating a trade. The thirty-year maturity runs from the date of the first payment to principal. In other words, in the case of a construction loan the final maturity would be thirty years plus the twenty-four months representing the period from the date of the note to the date of the first payment to principal. Of course, there must be monthly payments of interest during the period when no principal payment is needed. All loans made against property of any kind must be secured by a first trust deed.

The savings and loan association may make this type of loan to finance residential condominiums, co-ops, and cluster-type housing for one-family occupancy.

Not all associations want to make the 90 percent loans previously discussed. They feel that the 5 percent of total assets rule is too limiting and that they can serve more people by not making 90 percent loans during periods of tight money. During such periods many junior liens are given. Such a loan would not be eligible for 90 percent and would have to be made under the 80 percent program.

Housing for the Elderly

The Housing Act of 1968 made many changes in laws. One of the important areas was the financing of housing for the elderly. In connection with this type of housing, California savings and loan associations were authorized to enter the field. Under this Act, savings and loan associations may make loans not only to house the elderly, but also for rest homes and nursing homes. The loan must be amortized and cannot exceed 90 percent of the appraised value or cost, whichever is the lesser amount. The loan may be amortized over a thirty-year period. The first payment to principal does not have to be made for twenty-four months if the loan was to construct such a structure. The first principal payment for a loan used to buy existing housing for the elderly must be made after three months from the date of the note. In all cases the payments must be monthly after the first payment.

Urban Renewal

Under Financial Code Section 7153.5, savings and loan associations are allowed to make loans for urban renewal. Homes that need to be brought up to code may be used as collateral for loans. A loan of 80 percent of the appraised value may be made for a maximum period of thirty years. The first payment to principal need not be made for six months from the date of the note, and payments may be as infrequent as semiannually thereafter.

Loans on Improved Property

Up to this point we have been discussing residential property loans of various types and loans secured by money pledged in the savings and loan association. These loans make up about 97 percent of the loan portfolio of the average savings and loan association. Now let us consider the nonresidential loans for commercial, industrial, church, or club property, and other categories not under the residential classification.

Three types of loans on improved property are available from savings and loan associations. The most liberal is the amortized loan. Such a loan may be made for twenty-five years, with a maximum loan–to–appraised-value ratio of 90 percent if the association takes assignments of long-term leases as additional security. If the loan is to be on existing property, the first payment can be three months from the date of the note and monthly thereafter. The first payment may be twenty-four months after the date of the note and monthly thereafter if the improvements are to be constructed.

It is also possible to obtain unamortized loans for this type of property. A term loan of two years for an amount equal to 70 percent of the appraised value may be made with the understanding that the loan is to be paid at maturity, or a term loan of three years may be made for the amount of 60 percent of the appraised value of the property. Again the loan is to be paid at maturity.

In reviewing the regulations to this point, you will notice that the highest ratio of value to loan occurs when there is a relatively short period before principal and interest payments are started on a monthly basis. As the period for the return of the principal is extended, the ratio of value to loan decreases, for obvious reasons.

Loans on Unimproved Property

Few provisions are made by institutional lenders for the financing of unimproved property. Even when such provisions are made by law, few organizations are willing to accept unimproved property as collateral for a real estate loan.

Savings and loan associations are able to make loans for the purchase of unimproved property on which off-site improvements have been completed but before the foundations have been completed. The longest permissible term is twenty years, with no payments except for interest during thirty-six months of construction. After thirty-six months the payments to principal and interest must be monthly. The loan can be for 70 percent of the appraised value. If the loan is for the construction of the borrower's permanent home, the loan can be for a term of five years and for 75 percent of the appraised value. The principal payments must start not more than sixty days after the loan has been disbursed, and must be monthly thereafter with the amortization large enough to reduce the principal by at least 40 percent by the maturity date of the loan.

A state-chartered savings and loan may make unamortized loans on unimproved property where the off-site improvements have not been made. This type of loan can be for a period of two years with no payments to principal until maturity; however, the interest must be paid at least semiannually. The amount of the loan is limited to 95 percent of the market value. The association may also make loans on unimproved property where the off-site improvements have been completed. Such a loan is an amortized loan for a period of five years with the first payment due one month after the date of the note. The rate of amortization must be at least 1 percent per month, but by maturity the payment shall be accelerated if subsequent liens have been placed on the property. The loan-to-value ratio for this type of loan is 90 percent.

Unsecured Loans

A savings and loan association may make certain types of unsecured loans. It may make home improvement loans, either of its own programming, or FHA Title I loans insured by the FHA. The Title I loan may be secured or unsecured and must comply with FHA regulations. The association's program may be secured or unsecured. The term may be for twenty years with monthly payments after three months from the date of the note.

Federal Housing Administration Loans

A California-chartered savings and loan association may make any and all loans authorized by the Federal Housing Administration.

Veterans Administration Act Loans

A savings and loan association may make Veterans Administration loans provided that the maximum maturity does not exceed twenty-five years. The restrictions on the ratio of loan to appraised value, principal payments, and maturities correspond to the regulations explained in Chapter 14 under Veterans Administration loans; however, if the maturity is longer than twenty-five years, then at least 30 percent of the loan must be guaranteed by the Veterans Administration. Although these are the regulations that govern lending by California-chartered savings and loan associations, some loans have additional restrictions that cause them to be less desirable under certain circumstances to the savings and loan association. For instance, the 90 percent owner-occupied loan on property against which there is no second lien would appear to be an attractive loan; however, because only 20 percent of the total assets of the savings and loan association can be composed of such loans, they are reserved for clients who are most desirable and for property that is desirable from the standpoints of location, construction, and age.

A loan carrying similar restrictions is that which is made on an unamortized basis. Although such a loan is usually for a period of only three years, nevertheless only 10 percent of the unpaid balances of all loans in force may provide for no amortization during the inital three-year period. Even those loans that provide for quarterly or semiannual amortization cannot exceed 10 percent of the unpaid balances of all loans.

Another restriction on the savings and loan associations prohibits loans to any one borrower, or in any one transaction, or on any one project or tract, exceeding 10 percent of the total assets of the savings and loan association or of the net worth of that association, whichever is less. This provision is to protect the depositors, so that if any one contractor or tract should encounter extreme difficulty the savings and loan association will not have too great an exposure; however, if it becomes necessary to protect loans already made or to sell property that the savings and loan association has acquired through foreclosure, then it is possible to exceed the amount quoted above.

A further restriction applies to unimproved property loans and provides that a savings and loan association may not make loans against unimproved property for more than 5 percent of its total loan assets. A borrower who has borrowed against unimproved property and later desires to improve the property with a building, and who wishes to borrow from the savings and loan association for the construction of that building, does not have to have the land paid off at that time; however, the total loan on the improvements and the land loan cannot exceed 85 percent of the fair market value. Of course, the loan ratio for the improvements is controlled by the conventional limits.

One class of borrowers may not borrow from the savings and loan association. No association may make a real estate loan either directly or indirectly to any of its officers, directors, employees, or majority stockholders, nor can it make any loan to the immediate families of these designated people. The only type of loan that such persons can obtain from their association is a loan secured by shares or deposits.

Mobile Home Loans

One aspect of home financing was forbidden to savings and loan associations until November 19, 1969. At that time the federal and state legislatures realized that a very important segment of the housing industry was still outside the ability of the savings and loan association to aid. This was the mobile home industry.

The mobile home (manufactured housing) industry has been making such great growth that in 1981 one in every three new single-family residences sold was a mobile home; in 1959 only one in every twelve was a mobile home. These figures include from single-wide to triple-wide sectionalized mobile homes. In 1981 the cost of a mobile home could vary from $15,000 to $70,000, and for one that was customized could be as much as $125,000. These costs include delivery and set-up.

The name "mobile home" is a misnomer, since mobile homes are seldom moved once they have been set on a lot. That is why they are now being called manufactured housing in many instances.

The modern mobile home is a far cry from the old concept of "house trailers" hitched to the family car and pulled from one poor location to another. The modern mobile home is not a travel trailer. It is a unit pulled over highways to a modern complex, usually complete with swimming pool, shuffleboard court, billiard room, hobby area, and highly restricted spaces where it is placed on a foundation.

To help provide proper financing of mobile homes,

California-chartered savings and loan associations since November 1969 have been permitted to make loans secured by security agreements recorded on the mobile home being bought. The interest can be either added on, sometimes called gross rate, or simple interest with the interest being charged on the declining principal balance. For the purpose of such a loan a "mobile dwelling" shall be a vehicle, other than a motor vehicle, which is at least ten feet in width and forty feet in length and which contains facilities for year-round living for one family, including permanent provision for eating, sleeping, cooking, and sanitation.

Flooring Loans

Savings and loan associations may make flooring loans to a mobile home dealer for the purpose of purchasing, for inventory, a new mobile home dwelling. The amount of the loan cannot exceed 100 percent of the manufacturer's invoice price, plus 100 percent of the manufacturer's invoice price of installed optional equipment. The maximum term of such a loan shall not exceed twelve months from the date of the loan or purchase, including all extensions and renewals. Associations may also make loans to mobile home dealers for the purpose of purchasing used mobile homes for inventory. This would provide for the purchase of used mobile homes that are turned in on new mobile homes. The term of loans for the purchase of used mobile homes may not exceed nine months from the date of the loan or purchase of the mobile home. The amount of the loan may not exceed 75 percent of the appraised market value or other generally accepted valuation of each mobile home, including installed equipment whose wholesale value is listed in the current issue of *The Mobile Home Report Book*. All mobile dwellings on which loans are made or contracts of sale are purchased must meet the requirements and regulations of the Department of Housing and Community Development of the State of California, and must be manufactured by a company listed in the current *Blue Book*.

Retail Loans

The loans discussed above were loans to dealers. Savings and loan associations may also make loans to individuals purchasing mobile homes for their dwellings. Mobile home loans may be made for insurance or guarantee by HUD-FHA or VA under their mobile home financing program. In order to qualify, the loan must follow their guidelines. Conventional mobile home loans, advances of credit, or purchase of obligation may not exceed 90 percent of the buyer's total costs, including freight, itemized set-up charges, optional equipment sales and other taxes, and filing or recording fees imposed by law. Insurance premiums may be financed for the usual physical damage, and for vendors single interest coverage on the mobile home for an initial policy term not to exceed three years; no other insurance may be financed and included in the buyer's total cost.

The loan can be repaid over a period of twenty years by substantially equal monthly payments for a used mobile home. The loan-to-value ratio on a used unit is 80 percent if purchased and 75 percent if refinanced.

Rehabilitation of mobile homes. Savings and loan associations may make or buy loans to rehabilitate mobile homes as well as those discussed above. Such loans may be made with or without security. They must be to repair, remodel, or improve used mobile homes so that they will comply with minimum health and safety code standards.

The maximum loan for rehabilitation cannot exceed $5,000 and cannot be used to refinance an existing loan. It is paid by monthly payments over a period not to exceed ten years. The loan is evidenced by a simple interest note. There must be at least one written estimate of the loan and material costs to rehabilitate the mobile home. After the work has been completed, there must be a final inspection report.

Education Loans

A savings and loan association may also make education loans. These can be of its own planning or they may be guaranteed by the United States Government. The amount available per year varies from plan to plan. The time for starting repayment was changed in 1970 to nine months after graduation or after leaving school. To obtain an education loan the borrower must certify that money from the loan is to be used solely for educational expenses. A savings and loan association cannot make educational loans totaling more than 5 percent of its total assets.

Miscellaneous Limitations Applying to Various Loans

Unamortized loans carried in the loan portfolio of an association may not exceed 10 percent of the total of all loans in that portfolio. Although such loans do not usually exceed three years to maturity, it is still necessary that such loans not exceed 10 percent of the total loans. If the loan has been set up to call for quarterly or semiannual payments, it still falls under the 10 percent restriction.

Loans to one borrower or in any one transaction, or on any one project or tract, may not exceed 10 percent of the total assets of the savings and loan association or the net worth of that association, whichever is less. This provision is to protect the depositors, so that if any one contractor or tract encounters extreme difficulty the savings and loan association will not have such a great ex-

posure that it would be in trouble itself; however, if it becomes necessary to protect loans already made or to sell property that the savings and loan association has acquired through foreclosure, then it is possible to exceed the amount quoted above.

Loans to officers, directors, employees, or major stockholders of a savings and loan association cannot be made directly or indirectly by their own savings and loan association. The immediate families of those designated cannot borrow from the association. There is one exception to the restriction above. Any of those designated above can borrow against accounts that they may have in the association.

Appraisals cannot be made for a savings and loan association by an appraiser, officer, or member of any committee until he or she has been approved by the savings and loan commissioner to function for that particular association. All real estate loans made by a savings and loan association must be substantiated by an appraisal, and the loan-to-value ratio cannot exceed that which is provided by the Act. California is one of two states that has an appraisal force under the savings and loan commissioner. On every examination of an association's assets, spot checks are made of the appraisals furnished the association by its appraiser. If there is any large difference in the appraisal, the commissioner is empowered to require the association to set up a special reserve account for that loan.

Purchases of existing loans can be made by savings and loan associations provided that they qualify under the conditions set forth previously in this chapter and that they are loans the association could make on its own. Savings and loan associations may sell loans as well as buy them. California-chartered associations may sell all of a loan or any percent of it, depending on what arrangements are made between the selling association and the purchaser. The purchaser may be another savings and loan association, a bank, a pension fund, or an individual.

Payment of Interest

No sections of the Savings and Loan Act specify the periods at which interest shall be paid except Section 6705.1, which provides that interest shall be collected at least semiannually; however, Sections 7150, 7151, and 7169 refer by inference to interest payments that shall be made monthly. The practice in California, however, has been to charge and collect interest monthly.

FEDERALLY CHARTERED SAVINGS AND LOAN ASSOCIATIONS

Thus far we have been discussing only state-chartered savings and loan associations. We must now examine the types of loans permissible to a federally chartered savings and loan association.

Savings Accounts and Shares

For a federally chartered savings and loan association there is no limitation on the maximum term that a loan made against a savings account or share account can run, nor are there any requirements regarding payment of interest or principal. The maximum loan-to-value ratio for this type of loan is 100 percent. In comparison to a state-chartered savings and loan association, the federally chartered association can make a larger loan, since that permissible under state charter is only 100 percent, with state requirements for payment of principal and interest.

Loans on Single-Family Homes and Combination Home and Business Properties

Let us clarify the terms *homes* and *combination home and business property*. *Home* applies to a single-family dwelling. *Combination home and business property* applies to buildings containing one- to four-family residences, or a home with an office in the home, or a business unit at the front of the building with the home at the rear, or a business on one floor and the home on another in the same building.

A federal savings and loan association can make a loan secured by a first trust deed against a home or a combination home and business property for a maximum period of forty years. This type of loan requires a monthly payment of interest and principal and the maximum loan-to-value ratio is 90 percent. A 95 percent loan-to-value ratio may be made on a forty-year amortization basis; but the amount over 80 percent must be insured under a private mortgage insurance program. If the loan is over the 90 percent loan-to-value ratio, there must be a certification that this property is the principal residence of the borrower. There must be a certificate of principal residence if the loan-to-value ratio is over 80 percent and the security is on a condominium, a cooperative, a combined home and business property, or a lien on a one- to four-family unit.

It is also possible to make a fifteen-year maximum maturity loan secured by first trust deed on a home or combination home and business property if there is a semiannual payment of interest and at least an annual payment of principal. The loan-to-value ratio of this loan is 90 percent. The ratio can go to 95 percent, but anything over 90 percent requires private mortage insurance on that portion over 80 percent and a certificate by the borrower that it is his or her principal residence.

Using the same type of security, a federal savings and loan association may make a loan for a maximum of five years. There is no amortization required on this loan. There must be at least semiannual payment of interest, and the loan must be paid in full at maturity. The normal ratio of loan to value is 60 percent.

A federally chartered savings and loan association can also make a five-year maximum loan secured by a first trust deed on a home or combination home and business property provided that the interest is paid at least semiannually and the loan is paid in full at maturity. This type of loan must be presented to the board of directors, who may authorize a maximum loan-to-value ratio of 60 percent.

A federally chartered savings and loan can also make a 90 percent loan-to-value loan secured by a first lien to facilitate the exchange of property by the borrower. This type of loan has a maturity of eighteen months. Interest must be paid at least semiannually and the principal paid at maturity.

This type of loan would be helpful if a home was for sale because someone had been transferred to another community where they found a home but did not have the funds for a down payment. This type of loan would act as a bridge loan and would allow eighteen months for the other property to sell.

Construction loans.   A federal savings and loan association may make a construction loan and final loan to an owner-builder of a single-family structure provided that not more than 80 percent of the loan is paid out before the construction is completed. Such a loan may not be written for a maximum term of more than thirty years, and there must be a monthly payment of interest. A monthly payment of principal must also be made. The maximum loan-to-value ratio under this type of loan is computed in one of three ways. Of the two following formulas, the one giving the smallest loan will be the one used. First, 90 percent of the appraised value; second, 90 percent of the certified purchase price. The total amount of such loans carried on the books of a federal savings and loan association cannot exceed 20 percent of its total assets.

It is possible for noninstalment construction and rehabilitation loans to be made. These are usually the ones used by contractors who build or rehabilitate on speculation. If for construction, the maximum loan-to-value ratio is 75 percent and the maximum term for a single-family dwelling is eighteen months after the initial disbursement; for a two- to four-family unit the term is three years. The term may be extended one time by six months. The savings and loan association reserves the right to limit the number of units under construction at any one time.

For rehabilitation, the maximum loan-to-value ratio is 90 percent, unless all of the loan over 80 percent of the loan-to-value ratio is insured by a private mortgage insurance company. Then the loan can be made for 95 percent of the loan-to-value ratio.

If there are to be substantial alterations, repairs, or improvements, the maximum term for a single-family dwelling is eighteen months after the initial disbursement; for two- to four-family units the maximum term is three years.

A federally chartered savings and loan association was at one time restricted to loans within 50 miles of the main office of the association; this was changed to 100 miles from the branch making the loan, and is now changed to everywhere in the state in which the main office is located.

There are a few alternatives a federal savings and loan association can use other than the equal monthly payment amortization. They are the graduated payment mortgage (GPM), the adjustable rate mortgage (ARM)—also known as the adjustable mortgage loan instrument—and the reverse annuity mortgage (RAM).

All of these can be written to mature in forty years with a loan-to-value ratio of 90 percent. The ARM may be written with a loan-to-value ratio of 95 percent, but any amount over 90 percent requires that the loan amount over 80 percent of the loan-to-value ratio must be insured by a private mortgage insurance company. Also, all details of the ARM must be fully disclosed to the borrower: (1) Monthly payments cannot be adjusted more frequently than monthly. (2) There must be thirty to forty-five days prior notice of any change in payments. (3) The index upon which the changes are based must be agreed upon. (4) The index cannot be controlled by the lender. (5) The amount of change has no limit. (6) The change can be in monthly payments, the loan balance, or the term of the loan. (7) Negative amortization may occur if the payments are adjusted every five years to maintain amortization. (8) The loan can be paid off before maturity without penalty.

The reverse annuity mortgage is a loan made to clients whose income is fixed, usually retired people with obligations that exceed their income or that make it difficult for them to continue living in their home. This type of loan makes it possible for them to retain their home and, using their equity, to receive additional monthly income. The amount of the loan and the monthly payments is based on the age of the borrowers, the amount of the equity, and their need. The maturity of the note is based on certain events: (1) selling the house, (2) depleted equity (in which case the house is sold, the loan paid off, and any funds left over go to the borrowers), (3) the death of the borrowers.

In order for this type of loan to be made, the savings and loan association must present the program to the Federal Home Loan Bank Board for approval. If it does not raise any objections within sixty days, the savings and loan association can go ahead with the loan. The applicants have seven days after the commitment to change their minds and withdraw the application. The loan can be paid off at any time without penalty.

The GPM loan must show at which periods the payments will increase and the rate of the increases. All of this must be fixed at the time of origination. As in the other programs listed above, the note must be secured by a first lien. There must also be a disclosure made which compares the GPM with the conventional loan, and the borrower must be given the right to convert the loan at a later date.

Flexi loans.   The federal savings and loan associations are able to make flexible payment loans. The maximum term is forty years, and the regular loan-to-value ratio is 90 percent. The term can be extended to 95 percent if the amount above 80 percent of the loan-to-value ratio is insured by a private mortgage insurance company. The repayment of the flexible loan is made in two stages—interest only paid monthly for a period not to exceed five years, after which time the monthly payments shall include interest and principal amounts necessary to amortize the loan in full by the maturity date. The payments shall be an equal amount with no one payment being more than the others. The borrower must occupy the property.

Cooperative unit loans.   A federal savings and loan association may make loans on a cooperative unit. The maximum term is forty years, and the loan-to-value ratio can be 90 percent; however loans are allowed up to 95 percent if the amount over 80 percent is insured by a private mortgage insurance company. Payments are made monthly to interest and principal. Each payment should be in an amount adequate to completely amortize the loan by maturity. The loan is to be secured by security interest in stock, membership certificate, or other evidence of ownership, or assignment of borrower's interest in proprietary lease or occupancy agreement issued by the cooperative housing organization.

A cooperative unit that is being converted from a rental unit requires a certificate stating that the unit is the principal residence if the loan exceeds 80 percent of the loan-to-value ratio. The security is the same for the cooperative unit above. Maturity and payments are the same also.

Loans on multi-family dwellings and income-producing properties.   Under this caption is found single-family dwellings, dwelling units for four or more families, combination of dwelling units (including homes) and business property comprising 20 percent or less of total use; also included would be fraternity, sorority residence houses, living accommodations for college or hospital students and staff, and nursing or convalescent homes.

The maximum loan for these structures would be 90 percent of the loan-to-value ratio with a maximum term of thirty years. Payments could be semiannual and fully amortize the loan by maturity.

If the loan is to be partially amortized, payments could be for interest only, semiannual, and for a designated period. Then they could be increased to an amount that would fully amortize the loan by maturity. These payments could also be semiannual.

Under this type of loan it is possible for a savings and loan association to make noninstallment loans with a five-year maturity. Interest would be paid at least semiannually, and the loan-to-value ratio would be 75 percent. The principal would be paid in full at maturity. It is possible for this type of loan to be a three-year interest-only loan for construction or for rehabilitation. The construction loan is for 75 percent loan-to-value ratio with semiannual interest payments. The total loan is to be paid at maturity. The association may limit the number of structures under construction at any given time. There may be a three-year extension to the construction loan.

The rehabilitation loan is similar to the construction loan except the loan-to-value ratio is 90 percent. The loan must be for substantial alterations, improvements, or repairs.

Cooperative housing development. For the development of a cooperative housing development under a blanket loan, that is, a loan on the whole project, the maximum loan-to-value ratio is 90 percent, and the maximum maturity is forty years. The payments must be such that interest and principal will be paid monthly in substantially equal payments that will pay the loan off completely at maturity.

Unimproved Real Estate

A federal savings and loan association may make loans for the purchase and acquisition of unimproved real estate. The property must have potential for residential development. If it qualifies under this rather strict condition, a loan can be made for $66^2/_3$ percent of the value of the property for a period of three years. The interest is payable semiannually and the principal at maturity.

Loans for Development of Land and Construction of Homes or Single-Family Dwellings

A savings and loan association with a federal charter can make loans for the development of real estate into lots and the construction of homes on those lots. The maximum term is six years from the date of the *note,* not the date of the first payment. The disbursement of the land acquisition funds may include a twelve-month grace period in which the development costs can be determined and the final loan amount set. On this type of loan the interest must be paid at maturity; however, monthly payments of 1 percent of the balance applicable to construction and the site with improvements must be made after eighteen months have passed since distribution of the funds. If a home and site sell before the eighteen-month deadline, the money from the sale shall be prorated to pay off the construction loan and the site improvement loan, and the property released. The loan may be 80 percent of the value of the real estate and the structures as a completed project; however, disbursement of funds cannot exceed 80 percent of the value of the construction in process or completed and not sold; 70 percent of the value of the remaining lots or sites in process or completed; and 70 percent of the value of the remaining property. Loans of this type cannot be made by the association unless the general reserves, surplus, and undivided profits of the association equal at least 5 percent of the savings deposits.

Farm Loans

A federal savings and loan association may make two types of loans secured by a first lien on a farm. The first is a loan for 90 percent of the reasonable appraised value of the property. The maturity of such a loan is forty years. The second is a loan for 95 percent of the reasonable appraised value; however all amounts over 80 percent of the appraised value must be insured by a private mortgage insurance company. One such insurance company is the Mortgage Guarantee Insurance Corporation, commonly called "Magic." In order to qualify for this type of loan, the borrower must certify he or she will live on the farm. The payments are substantially equal payments and will amortize the loan in forty years.

These loans can be for the purchase of a farm, the construction of one- to four-family dwellings, or for the purchase of or refinance of a commercial farm. Such a loan cannot be made for hobby or vacation property.

Commercial Loans

The Federal Home Loan Bank Board encouraged savings and loan associations in late 1981 to provide more loans secured by first liens on commercial property including business and industrial property. In order for the property to qualify, there must be a permanent structure making up at least 25 percent of the total value of the real property, or improvements making the real estate usable by industry or business enterprise in fee or leasehold. If there is such a leasehold, it must be extendable or renewable automatically at the holder's option for five years after the loan has matured.

Loans on qualified commercial real property may be made for 90 percent of the appraised value or sales price, whichever is the lesser amount. This loan would be fully amortized in thirty years. The payments could be substantially equal, semiannual payments. It is possible to have a flexible loan written so that interest only could be paid semiannually for five years, after which the principal is amortized over the following twenty-five years, interest and principal being paid semiannually.

Loans secured by first liens on this type of real property can be made on a flat basis, that is unamortized, for a maturity of five years for 75 percent of the appraised value. The interest is paid semiannually. This type of loan could be used to construct a building on commercial or industrial property.

Loans under FHA and Veterans Administration Act

A federal savings and loan association may make FHA and VA loans that comply with the requirements established by these agencies. The loans may be under the various sections. For detailed information on the FHA and VA loans, refer to Chapter 13.

Purchase of Loans

A savings and loan association may purchase a loan from the Federal Savings and Loan Insurance Corporation as long as the loan is secured by a first lien on improved property. The directors may authorize any percentage of purchase price to value, provided a portion of the loan is guaranteed by the Federal Savings and Loan Insurance Corporation under a contract made with the purchasing savings and loan association.

A federal savings and loan association may participate in, by purchasing, a loan secured by a trust deed or mortgage on property located anywhere in the United States; however, the participation may not exceed 50 percent of the total amount owing. The loan must meet all requirements of a loan as set forth by the governing bodies, including the association's board of directors.

Loans on Mobile Homes

Federal savings and loan associations may make loans on mobile homes. The requirements are similar to those for California savings and loan associations. To qualify for a mobile home loan the home must be at least ten feet wide and forty feet long and must provide living facilities suitable for year-round occupancy by one family. It must have permanent facilities for eating, sleeping, cooking, and sanitation.

A federal association may make loans for the purchase of inventory of both new and used mobile homes for dealers. This type of loan, usually referred to as a flooring loan, may be for 100 percent of invoice if new, and 75 percent of value if used. This type of loan is necessary since few dealers have sufficient capital to finance the purchase of inventory. Almost all good dealers manage to turn their inventory four times a year. This means that the average dealer should be able to clear the flooring on a new mobile home about ninety days from the date that mobile home is delivered to him or her and the flooring is established on that particular mobile home. Therefore, flooring notes should not be set to mature in more than ninety days. If the dealer has not been able to sell the mobile home within the original flooring loan term, the loan may be renewed for successive ninety-day periods, but under no condition should the loan extend for a longer term than nine months in total. This is a maximum period, since innovations may cause the unit to become obsolete. At each renewal the interest should be paid to a current position, and the principal should be reduced by at least 10 percent.

The association should make a check of the dealer's inventory at least once every thirty days to be certain that the dealer is not selling the units out of trust (that is, selling the unit, collecting the money for the sale, and, instead of paying off the flooring loan, diverting the money to personal use).

A savings and loan association may make loans for the purchase of mobile homes by individuals. These loans may originate with the dealer by means of a conditional sales contract, usually sold to the association with the dealer indicating that the association has recourse against the dealer in case of default and the dealer will repurchase the contract. The association has additional security in this way and the dealer is more cautious in the credits that he or she offers the association.

A federal savings and loan association may make loans for the purchase of new mobile homes. The maximum term is twenty years. The minimum square feet is 400. The maximum loan is 90 percent of the buyer's total cost.

A federal savings and loan association can make loans for the purchase of used mobile homes. The loan may be for the maximum of 75 percent of the wholesale value as established by a recognized Blue Book, plus sales tax. The term may be for a maximum of twenty years or less, determined by a formula reflecting the age of the model.

A federal savings and loan association may make loans on mobile homes that are insured by the FHA or guaranteed by the VA. Loans of this type must comply with FHA and VA regulations.

In connection with all mobile home loans, the association shall exercise sound practices. It is to set its own credit standards and make sure that all contracts are purchased with these standards in mind. The chattel paper shall include provisions for the protection of the association. It will specifically make provision for protection in respect to taxes, maintenance and repairs, and other possible government levies. The savings and loan association may make arrangements for paying taxes and government levies by setting up impounds for this purpose; however, this is not required.

Loans for the purpose of purchasing a mobile home may be made directly to an applicant. In a case such as this, the loan applicant finds the mobile home he or she wants and goes to the savings and loan association for the loan, rather than signing a contract of sale at the dealer's office.

On July 1, 1981, land-use laws were changed so that mobile homes, or manufactured homes, could be set on permanent foundations on residential lots as long as they had a similar appearance to those in the neighborhood. This means that a mobile home being placed on a lot held in fee simple or a lot held by a long-term lease (which is ten years longer in duration than the loan's maturity or which is renewable so that it has a term at least ten years longer than the loan) could be financed by a note and trust deed or by a security agreement.

In order to qualify under the new law, there are a few other qualifications for the mobile home to meet. It must be at least a double wide. It must have been constructed after 1976 and bear the HUD label. The mobile home unit itself must be complete at the time of appraisal. The mobile home must be connected to permanently installed utilities, which must be protected from freezing and independent for each property.

Loans on Housing for the Aged

Federal savings and loan associations have developed a special type of loan for housing projects for the aged, including housing accommodations for individuals or multiple housing, such as rest homes or nursing homes suitable for and actually limited principally to the occupancy of aged people. "Aged" has been specified to mean people over fifty-five. The maximum period for which such a loan can be made is thirty years. Payments of principal and interest must be made monthly. The board of directors can authorize a loan of up to 90 percent of the value of the complete project; however, the total loans of this type may not exceed 5 percent of the total assets of the savings and loan association, and all such loans must be within the regular lending area.

From time to time we have indicated that the board of directors of a federal savings and loan association may increase the loan-to-value ratio upon presentation of an application to the board. However, this can be done in another way, in which the board of directors, to facilitate the handling of loans, authorizes the management to exceed the permissible loan-to-value ratio by passing a resolution specifying the maximum loans that management can make without reference to the board of directors.

Under certain circumstances federal savings and loan directors might feel that they should adhere strictly to the maximums recommended by the Act, and not authorize the additional percentage that is allowed to them. During periods of tight money the maximum clearly would not be granted.

Improvement Loan

A federal savings and loan may make home improvement loans on a secured or unsecured basis for a term of twenty years and thirty-two days. The first payment to interest and principal must be no later than 120 days after the loan was made. The payments, including interest and principal, may be made in substantially equal quarterly payments; this is the maximum interval between payments. However, the note could call for a shorter interval between payments, such as monthly.

These loans may be made for alterations, repairs, additions, equipment, furnishings, or improvements.

Other Types of Loans

In 1970 new legislation made it possible for a federal savings and loan association to make loans for equipping real property. This probably refers to household appliances, rugs, drapes, and air conditioners; however, explicit regulations concerning such loans have not been issued. The same is true for loans on the construction of new second homes, authorized by the same legislation.

On January 2, 1982, savings and loan associations were allowed to make direct or indirect consumer loans for personal, family, or household purposes. Loans made indirectly through a dealer must be made through a dealer who has been approved by the savings and loan association's board of directors. The federal savings and loan associations have the right to originate, purchase, sell, service, and participate in consumer loans. There is a limit on the amount of loans that can be made to one borrower. It cannot exceed 25 percent of total assets or 5 percent of the association's net worth; however, only a $3,000 loan may be made unsecured to one borrower. This amount will be adjusted annually based on the November-to-November consumer price index.

A federal savings and loan association may make loans secured or partially secured if the proceeds are to be used solely for the expense of college, university, or vocational education. The student does not have to be the borrower. The loan must be paid at maturity.

Savings and loan associations have been looking for extra funds to meet the demand for loans. The funds needed are those over and above the savings deposits on their books. They have been able to find a few sources not previously tapped. One of these has been the selling of trust deeds or mortgages, or participation in trust deeds or mortgages to individuals. This has accomplished two things. First, it has brought new money into the savings and loan associations to be used for additional loans. Second, it has increased the return on the investor's investment, and this makes a new friend for the association.

In addition, legislation has made available to the Federal Home Loan Bank funds that can be loaned to individual associations at reduced interest so that the association can make loans at a reduced interest rate. This is not only a move to enable additional real estate loans, but also a means of increasing the construction of new homes, which are in demand.

A comparison of the loans permissible from federally chartered and state-chartered savings and loan associations will show that they are very similar in many respects. However, in some instances a better loan may be obtained through a state-chartered savings and loan association than through a federally chartered one, or vice versa.

A further examination of the loans permitted savings and loan associations, whether federally or state-chartered, will confirm that these institutions are specialists that have worked for many years with real estate loans and have developed a complete range of services that make it possible for a person to obtain almost any type of financing.

Because of the high rate of return on savings deposited with them, and because of their ability to make loans that others do not make, savings and loan associations charge interest rates somewhat higher than those of insurance companies or commercial banks. However, a review of their outstanding loans will reveal that savings and loan associations certainly have a vital place in the world of real estate loans.

During 1979, 1980, and 1981, the amount of money and credit was restricted in an effort to control inflation. This resulted in intense competition for the money and credit that was available. Money market certificates, money market funds, and certificates of deposits (short- and long-term) became ways for depositors and investors to increase the yield on their savings or idle funds. Banks and savings and loan associations found themselves losing funds from their regular savings accounts, which paid 5.25 percent and 5.50 percent, respectively, to the various funds and certificates that paid up to 16 percent, depending on the yield on U.S. Treasury bills at the time of purchase of the funds or certificates.

In order for a bank or savings and loan association to break even on its loans, it must obtain at least 2 percent more than the cost of money. This cost includes interest on deposits, administration, and supplies. Thus, loans had to yield at least 18 percent in order for the lending institutions to break even.

Many of the loans in effect today were written eight or ten years ago to yield 8.5 to 10 percent. These were long-term loans (twenty-five to thirty years). This was satisfactory when interest on deposits was from 5 to 5.5 percent. The savings institutions relied on the due-on-sale clause in their trust deeds to be able to update interest yield, since most property changed hands every four and one-half to seven years. The *Wellenkamp* decision discussed previously changed all that, since institutions could no longer call a loan when the property was sold. As a result, many savings and loan associations found themselves losing money, and some had to merge with stronger associations in order to protect depositors.

On June 28, 1982, a decision was handed down by the Supreme Court in the *Fidelity Savings and Loan Association* v. *LaCuesta* case that stated that the *Wellenkamp* decision did not apply to Federal savings and loan associations. This means that as of June 29, 1982 Federal savings and loan associations can enforce their due-on-sale clauses.

The banks did not have quite the same problems as the savings and loan associations did since they were able to make other types of loans that had higher yield than their old real estate loans. These loans included construction loans on which the interest, in many cases, was 2 percent over the prime rate, which reached 21 percent. This increased the cost of the completed building and added to the inflation rate.

In 1981, the United States Government continued to be the biggest competitor for the $196 billion in savings, reflecting business-related earnings, personal savings, and state and local pension fund contributions. Federal borrowing took 78.8 percent of the available savings in 1981, or $154,448 million. This left only $41,552 million for the private sector, not counting the reserves that depository institutions must establish. This continuing need of the federal government for funds is the main reason for the high cost of money. It is hard to comprehend the cost to the government for interest on the national debt of $1,027,846 million as of January 4, 1982. The interest alone on this debt for the month of December 1981 was $8,587 million. The legal debt limit for the federal government is $4 billion, but about two times a year Congress extends a temporary debt ceiling. To give you some idea of how fast the unbalanced budget is increasing the national debt, it amounted to $581.481 billion on January 27, 1976; $720.644 billion on January 23, 1978; and $1,027.846 billion on January 4, 1982.

With the federal government taking such a high percentage of the available savings and thus driving up interest rates, it has become necessary for the private sector to find some way of overcoming the effects of the *Wellenkamp* decision in order to increase the yield on loans that were assumable and/or increasing the cash flow.

Some savings and loan associations have taken an idea

from the Federal National Mortgage Association. They offer to rewrite a low-interest loan at 1 to 3 percent below the current market interest rate depending on the nominal rate in the loan. The old loan must be one that is already on the savings and loan association's books. It is true that there will still be a loss on the loan but it could reduce that loss by 3 to 5 percent.

Other savings and loan associations are mailing letters to holders of older loans that have nominal interest rates from 6 to 10 percent. They ask their clients how they would like to cut their interest rate by about half. This would mean a loan that was written to pay 8 percent would actually only cost about 4 percent. This could be done by the simple process of each month making a payment slightly more than double the amount of the named payment.

As an example, consider a loan of $40,000 for twenty-five years at 8 percent. The monthly payment would be $308.74. The loan is fifteen years old and has ten years more to maturity. At this point in time, the balance is $32,320. By increasing the monthly payment to $655.45, the loan would pay out in five years, and the total payments would amount to $39,300.

If the loan payment of $308.74 was continued for ten years, the total payment would be $47,044. The interest on the five-year program would be $7,007, whereas the interest cost on the ten-year program would be $14,724—a savings of $7,717 under the five-year program, thus reducing the rate of interest to approximately 4.16 percent.

This program is a benefit to the borrower in that the loan is paid off twice as fast at a lower cost and benefits the lender by giving a large payment to principal each month, so that the lender has additional funds to lend at a higher rate of interest.

On September 30, 1981, the Federal Home Loan Bank, which controls approximately 4,000 federally insured savings and loan associations, gave them permission to sell their low-yielding loans at a loss. However, instead of reporting the loss at the time of the sale, this ruling allowed the loss to be reported over a period of time for tax purposes. This ruling also allowed savings and loan associations to balance the cost of money with the interest earned on the new loans they will be able to make. There are about $5 billion in old loans that could be affected by this ruling.

There has been another plan proposed by the Federal Home Bank Board that would allow a savings and loan association to form a partnership with investors looking for a tax break. The savings and loan association would contribute old notes and trust deeds bearing low interest rates. The investors would contribute cash. The loans would then be sold by the partnership at a loss, with the investors taking the loss as a deduction on their income

tax returns. The savings and loan association would have no losses, and any gains would be split by the partnership. The savings and loan association would have new money for new loans at the current rate of interest.

There is a program by which savings and loan associations can swap their low-interest loans at face value, less a small service charge, for securities known as mortgage participation certificates issued by the Federal Home Loan Mortgage Corporation. These, in turn, can then be used as security to borrow from the Federal Home Loan Bank. They can also be sold to investors, such as retirement funds, that want the investment but not the expense or problems of servicing a loan.

On May 22, 1980, the Federal Home Loan Bank increased the amount savings and loan associations could borrow from outside sources from 10 percent of the total savings deposits to 50 percent of its assets. This increased ability provided additional funds for loans.

These are some of the ways savings and loan associations have coped with the money and credit crunch of 1979, 1980, and 1981.

QUESTIONS

1. Savings and loan associations located in California can make loans secured by real estate within
   a. 50 miles of the head office
   b. 100 miles of any branch office
   c. 100 miles of the head office
   d. anywhere within the boundaries of California

2. Savings and loan associations have been a major source of
   a. farm loans
   b. multifamily dwelling loans
   c. single-family dwelling loans
   d. commercial property

3. Which of the following make the most real estate loans?
   a. banks
   b. mutual savings banks
   c. insurance companies
   d. savings and loan associations

4. Which of the following loans may a federal savings and loan association make without mortgage insurance?
   a. 60 percent of the loan-to-value ratio
   b. 75 percent of the loan-to-value ratio
   c. 90 percent of the loan-to-value ratio
   d. all of the above

5. Which of the following institutions invest most of their funds in home loans?
   a. savings and loan associations
   b. commercial banks

c. insurance companies
d. all of the above

6. Which of the following loans can a savings and loan association not make?
   a. FHA loans
   b. Veterans Administration loans
   c. combination residence and commercial property loans
   d. none of the above

7. The maximum term a loan made by a savings and loan association may have is
   a. forty years
   b. thirty years
   c. twenty-five years
   d. twenty years

8. Which of the following loans are not available from savings and loan associations?
   a. loans on mobile homes
   b. loans to mobile home dealers for inventory
   c. loans for consumer products such as furniture, dishwashers, washing machines, and so forth
   d. none of the above

9. Savings and loan associations can make loans up to 95 percent of the loan-to-value ratio if
   a. all amounts over 75 percent of the loan-to-value ratio are insured by private mortgage insurance
   b. all amounts over 70 percent of the loan-to-value ratio are insured by private mortgage insurance
   c. all amounts over 80 percent of the loan-to-value ratio are insured by private mortgage insurance
   d. none of the above

10. Savings and loan associations can make
   a. flat notes secured by trust deeds or mortgages
   b. adjustable rate mortgages
   c. graduated payment mortgages
   d. all of the above

BIBLIOGRAPHY

California Savings and Loan League, "California Savings and Loan Commission Regulations." Published by the League.

United States Savings and Loan League, "Comments and Rulings June 1981." Published by the League.

United States Savings and Loan League, "Savings and Loan Fact Book 1980." Published by the League.

6

Life Insurance Companies as Real Estate Lenders and Owners

Although life insurance companies making real estate loans do not face area restrictions as do savings and loan associations, life insurance companies are responsible for only the third largest dollar volume of loans in the United States. Life insurance companies' assets throughout the United States rose to a record $432,282 million at the end of 1979, an increase of $42,358 million over 1978. In the previous ten years, there was an increase of $235,074 million, or 119 percent.

Assets of life insurance companies include funds earmarked by the companies for their future obligations to policyholders. Investments representing the assets of the company are made in a wide range of areas including homes, farms, government, business, and industry. Table 6-1 shows the distribution of the investments. Although the total assets have increased 575 percent since 1950, the proportionate spread of the investments has remained fairly constant except for investments in government securities, which have fallen from 25.2 percent in 1950 to 6.9 percent in 1979. The decrease in investments in corporate bonds was 2.8 percent, while there was an increase in corporate stocks of 5.9 percent. There was an increase in holdings of mortgages of 2.3 percent. Policy loans increased by 4.9 percent, and miscellaneous assets by 2.2 percent.

MORTGAGES

Construction is a sign of economic growth and new buildings in various stages of completion are sure signs of economic progress. However, construction costs money; before any work can be done arrangements must be made to obtain that money, either from funds saved by the owner or from funds borrowed from some institution or individual. Life insurance companies are one of the largest repositories of savings in the United States, and it is only natural that they should, through deeds of trust and mortgages, provide a sizable portion of the money to be used in construction. Deeds of trust from life insurance companies make it possible to build homes, apartment houses, office buildings, stores, churches, shopping centers, factories, and recreational facilities; and, by enabling individuals to use someone else's money in this construction, such deeds of trust free personal funds for those purchases of other essential and nonessential items that also add fuel to the national economy.

Life insurance companies hold about 10 percent of the total mortgage debt of the nation. While the total ratio of assets to mortgages has leveled off in the past few years, the dollar amounts have nevertheless been climbing continuously since the end of World War II. By allowing so many of their assets to be invested in trust deeds and mortgages, life insurance companies have stimulated the economy. These capital investments have provided money for many additional jobs. However, the predominant type of loan will vary with the going rate of interest on conventional, FHA, and Veterans Administration loans, and on bonds. If bond interest is so high that there is no advantage in loaning money on real estate, the insurance companies will invest in bonds. However, when the bond rate drops to the point where the company will show more profit by making a real estate loan and paying for the servicing of the loan than by clipping bond coupons, then the company will return to making real estate loans. Such investment changes have happened several times in the past and have resulted in tight money in California and throughout the nation.

Mortgages held by insurance companies are divided into four basic types: farm loans, which accounted for $12,184 million in 1979; nonfarm FHA, with $6,372 million, nonfarm VA, with loans of $2,975 million, and nonfarm conventional, with loans totaling $96,890 million (for a total mortgage investment of $118,421 million for 1979). Since 1964 there has been a steady decline in the amount of VA loans, and 1966 was the peak for FHA loans with a steady decline since that time. Farm loans

TABLE 6-1   Distribution of life insurance company assets

YEAR	GOVERNMENT SECURITIES	CORPORATE BONDS	CORPORATE STOCKS	MORTGAGES	REAL ESTATE OWNED	POLICY LOANS	OTHER ASSETS
1960	$11,815	$ 46,470	$ 4,981	$ 41,771	$ 3,765	$ 5,231	$ 5,273
1964	12,509	55,454	7,938	55,152	4,528	7,140	6,749
1968	11,096	68,310	13,230	69,973	5,571	11,306	9,150
1972	11,372	86,140	26,845	76,948	7,295	18,003	13,127
1974	11,965	96,652	21,920	86,234	8,331	22,862	15,385
1976	20,260	120,666	34,262	91,552	10,476	25,834	18,502
1979	29,719	168,990	39,757	118,421	13,007	34,825	27,563

All figures in millions of dollars.

Source: *Life Insurance Fact Book* 1980.

and nonfarm conventional loans have shown a steady increase. By 1980 multifamily apartment and commercial property accounted for 76 percent of the mortgage holding of life insurance companies, compared with 14 percent for one- to four-family property. Farm mortgages accounted for over 10 percent.

See Table 6-2 for the figures given by the Federal Reserve Bank for the distribution of loans.

The life insurance industry placed a new emphasis on mortgage loans in the fall of 1967 when it committed itself to make loans up to $1 billion to help alleviate the problems of the urban community. A second $1 billion was pledged in 1969, and by the end of 1969 mortgages or commitments totaling $1.3 billion had been made. This was during a time of extreme money and credit shortage.

It is interesting to note that in dollar volume insurance companies hold more loans on California real estate than they do in any other state. The total in 1979 was $14,742.3 million. Texas was second with a total of $11,378.9 million; Illinois third with $5,611.5 million; and Florida fourth with loans totaling $5,489.2 million. The order changes somewhat in the case of FHA loans: California, Texas, Florida, and Ohio. The sequence for VA loans is Texas, California, Colorado, and Illinois. For conventional loans the sequence is California, Texas, Illinois, and Florida.

Life insurance companies began to withdraw from the home loan business in the mid-1970s. They were interested only in large home loans during that time. As interest rates continued to climb they withdrew even further

from home loans and became primarily interested in loans on commercial, industrial, and large apartment complexes. They also began to invest their funds to a greater extent in real property such as shopping centers, office buildings, industrial complexes, commercial buildings, and large apartment complexes. During the period 1979–82, they were not making any home loans but they were the first to get into participation loans on large properties of all types. (For an understanding of participation loans, refer to Chapter 4 on Creative Finance.)

RESTRICTIONS

Insurance companies other than those operating in California have been included in this chapter because any insurance company authorized to sell life insurance in California may make loans against real estate in California and invest in bonds secured by real estate in California or in corporate stocks of California. All insurance companies that lend money in California are subject to the regulations of the state of California governing the manner in which loans may be made against real estate, and if such a company has its head office outside the state of California, it is also governed by the laws of the state in which it is located and under which it is chartered. In case of conflict, the more stringent of the two rules is the one enforced by the insurance commissioner's examiners.

Life insurance companies that have been incorporated or are operating in the state of California are restricted to mortgage loans of 90 percent of the market value of

TABLE 6-2   Distribution of real estate loans by life insurance companies

YEAR	1- TO 4-FAMILY	MULTIFAMILY	COMMERCIAL	FARM	TOTAL
1979	$16,193[a]	$19,274	$71,137	$12,180	$118,784
March 31, 1980	16,850	19,590	73,618	12,413	122,471

[a]All figures given in millions of dollars.

Source: *Federal Reserve Bulletin,* June 1980.

the property used as security, if such property is improved by a single-family residence. A conventional loan such as this is not to be confused with the loans insurance companies may make or purchase that are guaranteed by the Federal Housing Administration or by the Veterans Administration. A loan on any other type of property for which an insurance company may take a trust deed is limited to 90 percent of the market value of that property. No state restriction is imposed as to the maximum number of years for which a loan may be made; however, company policy usually holds the term to twenty-five years with a maximum of thirty years. A loan with such a maturity requires periodic amortization. The state law does not specify that there be an amortization, but company policy usually dictates such procedure.

The Life Insurance Act of California and actuaries connected with maximum loans refer to 90 percent of the *market* value of the property. The Act does not specify at any point that the sales price must be considered. If there is any unusual discrepancy, however, between the appraisal of the property and the sales price, the insurance commissioner's agents will certainly criticize any excessive loan based on an appraisal greater than sales price. After the property has been owned for some time, an appraisal may be given that would reflect a higher value than had been paid previously for the property. The appraisal policies in most life insurance companies are conservative, however, and in most instances the appraised value would be somewhat less than the market value. Most insurance companies making home loans recognize areas in the community in which loans will be made to a high percentage of value. In other areas it is possible that no loan or at least a reduced loan-to-value ratio would be made.

The income of the borrower is an important factor in determining whether a loan will be made by a life insurance company. In recent years, some companies have required that the cost of the house not exceed 2.5 times the amount of the applicant's annual income, and that the most an applicant should allow for his or her monthly payment is 20 to 25 percent of his or her monthly take-home pay. This payment should include fire insurance and taxes.

It is important to remember that the only California law concerning real estate loans made by life insurance companies has to do with the ratio of market value of the property to the loan.

Because of the nature of its income, an insurance company can program its investments well in advance, and it is therefore not unusual to find insurance companies making long-term loans to people of desirable ability and reputation. The demand against life insurance company funds is small compared with that of commercial banks, and therefore a high percentage of the cash position of

the company may be loaned out. However, in 1979, 1980, 1981, and 1982, numerous policyholders borrowed against the cash value of their life insurance policies at low interest rates in order to invest that money in money market funds and money market certificates that returned much higher interest rates than were paid by the insurance company.

Once a real estate loan is made, the insurance company prefers to see it on the books for the life of the loan; most life insurance company contracts penalize a borrower for prepayment of his or her note and trust deed.

Real estate loans made by life insurance companies are generally for the following purposes:

1. To purchase, occupy, or invest in property.
2. For construction or improvements; however, life insurance companies, although not restricted from making construction loans, usually prefer to make a loan on a completed building to avoid the problems of construction. Therefore, they usually issue a take-out letter certifying that after the improvement has been completed they will pay off the construction loan and take over the obligation.
3. To refinance existing indebtedness.
4. To achieve a lower interest rate or longer term.
5. To provide additional funds for other use.

Interest charged by life insurance companies on their loans is usually slightly less than that charged by banks and considerably less than that charged by savings and loan associations, because the money with which they have to work costs them less; therefore, it is not necessary for them to obtain high interest rates.

CONSTRUCTION LOANS

Construction loans, because of the many problems involved, are potential losses unless they are handled efficiently and knowledgeably. All loan companies, whether banks, insurance companies, or savings and loan associations, must have an assured first lien on the property on which a building is to be constructed, which means that absolutely no work can be done on a lot prior to the recording of the deed of trust or mortgage upon that lot.

To be sure that no work is done, an inspection must be made of the property just before the mortgage or deed of trust is filed with the county recorder. This inspection is only the first of many that will be made during the course of the construction. It is possible to have a title company do the inspection, in which case it will issue an American Land Title Insurance Association policy, commonly called an ALTA policy. This policy will certify that it has inspected the property, that there are no encroachments from the adjoining property, that there are no unrecorded encroachments of easements, that the property is ready to receive a building, and that it is insurable by the title insurance company.

After this examination the lender will make at least four, and sometimes five, additional inspections of the property, as five stages of construction are accomplished. The first is usually after the concrete foundation has been installed and back-filled, when measurements are made to determine that the foundation corresponds to the plans and specifications. It will also be checked for rock puddles and other construction weaknesses. At this time some companies request the title insurance company to inspect the foundation and issue an endorsement to their policy certifying that the foundation is on the proper lot. The next inspection is usually made after the subfloor is down and the framing up. The third inspection is made after the rough plumbing and the electrical work have been installed, the roof is on, and the exterior sheeting is in place. There is another inspection after the house is completely enclosed and ready for painting, and then a final inspection when the house is finished and ready for occupancy.

After completion the owner is allowed ten days in which to file a valid notice of completion, after which the subcontractors have thirty days in which to file a lien against the property if they have not received payment for their labor or materials. The general contractor has sixty days in which to file a lien against the property should he or she not receive payment for labor or materials. At the end of this time the lending company must examine the records to determine whether a lien has been filed against the real estate. If not, the final disbursement can be made. Should the lending company desire to forego this inspection, it may request the title insurance company handling the transaction to make such an inspection and issue an endorsement to their policy showing that no liens have been filed against the property.

Because construction loans are so technical and require so much supervision, it is no wonder that life insurance companies prefer to make few such loans. In most instances the company is located miles from the property for which a loan is made; consequently, close supervision is not only difficult but at times impossible. Therefore, when construction is contemplated it is not unusual for a life insurance company to issue a take-out letter indicating that once the property has been completed according to approved plans and specifications, the company will make a loan on the property for the amount designated. Armed with such a letter, the owner usually approaches a bank or savings and loan association and arranges an interim-financing loan for the construction of the building. When the building is completed, the life insurance company pays the construction loan and takes the loan on the completed property into its books.

HOME OFFICE OPERATIONS

Real estate loans of small life insurance companies are often restricted to the immediate vicinity of the home office. In such cases there is a real estate loan division in the home office where the loans are processed, serviced, and carried. The home office determines what company loan policies will be, including the kind of property on which loans will be made and the geographical areas in which the insurance company is interested in making loans. The home office establishes some sort of committee to review loan applications and recommend whether to make or deny the loan.

The insurance company must also have a department to process and follow up real estate loans that the insurance company makes, to establish and maintain records, and to see that company assets are not wasted through undue delinquency of loans.

Loan applications through the home office are usually made directly by the applicant, who is referred to the company by field representatives or by independent mortgage brokers. In some instances, life insurance companies purchase groups of loans from mortgage bankers and other institutions.

FIELD OFFICE OPERATIONS

An insurance company will often decide that it is interested in making a block of loans in an area that promises economic appreciation. In such cases the company will open a branch office and establish a staff for processing applications, establishing loans on the insurance company's books, and servicing the loans made by the branch office.

The Prudential Life Insurance Company established such an office in Sacramento shortly after the end of World War II. The office was completely staffed, from appraisers through lending officers. The company had ascertained that the Sacramento area promised to be an area of economic advancement and wished to have a portfolio of loans in this area totaling a certain amount. The branch office was maintained until this amount was obtained.

LOAN CORRESPONDENTS

Should a life insurance company decide that it desires to make only a few loans in a certain area, it can appoint a loan correspondent. This correspondent can be an employee of the life insurance company, but in most cases the insurance company prefers to appoint outside individuals or companies.

It is not unusual for an outside individual or company

to represent many life insurance companies. The function of a correspondent is to act as a finder for loans for the insurance company, for which service the correspondent is paid a finder's fee. In some instances as soon as the loan is found, the correspondent's job is finished, and the life insurance company processes all the documentation and takes the loan into its home office real estate loan department. In such cases a mortgage broker can perform the function adequately for the insurance company.

In other instances a mortgage banker or company is designated as correspondent, and not only does that organization find the loan, but it actually makes the loan, including disbursement of the money. Periodically the loans that the mortgage banker or company has made are assigned to the life insurance company. At this point the transaction takes one of two directions. Either the insurance company takes the loans completely onto its books and establishes them in its real estate loan department, maintaining all records and documentation on the loans; or the mortgage banker or company continues to effect collection of the loans, maintains an inspection of the property to see that the life insurance company's asset is not wasting, and sees that fire insurance is paid, that the taxes are kept current, and that the loans are not allowed to become delinquent. For this service the life insurance company pays a servicing fee to the mortgage company or bank.

Most insurance companies at one time or another have used the above methods of acquiring loans. However, the system used is usually dictated by conditions in the location in which the loans are being acquired, and by the number of loans desired in each location. If a great number of loans is to be made in an area, the branch office–type of operation seems to be the most desirable. If there is to be a sampling of loans, the loan correspondent seems to be the most economical.

SERVICING AND FINDER'S FEES

Servicing and finder's fees vary from time to time according to the needs of the life insurance companies and their desire for additional loans. Usually an agreement for servicing is established at the time a new block of loans is submitted by the mortgage banker or mortgage company to the insurance company. The life insurance company may also contract for a block of a certain dollar volume of loans for which it agrees to pay certain servicing and finder's fees.

Immediately after World War II, when there was a surplus of uninvested money, finder's fees averaged 1 percent. Servicing fees have since ranged from 0.2 percent to 0.7 percent.

OWNERSHIP OF EQUITIES

Before closing the chapter on life insurance companies and the real estate loan market, we should consider one additional facet—the ownerships of equities in various types of commercial and residential properties that life insurance companies have been taking in recent years. The Metropolitan Life Insurance Company has made investments in high-rise apartment houses in San Francisco, carrying the ownership of such apartments on its books as real estate owned. Other life insurance companies have invested as purchasers in shopping centers and commercial buildings, and consequently are managers of these types of real estate.

In some instances there has been a desired appreciation in value of this property because of the conditions under which the property was originally purchased and the economic and population growth of the area in which the property was located.

QUESTIONS

1. Life insurance companies prefer to make real estate loans as follows:
   a. many small individual loans
   b. construction loans
   c. large loans
   d. none of the above

2. Life insurance companies obtain loan applications from
   a. mortgage bankers
   b. mortgage companies
   c. field office operations
   d. all of the above

3. Life insurance companies during 1979–82 were interested in making
   a. many home loans
   b. participation loans
   c. short-term loans
   d. loans in states in which they sold no life insurance

4. Loans made by life insurance companies on commercial real estate through March 31, 1980, exceeded those made on one- to four-family dwellings
   a. by 36 percent
   b. by 40 percent
   c. by 46 percent
   d. by 50 percent

5. Loans made by life insurance companies on commercial real estate exceeded those made on multiple-family dwellings through March 31, 1980, by
   a. 44 percent
   b. 40 percent
   c. 39 percent
   d. 35 percent

6. Loans made by life insurance companies on commercial property exceeded those made on farms through March 30, 1980, by
   a. 50 percent
   b. 40 percent
   c. 35 percent
   d. 32 percent

7. An insurance company's loan correspondent may be
   a. a mortgage company
   b. a mortgage banker
   c. an individual
   d. any of the above

8. An insurance company's real estate loan policy is determined by
   a. only the laws concerning real estate loans in the states in which the company is incorporated
   b. only the laws of the state in which the security property is located
   c. if the property is located in a state other than that of incorporation, the stricter law is used
   d. none of the above

9. An insurance company may make loans on real estate
   a. in any state that it wants to
   b. only in the state in which it is incorporated
   c. only in the states in which it is licensed to sell insurance
   d. only in states specified in its charter

10. The Life Insurance Act of California indicates that life insurance companies may make a maximum real estate loan of
    a. 90 percent of the value of the real estate
    b. 85 percent of the value of the real estate
    c. 80 percent of the value of the real estate
    d. 75 percent of the value of the real estate

BIBLIOGRAPHY

Institute of Life Insurance, "Life Insurance Fact Book 1981." Published by the Institute of Life Insurance, annually.

Federal Reserve Board of Governors, "The Federal Reserve Bulletin," June 1980. Published monthly by the Federal Reserve Bank.

7

Banks as a Source of Real Estate Financing

In the past 120 years California has grown from a sparsely settled area to the most populous state in the nation; from cattle raising and dry-land farming to production of a diversity of agricultural products, in quantity and quality that put it high on the list of the most productive states; from an area of no industry to a state famous for its industrial development.

Behind this growth stands a strongly built, well-organized, and well-conducted banking system that has become increasingly active in making real estate loans. (Refer to Table 7-1 near the end of the chapter.)

LOAN LIMITS

The great variance that used to exist between real estate loans allowed to California-chartered and to federally chartered banks no longer exists. There are a few areas of minor differences in the legally permissible loans, but the practices each bank follows are the result of decisions by the officers of the loan committee and the board of directors of each bank. Of course, each bank must operate within the limits established for it by statute.

One factor determining real estate loan policy is the community in which the bank is located. If it is a rapidly expanding community, property values could be on the increase, with a heavy demand being placed against the bank for real estate loans. If the community is deteriorating, land values could be dropping, and a conservative approach to loans would be needed.

A second item the bank must consider in establishing a loan policy is the ratio of deposits to loans. If deposits are excessive, the bank will probably liberalize its policy so that the excessive money can be put to work and earnings realized.

A third item considered by the bank is the demand

for high-interest loans such as instalment loans. If there is a heavy demand for the high-interest loan, the bank would probably desire to satisfy this demand and to reduce the number of real estate loans it makes through additional restrictions placed upon the real estate loan applications. This action, of course, would increase the earnings of the bank. In making this decision the loan committee and the directors must determine the interest accrual level they want the bank to maintain.

Clearly, local conditions influence the real estate loan policies of banks, and it is important to know the local policies as well as the permissive legislation passed by the agency regulating the bank. In the case of a state-chartered bank, this agency would be the state of California, with the regulations being policed through the State Banking Department. With the federally chartered bank, the regulating agencies would be the comptroller of the currency, policing the statutes established by legislation, and the Federal Reserve Bank, which has the privilege to make examinations of the bank if it deems it necessary.

It is possible to determine whether a bank is state or national by examining its title. If it is a national bank, it must bear the word *national* in its title. If it is a state bank, it cannot have the word *national* in its title. There are at least two national banks that do not actually have the word *national* in their title because of abbreviation. One is the Bank of America, N.T. & S.A. At first glance, this would appear to be a state bank; however, the "N" stands for National and the full and legal name of the bank is the Bank of America, National Trust and Savings Association. Another bank whose name is confusing is the Bank of California, N.A., which stands for the Bank of California, a National Association. Most other banks have their titles spelled out, such as the Crocker National Bank and the Security-Pacific National Bank.

PERMISSIVE REGULATIONS OF NATIONAL BANKS

Unlike savings and loan associations, national banks do not have different types of loans in their permissive statutes for different types of properties, with a ratio of loan to value that depends on the maturity of the obligation. The statutes state that a national banking association may make real estate loans that are secured by first liens upon improved real estate. For property to qualify as improved there must have been a substantial contribution made to the value of the property by its development or by a permanent building.

Under this interpretation farm land is improved when no additional major improvements are necessary to make it useful as a farm. Past or present use may be considered when appraising to determine if the property is an improved property.

The Comptroller of the Currency has indicated that a residential or business property is improved when a sizable permanent improvement has been made to the property or when its value has been increased by such improvements within its immediate vicinity. Thus, real property can be considered improved if it is (1) a property upon which a house has been constructed on a permanent foundation and connected with the usual utilities; (2) a commercial recreational area of at least seventy-five campsites with picnic tables, tent bases, toilet facilities, fireplaces, dockage, and a beach; (3) a commercial property improved with a substantial and permanent commercial structure; or (4) a trailer park having thirty or more sites, with hookups for sewage, running water, and electricity.

Under the interpretation of improved property given above, it is possible to consider off-site improvements as improving the property if the value of the property has been materially increased by them. However, each parcel and case under these circumstances must be considered separately, and no generalization can be made as to whether they would qualify. However, a property might qualify if (1) a developed urban area is immediately available to it; (2) it is prime industrial property that has been made more valuable by installation of paved streets and utilities, and transportation facilities are available; (3) it consists of lots in a housing subdivision for which major improvements such as streets and the usual utilities have been installed; or (4) it is an undeveloped potential residential tract almost completely surrounded by a rapidly growing and developed residential tract that would be adjacent to a major university in its development stages.

You may recall that a banking association may make a real estate loan when the loan is secured by a first lien on the property. This means, of course, that the property must be held in fee simple by the owner and that the borrower, through a deed of trust, must be able to give as security for a note a lien against his or her property that is prior to the rights of all others to the property. Thus a property against which a person held a life estate interest would not be acceptable for a real estate loan unless the holder of the life estate joined in the note and deed of trust or subordinated his or her rights in the property to the lender.

Certain types of liens are permitted and assessed from time to time that have no substantial effect on the value or the use of the real estate. Liens for taxes and assessments charged to the property by government bodies such as counties, cities, or districts for the current year fall into this category, in addition to certain zoning restrictions, permits, rights of way, easements, and leases that might be filed after the deed of trust.

If a person holds property as fee simple, it is possible for him or her to withhold certain portions of the fee and still have the loan be acceptable to a national bank, as might occur in the case of a mineral, petroleum, or gas reservation. This portion could be reserved by the borrower him- or herself as separate from the deed of trust or it could be held by a third party and still be eligible for a real estate loan under the national statutes.

Having considered what constitutes an improved property and a first lien, we can now examine the terms under which real estate loans can be made by national banks. As stated previously, these terms apply to all forms of loans, whether residential, farm, industrial, or commercial, insofar as the maximum term in years and maximum loan-to-value ratio are concerned. A national bank may make a real estate loan on a flat basis up to 50 percent of the value of the property if that loan is paid within five years.

All other real estate loans made by national banks must be amortized. As we have seen, amortization is a reduction of the principal of the debt during the life of the loan, on a regular schedule of payments. Under amortization, a national bank may make a real estate loan up to 50 percent of the appraised value of the property for from five to ten years if there is an amortization schedule with instalment payments sufficient to amortize at least 40 percent of the principal of the loan within ten years, or if the payments are adequate to amortize the entire principal of the loan within a period of not more than twenty years, or if the instalment payments are such that the entire loan will amortize within the period ending on the maturity date of the note.

To proceed to the next highest ratio, a national bank may make a loan of $66^2/_3$ percent for up to ten years (1) if the amortization schedule is such that 40 percent or more of the principal will be retired within the ten-year period; (2) if the amortization payment is sufficient to pay the entire principal of the loan within a period of not more than twenty years; or (3) if the amortization schedule is such that the entire principal of the loan will be paid within the period ending on the date of the note's maturity. A $66^2/_3$ percent loan may be made for ten to twenty years (1) if the amortization is sufficient to pay the entire principal of the loan within a period of not more than twenty years; and (2) if the amortization schedule is sufficient to pay the entire principal of the loan within the period ending on the date of the note's maturity.

The maximum loan is 90 percent and the maximum amount of time under this note is thirty years; within this thirty-year period the amortization must be sufficient to pay the entire principal of the loan within the period ending on the date of the note's maturity.

We have been discussing loans known as conventional bank loans. Two other classifications are considered only briefly at this point, since they are covered in detail later in this book: FHA- and Veterans Administration–guaranteed loans. Both of these are federally insured and as such are exempt from consideration for computing the ratio of loans to deposits as far as banks are concerned. Because they are insured and exempt from the consideration of computation in the ratios of loans to deposits, such loans are also exempt from the other statutes for loan requirements; consequently, these loans are made along the lines established by the Federal Housing Administration and by the Veterans Administration.

One other type of loan can be made, but it has not received much publicity in California. It is a loan upon which a private insurance company issues mortgage insurance or a guarantee that the loan will be paid. Of course, there is a fee in connection with this guarantee, and it is necessary that the bank keep in its files a record of the insurance the private company has issued. Under these circumstances a bank may loan 90 percent of the appraised value of the property for a period of thirty years.

In 1974 it became possible for national banks to make loans secured by real estate that does not comply with the normal restrictions and limitations, as long as the total amount of such loans does not exceed 10 percent of the amount that a national bank may invest in real estate loans.

Real Estate Loans on Leasehold Property

A national bank may make a real estate loan upon a leasehold provided that the lease does not expire within ten years after the maturity date of the loan. For a national bank to make such a loan, the leasehold must be improved according to the same definition that applies to improvements for real estate. Also, the security offered under

the leasehold must be a first lien upon the leasehold. In this regard the lease must not be more strict than those normally used in the area, and the lease should permit acquisition of the leasehold by the lending bank through voluntary conveyance or assignment and also provide for acquisition through sale under judicial process in such a manner that the recovery of the property or its value would not be jeopardized. The instrument used for such a lien must be a mortgage or a trust deed. As stated before, the loan must mature at least ten years before the date on which the lease is due to expire, or at the time of expiration there must be at least a provision for renewal of the lease for an additional ten years. The payments on the note secured by the lien must be amortized to qualify.

Construction Loans

Construction loans made by national banks are not considered real estate loans but commercial loans, unless the loan is to be a combination of construction and permanent real estate loan, in which case the loan may be domiciled in the real estate loan department immediately.

For interim-financing purposes a construction loan by a national bank is considered a commercial loan. When such a construction loan is made for industrial or commercial buildings, it may have a maturity of not more than thirty-six months where there is a firm letter of takeout, which becomes a binding agreement by a financially responsible lender to pay off the bank's construction loan.

Construction loans for residences and farm buildings may have a maturity of not more than eighteen months and are also considered as commercial loans whether or not secured by a first trust deed. Should it become necessary for construction loans to be held longer than eighteen months, the loans should be brought into a position where they qualify as real estate loans or, if they already qualify, they can be transferred to the real estate loan division and paid off as normal real estate loans.

When a national bank is making a combined construction and permanent real estate loan, the maximum maturity may be extended to thirty years. This is true whether the loan is for commercial, industrial, farm, or residential property.

Loans on Forest Tracts

A national bank may make real estate loans secured by liens upon forest tracts that are properly managed in all respects. Such a loan must be secured by a mortgage, deed of trust, or other such instrument. Any national bank may sell or purchase any such obligation. The maximum loan is $66^2/_3$ percent of the appraised value of the growing timber, lands, and improvements thereon. The note shall be written in such a manner that at no time will the amount outstanding be in excess of $66^2/_3$ percent of the appraised value of the remaining property, including the timber. Under no circumstances, however, shall the loan be made for more than three years if a flat note, and fifteen years if an amortized note, secured by a first lien, calling for at least payments of $6^2/_3$ percent of the principal annually. Where it is possible under state law, a security agreement should be taken on the timber as well as a deed of trust on the property.

Home Improvement Loans

Home improvement loans, first introduced to banks by the FHA Title I Home Improvement Loan, amounted to a long-term personal loan. The interest rate on the old Title I loan was limited to a 5 percent gross rate charge. As time passed and interest rates increased, banks found that the experience on the Title I loans was excellent, but the return on the loans was not adequate in comparison with the other instalment loans. As a result, banks developed their own home improvement loan using about the same credit pattern as that established for the old Title I loan. This was a loan to a person having an equity in his or her home and a good credit history. The loans were originally for a period of three years. As home improvements increased in cost, the term increased to five years, then to seven, and then to ten years. With the increase in the term, banks felt that they should have some protection; they used the "agreement not to encumber" as a means of placing a cloud on the title of the property by recording the agreement. In this way it was necessary for the bank to be paid off before title to the property could pass in case of a sale. In 1967 the courts decided that such an agreement was an "equitable mortgage" and could not be taken since it would be a second lien on the property and a bank could not take a second lien to secure a loan. In 1969 changes were made in Section 24 of the code under which national banks make their real estate loans to allow a national bank to take a second lien for the purpose of securing a home improvement loan.

Equity Loans

In 1976 many banks began using junior liens, seconds only, for advances against equity held in real property. Most banks limit these equity loans to a maximum of $100,000. The tight money period from 1979 to 1982 found many property owners using the equity in their property as security for a junior lien loan. There are no restrictions on the way the money is to be used. Some borrowers use money borrowed on their equity to pay college tuition for their children; others use it for a world cruise; and others for an investment.

Most banks are competitive in this type of loan. They will not make a loan that will cause total indebtedness,

including the first and second lien, to exceed 80 percent of the loan-to-value ratio. There are usually three maturities open to the borrower—a fifteen-year, fully amortized loan with monthly payments; a three-year maturity loan with monthly payments based on a thirty-year amortization; and a five-year maturity loan with monthly payments based on a fifteen-year amortization.

Loans secured by junior liens require a higher interest payment than those secured by a first lien, and the longer maturities usually require higher interest rates than shorter term loans. For instance, in January 1982 one bank required 19.5 percent plus 3 points for a fifteen-year, fully amortized loan, whereas a three-year loan required an interest payment of only 17 percent plus 3 points, and a five-year loan 18 percent plus 3 points. The interest rate is somewhat higher on equity loans for property that is not owner occupied.

Some banks are making junior lien loans in order for the buyer of real property to complete the down payment on the property. It is necessary for the buyer to pay down at least 20 percent of the purchase price or appraised value. As an example, it is less expensive for the buyer to assume a loan with a balance of $40,000 at 10 percent interest, obtain a junior lien for $40,000 for fifteen years at 19.5 percent, and pay cash in the amount of $20,000 on a property costing $100,000, than to obtain a first lien loan for $80,000 at 17.5 percent.

$40,000 at 10%	= $ 4,000	$80,000 at 17.5%	= $14,000
$40,000 at 19.5%	= $ 7,800		
	$11,800		
$11,800	= 14.75% interest rate.		

The term *appraised value* has often been used in establishing loan-to-value ratios for loan purposes; however, the examiners of both national and state banks feel that the term should be *appraised value* or *sales price*, whichever is smaller. Although the law is not written in this way, banks have been instructed to so interpret the law in order to have qualifying loans. The examiners take the position that if a piece of property has a sales price of $15,000 and sells for $15,000 but is appraised at $15,500, the appraisal is wrong, for otherwise the property would have sold for $15,500; and consequently their interpretation is that the ratio of loan to value should be upon the lower figure.

PERMISSIVE REGULATIONS OF STATE BANKS

A California state–chartered bank may make loans secured by a first lien on any real property, not just improved property. According to Section 766 of the California Bank Law, a first lien is not reduced by a lien of any tax assessment or bond levied or issued by any state, county, city, or other political subdivision, nor does the issuance of a bond to cover an assessment negate the first lien of a state bank unless any instalment or payment of the taxes, assessments, or bonds levied is past due. As soon as one of these becomes past due, the first lien of the bank is in jeopardy and must be corrected through payment of the delinquent tax lien.

A lien established through a contract for the furnishing of water, although the lien might be against the property, does not invalidate the bank's first lien unless a payment on such a contract becomes past due. A lease of the real property under which the owner receives all payments or royalties also does not invalidate the first lien of a state bank.

A lien for the issuance of a bond to be given in lieu of an assessment levied against the property does not negate the first lien unless the unpaid balance of the bond and the amount of the loan combined exceed the amount that would be permissible to loan in relationship to the sound market value of the property. A lien given to secure the payment of an assessment to meet the requirements of the laws of the United States in respect to any irrigation project in any state or territory of the United States does not invalidate the first lien unless the combined total of the loan made by the bank and the unpaid balance of the assessment is greater than the percentage of the sound market value of the real estate permitted to be loaned under the Bank Act.

Like the National Banking Law, the State Banking Law requires that ownership of the property be held in fee simple and assignments of petroleum, mineral, or gas rights do not affect the validity of the first lien; however, such assignment out of the fee simple would affect the appraisal of the property and would therefore affect the maximum loan that could be made against the property.

As is the case with national banks, the term of the loan determines the permissible ratio of the loan to the fair market value of the property. A state bank may make a real estate loan if the loan does not exceed six months on a flat basis and 85 percent of the sound market value of the property. The state bank may make a flat real estate loan for 60 percent of the sound market value if the maturity of the flat loan does not exceed ten years. A state bank may also make a loan for 90 percent of the sound market value of the property if the first payment is made within sixty days of the date of the note and if a monthly instalment is paid. The maturity may be for thirty years. If the loan is to be on a farm or productive agricultural land, a state bank may make a loan of 90 percent of the sound market value to be repaid over a period of thirty years if the payments are made in at least annual instalments.

A state bank can make a loan to build a home for the owner on a farm or a lot for a term of thirty years and for 90 percent of the sound market value of the property and the completed structure. The loan must be secured by a first lien. There must be substantially equal monthly payments over the term of the loan; however, the payments do not need to begin before one year from the date of the note.

A state bank holding a first lien against a piece of real property may take a junior lien against the same property, but all such loans may not exceed 75 percent of the sound market value of the property.

Construction Loans

A state bank may make a construction loan if the term of the loan does not exceed sixty months and the loan-to-value ratio does not exceed 85 percent of the sound market value, such value being determined by a proper appraisal. The loan must be secured by a first lien on the property and the proposed improvements. The improvements must be constructed according to plans and specifications submitted and approved before the loan is made. Before the loan is made, there must be a plan that provides for the payment of the loan or for the refinancing of the loan that is satisfactory to the bank.

The term of sixty months gives a builder adequate time to construct a large commercial building or a single-family unit. Loans for a single-family unit are usually written for shorter periods of time, such as six months to one year.

Equity Loans

State banks can make equity loans secured by second trust deeds. The first lien does not have to be held by the same organization that holds the second. Refer to equity loans under the section on national banks.

Leasehold Real Estate Loans

A state bank may make a real estate loan, taking as security a first lien on a leasehold upon which the lease does not expire or which has been extended or renewed so that it will not expire for at least ten years beyond the maturity date of the loan. It may make such loans if the amount does not exceed 60 percent of the sound market value of the property and does not run for more than ten years. This loan may be a flat note or amortized. The term of the loan does not exceed thirty years; in case of a farm, it is paid annually in equal or substantially equal payments; otherwise it is paid monthly. Monthly payments start within sixty days of the date of the note if a) the loan does not exceed 90 percent of the sound market value of the leasehold and improvements; or b) if the term of the loan does not exceed six months and the loan-to-value does not exceed 85 percent of the sound market value of the leasehold and improvements on the property subject to the leasehold.

Both state and national banks can buy existing notes and deeds of trust if they qualify within the statutes of the loan limitations imposed upon the state and national banks.

Loans Made from the Mid-1960s through 1982

A relatively new force entered the field of real estate lending in 1966 and continued with short periods of relief through the early 1970s: the actual shortage of money available for long-term real estate loans. In an effort to encourage FHA and VA loans, interest rates were increased to 8.5 percent. One-half percent was still required for mortgage insurance, and thus the borrower had to pay a net of 9 percent for an insured FHA loan. Many banks found it necessary to charge 9 to 9.5 percent for a conventional loan on better types of home loans, and they were not interested in loans on property that did not qualify under their highly restrictive requirements. It was not unusual to find 5 points required of the seller in order to obtain an 8.5 percent FHA or VA loan. Maximum loan-to-value ratio seemed to be 70 percent instead of the 90 percent allowed by law, and the property needed to be outstanding or the borrower a very good customer to qualify even for the 70 percent loan. A few flat notes were made, but the majority were amortized. The amortization period was for twenty-five years instead of the thirty years allowed by law, or from 50 percent to $66^2/_3$ percent of the economic life, whichever was less, in the case of residential property loans. Commercial and industrial property loans were made for a maximum of 50 percent of the value of the property and for a period of fifteen years. In the periods when money was most tight, loans on all but residential property were declined except under most unusual circumstances, and loans on multiple residences such as four-plexes and apartments were also declined.

Late 1971 saw a change in the money market and interest rates began dropping. By early 1972, 7 percent rates were available and the real estate loan market grew active again.

During the later part of 1974 a very strong disintermediation[1] was evident, and money for real estate loans became very scarce by mid-1975. Interest rates on real estate loans climbed to 10 percent, the maximum under California usury law; and loan rates asked by banks

and savings and loan associations, which are not subject to usury laws, climbed as high as 11 percent. FHA and VA loans received 9.5 percent interest. Before the interest was increased to 9.5 percent it was not unusual to see 8 or 9 points required to obtain a FHA or VA loan. At the end of 1975 there was a reintermediation[2] and money became more available. Real estate loan interest dropped to 9 percent and in some instances to as low as 8.5 percent by early 1976. FHA and VA loan interest also dropped. In early 1976 savings and loan associations and banks found themselves with more money to lend on real estate than they had had for several years, but interest rates charged remained at 8.5 to 9 percent through mid-1977.

In 1979 the Federal Reserve Bank Board began to control the expansion of the money supply rather than interest rates. This resulted in the old economic law of supply and demand taking over; interest rates started to climb. By 1981 it was not unusual to see real estate loans at 19.5 percent and HUD and FHA loans were authorized at 17.5 percent. These were reduced to 16.5 percent in late 1981. On January 14, 1982, Bank of America reduced its real estate loan rate on prime property to 16.5 percent. During 1979–82, many banks, savings and loan associations, insurance companies, and credit unions were forced to price themselves out of the real estate loan market. The cost of money was so great, they could not afford to make loans, except at very high interest rates.

Although banks rank behind savings and loan associations in quantity of real estate loans made, in California they have played a much larger role in the financing of real estate than in many other states. This is because of the large branch systems that continue to grow in California.

The Secondary Market

Under unusual conditions a bank will enter the secondary mortgage market, usually because it is located in an area that is not progressing rapidly as far as residential or other construction is concerned. As a result, time deposits accumulate in the bank, and some source of income must be obtained to pay interest on these time deposits. Under such conditions the bank will often inform a correspondent bank (one with which the bank carries commercial or savings accounts) that it wishes to invest a certain amount of money in real estate loans. The correspondent bank will then sell notes and deeds of trust from its portfolio to the bank desiring to make real estate investments. Both state and national banks are authorized

---

[1]*Disintermediation* is rapid and massive withdrawal of funds from savings and loan associations, banks, and insurance companies for investment in United States bonds and notes yielding much higher returns than are available through time certificates of deposit and normal savings accounts.

[2]*Reintermediation* is the rapid and massive deposit of funds into banks, savings and loan associations, and insurance companies because of lower interest on United States obligations.

TABLE 7-1   Overview of outstanding real estate loans

	1964	1975	1976	1977	1978	FIRST QUARTER 1980
Savings and loan associations	$101,333[a]	$278,693	$323,130	$381,163	$432,808	$479,078
Commercial banks	41,338	136,186	146,586	178,979	213,963	251,198
Life insurance companies	50,848	89,168	91,581	96,765	106,167	122,471
Mutual savings banks	40,503	77,249	81,554	88,104	95,157	99,151
Federal National Mortgage Association		31,824	32,904	34,369	43,311	53,990
Federal land banks		16,563	19,125	22,136	25,624	33,311
FHA and VA		4,970	5,150	5,212	5,419	5,833
Federal Home Loan Mortgage Corporation		4,987	4,269	3,276	3,064	4,235
Government National Mortgage Association		7,438	4,241	3,660	3,509	3,919
Farmers Home Administration		1,109	1,064	1,353	926	2,757
Individuals and others		119,315	124,858	138,199	154,173	182,762

[a]All figures are in millions of dollars.

Source: *Federal Reserve Bulletin.*

to act as loan brokers under these circumstances, and they are permitted to charge a fee for their services. The bank desiring to make real estate investments may also go directly to a mortgage broker and request that he or she obtain mortgages or deeds of trust for the bank to purchase on approval. Of course, the mortgage broker receives a commission for this function.

When a bank purchases loans from a correspondent, there is often an understanding that should there be a decrease in savings deposits and should the loans reach a proportion adverse to the bank's desires, the correspondent bank will purchase back enough of the notes and deeds of trust for the bank again to have a proper ratio of loans to deposits.

The branch banking system in California has made it possible for banks in small communities to make loans to community residents for real estate and commercial

investment, such loans being in excess of the loans that a unit bank could make. This is possible because a branch bank may use in one area funds that were accumulated and not needed in another area of the state. Such freedom of movement of funds has been of great advantage to the people of California.

Table 7-1 illustrates the relative importance of lending agencies active in the real estate loan market. The table shows growth in the real estate loans made by these agencies from 1964 through March 1980. This was a continuation of previous growth from 1946. The fourth agency shown on the table, mutual savings banks, is not too important in California since there are no mutual savings banks in the state. (They are located mostly in the Northeastern states and in Oregon, Washington, and Alaska.) They have been a lending factor in California, however, having placed through mortgage companies and

TABLE 7-2   Analysis of loans by type of security as of April 1, 1980

	1- TO 4-FAMILY[a]	MULTIFAMILY	COMMERCIAL	FARM
Savings and loan associations	73	8	9	10
Commercial banks	59	6	31	4
Life insurance companies	14	16	60	10
Mutual savings banks	65	17	17	0.05
Federal National Mortgage Association	90	10	None	None
Federal Land Banks	5	None	None	95
FHA and VA	33	67	None	None
Federal Home Loan Mortgage Company	76	24	None	None
Government National Mortgage Association	19	81	None	None
Farmers Home Administration	41	15	15	29
Individuals and others[b]	54	13	14	19

[a]All figures are in percents.

[b]Others include mortgage companies, real estate investment trusts, state and local credit agencies, state and local retirement funds, noninsured pension funds, credit unions, and U.S. agencies for which amounts are small.

Source: *Federal Reserve Bulletin.*

mortgage brokers more than $4,330 million in real estate loans.

Note that savings and loan associations lead in dollar volume, and that in 1964 life insurance companies were second. Although Table 7-1 does not show it, commercial banks moved to second place in 1969 and have held that position since.

It is interesting to note that the number of loans held by the Federal Home Mortgage Corporation and the Government National Mortgage Association declined from 1975–78 but increased in 1980; whereas the number of loans held by the Farmers Home Administration (FaHA) declined from 1975–78 and increased from 1979–1980. Loans held by individuals and others continued to increase.

Table 7-2 shows the type of security each of the major sources of real estate loans has taken.

QUESTIONS

1. The main source of real estate loans in California is
   a. savings and loan associations
   b. banks
   c. insurance companies
   d. all of the above

2. Banks made more real estate loans secured by one- to four-family dwellings than commercial property by
   a. 28 percent
   b. 30 percent
   c. 32 percent
   d. 38 percent

3. Banks made more real estate loans secured by one- to four-family dwellings than multifamily dwellings by
   a. 25 percent
   b. 38 percent
   c. 43 percent
   d. 53 percent

4. Banks made more real estate loans secured by one- to four-family dwellings than farms by
   a. 45 percent
   b. 55 percent
   c. 65 percent
   d. 67 percent

5. Banks can make loans against leaseheld improvements if the lease
   a. has six months longer to run than the note
   b. has five years longer to run than the note
   c. has ten years longer to run than the note
   d. has twelve months longer to run than the note

6. Banks can make home equity loans for any purpose if the total of the original loan and equity loan does not excceed
   a. 70 percent
   b. 75 percent
   c. 80 percent
   d. 85 percent

7. If you were looking for an organization to finance the sale of a multifamily dwelling, you should approach
   a. a mortgage banker making FHA loans for sale to the Federal National Mortgage Company
   b. a savings and loan association
   c. a federal land bank
   d. none of the above

8. If you were looking for an organization to finance the sale of a farm, the first one you should contact is
   a. the Federal Home Loan Mortgage Company
   b. a federal land bank
   c. a commercial bank
   d. the Farmers Home Administration

9. If you have commercial property that needs financing in order to make a sale, the first organization to contact would be
   a. a mortgage bank or a mortgage broker who is a loan correspondent for an insurance company
   b. a savings and loan association
   c. a commercial bank
   d. none of the above

10. Which of the following properties is not acceptable as security for a commercial bank real estate loan?
    a. a leaseheld improvement with fifty years to run on the lease
    b. a ranch that is fully improved
    c. a home on which there is a life estate interest
    d. a property that is held in fee simple but with a mineral reservation

BIBLIOGRAPHY

California State Banking Department, "Banking Law, Sections 750–776, 1220–1238, and 1380–82 as revised January 1981." Published by the California State Printing Office.

Federal Reserve Bank Board of Governors, "Federal Reserve Bank Bulletin." Published monthly by the Federal Reserve Bank.

Superintendent of Banks, "Banking Laws and Related Acts." Sacramento, California. California State Banking Department.

8

Basic Legal Concepts of Real Estate Financing

This is the first of two chapters dealing with the more significant legal aspects of real estate finance operations. Chapter 8 is concerned mainly with the basic concepts of real property as distinguished from personal property; the various recognized interests in real property; transfers and perfection of interests in real property; trust deeds, mortgages, land contracts, sales contracts, junior liens, and involuntary liens; necessity of deeds and security instruments being recorded; transfer of debtor's rights in the sale situation; escrows; variations of the trust deed and mortgage to accommodate special situations; and usury. Chapter 9 treats various ancillary agreements involved in financing real estate, such as construction contracts, leases, insurance policies, and title insurance. Although the secondary material is somewhat removed from the absolutely essential legal aspects of real estate finance, it can be significant in various types of financing situations.

Needless to say, these two chapters cannot replace a full course in real estate law. The intent here is to deal with basic legal concepts that must be understood by anyone who wishes to function effectively in the realm of real estate finance. Should the discussion of many aspects of real estate law seem brief and easy to understand, do not conclude that there is little substance to the law of real estate finance. Application of these principles to a specific financing situation can be complex and bewildering, as appellate court decisions indicate. The following minimal discussion of these topics is adequate for the purposes of the student of real estate finance, but it is no substitute for the advice of a lawyer when one is actually arranging the financing of a particular property.

REAL OR PERSONAL PROPERTY

Real estate finance is concerned with secured loans as differentiated from unsecured loans. An unsecured loan is backed solely by the debtor's promise to pay a certain sum to the creditor. If the promise is not kept, the creditor has no right to proceed against any specific property owned by the debtor until after he or she sues in court for the money owed and obtains a judgment against the borrower for the amount due. Even after such a judgment is obtained, the lender may recover nothing should the debtor have no assets that may be reached to pay the debt. This situation is obviously risky and therefore unsatisfactory to most lenders of substantial sums of money.

A secured loan involves two elements: the debt (usually evidenced by a promissory note) and the lien upon specific property. In the case of the typical real estate loan in California, a trust deed (in 99 percent of the loans) or a mortgage is executed and issued by the borrower at the time of the creation of the debt. This contract gives the lender the right to proceed against specific property of the borrower to secure payment of monies due. The secured creditor is thus in a preferred position, since he or she typically has the first opportunity to sell or take title to the specific property of the debtor in order to receive payment of the debt.

Anyone interested in real estate finance must understand the concept of property and of types of property interests that exist and that may be used as security for loan purposes. Without such knowledge it will be difficult to appreciate the value of the rights that a lender has as a secured creditor.

Broadly, *property* involves the power that one has over a physical object or one's sole right to something of value. The owner of property is virtually a dictator with regard to what will be done with his or her property. He or she can employ it to produce more wealth, sell it, lease it, hypothecate it, destroy it, or do nothing with it. The owner's absolute dominion over private property is limited by the state's power to tax, to appropriate by exercising the power of eminent domain, and to regulate on the basis of the police power and escheat.[1]

---

[1]*Escheat* is the procedure by which the state acquires ownership of property unclaimed by heirs after the owner's death, or otherwise unclaimed.

The early common-law judges considered real property to consist of physical objects attached to land and thereby permanent or attached additions to the soil. The greatest interest that could be owned in realty was a fee simple interest (commonly called a fee), which was recognized as the right of absolute control over a portion of the earth's surface, the subsurface to the center of the earth, and the airspace above the surface of the land for an infinitely great distance into space. At present there is a curtailment of airspace rights based upon the concept of reasonably necessary use of airspace. The right of the owner to airspace above the surface is usually limited by navigational necessity due to increasing air travel. This curtailment usually poses no problem, however, since even in extreme cases structures usually occupy only a few hundred feet of airspace.

Most states have defined the term *real property* in their statutes. Section 658 of the California Civil Code defines real property as "land, that which is affixed to land, that which is incidental or appurtenant to land, that which is immovable by law, except that for the purposes of sale, emblements, industrial growing crops and things attached to or forming part of the land, which are agreed to be severed before sale or under the contract of sale, shall be treated as goods." While this definition of the term *real property* is reasonably complete, some special kinds of property interests must be discussed separately for adequate understanding.

LEASES

The arrangement whereby the owner of property contracts to allow another to use his or her property for a period of time usually creates a landlord–tenant relationship. Such a contract is a *lease,* vesting the tenant with certain possessory rights in the property of another and the owner with the right to have this property revert to him or her at the end of the period specified in the lease. Leasing real property for a definite term creates a *leasehold,* otherwise known as an *estate for years.* Leasehold interests (the right of the tenant to possess and use the property of another) are usually considered to be *chattels* (personal property). However, if the lease contract is for a long enough period it may become an interest in real property, because of the long duration of the tenant's rights in the property. How long this period of a lease must be is difficult to determine. In some areas of California, a long-term lease means one running for fifty-two years or more. It is considered that the possessory and other rights held by the tenant under this type of lease continue for so long that the lessee's interest can be treated as an interest in real property. This means that the lessee has an interest in real property that can be used as security in real estate lending. Although there is a fine

line between a leasehold as an interest in real property and as an interest in personal property, it is felt that a leasehold of fifty-two years or more can be treated as an interest in real property.

Our primary goal in examining the nature of leasehold estates is to realize what is essential for a lease to create a property interest suitable as security for the promise to repay a debt. A lengthier discussion of leasehold hypothecation will follow later in this text. At this point we shall consider some leasehold interests other than the estate for years, that are, for obvious reasons, not acceptable as security for real estate loans. This knowledge may be vital in evaluating the management of an income property offered as security for a loan.

Under *periodic tenancy,* the tenant occupies the property for a certain period and pays rent for that period without agreeing to occupy the property for a definite period of time. The typical periodic tenancy is a month-to-month renting of space for residential purposes.

A *tenancy at will* is so informal and undefined a right to use the property of another that it can hardly be considered a typical landlord–tenant relationship. This type of tenancy is not for any definite or determinable period of time. There is only an agreement between the owner and the tenant that they intend to create a landlord–tenant relationship between themselves and that at some time the tenant will pay rent for the use of the premises.

A *tenancy at sufferance* develops when a tenant— once lawfully in possession of the landlord's premises— occupies the property illegally because of the expiration of the term of the lease. The tenant at sufferance, because he or she is holding the premises of another without permission, can be summarily removed at any time by the owner. As a practical matter, this arrangement is not really a bona fide landlord–tenant relationship.

The landlord and tenant, regardless of the specific arrangement between them, usually have certain basic responsibilities to each other. The landlord, at the required time, must place the tenant in possession of the leased premises, must allow the tenant to use the premises without interruption or harassment, and must have and maintain the leased property in usable condition for the tenant under the recently judicially created warranty of habitability (meaning in residential units that the essential requirements for habitability exist, such as a roof that does not leak; sound and operable electrical, plumbing, and heating systems; and sound floors, doors, windows, and ceilings). When the lessee is in possession of the specific premises leased and nothing attributable to the lessor is depriving the lessee of his or her reasonable expectancies as to the use of the space, the owner's basic obligations to the renter have been fulfilled. In residential unit leasing situations, the tenant's rights of possession and use are protected; his or her eviction is legally allowed only if done in accordance with the lessor's statutory remedies, such as the unlawful detainer action and the legal prohibition of a lessor's engaging in retaliatory eviction based upon the tenant's angering the owner by exercising legal prerogatives provided by law for the lessee's benefit. The tenant must pay rent in the proper amount when due, surrender possession to the landlord according to their arrangement, and not commit excessive damage (more than reasonable wear and tear) upon the premises. If permanent damage not attributed to reasonable use of the premises occurs at the hands of the tenant, this is waste, and the tenant is liable for all such injury to the property.

If the tenant attaches something of permanence to the property during his or her occupancy, it will usually belong to the landlord at the termination of the tenancy. If it is an item that can be removed from the premises without unduly damaging the property, the tenant can take it if he or she removes it before the termination of the tenancy. If personal property is rather firmly attached to residential property by a tenant, usually the landlord is favored in that it cannot be removed and taken from the premises without the landlord's consent.

The most significant questions concerning the removal at the end of the tenancy of personal property attached to the premises by the tenant arise in situations of commercial leasing. These cases are more important than residential ones, because personal property attached to leased commercial premises is usually of far greater value than that attached to residential premises. In the case of industrial and commercial property, the doctrine of trade fixtures applies. This means that the tenant, before the expiration of his or her lease term, may remove all trade fixtures attached to him or her to the property that make the leased space useful and more profitable than it would have been without them. The only items that cannot be removed by tenants are those so firmly attached as to become an integral part of the building or land. Obviously, if these trade fixtures that were a part of the original real property were removed, the property could suffer great damage and loss of value.

The problems involving the tenant's property interest in personal property attached to the landlord's property can be complex and important. The best general advice to the parties concerned with determining the rights and duties regarding such property is to define clearly *in the lease agreement* the property interests of the respective parties at the outset of the landlord–tenant relationship.

LIFE ESTATES

The *life estate* is a temporary ownership (interest) in real property. It is not a permanent interest, as is the fee estate, since the life estate lasts only as long as a des-

ignated human life. A life estate can be created by a statutory enactment, a deed, or a will. The usual concept involved is that the right to use and possess certain real estate is authorized by any one of the above means and that this right exists for the period of a specific human life. The required human life can be that of the grantee of the deed establishing such an estate or that of any other person who may be named in the instrument.

A deed with C as grantor conveying a certain described land "to A for the life of A" creates a life estate in A. After this deed is effective, A has the right to possess and use the land according to the terms of the deed and in accordance with the use being made of the property at the time of the creation of his or her interest in the property. C, the grantor, has a reversionary interest in the property. This means that upon the demise of A, C will again be vested with the fee interest in the property because he or she will again have, as before, the right to use and possession that was conveyed to A under the terms of the deed. For the duration of the life estate, the life tenant (A) has the following duties to the grantor (C): to avoid committing waste on the property; and to pay the current expenses of ownership, for example, taxes, insurance, a reasonable proportion of any special assessments on the property, and necessary maintenance.

In areas outside the community property states of the West and the South, the life estate is frequently created by the surviving wife's dower interest. This interest is typically an estate for life in one-third of all land that the husband owned at the time of the marriage, for the period of the marriage, and continued to own until the time of his death. The wife's dower interest is created by statute. Upon marriage, the wife has a life estate (dower) created automatically by the marriage in one-third of the husband's real property. For the duration of the marriage this automatic creation of the dower interest will occur every time the husband acquires a fee-simple interest in real property. The wife's interest will not be extinguished by the husband's conveyance unless the wife has joined as a grantor and thereby released her dower. Upon the death of the widow, the surviving children (who during the life of their mother as a widow had a remainder interest in the property) find that their remainder estate (conditional right to fee interest) has now become a fee simple estate in the property, since they now have the right of present use and possession. Dower does not exist in California, where the law of community property carries out the intent of the state with regard to providing a home for the widow and her children.

The creation of a life estate by deed can result in the existence of a reversionary interest in the grantor or a remainder interest in other persons. The establishment of a remainder interest following a life tenancy (as distinguished from the reversionary interest mentioned earlier) is accomplished through wording such as: "To B for his (or her) life and then to C in fee simple." Where a life estate is created by provisions in a person's last will and testament, the following language is likely to be found: "Our home at 2020 Third Avenue to my wife for her life and then to my son John." The result achieved here is for the wife to have a life estate and John a remainder—with John's interest developing into a fee-simple interest upon the death of the testator's wife.

In discussing the life estate, we have considered the duties and rights of the life tenant regarding the interests of the reversionary interest holder and the remainderman. From this understanding of the character of the life estate, we can see its obvious unsuitability as security for a loan. Despite the impracticality of accepting a lien upon a life estate interest in real property, knowledge of this type of property is vital to the education of a competent real estate finance person.

COMMUNITY PROPERTY

California is one of eight community property states in the United States. Mention has already been made of dower in the other states and its primary purpose of automatically creating a life estate in the husband's real property so that the widow will have the means of supporting herself and the children. Although the concept and legal details of community property are considerably different from dower, the essential intent of the state in providing for each right is the same.

Numerous legislative enactments and appellate court decisions have made the California Law of Community Property very complex. We can only sketch its basic outline here and mention some specific problems it creates with regard to real estate sales and financing transactions. To understand fully the basic structure of this law and to know what its effects will be in a given transaction, further study and legal advice will be necessary.

Under the California Law of Community Property, there are two distinct classes of property. *Separate* property is basically that property acquired before marriage, after termination of a marriage, or during marriage by gift, devise, descent, or bequest; it also includes the rents, issue, proceeds, and interest from such property in addition to all property acquired using this property as the means of payment. *Community* property, fundamentally defined, is that property acquired after and during marriage through the efforts of either spouse. All property acquired by the work of spouses is divided equally. For example, if the husband earns $3,000 a month from his employment, $1,500 of this is the community property

of his wife. Obviously, the division of community property between spouses or heirs involves only the property retained by a married couple after paying the expenses of living. Specifically, the following general classes of community property are recognized in California: earnings of the spouses; profits, rents, and issues from such property; and proceeds from the sale of such property.

The spouse owning separate property maintains virtually complete dominion over it, and the law does not require that any portion of this be allocated or used for the benefit of the other spouse. This absolute dominion over separate property continues so long as the owner can prove that it is separate and not community property. The typical way in which property will change from separate to community is through commingling with property that is community (especially in the case of the husband). After the identity of separate property has been lost (usually by depositing it in some type of joint bank account), it is almost impossible to prove its source and thus its ownership.

Use of real property for the purpose of arranging secured loans involves the question of what the spouses must do in the typical instance to hypothecate their property. Discussion of this subject must consider the special legal circumstances pertaining to separate property as distinguished from community property. The separate property of the husband can be used to satisfy his debts. Unless the husband consents, his property cannot be used to discharge obligations incurred by the wife alone. The wife's separate property is available mainly for the satisfaction of obligations she has created. For the wife's separate property to be taken in satisfaction of a debt secured by the hypothecation of community property, her express consent must be obtained in writing.

Except for the earnings of the wife during the marriage (which can be taken to pay for necessities of life during marriage), all community property is available to satisfy debt obligations incurred by the husband. Because of this legal situation of community property, when the wife and husband join as makers of a promissory note and as trustors on a trust deed, the community property interest in the real property subject to the trust deed is unquestionably liable for the debt.

The only real problems that might arise in making secured real estate loans would occur should the lender attempt to reach the separate property of the spouses to satisfy the debt. There would have to be a clear expression of consent on the part of the owner of the separate property before it could be taken to pay the obligation.

In the typical residential financing transaction, where a named couple is borrowing to purchase property, the only absolutely safe procedure is to have them both sign all contracts and lien instruments. During the accomplishment of this paperwork an attempt should definitely be made to have husband and wife act in concert, so that no disturbing marital disagreements arise before all the necessary legal obligations have been incurred by the couple for the lender's benefit.

EASEMENTS

Our main interest in this topic is to realize the necessity of adequate access to property if it is to have maximum utility. Unless this requirement is met, the usefulness and consequently the value of the property will be reduced. Whenever a parcel of land is considered as security for a loan, the lender must determine that there is suitable access to the property. Obviously, land that is completely inaccessible will not have a marketable title in terms of what is necessary before a lender will accept such property as security for a loan.

Generally defined, an *easement* is an interest in another's land that allows the owner of the easement to use that land in a certain limited fashion. The most common easement is a *surface easement,* which allows the owner of one parcel of land to pass over another's property to get to his or her land. This type of easement is usually appurtenant in that it is attached to one particular parcel of land and benefits that owner in the sense of providing access to his or her property. In the usual conveyancing or hypothecating situation, the appurtenant easement is automatically included as a part of the owner's interest in the fee and therefore is transferred by deed. For the same reason the type of easement is also subjected to the terms of a mortgage or trust deed upon the proper execution and delivery of such instrument.

Another significant easement is the *easement in gross,* in which the limited right to use another's property is not directly related to a specific parcel of land. This interest in land belongs to one owner for his or her use and enjoyment and does not serve any one parcel of land. A common example of this right is the utility corporation easement, in which a surface area is reserved for the erection and normal maintenance of electric power lines and poles or telephone lines and poles. An easement in gross can also exist in the form of a subsurface right for gas and water mains. The greatest significance of this type of easement is probably its effect of obscuring fee-simple property titles. This problem is often confronted by property owners and prospective lenders in the form of a utility company easement for power lines diagonally across a lot. Substantial construction is usually impossible in these cases, since construction of a building in the center of such a plot would unduly interfere with the easement owner's right to use the air and surface areas granted to him or her by the deed creating the easement.

LICENSES

A *license* is not an interest in land; it is discussed here for the sole purpose of distinguishing it from an easement so that a license will not be accepted as accomplishing the permanent access to land that can satisfactorily be done only by an easement. A *license,* granted by a private landowner, is a personal, revocable, and nontransferable grant of authority to use a portion of another's land for a temporary purpose. Since this is not an interest in land, none of the formalities of land conveyancing are required to create a license. This right is usually based upon a verbal expression of intent by the property owner. The granting to another of permission to fish upon one's land, and the right of a theater ticket purchaser to occupy a seat during the performance of a show are examples of licenses.

OWNERSHIP OF REAL PROPERTY BY SEVERAL PERSONS

The situation of multiple ownership of real property can evolve either automatically, according to a rule of law, or voluntarily, through the agreement of two or more persons to such an arrangement. In California the automatic creation of interests approximating such ownership is in accordance with the Law of Community Property. Since this body of law peculiar to California and seven other states has already been discussed, we will concentrate here on *joint tenancy, tenancy-in-common,* and *tenancy-in-partnership*. In the usual residential land sales transaction, the vendees ultimately take title in joint tenancy or as tenants-in-common. The tenancy-in-partnership is obviously restricted in its application to the transfer of title to a business or professional firm. Because of their greater importance in the typical residential land transaction, we are primarily concerned with tenancy-in-common and joint tenancy.

Tenancy-in-common is favored by law over joint tenancy. Therefore, unless two or more people taking title to real property clearly express an intent to create a joint tenancy, a tenancy-in-common will result from a conveyance of an interest in real property to them. The California Civil Code defines this tenancy as a co-tenancy without the right of survivorship. To create this kind of interest there must be unity of possession among the tenants and each must have the right to occupy the entire parcel of land along with the other owners. The lack of the right of survivorship among tenants-in-common is unquestionably the most significant and distinguishing feature of this tenancy. It means that in most cases, upon the death of one of the co-owners, the interest previously held by this person will usually have to be dealt with in probate court proceedings before it passes to another.

The result of probate proceedings is that the surviving tenants-in-common often find themselves involved in a tenancy with strangers (usually the heirs of the deceased former tenant-in-common). From an ownership and management point of view, this possibility may have disadvantages.

The tenants-in-common are independent of each other except for the established rights of possession and occupancy. Thus, a tenant-in-common can usually sell, lease, or hypothecate only his or her interest in the property. Unless he or she is acting as an agent for the other owners, he or she cannot subject their property interests to the claims of third parties. While relatively independent owners of a particular property, the tenants-in-common are each liable for a proportionate share of charges levied against the property, such as taxes and special assessments. If real property held in tenancy-in-common is offered as security for the repayment of a loan, it is important to understand the independence feature of this tenancy and to accept such property as loan security only when all the multiple owners join in a written agreement hypothecating the property.

One of the main reasons for vendees taking title to real property under this type of tenancy is the possible minimization of federal estate taxes upon the death of one of the owners. In appropriate circumstances, holding title to land as tenants-in-common can prevent the double taxation of the property. Under joint tenancy ownership, the property may be taxed as completely owned by the first decedent and taxed again upon the death of the surviving joint tenants who have succeeded to complete ownership of the property by surviving the longest. For purposes of real estate finance, in most cases involving the legal aspects of the tenancy-in-common, we are mainly concerned with recognizing the quality of interests created, their nature, and the mechanics of placing the entire property interests as security for the funds borrowed.

The joint tenancy, while not favored by the law in the sense that it is automatically created when two or more persons take title to real property simultaneously, is the most common device for vendees taking title to residential property. The basic reason for this greater use is the automatic succession by the survivor to a deceased joint tenant's interest in the property. For the typical married couple this security device is very tempting in the sense that it assures the survivor's ownership and control of the family home (assuming that no third-party rights develop that prevent this, such as unpaid taxes or default on secured loans against the property). Therefore, it is obviously the kind of tenancy most often encountered in the mortgage lending field. From the standpoint of the frequency of occurrence, it is much more important than the tenancy-in-common.

A special procedure, typified by the employment of

certain "magic words," must be followed if joint tenancy is to be created in California. Under common law in California, to create a joint tenancy there had to be unity of time, title, interest, and possession. Essentially this meant that the joint tenants had to have the same interest transferred to them under the same conveyancing instrument, starting at the same time, and held under the same undivided possession. Therefore, under the common-law requirements for the creation of this special advantageous tenancy, a grant of the interest in certain real property was necessary to all of the joint tenants under an instrument (usually a deed), and the conveyance had to result in the creation of the same rights and interests in the property. To distinguish a conveyancing instrument creating a joint tenancy from an instrument creating a tenancy-in-common, there had to be a definite expression that a joint tenancy with right of survivorship was intended to be created among the named grantees.

In California most of these ritualistic requirements have been eliminated by statute. The main requirement for creating a joint tenancy in California is that there be, in a conveyancing instrument, a definite expression of intent by the grantor of his or her intent to vest the grantees, as joint tenants, with title to certain described property. All that is necessary to create this kind of tenancy in real property is to convey it "to A and B, as joint tenants." The simplification of the requirements for creating a joint tenancy in this state means that a sole owner can create, through a conveyancing instrument to himself or herself and others as grantees, a joint tenancy among all the named grantees. By employing the same method, tenants-in-common can create a joint tenancy among themselves in the property they hold in common. The property rights and obligations of tenants-in-common (already discussed) and joint tenants are essentially the same.

A joint tenancy in California is terminated by the following means: (1) conveyance by one (or more) of the tenants of all his or her interest to one joint tenant; (2) death of one of two joints tenants; (3) conveyance by one of the joint tenants of his or her interest in the property to a third person (creating a tenancy-in-common between the grantee from the conveying joint tenant and the other joint tenant); and (4) joint tenants contracting between themselves to end the right of survivorship.

RESTRICTIONS, CONDITIONS, AND COVENANTS

In dealing with these topics we are concerning ourselves with the private, nongovernment approaches to limiting the use and development of land, which contrast with the employment of the police power under state governments in the form of zoning laws to restrict and limit the use made of land. The private approach to controlling land use is accomplished essentially by the enforcement of contracts in courts of equity. The public limitation of land use under zoning laws is distinguished from private controls in the sense that local government bodies or officials will act to limit the use of land. These actions are typically in the form of orders from officials to specific owners, or of ordinances enacted by the city council or county board of supervisors affecting a certain parcel of land within their jurisdiction. Zoning of land for a limited number of uses is lawful provided that a reasonable connection exists between the health, welfare, safety, and morals of the community and the zoning limitations. Also, the zoning category must not be so restrictive as to deprive the owner of virtually the entire benefit of ownership without protecting the vital interest in the public's general health and safety. More and more state supreme courts (such as New Jersey and Pennsylvania) are holding that zoning ordinances that absolutely prohibit the construction of rental apartments or that require large lots (two to five or more acres) for a single-family house violate the equal protection clause of the Fourteenth Amendment to the United States Constitution because they prevent less affluent people (typically members of minority races) from obtaining suitable housing accommodations in communities in which they would like to live.

Both private and public restrictions pertaining to land use are important to secured lending. The main significance of these land-use controls lies in their protection of the value of property by keeping inharmonious or obnoxious land uses out of a neighborhood. Also, their sanctioning of substantial income-producing activities on a parcel of land can provide the income necessary for an owner who has borrowed money to acquire or improve property to meet his or her obligations. Thus, if public and private land-use restrictions are not determined accurately (usually by means of a title examination or property appraisal), the land may prove not to be situated so that it can be used legally to produce the income necessary to meet loan obligations or so that its value is protected from the adverse influence of inharmonious land uses invading an area.

Compared with determining the existence, status, and force of land restrictions, conditions, and covenants, the determination of the existence, stability, and enforceability of local zoning laws is relatively simple. The main problem is that the comparative certainty of zoning laws exists mainly within the corporate limits of municipalities. In many urban areas where new construction is taking place, the land being developed is not within the corporate limits of a city or town with an established master plan and zoning ordinances based upon such a plan. Another aspect of the indefiniteness of land-use

control through zoning ordinances is that the government frequently changes the zoning classifications applicable to parcels of land. The question of allowable land use under government zoning ordinances must be answered in determining the financial feasibility of land development plans related to certain parcels of land, because the zoning determines the utility and hence to a great extent the value of such land. In developing areas the only practical way to limit land use and thereby enhance and protect the value of many parcels created by subdividing is through private restrictions. Although we must deal with this complex subject in a limited fashion, do not underestimate the importance of this area of real estate law, for it is directly related to the success or failure of real estate financing programs.

Restrictions upon land and its use that are enforceable in courts are based upon long-standing concepts of public policy established and sanctioned by appellate courts and statutory enactments. The main support for enforceable land-use restrictions is their reasonableness, in the sense that they serve a legitimate useful purpose of protecting or preserving interests recognized by the courts.

This discussion of restrictions, conditions, and covenants covers lawful and unlawful prohibitory provisions and examines the basic mechanics involved in creating such private land-use regulations. The examination of enforceable and unenforceable land-use restrictions is designed to provide a general understanding of the possible scope of such prohibitions.

Before discussing these topics, we should realize that restrictions upon land use in the case of the subdivision of a tract of land are usually created by covenants. These covenants "run with the land," which means that the land itself—not just a particular owner—is burdened with the limitations. *Conditions* are distinguishable from *restrictions* on land in that the condition is operative when a prohibited use is made of the land and has the effect of depriving the violating owner of title to the land. This means that the owner not observing such land-use conditions runs the grave risk of losing title to his or her property, whereas the violator of a restriction created by a covenant running with the land merely faces the possibility that a court of equity will issue an order for him or her to comply with the land-use restriction.

The California courts have allowed owners to create and enforce land-use restrictions such as prior approval of building plans and specifications by a review committee before construction may be undertaken; only single-family houses to be built on land; only commercial use to be made of land; only buildings of a certain size to be built; certain setbacks from the perimeters of a lot must be observed, that is, these areas are not to be occupied by buildings; and a certain style of architecture in any building constructed on the land.

In California the following land restrictions are not enforceable: prohibitions on land conveyancing that absolutely prevent the owner from disposing of the property; restrictions prohibiting conveyance to members of certain religious groups or races; and restrictions on the use of land that are determined to be unreasonable, for example, they are uncommon and the burden imposed upon the use that could otherwise be made of the land is disproportionate to the benefit derived from the restriction.

The chief requirement for an effective restriction upon land use to be created by a covenant in a deed is that the grantee (owner or owners subsequent to the creator of the restriction) must have had notice of the burden placed upon the land at the time the property was conveyed to him or her. This notice may be actual (grantee has personal knowledge of the restriction), or it may be constructive (restriction is found in a recorded deed although the grantee does not have actual knowledge of the provision). If the restrictive covenants are to be enforceable by owners subsequent to the grantor creating them, there must be an expression of intent that all lot owners deriving title through the creator of covenants will have the right to proceed to have a court enforce the restrictions against any owner violating them. This requirement of express stipulation usually involves the grantor in the creation of a rather comprehensive plan of restrictions that will presumably benefit all the lots in a subdivision. The mechanics of making the lots in a subdivision subject to restrictive covenants running with the land consist of recording a map of the area to be covered by the comprehensive restrictions along with a statement declaring the restrictions. Each deed issued to a grantee by the grantor creating the restrictions should contain a statement that the land conveyed by the deed is subject to land-use restrictions and should indicate where the description of restrictions can be found among the county recorder's records.

The mere act of creating land-use restrictions will not assure that a court, when petitioned to enforce them, will actually do so. Restrictive land-use covenants can be eliminated or rendered ineffective in several ways. If the grantor wishing to restrict the use made of land does not include the restrictions in most of the deeds, the restrictions will not be regarded as effective in creating a general land-use plan and will therefore be considered unenforceable. Some restrictive covenants provide that a certain number of the owners of lots subject to such limitations may agree to abrogate one or more provisions of such a limiting scheme. When this requirement is complied with, the restriction so acted upon is eliminated. General lack of enforcement will lead to a situation in which it is doubtful that a court of equity will, at a subsequent time, enforce the breached land-use limitations. Under the cir-

cumstances of such an extensive period of lack of enforcement, the court would usually consider it inequitable to effectuate the limitations. If a court can reasonably determine that conditions in the area subject to the limitations have changed to such a degree that the benefits originally intended to be derived from the restrictions cannot be achieved, it will not enforce the restrictions. For example, suppose that subdivided land parcels originally subject to restrictions limiting land use to agricultural activities are subsequently allowed to include—through nonenforcement of applicable restrictions—fairly numerous commercial and industrial developments. Under these circumstances, a court may well hold that general area land-use conditions have changed so much from the original restrictive plan that it is unreasonable to enforce the restrictions. The basic reason for such a judicial conclusion would be that as a practical matter the allowed breaches of the original limited land-use plan resulted in so much of this land being used for nonagricultural purposes that it was no longer possible to preserve the agricultural status of the regulated land parcels.

The California appellate courts have held that land-use restrictions do not apply to the state or its subdivisions. Thus, there is no enforcement of the land-use limitations against school boards, cities, or departments of the state government.

Conditions in deeds that have the purpose of controlling land use in the sense of limiting it achieve the same purpose as restrictive covenants. The main differences are the method of enforcement and the general scope of their operation. As already mentioned, the usual method of enforcement is for the grantor or his or her successors in interest, who have the right and therefore the power to obtain compliance by the grantee or his or her successors, to seek a court order that will force the reconveyance of the property back to them because of the violation. The scope of operation of this type of land-use restriction is much more limited in the sense that it typically operates upon only one parcel of land. Thus, compared with a comprehensive land-use plan based upon a set of land-use restrictions affecting many lots, this type of land-use limitation is not too significant in general real estate operations.

Any type of private limitation upon the owner's right to use land in a reasonable fashion runs contrary to the strong public policy of maximum latitude in using land. Therefore, the creation and enforcement of such limitations is not favored by the law. As a result, very technical requirements for the creation of such limitations have to be followed precisely if one wishes to bring them into existence. After they have been formally created, they must be preserved by constant vigilance on the part of those who would like to enforce them. Because of the exacting technical requirements for creating such limitations and the long-term supervision necessary, it is not surprising that there are many cases in which the intent to create such land-use controls came to naught.

From the standpoint of creating difficulties for succeeding generations, there are few things more harmful that can be done in the area of land titles than to create needless and useless restrictions upon the right to use land. Therefore, a thorough examination of the actual need for land-use restrictions is strongly urged before any are created. If restrictions upon the right of owners to use land serve a useful purpose, only the minimal restriction should be employed. Following these policies will avoid the possibility of future litigation to remove existing but useless limitations upon land use.

TRANSFERS OF PROPERTY INTERESTS

The transfer of title to real property from one owner to another is complex and formal compared with the transfer of title to personal property. With transferring title to real property in the typical sales transaction, it is absolutely essential to have all agreements and commitments reduced to writing. Thus, the contract to buy, the deed whereby title is transferred, the escrow agreement, and the promissory note and trust deed creating a secured indebtedness are all in writing.

In most sales situations the ultimate conveyance of title to the property sold is based upon the contract of sale between the seller and the buyer. This agreement provides (in its essential aspects) that the buyer will purchase, by a certain or determinable date, a specific parcel of land, at a stated price, and in accordance with a specified financing plan. The seller agrees to sell, by a certain date, the described parcel of land, at the agreed-upon price, and to accept the method of financing the payment of the price. Most sellers prefer to obtain a deposit of money from the prospective buyer when he or she makes the offer to buy. This deposit is subject to forfeiture as liquidated damages if the buyer breaches the contract after the seller accepts the offer. Thus, even though a California court will not enforce a forfeiture clause that allows the seller to obtain compensation for breach of contract in excess of his or her actual loss due to the breach, these standard clauses in most California contracts serve a useful purpose. They act as a threat of immediate loss if the buyer fails to perform on the contract he or she is now a party to. The deposit of money at the time of the buyer's offer to purchase is not essential to making the offer, but it is desirable in the sense that it may constitute the necessary coercive element that prevents the nervous buyer from "jumping the traces" and not actually buying the property. Other detailed spec-

ifications creating obligations for the seller and buyer may be included in the contract. In the residential sale situation, these other details usually relate to existing mortgages or trust deeds and to disposition of draperies, blinds, TV aerials, and the like. That property is transferred from one owner to another will not automatically terminate existing secured indebtedness on the property. At the time of title transfer, these obligations may usually be discharged by payment or assumed by the buyer, or the buyer may take title subject to the debt. (Assumption and taking title subject to the debt are discussed in detail later.)

As soon as the contract for the sale of an interest in land is created by the owner's acceptance of the prospective buyer's offer to purchase, certain equitable interests are automatically created. Equitable conversion occurs, which means (based upon the rule of equity that what *should* be done is regarded as *being* done) that the vendee has the right to the land (and, as far as equity is concerned, owns it) and that the vendor has the right to the money to be paid by the buyer for the land. Under the common-law application of this principle, the vendee has to bear any loss due to damage to the property being sold under the contract. For example, if most of the value of the property was in the improvements, the vendee could be required to buy a property that was comparatively worthless because of destruction of the building by fire between the time the contract was created and the time for transfer of title by deed. This difficult situation has been alleviated in California by legislation that provides essentially for the vendor to bear the risk of any such loss occurring during this interim period, provided that he or she is in possession of the property and has title to it.

It is most important that the contract state in plain, understandable language exactly what the intent of the parties is as to the land in question. We cannot now delve into the intricacies of contract interpretation by the courts; however, it should be realized that much of the litigation over contracts relating to the sale of land involves determining exactly what obligations were incurred by the parties under the contract. It is inexcusable to write a contract so vague and indefinite that it constitutes no solid binding agreement or is subject to several possible reasonable interpretations. Contracts for the sale of land are construed in their entirety by courts so as to determine from their contents what the intent of the parties was as to the rights and duties to be created under the agreement. (In most agreements any verbal statements cannot be considered part of the contract, because the parol evidence rule prohibits a court from construing a written contract from such statements.) This basic task of the courts in such lawsuits emphasizes the duty of anyone completing such contracts of sale to have all the necessary facts at hand so that the parties, the land, time for performance, price, and financing can be described in such plain, understandable language that no one can legitimately and reasonably question the rights and obligations created by the contract.

The parties to a contract of sale involving land are known as the *vendor* (seller) and the *vendee* (buyer). When these parties have completed their obligations to each other in the sale situation, a deed is completed and delivered from the seller to the buyer. This deed from the *grantor* (seller) to the *grantee* (buyer) effects the primary purpose of the transaction: to transfer title to the specific parcel of land from the grantor to the grantee for an agreed price.

In California the *grant* deed and the *quitclaim* deed are the two types of deeds most commonly used in the sales transaction. It is also possible to employ the *warranty* deed in conveyancing. The grant deed is used most often since there are some warranties made under its terms by the grantor in favor of the grantee. (Remember that most of the protection of the grantee in California as far as marketable title is concerned is derived from title insurance policies.) The quitclaim deed is not often used in sales transactions because it is not truly a conveyance and makes virtually no warranties by the grantor to the grantee.

The quitclaim deed is essentially a release of any interest that the grantor may have in certain property described in the deed. The grantor does not warrant that he or she has title to the property, not does he or she undertake any other obligation to the grantee. This type of deed will transfer any interest (legal or equitable) that the grantor may have at the time the deed is completed and delivered. Hence, interests that are equitable in nature (recognized by a court of equity but not necessarily traceable to a chain of title based upon an unbroken chain of recorded deeds) may be transferred through the use of the quitclaim deed. Therefore, a vendee may transfer his or her rights in property based upon a contract of sale before he or she has received legal title through delivery to him or her by the vendor of a properly executed deed. The usual purpose for using a quitclaim deed is to clear the title to land by having a person who might possibly retain some interest in the parcel release it by executing and delivering such a deed.

Because of its almost universal use in California land sales transactions, the grant deed is the most significant conveyancing instrument used in the state. This deed is distinguishable from the quitclaim deed by its use of the word *grant* and by two warranties found in the deed that bind the grantor and his or her heirs: namely, that previous to the execution and delivery of the deed the grantor has not conveyed the same property interest to anyone else, and that at the time of the conveyance the property so conveyed is not subject to any liens, claims, or encumbrances made by the grantor except those accepted by the grantee. It is significant that these two warranties are concerned only with activities of the grantor and therefore do not cover defects in the title due to the activities of third persons. The warranties by the grantor to the grantee under the grant deed are obviously limited as to their coverage. It is therefore essential that the grantee have some other assurance of a good title to the property for which he or she is paying. This additional assurance is usually a title insurance policy, which provides protection in the form of an insurance contract wherein the insuring company (as in generally the case with insurance companies) commits itself to pay for certain damage suffered by the insured party. The typical title insurance policy usually covers only certain specified contingencies and is not a universal cure-all for defects in land titles. (Title insurance contracts will be discussed in greater detail later.)

The warranty deed may also be used in California conveyancing. Under the warranty deed (used only when a stipulation in the contract of sale obligates the vendor to convey by such a deed), the grantor and his or her heirs, successsors, and assigns warrant that the grantee will enjoy quiet possession, title to the described premises, and defense of his or her title by the grantor and his or her heirs, successors, and assigns against all lawful claims of third parties affecting the grantee's interest in the property. The value of these warranties is dependent upon the substantial question of the ability of the grantor to bear the burden of paying for the required title defense. Warranty deeds are not common in California now because of the virtually universal use of the grant deed and an accompanying title insurance policy to protect the grantee's interest in his or her property.

To transfer effectively an interest in land, a deed must contain a specification of the grantor and grantee, a written statement describing the interest conveyed, a subscription (the grantor's signature at the end of the writing indicating intent to convey), and delivery and acceptance of the instrument by the grantor and grantee, respectively. When these requirements have been complied with, the transfer of property from the grantor to the grantee is complete. Note that there is no requirement that the deed be recorded to complete the conveyance of property by deed. Recording of documents such as deeds that affect the status of property titles is not a legal requirement. Such instruments are recorded to protect the grantee or secured lender from the possible claims of third parties that may deprive them of part or all of their interest in a certain parcel of property. There is no place in the prudent conduct of real estate financing operations for the unrecorded deed or trust deed. (Recording is discussed in detail later.)

THE ESCROW AS A MEANS OF EFFECTING REAL ESTATE TRANSFERS OR FINANCING

Under the terms of a contract for the sale of an interest in land, the parties incur obligations that are concurrent as to time of performance. If the parties to the agreement are honest and of knowledgeable good will, there is usually no problem in completing the transaction. The vendor-grantor will convey the interest that the vendee-grantee is to receive. The required price will be paid or financed in accordance with the agreement so that upon delivering the deed, the vendor is compensated for the property interest sold. If this ideal situation does not exist (and actually it seldom does) because the parties involved cannot or will not perform in accordance with their voluntarily assumed obligations, it is obvious that many difficulties can arise. If the buyer does not produce the funds to pay the seller for the interest being sold, and if the seller does not have a marketable title (a title reasonably clear of lawful claims by third persons so that the grantee obtains quiet enjoyment and possession of the property) at the time of conveyance, the parties are not going to receive their just expectations under the contract. Also, if the grantor will not deliver the deed to the grantee before the grantee pays for the property and if the grantee will not pay the required price until he or she gets title by taking delivery of the deed, the parties are obviously at a standoff and the contract will not be performed. (And who can blame complete strangers for some lack of faith?) To overcome these difficulties the escrow concept was introduced and widely adopted in California.

It is not necessary to establish an escrow to complete a land sales transaction in California; however, if vendor and vendee seek to complete the performance of the sales contract without this third-party participation, they must themselves perform or arrange for another to perform the duties of an escrow holder in the California conveyancing situation. Because of the wide acceptance of the escrow holder as the proper agency for the completion of the mechanical aspects of a land conveyancing based upon a sales contract, it is virtually impossible in the vast majority of cases to ignore this step in the transfer of a property interest. To safeguard the interests of the parties to most real estate sales transactions in California, a competent, efficient escrow holder should be selected and burdened with the details of completing the transfer of title and payment by the parties.

The duties of escrow holder are obviously determined by the specific aspects of the transaction. Although many standard tasks must be done before transfer of title is accomplished and payment is received, unique requirements may certainly develop in each escrow. Since we cannot deal here with all aspects of escrows, we will concentrate on only the fundamental aspects usually found in the typical sales transaction.

By understanding the function of the escrow we can better comprehend what it is, how it is created, and the mechanics of carrying out the duties placed upon the escrow holder by the escrow instructions.

The term *escrow* is defined in Section 17003 of the California Finance Code as

any transaction wherein one person, for the purpose of effecting the sale, transfer, encumbering, or leasing of real or personal property to another person, delivers any written instrument, money, evidence of title to real or personal property, or other thing of value to a third person to be held by such third person until the happening of a specified event or the performance of a prescribed condition, when it is then to be delivered by such third person to a grantee, grantor, promisee, promisor, obligee, obligor, bailee, bailor, or any agent or employee of the latter.

To create an escrow it is necessary to have an enforceable contract between two parties (typically vendor and vendee in a sales situation) who are obligated to sell, convey, and purchase a certain interest in land. After such a contract comes into existence providing for the creation of an escrow and designating a specified corporation, or real estate broker, as the escrow holder, the parties join in the completion of another agreement—escrow instructions. These instructions (usually drawn up by the escrow holder on the basis of the terms of the contract between the vendor and vendee) specify the details of the obligations of the respective parties and constitute the "road map" to be followed in completing the transaction. In the typical transaction the vendor has the obligation to complete and deliver to the escrow holder the required deed and to secure for the grantee the appropriate policy of title insurance, which is also evidence of the marketability of the title. The vendee has the basic obligation to pay the price agreed upon in the contract, which means that he or she usually pays some cash to the escrow holder and borrows some money to make up the difference between his or her cash payment and the purchase price due. To borrow the money he or she must often execute a promissory note secured by either a mortgage or a trust deed. If the note and trust deed are necessary, they are delivered, along with the required cash, into the hands of the escrow holder. After these documents and monies have been delivered to the escrow holder, the escrow is "closed," which simply means that the escrow holder "crosses hands" in the sense of delivering the deed to the vendee and the required amount of cash and any promissory notes and liens securing the debt to the vendor. In its simplest form, this is the creation, operation, and conclusion of an escrow in the usual sales transaction. The only departure from this description in actual practice is that the documents required to be produced by the various parties may be executed by the escrow holder and signed at its office.

At the commencement of an escrow the escrow holder is an agent for both parties to the transaction. The basic responsibility of the escrow holder is to carry out the instructions given to it without negligently or willfully causing loss to any of the parties to the transaction. After documents and monies have been entrusted to the escrow holder, it becomes, regarding the delivery of those items to the parties entitled to receive them, solely their agent. The change that evolves in the agency status of the escrow holder affects the liability aspect of the situation, if for some reason the parties do not receive what they are entitled to from the transaction. If the parties to the escrow have delivered to the escrow holder whatever they are obligated to produce, and then it is passed on to the correct party, the loss (presumably through negligence or willful action, both of which result in liability for the person causing the failure to perform) falls upon the escrow. As far as the parties to the transaction are concerned, once they have made proper delivery to the escrow, they have performed and are under no further legal obligation to the other party. Prior to such delivery any failure to produce monies or documents creates liability for the party responsible for the particular performance.

The escrow holder in its agency capacity is under strict control of the parties to the contract, which means that any departure from the terms of the escrow instructions or from the custom and usage of local escrow practice must, to be valid, be agreeable to all parties to the transaction. Admittedly, however, some escrow clerks do not act in accordance with their legal place vis-à-vis the parties to the transaction.

What, in fact, does an escrow holder do to complete the performance of its duties in a typical situation? To effect the completion of the transfer of title to the property, the escrow will (1) request a preliminary title report (usually from the title company that is to issue the policy of title insurance); (2) arrange for the title insurance policy to be issued; (3) notify the seller and the buyer of the documents or money to be paid into the escrow and proceed to arrange for the completion of said documents; (4) obtain a beneficiary's statement showing the current status of the obligation, if there is a loan in existence that will remain in effect with the buyer taking over the debtor's obligation; (5) determine exactly how much cash will have to be paid into escrow to complete the transaction, by prorating all incidental items such as interest, taxes, and insurance premiums to the date when title passes to the vendee; (6) determine the cost to each party of completing the transaction by computing such items as cost of recording documents, escrow fee, and title

insurance premium; (7) be responsible for having the appropriate documents recorded in the proper order; and (8) prepare the statement of account that will formally indicate to the parties the nature of their respective obligations.

This is a brief description of the escrow, its creation, and its function. Escrows can be established for virtually any legitimate business transaction containing the element of concurrent performance. Escrows are frequently established for the purpose of making new loans on real property or of refinancing old ones. The escrow serves as an agency between the parties for the purpose of determining that the funds to be borrowed are available, that the title of the property owned by a loan applicant is marketable and thus suitable as security for debt, and that the promissory note and trust deed will be properly executed and issued. Theoretically, it is not necessary to establish an escrow for the purpose of transferring title to real property or of arranging a secured loan, but as a practical matter doing so is so customary and useful as to be virtually unavoidable in California.

RECORDING

Although not essential to the validity of such instruments as deeds, mortgages, and trust deeds, recording is necessary in California if one is fully to protect his or her interests in real property or secured loans. Recording of documents that establish title or a lien on real property is the method that has been developed to notify the public of the interests held by various persons in a particular property. The basic problem before the practice of recording was established was the determination of rights when an owner of property had sold the same parcel of land two, three, four, or more times. Who had title to the property in such a case? Before the development and use of recording, the English courts solved these disputes with the legal principle that after the first sale of his or her property the seller had nothing left to sell. Thus, the second, third, and fourth "buyers" had no rights in the property, which meant that their only recourse to prevent loss was to have the seller return to them whatever consideration they had given him or her. From the standpoint of maintaining the public trust in real estate and preventing fraud, this solution was not really satisfactory, because it left the seller in complete control of the situation; he or she was often the only source of information for the buyer as to whether any other parties had title or security rights in the property. The implementation of the recording system in this country placed a new burden upon the purchaser or lender in transactions involving real estate: if he or she did not comply with the recording statute and file documents stating his or her interests in the property with the county recorder, he or she might well lose those interests to another party who did comply with the recording statute.

The most significant result of recording is that it gives constructive notice of the interests in real property when documents stating title to such property are filed with the recorder of the county in which the property is located. Therefore, whether or not a purchaser or lender actually knows of the interests that others may have in the property, he or she is charged with such knowledge and therefore cannot perfect any superior rights in the property that would minimize or eliminate the interests of those who have previously recorded their instruments. This situation requires that there be a search of the title to real property every time that a purchase is considered or a loan is to be made with the property serving as security for the debt.

Recording results in *constructive* notice to the public of interests in property, but there is also the concept of *actual* notice of interests in land. Although there may not be personal knowledge of outstanding interests in all instances of actual notice, actual notice is not constructive since it is not based upon county recorder office records. Actual notice results from the occupancy of property by persons other than the alleged owner. Thus, if a prospective purchaser or lender went to the property and found someone other than the seller or borrower in possession of it and with an interest in the land, the party contemplating dealing with the property would have notice of the other person's interest in it. This concept of actual notice illustrates the importance of actually inspecting real property before purchasing or lending on it, so that one's interest in the property will not be superseded by a prior claim.

Basically, the documents that can and should be recorded are those that affect the title or possession of real property: specifically, instruments such as deeds, mortgages, trust deeds, contracts of sale, leases, option agreements, court judgments, and conditional sales contracts or leases affecting title to property once personal but now a fixture due to its attachment to land.

A basic requirement for any instrument to be recordable is that it be executed (signed) in the presence of a notary public, a requirement formally known as the acknowledgment of the instrument. The purpose of this acknowledgment is to obtain assurance that the party to the instrument is truly the person indicated to be the executor of the document. Performance of an acknowledgment before a notary public assures that the correct party is completing the document, since persons selected and commissioned as notary publics are chosen primarily because of their honesty and good reputation in the community.

The recording statute in California (and in most states) is designed to protect the interest in real property of the bona fide purchaser. The bona fide purchaser has in good faith, without notice of other parties' interests in the property, given value for the real estate. The California recording statute protects this type of purchaser only—and only if he or she records his or her document before some other party records who has subsequently received an instrument that affects the title to the property. In California an unrecorded instrument is effective between the immediate parties to the transaction, but it cannot prevent third parties from possibly perfecting some superior interests in the property.

The operation and effect of the recording statute in California can be comprehended more fully by considering some examples. If A, owning land, conveys it to B on July 1, the deed does not have to be recorded to effect this transfer to title. If the title to the same land is conveyed by A to C on July 2 without either party recording, B still has the superior claim to the property. But if C records his deed on July 3 and B has not yet recorded his deed, C has the superior claim to the property. In the latter circumstance, C owns the property and B has no enforceable claim or interest in the property. C, by being a bona fide purchaser of the property and recording first, is the party whose interests will be protected over those of B. B has not followed the provisions of the recording statute and suffers the penalty of deprivation of his or her purchased interest in the property. If a trust deed is involved the same result is achieved. The party who made the first loan on the property but who did not record it first would find that a subsequent lender who recorded his or her trust deed first would have a prior lien on the property; the first lender would have to take a lien of secondary priority.

The actual act of recording is a purely mechanical process. An instrument to be recorded must be filed with the county recorder of the county in which the property is located. The actual recording is the county recorder's copying the document into the official record book and indexing it under the names of the parties to the transaction. The permanent records maintained in the recorder's office may be handwritten, typewritten, or photographic reproductions of the instruments on microfilm. In conducting a title search under the first method of recording the title, the searcher will examine copies of the documents in large permanent books, whereas in the microfilm system the search will consist of viewing microfilm displayed on special visual display machines. For the legal effect of recording to be achieved in California, the instrument, in addition to being copied and filed in the record system, must be indexed so that it can be located in the chain of title by anyone conducting a search for any particular parcel of land. The county recorder is the agent of the party recording an instrument and is responsible for errors in copying the document or in indexing. The constructive notice derived from recording affects the right of third parties only to the extent that instruments are correctly spread upon the official records.

Priority of title, or liens on real property will be determined in most cases by the order of recording. Thus we are dealing with a chronological situation in the sense that a first trust deed is truly a prior lien because it is recorded first. A second trust deed is usually superseded in priority by some other trust deed simply because it was not recorded first.

The terms of a security contract may affect and determine the priority rights of liens on real property. The typical agreement, known as a *subordination agreement,* provides that under certain circumstances a first lien (determined by the time of its recording) may become inferior (subordinated) to a lien created later. A subordination agreement arises in the sale of land that is to be improved at a later time. The vendor of the land finances the sale of the property by accepting only partial payment of the purchase price at the time of title transfer and takes a promissory note secured by a first trust deed on the property. If the usual trust deed is used in this situation, any lender making a secured loan to cover the cost of constructing improvements on the property would be in the position of a second trust deed holder, since the seller's lien was recorded first. This position would be untenable for most lending institutions, since statutes regulating lending by most insurance companies, banks, and savings and loan associations do not allow them to make any real estate loans that are not secured by first liens (first trust deeds). Also, aside from this legal requirement, many of the managers of such sources of real estate credit would not be interested in making loans secured by a second lien, since they would be in an inferior position in that, if there were foreclosure upon the property, they would be entitled to proceeds from its sale only if the property sold for enough to pay the debts secured by both the first and second liens. In a declining real estate market (when foreclosure sales are most likely to occur), the selling price of the property obviously may not be enough to retire both debts. Therefore, something has to be done to enable the purchaser of unimproved property to borrow the money necessary for improving the property.

The solution to this dilemma is the subordination agreement, which is simply a clause incorporated into the first trust deed providing that if there is borrowing by the trustor or his or her heirs, successors, or assigns, the lender making the construction loan will have a first lien upon the property. For his or her own benefit, therefore (because improved property will presumably be more valuable than unimproved property), the seller of raw land gives up his or her priority to facilitate the sale and development of the property.

This discussion of the subordination agreement illustrates a very important aspect of voluntary liens on real property. Such liens are essentially contracts between the lender and the borrower; therefore, the parties have considerable latitude in arranging the terms and conditions of the obligation. It is important to realize that the rights and duties of parties to a loan agreement are based largely upon the terms of the promissory note and the mortgage or trust deed. Of course, the parties will also find their situation governed by the statutes of California and the controlling appellate court decisions, but they can never prudently neglect consideration of the terms of the loan found in the note and lien document.

Thus far we have been concerned primarily with the recording statute as it applies to instruments that are usually created voluntarily. The recording statute also applies to involuntarily created interests in real property that are based upon written instruments. Most of these involuntary liens are based upon statutes or principles of law formulated and set forth in appellate court decisions. These liens are usually unique, therefore, since they recognize some special interest of the lien holder. Tax liens and mechanic's liens are examples of these special liens. Because of the unique characteristics of these interests in real property, they will be discussed separately after further consideration of California mortgages and trust deeds.

ADVERSE POSSESSION, PRESCRIPTION, AND IMPLIED DEDICATION

One could be engaged in the real estate sales or finance field for a lifetime without encountering an adverse possession problem. Nevertheless, one should be acquainted with this property concept, which is firmly rooted in Anglo-American law. When an adverse possession problem arises, the result is usually loss of valuable property interests in addition to the cost of litigation.

The legal reason for the concept of someone gaining title to another's property by possessing it in open defiance of the owner's property rights is the statute of limitations on trespass actions. When someone takes illegal possession of someone else's property, the property owner is allowed a certain period of time in which to begin a court action to have this person removed from the premises as a trespasser. Under adverse possession, when the statutory period for this proceeding has expired and when the occupier of the land has completed the additional requirements for him or her to obtain title to the land, the true owner is dispossessed of the property and deprived of his or her title to the land. Obviously, a real property owner must be continually aware of the use being made of his or her land and of who is occupying the land.

In California, a person wishing to perfect title in the land of another must occupy the property—possess it exclusively, openly, notoriously, hostilely, and continuously—for five years, under a claim of right or color of title, and must pay the taxes levied against it for a continuous period of five years. If any one of these requirements is not met for the five-year period by the adverse possessor, the true owner retains title to his or her property because the other party has failed to meet the strict requirements for perfecting title in another's land by adverse possession.

The main danger from adverse possession is the possible loss of title to all or a portion of a parcel of land. This results in a decrease in the value of property and undermines a secured loan, since upon foreclosure the property will not sell for as much as it would have if this adverse interest had not been perfected. In California adverse possession does not occur often because most occupiers of other people's property do not or cannot comply with the requirement that they pay the property taxes as they fall due during the five-year period.

A greater danger to the integrity of land titles is the perfection of easements in real property by prescription. This concept is essentially the same as adverse possession except that the illegal user of someone's property obtains an easement, not a fee-simple interest, in the owner's land. Additional differences are (1) there is no requirement to pay taxes on the easement way (because none are usually levied—but if taxes are levied they must be paid to develop prescriptive rights) and (2) the trespasser does not have to maintain a semblance of continuous possession of a certain area. The person traversing the land must simply use the property whenever he or she desires and with some degree of regularity on a continuous basis for the five-year statutory period. After an easement has been perfected by prescription, the easement holder has an interest in the land that cannot be taken from him or her unless he or she consents or is deprived of it by the exercise of the power of eminent domain. Obviously, the perfection of such an interest in property significantly obscures the title.

Adverse use by the general public resulting in implied dedication of the used property to the public (essentially a public easement over the surface of such land) was developed into a specific rule of law in the California Supreme Court decision of *Gion* v. *Santa Cruz* (2 C.3d 29, 84 C.R. 162, 1970). In this case an oceanfront lot in Santa Cruz, California, was owned by private individuals, but was used on a continuing basis by members of the general public over a period of years. The various owners of this parcel of land over several decades did not effectively object or act to prevent the city of Santa Cruz from improving the land by installing guard rails, paving, and trash receptacles. This use (adverse to the owner) by the city and the general public continued for more than five consecutive years, and the owners took no effective action to stop it. The California Supreme Court held that the owner's fee interest in the parcel of land was subject to a surface easement in favor of the city of Santa Cruz and members of the general public for recreational uses. Because such use by any nonowner of any privately owned land could occur during any consecutive five-year period, this decision cast a cloud over much privately owned land in California—especially land on the Pacific coastline. In 1971 the California legislature enacted legislation intended to limit the scope and effect of the *Gion* v. *Santa Cruz* rule on implied public dedication of privately owned land. The new law provided that no use of privately owned real property like that occurring in the *Gion* case shall ever result in the public or a government body obtaining an established legal right to continue permanently to use such property in this manner unless the owner of the property offers in writing to dedicate his or her property for public use (Calif. Civil Code, Sec. 1009[c]). The situation that now exists is that public use before 1971 of privately owned land will still result in public dedication of such property; however, if any of the required public use of privately owned property occurred after 1971, the result will not be automatic public dedication of the property.

Deprivation of interests in property by adverse possession, implied dedication, or prescription may not be insured against in title insurance policies. This greatly increases the danger of loss from this source to property owners or lenders. Therefore, it is very important that the possible existence of an unmarketable title due to such interests be considered in every purchase or loan transaction.

PROMISSORY NOTE

Evidence of the debt owed in real estate financing transactions is typically in the form of a *promissory note*. Because this contract is a negotiable instrument, dealing with and collecting on the basis of this obligation are controlled by the negotiable instruments law. Persons engaged in making real estate loans should therefore be reasonably familiar with this specialized body of law.

Since the promissory note is a contract, the parties are in a position to exercise considerable latitude in establishing the terms of the debt to be repaid. The actual formulation of the provisions of the note is derived from a bargaining procedure. The lender obviously desires to be placed in a position in which he or she will enjoy maximum safety of principal and return, whereas the borrower wants to gain as much latitude as possible in terms of relief from penalties and expense in case of default and of opportunity to refinance the debt. Most prospective borrowers are in a poor position to demand advantageous terms in the debt contract. (However, the condition of the money market may sometimes create considerable competition among lenders to make loans, so that the borrower can obtain advantages not otherwise available.) Both lenders and borrowers are affected by the custom of the community with regard to the provisions of notes used to lend money in various sections of the country.

To understand the possible variations in promissory notes used in financing real estate, one should examine the note contracts used by various lenders. There are some differences in almost all notes, as well as a number of provisions that are common to virtually all such contracts. We shall concern ourselves, therefore, with the typical significant provisions found in promissory notes.

The promissory note used in real estate financing usually provides for the total amount of money due; periodic payments to be made if the loan is an amortizing one; the interest rate; the maturity date; identification of the *debtor* (maker) and *creditor* (payee); penalties for late payment; the cost of collecting through litigation to be borne by the debtor; conditions under which the due date of the debt may be accelerated by the holder of the note; and provision whereby the debtor can pay the debt prior to the established maturity date. This last provision, commonly known as the prepayment privilege, is usually highly prized by the borrower, because it allows him or her a degree of flexibility in dealing with the property. This flexibility usually takes the form of refinancing the debt, which can be done when the prepayment provision is in the note since the debtor can force the holder of the note to accept full payment of the obligation prior to the actual date of maturity. In many cases this right of the debtor facilitates his or her selling the property by allowing a prospective purchaser to obtain a larger loan against the property than may exist, or to borrow money at a lower rate of interest than would have to be paid if the buyer took over the existing obligation. In actual practice, lenders do not like to give the borrower the right of prepayment; if allowed, it is usually limited by provisions to the last one-half or one-third of the loan term. The limitation may also take the form of limiting prepayment to an annual amount of not more than a certain percentage of the total amount borrowed. The lender may also specify a price to be paid by the debtor if he or she exercises the prepayment right; this amount is often measured by a percentage of the total amount of money borrowed.

Over the years secured real estate lenders have placed what are called *acceleration clauses* in the contracts they use to make such loans. These clauses specify that under certain circumstances, at its option, the lender may accelerate the time of payment of the entire unpaid loan principal. Typical justifications for acceleration of the trustor's payment of the total unpaid debt balance are default on obligations by the trustor (failure to make timely payments of principal and interest, committing waste, not paying real property taxes or special assessments, or not paying fire insurance premiums); sale or transfer of the trustor's ownership in the collateral property; and increasing the amount of secured debt against the collateral property. Recently there has been significant litigation in California over the enforceability of due-on-sale and due-on-further-encumbrance-by-trustor acceleration clauses. The validity and enforceability of the due-on-sale acceleration clause were considered by the California Supreme Court in the case of *Tucker* v. *Lassen Savings and Loan Association* (12 C.3d 629, 116 C.R. 633, 1974). The trustors had purchased a residential property using purchase money funds borrowed from the savings and loan association to pay part of the price, and had then sold the collateral property using a land contract to accomplish the sale. Under the terms of the land contract the trustors retained ownership of the legal title to the collateral property until the buyers paid the sale price in full. The lender considered the land contract transaction a sale of the collateral property and sought to enforce the due-on-sale clause in the purchase money loan agreement. The California Supreme Court held that, under the particular facts of this case—that is, a purchase money trust deed trustor selling under a land contract—the due-on-sale clause was unenforceable because it constituted an unreasonable restraint on alienation (of the owner's right to sell real property), since the trustor retained an ownership interest in the collateral property and an obligation to make the trust deed loan payments under the land contract. The court further held that the lender had not demonstrated how the land contract sale jeopardized its position as a secured real estate lender to the extent that the due-on-sale clause had to be enforced to protect its legitimate interests in the original loan transaction. After *Tucker* v. *Lassen Savings and Loan Association,* due-on-sale clauses in California trust deed loan contracts were still enforceable at the option of the lender—if the sale transaction was an immediate final sale of the collateral property by the trustor or if the land contract was used to sell the collateral property and the lender could prove that its position as a secured lender was jeopardized by this transaction. The legal status of the enforceability of due-on-sale clauses in California residential purchase money trust deeds remained as established in the *Tucker* v. *Lassen Savings and Loan Association* decision until 1978, when the California Supreme Court decided the landmark case of *Wellenkamp v. Bank of America, National Trust and Savings Association* (148 C. R, 379, 21 C 3d 943, 582 P.2d 970). A summary of this important decision affecting residential purchase money loan trust deed and mortgate due-on-sale clauses follows.

WELLENKAMP v. BANK OF AMERICA, NATIONAL TRUST AND SAVINGS ASSOCIATION

Synopsis

The purchaser of real property (Cynthia Wellenkamp), which property was subject to a deed of trust sought an injunction against enforcement of due-on-sale clause in the trust deed and a declaration that exercise of such clause without any showing that the lender's security had been impaired as a result of the sale to the plaintiff Wellenkamp constituted an unreasonable restraint on alienation (the policy in California and other states is to maximize the transferability of real property among the citizenry through sale).

The Superior Court

Dismissed the purchaser/plaintiff Wellenkamp's complaint and the plaintiff appealed to the California Supreme Court.

The California Supreme Court, Manuel, J. held that: (1) if the requirements for a declaratory judgment are met, the court should declare the rights of the parties and (2) *a due-on-sale clause contained in a promissory note or deed of trust cannot be enforced upon the occurrence of an outright sale unless the lender can demonstrate that enforcement of it is reasonably necessary to protect against impairment of its security or risk of default.* Therefore, *the decision of the Superior Court is reversed,* (3) although circumstances may arise in which the interests of the lender may justify the enforcement of a due-on-sale clause in the event of an outright sale, the mere fact of sale in itself is not sufficient to warrant enforcement of the clause, and the restraint on alienation resulting therefrom, in the absence of a showing by the lender that such circumstances exist, (4) in the instant case the party seeking enforcement of the due-on-sale clause is an institutional lender. We limit our holding accordingly. We express no present opinion on the question of whether a private lender, including the vendor (seller) who takes back secondary financing (a second trust deed) has interests which might inherently justify automatic enforcement of a due-on-sale clause in his favor upon resale of the collateral property.

When this decision is effective: Given the importance of the stability of real estate titles and the interest in preserving completed real estate financial arrangements,

we hold that this decision shall not apply when the lender, prior to the date that this decision becomes final, has either enforced the due-on-sale clause, resulting in the sale of the subject property by foreclosure or in discharge of the accelerated debt, or when the lender has waived enforcement of the due-on-sale clause in return for an agreement with the new buyer modifying the existing financing, e.g., buyer agrees to a higher than contract interest rate in exchange for being able to assume the unpaid balance of an existing trust deed loan on the property purchased.

As to all other due-on-sale clauses in mortgages or trust deed loans on residential real estate, this decision applies to them if they are still in existence—no matter when the loans were made.

Facts

In July 1973, Mr. and Mrs. Mans purchased a parcel of real property in Riverside County, California, which they financed by a purchase money trust deed from defendant Bank of America, National Trust and Savings Association—in the amount of $19,100 (at an 8 percent per annum interest rate), giving the bank a promissory note secured by the trust deed. The deed of trust contained the standard due-on-sale clause which provided that if the trustor "sells, conveys, alienates, . . . said property or any part thereof, or any interest therein . . . or becomes divested of title or any interest . . . the beneficiary . . . shall have the right at its option, to declare said note . . . secured hereby . . . immediately due and payable without notice . . . ." The Mans's trust deed named defendant Continental Auxiliary Company as trustee.

In July 1975, plaintiff Cynthia Wellenkamp purchased the property from the Manses. She paid the Manses the amount of their equity in the property and agreed with the Manses to assume the balance of their loan from defendant. A grant deed transferring title to plaintiff Wellenkamp was recorded on July 19, 1975. Defendant Bank of America, National Trust and Savings Association was given prompt notice of the transfer of title to Wellenkamp as well as her check for the July payment on the Mans's loan. Bank of America, National Trust and Savings Association thereupon returned this check to Wellenkamp with a letter notifying her of its right to accelerate upon transfer of the property by the Manses. The letter offered to waive Bank of America, National Trust and Savings Association's right to accelerate in return for Wellenkamp's agreement to assume the Mans's loan at an increased rate of interest (an increase from the original 8 percent to $9\frac{1}{4}$ percent per annum). A printed assumption agreement was enclosed with Bank of America, National Trust and Savings Association's letter for Wellenkamp to sign. Wellenkamp did not agree to the increase in the interest rate and Bank of America National Trust and Savings Association filed notice of default and election to sell under the trust deed. Wellenkamp then filed the present action in which she sought an injunction against enforcement of the due-on-sale clause and a declaration that exercise of such a clause, without any showing that Bank of America, National Trust and Savings Association's security had been impaired as a result of the sale of the property to Wellenkamp constituted an unreasonable restraint upon alienation in violation of California law.

Further Reasoning and Justification for the Decision

Outright sales of real property commonly involve different types of financing arrangements, depending upon the circumstances existing at the time of the sale. Thus, when new financing is available and economically feasible, a buyer will be able to arrange to pay the seller the purchase price in full in an "all cash to the seller" arrangement. When, however, new financing is unavailable for real estate loans are in short supply, new financing may be difficult, if not impossible, to obtain, the buyer may arrange as did Wellenkamp herein, to pay the seller only the amount of the seller's equity in the property agreeing to assume or take "subject to" the existing deed of trust, in a "cash to loan" arrangement.

The availability of financing often depends upon general economic conditions and in times of inflation when money is "tight" the funds available for real estate loans are in short supply and if available—only at high interest rates—therefore, under these conditions, it may be practically difficult—if not impossible—for purchase money loans to be obtained by residential buyers. *Under these conditions the only way a trustor-seller could sell the property would be if assumption were allowed by the institutional lender—and if such assumptions were not allowed—the due-on-sale clause would constitute an unjustified and therefore illegal restraint on alienation of real property and therefore not legally enforceable.*

Justice Clark Dissenting

Holding that exercise of a due-on-sale clause upon outright sale of real property unreasonably restrains that sale, the majority of the court in its opinion either misreads or rejects the very decisions on which it relies, particularly *Tucker* v. *Lassen Savings and Loan Association,* 116 Cal. Reptr. 633, 12 Cal 3d 629 (1974). Additionally, the majority rewards in its opinion the owner of encumbered property with the award of a bonus in that he can now sell his property for something in excess of what he could sell it for if unencumbered.

We have come full circle. In attempting to take away contractual rights of lenders in order to assist borrowers in selling encumbered properties, the majority opinion has devised a scheme which affords yesterday's borrower a clear advantage over today's seller who comes to the marketplace with his property free from encumbrance. But this beneficence may be shortsighted. For, in attempting to assist the Wellenkamps, the majority opinion must necessarily restrict if not dry up mortgage funds otherwise available to the next generation of borrowers.

The majority opinion errors first in concluding that a due-on-sale clause unreasonably restricts outright sale of property; errs again in concluding there is little or no justification for the clause, contrary to our earlier holdings. We err again in failing to recognize that lenders and borrowers, owners, and prospective owners should be allowed to run their own affairs with minimal governmental intrusion—particularly from this branch.

The *Wellenkamp* decision was followed by *Fidelity Federal Savings and Loan Association* v. *de la Cuesta,* 175 Cal. Rptr. 467, 121 Cal App 3d 328, (1981)—a summary of which follows.

FIDELITY FEDERAL SAVINGS AND LOAN ASSOCIATION v. DE LA CUESTA

Justice Blackman delivered the opinion of the court and was joined in the majority decision by Burger, C.J.; and Brennan; White; Marshall; and O'Connor. A synopsis of this opinion follows:

Section 5(a) of the Home Owners Loan Act of 1933 (HOLA) empowers the Federal Home Loan Bank Board (Board) under such regulations as it may prescribe, to provide for the organization, operation, and regulation of federal savings and loan associations. Pursuant to this authorization, the Board issued a regulation providing that a federal savings and loan association "continues to have the power to include . . . in its loan instrument" a due-on-sale clause, i.e., a provision that permits the association to declare the entire balance of the loan immediately due and payable if the property securing the loan is sold or otherwise transferred without the association's prior written consent. A preamble to the regulation stated that the due-on-sale practices of federal savings and loan associations shall be governed "exclusively by federal law" and that the association "shall not be bound by or subject to any conflicting state law which imposes different . . . due-on-sale requirements." Appellees (de la Cuesta) each purchased California real property from one who had borrowed money from appellant Fidelity Savings and Loan Association (Fidelity). The borrowers had given Fidelity deeds of trust on the property; each deed contained a due-on-sale clause. Fidelity, not having received prior notices of the purchases, proceeded to enforce the due-on-sale clauses to accelerate payment of the loans, and when they were not paid, instituted nonjudicial foreclosure proceedings. Each appellee (de la Cuesta) then filed suit against Fidelity in California Superior Court, asserting that Fidelity's exercise of the due-on-sale clauses violated the principles announced in *Wellenkamp* v. *Bank of America National Trust and Savings Association,* 21 Cal. 3d 582, 582 P.2d. 970, which limited a lender's right to exercise such a clause to cases where the lender can demonstrate that the transfer of the property has impaired its security. The Superior Court consolidated the actions and granted Fidelity's motion for summary judgment on the ground that the Federal Government had totally occupied the regulation of federal savings and loan associations. The California Court of Appeal reversed, holding that *Wellenkamp* was controlling and that federal law had not expressly or impliedly preempted state due-on-sale law.

Held

The Federal Home Loan Bank Board's due-on-sale regulation preempts conflicting state limitations on the due-on-sale practices of federal savings and loan associations, and thus bars application of the *Wellenkamp* rule to such associations.

(a) The general principles governing preemption of state law that conflicts with federal law are not inapplicable here simply because real property is a matter of special concern to the states. And federal regulations have no less preemptive effect than federal statutes. Where Congress has empowered an administrator to promulgate regulations, regulations intended to preempt state law have that effect unless the administrator exceeded his statutory authority or acted arbitrarily.

(b) The language of the Board's regulations and especially the preamble thereto clearly show the Board's intent to preempt the *Wellenkamp* doctrine. The conflict between that doctrine and the regulation does not evaporate because the regulation simply permits, but does not compel, federal savings and loan associations to include a due-on-sale clause in their contracts and enforce that clause when the security property is transferred. While compliance with both the regulation and the *Wellenkamp* rule may not be a physical impossibility, that rule forbids a federal savings and loan association to enforce a due-on-sale clause at its option and deprives the association of the flexibility given it by the Board. The rule therefore creates an obstacle to the accomplishment of the regulation's purpose.

(c) The Board acted within its statutory authority in issuing the preemptive due-on-sale regulation. Both the language and legislative history of the Home Owners Loan Act indicate that the Board was authorized to regulate the lending practices of federal savings and loan associations. Congress delegated power to the Board expressly for the purpose of creating and regulating these associations so as to ensure that they would remain financially sound and able to supply financing for home construction and purchase. Consistent with that purpose, the Board reasonably exercised its authority in promulgating due-on-sale regulation.

Justice Rehnquist, with Whom Justice Stevens Joins, Dissenting

The Court today concludes that in section 5(a) of the Home Owners Loan Act of 1933, 12 U.S.C. Section 1464(a), Congress authorized the Federal Home Loan Bank Board to preempt by administrative fiat California's limitations upon the enforceability of due-on-sale clauses in real estate mortgages held by federal savings and loan institutions. The Court reaches this extraordinary result by concluding that due-on-sale clauses relate to a savings and loan's mortgage-lending practices which "are a critical aspect of its operation" over which the Board unquestionably has jurisdiction." Because I conclude that Congress has not authorized the Board to promulgate a regulation such as 12 CFR section 545.8-3(f), I dissent.

DAWN INVESTMENT COMPANY v. SUPERIOR COURT OF LOS ANGELES COUNTY

Here the sellers of nonresidential investment–commercial type real estate—who were co-beneficiaries of a deed of trust securing a purchase money promissory note debt contract were a corporation wholly owned by a married couple and the mother of the husband who owned the corporation. In the course of selling the property in 1977, as part of financing the sale price, the sellers took back from the buyer a promissory note secured by a second deed of trust which contained a standard due-on-sale clause. Three years later these buyers (debtors on the purchase money trust deed) sold the property and took back from the buyer an all-inclusive deed of trust. Upon learning of the transfer of title to new owners in 1980, the 1977 sellers (and trust deed beneficiaries) notified the 1980 sellers and buyer that they were exercising their rights as secured lenders under the due-on-sale clause and demanded immediate payment in full of the debt they held. After receiving this demand for payment, the sellers of the property in 1980, in order to prevent foreclosure on the property by the 1977 trust deed beneficiaries, sued the trust deed beneficiaries in Superior Court seeking injunctive and declaratory relief.

In upholding the 1980 seller trustor's and buyer's right to have the existing 1977 trust deed debt assumed when the property was sold, the California Supreme Court reasoned and stated as follows: "The assumability of existing purchase money trust deed loans upon the subsequent sale and transfer of title of the property established in *Wellenkamp* v. *Bank of America, National Trust and Savings Association* (which was in that decision limited to purchase money financing of residential property where the loan was made by a financial institution) is also applicable to purchase money financing of investment–commercial type property. The test for reasonableness of a restraint on alienation involves balancing the quantum of restraint against the justification for it. Applying this test we determine that there was no valid basis for any distinction between a due-on-sale clause in a deed of trust on an owner-occupied residence and a deed of trust on an investment or commercial property."

The Court made a definite statement that the *Wellenkamp* v. *Bank of America, National Trust and Savings Association* rule prohibiting institutional purchase money residential lenders from automatic enforcement of the due-on-sale clause applies to private purchase money lenders also. To support this ruling the court noted that while private purchase money trust deed financing is usually for a relatively short term and that the quantum of restraint is thus less than in the case of long-term financing, the justification for restraint in the case of short-term financing is also less. In further support of this holding that due-on-sale clauses in private person purchase money trust deeds are not enforceable it concluded that no substantial reason has been shown to treat private lenders differently than institutional lenders regarding this matter.

To summarize: The status of enforcing due-on-sale clauses in purchase money trust deeds in California is that under the *Dawn Investment* case due-on-sale clauses in loan contracts where the loans are made by private persons and state-chartered institutional lenders purchase money trust deeds are not automatically enforceable in this state.

If a lender can show, by presenting adequate evidence, that allowing the debt assumption to occur the lender's risk of financing loss will be increased substantially over what it was before the debt assumption by the new owner-buyer took place, then the due-on-sale clause can be enforced by the lender. Such evidence allowing enforcement of the due-on-sale clause is not often available to the lender, so the usual result is that buyers of property can legally assume such existing loans as part of the purchase price financing plan.

In the case of *La Sala* v. *American Savings and Loan Association* (5 C.3d 864, 97 Cal. Reptr. 849, 489 P2d 1113), the California Supreme Court established the legal principle that the typical due-on-encumbrance clause is not automatically enforceable just because another trust deed loan has been placed against the senior trust deed collateral property. For this acceleration clause to be enforceable, the senior trust deed beneficiary must show that enforcement of the clause is necessary to protect the legitimate interest of the lender; failing this, the clause is an unlawful restraint on alienation and therefore unenforceable. In this decision the court set forth examples of additional encumbrances warranting enforcement of the clause: conveying the trustor's interest by placing another lender in the position of mortgagee in possession; using another trust deed to disguise the actual sale of the property; and so diminishing the trustor's equity in the property with other loans as to eliminate the debtor's equity in the collateral property. (Since most second trust deed lenders make such loans on the basis of a sufficiently large trustor's equity remaining in the collateral property after the second loan is made, such additional borrowing by most trustors will not now provide a legal basis for the beneficiary of the first trust deed implementing this acceleration clause.)

In California, when a loan is determined to be usurious, no illegal interest can be collected from the borrower by the lender. Also, under certain conditions, the victimized debtor can collect damages from the lender in an amount triple the legal rate of interest due.

There are maximum interest charges established in California for various institutional lenders. Also, there are strict requirements limiting the size of fees that can be charged borrowers by loan brokers who perform the service of obtaining real estate loans. The limitations upon service charges and the interest legally chargeable will be considered specifically in those chapters dealing with the various lenders and loan agents.

SECURITY DEVICES

We shall now deal with voluntarily created security devices that facilitate the extension of credit in real estate transactions. Although our primary concern is with the trust deed, consideration will be given to the mortgage and to the land contract.

Mortgages and Trust Deeds

Before extending credit to a borrower, the lender must consider certain preliminary matters that have a direct bearing upon the decision whether to grant the loan. The prospective creditor considers the borrower's credit standing, character, and capacity to repay the loan, and the value of any property that may be hypothecated to the lender as specific security for the loan. In the United States the real estate mortgage is the instrument customarily used to place the lender in a position in which he or she has a preferred claim on specific property owned by the debtor; such property may be subject to a lien for the benefit of the creditor. The deed of trust, used primarily in the western United States, constitutes another recognized method of accomplishing the hypothecation of property for the creditor's benefit.

Effect of a mortgage or trust deed. If a lender makes a loan and takes from the borrower only a promissory note, he or she is an unsecured creditor, which means that he or she, the lender, is able to proceed against the debtor personally for the collection of the obligation. Such legal recourse may be adequate for the lender, in that the debtor may voluntarily repay the sum due on the retirement date, or may have assets that can be reached through the usual processes of litigation. However, experience in real estate finance has made the usual lender reluctant to be placed in the position of an unsecured creditor. To assure the safety of their loans, creditors want to be able to sell property to regain the loan amount if the debtor does not repay according to the terms of the debt. Many lenders are required by law to have an enforceable first lien on real estate before they can finance real estate transactions. Such regulated lenders include commercial banks, savings and loan associations, life insurance companies, and mutual savings banks. Because of this series of factors affecting real estate lending practices, the secured real estate loan is the rule rather than the exception.

General comments on the real estate mortgage. To appreciate fully the intricacies of the trust deed as it is employed in Western states such as California, we should first examine the characteristics of the mortgage.

The parties to a mortgage are the *mortgagor* (borrower) and the *mortgagee* (lender). The mortgage is executed in writing by the borrower in the form of a defeasible (annullable) grant of the property mortgaged to the mortgagee. The interest of the mortgagee in the property derived from this grant (usually a lien in states such as California) is usually terminated by the borrower's repaying the debt in accordance with terms of a promissory note.

In some states including California the life of the mortgage (and therefore the effectiveness of this right in behalf of the lender) is dependent upon the enforceability of the debt contract. A number of other states do not limit the life of the mortgage to the life of the promissory note. Thus, it is obvious that in California the mortgagee or his or her successor in interest must enforce his or her rights within the term of the note or they are forever barred from enforceability in the courts.

The majority of American states, including California, subscribe to the "lien theory," under which the legal title to the property hypothecated to secure the debt remains with the borrower. The mortgagee has a lien on the property that can be enforced against the property only when the debtor defaults on his or her obligations to the mortgagee set forth in the terms of the promissory note and the mortgage.

If a mortgagor borrows money for the purpose of acquiring real estate, he or she will ordinarily issue a promissory note and a mortgage to his or her mortgagee, who in turn will record the mortgage in the county recorder's office of the county in which the property is located. Priority of the mortgagee's claim on the hypothecated real estate is therefore governed by the local recording act. Upon satisfaction of all obligations to the mortgagee, the promissory note is surrendered to the mortgagor by the mortgagee. The mortgagee also causes the title of the property to be cleared by recording a document showing retirement of the debt and termination of the mortgage. (In some states, annotation may be inserted in the margin of the mortgage record in the county recorder's office to show termination of the mortgage lien as a matter of public record.) Thus, we have a brief outline of the mortgage loan transaction in which the debtor completes the repayment of the debt according to the terms of the promissory note and the mortgage.

In the case of an unsuccessful mortgage loan in which the debtor is unable to repay the debt or to carry out other obligations specified by the promissory note and the mortgage, the procedure for dealing with the property is complicated by litigation. The mortgagee or his or her successor in interest must bring a lawsuit against the mortgagor and anyone else with a lien claim to the property. For illustration, let us assume that $90,000 has been borrowed from a lender, with a promissory note and mortgage issued by the debtor in favor of the lender. The promissory note is due July 1, 1985. On July 1, 1985, the debt is not paid. Nor is it paid the following day or week. Clearly the debtor has defaulted. In proceeding against the property on which he or she has a lien, in California the lender will

1. Bring a lawsuit against the debtor in a court of equity, requesting appropriate relief (sale of the mortgaged real property and application of the proceeds to the debt due).
2. Prove at the trial the validity of the promissory note and of the mortgage, and prove default on the obligation by the debtor.
3. On the basis of the lender's proof, the court will decree that a foreclosure sale be held by a court-appointed commissioner.

4. Notice of the description of the property and the time and place of the foreclosure sale must be given in a public place (the courthouse door, for example) for twenty days preceding the sale. This same notice must be given in a newspaper of general circulation once a week for the same period. The sale of the property must be to the highest bidder.

Procedures that may take place after the date of the foreclosure sale include the following:

1. The mortgagor (or successor in interest) may redeem the land sold in a foreclosure sale at any time during the twelve-month period immediately following the sale by paying the entire debt due the mortgagee.
2. If the period of redemption expires without the debtor or his or her successor redeeming, the purchaser at the foreclosure sale has title to the property, unless some other interest has developed that is superior to his or hers or there is some equitable reason for extending the period of redemption.

Summary of Mortgages in the State of California

1. There are two parties to the mortgage: the mortgagor and the mortgagee.
2. The duration of the effectiveness of a mortgage as a lien on real property is measured by the life of the debt.
3. The redemption right of the defaulted mortgagor can be eliminated permanently in the usual case only by expensive and lengthy litigation. This legal procedure involves at least one to two years' delay before the rights of the mortgagor are terminated.

The trust deed.   The trust deed is a security device giving the lender the status of a secured lender similar to that of the mortgagee.

In contrast to the mortgage, the deed of trust involves three parties in the hypothecation of real property for the lender's benefit: The trustor has hypothecated his or her property under the terms of the trust deed.

The trustee holds the title to the property of the trustor for the benefit of the beneficiary.

The beneficiary has extended credit to the trustor according to the terms of a promissory note evidencing the obligation that is to be repaid. The payment of this debt is assured by the personal credit of the debtor and by the value of the hypothecated real estate. In the event of default on the obligation by the trustor, the beneficiary may sell the hypothecated real estate under the terms of the deed of trust.

It may appear from Figure 8-1 that the trustor does not have title to his or her property, if one takes at face value the representation that the trustor has conveyed title to his or her property to the trustee for the benefit of the beneficiary. This apparent full and complete conveyance would logically lead to the conclusion that the

FIGURE 8-1

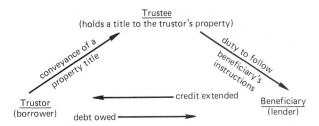

trustor does not own any interest in the property for the duration of the obligation to the beneficiary; however, such a conclusion is incorrect. Under California law the trustee has only that interest in the trustor's property which is necessary for him or her to fulfill his or her responsibilities to the trust deed beneficiary. Therefore, the trustee has title to the property only in the sense that it is security for the repayment of the obligation due the beneficiary.

Exactly what, therefore, is the quality of title that the trustor has to the hypothecated property? The trustor in California has essentially the full legal title to the property. He or she can sell it, encumber it further, lease it, or do other things that signify typical ownership powers over property and that are not inconsistent with the rights of the beneficiary in the property. He or she has full insurable interest in the property and is liable for the local real property taxes.

Trust deed procedure when there is no default. The trustor executes a promissory note for the amount of the loan to him or her. He or she also executes a trust deed on his or her property that is being used as security for the loan. The trust deed is recorded in the county recorder's office of the county in which the property is located.

For the duration of the obligation to the lender, the trustor makes to the beneficiary those payments of principal and interest specified in the promissory note. He or she also attends to his or her other obligations under the terms of the trust deed. These obligations often include paying taxes, insuring improvements on the land for the beneficiary's protection, and maintaining the property so that it will not lose value through deterioration.

At the end of the term of the loan, the trustor will have made all of the payments to the beneficiary called for in the promissory note, and the following procedures then occur. The trustor obtains the promissory note. The beneficiary notifies the trustee in writing that the obligation has been satisfied and therefore the trustee's interest in the property should be reconveyed to the trustor. The trustee reconveys and has the reconveyance recorded in the county recorder's office of the county in which

the property is located. After recording, the reconveyance is delivered to the trustor.

It should be noted that some trustees retain possession of the promissory note that is surrendered to the trustor. They require that the trustor deliver it to them accompanied by the beneficiary's request for reconveyance. Under this procedure for concluding the loan transaction, the trustor receives only the reconveyance of the trustee's interest.

Trust deed procedure when default occurs. This trust deed comes into existence accompanied by a promissory note, as does any trust deed. However, in this case the debt evidenced by the promissory note is not paid on the date it is due. To collect the money due him or her, the beneficiary must give the trustee notice of the default and must request that he or she proceed to have the property sold to satisfy the obligation owed by the trustor.

Commencing with the time of default, the following procedures take place to provide the beneficiary with the protection to which he or she is entitled as a secured lender:

1. The beneficiary notifies the trustee in writing that a default has occurred.
2. The beneficiary demands that the trustee exercise his or her power to sell the property under the title to the property vested in him or her at the time of the execution of the trust deed by the trustor.
3. The above demand is accompanied by the delivery of the promissory note and trust deed to the trustee by the benficiary.
4. The trustee then records the notice of default in the county recorder's office in the county in which the property is located. (This notice must be recorded at least ninety days before the notice of sale of the property is given.)
5. Notice of the default is given to the trustor.
6. Under a California statute, notice of the default must be sent by registered mail to each person who has recorded a request for such notification within ten days from the recording of the notice of default.
7. This notice of the trustor's default—normally on a first trust deed—is given primarily for the benefit of second trust deed holders who wish to know of the status of the first trust deed so they may protect their property interests.
8. During the entire ninety-day period following the recording of the notice of default, the trustor, his or her successor, or a holder of a junior lien may reinstate (restore the status of) the defaulted trust deed by forwarding to the beneficiary all sums due on the obligation. This payment must include all costs connected with the procedures that have taken place to the date of the payment. The entire amount of the trustor's debt to the beneficiary does not have to be paid.

   If such payment is made to the beneficiary in a timely fashion, the sale proceedings are abandoned by the trustee and the trust deed is restored to its standing prior to the default.

If the default is some other dereliction on the part of the trustor rather than failure to pay the beneficiary, the amount required to remedy such failures reinstates the trust deed.

If the reinstatement of the trust deed does not occur through the procedure outlined above, the sale of the property proceeds as follows:

1. The trustee executes a notice of sale containing such information as the description of the property and the time, place, and reason for the sale.
2. This notice of sale must be published for twenty days following the ninety-day period that began with the recording of the notice of the trustor's default.

   After the twenty days, during which the notice is posted on the premises to be sold, published in a newspaper of general circulation at least three times, and posted in a public place such as the county courthouse, the sale of the property can be held by the trustee.
3. The property is put up for bid (according to the usual practice) approximately twenty-two days or more after the date of the original publication of notice of sale. The sale takes place at a specified location in the county in which the property is located.

   The sale must be conducted in a fair manner to obtain the highest possible price from a qualified bidder.
4. After the completion of the auction (the sale may also be private if a fair price is obtained), the highest bidder receives a trustee's deed to the property.

   The trustee's deed conveys to the purchaser the title to the property formerly held by the trustor.
5. The sale of the property by the trustee is an irrevocable final sale that cuts off the trustor's interests completely, except if a real default has not occurred and if the trustor had made substantial unsuccessful efforts to cure the apparent default. In such a case a court of equity will sometimes allow the trustor to retain the property upon curing the apparent default within a reasonable time.

Sale of trust deed by beneficiary.   Since the promissory note and trust deed constitute property, they can be sold by the owner. To effect such a transaction, the beneficiary would negotiate the promissory note to the purchaser and would then assign the trust deed to him or her.

Deficiency judgments—mortgages and trust deeds.   The basic policy and rule of law in California is that no deficiency judgment is allowed against a trustor on purchase money trust deeds or mortgages (liens created when money is borrowed to buy real property) when: (1) the seller extends credit to the buyer, or (2) the number of residential units on the property is four or less, the trustor lives there, and the loan is a third-party loan in that a stranger to the sales transaction (such as a financial institution) extends the credit to the buyer-bor-

rower. An exception to this policy and rule of law was established by the California Supreme Court in the case of *Spangler* v. *Memel* (102 C.R. 807, 1972). This case involved a large two-story house on a commercially zoned lot on Sunset Boulevard in Los Angeles, purchased by Mr. and Mrs. Spangler and then resold by them to Mr. Memel, who planned to raze the house and build an office building on the site. The terms of the sale of the property to Memel included a $63,900 purchase money trust deed with the Spanglers as beneficiaries, coupled with a subordination agreement whereby the Spanglers agreed to subordinate their first lien priority purchase money trust deed up to $2 million in construction loans. Memel built an office building on the site and tried to rent space in it, but was unsuccessful in the rental program. The two trust deeds against the property went into default. The sale price received for the property at the foreclosure sale was less than the total balance of unpaid secured loans. The Spanglers sued Memel for a deficiency judgment based upon the unpaid debt secured by their second priority purchase money trust deed. In allowing the Spanglers, holders of the purchase money trust deed, to obtain a deficiency judgments against Memel in this case of a nonresidential property development purchase money trust deed, the court stated:

Effective prevention of overvaluation in a sale of property for commercial development utilizing a subordination clause lies in forcing the purchaser-developer to make realistic assessments of the likelihood of the project's success and in inducing him to exert his highest effort in carrying it out. We think this can be accomplished by placing the risk of failure upon the purchaser-developer where it in reality belongs, by permitting the sold-out junior lienor-vendor to recover a deficiency judgment in an action on his promissory note. We are of the opinion that the purpose of preventing overvaluation in this context is best subserved by not applying Section 580b.

Another facet of the difference between the sold-out junior lienor in the subordination clause context and the standard purchase money situation deserves comment. In the subordination clause context, the amount of construction loan is usually extremely large. This is illustrated by the case at bench where the subordination clause provided that the vendor would agree to subordinate for construction loans up to $2 million, and a loan of $408,000 was actually obtained. It is clear that the typical vendor in this context cannot possibly raise the astronomical sums needed to buy in at the senior sale and thereby protect his junior security interest. The only possible protection available to the vendor other than careful and sometimes fortuitous choice of purchasers is to allow a deficiency judgment against the commercial developer.

We, therefore, conclude that when in the sale of real property for commercial development, the vendor pursuant to the agreement of sale, subordinates his purchase money lien to the lien securing the purchaser-developer's construction loan and thereafter, upon the default of the purchaser-developer, loses his security interest after sale or foreclosure under the senior lien, Section 580b should not be applied to bar recovery by the junior vendor-lienor of the unpaid balance of the purchase price of the property.

When the power to sell the hypothecated property is exercised in a default situation under the terms of a trust deed or a mortgage that gives the mortgagee power of sale upon default, no deficiency judgment is allowed the lender.

If there is a judicial foreclosure of an ordinary trust deed or mortgage (not a purchase money lien), the beneficiary will be allowed to obtain a deficiency judgment if one is warranted. (Under California law, the beneficiary of a trust deed can elect to have the property sold upon default, which is the usual remedy, or he or she can have the trust deed foreclosed as if it were a mortgage.) A deficiency judgment would be warranted if the property sold for a price less than the amount of the debt due to the beneficiary or mortgagee. For example, if the debt due was $90,000 and the property sold at the foreclosure sale for $70,000, the beneficiary would be entitled to a deficiency judgment of $20,000.

Any surplus remaining from the sale of property under trust deed or mortgage procedure is paid to the debtor.

QUESTIONS

1. Legal interests in land are
   a. an easement
   b. a license
   c. a periodic tenancy
   d. any term tenancy
   e. all of the above

2. Concerning restrictions, conditions, and covenants, the following is (are) true:
   a. They generally constitute a private, legal approach to controlling land use in an area where they are applicable.
   b. Practical and appropriate land-use covenants, conditions, and restrictions can have the effect of enhancing and protecting the market value of land locations in such a restricted area.
   c. Restrictive covenants, conditions, and restrictions are, if properly created and enforced, legally enforceable in the state of California.
   d. In California, private covenants, conditions, and restrictions are not enforce-

able against the government of the state of California.
   e. All of the above.

3. Concerning recording documents affecting the status of the title to specific parcels of land, the following is (are) true:
   a. For a deed conveying title to a property to be legally effective, it must be recorded.
   b. The recording of such documents is legally the basis of giving constructive notice of the contents of the documents to the general public.
   c. The recording statute in California is effective in protecting the legal rights in the title to such property of any purchaser.
   d. The chronological order of recording lien documents affecting the title interests of various parties in such property is the only method of establishing relative lien priority between two or more persons.
   e. All of the above.

4. Ownership-type interests in land legally owned by others can be obtained by a nonowner through adverse possession and perfecting an easement by prescription. Concerning these methods of acquiring ownership-type interests in the land of another, the following is (are) true:
   a. This cannot be done in the state of California.
   b. This can be done only when the land is used for agricultural purposes.
   c. No trespassing is allowed in these methods of acquiring property interests in land.
   d. The nonowner perfecting property interests in the land of someone else through these methods involves the running of the statute of limitations against trespassers.
   e. All of the above.

BIBLIOGRAPHY

BOWMAN, ARTHUR G., and W.D. MILLIGAN, *Real Estate Law in California* (6th ed.), Englewood Cliffs, NJ: Prentice-Hall, 1982.

KRATOVIL, ROBERT, and RAYMOND J. WERNER, *Real Estate Law* (7th ed.), Englewood Cliffs, NJ: Prentice-Hall, 1979.

9

Operative Legal Aspects of Real Estate Financing

MISCELLANEOUS CLASSIFICATIONS OF TRUST DEEDS

Although the California trust deed has already been discussed in some detail, some specialized aspects of this financing device remain to be considered. The names of these specialized trust deeds denote their functions. (These special designations are also appropriate for mortgages issued for the same purposes as the trust deeds.) These trust deeds are essentially the same as any others—only the purpose and provisions of the contracts necessary to accomplish these ends distinguish them from the common garden variety of trust deed.

Purchase Money Trust Deed

The *purchase money* trust deed is issued by the borrower who is obtaining credit for the purpose of purchasing real estate. The beneficiary can be the seller of the property or a stranger to the sales transaction who is lending funds to the vendee. A principal distinguishing characteristic of this type of trust deed is that no deficiency judgment is usually obtainable from the trustor by the lender (beneficiary) who made the loan to the purchaser in cases where the lien is on a residential property containing no more than four units and occupied at least in part by the purchaser-borrower (living in at least one unit out of four). The property is therefore the primary assurance of payment, and, when it has been disposed of at a properly conducted foreclosure sale, the rights of the creditor have been exhausted. Most trust deeds issued in California today are purchase money trust deeds. Therefore, a lender (purchaser of a trust deed) is very much concerned with the existence of a margin of safety in terms of a reasonable trustor's equity; so that, should foreclosure be necessary due to default, the property would be likely to sell for enough to retire the obligation. An equivalent to such equity in terms of protection for the owner of the

trust deed is some form of insurance requiring the insurer to repay the obligation should the debtor default.

Package Trust Deed

The *package* trust deed is an extension of the coverage and use of the secured real property loan. In the traditional financing situation, the lien is on what is unquestionably real property, in other words, land and improvements permanently attached thereto. In the package financing situation, the person buying real property also borrows money for useful items such as appliances, carpeting, drapes, air conditioning equipment, and the like. The fundamental purpose is to provide a means of financing virtually everything reasonably necessary for the residential purchaser to live comfortably in his or her new home.

A number of problems are connected with this type of specialized financing. One involves protecting the lien on the property from the interests of third parties that might defeat the preference that has been achieved. This problem exists because, for the additional items purchased with the borrowed funds, the trust deed must apply to real property. Therefore, the extra items usually have to be so situated as to be fixtures, and hence part of the real property. Increased construction of various built-in items in houses had made it legally feasible to lend money for more items essential to the enjoyment of residential property, but not traditionally considered to be real property.

If they have the legal authority to do so, lenders can lend funds for the acquisition of personal property. The trust deed covering such items of personal property must be so recorded as to give notice of the lender's lien on the property. Although this concept is relatively new in real estate finance, it is growing at various rates in different sections of the country according to public understanding and acceptance. Another factor slowly facilitating the growth of package financing is the comprehension by lenders of its advantages. Such lending obviously increases business. An additional measure of protection for the comparatively large loan made is that the lender is definitely aware of most of the debt incurred by the borrower to equip the property and is in a position to safeguard the debt position of his or her borrower because he or she holds a large portion of the borrower's outstanding obligations.

Blanket Trust Deed

As the term suggests, the *blanket* trust is a lien on more than one parcel of land. This financing contract is used most frequently by subdividers or developers who have purchased a single tract of land for the purpose of dividing it into smaller parcels for sale or development. The lien on the property from the original sale provides that, upon the payment of designated amounts, the creditor will release certain portions of the property from the trust deed. The seller of the tract usually provides that he or she is entitled to receive payments somewhat larger than the proportionate value of the land released from the lien. This provision is advantageous to the beneficiary of the trust deed because it usually leaves as security land that is worth more than the remaining balance of the debt. If a seller of ten acres of land for $100,000 (with a $20,000 down payment) requires a payment of $10,000 before allowing a partial reconveyance of one acre by the trustee, he or she is still owed $70,000, but the land still subject to the lien is presumably worth at least $90,000.

The blanket trust deed also facilitates the lending of money on real estate when a single property of the borrower is apparently not valuable enough to constitute adequate security for the debt. Under such conditions the lien could be made applicable to two or more parcels of land owned by the borrower. This use of the blanket trust deed and its applicability in the subdivision situation indicate its flexibility and therefore its considerable usefulness as a tool of real estate finance.

Construction Loans

The construction loan is essential to the real estate industry because it makes possible the improvement of property. It is a practical necessity, because most individuals seeking to improve their land do not have the thousands of dollars necessary to pay for the improvements as they are constructed; and few building contractors possess such vast financial resources that they can pay for the costs of construction when payments are due. Intermediate financing is therefore a vital bridge between raw unimproved land and the best use of such property in terms of improving it properly.

Construction loans may be cast originally in perma-

nent form with the lender who will carry the loan for its full term. Such an arrangement involves a standard promissory note secured by a trust deed; therefore, nothing in the terms of the loan agreement indicates that the loan is for the purpose of providing construction funds. This arrangement is not a typical construction loan.

Another arrangement for this type of loan is for the lender to accept a builder or developer as a borrower and make the loan to this person or firm in an amount sufficient to cover construction costs. This loan may be permanent upon the sale of the improved property to a buyer whose credit is acceptable to the lender. If the prospective ultimate owner of the property is not acceptable as a debtor, the lender may, under the prerogative usually reserved to him or her in the loan contract, refuse to allow that party to assume the loan. Therefore, retirement of the construction loan will be necessary before any sale to that particular purchaser. When a buyer does not qualify in terms of the lender's credit requirements, an amount will have to be borrowed sufficiently large to pay off the outstanding debt incurred for construction financing and for the placing of a purchase money loan on the property. This is the most common type of arrangement for the financing of construction.

Loans can be made for construction purposes alone. This type of loan is made for a relatively short period of time. The builder who cannot sell the property during this period of time is indeed in trouble. He or she has to either take out a permanent loan that can be assumed by a qualified buyer or seek an extension of his or her originally temporary financing. This type of loan is usually secured by a recorded lien that is eliminated as soon as permanent financing enables the debt to be paid in full.

Junior Trust Deeds

The *junior* trust deed is superseded in priority by one that is prior in right, which means that if the obligor does not comply with his obligation under the terms of the loan and thereby defaults, the junior lien will not be paid first. If upon foreclosure the sale of the property subject to the lien does not produce enough money to pay off the first and second liens, the second (junior) lien, if it is a purchase money lien, may become an uncollectable debt. If it is not a purchase money obligation, the creditor may sue on the note and obtain what amounts to a deficiency judgment against the debtor.

The time of recording of trust deeds usually determines their priority and the right to be paid upon foreclosure. This priority may also be governed by terms of a loan contract, which may effect the subordination of a first lien to one made at a later time to finance a worthy undertaking such as the construction of improvements on the premises.

The holder of a junior lien is in a relatively better position to protect his security interest in California than in many other states. Recognizing his secondary position, he can record in the county recorder's office of the county in which the property is located a request that he be notified of default on the first trust deed and of the implementation of foreclosure procedures. Upon receiving this notice, should he feel that the property is valuable enough that it is worthwhile to protect his interest in it, this lien holder can cure the default on all the prior trust deeds and thereby prevent the foreclosure upon the property. If the loans were secured by mortgages rather than trust deeds, the junior lien holder would have to pay off all the obligations secured by prior liens in order to protect his or her interest in the property.

In most situations there is no question of the additional risk the junior lien holder assumes compared to a first lien holder. Therefore, the yield on second trust deeds is often large compared with that of other, more secure investments. The ultimate security for the junior lien holder is the good credit rating and strong financial position of the debtor, along with a substantial owner's equity in the property. Junior liens held on property located in remote areas or in areas subject to excessive speculation are obviously very risky and are generally worthless because of the almost infinitesimal value of such security.

Open-End Trust Deeds

Open-end trust deeds are secured loans that provide for sums of money to be lent to the same borrower at various times. In operation this type of loan actually amounts to a continuing source of credit for the borrower. The courts have referred to this type of loan as a trust deed or mortgage for future advances. This type of financing plan is usually used in a complex lien situation, involving loans made to facilitate improvement on a specific property. As the property is improved, other interests that can and usually do come into existence may affect the priority of this loan. Mechanic's liens are usually the biggest worry of the lender making this type of loan for construction purposes. The major problem is for the lender to preserve his or her standing as the first lien holder on the property.

Formerly, when the lender in this situation had the option to advance funds or to refuse such advances, the priority of the lien securing such advances did not date from the time of the recording of the trust deed, but was determined by the date on which the advance to the borrower was made. Thus, the priority originally enjoyed as to a previous advance might easily be lost during the time necessary for construction of improvements. For example, if an optional open-end loan was established

with the first advance made at the time of recording on February 1, and a right of mechanic's lien accrues before the next advance is made on March 15, this later advance would be secured not by a first lien on the improved property, but by a junior lien. The mere possibility of this makes the open-end loan with optional advances generally undesirable from the lender's standpoint.

For the benefit of the parties to construction loans, the rather precarious priority position of loans providing for future optional advances has been improved somewhat by the California legislature. The California Code of Civil Procedure, Section 1188.1, provides that future optional advances for purposes of construction, under certain limitations, may have the same priority rights as obligatory advances. The optional advances protected by the first lien cannot exceed the amounts of obligatory advances to be made by the lender. Presumably only a small degree of protection is given to these advances, since they are limited in amount and would usually consist of payments made outside an obligatory loan payment schedule to retire mechanic's liens that have been filed. Such preferred treatment of the priority of optional advances applies *only* to loans made for construction of improvements on the property.

The lender can prevent prior liens from "slipping in" when advances are made to the borrower by making mandatory his or her obligation to provide money at various times. With obligatory advances all the payments are secured by a first lien, since the originally recorded trust deed is constructive notice to the public of the lender's obligation to make the scheduled future advances.

The open-end trust deed is a versatile financing tool. Although its greatest use is in the construction loan field, it can be employed in other circumstances in which a borrower can best use a loan made in installments. From another viewpoint, the lender may not wish to relinquish control over the funds until they are actually needed by the borrower.

Term Loans

Before the Great Depression the *term* loan was common. This promissory note provided that a loan of a certain amount would be made for a definite number of years, usually for what would today be considered an unusually short period. Few loans were for more than five years. The obligations of the debtor during the period of the loan were to pay the interest as it came due under the terms of the note, to protect the title from superior party interests, to avoid committing waste on the property, and to insure the improvements for the benefit of the lender. The debtor was obliged to pay the principal of the debt only on the due date. The payment of the principal was usually made only if the debtor had prospered and if he or she had made some provision for retirement of the debt on the due date by setting aside funds. The principal was often not paid when due, and the obligation was renewed for another period by the creditor. Renewal was usually allowed only after the debtor had paid a fee for the privilege. Provided that the financial future of the debtor, the value of the hypothecated property, and general economic conditions affecting the region were reasonably secure, such periodic renewal of the obligation would probably continue, since the primary business of financial institutions was and is to conduct profitable operations making loans that are repaid. When any one of these favorable conditions terminated, the loan would usually not be renewed. Calling of term loans generally occurred during times of widespread economic distress, resulting in numerous foreclosures upon real property so that lenders might collect the principal of the loans they had made. To some extent, therefore, the first-mortgage term loan coupled with second and even third mortgages brought about a substantial number of loan foreclosures in the 1930s and thereby contributed to the extent of the real estate collapse during that period.

One of the major problems of the first-mortgage term loan accompanied by substantial secondary financing was that it could and too often did exceed the possible sale price of the property upon foreclosure. Therefore, in the 1930s, when there was an agonizing reappraisal of real estate lending practices, both the term loan and large secondary financing were discredited as prudent means of financing real estate. Secondary financing was legally eliminated by the Federal Housing Administration. Conventional lenders recognized the great dangers incident to the combination of the first-mortgage term loan coupled with substantial secondary financing. The most popular real estate loan to arise from the reappraisal was the self-amortizing loan.

Amortized Loans

The terms of an *amortized* loan can vary because of the latitude allowed the parties in specifying the exact provisions of the debt obligation. The exact terms of the debt contract may be affected by the legal requirements with which lending institutions must comply. The rate of interest, the age of the borrower, the age and condition of property improvements, the term of years for which the loan is written, the amount borrowed, and any particular contract provisions desired by a certain lender may all serve to determine the specific rights and duties under a loan contract.

The amortizing scheme of debt repayment protects the positions of the lender and the borrower in several ways. For the lender it creates increased assurance of repayment by continually increasing the equity of the debtor in the

property and by forcing him or her to provide for periodic repayment of the obligation over the period of the loan. For the borrower this plan provides a training program in debt payment, a series of obligations that can be met because they are relatively small compared with the large obligation coming due in the term loan situation; also, the growing, valuable equity in the property motivates him or her not to default. This equity can also be sold or used as a basis for refinancing the obligation. The monthly payment, direct-reduction loan is now probably the most common type of real estate loan made. The debt reduction can be established at any level the parties wish. It can be set at a monthly level providing for the payment of interest due plus a minimum of 1 percent of the principal. It can be set at a level sufficient to pay the interest due every month and the principal borrowed over the life of the debt. Under the latter type of loan agreement, the debtor typically pays the same specific sum every month over the life of the loan. During the repayment period the amount of the monthly payment used to retire the principal increases and the interest paid decreases because of the constant reduction in the size of the debt.

Because of the lattitude allowed the lender and the borrower in establishing the terms of a loan obligation, and because of the usual comparative ignorance of most borrowers in residential loan situations, debts very disadvantageous to the borrower can be created.

In California problems have arisen with debts calling for a balloon payment. This instalment on the debt is one much greater than any of the previous payments due the creditor by the debtor. This type of loan contract provides for relatively small monthly payments (paying the interest due, but retiring none or little of the principal) and an enormous final payment. The provisions of this loan are, in effect, a return to the old term loan. Because of the tendency of this type of obligation to precipitate defaults by borrowers whether used in a first or a second trust deed, there has been some concern in California about the use of this kind of financing. (As of 1974 the state of California prohibited use of a second trust deed loan balloon payment where the repayment period was six years or less and the collateral property was the dwelling unit of the trustor.)

INVOLUNTARY LIENS

Tax Liens

The primary interests in tax liens are those of the local property-taxing authority, the federal government, and the secured lender, whose interest may be affected adversely by the perfection of these liens.

Protection of its revenue has long been one of the primary interests of government. Consequently, taxing authorities are commonly in a legal position to place liens against property when taxes are not paid promptly. No matter when they are filed, tax liens often take priority over any other liens already in existence. Thus, the law governing the priority of these liens often has the effect of eliminating the usual rule of lien priority.

In California, municipal and county property tax liens are given priority over previously perfected private interests such as trust deeds and mechanic's liens. Because of the preference of the tax liens, trust deeds and mortgages provide that one of the obligations of the trustor is to pay the property taxes before they become delinquent. Failure to pay such taxes constitutes a default by the debtor. An arrangement is often created whereby the holder of the trust deed can pay the taxes to protect the title to the property and can then hold the trustor responsible for reimbursement of the amount so expended. The priority of the property tax lien is also the reason for the frequent establishment of a tax service at the borrower's expense when a loan secured by a trust deed is made. This service makes an annual check to see whether all taxes due, which if unpaid would be a lien against the property, have been paid promptly by the trustor. If the taxes become delinquent the service will notify the holder of the trust deed, thus enabling the creditor to take whatever action is authorized and appropriate for the occasion.

Special assessments against a particular property, if not paid on time or let to bond, can become a superior lien against the property in the same way and to the same extent as the unpaid property tax. Therefore, the holder of the trust deed has an equal concern about unpaid property assessments on property constituting security.

California state taxes that are not directly levied upon a parcel of land usually do not have the priority rights of delinquent real property taxes or of special assessments. Therefore, the danger to the desired preferential position of the lender is not nearly as great in this case.

To protect its revenue the government of the United States has enacted legislation to give federal tax liens for unpaid taxes significant priority in claiming interests in the property of delinquent taxpayers. It is difficult to state succinctly the established rules of law in this area, because of varying interpretations of relevant statutes by the federal courts. The issue of priority between federal tax liens and private liens such as real estate mortgages and trust deeds arises when the lender has first made such a secured loan, the federal tax lien is subsequently created, and then the property is sold at a foreclosure sale because of the default of the debt contract secured by the first trust deed. Before recently enacted remedial legislation, the federal government's lien could be secret (not a matter of public record) and yet in later litigation over lien priorities be determined to be the prior lien.

This situation was corrected by statutory enactments that require the federal government to file documentary evidence of such a lien in the federal district court with jurisdiction over the real property or in the state office where liens against real property can be filed (the county recorder's office of the California county where such property is located). At the present time—given the situation of a real estate trust deed being recorded, a federal tax lien filed as a matter of record, default, and foreclosure of the trust deed by the lender—the beneficiary will have a first lien priority because its lien was first as a matter of record and fully perfected. There was nothing left to do to make it an effective lien. Where a secured real estate loan requires the lender to make obligatory advances over a period of time (as in a construction loan situation), such advances made within forty-five days of the filing of a federal tax lien will retain their first priority based upon the time priority of the trust deed being recorded before the filing of the tax lien. If such advances are made after forty-five days have elapsed from the date of the filing of the federal tax lien, the federal tax lien will have lien priority over such obligatory advances. This means that the lender in those obligatory loan advance situations will want to check the county recorder's office and the federal district court records in the area of a state where the collateral property is located before making successive loan advances.

Here are some further comments on the effect of federal tax liens on trust deed and mortgage loan priority:

The Federal Tax Lien Act of 1966 (Public Law 89–719) provides, among other things, that written notice of a nonjudicial sale be given to the secretary of the treasury or his delegate as a requirement for the discharge of a federal tax lien recorded more than thirty days before the sale or the divestment of any title of the United States, and establishes a right in the United States to redeem the property within a period of one hundred twenty days from the date of such sale.

When a federal tax lien inferior to the deed of trust being foreclosed has been recorded more than thirty days before the sale date, notice must be given to the federal government in order that the lien be eliminated by the sale. If the lien was recorded thirty days or less before the sale, no notice is required. Although the trustee's sale will eliminate such lien, the right of redemption must still be considered.[1]

Presently lien priorities between private real estate mortgages and trust deeds and federal tax liens are in a state of flux, although there has been some improvement in the priority status of the private lender by federal legislation enacted in 1966. Federal tax liens can, under certain circumstances, still attain superior priority over

---

[1]Arthur G. Bowman, *Real Estate Law in California*, 4th ed. (Englewood Cliffs, N.J.: Prentice-Hall, Inc., 1975), p. 438.

private real estate loan liens, but the prudent lender, by checking the record title of collateral property, can now know more exactly than before the lien priority status that it has in a given property.

Attachment Liens

Although not too common in the everyday affairs of the real estate industry, the *attachment* lien can be significant because it causes a cloud on the title to property. The attachment lien is a right provided by statute in California for the plaintiff in a lawsuit so that he or she may be reasonably assured that the defendant has assets within the jurisdiction of the court that can be used to satisfy any judgment that may be obtained. When a person commencing a lawsuit attaches the property of the defendant, certain property (either real or personal) is seized or retained in the custody of the county sheriff, who proceeds against it under the court's writ of attachment.

This rather extraordinary process can be implemented only when conditions indicate that there is no existing security for a lien, that the defendant apparently has no property located within the jurisdiction of the court, or that the defendant may, before the conclusion of litigation, dispose of his or her available property or leave the jurisdiction of the court with any property that could be taken to satisfy any judgment awarded the plaintiff. To perfect this lien the plaintiff, upon commencing a lawsuit under circumstances allowing the issuance of this writ, applies to the court for the issuance of the attachment order; offers proof of the allegations indicating why the writ should be issued, and upon the attachment order emanating from the court usually posts a bond or deposits cash in court to protect the defendant if the writ is in fact wrongfully issued. Finally, the sheriff proceeds to locate the property that can be attached. (Property exempt from creditors' claims under the California Debtors' Exemption Statute cannot be attached.) After seizure the defendant-owner is allowed to prevent the writ from becoming a lien against his or her property pending the trial of the lawsuit by depositing money or posting a bond in an amount satisfactory to the court. If the money is not deposited nor the bond posted with the court, the writ of attachment is perfected against specific real property by the filing as a matter of record of a copy of the writ and the posting of the same upon the premises or serving notice upon the occupants of the real property.

Personal property can also be attached, and it may be more desirable to attempt to seize this property under a writ of attachment than real property because of the relative ease of seizing personal property such as bank accounts, the contents of safe deposit boxes, and automobiles.

Judgment Liens

The *judgment* lien is another lien on real property that will seldom be encountered in real estate financing transactions. This type of lien comes into existence after a defendant has lost a lawsuit and the plaintiff has obtained a court order (judgment) requiring that the defendant pay the sum of money set forth in the order. For this court order to become a lien on all nonexempt real property owned by the defendant in the county, an abstract of the judgment must be filed in the county recorder's office. When this is done in a timely fashion on behalf of the plaintiff, the lien commences and lasts for ten years from the date of recording. The lien will also attach automatically to any nonexempt real property acquired by the judgment debtor during the ten-year period. The judgment debtor may prevent the lien from becoming effective by appealing from the judgment of the trial court and by depositing with the court rendering the judgment an amount of money or bond determined to be sufficient to protect the interests of the judgment creditor if the judgment is sustained by the appellate court.

The priority, and therefore the practical value, of this lien to the judgment creditor is determined by the time of the recording of the abstract of judgment. Therefore, if a first trust deed or any other lien is already a matter of record, the judgment lien is junior to it. Should such prior lien be implemented when the property is sold, the only time the judgment lien will have any immediate value to the creditor will be if the sale results in a surplus after the prior secured lien has been paid.

Execution Liens

The *execution* lien is related to the judgment lien in that the levy and execution upon property of a debtor who has not heretofore paid the judgment debt is the procedure for implementing the judgment and securing the payment to the plaintiff who instituted the lawsuit. The levy and execution on property are performed by the sheriff under the order of the court issuing the judgment in favor of the plaintiff after the court (or jury, if there was a jury trial) renders such a verdict.

The execution lien situation has two aspects. If the judgment already issuing from the court in favor of the plaintiff has been elevated to the status of a judgment lien, the execution process simply implements that already existing lien. If the judgment is not a lien against real property of the defendant that can be taken to satisfy the debt, the execution is implemented and becomes a lien against the property of the debtor through the same recording process used in the perfection of the writ of attachment. Under court order and supervision the real property will be sold according to the prescribed procedures. After the sale of real property by levy and execution, the owner-debtor has one year to redeem the property by paying the sale price received for the property plus interest and reasonable expenses incurred by the buyer for taxes, assessment, insurance, and maintenance.

Mechanic's Liens

Mechanic's liens are a complex subject; therefore, we will merely outline briefly the essence of the mechanic's lien and concentrate most of the discussion on its immediate effect upon the legal position of the trust deed holder when filed against property that has been hypothecated for his or her benefit.

In authorizing the mechanic's lien, a value judgment was made that became the policy of the state of California and that is implemented under its Constitution and statutes. The value judgment was that those parties furnishing labor or material that improves and therefore benefits real property should be able to proceed against the property that has benefited from their efforts and resources. The complexities enter this picture when consideration is given to the perfection of the command in the California Constitution that mechanic's liens shall be available to provide compensation for unpaid laborers or suppliers of material.

We shall concern ourselves with (1) identifying the parties who can file such liens; (2) the procedures for establishing such a lien; (3) the enforcement of these rights; and (4) what can reasonably be done to protect real property from being used to satisfy the demands of mechanic's liens claimants.

The California Civil Code, Section 3110, provides that

Mechanics, materialmen, contractors, subcontractors, lessors of equipment, artisans, architects, registered engineers, licensed land surveyors, machinists, builders, teamsters and draymen, and all persons and laborers of every class performing labor upon or bestowing skill or other necessary services on, or furnishing materials or leasing equipment to be used or consumed in or furnishing appliances, teams, or power contributing to a work of improvement shall have a lien upon the property upon which they have bestowed labor or furnished materials or appliances or leased equipment for the value of such labor done or materials furnished and for the value of the use of such appliances, equipment, teams, or power whether done or furnished at the instance of the owner or of any person acting by his authority or under him as contractor or otherwise. For the purposes of this chapter, every contractor, subcontractor, architect, builder, or other person having charge of a work of improvement or portion thereof shall be held to be the agent of the owner.

Some general technical requirements must be fulfilled by lien claimants before they are legally able to file this type of lien. Those persons contributing to the improvement of real property who must be licensed to carry on the vocation legitimately in California must be duly licensed at the time they contract for and perform their function or they are usually not entitled to a mechanic's lien. Suppliers of materials, to be entitled to this kind of lien against property, must contract to furnish and actually furnish the required material for the improvement of a specific property. This lien is provided for those who have contributed to a "work or improvement" on the property sought to be subjected to the lien. An improvement as contemplated by the statute may consist of construction, alteration, addition to, or repair of property. The term also encompasses the razing and removal of buildings and the grading of land. If what is done does not constitute an improvement in accordance with the legal definition, the benefit bestowed upon the property cannot be the basis of a mechanic's lien.

The use and satisfaction of the mechanic's lien involves the following basic steps:

1. The work to be performed or the materials to be furnished are contracted for by a properly qualified party (meeting all requirements for licensing and contracting in California).

2a. Within twenty days of the first furnishing of labor, equipment, or materials, anyone except one under direct contract with the owner or one performing actual labor for wages thus improving a property and wishing to perfect a mechanic's lien on this property with a priority based upon such action must give a preliminary written notice of these events to the property owner, construction lender, and general contractor.

To comply with this statutory requirement so as later possibly to file and foreclose on a mechanic's lien if not paid for the improvements, the written notice must specify a general description of the equipment, labor, or materials furnished to a property; name and address of the person contracting with the potential claimant; name and address of the potential claimant; a description of the property improved by the described labor, equipment, or material; and an allegation that if all labor, equipment, and material furnished for a property are not paid for in accordance with contracts for them, a mechanic's lien may be filed against the improved property to satisfy the unpaid debt.

The copy of the required twenty-day preliminary notice delivered to any construction lender involved in such a project has to set forth an estimate of the total price of materials, equipment, or labor furnished under the contract for the improvement of the property.

(If more than twenty days elapse after the commencing of the improvement of property by furnishing labor, material, or equipment without delivering this written notice to the parties entitled to receive it [delivery may be in person, by messenger, or registered or certified or first class U.S. mail], the furnisher of such elements of property improvements loses priority over security liens perfected between the end of the twenty-day period and when the twenty-day notice is finally delivered. A mechanic's lien claimant is required to file such twenty-day preliminary notice and must do this if the lien for the improvements wrought in a property is to be enforceable in California courts.)

2b. When the materials have been furnished or the work on the premises has been completed, the unpaid claimant has a certain period to file the mechanic's lien. The time allowed for this filing depends upon the legal situation of the claimant and upon whether a notice of completion has been filed by the party having the improvements made to the property.

2c. The original contractor (a party who has contracted with the owner or his or her agent to complete the entire job, that is, to furnish all necessary materials and labor for the job or a specialized aspect of it, such as electrical wiring or plumbing) may file a mechanic's lien within sixty days after the recording of the notice of completion in the county recorder's office of the county in which the property is located.

2d. Any person other than the original contractor may file a lien within thirty days after the recording of the notice of completion in the appropriate county recorder's office.

2e. If no notice of completion is filed by the party having the work done, any and all furnishers of material or labor for the improvement of the property have ninety days from the completion of the improvement to file a mechanic's lien. The critical question is, when has the work of improvement been completed? While no definite answer can be given to this question, there is substantial agreement that the work on the improvement has been completed when (1) the owner or someone under his or her authority has occupied the premises and the work is no longer going on; (2) the property has been accepted on behalf of the owner; (3) no labor has been performed on the premises for a period of sixty consecutive days; and (4) all labor has ceased on the improvement for thirty consecutive days and the owner has filed a notice of cessation.

3. The mechanic's lien is terminated (1) by payment being made to the claimant, who releases the lien; (2) by the claimant proceeding to commence foreclosure proceedings in court within ninety days of the filing of the lien; (3) if the lien claimant does not commence foreclosure litigation within ninety days after the filing of the lien in the county recorder's office, in which case the lien will automatically expire.

From the standpoint of real estate lending, the mechanic's lien poses probably the greatest threat to the first priority necessary for the typical secured loan. This threat is common, because much of the property accepted as security for a loan has only recently been improved— for example, the construction of a tract of houses for sale. The lender naturally wants to assure the preference of the first trust deed securing the loan.

The priority of the mechanic's lien commences from the time that construction was begun on the property. What constitutes commencement of the improvement of the property is certainly a vital question. According to various California appellate court decisions, work has

commenced when a person observing the lay of the land could, as a reasonable individual inspecting the property, readily see that construction was underway, because of the materials placed on the property, the clearing of natural foliage growth, excavating, and the conduct of activities normal to property improvement.

Although the mechanic's lien cannot be filed until a certain number of days after the completion of the improvement, its priority is determined from the date that work commenced on the property. This means that any lender lending money on improved property or on property to be improved should determine immediately, before actually effecting the loan, that no work of improvement is underway on the premises. Therefore, an inspection of the property immediately before recording the trust deed is usually required. Another way of protecting the first priority of a trust deed is to determine, before the loan is actually made, that all laborers, contractors, and suppliers have been paid and have in effect waived their right to file a mechanic's lien against the property. In construction lending, a portion of the loan may be withheld until evidence of payment of all laborers and materialmen is produced to the lender's satisfaction.

If a mechanic's lien is enforced by a claimant through a foreclosure action, a court judgment in favor of the claimant will be used to force the sale of the property. The court rendering the judgment will order the sheriff to conduct the sale. After the sale to the successful bidder, there is a one-year period of redemption during which the owner can redeem the property by payment of the debt, interest due, and costs incident to the proceeding.

Stop Notices in California

The California statutes pertaining to liens against improved real property to compensate the improvers of such property for the labor and materials used to make it more valuable provide for the filing of stop notices in addition to mechanic's liens. The stop notice is a device used by subcontractors improving real property by furnishing labor or materials to proceed against construction funds held by a construction lender. Section 3103 of the California Civil Code reads, "Stop notice means a written notice, signed and verified by the claimant or his agent stating in general terms the following: (a) the kind of labor, services, equipment, or materials furnished or agreed to be furnished by such claimant, (b) the name of the person to or for whom the same was done or furnished, and (c) the amount in value, as near as may be, of that already done or furnished and of the whole agreed to be done or furnished." To be effective in creating a lien against those funds in possession and control of the property owner or a construction lender such as a commercial bank or savings and loan association, the notice must be served personally; by agent; or by registered, certified, or first class U.S. mail. The effect of serving the stop notice when unexpended funds to be used for paying the cost of construction are still under the control of the property owner or a construction lender is established by statutes in California. Section 3161 of the California Civil Code provides that

It shall be the duty of the owner upon receipt of a stop notice . . . to withhold from the original contractor or from any person acting under his authority and to whom labor or materials or both, have been furnished, or agreed to be furnished, sufficient money due or to become due to such contractor to answer such claim and any claim of lien that may be recorded therefor, unless a payment bond has been recorded pursuant to the provisions of Section 3235, in which case the owner may, but is not obligated to, withhold such money.

Section 3162 of the California Civil Code provides that

Upon receipt of a stop notice . . . the construction lender may, and upon receipt of a bonded stop notice the construction lender shall, withhold from the borrower or other person to whom it or the owner may be obligated to make payments or advancement out of the construction fund, sufficient money to answer such claim and any claim of lien that may be recorded therefor, unless a payment bond has been recorded pursuant to the provisions of Section 3235 at any time prior to the serving of the first stop notice or bonded stop notice.

To enforce a stop notice through litigation in a California court the following requirements must be fulfilled: (1) the stop notice claimant shall have given the owner or construction lender the required preliminary twenty-day notice (in the form similar to the mechanic's lien twenty-day preliminary notice); (2) the stop notice must be properly served on behalf of the claimant; (3) the stop notice must be served by the claimant upon the owner or construction lender in a timely fashion, that is, within thirty days after the recording of a notice of completion or within ninety days after the cessation of work of improvement on the property where no notice of completion is recorded; and (4) the lawsuit to enforce the stop notice against the construction fund must be commenced within the ninety days following the serving of the owner or construction lender with the stop notice.

If the requirements for perfecting and enforcing a stop notice lien against a portion of a construction fund are fulfilled by such a claimant, this remedy—in addition to the filing of a mechanic's lien against the improved property—is available to him or her. The main protection the construction lender has against being required to honor stop notice claims exceeding the allotted construction funds is (1) to accept only known dependable general and subcontractors on a job; (2) to make sure that work

alleged to have been completed by subcontractors has in fact been completed at the time of construction fund disbursements; (3) to require owner-borrowers to have substantial equities in properties being improved with borrower funds; (4) to determine that disbursed construction funds are in fact used to pay for labor, material, and services necessary to improve the property that is collateral for the construction loan; (5) at all times to retain more than the cost of completing improvements in a construction fund; and (6) to require completion bonds of general contractors and subcontractors who are participating in the construction process.

Limiting Liability for Construction Costs Protected by Mechanic's Liens and Stop Notice Liens in California

Under Section 3124 of the California Civil Code, the owner of real property to be improved by the addition of labor and materials may limit his or her personal liability and that of the improved property through recording, in the office of the county recorder of the county where the property is located, a copy of the construction contract that exists between the owner and the original contractor (general contractor) before the commencement of construction work.

Liability of Construction Lenders to Buyers of Single Family Residential Property

On December 12, 1968, in its decision on *Connor* v. *Great Western Savings and Loan Association* (73 C.R. 369, 447 P2d 609), the California Supreme Court held that under the circumstances of this controversy a construction lender was liable to the purchasers of defective single-family detached houses that had been built with its funds. Briefly stated, the facts in this case were (1) an inexperienced, woefully undercapitalized land developer bought a sizable tract of land in Ventura County with substantial financial assistance from Great Western Savings and Loan Association; (2) virtually the entire cost of converting raw acreage into town lots for subdivision purposes was financed by Great Western; (3) virtually the whole cost of building model houses and houses sold or to be sold was financed by Great Western; (4) in addition to providing nearly all of the capital to develop this housing tract, Great Western had the legal right to first refusal of all buyer first trust deed loan applications generated from sales activity at the tract, and if Great Western did not have an opportunity to make such a loan to buyers of houses because they obtained the purchase money loan elsewhere, the developers had to pay Great Western a sum equal to the fees and interest obtained by the lender who did make the loan to the purchaser; (5) Great Western's agents inspected the houses being built to determine that they were in conformance with the approved construction loan plans; (6) the houses were built upon expansive adobe soil that could have been discovered before construction began and precautions taken to prevent the damage that ultimately occurred to the houses (expansion of the soil and the resulting pressure destroyed concrete slab foundations supporting each house, causing an average of $6,000 damage to each house); and (7) neither the financially distressed developer-borrower nor the families buying the houses with only 5 to 10 percent down payments were able to spend the thousands of dollars required to repair the extensive damage to the $14,950–$15,950 houses. In holding the construction lender liable for the damage suffered by the people who had purchased the houses, the California Supreme Court stated at pages 376, 378, and 379, 73 C.R. 369:

Even though Great Western is not vicariously liable as a joint venturer for the negligence of Conejo [name of development concern], there remains the question of its liability for its own negligence. Great Western voluntarily undertook business relationships with Conejo to develop the Weatherfield tract and to develop a market for the tract houses in which prospective buyers would be directed to Great Western for their financing. *In undertaking these relationships Great Western became much more than a lender content to lend money at interest on the security of real property*. It became an active participant in a home construction enterprise. It had the right to exercise extensive control of the enterprise. Its financing, which made the enterprise possible, took on ramifications beyond the domain of the usual money lender. It received not only interest on its construction loans, but also substantial fees for making them, a 20 percent capital gain for "warehousing" the land, and protection from loss of profits in the event individual home buyers sought permanent financing elsewhere.

Great Western had a duty to exercise reasonable care to prevent the construction and sale of seriously defective homes to the plaintiffs. The countervailing considerations invoked by Great Western and Amici Curiae are that the imposition of the duty in question upon a lender will increase housing costs, drive marginal builders out of business, and decrease total housing at a time of great need. These are conjectural claims. In any event, there is no enduring social utility in fostering the construction of seriously defective homes. If reliable construction is the norm, the recognition of a duty on the part of tract financiers to home buyers should not materially increase the cost of housing or drive small builders out of business. If existing sanctions are inadequate, imposition of a duty at the point of effective financial control of tract building will insure responsible building practices. Moreover, in either event the losses of family savings invested in seriously defective homes would be devastating economic blows if no redress were available.

Those in the business of financing tract builders could therefore reasonably foresee the possibility that they might be under a duty to exercise their power over tract developments to protect home buyers from seriously defective construction. Moreover, since the value of their own security depends on the construction of sound homes they have always been under a duty to their shareholders to exercise reasonable care to prevent the construction of defective homes. Given that traditional duty of care, a lending institution should have been farsighted enough to make such provisions for potential liability as would enable it to withstand the effects of normal retrospective effect. [Italics added.]

Connor v. *Great Western Savings and Loan Association* does not create a blank check type of liability on the part of institutional construction lenders in California. The key concept resulting in construction lender liability to buyers of defectively built houses that it financed is that the lender, by virtue of its deep involvement in operating and financing residential development, "became much more than a lender content to lend money at interest on the security of real property."

A later appellate court decision in California, known as *Bradler* v. *Santa Barbara Savings and Loan Association* (79 C.R. 401, August 27, 1969), defined more specifically the liability of the construction lender who lent funds to a builder who built and sold a house to a buyer that, after the conveyance of title to the purchaser, proved to be a substantially defective structure. In this case, the buyer seeking recovery from the construction lender for damage to the house's foundation from expansive adobe soil cracking alleged, in addition, that (1) the lender had approved the plans for the house, the building specifications, and the construction methods used by the builder; (2) the lender had supervised and inspected construction processes; and (3) the lender had approved the completed house. In holding that the lender was not liable to the buyer for damage from structural defects in his house, the court emphasized that one construction loan was made and that the lender acted like the usual construction lender, hence there was no liability under the legal standards for such liability as was established in the *Connor* decision. Specifically, the appellate court at page 407, 79 C.R. 401 stated that

Santa Barbara Savings and Loan Association's alleged participation as a lender was that of the usual and ordinary construction and purchase money lender, content to lend money at interest on the security of real property. Approval of plans and specifications and periodic inspection of houses during the construction is normal procedure for any construction money lender. The allegation that it supervised construction is a conclusion and will be disregarded. Unlike *Connor*, its financing did not take on "ramifications beyond the domain of the usual money lender." Unlike *Connor*, it was not financing the development of a large tract wherein it sought to receive substantial fees for making construction loans. Unlike *Connor*, it did not receive a fee for "warehousing" land. Unlike *Connor*, it received no guarantee from loss of profits in the event a home buyer sought permanent financing elsewhere. Unlike *Connor,* it was not "preoccupied with selling prices and sales."

A further definition of the legal boundary of liability of construction lenders to buyers of defectively built houses constructed with the borrowed funds is found in Section 3434 of the California Civil Code (enacted September 4, 1969), which provides that

A lender who makes a loan of money, the proceeds of which are used or may be used by the borrower to finance the design, manufacture, construction, repair, modification, or improvement of real or personal property for sale or lease to others, shall not be held liable to third persons for any loss or damage occasioned by any defect in the real or personal property so designed, manufactured, constructed, repaired, modified or improved or for any loss or damage resulting from the failure of the borrower to use due care in the design, manufacture, construction, repair, modification or improvement of such real or personal property, unless such loss or damage is a result of an act of the lender outside the scope of the activities of a lender of money or unless the lender has been a party to misrepresentations with respect to such real or personal property.

By adhering to the legal standards that will prevent the institutional lender from being liable to buyers of defectively built houses constructed with the borrowed funds, officers of such lenders can avoid this possible cause of great financial liability.

MISCELLANEOUS LEGAL INSTRUMENTS RELATED TO FINANCE

Construction Contracts

Construction contracts are related to real estate finance because much construction in this country is accomplished with borrowed money. This significant dependence of construction activity upon the extension of credit often creates a need for coordinating the provisions of a loan with the terms of a construction contract.

Like other contracts, the construction agreement is in a broad sense limited as to its provisions only by the needs and ingenuity of the parties. We are primarily concerned, however, with the essential provisions of such contracts. The parties to this type of arrangement must incorporate the entire agreement between them into a writing that will be the contract between them. The expression of intent on the part of each party should be unambiguous. Most of the usual rules of law as to whether the agreement need be evidenced by a writing and as to the interpretation of language apply to such agreements. Because of the complex undertaking they provide for, most building contracts are of necessity reduced to writing. (It is not at all uncommon for construction contracts—including the specifications for materials to be used and standards of workmanship—to run into hundreds of pages in the case of multistoried buildings.)

In this type of contract three parties are usually substantially concerned with the terms of the agreement: (1) the owner for whom the building is being constructed; (2) the general contractor; and (3) the architect who has been commissioned to design the building for the owner. A lender making a construction loan will typically have an interest in this contract because the disposition of the funds loaned, the timely completion of a quality improvement, and the achievement of a proper and sufficient lien securing the loan on the improved property are all of vital concern to him or her.

Fundamentally, the owner wants to see the timely completion of a proposed structure for the agreed price in accordance with the design and quality specifications that have been developed by the architect.

The architect has designed a building for the owner and has usually accepted the responsibility of supervising the construction of the building. In this supervisory capacity the architect is often the agent of the owner who is to see that the structure is completed in accordance with the planned design and that the construction meets the minimal quality standards required in the contract.

The contractor is to a certain degree responsible for the erection of the specific building described in the contract. He or she is bound to complete this task within a specified or determinable period and for a definite consideration. Therefore, he or she is interested in keeping the expense of construction to a minimum while substantially performing the contract. Any extra expense due to changes by the owner in size, materials, or design is an additional expense for which the contractor will want to be sure that the owner is responsible.

The construction lender is interested primarily in seeing that the terms of the contract are complied with, that there is opportunity for inspection of construction at critical times, that periodic payments of the borrowed funds are made when due, and that there are no liens prior and superior in right to his or her lien on the property that is security for the loan.

Sales Contract

Although we have discussed the sales contract in conjunction with the land contract, it is worthwhile to review the essentials of this contract and the opportunity for enforcing it in California. This type of contract (deposit receipt) should always be reduced to writing if it is to be enforceable in court under the California Statute of Frauds. Under the provisions of the sales contract, an owner of land obligates himself or herself to convey his or her ownership interest in specific real property, for a definite price, by a certain time, using a specified type of deed, to an ascertained buyer. The buyer commits himself or herself to pay the agreed price for the seller's property, take title, and perform the contract in accordance with the time limits of the agreement.

If there is a breach of this contract and there is no fraud on the part of the plaintiff, and an adequate consideration has been promised and tendered, the party who desires to have performance may go into a court of equity and obtain an order of specific performance. This right to specific performance is an extraordinary remedy of equity; it may be obtained by either the seller or the buyer in the land-sales contract situation when he or she has made and performed a contract equitable to the other party who has breached the agreement. The basic reason for this extraordinary remedy in the case of the sale of land is that equity regards every parcel of land as unique, and therefore money damages will not really restore the party injured by the breach of contract to the equivalent of the position he or she would have been in had the agreement been performed. The remedy of specific performance of the contract may be waived by the party suing, due to breach of contract and money damages obtained instead.

Despite the provisions of the sales contract calling for the buyer to forfeit any money paid to the seller should the buyer breach the agreement, the California courts will enforce such a clause only to the extent of allowing the seller to retain monies equivalent to the loss actually suffered by the nonperformance of the agreement.

Leases

The *lease* is a contract wherein the owner of real property (the landlord or lessor) agrees to surrender possession to a person (the tenant or lessee) who usually agrees to give consideration known as rent for this privilege that the owner grants him or her. The controlling rights and obligations of the parties to this kind of contract are ordinarily derived from the common-law rules and statutes that automatically create them and from specific provisions developed through the bargaining that usually takes place prior to any agreement between the parties. We shall first consider the basic terms of leases and then proceed to discuss the provisions most often incorporated into lease agreements.

Whenever there is an expression of intention in the form of agreement to lease property, certain rights and duties will be created. The owner of the property is obligated to provide possession of the premises for the tenant at the specified time and to assure that he or she will not interfere with the tenant's quiet enjoyment of the property. If the lessee in possession does not obtain quiet enjoyment of the premises, he or she has probably been constructively evicted by the lessor and can then vacate the premises without incurring any liability for

rent payments not made after his or her departure. These are the few essential obligations of the landlord to the tenant under the common law. The statutes of California create other specific obligations for the landlord concerning the condition of the premises insofar as it is relevant to the health and safety of tenants. These regulations (whose violation is usually a misdemeanor) may be found in municipal codes or in the state statutes, depending upon the geographical location of a particular property.

The tenant's basic obligations to the lessor are (1) to pay the required rent when due; (2) not to injure or damage the leased property beyond reasonable wear and tear (technically known as the obligation not to commit waste on the premises); and (3) to return possession of the premises to the landlord at the proper time. Under a term lease the tenant has the duty to vacate the premises in favor of the owner in accordance with the termination date of the lease. In the case of periodic tenancy he or she has the obligation to surrender possession when proper notice of termination of the tenancy has been given by the landlord, and conversely, if the tenant wishes to end the tenancy properly, in a legal sense, he or she has to give timely notice to the landlord indicating his or her intent to conclude the landlord–tenant relationship.

The typical residential lease contract may provide for rights and duties that to a varying degree are advantageous to either the landlord or the tenant. The prudent landlord will usually want to restrict the number of people who may permanently occupy the premises; limit animals and birds kept on the premises; obtain advance payment of the rent that is due; collect a cleaning and breakage deposit upon the initiation of the lease; severely limit the tenant's right to sublet (rent a portion of or all the premises to another for part of the lease term); require the tenant to pay the costs of operating the property; restrict the opportunity to assign the lease to another (contract with a third party, allowing that person to use and enjoy the entire property for the remainder of the lease term); reserve the right to enter and inspect the premises under certain specified circumstances; and provide penalties for late payment of rent to maximize the likelihood of timely payment of rent. Usually the interests of the tenant are diametrically opposed to those of the landlord regarding the inclusion of provisions such as these in the lease. Whether they will be included depends upon the strength of the parties' relative bargaining positions and their skill as negotiators.

Insurance Policies

Owners of any kind of improved property usually insure the improvements against damage or destruction by fire, the elements of nature, and certain types of willful or negligent human action.

Insuring oneself against personal liability for injuries suffered by people on the premises is also common. Injury to a person while he or she is on your property does not automatically create legal responsibility and hence liability for the harm suffered. However, if a lawsuit is filed based upon such an occurrence, the insured obtains the benefit of being represented in court at the expense of the insurance company.

It is important to realize that all insurance policies are contracts that specify the contingent responsibility of the insurer and the rights and duties of the insured. Therefore, unless certain rights are specified for the insured against the insurance company, the policy is not effective in the sense of providing protection for a damaging event.

Insurance policies protecting the interests of the owner and the secured lender from loss due to destruction of improvements are important facets of real estate lending. This is true because a considerable portion of the value of real estate as security for the repayment of a loan often lies in the improvements. Typically, under the terms of a loan agreement, the borrower is obligated to insure the improvements for the benefit of the creditor.

Termite Report

In California, as in other portions of the southwestern United States, termite damage to wood used in buildings is a common problem. Since the existence of termites and the damage they can do is fairly common knowledge, a considerable number of purchasers of real property want to be as sure as possible that improvements on the property they are purchasing are free from termites. This desire on the part of vendees often leads to so-called termite clearance provisions in contracts of sale and hence in escrow instructions. The contract will usually provide that the seller, before the transfer of title to the vendee, must produce evidence assuring the absence of termites from the improvements. This evidence is typically in the form of a statement from a licensed pest-control operator that the property has been examined and that no visible evidence of termite infestation has been found. The vendee will ordinarily try to obtain a commitment in the contract obligating the seller to bear the cost of curing termite infestation and damage before the purchaser can be required to complete the performance of his or her obligations under the contract and take title to the property.

Whether a termite clearance clause in a contract for the sale of real property or escrow instructions will afford the desired protection to the vendee depends upon whether it is clearly drafted so as to place a definite obligation upon the vendor to assume this responsibility. If the clause is omitted from the contract or is defectively drawn, the vendee is obligated to take title to the property, termites and all, since the rule of *caveat emptor* usually applies in the sales contract situation.

Title Insurance

There are various ways of determining the nature and quality of the title to real property. The predominance of the use of title insurance policies in California makes irrelevant any discussion here of other means of determining the quality of title. The title insurance policy, fulfilling the essential function of determining the status of a land title and also of insuring certain designated parties from loss due to the occurrence of specified contingencies, plays a vital part in secured real estate lending.

The primary purpose of title insurance in the lending situation is to provide protection to the lender from loss of his or her security due to the establishment of prior third-party rights in the property.

Historically, the determination of title quality and protecting the interests of those directly concerned with a marketable title proceeded from the abstract lawyer's opinion practice, to the certificate of title, to guarantee of title by an abstract company, and finally evolved into the issuance of modern title insurance policies by insurance corporations regulated by the state of California.

A title insurance policy should be issued in every real estate sales or loan situation. In the case of purchase money loans, the title search on behalf of the purchaser who may be borrowing from a lending institution to purchase the property will often result in the issuance of two title insurance policies. One policy is for the purchaser; the other, usually providing for great protection in case of defective title, is issued to the lender. To appreciate and understand fully the protection afforded the insured to whom a title insurance policy is issued, we must distinguish between the two basic types of policy widely used in California.

The California Land Title Association Standard Coverage Policy is the one traditionally issued for the protection of the purchaser's interest in the land-sale situation. Like any other insurance policy, it provides that the insurer will indemnify the designated beneficiary for any loss brought about by enumerated causes. The responsibility of the insuring corporation also includes the obligation to incur the cost of any litigation conducted in defense of the insured's interest. This type of policy insures against loss due to the following risks that are a matter of public record (whose existence could have been determined by examination of the correct county recorder's records): (1) mistated priority of liens securing loans, (2) unmarketable title, (3) insured not holding title as of a specific date, and (4) defects in liens or encumbrances. While primarily insuring against loss due to title defects ascertainable from the public records, this type of policy usually provides protection from off-record defects such as (1) forgery of the name of a party to a document in the chain of title, (2) incompetency of a person issuing a document vital to marketability of title, and (3) legal status (married, unmarried, bankrupt, alien) of the individual.

It is possible to negotiate with a title company and upon the payment of an additional premium to expand the protection afforded the insured under the policy. This increased protection is established by special indorsements to the policy made by the company.

The American Title Association policy, providing greater protection that the CLTA policy, was developed to meet the higher standards of title protection required by real estate lending institutions. This additional coverage has greatly facilitated the lending of money on California real estate by out-of-state lending institutions. The ATA policy provides the same protection of the insured's interest in the property as the CLTA policy and also includes insurance against possible loss from certain off-record defects in the title.

The lender who demands and obtains protection by the issuance of a CLTA policy with indorsements providing for extended coverage or by an ATA policy has about the most complete protection possible from losses due to recorded or off-record third-party interests in the land. The purchaser insured by the CLTA policy is not usually insured against loss due to faulty titles caused by off-record defects.

Lenders have a crucial interest in maximizing the assurance of the marketable title of hypothecated land. They have achieved increased protection from loss due to defective land titles by using special title insurance policy provisions. Their demands for increased protection have been met by indorsements to the CLTA policy or by specific provisions in the ATA policy. The special title insurance requirements of lenders brought about title insurance protection against the following defects in land titles:

1. Defects, liens, and encumbrances not disclosed by the public records
2. Easements established by use and not disclosed by the public records
3. Rights of parties in possession not disclosed by the public records
4. Mechanic's liens that have gained priority by reason of commencement of work prior to recording of the mortgage or deed of trust
5. Water rights, mining claims, and patent reservations
6. Location of property lines according to accurate survey
7. Existing covenants, conditions, or restrictions under which the lien of the deed of trust can be destroyed or subordinated
8. Present and existing violations of enforceable covenants, conditions, or restrictions
9. Final court orders or judgments requiring removal from land contiguous to the hypothecated land of any encroachment or interest benefiting the security

10. Existing tax liens or assessment liens that are prior to the deed of trust, except as indicated in the policy of title insurance
11. Bankruptcy proceedings or United States tax liens affecting the title to the property except as indicated in the policy

The cost of title insurance policies depends upon the face value of the policy and upon the extensiveness of the coverage provided. The face value of the policy is usually governed by the size of the interest that the insured has in the property. Thus, the purchaser of real property will have a title insurance policy issued to him or her in the amount of the purchase price. The lender will naturally desire the issuance of a policy in an amount equivalent to the loan that has been made. The ATA policy or the specially indorsed CLTA policy will usually cost more because of the increased work necessary to issue the policy and the greater risk created for the insurer.

In California today, prudence in either purchasing real property or accepting it as security for the repayment of a debt demands a title search with the issuance of an appropriate policy of title insurance for the benefit of the vendee or the lender.

Transfer of Rights and Duties in Mortgages and Trust Deeds

The general rules of law that apply to mortgages and trust deeds are essentially the same. Therefore, we shall discuss trust deeds (because they are far more significant than mortgages in terms of frequency of use), knowing that the legal status of the mortgage is virtually the same as that of this more commonly used instrument.

There are two important aspects of this general topic: the transfer of property rights in the promissory note and trust deed from one holder to another, and the sale of a trustor's interest in real property with the debt that exists continuing as an obligation to be paid by the vendee.

To accomplish the sale of a trust deed, the seller must comply with the negotiable instruments law as it governs the transfer of property rights in notes and with the law of contracts (as to the trust deed) governing assignment of contractual rights. That the note is the more significant property in the trust deed situation is illustrated by the fact that whoever is entitled to the note can also, because of this ownership, demand and obtain, through legal process if necessary, the trust deed. If a person is legally possessed of only the trust deed, it does not necessarily follow that he or she is entitled to the note. Negotiation of a note secured by a lien transfers the entire "property package" to the purchaser. Assignment of the trust deed alone does not transfer any property rights in the debt, so such assignment accomplishes nothing. The assignee of the trust deed, since the property rights in the note have not been transferred to him or her, gains no rights in the debt.

The promissory note is transferred (depending upon whether it is bearer or order paper) by indorsement and delivery or by delivery alone. The trust deed is transferred by an assignment to the transferee of the note. The documentary evidence of the assignment may be recorded, which will result in constructive notice of the new owner's interest in the property under the trust deed, and in some additional protection of this interest.

The transfer of the trustor's interest in property with the purchaser obligating himself or herself to pay some or all of this debt is a very important aspect of dealing with trust deeds. We are usually dealing with contractual relationships among three parties—the lender, the original borrower, and the purchaser from the borrower. Therefore, the rights and duties of the respective parties will be governed primarily by the terms of the contracts between them, by the relevant California statutes, and by their actions in these transactions. When real property with a trust deed against it is sold, the loan may be assumed by the vendee or he or she may purchase the property "subject to the trust deed." The use of these technical words is very significant in that they effect very different legal rights and obligations for all parties to the transaction. Therefore, it is incumbent upon anyone engaging in real estate finance activities to know the different legal effects achieved by these clauses.

When the vendee purchases property from a trustor "subject to the trust deed," he or she has not assumed the unpaid balance of the debt as a personal obligation. Thus, if a foreclosure proceeding is conducted because of default, the property is primarily liable for the debt and there can be no proceeding against the vendee to obtain deficiency judgment. Because of the limited personal liability of the vendee taking title to property "subject to the trust deed," it is to his or her great advantage to negotiate to achieve this benefit.

When the vendee purchases property from a trustor and "assumes the trust deed," the result is to make the new owner personally liable for the unpaid balance of the debt. Thus, if the trust deed is one other than a purchase money trust deed, this vendee could be held personally liable for any deficiency resulting from the sale of the property, should a foreclosure sale produce an amount of money insufficient to retire the debt.

After the transfer of title by the trustor with the debt he or she created still in existence, this party remains liable to the holder of the promissory note for the unpaid balance to the extent that this liability existed initially. This means that the original borrower is in the legal position of a surety for the debt. Hence, he or she has a contingent obligation to pay the debt if the vendee who purchased the property from him or her defaults on the obligation to pay the remainder of the obligation. Possible liability of the original borrower is eliminated as a practical matter if the trust deed debt is a purchase money loan, because in California deficiency judgments cannot be obtained against persons liable on purchase money loans.

For there to be a provable purchase of property by a vendee taking title "subject to the trust deed" or "assuming the trust deed," there should be a writing expressing this intent. The written statement can appear in the contract of sale or in the deed used to convey title from the trustor-grantor to the vendee. Written evidence is necessary here because of the requirements of the California Statute of Frauds.

Land Contracts

The land contract is essentially a device for the extension of credit by the seller to the buyer of real property. It is also a contract whereby the vendor is traditionally obligated to convey marketable title to the property upon the occurrence of certain specified events. Thus, this agreement has appropriately been called a contract for a deed. Despite this dual functional aspect of the land contract, we shall direct most of our attention to the financing arrangements, largely disregarding the sale portion of the agreement.

Since the parties to this type of arrangement are, in fact, entering into a contract, they have considerable latitude to establish specific rights and duties in accordance with the provisions that seem to suit their purposes. Because of the great opportunity to contract on terms satisfactory to them, they can achieve many variations in the land contract. We are necessarily confined to discussing the usual provisions of such contracts and to commenting upon the rights and duties of the parties as established under the typical agreement.

These contracts provide for the sale of a certain described parcel of land; delivery of possession to the vendee; identification of the seller and the buyer; time for performance; the type of deed to be used; quality of title obtained by vendee; seller to have title insurance policies issued to buyer when deed is delivered; price to be paid; terms of payment; liquidated damages clause; no recording of the contract by the vendee; when the buyer will be entitled to a grant deed and to issue a promissory note secured by a trust deed for the unpaid balance; forfeiture clause; that upon default by the buyer a landlord–tenant relationship is created between the vendor and the vendee with occupancy of the premises to be at the will of the seller; the care that the vendee is to exercise over the property to protect its physical condition; insurance of improvements by the vendee for the benefit of the vendor;

vendee to pay all property taxes and assessments levied against the property; and buyer to pay for cost of any litigation incurred by the seller to enforce the contract. Because there is no substantial legal question about the meaning of a number of these clauses or about their enforceability, we shall not dwell at great length upon clauses involving expression of the parties' intent to buy and to sell; delivery of possession to the vendee; identification of parties; time for performance; type of deed to be delivered to the grantee; quality of title; issuance of a title insurance policy; price to be paid; rate of interest to be paid by the buyer to the seller; when the buyer will be entitled to a grant deed from the seller; insurance of improvements by the vendee for the vendor's benefit; vendee's obligation to pay all taxes and assessments levied upon the property; and buyer's obligation to pay the cost of any lawsuits required by the vendor to enforce the contract. The legal status of those crucial clauses in the contract that provide for the vendor's rights—clauses that have made the land contract so advantageous from the seller's standpoint—has been questioned frequently in the courts during the last thirty years. The problem created by the results of this litigation is whether the clauses will be enforceable in court for the benefit of the seller, or, in other words, does the language of the contract mean what it says when tested in litigation? In California the trend in the courts has been to construe these clauses so as to provide protection for the vendee that is not specifically set forth in the contract. The result has been a nullification of the specified legal rights and prerogatives established in these contracts for the benefit of the seller.

Before examining these critical clauses in the contract and determining their legal status, we shall investigate the economic and sales justification for the use of the land contract. Exploring the practical aspects of the use of this security device should enable us to comprehend what real effect the various statutes and appellate court decisions have had on the usefulness of this contract. Historically, the land contract has most often been used under conditions that are adverse from the standpoint of obtaining financing from traditional institutional sources. These adverse conditions have usually consisted of the buyer's being a poor credit risk (because of his or her poor past credit record, existing obligations, lack of ability to manage money, or minimal income potential); of the unsuitability of the property as security (either because of its being unimproved and therefore not legally or economically acceptable as security by most loan sources, or because the sale price at which the buyer is purchasing the property is excessive in terms of the determined value of the property); of generally adverse economic conditions that have limited severely the supply of lendable funds, thereby leaving the land contract in a comparatively attractive position as a means of providing the necessary credit; or of a sale in which the initial cash payment by the buyer is so small as to create almost no equity in the property. In this last situation (if the debt obligation is not eligible for insurance for the lender's benefit by public or private organizations), the vendor considers himself or herself to be in such a precarious position should the debtor default that he or she cannot see how the costs of foreclosing a lien could be met without considerable expense to him or her. What the vendor wants in such a situation is sale of the property under conditions giving him or her the power to divest the defaulting buyer completely of his or her rights in the property summarily and at virtually no expense to himself or herself. Thus, the land contract, in this situation in which it has most often been employed, amounts to a banana peel under the heel of the defaulting buyer that will allow the elimination of his or her interest with a minimum of time and expense. Under this initial traditional concept of the land contract, the seller held all of the rights and powers, with the position of the buyer (until he or she obtained title) being that of the owner of a tenuous equitable interest in the property that could be eliminated by the seller for any number of reasons. Under the terms of the contract, the seller was in virtually a "heads I win, tails you lose" position relative to the buyer.

However, considering the position of the seller in this rather risky sale (risky from his or her standpoint because no reasonable buyer's equity existed that would motivate or enable the buyer to comply with the contract terms) wherein the chance of buyer default was great, it is difficult to blame the seller for attempting to maximize his or her protection under the contract. The seller did not want to be in a position in which legal interests of record, brought into existence by this type of sale, would obscure the title to his or her property. If this were allowed to happen, probably the only ways the vendor could clear the title to land for subsequent sale after the vendee's default would be to begin an expensive, time-consuming, quiet title action or to obtain a quitclaim deed from buyers who were likely to be disagreeable and disgruntled at having lost their investment in the property. Neither of these alternatives would be attractive for the seller trying to conduct the business of selling land for a profit.

In response to complaints by buyers concerning the apparent one-sidedness of these contracts, the California courts took under consideration the equities of this contractual relationship. Over the years there has been a significant modification of the effect of those clauses in land contracts that were vital to the preservation of the dominating interests of the seller. By comparing the previous rights of the sellers with the disposition made of these specific contractual provisions by the courts, we will gain insight into the present legal effect of such clauses.

Before the appellate court decisions in favor of the vendee, the vendor could usually cancel the contract upon default and immediately terminate the vendee's interest and regain possession of the property from him or her, retain as liquidated damages any monies paid by the vendee up to the time of default, prohibit recording of the contract by the buyer, and obtain a deficiency judgment against the debtor under certain conditions. What has happened to these earlier enforcement capabilities of the vendor? The provision of the contract prohibiting the vendee from recording the contract is usually unenforceable now, since it is contrary to public policy. The right of the seller to obtain money damages for the buyer's breach of contract is now limited to the reasonable rental value of the property while possessed by the purchaser plus the cost of enforcing the contract through legal processes. This means that there is now, under the California Code of Civil Procedure, Section 580b, no possibility of the seller obtaining a deficiency judgment against the defaulting debtor. Judicial interpretation of the California Civil Code, Section 3275, has determined that the vendor may not immediately dispossess and thereby forfeit the property interest of a willfully or inadvertently defaulting debtor who is purchasing by land contract. The debtor now has the right, after default, to have the vendor reinstate the contract on his or her behalf if and when the default has been cured. (Presumably the vendee must correct the default within a reasonable time, probably within at least one to two years.) These interpretations regarding the debtor's rights have created what amounts to an equity of redemption for the defaulting vendee. A question therefore arises as to the difference between the land contract and the mortgage or trust deed that is made effective as a lien against the property by proceeding through the lengthy and time-consuming court foreclosure proceeding. One must agree that this new equity of redemption has eliminated the primary advantage that used to exist for the vendor under the land contract financing device. However, the unscrupulous vendor might bulldoze the timid, unknowing vendee off the property and out of his or her interest, thereby enjoying the rights the contracts provide for him or her.

The land contract has so many disadvantages and limitations incident to its use today in California that it should probably not be used in most cases. From the vendor's standpoint, the main disadvantages in using this financing instrument now are (1) the liquidation damages clause is limited; (2) the contract can be recorded and thereby can create the necessity of litigation to achieve a marketable title after a vendee's default; and (3) the

debtor now has an equity of redemption, so the creditor has no right to summarily dispossess and eliminate the interest of the knowledgeable litigious vendee. In most transactions, the vendor is now much better off in California using the trust deed with the trustee's power of sale provision rather than tangling with the land contract as presently enforced in the courts.

The nullifying of the vendor's rights under the contract has not eliminated all the disadvantages for the vendee. The most significant disadvantages remaining for the vendee under the land contract are (1) his or her ability to sell interest in the property may be restricted; (2) his or her interest under the land contract is nebulous in the minds of many prospective purchasers and lenders, and therefore its value to him or her is questionable before he or she obtains a deed from the vendor; and (3) when he or she has performed the contract to the full extent and is entitled to a deed, he or she may not be able to locate the grantor or the title conveyed may not be marketable. Undoubtedly, with all of these disadvantages for the vendee under the land contract, he or she is wise to use the trust deed instead as a means of financing most property sales transactions.

Sales Contracts

The *sales* contract is primarily an agreement for the transfer of an interest in real property, enforceable if necessary in the courts. However, under certain circumstances it can have some aspects of a financing arrangement. If the obligation to pay the specified purchase price is not secured (according to the terms of the contract) by a specific lien on the property, this contract will create what is known as a vendor's lien. Also, the vendee has, prior to conveyance of title, a lien on the property in the amount of the portion of the purchase price paid to and received by the vendor. If for some reason a defective and therefore unenforceable trust deed or mortgage is issued to the vendor by the vendee, the vendee can have a court of equity, on the basis of the sales contract, create a specific lien on the property sold.

Other Real Estate Financing Arrangements

The period from 1966 through 1970 was characterized by a stifling shortage of real estate credit compared with effective demand for it. This was also a time of unprecedented inflation, with the annual increase in the cost of living ranging from 5 to 7 percent. These two conditions brought about drastic changes in the real estate lending practices of major institutional sources of real estate credit. The two main changes in real estate loan practices by financial institutions were to increase interest rates on secured real estate loans to historic highs and to participate in the legal rights of the property owner borrowing funds. During the height of the so-called money crunch of the late 1960s, in many states interest rates went up to the legal maximums allowable under state usury laws. States with unacceptably low maximum interest rates on real estate loans suffered a grave shortage of real estate credit because the available funds would be lent by national institutional real estate lenders only in those states where the highest yields were to be obtained on such loans. The other effect of this crisis in real estate credit was to produce the "piece of the action" equity participation secured real estate loan. In this loan contract the lender collected interest on the funds lent and in addition either acquired title to an interest in the collateral property or shared in prerogatives of ownership, such as a percentage of the gross rentals collected from an income-producing property. Such loan agreements depended upon an excruciating shortage of real estate credit and a likelihood that substantial profits were to be made on a particular parcel of real estate by the owner-borrower even if he or she gave up a portion of his or her ownership of the property.

The unique real estate loan contract arrangements developed during the late 1960s are (1) contingent interests for lenders; (2) lender receiving an ownership interest in the collateral property as a further inducement to make the loan; (3) sale leaseback; (4) sale buyback; (5) wraparound mortgage (called all-inclusive deed of trust in California); and (6) joint venture front money transactions.

The contingent interest arrangement for real estate financing meant that, in addition to receiving loan fees and interest on money lent, the lender was further compensated under the debt contract by a percentage of the gross income from a collateral property, or a percentage of the net income derived from the property, or variations of these compensation formulas.

Besides being compensated for making a real estate loan by interest and loan fees, a lender might acquire actual ownership in the borrower's property hypothecated as security for the loan by being made a tenant in common with the owner, owning stock in the borrowing corporation. He or she might be conveyed an interest in the partnership owning the property in question. Through this ownership position in the collateral property, the lender would possibly obtain a higher yield from its loan and also participate in increases in the market value of the property in the future.

In the sale and leaseback arrangement, the borrower sells the property (which is collateral for a loan) to the lender, and the lender immediately leases the property back to the seller-borrower. Through this device the les-see-borrower can in effect obtain 100 percent financing on the land and the maximum legal loan-to-value ratio loan from an institutional lender on the leasehold and improvements made on the property. It is also possible to provide the lessee-borrower with an option to repurchase the property from the lender at a later date.

In the sale and buyback arrangement, the would-be borrower sells the property that he or she is to finance to the institutional lender, who then sells it to the borrower on a long-term land contract. The down payment required on this land contract is small (10 percent of the purchase price), and the term of the contract can be for a very long time.

The wraparound mortgage is in effect a second mortgage lien on a property. It has usually been used where it is impossible to retire an existing loan on a property because of restrictive prepayment conditions in the debt contract, or where it is undesirable to do so because of the relatively low rate of interest on the existing debt. As a desirable setting for the wraparound loan, the property has appreciated in value very markedly and the borrower-owner has an excellent credit rating. Under the wraparound loan arrangement, the lender making this loan assumes the obligation to carry out all legal duties to the creditor holding the first loan. Although the lender in the wraparound loan arrangement obtains a promissory note from the borrower for the total amount of indebtedness to be placed against the property, the only sum lent is the difference between the unpaid outstanding balance of the first loan and the total sum to be placed as a lien against the property. An example of the wraparound secured real estate loan situation follows. An income-producing property with a market value of $1,500,000 has a 5.5 percent loan with a balance of $500,000 against it. The owner-debtor of this shopping center seeks to borrow $500,000 more against this property. The wraparound lender obtains a promissory note in the amount of $1,000,000 bearing 13 percent interest secured by another mortgage, actually disburses only $500,000, and assumes the duty of making the payments on the first mortgage loan of $500,000.

The last real estate financing technique to gain prominence during the late 1960s is the joint venture front money arrangement. Here the party providing needed funds for a real estate development venture does not take the position of a creditor in the transaction. The furnisher of funds for development takes the position of a partner in a partnership, a shareholder in a corporation, or one of the parties to a contractual joint venture. The furnisher of funds under these arrangements is usually assured a first priority in using the profits from the enterprise to return its original investment. After the return of capital has been achieved, the provider of capital shares in the profits from the enterprise to return its original investment. After the return of capital has been achieved, the provider of capital shares in the profits from the development according to a formula established in the joint venture agreement. The gravest risks in this type of real estate credit extending technique are the possible liabilities that may be incurred by becoming a participant in the venture and the possibility that the development project will not be adequately profitable so to return the capital provided to the developer plus generating an adequate yield on the investment. In the operation of this real estate financing device, the developer who needs the funds for a project provides the time, effort, and skill to manage the enterprise, and very little capital.

As funds for real estate loans become more plentiful in relation to effective demand for them and as interest rates decline, the tendency is to move away from the widespread use of these unique arrangements and back to the making of simple secured real estate loans based solely upon a debt contract and a mortgage or trust deed lien.

LEGAL ASPECTS OF COOPERATIVE APARTMENTS AND CONDOMINIUMS IN CALIFORNIA

We stressed in earlier chapters that the real estate finance professional must always be research-minded and aware of new developments. The rapid increase in the number of condominium housing units constructed in California during the 1960s and 1970s confronted the real estate and finance industries with new concepts that had to be evaluated if the best decisions relevant to sales and financing of these properties were to be made.

The purposes of this short discussion are (1) to compare the landlord-owned and -operated apartment house with the cooperative and with the condominium; (2) to compare the legal framework of commonly used cooperative arrangements with the condominium; (3) to determine the advantages and disadvantages of each type of property ownership; (4) to set forth the financing possibilities for each property; and (5) to describe the operations of the traditional cooperative and of the condominium.

Although this discussion is concerned with apartment properties, do not conclude that the only feasible use of the condominium concept is for apartments. There is every indication that its most significant employment in the future may be in commercial and industrial land development, because in these types of land use, the possible disadvantages and problems existing in apartments may well be minimized and the advantages accruing to the owner increased. This discussion is limited to residential land use because in this type of property the cooperative and condominium approaches have been used most often.

The legal problems of cooperatives and condominiums and the solutions to them are governed to a considerable extent by the economic, social, and psychological environment in which people use properties. Therefore, we shall consider these factors before examining the legal structure of cooperatives and condominiums.

The creation and maintenance of the value of these properties will probably be governed by essentially the same principles of property value that apply to the landlord-owned apartment house. Unless there is considerable population pressure from people who are economically able and personally willing to live in privately owned apartments, cooperatives, or condominiums, the improvement of land with buildings will not necessarily make the entire property more valuable. People must be sufficiently abundant to create and maintain a market for the available space, and they must have the earning power and disposable income necessary to purchase ownership interests in such properties. As in most real estate sales, purchasers can truly become buyers only if they can borrow the greater portion of the purchase price.

Cooperatives and condominiums will usually succeed only where a traditional apartment house would also be a feasible, prudent investment. The point is that cooperative and condominium success requires that people who can afford to and who desire to reside in such an apartment be present in adequate numbers to create effective demand for nearly the entire supply of such space available at any given time. A cooperative or condominium located in the wrong place from the standpoint of effective demand for space not yet existing will be a financial failure. Such a property can also suffer from lack of the necessary effective demand if people are present who are financially able, but who do not desire to reside in such a property as owners. This last circumstance can exist in major cities if the prospective occupiers of such space believe that economic, social, or psychological disadvantages exist. These disadvantages do not have to exist in fact; the damage to the potential success of such properties will be achieved if, through ignorance, the belief that they do exist arises and continues for some time.

An enormous educational task faces the developers and promoters of the condominium—to attain reasonable public acceptance of this type of ownership. To develop the public acceptance, and therefore demand, so vital to the success of condominiums, the real estate industry must produce enough trained, ethical, sophisticated salespeople to sell the quantity of such space created.

If these economic, social, and psychological elements of cooperative and condominium living are not recognized and dealt with adequately, no legal legerdemain will save such projects from financial disaster. The law can solve some of the problems, but not all.

It is much more difficult to achieve public understanding of what is being sold in marketing condominiums than in marketing cooperatives. There is some apprehension in real estate finance circles that public ignorance of the nature of condominiums will prevent general public acceptance of them, and thus that financing this type of property should be avoided; but if there is no support of the sale of these units by financial institutions lending to buyers, the chances for their being a success (in that they are sold widely to the general public) will be small. Such defeatist attitudes must be overcome if these housing concepts are to progress.

Except for people in special circumstances (such as some retired individuals who want to minimize their concern with a residence, yet own it) the strong demand for cooperatives and condominiums will be in areas in which land is very scarce, and, when available, high-priced. Under these circumstances outstanding employment opportunity, significant transportation advantages, amenities, or all three create effective population pressure to the extent that financially capable buyers will accept a cooperative apartment or condominium. Where these special magnets attract the necessary quality of people, cooperatives and condominium residences in considerable numbers will probably be readily salable. In short, location is usually much more important to the success of these special properties than to the marketing of the traditional single-family house.

Traditional Apartment Houses

The cooperative apartment and the condominium are supposed to be improvements for the tenant over his or her situation in the landlord-owned and -operated apartment house. Exactly what does the traditional mode of living involve? Briefly, the owner (landlord) leases certain space to the occupant (tenant) for a period of time, for consideration called rent; the owner often maintains the premises in accordance with certain established standards. The renter must pay the rent, take reasonable care of the premises, and surrender possession when the owner is legally entitled to it. Despite all the money he or she pays the landlord for the privilege of occupying the space, the renter does not perfect any ownership interests and may be subject to the whims of a capricious landlord. All the tenant can usually say is that for the price paid he or she had the use of certain space for a period and that he or she did not go into debt for living quarters.

Cooperative apartments and condominiums, if they are to be successful, should offer a person something he or she will not achieve from the rental apartment arrangement. Whether the particular offerings of those types of housing are attractive will depend upon the likes and dislikes of the individual. A person who does not like any responsibility for building and grounds maintenance, shuns large debts typically running on for a decade or more, and detests being anchored to one spot will not like the cooperative and condominium concepts. Exactly how many persons desire these particular features is really not known; apparently, however, millions of Americans in the twentieth century assume that their shoulders are strong enough to carry these burdens.

Cooperative Apartments

In California a cooperative apartment can be established and owned under three different legal arrangements: tenancy in common, business trust, or corporation. The corporate form of cooperative is the most common arrangement used in this state, for practical reasons: (1) ease of comprehension by the public; (2) centralized management power and operation by a legal entity; (3) limited liability for apartment owners; (4) long duration of building ownership by the corporate entity; and (5) an established, fairly well settled body of corporate law, which facilitates the answering of many questions occurring when the corporation is applied to this special situation.

Despite the obvious preference for the incorporated cooperative apartment in California, the tenancy-in-common cooperative has also been used here. Under this arrangement the purchaser of an apartment receives a deed conveying to him or her an undivided fractional interest in the land and building, subject to a reservation by the grantor of the exclusive right to occupy and use all designated separately identified space units in the building as shown on the plat made part of the deed by attachment. Excepted from this reservation are the rights of occupancy and use that are conveyed to the grantee. The deed to the apartment purchaser will specifically grant him or her the exclusive right to occupy a particular apartment properly identified on the plat attached to the deed. (This plat is legally adequate to accomplish the conveyance to the grantee of his or her apartment if it is a plan of a particular floor of the building showing the location and apartment number of each apartment on a certain floor, room arrangement, and dimensions of all spaces included in the apartment.)

The ownership interest the purchaser obtains under the deed usually used to convey the interest is a fee in the space taken up by the apartment outlined in the plat attached to the deed. Except for limitations on the area of the property and on the right to transfer title, any restrictions on ownership found in deeds or other recorded instruments should be similar to those applying to a fee interest in a parcel of land. This property interest could be used as a security for a loan if it were acceptable as such to a lender.

Business trust and corporate co-ops. The business trust can be used for a variety of purposes including the establishment and operation of an apartment building. In using the trust for cooperative apartment ownership and operation, the following steps and procedures are employed: (1) the trust is created; (2) the trustees take title to the property; (3) the trustees issue certificates of beneficial interests either to a developer who, when selling an apartment, assigns the requisite number to a buyer, or to the actual purchasers of the individual apartments; (4) the trustees assign to beneficial interest certificate holders (by a contract assignment or by a proprietary lease) the right to occupy specific space in the building. In this legal setting, the rights and duties of the trust beneficiaries (owners of the apartments) are set forth in the declaration of trust, which is the contract establishing the trust. The most significant provisions of the declaration of trust typically provide that (1) the pledging of any beneficial interest of hypothecation is to be by the usual lien procedures; (2) the beneficiary is to surrender possession of his or her space upon termination of his or her rights in accordance with the declaration of trust; (3) the owner is not to use his or her space for purposes prohibited in the bylaws or the trust declaration; (4) the owner is to pay his or her pro rata share of operational expenses; (5) the owner can effect a transfer of his or her interest in the building only if he or she complies with the terms of the trust agreement and obtains approval of the trustees; and (6) upon an owner's failing to meet his or her payment obligations, the trustees may dispose of the interest the delinquent debtor held in the property by sale and apply the proceeds of this sale to the delinquency.

For the trust beneficiaries (owners of a cooperative apartment house) to have the privilege and protection of no personal liability based upon ownership or operation of the property, the trustees must have and maintain complete ownership and managerial control of the property. Whenever an owner effectively participates in the management of this property, he or she is risking the loss of this preferred status.

A trust declaration can provide for the trustees to establish bylaws regulating the use of the various spaces and the conduct of all people residing in the building. These bylaws (assuming that they are deemed reasonable for the purposes and objectives of the trust) may be established in such a way as to be enforceable through some form of punitive action by the trustees, for example, fine or forfeiture of interest in the trust property.

Property owned by a trust can be financed for acquisition or improvement purposes by the trustees' borrowing funds to serve the purposes of the entire property; or individual owners could conceivably borrow and use their property interest as security for a necessary loan.

The complexion and operation of the cooperative apartment enterprise organized as a corporation is much more easily understood than the others, because many people are generally familiar with the legal framework of a corporate business. The cooperative established and operated as a corporate entity involves the following steps and practices: (1) entrepreneurs organize a corporation for their avowed purposes; (2) the land—or land and building—is sold to the corporation (which, if it intends to construct the required building itself, will adhere to basic patterns of construction financing for conventional loans, and, if FHA loan insurance is involved, will comply with the appropriate regulations); (3) assuming that an apartment building exists, the corporation leases apartments to tenants who are required to be shareholders in the corporation; and (4) the apartment owners, under the terms of their proprietary leases and stock contracts, accept certain restrictions on the right to transfer their interest; obligate themselves to pay monthly certain sums to pay interest, retire debt principal, and maintain the property; and agree to observe certain established standards of conduct on the premises.

The amount of corporate stock purchased by each owner is determined by the sale price of the individual apartment. The sale price of the apartment will (initially) determine the liability of the owner for monthly payments and special assessments. Purchase of the stock does not confer the right of occupancy upon the owner of stock. To be truly an owner of this type of cooperative apartment, the stockholder must lease a specific apartment from the corporation by proprietary lease. This lease has many of the attributes of a standard apartment lease with the additional requirements that pertain to the special situation.

In determining the rights and duties of the owners and of the corporation in the incorporated cooperative situation, the articles of incorporation, bylaws, stock certificate contract, and proprietary lease are of the utmost importance. The complete picture of the organization and of operation of this type of property cannot be obtained until these sources have been examined.

The bylaws, stock certificate contract, and proprietary lease usually contain the majority of specifications pertaining to the conduct standards, ownership rights, and financial duties of the owners.

The financial arrangements for a corporate cooperative undertaking are usually made by the corporation upon decision by the board of directors. The usual secured real estate loan that is arranged covers the entire building and thereby constitutes one lien on the whole property. The result is that there is only one financing plan for the purchaser of a cooperative apartment—the one originally brought into existence by the corporation. There is only one financing plan because every purchaser of stock in the corporation can buy his or her apartment only within these already established limitations. For example, if an incorporated cooperative apartment house is being sold and a mortgage in the amount of 75 percent of the value of the property has been arranged by the directors, every purchaser of an apartment must arrange for a down payment of 25 percent of the purchase price of his or her property. If, as is often the case, the loan is of the amortizing type, the required down payment (assuming initial property value continues or increases) will increase constantly as the principal of the debt is retired with every payment. A substantial financial obstacle may arise here, in that the required down payment is formidable initially and may well become too large for most buyers as the loan is reduced. This may obviously have a repressive effect upon the sale of the property to many prospective purchasers.

In this type of cooperative all owners are in identical situations as far as their property interests are concerned. The mortgage is on the entire property, any special assessments by local government will typically be against the entire premises, and the local property taxes are levied against the whole property. Thus, if an owner does not make a payment of money to the corporation for taxes, the mortgage, or special assessments, there is the distinct possibility of a default or delinquency occurring because all monies due cannot be paid on time. During the Great Depression, foreclosure sales of incorporated apartment houses occurred because of nonpayment of monthly assessments by shareholders. These foreclosures, caused by the fall in the price level of the real estate market, often eliminated completely the ownership equity of many nondefaulting apartment owners. Since the federal government is considered to have the primary economic duty to the nation of preventing another major economic debacle, many analysts believe there is no longer any real threat to owners' interests in such properties.

Life in an apartment building is commonly at close quarters, a situation that can create social and psychological problems for many of the people living there. The greater the day-to-day contact forced upon building residents by a particular architectural design, the more acute such problems may become for those residents. Architectural design minimizing the enforced daily contact between residents will probably maximize the attractiveness of this type of housing for the large number of people who will associate with compatible neighbors but who do not like to have people personally obnoxious to them forced into their lives. Because of this situation and the financial stakes involved in such housing, the opportunity for selecting one's neighbors assumes great importance in the case of cooperative and condominium housing.

There are various ways to limit the ability of the owner of a cooperative apartment to transfer his or her property interest. Accomplishing such restraint is a technical task calling for an artfully worded statement fulfilling the purpose in mind without violating the strong public policy against most restrictions on the transfer of property. Essentially, the limitation must be of limited effect, must be reasonable, and must clearly accomplish a legitimate objective that has value to recognized property interests so that a court can find a beneficial aspect of the restraint on property. In the corporate cooperative the restriction is established and made effective by requiring the apartment owner who sells his or her property to obtain the approval of the board of directors before the transaction can be completed by the transfer of the corporate stock and proprietary lease rights to the prospective vendee. The stated purpose of such a limitation is to preserve a corporate community of congenial owners who are interested in the general welfare of the corporation and whose financial resources are adequate to preserve the integrity of the corporate enterprise by enabling the corporation to collect the funds necessary for operation. A substantial body of corporate law sustains the right of corporate owners to keep destructive, inharmonious elements out of the firm to protect and preserve the organization. This protection of business corporations is usually obtained by first-refusal provisions in stock contracts requiring that any shareholder desiring to sell his or her stock must first offer it to the corporation or to other shareholders before transferring it to an outsider. The corporate cooperative restrictions upon the sale of apartments are also aided by an established body of law upholding leasehold restraints. Leases often contain provisions restricting the lessee's ability to sublet or assign his or her interests in the lease. In the case of breach of these limiting provisions of the contract, the lessor will often have the right of re-entry to terminate effectively the lessee's interest in the property and thus to protect his or her stake in the property.

This established and legally settled means of reasonably restricting the apartment owner's right of transferring his or her property interest to another is one of the strongest factors in favor of the corporate cooperative. This is not to say that restraints on alienation of comparable effectiveness cannot be developed for the condominium or trust arrangements; however, especially with regard to the case of the condominium, the law is relatively unsettled and untried as to this aspect of the organization. Also, in the condominium one is dealing solely with interests in real property, not with a combination of real property and ownership of a business organization. Therefore, because of the relatively few court decisions on questions of the enforceability of restrictions on real property interests in condominiums, it is concluded that most appellate courts would be more likely to invalidate these restrictions than they would those based upon the established corporate cooperative arrangement.

In the business trust cooperative, restrictions can be based upon the transfer of the property represented by the certificates of beneficial interest and the proprietary lease or grant employed to transfer possessor rights to the owner. Restrictions upon interests in a business trust are well established in the law and therefore readily upheld.

In the California tenancy-in-common cooperative arrangement, the situation is similar to that in the condominium with regard to limiting the right of the owner of an apartment to dispose of it by sale. However, there is no reason to believe that a limited restraint cannot be developed on transfer of this ownership interest that will be upheld by the courts.

Condominiums, a History

The California Civil Code, Section 783, defines a condominium as "an estate in real property consisting of an undivided interest in common in a portion of a parcel of real property together with a separate interest in space in a residential, industrial, or commercial building on such real property, such as an apartment, office, or store." A condominium may include in addition a separate interest in other portions of such real property. Such estate may, with respect to the duration of its enjoyment, be (1) an estate of inheritance or perpetual estate, (2) an estate for life, or (3) an estate for years.

There are some indications that condominiums existed in Rome when the Roman Empire was at its height, although the concept used was probably not the same as that used in the United States today. Nevertheless it is fairly certain that the modern concept originated many years ago in Europe, where it is still found today. It moved from Europe to South America, where there is a separation of the land from the air space (as is required today under the Federal Housing Administration concept in the United States).

From South America it moved in the 1950s to Puerto Rico, where, because of land shortage and growing population, land prices were rising and it became increasingly necessary to have a higher use of the land than that which could be established through individual and sprawling construction. Condominiums have been successful in all these countries because individuals want to own their homes. With condominium structures it is possible for people to buy their homes, having an apartment

within a building in which there are common ownerships of such things as walls, roofs, foundations, stairwells, elevator shafts, and lobby space. Condominiums did not gain immediate popularity in the United States, probably because there was no need for such a high-intensity use of land; a person could buy land, build upon it, and own both land and structure. However, with the development of cities and the increase in land cost because of the scarcity of land, the door has been opened for the use of condominiums, particularly in the luxury apartments toward which there has been a trend since World War II.

The first United States condominium was set up in 1947 by a group of twelve servicemen who had returned from World War II and desired to live in an apartment house in New York. The servicemen had to have ownership of these apartments for their loan to qualify under the Veterans Administration GI Bill, and such qualification was impossible unless the ownership of each apartment belonged to the individual serviceman. Because the bundle of rights theory holds that ownership of land includes the ownership of the air above it, the title insurance company stated that it would be able to insure the air space above the land, provided it could be reduced and held in possession. To accomplish this each of the owners of the apartment building became a tenant-in-common as to $1/12$ of the land and buildings, excluding twelve cubes of air representing the interior measurements of the individual apartments. Each individual then received title to his cubicle of air as it was legally described.

There are three methods by which a unit of air space can be described. One method is to draw up a subdivision plan and record a plat of a subdivision of air space called the plots, representing the individual unit by means of a drawing just as if it were a description of a unit of land lying on the surface of the earth. Each one of the plots is given a number just as if it were a subdivision of land, and conveyance would be by means of number as shown on the plat. A problem could develop in this type of description if the building is constructed after the subdivision of the air is filed and if in the construction the builder did not follow the plans in exact detail as to elevation. The problem would then be encroachment of air cubes on one floor upon those on the next.

A second means would be by a floor plan certification. In this method a survey is made of the land, showing the location of the building, and then a floor plan is provided, showing the location of the unit of air as to dimensions and as to elevation in relation to the ground floor. In this case the architect who followed the construction of the building would have to certify that the construction followed the plans and specifications provided.

A third method is through the apartment survey. A survey is made of the land and the building is plotted upon the survey. A space survey is then made upon each unit on each floor to show the elevations of the floor and the ceiling surfaces. The dimensions of the inside surfaces of the walls and their location with reference to the land boundaries are projected vertically. Title insurance companies will insure descriptions following any of these three methods.

Thus, it is possible to establish a condominium program and to have an insured loan on an air space as defined and on the common property. How is such a condominium formed? First, a declaration by the owner of the property to establish a condominium must be recorded with the county recorder, and, if it is to be FHA-insured, with the director of the Federal Housing Administration. The declaration must describe the land, the units, and the common elements of the property. It should state that the units and the common portions of the property go together as an entity: one cannot be conveyed without the other at any time. Such a declaration will usually include for the co-owners the right of first refusal on the purchase of an apartment before it is placed for sale on the market. The declaration should indicate the nature of the common elements and should show the respective undivided interests of the owners in these elements. It should provide for funds for the maintenance of the common elements. The owners should give easements for maintenance of electrical wiring, heating conduits, plumbing pipes, telephone lines, and other utilities necessary for the upkeep and use of the property.

The next document to be developed is a set of bylaws equally binding upon all parties and owners. They should provide for the election of a manager or management board with the authority to make decisions concerning the normal operation and maintenance of the building and its common elements. They should establish a regular meeting date and a method of paying the cost of the operating expenses. In most instances, since a set of bylaws is usually necessary for the operation and house rules, the bylaws should provide for the establishment of such rules by the management committee, the officers, or the manager. One of the main problems that develop in a condominium is the assessing of common expenses for administration, maintenance, repairs, replacements, and yard work where such is required. Taxes are assessed against each unit as if it were separate property, and mechanic's liens can be filed against one unit without affecting an adjacent unit.

Insurance is usually covered under a blanket policy, with each unit being covered by an endorsement showing each individual condominium's owner, and in case of mortgage there is a loss-payable endorsement to the mortgage. As a rule the owners must provide their own risk insurance for furniture and personal effects. In case of fire, should the total loss not be covered, an assessment would be made against the individuals prorated as to the

effect upon each one. In states in which homesteads are allowable (that is, state law prohibits creditors taking a family home to satisfy debts), it is possible to homestead an ownership in a condominium.

The California condominium has certain characteristics, problems, and requirements that have a direct bearing upon the ownership rights, duties, and implementation of this type of property development scheme. The establishment of a condominium is based upon three essential documents: the declaration, the bylaws, and the deed to individually owned spaces ("apartments" in our discussion). Financing the purchase of a condominium property is accomplished by the purchaser executing and issuing a promissory note secured by a trust deed to create a secured loan that is not substantially different from a loan on an ordinary house.

Let us now examine the provisions of the three basic documents and learn how the provisions of each document contribute to the creation of the entire condominium arrangement.

The declaration (or master deed) is the heart of the condominium plan. This recorded document is in a number of ways comparable to covenants running with the land that control the use that can be made of land in the typical residential subdivision. After the recording of the declaration, the operative provisions that establish the condominium are incorporated by reference into all deeds issued to vendees. (Incorporation by reference of provisions of the declaration into a grant deed is accomplished by simply reciting the paragraph of instrument, the page, and the volume number of the county recorder's records where the recorded declaration can be found. This serves to charge the party to be bound by such provision with the legal obligation to observe it.)

The master deed will usually set forth provisions pertaining to (1) a legal description of the land; (2) a legal description of each unit and a description of the common elements; (3) the establishment of an association of owners; (4) a method for sharing common expenses; (5) the unity of the ownership of a unit and of related ownership of the common portions of the building, which are an entity not to be conveyed or mortgaged separately; (6) the number of votes assigned to each unit in the building; (7) how the building is to be managed; (8) restrictions on the individual owner's right to partition his or her property interest; and (9) the grant by the respective apartment owners to the owners' association of a right of first refusal or preemptive option enabling the association to purchase any units whose owners wish to sell them. (This last provision often found in the declaration is the condominium version of the restriction on the sale of corporate stock and of transfer of interest in the proprietary lease, which we discussed in conjunction with the corporate cooperative apartment.) This right of the group of owners of apartments to purchase the interest of any one owner who is selling his or her property is designed to assure the compatibility of the ownership group and the general financial security of the total community that is interested generally in the entire property.

The bylaws pertaining to the operation of the condominium are similar in their provisions and functions to other organizational bylaws. For obvious reasons it is vital that these bylaws, which are the rules for operating this property and which establish minimal standards of conduct, should be legally binding upon the residents of the building. Of course, the specific provisions included in the bylaws for a building depend upon the particular situation, the problems of the property, and the owners of the apartments. Basically, most condominium bylaws should provide for (1) rules of conduct for people in the building or a method for the establishment of such regulations; (2) the selection of an administrative board to assume the ultimate managerial responsibility for the property; (3) how and when meetings of the board or of all owners will be called; (4) notices that can and will be given to residents under certain circumstances; (5) deciding upon expenditures for maintenance and repair of the premises; (6) apportionment of such building expenses; (7) regulation of the use of the common areas of the buildings; and (8) the method of collecting sums for building operation and maintenance expense and of enforcing the obligations created for the individual apartment owners. To allow the bylaws to be changed with a minimum of trouble and expense and yet maintain their legal enforceability, reference to their existence should be made in the master deed, with each purchaser of a unit receiving a copy of them along with any amendments. To be acceptable to lenders most condominium convenants, conditions, restrictions, and bylaws prohibit lenders who acquired title to such units by foreclosure from being financially liable for special assessments by the owners' association board of directors during such typically temporary lender ownership.

The bylaws and the other obligations of owners are typically designed so that they apply to any subsequent owners of the property. This continuation of responsibilities under the bylaws and the declaration could create problems for financial institutions taking over such a property interest after a borrower has defaulted on his or her debt. The gravest problem is the possibility that the members of the association may levy excessive assessments on the lender during the period of the institution's interest in the property.

The deed used to convey the interest purchased by the individual buyer is of the type usually used to transfer fee interests in property. In California this is usually a grant deed. The deed is relatively short and simple because the full and complete legal description of the property, regulations, restrictions, and covenants contained in the declaration can be made effective and binding when incorporated into this instrument by reference. A policy of title insurance will be issued on behalf of the purchaser in the typical sales transaction.

Financing the individual condominium unit is a transaction similar to that of a secured real estate loan on a fee interest in the typical residential surface subdivision. The borrower has an interest in real property that will be hypothecated for the benefit of the lender. The lien of the lender will be upon the fee interest in space as served by the rights in common areas that the condominium dweller owns. Because of the legal separateness and individuality of the property interest of every condominium owner, each one does have the opportunity to arrange for financing that fits his or her particular circumstances. Each condominium unit is completely divorced from every other one as to taxation, assessment, and real estate loan liens, thus enabling the title to each unit to be analyzed and determined separately from any other property interest in the building.

Not until California law made separate local property taxation of each unit mandatory on the part of the tax assessors could condominium titles be readily accepted as security for real estate loans by most lending institutions. Until separate tax liability of each property became a legal reality, there was always the possibility that the lender's secured loan would lose its priority if the entire property was taxed as a whole. If this was done, each property would be responsible to the tax collector for any amount of taxes unpaid due to the delinquency of any apartment owner. Such a situation would virtually repeat the situation of the corporate property during the Depression of the 1930s, when any failure by an apartment owner to pay his or her proportionate share of taxes could create a default ultimately leading to the sale of the whole property for delinquent taxes. With the legal implementation of separate assessment and tax liability, one of the major hurdles to financing condominiums by conventional and FHA-insured loans was removed.

The sale of condominiums usually involves the sale of a subdivision in California. This necessitates compliance with the relevant sections of the California Real Estate Law. There is also the possibility that the sale of such property, particularly before construction is completed, may constitute the offering for sale of security interests in California and thus require compliance with the security ("Blue Sky") laws of the state.

As previously mentioned, one of the greatest obstacles to the sale of cooperative housing (of which condominiums are a part) was the lack of available financing in the sense that the required down payment could be substantially minimized, thereby expanding the size of the market for such property. The Housing Act of 1961 encouraged the sale of condominium properties. Under Section 234 of this Act, the Federal Housing Administration is authorized to insure loans secured by first liens, "given to secure the unpaid purchase price of a fee interest in, or a long-term leasehold interest in, a one-family unit in a multifamily structure and an undivided interest in the common areas and facilities which serve the structure." Since we are primarily concerned with the legal aspects of the condominium, there will be no lengthy discussion of the establishment and servicing of this type of loan. For further investigation of this type of loan, examine the relevant section of the National Housing Act, as well as the Federal Housing Administration regulations affecting such a loan.

The National Housing Act of 1961 placed condominium financing under the insurance provided by FHA. To be eligible for mortgage insurance, a family unit must be in a multifamily structure that is or has been covered by a project mortgage insured by the FHA, and the multifamily structure must have been committed to a plan of apartment ownership by a deed or other recorded instrument approved by the director of the FHA before its execution. Such a deed shall provide a description of the land and the multifamily structure and their respective areas, and a description of each family unit in terms of its units, location or rooms, main entrance doors, immediate place with which it communicates, and any other data necessary for its certification. A description of the common areas as well as the common facilities must be provided. There must be a clear expression of the purpose for which the multifamily structure and each of the family units are to be used. The deed shall also state the basic value not in excess of the FHA appraised value, and the value of the multifamily structure in each family unit according to basic values, the percentage pertaining to each owner, and the expense and the profits of rights in the common areas and facilities. It should provide information on all items related to the administration of the property by the association or the cooperative of owners. The deed should state that the plan for apartment ownership and the provisions relating to the administration of the property cannot be changed without prior approval by the FHA. The mortgagee will certify that the individual deed for the family unit to be covered by an FHA-insured mortgage complies with all legal requirements of the jurisdiction, that ownership thereunder is subject to the plan of apartment ownership, that the mortgagor has good and marketable title to the family units subject only to the mortgage, which is a valid first lien upon the same, and that the local property taxes are assessed and levied against each family unit as a taxable entity and are not assessed and levied against the multifamily structure as a whole.

The maximum mortgage amounts under the condominium Section 234 are $45,000 per unit, or 97 percent of the first $25,000 of the appraised value of the property as of the date the mortgage is accepted for insurance; 90 percent of the value between $25,000 and $35,000; and 80 percent of the excess up to a total loan of $45,000. If a condominium unit is bought by a nonoccupant (first owner), the maximum loan shall be 85 percent of the amount computed under this section for an owner who is the occupant.

The loan application is made through a mortgagee by the applicant for commitment of insurance. Forms 2800 and 2900 are prepared, together with verification of deposits and verification of employment; a signed or certified copy of the purchase agreement is forwarded to the FHA together with the declaration of intent to establish a condominium; and an application fee of $25 is collected. If the application is approved, the commitment is issued and the lending institution processes the loan in its usual manner.

To summarize the characteristics of these various approaches to urban living, we list below the most significant factors pertaining to ownership or occupancy of the various housing units that have been discussed.

1. *Landlord-owned apartments*
   a. The occupant leases property for a period of time during which he or she is entitled to quiet possession and reasonable use of the premises.
   b. The occupant is obligated to pay rent for any established lease term, to avoid committing waste, and to surrender possession of the premises to the landlord when he or she is legally entitled to it.
   c. The occupant usually does not incur any expenses of occupancy that are deductible from federal or state income taxes.

2. *California tenancy-in-common cooperative*
   a. The purchaser owns under a deed an undivided interest in the land and buildings accompanied by the exclusive right to occupy a particular apartment.
   b. The apartment occupant owns an interest in real property.
   c. The owner incurs liability for property taxes, assessments, insurance, and usually for the obligations connected with retirement of an amortizing loan. These obligations may be proportional to overall tax and debt obligations, or, if there is a separation of ownership and liability of the individual owner's interests for tax and loan purposes, such financial repsonsibilities may be individual rather than collective.
   d. The property owner will usually be entitled to deduct certain expenses of ownership from federal and state income taxes.
   e. There has been no definite determination in California of the exact quality and nature of the individual owner's property interest in this type of cooperative apartment scheme. Therefore, it has been difficult to make the general public realize what they

are actually buying when acquiring such an apartment. The tendency has been to turn to more comprehensible types of cooperative plans, such as the corporate cooperative.

f. There are usually first refusal restrictions upon the transfer of ownership rights of the individual apartment owner.

3. *Business trust cooperative*

a. The owners of these apartments acquire an interest in the property held by the trust and evidenced by certificates of beneficial interest. These units of beneficial interest evidenced by the certificates are issued in proportion to the sale price of the apartment unit.

b. Usually the trust owns and finances the entire building containing a number of units. Consequently, the owners of individual apartments do not usually have debt obligations owed directly to local taxing agencies or lenders. The trust owes taxes, assessments, and loan payments. These financial responsibilities are met by the trustees' collecting proportional payments from the individual apartment owners and using these funds to meet the obligations against the entire property.

c. Provided that the holders of certificates of beneficial interest in the trust property do not actively participate with the trustees in the management of the enterprise, they are not personally liable in contract or tort due to the ordinary operations of the property.

d. There are usually first refusal restrictions on the apartment owner's right to transfer interest in the trust property.

4. *Corporate cooperatives*

a. The first step in the establishment of this type of cooperative is to form a corporation under the laws of the state.

b. The corporation proceeds to acquire title to either unimproved or improved land. (If the land is unimproved, the corporation will proceed to develop a design for a building, arrange for construction financing, and contract for completion of the building containing the apartments. The usual construction financing procedures will probably be followed, with a permanent loan being arranged to replace the initial temporary credit arrangement.)

c. The apartments will be sold by the corporate owner. (This may be done before construction, concurrently with it, or after completion of the building.)

d. The owner of an apartment purchases stock in the corporation in the amount of the inital price paid for his or her space. His or her right of occupancy is not based upon stock ownership, but is derived from a proprietary lease from the corporation as lessor to him or her as lessee.

e. The board of directors of the corporation manages the building and oversees the meeting of corporate responsibilities for taxes, assessments, insurance, and loan payments.

f. The only means of financing the purchase of this type of apartment unit lies within the boundaries of the loan contract between the corporation and its lender.

g. The apartment owners could have third parties perfect interests in the property prior to and adverse to theirs if they all do not pay their assessments in full and on time. These adverse interests will usually be based upon delinquent taxes and assessments or trust deed foreclosure actions.

h. The owner of such property is usually entitled to deduct certain expenses of residential ownership (real property taxes and interest) from federal and state income taxes.

i. The right to sell the corporate stock or to transfer interests based upon the proprietary lease is limited by first refusal provisions requiring the possible sale to the corporation if the owner's prospective vendee does not meet the legitimate financial and social requirements for an owner of such property.

j. The owner of this corporate stock has the protection of limited liability that all corporations usually enjoy.

5. *Condominium apartments*

a. Unimproved or improved land is acquired by an owner who desires to sell portions of the property in the form of apartment space.

b. The plan for a condominium is based upon a declaration. When this instrument is recorded it becomes a plat and a means of applying certain necessary rights and duties to all units in the property.

c. Bylaws are developed under authority provided in the declaration. These bylaws govern the conduct of residents on the premises and establish a scheme for operating the property on a day-to-day basis.

d. The property interest acquired by the purchaser in this property is usually a fee interest in a certain air space. The fee interest is held in conjunction with rights in common areas of the structure that are accessible and usable by all residents as incident to the enjoyment of their fee interest.

e. The individual apartment owners are responsible for protecting their property interest from the perfection of superior rights in it by third parties. This means that each owner assumes obligations for real property taxes, assessments, insurance premiums, and debt payments very similar to those of the purchaser of the typical tract house. In addition to these obligations, there will be some maintenance and repair expense connected with these properties. An association of owners is normally formed to oversee the care of the property and to assure that the financial support necessary to maintain the property is forthcoming. This burden will be shared according to an established formula by the various occupants of the property. The potential for substantial increases in monthly homeowner assessments by the board of directors of a condominium complex is one very real financial hazard to owning or making long-term loans on such property. (This potential financial risk to ownership also applies to cooperative apartments.) Incompetent, dishonest, or financially capricious management of a condominium complex by a board of directors can result in increasing the entire cost of operating such a property to the point where many original owners and potential buyers of units cannot afford to own such property or to justify its ownership. If this occurs the market value of the units in the complex may be adversely affected, causing financial loss to both owners and lenders. Because of this problem, buyers and lenders should determine the quality of management and the soundness of the financial condition of a condominium owners' association before buying or making purchase money loans on units in such a property.

f. The right to transfer one's property interest in the condominium unit is limited under the terms of the declaration. The typical restriction takes the form of a right of first refusal reserved for the benefit of the owners' association so that they can protect their interests in the property from financially irresponsible or socially incompatible owners.

State of California Legal Protections for Condominium Owners and Lenders

The condominium concept of real property ownership in the United States is a unique type of property ownership arrangement that is used mostly for ownership of residential units. Compared with owning a house on a lot or renting an apartment, ownership of a condominium unit is a relatively complicated legal and organizational situation. Examples of its complexity include the following:

1. Each owner's property rights consist of the purchased and solely owned unit; a proportionate interest in the common areas of the complex; and easement and service rights in specific common areas—hallways; elevators; electric, water, and sewer service lines.

2. The owner does not solely and directly control what is done with his or her residential environment. An owners' association board of directors (actually corporation directors elected to office by the owners of units in the complex) has the legal power to make and enforce important decisions concerning how much monthly homeowner fees should be; whether there should be special assessments, and, if so, their amount; who shall operate the complex; what the house rules should be; when and for how long the tennis courts should be open; what the proper water purity and temperature of the swimming pools should be; how much money should be spent on security guards; whether items in common areas such as carpeting and furniture should be replaced, and, if replaced, their cost.

3. Whoever runs a condominium complex determines whether it is an affordable, pleasant place to live, and the directors of the owners' association run condominiums and have the immediate legal power to make them affordable and pleasant or to price them out of the market.

4. Determining who the directors of an owners' association are to be is done through shareholder (current unit owners) voting to elect members of a corporate board of directors. This can often be a competitive, acrimonious process since the various factions that exist among the owners' usually campaign for their respective slates of directors.

5. Since condominium complexes often have a high unit density per acre, living close to people in such an environment requires effective enforcement of reasonable house rules to allow maximum use and enjoyment of individual units without depriving others of peace, quiet, and legitimate enjoyment of their property.

The legal, physical, and interpersonal complexities cited above have increasingly led to disputes among unit owners, which sometimes have led to expensive, time-consuming litigation. (General experience indicates the wiser, quicker, and much less-expensive methods of settling in-house condominium disputes among residents are negotiation or arbitration, rather than suing each other in a court of law.) Because of the relatively complex legal, physical, personal, and financial aspects of residential condominium ownership, the state of California has taken a formal interest in regulating what are considered to be critical legal, operational, and financial aspects of owning this type of property in order to provide minimum guidelines in the operation of these complexes and to protect the public. This state interest in individual property rights and the operation of the corporate owners' association manifests itself in Title 10 of the California Administrative Code, Regulations of the Real Estate Commissioner. It concerns the legal aspects of owning an interest in real property that is a condominium; the governance of the property by an owners' association board of directors; changes in costs of operating a condominium complex that are paid by individual unit owners; and changes in the covenants, conditions, and restrictions, owners' association articles of incorporation, and the corporation bylaws. Title 10 regulations are assumed to supersede conflicting provisions in the existing covenants, conditions, restrictions, articles of incorporation, and bylaws of such associations.

These regulations are significant to condominium owners and lenders because they are the legal standards for the rights and duties of owners and lenders and for the powers of owners' associations' board of directors in California. The continued financial affordability of owning a condominium unit and the financial viability of a complex's owners' association are vital to maintaining and possibly increasing the market level of value for the units in a development. Knowledge of and the ability of management and individual unit owners in the condominium property situation to apply these rules and regulations in the operation of such a property arrangement are vital to the continued success of this unique and useful real property ownership arrangement.

Converting Rental Apartments to Condominiums

It is legally possible to convert existing rental apartment complexes to the condominium form of real property ownership and to sell the individual units. To accomplish this change in the nature of ownership for each unit in a rental apartment complex, the owner of such a property needs to (1) Have the apartment units surveyed to develop a complete, accurate legal description for each unit. (2) Go to the local government agencies regulating land use that have jurisdiction over the property to be converted and obtain their approvals. These approvals usually include rezoning, zoning variances, and approval of a subdivision map for the new condominium subdivision. (3) File the necessary documents with the California Department of Real Estate, which then issues a public report allowing the owner to sell the units legally. (4) Arrange for funds to pay expenses of ownership during the conversion period such as real property taxes, any existing mortgage payments, and the cost of refurbishing or modernizing the units to be sold. (5) Give existing tenants notice of the conversion. Sometimes under conversion statutes applicable to rental apartment complexes, this advance notice has to be given a year in advance of termination of the rental apartment, provided the owner can legally require the tenants to either buy a unit or cease to be renters and vacate the premises. (6) Allow existing tenants the privilege of buying the unit they are renting at a price somewhat less than the sale price schedule for that and similar units if they buy the unit within a given period of time. (7) Replace the single large mortgage loan, if it exists—which does not allow partial reconveyances of title by the trust deed trustee, since individual apartments are sold and title conveyed to the buyers—with a trust deed loan arrangement, such as a blanket trust deed, which does allow partial conveyancing of units. (8) Arrange for take-out loan commitments for relatively long-term purchase money loans so that prospective buyers of the converted units will be able to borrow a substantial portion of the sale price of the units.

The level of activity in converting rental apartment complexes to condominiums increased substantially after 1975. The people who engaged in this did so because of the substantial profit per unit that could be made. Owning one's own home is a strong desire on the part of most Americans and, with the prices of houses escalating into the realm of the unaffordable, the most affordable home for most households soon became a condominium apartment.

In the late 1970s and into the 1980s more and more local governments placed increasingly severe restrictions that were expensive to comply with on the owners of rental apartments who were converting them to condominiums. This local government action was done under the legal authority of their police power and in order to severely slow down the decrease in the number of rental apartments due to the conversion process. Local government officials often felt, especially during the increasingly severe housing shortage that developed in the latter part of the 1970s and continued on into the 1980s, that more and more the only generally affordable housing available to a substantial portion of households was rental apartments. Since the rate of new rental apartment construction was much lower than it had been during the 1950s and 1960s, these government officials sought to preserve the number of rental apartments in their communities, even though the ordinances severely limited or virtually prohibited the conversion of rental apartments to condominiums and thus infringed upon the property rights of rental apartment owners.

Rental apartment complexes that are economically feasible to convert to condominiums are typically (1) located in desirable neighborhoods; (2) quality-built and well-designed structures with good floor plans, fully equipped with modern equipment and appliances, and effectively sound proofed; (3) equipped with suitable recreational facilities; and (4) equipped with adequate parking facilities, with each unit allocated its own exclusive parking space.

Americans still have a great desire for homeownership, and one of the most affordable homes has been and will likely be in the future the quality rental apartment converted to a condominium and sold with acceptable financing terms.

Time-Sharing Projects

Over the years the legal concept of condominium ownership has evolved through (1) building a structure originally as a condominium with individual apartments part of a subdivision or (2) converting rental apartment complexes to condominium apartments and selling them to time-sharing projects. The time-sharing concept of property ownership started in resort-type areas where the occupancy rights of each condominium apartment were divided into periods of exclusive owner occupancy—usually on a week-by-week basis. The property right for the use of a condominium for a week or several weeks could be for the duration of a specified period of time, for example, twenty, thirty, or more years or on into perpetuity like a fee interest.

The major marketing tactic used to market time-sharing interests is to emphasize that hotel rates are always increasing and that the vacationer may want to be able to vacation in such places as Las Vegas, Hawaii, Aspen,

Lake Tahoe, or on the coast of Southern California. The marketing tactic emphasizes that the buyer, in purchasing one or two weeks in a time-sharing condominium, is "freezing" the cost of staying in his or her favorite vacation spot. The usual costs of condominium apartment ownership also exist in the time-sharing arrangement—owners' association monthly fees, potential special assessments, real property taxes, and periodic mortgage payments if a loan is obtained to buy the time-sharing interest.

A significant difference between the time-sharing arrangement and the usual condominium ownership is that, in the former, fifty weeks of use are sold and twenty-five people buy two weeks each, the owners' fees are paid by twenty-five different owners rather than by just one owner.

Time-sharing interests in condominiums are defined in the California Business and Professions Code, Section 11003.5, as follows:

a.　A "time-share project" is one in which a purchaser receives the right in perpetuity, for life, or for a term of years, to the recurrent, exclusive use or occupancy of a lot, parcel, unit, or segment of real property, annually or on some other periodic basis, for a period of time that has been or will be allotted for the use or occupancy periods into which the project has been divided.

b.　A "time-share estate" is a right of occupancy in a time-share project which is coupled with an estate in the real property.

c.　A "time-share use" is a license or contractual membership right of occupancy in a time-share project which is not coupled with an estate in the real property.

The sale of time-sharing interests are regulated by the California Department of Real Estate under Section 11004.5 of the California Business and Professions Code. This statute provides that when twelve or more time-sharing estates or time-sharing uses having terms of five years or more—or terms of less than five years—with options to renew and when the time-sharing rights involve use of a dwelling unit in a structure, they constitute "subdivided lands" and a "subdivision." For time-sharing units that are within this statutory definition of a subdivision, the developer must obtain a Department of Real Estate public report before being able to legally sell property interests in California. The sale of condominium time-sharing units is considered to be the sale of interests in real property, and therefore, under the usual sales commission compensation arrangement, salespersons selling such properties are required to have a California real estate license. Other limits placed on the creation of time-sharing are ordinances by local governments severely limiting or prohibiting the creation and sale of time-sharing units in various communities.

Time-sharing sales efforts have been most successful when the condominium units are located in desirable and easily accessible locations. Therefore, in a practical economic sense, locales in the United States where time-sharing interests can be successfully marketed are limited in number.

To increase the attractiveness of time-sharing interests to potential buyers, developers can arrange to have their complexes participate in a listing of time-sharing units. The owned weeks can be traded from location to location by owners of various weeks. Thus, if you own the last week of December at a Lake Tahoe time-sharing condominium and you prefer to play golf during your week instead of ski, you can, through the time-sharing exchange service, trade your week for the week someone else owns in a Scottsdale, Arizona, condominium.

Investing in time-sharing unit properties or financing them is a very specialized field of real estate activity. It is expected that the development and marketing of condominium time-sharing interests will continue to be limited to the better known, more desirable and affordable resort areas.

This discussion of cooperatives and condominiums is merely an overall view of the structures and the problems of these types of properties. In the future there will be much discussion of these concepts, especially of the condominium. There are a number of important practical problems incident to the condominium that could become critical if the building is severely damaged or destroyed or if unreasonable, capricious people acquire an ownership interest in the property. The ultimate resolution of such problems will be found in the provisions of the agreements between the parties, in state statutes, and in judicial interpretations of both these sources of authority. If a reasonable, forward-looking approach is taken to condominium development, it has great potential for residential, industrial, and commercial properties in urban areas.

JUNIOR LIENS

Nature and Characteristics

A *junior lien* is a deed of trust or mortgage given by a borrower, using as security real estate against which a first lien has already been given. A junor lien may be a second, third, fourth, fifth, or even a sixth obligation secured by a mortgage or deed of trust.

The order in which a deed of trust or mortgage appears against the property is determined, not by the date of the instrument, but by the date on which the instrument is recorded. The deed of trust or mortgage recorded first holds the prior lien. Thus, a note secured by a deed of trust held as an unrecorded document may find itself in a secondary position even though this was not the intent of the borrower or lender; in this way a subsequent loan recorded before the intended first deed of trust or mortgage would become the first lien.

A junior lien document need not indicate that it is a junior lien, although in some instances its status as a junior lien is stated in the body of the instrument at the time it is prepared.

The holder of a junior lien has the right to foreclose against the property in case of a default. In case of such a foreclosure, consideration must be given to the first lien. If there is considerable equity in the property, it is possible that at the foreclosure sale a bid will be given that will allow both the first lien and the junior lien to be cleared. If the bid is such that there is a surplus after paying all expenses and obligations, this amount will revert to the individual in default and against whom foreclosure was brought.

In most cases of a foreclosure of a junior lien, the holder of the junior lien wants to be able to assume the payments on the first lien. If he or she cannot do this, he or she must be in a position to bid a sufficient amount to clear the first lien and to satisfy the expenses of the foreclosure. Clearly, junior liens are more hazardous than first liens; consequently, the interest rate is higher and as a rule the note is written for a shorter period.

If the holder of the junior lien does not check frequently with the holder of the first lien, a default can occur in the first lien without the holder of the junior lien being aware of the default. In that case the first lien may be foreclosed without the holder of the junior lien even knowing that the loan was in trouble. There are cases on file in which the junior lien has been kept in a current position but the first lien has been allowed to go into default. To forestall such a situation, the holder of the junior lien should record a request for notice of default and sale with the county recorder in the county in which the property is located. With this request filed, the holder of the junior lien will be notified should a default occur that leads to foreclosure procedures. Of course, the default of the first lien constitutes a default of the second lien although it may be in a current position as far as payments are concerned.

Should a first lien be foreclosed without the holder of the second lien appearing to protect himself or herself by bidding on the property, and should a sale be made, all subsequent junior liens are eliminated and any interest that the holders of the junior liens might have in the property is lost.

In the case of junior liens, it is necessary to know whether the lien is for a purchase money obligation or whether it is merely for additional funds for use of the owner of the property. If it is not for a purchase money contract and the first lien is foreclosed without adequate

funds being obtained to discharge the second or junior lien, the holder of the junior lien has the right to bring suit against the borrower on his or her personal property. If the junior lien is for a purchase money obligation, the holder of the junior lien does not have such a right.

It used to be illegal for institutional lenders such as savings and loan associations and commercial banks to make a real estate loan secured by a junior lien unless they also held the first lien on the property at the time the second trust deed loan was made. In 1977 this situation was changed: These institutional lenders can now make such loans. Commercial banks now commonly call such second lien priority loans "home equity" or "homeowners" loans. Typical terms are a maximum amount of $25,000 or 80 percent of the market value of the single-family residential property minus the outstanding amount of the existing debt secured by the first trust deed. The loan repayment term can range from five to twenty-five years, and the usual interest rate is from 10 to 17 percent per annum. Such loans from banks ordinarily have no repayment penalty provision. In making such second trust deed loans, the bank considers the borrower's financial ability to repay both the existing first loan and the contemplated additional junior lien debt. Commercial banks have long had the authority to make home improvement loans that are in effect junior loans against such property. Where a bank also holds the existing first trust deed loan against a residence, in the process of making another loan to the borrower on the property, it will often prepare a notice of additional advance against the previously recorded deed of trust or mortgage, rather than a new deed of trust or mortgage for recording. This notice of additional advance must be recorded so that subsequent lenders may be on notice that such an advance has been made.

Importance of Junior Mortgages

Prior to the advent of the FHA, junior mortgages were a common and well-accepted manner of financing property. Such mortgages were necessary because of the relatively low loans that were possible in relationship to the value of the property. Also during this time, because of the lack of an amortization procedure, most junior mortgages were on a flat basis, as were the first mortgages.

It was common practice for no payment to be made on the junior mortgage until the first mortgage matured and was paid off, at which time the junior mortgage became the first mortgage.

In the Great Depression so many losses were suffered by holders of second trust deeds or second mortgages that such financing fell into disuse; not until after World War II did the second mortgage again become a popular adjunct to the real estate financing field. However, the character of the second or junior lien has changed considerably since the mid-1930s. Today almost all first liens require a monthly amortization of principal, and most are based on a long-term maturity. Partly because of this practice the second or junior lien should also be amortized; otherwise, because of the length of the first lien, exposure to risk would be so great that most investors would be unwilling to accept it. Consequently, present-day junior liens are usually amortized with a monthly reduction in principal amount, as are first liens. In this way the owner's equity increases each month and the risk to the lender diminishes.

Studies made in 1975 showed that junior liens of some kind were involved in three out of four sales. From 1979 to 1982 the ratio was much higher due to the extensive use of creative financing.

Junior Lien Financing

Basically, junior financing originates in four ways: (1) as a direct loan to the homeowner for his or her use; (2) as a direct loan to the homeowner for improvements to his or her home; (3) as a loan given by the seller of property to the purchaser to supplement the first trust deed so that the sale of property may be consummated; and (4) as a note and a deed of trust or mortgage given to a real estate salesperson for his or her commission or for a portion of his or her commission in connection with the sale of a property in which the cash changing hands is inadequate to pay the agent's or broker's commission.

Many emergencies arise in everyday life, requiring immediate funds: medical expenses, educational expenses, or even transportation replacement. Frequently repayment under the normal procedures would place an undue hardship upon the borrower. Also, the individual may not be able to qualify for a personal loan. Therefore, junior lien financing is used; it gives a smaller monthly payment, is spread over a longer time period, and is usually at a slightly lower interest rate than could be obtained if the financing were done on a personal loan basis.

Junior financing is also used for improvement to property. Such improvements are always expensive, and under a home improvement loan they require a discounted interest rate or gross rate interest spread over a short period. When the improvement to the property is an addition to the home, or the construction of an additional building, the monthly charge for repayment under a home improvement loan would be difficult for a person of modest means to maintain. The homeowner therefore goes to the junior financing market for his or her funds and is able to complete the desired improvements.

The third manner in which the junior lien originates is through the sale of property when the purchaser does not have adequate money to pay for the equity held by the owner. This source of financing is interesting because it involves equity that in some instances needs to be used at a later date by the seller. For a long time the fact that the seller would have to discount the face amount of a note to dispose of it, should the need arise, was not taken into consideration. This resulted in a hardship and a loss to the seller when it became necessary for him or her to convert the junior lien to cash.

For instance, assume a property with a value of $15,000, against which it was possible for the purchaser to obtain a conventional loan of $10,000. Mr. A paid Mr. B $1,000 in cash and gave a junior lien in the amount of $4,000. At that point Mr. B had received $1,000 in cash for his $5,000 equity and a $4,000 note secured by a junior lien against the property. Mr. B moved into another community and found a home that he desired to buy. However, to buy the house it was necessary for him to have $3,000 in cash. He had the $1,000 from his previous home and the $4,000 second lien. He approached the junior financing market for cash on his lien, only to find that for his note worth $4,000 he could obtain only $2,5000. Since he was desperate for a home, he sold the note for $2,500, thus suffering a loss of $1,500 which, in turn, was a loss of his prior equity. As such situations became common knowledge, the sales price of the original home was increased to take into consideration the discount that the holder of the second lien would have to accept, should he or she sell it. Thus, in our example, instead of the property selling for $15,000, it would have sold for $16,500, and when it became necessary for the junior lien holder to cash in the note, he or she would have obtained the full amount of the equity that he or she had in the home.

Any second mortgage agreement between buyer and seller should consider several points for the protection of the seller. First, the contract term should be relatively short, usually not over five years. Second, the interest rate should approximate 16 percent. Third, the repayment schedule should provide for as large a payment as the buyer can safely handle. Fourth, the contract should provide for an acceleration clause in case the new owner should decide to sell the property. This would allow the loan to be called immediately. Fifth, the down payment should be large enough to cover the broker's commission and closing costs. Sixth, a demand for notice of default should be recorded. Seventh, the fire insurance policy should name the seller "as his or her interest appears."

It would be appropriate to mention here that since second trust deeds are not permitted in the original financing under FHA or VA loans, the use of junior financing in connection with the sale of a home must be limited to those homes upon which conventional financing is made. These are usually older homes or homes in areas in which the FHA or VA may not guarantee loans.

The final type of junior financing is a note given in lieu of cash for a commission. This again involves property that is not qualified for FHA or VA loans and on which there is not adequate down payment to cover the commission due to the agent or broker.

SOURCES OF JUNIOR FINANCING

Individuals are by far the greatest source for junior financing. An individual does not have government restrictions upon the amount of loans he or she can make, upon the loan-to-value ratio, or upon the term for which the loan can be drawn. A great number of individuals who have accumulated savings and who are looking for a high rate of return will use their savings for junior lien financing. Some individuals will even borrow to make junior lien loans; however, they must have a financial position that is sizable and liquid. The lending institution will analyze the existing junior liens that the individual has and determine whether they are strong or weak. If the lien is weak they may consider it a liability rather than an asset and consider the amount of the first lien that it would be necessary for the individual to assume, should it become necessary to be protected on his or her second.

Another source of junior lien financing is savings and loan associations. While such loans have in the past been restricted in the sense that the borrower must already have owed the association on a first lien loan before he or she was allowed to borrow on a second lien, as of 1977 that situation changed. As of that year savings and loan associations were authorized to make junior lien loans often comparable in amount, terms, and criteria for making such loans to those offered by commercial banks in California. There are some differences in amounts and terms from lender to lender and borrower to borrower.

Certain other organizations are also in the business of making junior lien loans. One type of organization comes under the Industrial Loan Law; a good example of this is the Fireside Thrift Company, with offices in northern California. This organization makes personal loans as well as real estate loans and accepts deposits with the understanding that they will be loaned to qualified borrowers. When an applicant approaches such an organization for a loan, an appraisal of the property is made and 75 percent of the quick sales price is determined. From this amount the first lien is subtracted, and the organization will lend the difference, except for $2,000. The owner is required to have at least a $2,000 equity in the property. In other words, an appraisal determines that a property is worth $45,000 on a quick sale; 75 percent of this amount is $33,750. There is already a first lien for $20,000, giving the owners an equity of

$13,750. Since they must retain an unencumbered $2,000 equity, they would be able to borrow only $11,750. In 1982 these organizations were able to make loans having maturities from one to eight and one-half years in length, depending on the property and the borrower. The interest charged was from 21 to 23 percent. No points were charged on loans under $10,000, and there were no prepayment penalties.

This type of organization can make loans secured by either first or second liens. The interest is high, but they are a good source of swing loans.

An organization operating under the Industrial Loan Law can make a loan in two ways. It can make a regular real estate loan, in which case it will obtain a preliminary report, record the deed of trust, and obtain a title insurance policy charging the expenses of the loan to the borrower. Or, if the lending officer feels that such expense and formality are not necessary, the organization can take a deed of trust and record it without obtaining the title policy or preliminary report.

Mortgage brokers who specialize in the sale of junior liens are another source of junior financing.

Interest Rates and Terms

Junior financing involves a greater risk than first trust deed financing; consequently the interest rate is always higher. This follows the axiom of the greater the risk, the greater the yield. When a second trust deed or any junior lien is sold, it is usually sold at a discount from its face value. This discount allows the holder to realize a higher yield than the named interest in the note; however, it is illegal for an individual making a junior lien loan to extract a discount from that note. Such a discount is considered a violation of the usury law.

The terms for most junior liens are short, usually five years or less. In most instances there will be a balloon payment, which the holder of the lien will sometimes refinance. Most junior liens are also on an amortizing basis, although in recent years some property has been sold with a flat note being taken by the seller for a five-year period on an interest-only basis. Such a note has often been accepted with the understanding that at the end of five years the property will be refinanced and the secondary lien paid off.

Secondary Market for Junior Liens

There is a secondary market for junior liens because of the high yield on these loans. The secondary market consists of individuals and organizations established primarily for the purpose of purchasing junior liens. Real estate brokers may also act as loan brokers, in which case they must comply with the real estate law. Refer to Article 7 of the California Real Estate Law for the regulations under which real estate loan brokers must operate.

In some communities a real estate loan exchange has been organized. Invitations for bids on the mortgages and trust deeds are extended and such offers are made to the holders of the notes. If the offer meets with the holder's approval, the assignment of note and deed of trust is made to the new purchaser and the exchange receives a commission for the transaction. Such organizations act only as intermediaries and are not subject to the Real Estate Loan Brokers Act.

QUESTIONS

1. Miscellaneous classifications of trust deeds in California include
   a. purchase money
   b. package
   c. blanket
   d. junior
   e. all of the above

2. One result of the tremendous financial losses on mortgaged residential real estate during the Great Depression of the 1930s was that
   a. the term loan repayment schedule to pay off such debts was initially adopted generally in the United States
   b. the variable interest rate mortgage became very popular
   c. foreclosing upon residential mortgages where homeowners were the mortgagors was generally outlawed
   d. the amortized mortgage debt repayment schedule came into general use
   e. all of the above

3. Unpaid improvers of real property (material suppliers, general contractors, subcontractors, and laborers) may seek legal recourse for payment if not voluntarily paid for their improvements of specific projects by filing a lien against the property they improved. This lien is known as a mechanic's lien. Important legal aspects of the enforceability of the mechanic's lien are
   a. that the mechanic's lien claimants have a state of California contractor's license that is valid when contracting for a job and throughout the entire construction period
   b. that a preliminary twenty-day notice be properly delivered to the owner for whom the improvement work is being done and to any construction lenders
   c. that the mechanic's lien claimants file mechanic's liens in the county recorder's office of the county where the improved property is located within the

limited filing time provided by law after completion of all improvements
   d. that the improver of the property who seeks to file a mechanic's lien against it due to nonpayment for work or materials actually comes within the legal definition of an improver of real property in California
   e. all of the above

4. The following is (are) true concerning real estate construction contracts:
   a. They have no relationship to real estate construction loan agreements.
   b. If the owner of the land being improved and the architect who designed the structure agree that besides designing the structure the architect should supervise the construction, the architect is typically an agent of the owner in dealing with the general contractor and subcontractors.
   c. Requiring performance bonds as a condition precedent for accepting a general contracting firm as the general contractor for a construction job does not make any financial sense for the property owner.
   d. There are no legally defined performance standards applicable to the performance of general contractors in constructing buildings.
   e. All of the above

5. A junior lien is
   a. any note and deed of trust or mortgage given by a borrower using as security real estate against which a first lien has already been given
   b. a note and deed of trust given as security by individuals who have not reached their majority
   c. a lien that is second after the first lien
   d. a first lien against real estate given by a corporation in the name of an individual

6. Most junior liens made in the period from 1979–1982 were secured through
   a. savings and loan associations
   b. banks
   c. individuals
   d. mortgage bankers

7. The following are the substantial differences between a first trust deed and a second trust deed under normal conditions:
   a. A second trust deed is usually for a shorter term.
   b. A second trust deed is usually for less money.

c. A second trust deed usually yields higher interest.

d. All of the above.

8. A junior lien can be foreclosed if
   a. the payments are at least 120 days past due
   b. there has been an error in computing the annual percentage rate and it has been stated incorrectly
   c. the holder of a lien having precedence over the junior lien files a notice of default
   d. the borrower dies

9. A junior lien may be used to
   a. provide the owner of the property with funds that can be paid over a longer period of time than an unsecured loan
   b. provide for closing a gap between the sales price, first mortgage, and down payment
   c. provide funds to pay a real estate commission when the buyer does not have enough cash to close a sale
   d. all of the above

BIBLIOGRAPHY

BOWMAN, ARTHUR G., and W. D. MILLIGAN, *Real Estate Law in California* (6th ed.), Englewood Cliffs, NJ: Prentice-Hall, 1982.

KRATOVIL, ROBERT, and RAYMOND J. WERNER, *Real Estate Law* (7th ed.), Englewood Cliffs, NJ: Prentice-Hall, 1979.

10

Loan Applications, Processing, and Closing

PRIMARY FUNCTION OF A REAL ESTATE LOAN DEPARTMENT

The primary function of any real estate loan department is to acquire good loans secured by deeds of trust on desirable property owned by people or corporations of integrity who are able and willing to pay off their obligations over a period of time. The origin of the loan applications will vary with the type of organization making the loan.

Banks and savings and loan associations, because of close proximity to their depositors, enjoy direct application from their clients. They may also receive referrals from real estate brokers in connection with sales being made and, under certain conditions and when money is extremely plentiful, they may even use mortgage brokers. Life insurance companies, except for field offices, depend largely upon the mortgage broker and the mortgage banker for the placement of their funds.

All funds used for loans are someone's surplus that has been saved through the individual's efforts to accumulate a backlog of capital. These funds can be represented by savings accounts in banks or savings and loan associations, or by the premiums that have been paid to insurance companies and are available to the insurance companies for investment; they can be funds, such as retirement deposits for future benefits, that have been paid by individuals in certain organizations; or they can be funds set aside by any one of numerous methods available, as in cases of institutional lenders and retirements funds.

There are legal restrictions on the types of investments and loans that can be made. In the case of the individual who has accumulated sufficient monies to enter the real estate field and make loans against deeds of trust or mortgages, the only restrictions are those established by good judgment as to the property and the borrower. The loans that he or she obtains usually originate with real estate brokers or with referrals from bankers whom he or she has advised of an interest in making loans secured by deeds of trust that may not quite meet the standards of the bank.

Institutions and individuals who wish to make real estate loans are interested in revenue from the funds they have accumulated; therefore, it is natural for them to consider the possibility of loans as well as bond investments. In considering loans it is natural for them to take security when it is available. Since many of these loans are to be long-term loans, a nonwasting type of asset should be used as security. We therefore find institutions and individuals taking first trust deeds against property and, in some instances, junior liens.

In making loans of this type the organization or individual is interested in the income from the principal, not in buying real estate. Often a broker trying to sell a loan to an institution will ask the lending officer if the institution would like to have the piece of property for the amount of the loan. This proposal sounds attractive, but when the lender tries to acquire a property under such circumstances he or she invariably does not acquire the property for the cost of the loan, since the very process of foreclosing is expensive. In many instances, foreclosing results in much adverse advertising and criticism. The very necessity for a foreclosure indicates that no market exists for that piece of property at the price that would satisfy the first deed of trust and other obligations against the property. If there were such a market, the borrower would have sold the property. At the trustee's sale, therefore, the lender would probably receive the property on its own bid and would then find it necessary to carry the property as a nonproductive asset. After foreclosure and before selling the property, the lender might have to remodel the property completely, since foreclosure would indicate an economic problem of the borrower, who probably would have allowed the property to depreciate long before the lender had to foreclose. Even after remodeling, the length of time the lender might be forced to carry the property as a nonproductive asset would depend upon the economic conditions of the area. Certainly a lender does not want to buy real estate under these circumstances. If he or she is looking for investments in real estate he or she will purchase on the open market the type of real estate that will be beneficial.

To be protected and to be able to analyze the applications received, the lender customarily accepts a formal written application and then makes an appraisal of the property to determine its current market value.

SUPERVISION OF LOANS

The second important function of the real estate loan department is the supervision of loan applications received and loans made.

The approval of a loan is granted only after a thorough investigation of the individual from the information detailed on the application and after a review of the appraisal to see that the amount of the loan is within the lender's legal limits. After the loan has been approved and the funds disbursed, the problem of servicing the loan arises. Proper servicing often makes a highly satisfactory loan of one that promised to be only mediocre. On the other hand, improper servicing often allows a loan that should have been most satisfactory to become a problem.

One of the first obligations of loan servicing is to see that the monthly or current payments are made by the borrower and are currently processed into payments to interest and principal. In some cases the lender requires not only that the borrower pay the interest and the principal in periodic payments, but that a proration of the taxes and insurance be included in those payments. In such a case the lender must establish for the borrower a trust fund to which these payments are credited, so that when fire insurance and property taxes fall due, sufficient funds will be available to satisfy these obligations without calling upon the borrower for additional payments. Each year the lender must review the charges on fire insurance and taxes to be sure that the amount being impounded is sufficient to cover the charges when they fall due. If sufficient funds are not available, he or she must notify the borrower that an additional payment is necessary each month to build up the trust fund.

The real estate loan department in its servicing program must also be sure that the property is adequately covered by fire insurance and by comprehensive insurance. In some areas in which other hazards are normal, the lender may require additional insurance, such as earthquake or flood insurance. The lender must then be sure that such coverage is in force at all times and that it is adequate to cover the amount of the loan in case of loss.

In some cases of 100 percent financing it is difficult to obtain insurance for the full amount of the loan, since the cost covers not only the improvements on the property but also the real property itself. In these cases, the insurance should cover at least the amount of the loan less the appraised value of the land.

In California, delinquent taxes can threaten ownership of property and the property can revert to the state or to the district assessing the ad valorem tax after five years of tax delinquency. The lender must therefore be certain that the taxes are paid at all times, which is accomplished by a search of the records and by a review of the publication of tax delinquencies. Many organizations are now using agencies such as the California Tax Service, which will review, for a fee, the records of the various taxing agencies and determine any delinquency on the property against which the lender holds a deed of trust. If such a delinquency occurs, the lender is notified and it becomes his or her responsibility to see that the tax delinquency is cured. The fees that such agencies charge are certainly reasonable, considering the accuracy achieved and the time saved.

A third responsibility under the servicing of a real estate loan is a periodic inspection of the property to determine that it is being properly maintained and that no undue depreciation is occurring. All deeds of trust provide for periodic inspections of the property and for ready access to the property. Inspection can cure several potential dangers. In some instances the cancellation of a fire insurance policy can be forestalled by requiring over-abundant high weeds to be trimmed. If the property is empty and the fire insurance policy contains no provision for a vacancy factor, the fire insurance may possibly be cancelled. Therefore, as a portion of the servicing program, frequent and periodic inspection of the property should be made. In any event, a prompt inspection should be made whenever the property loan becomes delinquent. When foreclosure seems likely, a new appraisal should be made of the property to determine whether the lender is still adequately secured.

A fourth servicing duty occurs when the property is sold without being refinanced. At the time the new owner takes over the property, all the records in the office must be changed to show the new owner's name. However, a cross index should be maintained to show that this property at one time belonged to the original owner, so that, should any question arise concerning this particular individual or the property owned by him or her, it can be determined that he or she no longer has an interest in the property and that it is now owned by the person assuming the mortgage. Insurance papers must be reviewed to be certain that the proper endorsements have been obtained. Tax records must be changed so that the lending agency will continue to receive notification of taxes when they become due. In cases of FHA or VA loans, the servicing agency or the servicing department must file with the FHA the notification of an assumption by the new borrower.

A fifth obligation of the servicing department is to see that in cases of serious delinquency steps are taken to protect the lender, even to the point of foreclosure. As a rule, people will pay their real estate loan before they pay other obligations, since it is most important that they have a roof over their heads. Therefore, the lender usually finds that when a serious delinquency occurs, it is not the only delinquency. There are often many other creditors, many of them making demands impossible for the borrower to meet, and possibly even filing liens through suits against the property. The lender, of course, has no obligation to such creditors; however, they do complicate matters and since an extended delinquency deprives the lender of the income to which he or she is entitled from the loan, good servicing sees that such a loss does not become extensive, either by filing foreclosure as soon as feasible or by bringing pressure to bear so that the delinquency is cured.

To hold such losses to a minimum, the lender is very interested in the property against which he or she is loaning and in the individual to whom the loan is made. For self-protection and to obtain information about the property and the borrower, the lender customarily takes formal applications for real estate loans.

REAL ESTATE SETTLEMENT PROCEDURES ACT

On June 20, 1975, the Real Estate Settlement Procedures Act (RESPA) of 1974 (Public Law 93533) became effective. It was an attempt by Congress to reduce real estate loan costs by requiring the lender to give a full and accurate estimate of all closing costs at least twelve days before closing. The Act also required that a booklet be given to every loan applicant at the time of the loan application, to inform the prospective buyer-borrower of a one- to four-family residential dwelling of the nature and costs of the settlement procedures. The advance disclosure of costs must be given at the time the loan is committed. The theory was that the buyer-borrower would then have twelve days to look for a better loan with lower closing cost. The twelve-day wait was required even if the borrower was satisfied with the proposed transaction.

In the case of a residence that was not owner-occupied (by the seller), the Act required that the purchase price

paid by the seller and the date of acquisition be disclosed to the buyer, if the property had been owned by the seller for over two years. It also stated that the advance disclosure and a copy of the truth-in-lending disclosure be given before the signing of any documents such as a note or deed of trust. The Act then required that a closing statement showing actual costs be delivered to the borrower within three days of closing.

The Act had no sooner gone into effect before it became evident that parts of it were causing more problems than it was curing. Lender costs because of lost time were translated into increasing costs to the borrower, and information concerning property owned for more than two years was difficult to obtain because of resistance from sellers and real estate sales people. Because of these problems, the Act was revised and the amendments became effective on January 2, 1976.

The new Act does not provide for advance disclosure; however, the lender must give a good-faith estimate of the amount, or range, of charges for certain closing costs at the time of the application for the loan or no later than three business days after the application has been made. The lender must give HUD Form 1 (Uniform Settlement Statement) to the borrower one day before settlement so that he or she will have an opportunity to review the charges on the statement at that time.

The lender may require that certain people or firms be used for legal work, title insurance, or title examination, and that the borrower pay for these services. In such cases the lender must tell the borrower of this requirement, give a cost estimate of the service, and state whether the people or firms do business with the lender.

It is no longer necessary to notify the buyer of non–owner-occupied property of the date of acquisition if the seller has owned the property more than two years, or to notify him or her of the purchase price. The cost of improvements does not have to be disclosed. The new RESPA booklet, made available on July 1, 1976, must be given to the loan applicant at the time of the application.

Loan trust funds can be established by the lender at the time the loan is closed, but for no more than the amount needed for the payment of the insurance and taxes plus two months' deposit.

The lender cannot charge a fee for the preparation of the uniform settlement statement or the truth-in-lending statement. Since the uniform settlement statement shows all the charges made, it is no longer necessary to show them on the truth-in-lending statement. The annual percentage rate must be given along with the total of the payments and the finance charge on all but purchase money loans. The APR is all that has to be disclosed on a purchase money loan.

Some loans are exempt from RESPA, such as junior

liens, home improvement loans, loans secured by liens on other than a residential unit, loans on property larger than twenty-five acres, loans to refinance an existing loan, construction loans, loans to buy vacant land, loans on homes less than one year old, and home loans eligible for sale to FNMA, GNMA, or FHLMC.

Organizations that must comply with RESPA include any lending agency that makes over $100,000 per year in real estate loans; and any agency connected with any part of the federal government, such as the Federal Reserve Bank, the Comptroller of the Currency, the Federal Deposit Insurance Corporation, and the Federal Savings and Loan Insurance Corporation. Thus, state- and federally chartered banks that are members of the Federal Deposit Insurance Corporation, and state- and federally chartered savings and loan associations that are covered by the Federal Savings and Loan Insurance Corporation are affected.

NATURE AND PURPOSE OF A LOAN APPLICATION

The *application* as given to a real estate lender is a formal declaration of the applicant for the loan. It is one side of the contract, saying, in effect, that for a loan of a certain amount, the borrower will deliver title insurance on the property described in the application, a deed of trust, and a note secured by that deed of trust that constitutes a lien on the property, subject only to the taxes that might be due but not payable, to rights of way, to normal easements and other acceptable liens. The borrower also states that in consideration of the loan he or she will make certain payments over a period of time.

If the lender accepts the application, it becomes a contract, and the loan is processed. The application provides the lender with preliminary information from which he or she is able to draw certain conclusions concerning the applicant and the property. In many instances it will show whether such a loan is possible or practical, and it will often forestall additional work.

The application provides the borrower and the lender with a permanent record of the borrower's statement and of the initial steps taken in connection with the loan application. In case of fraud or misstatement, such information could mean the difference between a loss and a profit on a real estate loan.

BASIC CONTENT OF THE APPLICATION

A real estate loan application is usually divided into three parts. The first is the application for the loan, including the amount requested, the monthly payments, the term, and the interest rate. The second part of the application gives a complete description of the property, including the street address (for the convenience of the appraiser), the legal description (to be used in ordering a preliminary title report), and a description of the improvements. The third part asks for information about the applicant complete enough so that a credit report can be ordered from it. The appraisal, although not completed at the time of the application and not a part of the application, is as necessary to the application as the other three.

The first item on the application is usually the applicant's name. If the application is for a purchase money loan, the name on the application should be exactly the same as that under which the individual anticipates taking title at the time of the sale. If the applicant now owns the property but is borrowing for some purpose other than purchase, the applicant's name should be the same as that under which the title is vested at the present time. The lending institution will therefore be sure to have the note and the deed of trust drawn in the proper form so that no question can be raised to place a cloud upon the title regarding the legality of the documents used.

The application should also be dated as of the date it is made. At this point it should include a formal statement of the applicant and detailed request for the loan, which could read something like this:

An application is hereby made for a loan of _____ dollars to bear interest at the rate of _____ percent per year, to mature in _____ years, to be repaid in installments of _____ dollars per month or per year plus (or including) interest and to be secured by a first trust deed to the following real estate, situated in the city of _____ , county of _____ , California.

When such a statement is made, there can be no misunderstanding at a future date should the borrower claim that the loan being tendered to him or her is not the one for which he or she applied.

The formal statement could also indicate the purposes for which the loan was being requested.

Now that the name of the individual, the amount of loan, and the terms under which it is to be repaid are known, the property itself should be described. The first description is usually of its location. If there is a street address, it should be shown. It is helpful to the individual looking for the property for purposes of appraisal or identification if the application indicates on which side of the street (according to compass direction) the property is located. If there is no street address, the person taking the application should indicate the distance from the closest intersection and should give either some indication of a landmark or a brief description of the property so that the appraiser can recognize it when making his or her inspection. This description might read as follows:

This property is located 850 feet south of the intersection of Main Street and Tenth Avenue; it is on the west side of the street; the house is white stucco with a green composition roof, and there is a pink mailbox at the roadside.

Following the street address is the legal description of the property as it is recorded and described in the county records. It is easy to see a piece of property and say "There it is" or "It extends from the road to the fence at the rear." However, it is described differently in the county records. This description could be of several different types, for example, the lot, block, and tract:

Lot 5, Block 2, in the City of Bottletown, County of Amador, State of California, as per Map recorded in Book 55, Page 42 of Maps, in the office of the Recorder of said County.

The property might also be described with reference to the government survey of sections and townships, in which case the legal description might read as follows:

The west one-half of the northeast one-quarter of the southeast one-quarter of the northeast one-quarter of Section 8, Township 9 North, Range 6 East Mt. Diablo Base and Meridian.*

The legal description could also be a metes and bounds description, in which case the description might be similar to this:

All that portion of lot 173 as shown on the official Map of Orange Vale Colony, filed in the office of the County Recorder of Sacramento County on September 18, 1895, in Book 3 of Maps, Map No. 20, more particularly described as follows:

Beginning at a point in the center line of Hazel Avenue which said center line is the east line of said tract No. 173 which point of beginning is south a distance of 330′ from the northeast corner of tract 173 and the point of intersection of the center line of Hazel Avenue and Central Water Avenue; thence running westerly on the line parallel with the north line of said tract 173 a distance of 660′ to a point in the west line of said tract 173, then southerly along the west line of said tract 173 a distance of 156′ to a point, said point being located northerly 174′ from the southwest corner of said tract 173; thence south 174′ and parallel with the west line of said tract 173 to a point in the south line of said tract 173, then east 184.5′ along the south line of said tract 173 to the southeast corner of said tract 173 and a point in the central line of Hazel Avenue, thence northerly along the east line of said tract 173 and the center line of said Hazel Avenue a distance of 330′ to the point of beginning.

With a legal description such as one of these, it is possible to determine all the vested interests as well as

*See figure 10-1 at the end of this chapter for ways to compute the area contained in such a description.

any liens that might exist against the property. This determination is made by referring the legal description to a title insurance company and obtaining a preliminary report of title, or, if one knows how, by a personal search of the records. However, today almost everyone uses a title insurance company. This company's preliminary report, although not insuring the title to be as it is reported, is a good indication of the items that may have been placed against the described property. For instance, there might be a payable street assessment or unpaid city or county ad valorem taxes. If the taxes have been paid the preliminary report will show them as such and will show the amount. If someone has loaned money against the property, it will show as an exception to the title. Leases against the property will also be shown. It is possible for owners to grant a right of way or easement across land; if such an easement or right of way has been granted, the preliminary report will reveal it and the lender and the appraiser must consider their effect on the property. After an inspection of the preliminary title report, the lender can tell whether the property would be acceptable to him or her as security.

The loan application should include a question as to whether there is a first lien on the property and also one as to any junior liens that might be on the property. Thus, if there is a contract of sale that is not recorded, it will show up on the application. An undisclosed contract of sale might also be revealed should the appraiser find someone other than the borrower or the seller in control of the property.

The application should also ask whether any improvements have been made on the property within the last ninety days, which would give some indication whether there could be any mechanic's or labor liens on the property.

There should also be a short description of the property and improvements. If it is a single-family dwelling, the type of construction and the number of rooms, stories, bedrooms, and baths should be indicated. If it is a multiunit residential property, the number of rooms and stories and the type of construction would again be pertinent.

If it is commercial, industrial, or other nonresidential property, there should be a brief description of the property and improvements. If leased, the terms of the lease, as to both the rent and the length of lease, should be stated. The application should also reveal the length of time the lease has to run.

If there are buildings separate from the residential dwelling or from the buildings described above, they should be described briefly.

The application should then indicate the length of time the borrower has owned the property, if he or she owns it, the purchase price paid when it was purchased, and the manner in which it was acquired, whether by full payment of cash, by exchange, or by some other means. If the borrower is purchasing the property at the present time, the purchase price should be shown, together with the down payment that is proposed.

If there is to be a junior lien, the conditions of the junior lien should be enumerated, giving the terms, the monthly payments, and the amount involved. The information is desirable so that the lender will know whether the individual will have sufficient income to cover all expenses involved.

If the property is multifamily residential property or commercial income property, other information should be made available to the lending institution. First, there should be a schedule of income that is expected or that is now being received. Operating expenses should be shown, including management, wages, gas, oil, lights, power, water, supplies, telephone, laundry, elevator, repairs, and other miscellaneous expenses. Information should be given regarding the real estate ad valorem tax and personal property tax. The lender should also be interested in the insurance expense connected with producing the income, which could include fire insurance on the building and on furniture and equipment, liability insurance, earthquake insurance, flood insurance if required, and other types of hazard insurance. The lender is also interested in repairs and in maintenance such as roof repairs, papering, painting, plumbing, and furniture replacement. This information is necessary not only to the lender, but also to the appraiser, since he or she will be using it in the income approach to value when he or she makes the appraisal for the lender.

The first part of the application provides a good understanding of the property and its expenses. The second part of the application deals with the borrower. It is first of all desirable to know by whom the applicant is employed, and since his or her spouse may join in the purchase of the property or in the borrowing against it, unless the borrower is dealing with his or her sole and separate property, the lender will want to know by whom the spouse is employed, if the spouse is gainfully employed. The addresses of the employers of both applicants should be given, as well as the type of business in which they are engaged. The lender is interested in knowing how long each individual has held his or her present position, as this gives some indication of that person's stability. If the individual has not held the same job for at least two years, additional information of the same type should be obtained for previous employers, for at least a two-year period.

The application should reveal the annual income from employment for both the applicant and the co-applicant. Any other income, such as rentals, interest, royalties, or a second job, should also be shown for both of them.

Other personal information that should be on the application is the number and age of each of the applicant's dependents. This information helps the person analyzing the application to understand the potential net income available to the individual from his or her employment and other sources. Knowing the ages of the dependents helps determine whether the expense of the dependents will continue for a long or short period.

The application should reveal any monthly payments that the individual is now making. In the case of a home that is already owned, it should show the amount of the monthly payment now being made. In the case of a home purchase, it should show the amount of rent paid in the past or the home mortgage payment for the previous home. The monthly payment for furniture, automobiles, and clothing should also be listed.

The application should also reveal whether there is life insurance, and if there is, how much and the name of the company that is insuring the applicant. Any cash value to the policies should also show. If there are loans against the policies, this obligation should be shown so that the lender has some knowledge of whether funds are available to take care of the loan, should a protracted illness cause the wage earner to be without an income, or whether there would be sufficient funds to clear the indebtedness, should the wage earner die. It is always poor business from a public relations standpoint to foreclose on a widow or a church, and a lending institution would not want to find itself in a position requiring such foreclosure because of lack of life insurance. If the lending institution is a bank, its application will ask for the name of the bank with which the individual is doing business and for the types of accounts that he or she carries. If the account is not at the lending bank, it will probably request that the applicant consider moving his or her account to that bank. Through such accounts the bank accumulates sufficient money to make loans to other borrowers. In times of tight money the bank dislikes having to make loans to noncustomers, for fear no funds will be available should a customer desire to borrow money at a future date.

At least four credit references should be given to allow the lender to investigate the applicant's reputation for paying his or her obligations.

The application should provide information concerning the present financial position of the person in the form of a financial statement showing all his or her assets and liabilities. Assets might include such items as cash in the bank, notes and mortgages due to the applicant, stocks and bonds owned, other real estate owned, and cash value of life insurance. Liabilities would probably include notes payable, instalment notes payable with total amount of monthly payments, accounts payable, debts on real estate owned, and other liabilities.

From the personal data and the financial statement,

the lender can analyze the individual's character, capacity, and capital. The credit information reveals the character; income and monthly payments reveal capacity; and other assets owned show the capital. To obtain his or her past credit information, the lending agency will have to conduct its own investigation or request a retail credit association or other credit-gathering organization to make an investigation, using the information on the application.

IMPORTANCE OF PROPERLY SUBMITTING APPLICATION

A properly completed application will provide all the information necessary for the lender to make a thorough analysis. If it is fully completed it will not be necessary for the lending officer to contact the prospective borrower at various stages for additional information. It is important that the legal description be furnished at the time of the application; otherwise, once the loan has been approved, the officer will have to try to obtain the description, which is necessary to complete the request for a preliminary report from the title insurance company. The more time required to contact the borrower, the more time is wasted; therefore, it is important that *all* phases of the application be completed at the time the application is taken. Another reason for fully completing the application is that it permits the lending officer to determine whether by taking this loan the applicant will be overextending himself or herself. When the application is completed properly, it should be evident to the lending officer whether sufficient funds will be available, after all existing obligations are paid each month, to pay the proposed obligation. If there seems to be no possibility of such a payment being made, the completed application makes it possible to avoid wasting valuable time in further processing of the loan.

An application that is made in person and completed by the lending officer making inquiries of the applicant encourages development of an understanding between the interviewing officer and the applicant. This time, properly used by the lending officer, allows the applicant to justify his or her request and to convince the lending officer that he or she is taking an application for a loan that will be properly repaid should it be approved.

THE REAL ESTATE BROKER AND THE APPLICATION

The real estate broker need not take a formal application in connection with the real estate loan; however, by doing a little preliminary screening of buyers, he or she might be able to avoid wasting time in a hopeless cause and to save his or her time for an individual who will qualify

for a loan. In certain instances it is not unusual for a broker to work closely with a lending agency. By so doing the broker may establish conditional commitments in connection with some of the more desirable properties he or she has for sale. Lending agencies are happy to obtain conditional commitments on properties from the Federal Housing Administration, and other lending agencies and savings and loan associations have been known to work closely with some brokers in giving conditional commitments for conventional loans. To obtain such commitments the broker sometimes must advance the appraisal fee, which in turn can be refunded from the closing cost when the loan is finally made. With a conditional commitment, the real estate broker can inform the applicant of the amount of down payment that will be necessary for whatever agency has given the commitment and of the terms available through that agency. If the broker does not have a commitment, he or she should be familiar enough with the permissive legislation governing all agencies so that, by using the sales price as the maximum appraisal figure, he or she would be able to give some indication as to the amount of loan, the monthly payment, and the period for which the loan could be drawn. In the case of an FHA application, it is not unusual for the real estate broker to prepare all the application documents and present them to the bank for analysis and processing. A quick analysis by the real estate agent or broker of the information that is obtained by questioning the buyer should indicate whether he or she has a potential sale or whether the individual would be unable to qualify for any type of real estate loan. This will save time for both the broker and the lending agency and will win him or her a vote of confidence should the lender be asked for the name of a reputable real estate broker.

It is often helpful for the realtor to present the applicant to the lending officer. At that time the realtor can give any pertinent information that the lending officer desires, can help complete the application from his or her information concerning the property, and can answer any further questions from the applicant.

When the lending officer must ask confidential information such as salary, place of employment, and financial position, he or she will usually request that the realtor leave the room. However, if the real estate broker has done a good job, he or she probably knows all such information already.

LENDER'S INITIAL INTERVIEW

When an application has been completed by the realtor and presented to the lender, it is desirable for the lender, before further processing, to hold an interview with the borrower. This interview, as in the case of direct application from the borrower, is to determine the practicality of the loan and whether further processing is justified. At this time the lending officer will further query the borrower to determine whether the information is adequate and accurate. This will give the lending officer an opportunity for further questions and the chance to form an opinion of the applicant from personal contact.

At this time the lender can discuss the apparent strength of the collateral, indicating the maximum loan that could be expected and also indicating that this amount may very well be more than that of the final approved loan. The maximum loan value is based on the sales price or appraised value, whichever is smaller, and since the estimate is based on the sales price the actual loan might have to be for a smaller amount.

Real estate lenders are often criticized because their appraisal of the property offered as collateral is not as high as the applicant feels it should be. However, several things must be taken into consideration in appraising real estate for loan collateral purposes. First, such loans are long term, and it is necessary that the collateral stay in existence and maintain the necessary ratio of value to loan until the end of the loan. Second, since this is a value that must last for a long time, it is normal to consider present and future economic factors. If a depression is foreseeable, the lender's appraiser will naturally take this into consideration to keep a good loan on the lending institution's books. Next, the lending officer will discuss the applicant's income with the applicant and will try to obtain some information on previous employers and length of employment by them; from this information he or she will develop an opinion of the dependability of the individual.

At this point, the lending officer should have an insight into the applicant's ability, personality, and character and should be able to determine whether the loan application is one with which the lending agency wishes to proceed. The cost of the loan should now be discussed with the applicant so that there will be no misunderstanding when the lender's and the title company's charges are made. These costs normally consist of escrow fees, notary fees, loan office fees, appraisal fees, credit report, title policy, recording fee, fee for drawing the deed of trust, miscellaneous legal fees, fire insurance premiums, and California Tax Agency fees. After the applicant knows the expenses involved, the type of loan that he or she will be able to expect, and the monthly payment necessary to service the loan, he or she should be able to advise the lending officer whether to go ahead with the loan.

After the application has been received, the bank's first step is to request an appraisal of the property. The appraisal can be made by an independent organization at the request of the lending agency or it can be made by an official appraiser on the staff of the lending agency. After the appraisal has been completed and delivered to the lending officer, he or she will request that a credit analysis be made. Again, this can be made by the lending agency or, as in most cases, a report will be ordered from the local credit-gathering association, usually an agency of the Retail Credit Association or the Credit Managers Association. In the case of investigation of a corporation, a Dun & Bradstreet report will occasionally be ordered. If the credit analysis is favorable, the loan application is then reviewed by the loan committee and at this point is either formally accepted or rejected. If it is accepted, the applicant is so advised and the normal processing procedures are started. These entail (1) ordering a preliminary report from the title insurance company; and (2) drawing the necessary documents such as the deed of trust, the note, the security agreement (if necessary), the disclosure statement under Regulation Z, the disbursement order (which authorizes the lender to disburse the funds in any way necessary to obtain a first lien on the property), and any other documentation that the agency feels is necessary.

APPRAISAL REPORT

Real estate appraising will be covered in more detail in Chapter 12. At this time we shall review the items that the lending officer would expect to find in the appraisal report.

As a rule the appraisal report submitted in connection with a real estate loan is a form report that will include a total valuation of the property for loan purposes and that will separate land value and improvement value. If the application involves a sale, the appraised value will not necessarily be equal to the sales price. The appraisal report will contain a description and a location of the property to make sure that the property being described is the property upon which an application was received.

The improvements on the property will be described and comments will be made about their age and condition. There will be a reference to the neighborhood, the population, and the improvements surrounding the property. If the property is income property, there will be some analysis of the income, expense, and lease arrangements. The basic appraisal report should also include a statement regarding the taxes and assessments together with the assessed valuation of the property. It should indicate the availability of transportation and other desirable facilities such as churches, schools, parks, and shopping facilities. The appraisal should indicate the present zoning, and a judgment whether this zoning is the best use of the land involved. The appraisal should be accompanied by a photograph of the subject property.

CREDIT ANALYSIS

Increasing emphasis has recently been placed upon the borrower's ability to repay. Lending agencies are interested in proper servicing of their loans. It has therefore become increasingly important to analyze the credit risk that the borrower brings to the lender. Certain formulas have been established for this analysis as desirable, though not hard and fast, ratios of expense.

It is felt that the purchase price of a home should not exceed two and one-half times the buyer's annual income. Under this rule of thumb, a family with a combined income of $32,000 should not buy a home costing more than $80,000. However, there are exceptions to all rules. For instance, a family may have cash from the sale of a previous home that could be part of a down payment to lower the payments to a manageable amount.

Many lenders feel that a monthly payment for shelter (home loan) should not exceed 25 percent of the gross monthly income, or that total monthly payments, including shelter, should not exceed 33 percent of the gross monthly income. However, in 1980 and 1981, due to the inflated cost of housing and high interest rates, many lenders have approved loans that call for monthly payments of 30 percent of the gross monthly income. Nevertheless, the buyer must have few other obligations and good potential for increased income.

In calculating the total monthly payments, some companies permit a consideration for the veterans exemption on the tax schedules. However, if there is a secondary loan, the payments on it must also be included to determine what the gross amount of income should be. In connection with gross income, the lending officer will determine whether overtime wages are included in the gross income reported. If overtime is included, it is necessary to determine whether such income is a normal condition of the business in which the individual is occupied. If it is normal in that industry for an individual to work forty-eight hours, then the overtime would be allowed. However, if this is not a normal situation, the overtime will not be allowed unless it has been received for the past two or three years, in which case the organization may allow a 50 percent declaration of overtime to be included in the total monthly income.

Income from stocks, bonds, and rentals has a tendency to fluctuate; therefore, most companies allow only a 50 percent credit for such income. Since 1976 a wife's income must be considered, and it is now much easier for a single woman to obtain financing for a home.

After the financial statement has been analyzed, it may be necessary to consider some way of strengthening the application, which can sometimes be done by use of co-signers. Such strengthening is usually required when the applicant is very young and has the income for the loan but does not have the experience or the capital to supply him or her with a backlog for contingencies. Under these circumstances the same information is gathered from the co-signer, and it is most desirable that the co-signer be of blood relationship. A co-signer is sometimes also used when the applicant is elderly, to facilitate the closing of an estate and the continuation of a payment schedule should the applicant die. A co-signer on a note secured by a deed of trust can also add additional security to the note should a decline in property value necessitate foreclosure proceedings.

The information discussed so far pertains to financial ability, but the lender is also interested in the moral risk involved. He or she will be interested in whether the borrower treats his or her obligations honorably and makes payments when they fall due or whether he or she has a tendency to be lax in repayment. Information concerning the borrower's previous credit record gives a good indication as to what the lending agency can expect on a loan that it might consider. If the past record shows that he or she has always made the payments, the lender can expect to receive payments regularly on the note unless some unforeseen event occurs. If the previous record shows that the prospective borrower gave all or a few lending agencies a difficult time in collections, then the possibilities of the present lender having problems with his or her loan are almost certain.

Credit information can be obtained from certain sources. There are professional credit-gathering sources such as Dun & Bradstreet, Retail Credit Bureaus, and Credit Managers Associations. Besides these professional gatherers of credit information, the lender can obtain additional information from the acquaintances of the applicant, his or her bank, former creditors, or present employer. Some employers may be hesitant about giving information concerning employees; however, most employers are willing to verify that the individual is employed there, even though they will not verify the worker's salary.

When the lending institution has all its credit information together, it should be able to decide whether this individual will be able to qualify for the proposed loan. In reaching this decision, it will have used the "three Cs" of credit (capital, capacity, and character) using certain selected criteria such as the amount, stability, and trend of the effective income; the amount, stability, and trend of expenses; the other obligations that the borrower has acknowledged; the amount of down payment being made; past repayment record; the ratio of disposable income to housing costs; and other expenses such as medical, number of dependents, and social position the family feels it must hold.

NOTES

After the application has been approved, several documents must be prepared. The note and deed of trust are the two that form the basis of the loan. (Refer to Chapter 8 for the content of the note.) Some basic changes in the character of the note are developing, because of the great increase in the cost of money to the lender during the money shortage of 1974–1975, and because of the ever-rising average cost of single-family dwellings. (Refer to Chapter 4 for types of notes.)

CLOSING THE LOAN

Before the loan may be disbursed, the deed of trust must be recorded, or the title company must indicate that it is ready to record and ready for the funds. In this way recording and disbursement of funds occur almost simultaneously. In most instances in California such transactions are handled through title companies and escrow companies; in the case of a sale, they will have in their possession a grant deed to the purchaser; a reconveyance of the deed of trust or mortgage if there is one on the property; the deed of trust from the lending institution; and escrow instructions in connection with the disbursement of the proceeds of the loan.

Immediately before the recording, certain final checks should be made to be sure that the transaction will be legal. The capacity of the parties involved in the transaction should be explored to determine that they have the capacity to contract; that they are of age and mentally sound; that the interest rate of the note is in compliance with the usury statutes of the state;[1] that the title of the property after the documents are recorded will be in the condition required by the lending agency and by the purchaser; that the recipients of the funds or proceeds of the sale are properly identified; that the property is properly described; that the deed of trust is drawn to encumber the property correctly; that a proper receipt has been given for the proceeds of the loan; and, after all this has been accomplished, that the documents have been properly recorded.

After the closing of the loan, the lending agencies will want to make certain verifications to be sure that their file is properly documented. First, they will want to verify that the deed of trust has been recorded, and that the title

policy describes the deed of trust properly as to date, date of recording, and page and book of recording. The amount recited on the deed of trust should be the same as in the note, and the date of the deed of trust should be the same as that of the note. The deed of trust is signed with the exact name under which the title policy shows title to be vested and with exactly the same name as the note. The description in the deed of trust should be the same as the description of the property shown in the title insurance policy.

The fire insurance policy must show that it is on the same property described in the application, if by street number; if by legal description, it must be the same description as in the deed of trust. There must be adequate insurance to cover the loan and the policy must be signed by a duly authorized agent of the company.

The application must be signed exactly as the note and deed of trust. The appraisal amount must be adequate to qualify the loan under the basis of value-to-loan ratio.

Although there is a uniform commercial loan code, there has been an effort to pass a uniform real estate loan code for years but without success. The Federal National Mortgage Association was established to participate in the secondary mortgage market. It bought FHA and VA loans for years because the loan documentation was uniform in form from application to note and trust deed. But FNMA would not buy conventional loans because there were almost as many forms, applications, notes, and trust deeds as there were lenders. FNMA finally designed loan applications, notes, and trust deeds or mortgage forms and said, "If you want to sell your loans to us, use our forms." As a result, almost all applications, notes, trust deeds, and mortgages are uniform regardless of the lending institution.

FARM LOAN APPLICATIONS

One other type of loan application should be considered in connection with real estate loan applications—a real estate loan secured by a producing farm or ranch. The first part of the application for such a loan is similar to that for residential and income property, through the legal description of the property. At this point, some indication is given as to the total number of acres and how many of the acres are cultivated. Such information, of course, is pertinent to the farm and its productivity. Other important information is given in the description of the property. For example, the application would state whether the property is located on a paved, gravel, or dirt road; and it would indicate the number of miles and the direction of the farm from the nearest railroad town (or truck terminal, since trucking is taking over a great deal of the freight traffic that used to be handled by railroads).

The application would indicate the number of miles

---

[1]In California the legal rate is 10 percent or the Federal Reserve Bank's discount rate plus 5 percent, whichever is larger on the date the note is signed.

from a school and from a church. Although most farms have some sort of address—either a rural address that is a star route, or route 1, route 2, and so on—it is sometimes difficult, without a map of the routes, for an individual to find the farm being described. Therefore, minute details must be given so that the appraiser or inspector of the property will have no difficulty in finding the farm. Landmarks, colors of houses, schools, and directions are all useful to the person trying to find the property. The farm application should identify the occupant of the farm or ranch, state whether it is now operated or will be operated on a tenant or hired-help basis or whether the owner now occupies and operates it. If it is under tenancy in terms of lease, then the terms and the length of time the lease has to run under the present terms should be indicated. The applicant should indicate the length of time he or she has lived in the vicinity, and if the applicant has lived on this particular ranch, he or she should show the number of years of occupancy on the application. If the applicant has owned the property for some time and has made improvements, he or she should show the length of time the property has been owned; the cost of acquiring the property; the condition of the property at the time purchased; whether it was bare land or contained improvements; whether fruit trees, grain, hay, and so on, were on the property; and if so, the number of acres of each. If improvements have been made, he or she should show also the number of acres that have been improved and the cost of such improvements as land leveling, planting, installation of wells, irrigation systems, and so on.

If the applicant knows the types of soil found on the farm, they should be given. There should be an indication of the depths of the surface soils to hardpans, of whether there is gravel underlying, or of whatever the condition of the subsoil. There should be statements of any tendency to alkalinity, and if one exists, of whether it is white or black alkali and how heavy; any erosion or possibility of erosion should also be shown.

The applicant for farm land should also describe the source of water, whether well, river, or district, and the number of acres the present supply will irrigate. If water is supplied by an irrigation district or company, the applicant should state whether he or she holds ownership in the company or whether the applicant must purchase such ownership if he or she purchases the property. If it is necessary to purchase water, the annual charge per acre should be shown. Any district water taxes should be enumerated. If the source of water is a well, the depth of the well should be stated, as well as the size of the casing, the depth at which the water stands, and how far it is lowered by constant pumping. The applicant should also indicate any holdings of farm equipment such as

machinery, tools, and trucks. This information is necessary to determine whether the land is self-sustaining or whether the operator must hire a great deal of the work done in producing a crop.

Since the appraiser values the farm according to its productivity and capitalization of its productivity, historical record of that production must be given. If there is more than one crop, each crop should be delineated by name, quantity, number of acres, and total profit for which it was sold. The application should also reveal whether additional funds have been received from dairy livestock, poultry, and other products. It is useful in considering a farm application to have some indication of the amount of farm labor it was necessary to hire and of the total operational expense, again to determine whether the ranch or farm is a productive or merely a sustenance operation.

Another very important item concerning ranches in California today is county taxes. If the ranch or farm happens to be in proximity to a large community such as Bakersfield, Fresno, San Jose, Stockton, Sacramento, Chico, or San Mateo, the assessed valuation on the farm may be very high. Such taxes must of necessity have some bearing upon the capitalization of income, since they are an expense and must be paid for the farmer to have the income from and control of the property.

Although the improvements on a farm do not have the importance to the lender or the purchaser that the residential improvement has on a residential lot, it is nevertheless desirable for the lender to have some knowledge of the improvements on the farm. If there is a main dwelling or a barn, the lender is interested in its size, the number of rooms and stories, and when it was built. All other buildings and their condition should also be shown on the application.

It is very easy in present-day California to overimprove a farm as far as buildings are concerned, and unless the investment is justified through the capitalization analysis, the overimprovements do not significantly affect the value of property offered as security.

The personal information concerning the farm applicant is similar to that for a residential applicant except that most applicants will be received more favorably if they have been in the farm business for some time; however, the financial statement continues to be of great importance. If the individual is employed off the farm and will continue to do so, this information becomes important in the analysis of the applicant's capacity.

This is the kind of information that a lender will look for in a formal application presented to him or her for a farm loan. The better the real estate broker or agent understands the application presented, the better he or she will be able to determine to whom the application

FIGURE 10-1

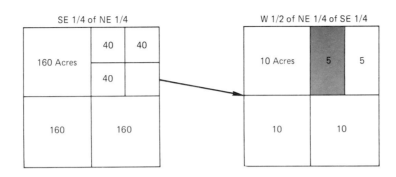

should be presented. If the applicant is making direct application, the more he or she understands the required problems and questions, the easier it will be for him or her to obtain the desired financing.

To compute the area of a government survey description, start with the last area given. The parcel is 5 acres and is located in the section as shown in Figure 10-1. It is possible to find the acreage by multiplying the fractions in the description and multiplying the answer by the acreage in a section (640). Using the above description:

$$\tfrac{1}{2} \times \tfrac{1}{4} \times \tfrac{1}{4} \times \tfrac{1}{4} = \frac{1}{128} \qquad 640 \times \frac{1}{128} = 5$$

This is a good shortcut but it does not show the parcel's relation to the whole section.

QUESTIONS

1. The major function of a real estate loan department is to
    a. make as many FHA loans as possible
    b. limit loans to certain areas
    c. make loans on desirable property to individuals, corporations, or organizations with a good credit reputation
    d. all of the above
2. A real estate loan application is
    a. a written request for a loan
    b. a document that allows the lender to render a judgment as to the credit ability of the applicant
    c. a document that reveals the financial capacity of the applicant
    d. all of the above
3. The real estate loan application must contain a legal description because
    a. it contains the street address of the property
    b. the appraiser needs it in order to appraise the property

c. the title company needs it before a preliminary report can be issued
d. none of the above

4. The ratio the lender uses in order to make a legal and desirable loan is known as the
    a. loan-to-value ratio
    b. loan-to-price ratio
    c. loan-to-assessed-value ratio
    d. value-to-loan ratio
5. Large loans on commercial properties are usually made at a lower interest rate because
    a. servicing is usually less expensive
    b. they usually remain on the books for the full term
    c. a smaller percentage of the value is loaned
    d. all of the above
6. If a real estate broker intends to sell a home using HUD-FHA, he or she will need a conditional commitment from HUD-FHA. This will be ordered from HUD-FHA by
    a. an authorized lender
    b. the broker
    c. the owner
    d. the buyer
7. In analyzing the borrower's ability to repay a loan, the lender desires a certain ratio of monthly payment to monthly income. Which of the following would be most desirable to the lender?
    a. 3 to 1
    b. 4 to 1
    c. 5 to 1
    d. 6 to 1
8. Before a real estate loan can be approved, among the items found in the client's file would be all of the following except
    a. a completed real estate loan application
    b. a credit report from a reliable credit reporting agency

   c. a recorded deed of trust
   d. an appraisal report

9. The application for a real estate loan must be completed in full at the time the application is made by the borrower except for
   a. the request for a loan
   b. the appraisal
   c. information concerning the property
   d. information concerning the borrower

10. When a real estate loan department is servicing a loan, its responsibilities are
   a. to see that the loan does not become delinquent
   b. to see that a delinquency is reported immediately if incurable
   c. to see that the insurance and taxes are paid in full
   d. all of the above

11

The Mathematics of Finance

The mathematics of finance does not necessarily apply primarily to real estate. However, in many instances direct application of the principles of mathematics can be made to the financing and to the questions arising from the purchase of real estate.

Many of the computations used are elementary and may already be known to you. However, this chapter will be a ready reference for the mathematics of finance.

PRORATION

Proration is proportional division or distribution. In real estate the term is usually used in connection with the proportional distribution of expenses in connection with taxes, insurance, bonded indebtedness, and other items whose expense should be distributed between the buyer and the seller. Since the expense to be divided is a whole, the mathematics in connection with proration becomes one of fractions.

A fraction has two parts, the *numerator* or portion above the line, and the *denominator* or portion below the line. In the fraction $1/3$, 1 is the numerator and 3 the denominator.

Fractions are of two types, *proper* and *improper*. A proper fraction is one that is a *part* of a whole, such as $1/3$, $1/2$, or $2/3$. An improper fraction represents *more than* a whole, for example, $4/3$, $5/2$, or $5/4$. An improper fraction can be changed into a *mixed number;* for example, $5/4$ becomes $1 1/4$. Before fractions can be added, they must all have a common denominator, and to facilitate solution the lowest common denominator is used. In the case of $1/4$, $1/2$, and $1/3$, the lowest common denominator is 12. One-fourth would become $3/12$; $1/3$ would become $4/12$; and $1/2$ would become $6/12$. Adding these three fractions, we add the numerators to arrive at a total of $13/12$. Since this is an improper fraction, it would probably be reduced to the mixed number $1 1/12$.

To subtract one fraction from another, it is again necessary to change the fractions to the lowest common denominator and then subtract the numerators to arrive at an answer. In subtracting $1/4$ from $1/3$, the lowest common denominator again is 12. Then $4/12 - 3/12 = 1/12$.

To multiply fractions, multiply one numerator by the other and one denominator by the other. Thus, $1/4 \times 1/3 = 1/12$.

To divide fractions, invert the divisor and multiply the resulting fractions. Thus, $1/4 \div 1/3 = 1/4 \times 3/1 = 3/4$.

Let us now apply the mathematics of fractions to a proration of a tax and insurance expense in connection with the sale of a parcel of real estate. Assume that a house was sold and cleared escrow on May 1, 1976. The sales price was $60,000. It is a new property that has never been on the tax rolls. The tax rate is 1% of the market value. From the information that has been given, let us determine the annual tax cost. To arrive at the assessed value, we multiply 1% times $60,000. Thus, $.01 \times 60,000 = 600$. Since there are twelve months in a year, the monthly cost of taxes would be $1/12 \times 600$. Multiplying the two numerators and the two denominators yields $50 per month. Since the tax year is figured on the basis of July 1 of the preceding year through June 30 of the present year, as of June 30, 1976, the seller would have lived in the house ten months of the taxable year and a proration of the expense of the tax would be $10/12$ of the total tax. Since we have already figured the tax on the basis of a monthly payment, the seller would owe ten times the monthly base of $50 or $500.

Another way of computing this would be to take the $10/12$ and reduce it to $5/6$ times the total amount of tax, or $5/6 \times \$600$, which also equals $500.

In prorating the insurance, the same process would be used. A three-year insurance policy for $60,000, assuming a fire rate of $1.25 per $100, would give a three-year premium of $750 since there are thirty-six months in three years; the monthly cost of insurance could then be determined by multiplying $\frac{1}{36} \times \$750 = \$20.83$ per month. Assuming the insurance policy was purchased January 1, 1976, the seller would be liable for the four months in which he had the benefits of the insurance coverage; thus, $4 \times \$20.83 = \$83.32$, the portion of the insurance costs that should be charged to him.

All escrows do not close on the first of the month. When they close later in the month it is necessary to prorate on the basis of days used. For escrow and real estate loan purposes, proration and interest charges are computed on a three hundred sixty–day year and a thirty-day month.

In the insurance example we found that the cost per month was $20.83. To find the per-day cost it would be necessary to use the following equation: $\frac{1}{30} \times \$20.83 = .69$, or 69 cents per day. If the escrow had closed on May 6 instead of May 1 the seller would have owed an additional five days, or $3.45. The total owed by the seller would then have been $86.77. The same principle would apply to proration of taxes and interest, as well as to income collected in advance.

Now let us assume that the organization financing the sale requires that a loan trust fund or impound be set up for the accumulation of taxes and insurance. Under these circumstances the financing institution would expect the escrow organization to collect $83.32 plus $500 for taxes for the initial payment into the impounds, and it would then charge $20.83 per month plus $50 for taxes when the monthly payment of principal and interest was made. At the end of the time covered by the policy the funds necessary to purchase new insurance and pay taxes would be in the impound or the trust fund. There are two ways in which the institution might request the impound for the taxes to be collected by the escrow organization. First, it could require that the full amount of $583.32 be collected by the escrow company and forwarded to the financial organization for credit to the impounds, and it could continue to charge $70.83 per month, in which case by July 1 the amount of taxes for the year 1975–1976 would have been collected and available for payment. However, this is not the normal way in which it would be handled, since the taxes are usually paid just before December 10, at which time the first instalment becomes delinquent, and just before April 10, at which time the second instalment becomes delinquent. Since approximately one-half of the taxes would be delinquent in December, the financing institution would multiply $600 by $\frac{1}{2}$ to find the amount due in December: they would need $300 in their loan trust fund by December 10. Since the escrow closed on May 1, the first payment on the note would be due in June, usually by June 10, and they would therefore have collected by December seven pay-

ments of $50 totaling $350, or $50 more than necessary to make the first payment. By April 10, when the second instalment of $300 was due, the financial institution would have collected four more payments of $50, or $200. The total in the impound fund, including the balance of $50 left over from the first payment, would be $300. Therefore, at the time of the close of the escrow on May 1, 1976, the financial institution would not request the escrow company to collect an additional amount in order to have the full amount necessary to pay all the taxes before they became delinquent.

INTEREST RATE AND PRINCIPAL

Interest is rent paid for the use of money; rent, of course, is the fee paid for the use of anything owned by another. We might say, therefore, that interest is a fee paid for the use of money and that the interest *rate* is the fee expressed as a percentage of the money used. *Principal* is the amount of money used, often referred to as the amount of money owed.

Interest can thus be computed by using the following formula:

$$\text{Interest} = \text{Principal} \times \text{Rate} \times \text{Time}$$

As an example: A borrows from B $1,000 for one year at 7 percent. Using the above formula, we find

$$\text{Interest} = \$1,000 \times 0.07 \times 1 = \$70$$

Therefore, interest equals $70.

Using approximately the same basic formula, we would be able, by making adjustments in the formula, to find out what the principal amount was, if the interest, the rate, and the time were known. Thus:

$$\text{Principal} = \frac{\text{Interest}}{\text{Rate} \times \text{Time}}$$

Using the same problem, principal $= \dfrac{70}{0.07 \times 1}$. This then would become $70 \div 0.07$. Since there are two decimals in the divisor, we add two places to the dividend and find that principal equals $1,000.

By making a slight adjustment in the basic formula, we can find the rate by dividing the interest by the principal times the time:

$$\text{Rate} = \frac{\text{Interest}}{\text{Principal} \times \text{Time}}$$

In this way, using the same example,

$$\text{Rate} = \frac{\$70}{\$1,000 \times 1}$$

$$= \frac{70}{1,000}$$

$$= 0.07$$

Therefore, the rate would be 7 percent.

Where the interest, principal, and rate are known, it is possible to determine the time by using the same basic formula with adjustments.

$$\text{Time} = \frac{\text{Interest}}{\text{Principal} \times \text{Rate}}$$

Using our same example,

$$\text{Time} = \frac{\$70}{\$1,000 \times 0.07}$$

$$= \frac{70}{70}$$

$$= 1$$

Therefore, the time would be one year.

One can quickly calculate 6 percent on a monthly basis, by remembering that 6 percent per year is equal to 0.5 percent per month; consequently, interest for one month could be computed quickly by pointing off two places in the principal amount and multiplying by $^1/_2$. If it were interest for two months, it would be necessary only to point off the two places and the result would be two months' interest at 6 percent. Another way of computing interest for a month at 6 percent is to multiply the principle amount by 0.005. Interest for one month on $2,500 would then be figured as follows:

$$\$2,500 \times 0.005 = \$12.50$$

There is a shortcut for computing interest for one month when the rate is 7.2 percent or 8.4 percent per year. For monthly interest charge at 7.2 percent per year, multiply the principal by 0.006. $2,500 for one month at 7.2 percent would be

$$\$2,500 \times 0.006 = \$15.00$$

If the interest rate is 8.4 percent per year, multiply the principal by 0.007. An annual percentage of 9.6 would be multiplied by 0.008 to get the monthly interest charge.

NOMINAL INTEREST

The *nominal* interest rate is the rate specified in the note. However, depending upon the way in which the interest is paid or collected, the nominal rate may not be the effective interest rate. The *effective* interest rate is the rate actually paid by the borrower for the use of the money. The effective interest rate is higher when the interest is collected as a discount interest with monthly payments made, or when a gross rate, sometimes called add on, interest is collected and monthly payments are made. When a loan is paid off in periodic payments, such as monthly payments, the note is referred to as an amortized note or amortized loan.

DISCOUNT INTEREST

Discount interest is collected in advance and deducted from the amount of principal paid to the borrower. For example, assume that an individual borrows $100 for which he or she agrees to pay 6 percent discount interest. The bank would write a note for $100, pay the individual $94, and collect, over the period of repayment, $100.

The nominal rate of interest, the amount named in the note, is 6 percent. However, what is the effective rate of interest? To compute the effective rate of interest, we divide the interest by the principal, multiply the result by twice the number of payments per year divided by the total number of payments in the contract, and add one. To state this as an effective formula, we might use the following letter symbols:

E = effective interest

I = interest paid

P = money received by borrower

M = number of payments per year

N = total number of payments in contract

With this legend established, the formula would be

$$E = \frac{I}{P} \times \frac{2M}{N + 1}$$

Assuming twelve monthly payments, let us now determine the effective interest under a discount interest plan. Our formula would show

$$E = \frac{6}{94} \times \frac{2(12)}{12 + 1}$$

$$= \frac{6}{94} \times \frac{24}{13}$$

$$= \frac{144}{1,222}$$

$$= 0.118$$

Although the nominal interest is 6 percent, because of the manner in which it is collected, the effective interest earned by the lender is 11.8 percent.

GROSS RATE INTEREST

In the case of *gross rate* interest, the amount of the interest for the period of the loan is added to the principal, and monthly payments are made against the resulting total until the total amount is paid in full. Using the same example of a $100 loan at 6 percent for one year with monthly payments, and using the formula above, let us determine the effective rate under the gross rate charge.

$$E = \frac{6}{100} \times \frac{2(12)}{12 + 1}$$

$$= \frac{6}{100} \times \frac{24}{13}$$

$$= \frac{144}{1,300}$$

$$= 0.111$$

The effective interest earned by use of the gross rate interest charge would be 11.1 percent compared with 11.8 percent under the discount rate of interest. The effective rate can also be different from the nominal rate in cases of a flat loan or of a loan that has a constant amount due and is paid in full at maturity, and whose interest has been subtracted before disbursement of the principal to the borrower. A loan of $100 at 6 percent discount would yield $94 to the borrower if the loan were for one year and $88 to the borrower if it were for two years. The formula for figuring effective interest under these circumstances, using the legend above, would be

$$E = \frac{I}{P} \div 2$$

Assuming a two-year loan as stated above,

$$E = \frac{12}{88} \div 2$$

$$= 0.137 \div 2$$

$$= 0.068$$

It is interesting to note that in this particular type of transaction, the effective interest becomes larger as the time is extended; for instance, the effective interest for one year is 6.3 percent, for two years 6.8 percent, and for three years 7.3 percent.

Let us consider another aspect of effective interest. An investor will often purchase a note, secured or unsecured, at a discount. The body of the note gives the nominal rate, but what is the actual yield to the investor? Consider a typical situation. Mr. A, a known investor, is offered a flat note of $3,000 at a 20 percent discount. The note calls for interest at 8 percent per year. It will mature in five years from the date the investor purchases the note. What is the effective rate of interest the purchaser will realize?

The first step is to find the amount of interest the purchaser will receive in interest each year from the named interest rate. The note is for $3,000 and the interest rate is 8 percent, so $3,000 × 0.08 = $240, the amount of interest for one year. The discount was 20 percent of the face amount of the note, so $3,000 × 0.20 = $600. The purchaser therefore paid $2,400 for the $3,000 note and will receive $3,000 at the time the note matures. The note will mature in five years, so in five years he will earn another $600, or $120 per year. As a result of the interest earned each year, $240 and the proration each year of the discount amount to $120, the purchaser's annual income is $360. His investment is $2,400, so the effective interest would be $360 divided by $2,400, or 15 percent. This is the effective interest rate the investor realizes from his $2,400 investment.

DECLINING-PRINCIPAL LOAN

A *declining-principal loan* is one in which the interest charge is figured on the unpaid balance during the amortization of the loan. The loan payment usually consists of a fixed amount paid to principal plus an interest charge during the periodic amortization. An example of this type of loan would be a loan for $1,200 payable at $100 per month plus interest on the unpaid balance at the rate of 1 percent per month. Since the payment of interest is 1 percent per month, the nominal interest expressed in an annual interest rate is 12 percent. The question that often arises regarding such a note concerns not what the effective interest is, but how much interest will be paid during the term of the note. This amount can be computed by multiplying the amount of the loan times the annual interest rate. This amount is then multiplied by the number of payments in the contract plus one, and divided by twice the number of payments per year. Expressed by a formula, this would read

$$I = PR \times \frac{N + 1}{2M}$$

Now, using the figures that we used in our example.

$$I = 1{,}200(0.12) \times \frac{12 + 1}{24}$$

$$= 144.00 \times \frac{13}{24}$$

$$= \$78.00$$

Therefore, $78 interest would be collected over the life of the contract.

MORTGAGE YIELDS

Mortgage yield is the effective interest return that an investor enjoys from a loan secured by a first deed of trust or real estate mortgage. There is no difficulty in ascertaining the net yield on a note secured by a deed of trust that calls for a nominal rate of annual interest paid on the declining principal. When the note is for $1,000, the interest rate is 5 percent, and the investor has loaned a full $1,000, the mortgage yield is 5 percent. However, a problem arises when legislation sets a maximum interest rate, as in the case of FHA and GI loans where the maximum interest rate is lower than that expected on the current market. In an effort to bring the yield to a desirable level, the system of real estate *points* was inaugurated. Real estate points are actually nothing more than a percentage discount of a balance of a note expressed as numbers rather than as percentages. Thus, when a person indicates that he or she will charge 2 points for making a loan, it means that he or she will charge 2 percent of the existing balance of that loan to make it. In other words, if a person charges 2 points on a $1,000 loan, he or she will charge 2 percent of the $1,000 and disburse $980 in return for a $1,000 note.

Points or discounts such as this are often taken when an individual holds a note that he or she wishes to sell and finds that the interest named in the note is smaller than the going rate. When this occurs, the purchaser will attempt to bring the nominal rate to a current effective rate by charging a discount on the note, again called points.

A discount may also be taken by a purchaser of a mortgage loan when the mortgage has some risk attached to it such as a second mortgage or deed of trust. In this case the remaining balance on the note may be discounted as high as 50 percent, which means that a note for $1,000 could be purchased for as little as $500. The mortgagor would find it necessary to pay the mortgagee, or the trustor the beneficiary in the case of a trust deed, the full amount still due on the note. This would change the effective rate considerably, and it creates a problem for which another formula has been designed.

For the purposes of this formula,

E = effective interest rate

D = discount amount

B = balance due on the note

R = nominal rate of interest

N = number of years left on the note

A = net amount advanced.

The formula would thus read

$$E = \frac{\dfrac{D}{N} + \dfrac{B}{2}(R)}{\dfrac{A}{2}}$$

This formula will give a close approximation of the yield but not an exact figure, since it deals with averages. This formula is our old friend $R = I/P$ (rate of return is equal to interest received divided by the principal). The balance divided by two gives the average principal during the life of the note, and this amount multiplied by the rate gives the average annual return on the principal. The discount divided by the number of years the note has to maturity gives the average earnings from the discount each year. The total of these is equal to the average annual income from the note. When this amount is divided by the average amount of investment (the average is used since payments are received and therefore the total original investment is not the investment for the full term), the rate of return is found.

As an example, let us assume that we wish to find the effective rate on a deed of trust note that matures in five years with an annual payment plus interest at 5 percent on the unpaid balance of $5,000. The owner, who wishes to sell this note, finds an individual interested in buying it at a 10 percent discount. Our formula gives

$$E = \frac{\dfrac{500}{5} + \dfrac{5,000}{2}(0.05)}{4,500 \div 2}$$

$$= \frac{100 + 125}{2,250}$$

$$= \frac{225}{2,250}$$

$$= 10 \text{ percent}$$

Effective interest after such a discount would be 10 percent.

By a slight modification in the formula it is possible to determine the amount that should be advanced in order to have a specific effective rate of return, knowing the nominal rate, the effective rate, the effective rate desired, and the balance due on the note. Once again, let us assume that an individual wishes to sell a $5,000 note that matures in five years with annual payments and 5 percent interest on the declining balance and that an effective rate of 7 percent is desired. How much should be advanced against such a note to realize the effective rate of 7 percent? In this case, our formula would read

$$A = B - \frac{NB}{(2 + NE)} (E - R)$$

Substituting figures for the formula, we obtain

$$A = 5,000 - \frac{5 \times 5,000}{2 + (5 \times 0.07)} (0.07 - 0.05)$$

$$= 5,000 - \frac{25,000}{2.35} (0.02)$$

$$= 5,000 - 212.77$$

$$= 4,787.23$$

If the purchaser paid $4,787.23 for a note with a nominal rate of 5 percent and carried the note until maturity, he or she would realize an effective rate of 7 percent.

How does a longer term affect the computations? Let us assume that a person wants to purchase a note for $25,000 that has thirty-five years to run to maturity, and that has a nominal rate of 7 percent. The purchaser wants

to discount the note so that he or she would receive an effective rate of 15 percent. By using the formula above,

$$A = 25,000 - \frac{35 \times 25,000}{2 + (35 \times 0.15)} (0.15 - 0.07)$$

$$= 25,000 - \frac{875,000}{7.25} (0.08)$$

$$= 25,000 - 9,655.17$$

$$= 15,344.83$$

The net value of the note under the above circumstances would be $15,344.83.

BALLOON PAYMENTS

When the final payment of an amortized loan is considerably larger than the normal payment, that payment is called a *balloon payment*. Thus, if a contract calls for a $50 per month payment including interest for 11 months and a twelfth payment of $500, the $500 is a balloon payment. In the case of discount notes and gross rate notes, the balloon payment is easily computed. However, in the case of real estate loans, it is somewhat more difficult. As with many of the other answers that we obtained by using formulas, this answer can also be obtained by the use of annuity tables that show the present value of $1, in conjunction with a loan payment amortization schedule. Unfortunately, the annuity tables, which show a monthly payment breakdown, are not easily available and are usually not near when the need arises to compute the problems. However, almost all real estate brokers and all real estate loan officers have a book of equal monthly loan amortization payments with which it is possible to compute a balloon payment. Let us assume a loan of $5,000 with interest at 6 percent payable at $51.84 per month with the whole note maturing in five years. How much will the balloon payment be at the end of the fifth year? In other words, how large will the outstanding principal balance be at that time? By referring to the monthly payment amortization schedule using the 6 percent rate with a $5,000 balance, we find that $51.84 would pay off a $5,000 note in eleven years. This means that at the end of five years, there would still be six years to run. Now, referring to the amortized schedule again, in the six-year period and the 6 percent table, we look for a payment of $51.84. The schedule shows that $51.38 for six years at 6 percent will pay off $3,100 while $3,200 would require a payment of $53.04; therefore the amount that would be paid off by $51.84 is between $3,100 and $3,200. Now consider these two columns of figures:

PAYMENT	PRINCIPAL
$51.38	$3,100
51.84	unknown
53.04	3,200

The difference between $3,100 and $3,200 is $100, whereas the difference between $51.38 and $53.04 is $1.66. The unknown figure bears the same relationship to $3,100 that $51.84 bears to $51.38, and $3,200 bears the same relationship to $3,100 that $53.04 bears to $51.38. Therefore,

$$\text{Balloon} = 3,100 + \frac{(51.84 - 51.38)}{1.66} \times 100$$

$$= 3,100 + \frac{0.46}{1.66} \times 100$$

$$= 3,100 + (0.2771 \times 100)$$

$$= 3,100 + 27.71$$

$$= 3,127.71$$

Therefore our unknown balloon payment is $3,127.71.

SIMPLE INTEREST

Simple interest is computed on the original principal without any provisions for additional interest to be paid on interest. For instance, simple 6 percent interest on a note of $1,000 for two years would be $60 per year, or $120. The interest could be payable quarterly, annually, or in some instances even at maturity.

COMPOUND INTEREST

Compound interest is interest that carries with it a provision that interest be computed not only upon the principal but also upon the unpaid interest. For example, on $1,000 for three years at 6 percent compound interest, the interest for the first year would be $60. If interest was not paid at the end of the first year, then the interest for the following year would be computed on $1,060 and would be $63.60; if the interest was not paid at that point, then the interest for the third year would be figured on $1,123.60. The final year's interest would then be $67.41, and at maturity the note would be for the full amount of $1,191.01.

CAPITALIZATION

Capitalization is the establishment of a value of a capital asset, by dividing the anticipated income from the asset by the desirable rate of return from such an asset. This procedure can easily be converted to a formula.

V = value

I = income

R = rate of return

D = rate of depreciation

N = net income

Our simple formula would be

$$V = \frac{I}{R}$$

Therefore, if we have an $8,000 income from an item and an 8 percent return is anticipated, our formula would show $V = 8,000 \div 0.08$ or $V = \$100,000$.

For simple calculations this formula may be adequate. However, certain expenses connected with producing an income should be subtracted from the income before it is actually used for capitalization purposes. Of course, in such a simple capitalization formula, we expect that the income will continue into infinity and have made no provision for depreciation of the item, slackening of income, or replacement of the item. Let us assume then that in order to produce the $8,000 of earnings, $2,000 of expenses were incurred and that the item has a life expectancy of fifty years. This means that each year, using a straight-line depreciation, a 2 percent depreciation should be charged. Our formula then should read

$$V = \frac{N}{D + R}$$

Using the figures in the problem, $V = 6,000 \div 0.02 + 0.08$; $V = 6,000 \div 0.10$; therefore, $V = \$60,000$. For further application of the capitalization theory, see Chapter 12.

Capitalization, using the above formula, came under fire in the days of the extremely high interest rates. Some appraisers are still using the formula. Some are computing an estimated depreciation and including that figure in the expenses. Some feel that the first year's estimated appreciation should be included in the net income in order to show a realistic capitalization figure for appraisal purposes.

SQUARE FOOTAGE

The ability to determine the square footage contained in a building or parcel of land is important in the appraisal process. The area, square footage, of a rectangle is found by multiplying the width (frontage) by the length (depth). The formula would be

$$A = F \times D$$

In a description of a parcel, the width is always given first. What could be the area of a parcel 210 feet × 400 feet?

$$A = 210' \times 400'$$
$$= 84,000 \text{ square feet}$$

An acre contains 43,560 square feet. How many acres in the parcel above?

$$\text{Acres} = 84,000^{\square'} \div 43,560^{\square'}$$
$$= 1.928$$

An acre of land in that area is selling for $50,000. What should the price be on the parcel?

$$\text{Price} = 1.928 \times \$50,000$$
$$= \$96,400$$

What is the depth of a rectangular parcel containing 3 acres? The frontage is 250 feet.

$$\text{Square footage} = \text{width} \times ?$$
$$= 3 \times 43,560^{\square'}$$
$$= 130,680^{\square'}$$
$$130,680 = 250 \times \text{depth}$$
$$\frac{130,680}{250} = \text{depth}$$
$$\text{depth} = 522.72 \text{ feet}$$

The ABC grocery store has an opportunity to lease a building in a shopping center that is 200 feet by 100 feet. The lease would allow it to sublease the part not used by the store. The master lease calls for the rent of $1.50 a square foot per month. It proposes to use the area as shown in Figure 11-1.

The store would lease the whole building at $1.50 a square foot per month and sublease portions B, C, D, E, and F at $2.25 a square foot per month. What would

be the total rent paid by the store? What would its net rent be?

$$\text{Area} = 100' \times 200'$$
$$= 20,000^{\square'}$$
$$\text{Total rent} = 20,000 \times \$1.50$$
$$= \$30,000 \text{ per month}$$
$$\text{Area} = 100' \times 70'$$
$$= 7,000$$
$$\text{Rent collected} = 7,000 \times \$2.25$$
$$= \$15,750$$
$$\text{Net rent} = \text{rent paid less rent collected}$$
$$= \$30,000 - \$15,750$$
$$= \$14,250$$

What was the net cost per square foot of the area used by the ABC grocery store?

$$\text{Area used} = (100' \times 100') + (100' \times 30')$$
$$= 10,000' + 3,000' = 13,000^{\square'}$$
$$\text{Net cost} = \$14,250 \div 13,000^{\square'}$$
$$= \$1.096 \text{ per square foot}$$

The area of a right angle triangle can be found by using the following formula:

$$A = \frac{W \times D}{2}, \text{ where}$$

$A = \text{area}$

$W = \text{width}$

$D = \text{depth}$

A parcel of land is in the form of a right triangle. The width is 25 feet and the depth is 100 feet. What is its area?

$$\text{Area} = \frac{25' \times 100'}{2}$$
$$= 1,250 \text{ square feet}$$

You own a corner lot which is zoned Commercial. It has a frontage of 100 feet on the main road and 75 feet on a minor road. There has to be a 50-foot setback from

FIGURE 11-1

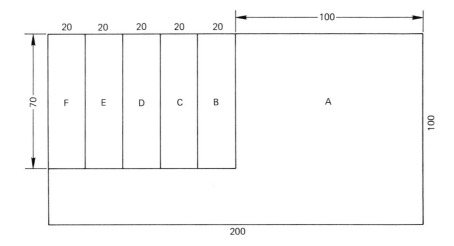

the main road, the lot faces north on this road and east on the minor road, and a 25-foot setback from the minor road. A setback of 20 feet is required from the south boundary of the lot, and a 10-foot setback from the west boundary of the lot. What would be the dimensions of a building that could be built on your lot?

The 50-foot setback from the main road plus the 20-foot setback from the south lot line would leave only 5 feet for the depth of the building. The 25 foot setback from the minor road plus the 10 feet from the west lot line would leave 65 feet for the width of the building.

The building would be 65 feet by 5 feet and would contain 325 square feet. A lot that looked quite valuable on the surface turns out to be of no value for a lot on which a building could be constructed. See Figure 11-2 for a plat of the lot.

SALES PRICE

Quite often sellers indicate that a certain net amount is desired and that the commission has to be included in the listed price. How is the sales price determined? As

FIGURE 11-2

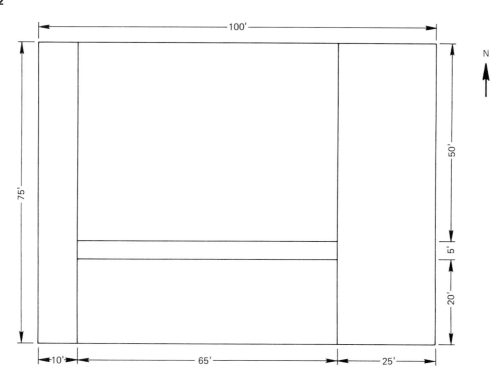

178   The Mathematics of Finance

an example, assume that the sellers tell the broker they desire $70,000 net for their home. The broker informs them the commission will be 7 percent. The sellers say they don't care what the commission is so long as they receive $70,000. What would be list price have to be in order for them to receive $70,000? Ignore closing costs.

Since the commission is to be 7 percent, then $70,000 would have to be 93 percent of the whole, so

Sales price = $70,000 ÷ 0.93

= $75,268.82

To prove our calculations, solve for the commission:

Commission = $75,268.82 × 0.07 = $5,268.82

Net to seller = $75,268.82 − $5,268.82

= $70,000

Builder B sells a home for $87,500. He made a 25 percent profit. What was his cost?

Cost = $87,500 ÷ 1.25 (125%)

= $70,000

A lender's opinion of the value of a property on which he or she will or has made a loan can be determined if the annual interest rate and the amount of one year's interest is known as well as loan-to-value percentage is given (loan-to-value ratio). Consider a loan at 14 percent interest, 80 percent loan. The interest paid the first month was $700. What was the appraisal?

Interest = $700 × 12

= $8,400 interest for one year

$8,400 ÷ 0.14 = $60,000 the amount of the loan

Appraised value = $60,000 ÷ 0.80

= $75,000

PRORATION

At the time a real estate transaction closes there are various expenses, some prepaid by the seller and some that are due but not payable, that must be allocated (prorated) between the seller and the buyer. These would include such items as insurance, taxes (paid or due but not paid), interest on notes assumed, bonded interest and indebtedness, and so forth. In computing them there are certain procedures that have been established in prorating expenses.

1. In almost all cases proration is based on a 360-day year.
2. Expense occurring on the day of closing and thereafter is charged to the buyer.
3. Determine the person to charge and for what period of time. In order to do this, the date of closing escrow must be known as well as the date to which the item is paid. If the item is paid beyond the date of closing the buyer pays. The seller pays if the item is payable up to the day prior to the closing.
4. Determine the amount of money to be charged.
5. Property taxes cover the year from July 1 through June 30 of the following year.

Proration of taxes is obtained by dividing the annual tax by twelve and that amount by thirty to obtain the daily cost. Remember the day of closing is charged to the buyer. For example, the taxes on a parcel amount to $2,275 for the year; the first installment of $1,137.50 has been paid by the seller; the escrow is to close on August 14. What would the proration be?

$2,275 ÷ 12 = $189.58 per month

$189.58 ÷ 30 = $6.32 per day

$189.58 + $82.16 = $271.74
(1 month)   (13 days)

$1,137.50 − $271.74 = $865.76

The buyer would be responsible for $1,137.50 for the year's taxes, and would have to pay into escrow $865.76 to reimburse the seller for taxes paid but not used.

Insurance premiums are computed on either a twelve-month or thirty-six-month premium depending on how the policy was written. Thirty-six months used to be the term of the normal insurance policy, but many are being written on a twelve-month term. Assume a policy written on January 10 for twelve months with a premium of $1,010; the closing date is August 14.

$1,010 ÷ 12 = $84.17 per month

$84.17 ÷ 30 = $2.81 per day

$589.19 + $8.43 = $597.62
(7 months)   (3 days)

Buyer would pay in escrow

$1,010 − $597.62 = $412.38

Interest on an assumed loan is another item that must be prorated. Assume that there is a $74,595.63 balance on a loan that is to be assumed. The interest at 14 percent has been paid for July. The closing date is again August 14. Who pays the escrow for the interest, and how much?

Interest = \$74,595.63 × 0.14

      = \$10,443.39 per year

      = \$10,443.39 ÷ 360

      = \$29.01 per day

      = \$29.01 × 13 days

      = \$377.13

Thus the seller would have to pay \$377.13 into the escrow account.

FINANCIAL STATEMENT

Although the financial statement is not as important in real estate lending as it is in commercial lending, it is a vital part of any application for a real estate loan since it is a means of determining the financial condition of the borrower through a mathematical analysis of the figures it includes.

Typical questions that might be answered by an analysis of the financial statement follow.

1. *Is the investment in term assets excessive in relation to current assets?* An investment that is top-heavy in fixed or term assets can sometimes lead to a shortage of working capital (current assets minus current liabilities), which in turn can cause slowness in the payment of current liabilities and a reduction of earnings through inability to take discounts.

2. *Are the total liabilities excessive in comparison to the capital account or the owner's equity?* Although it is true that very few individuals can show a capital account equal to their total liabilities, such a high ratio is still desirable since a drop in any of the capital assets would surely jeopardize the position of the creditors.

3. *Has the income pattern been stable? Is it increasing or is it on the decline?* This comparison is probably one of the more useful, since it will indicate the likelihood of prospects meeting their monthly payments. Is there a chance of a default in long-term indebtedness? Certainly if such a pattern has been on the increase, all things being equal, we can expect it to continue. Therefore, the determination of growth or decline in the income pattern is most important when making an analysis of the financial statement.

The financial statement actually includes several documents. The *balance sheet* may be prepared at any given time and reflects the financial position of the individual, company, or organization at that time. It contains a record of assets and liabilities plus the reconcilement of the capital account. Since the assets must balance with the liabilities plus the capital account, the statement has become known as the balance sheet.

Under assets are shown current assets such as cash, accounts receivable, stocks and bonds that are readily converted to cash, and inventory and other items that may easily be converted to cash. The balance sheet also includes fixed assets, which take longer to convert to cash, and which might include real estate, heavy equipment, deposits with agencies, leasehold improvements, other assets of improvements, and other assets of nonliquid form.

The other side of the balance sheet contains the liabilities. These, like the assets, are divided into current and fixed categories. Current liabilities include items such as accounts payable and the portion of notes payable due within one year, while fixed liabilities include real estate loans, the totals of notes payable that exceed one year, and other liabilities. The difference between total assets and total liabilities is the capital or equity of the business. Capital can be divided into paid-in capital, which is stock issued by the company; surplus, or earnings that have been placed into an account but not taken into the capital; reserves for losses against earnings that have not been distributed to capital; and undivided profits.

A second financial statement of interest to the statement analyst is the *operations statement,* sometimes called the profit and loss statement, which is used to measure the results of the operation of a business in terms of profit or loss. This statement consists of two parts—income and expense.

Income includes sales. The cost to the producer of goods sold is determined by subtracting the closing inventory from the beginning inventory and adding to this the cost of purchases for the period. The resulting figure subtracted from the total sales income gives the gross profit enjoyed by the organization. From the gross profit are subtracted operating expenses such as wages, light, power, heat, water, advertising, entertainment, travel, interest, maintenance, and repairs. Subtracting the operating expenses from the gross profit gives a net operating profit, to which is added other income such as refunds on returned inventory, purchase discounts, and income adjustments. From this figure are subtracted other expenses such as sales discounts allowed and refunds on returned merchandise, and the result of this subtraction is either a net loss or a net profit for the period. It is this figure upon which federal and state income tax computations are based. The taxes are deducted from the net profit or loss and the resulting figure carried forward as an addition to or subtraction from the capital account.

A third financial statement that it is useful to analyze is a statement of *cash flow,* sometimes called the statement of application of funds. The purpose of this statement is to show the changes in the available working capital and the flow of this capital. It is a projection of anticipated income and anticipated outgo by months. A thorough analysis of this statement will reveal times when loans will be necessary and when, through the normal course of business, it will be possible for these loans to be repaid.

Now that we understand financial statements and their contents, let us consider how the analyst uses them. First, it is desirable to have several years' statements to work from so that spread sheets (sheets that contain all elements of the balance sheet, year by year) can be prepared and a quick analysis by observation made. With several years' financial statements on a spread sheet, it is easy for the analyst to see whether the capital account and the working capital are increasing. Working capital is the difference between current assets and current liabilities. If the total current assets are $20,000 and the current liabilities are $15,000, the organization has a working capital of $5,000. It is also desirable to have available a reference to the national averages for the type of business that is being analyzed. Robert Morse Associates publishes such a book on national averages, as does the National Cash Register Company; such books compare firms within the same industry that are making comparable sales. In other words, it is possible to compare an organization making $250,000 per year gross sales with another also having a $250,000 per year gross sales average. Certainly it would not be fair to compare a business with $250,000 per year gross sales to a business with $1,000,000 per year gross sales. If possible, it is also desirable to compare the business with the trend in its area to see whether it is following the trend, and if not, why not.

Since most of the national averages have been converted to percentages, it would facilitate matters to change the dollar balances shown on the financial and operation statements to percentages for easy comparison. It is wise to remember that for every average there must be figures below as well as above the average. Therefore, although a particular business does not follow the average exactly, the average does provide a criterion by which to judge.

IMPORTANT REAL ESTATE RATIOS

Current Ratio

Of the ratios that should be analyzed in connection with the operation and balance sheets, probably the best known and most used is the *current ratio*. It is used to measure relative liquidity of the statement. Certainly a firm that has a current-assets-to-current-liabilities ratio of 2 to 1 is in a much better position to meet its current liabilities than a firm with a current ratio of 1 to 1 or even possibly an inverted ratio of $3/4$ to 1. A ratio of 2 to 1 would indicate that the value of the assets would have to drop

below 50 cents on the dollar before the organization would be unable to meet its obligations. A current ratio of 3 to 1 would indicate that there were three times more current assets than current liabilities and that the value of the assets would have to drop to $33^1/_3$ cents on the dollar before the firm would not be able to meet all its current liabilities.

Ratio of Net Income to Interest Charges

This ratio is of importance to the analyst, just as are all other expense items in ratio to the net income. An expense item that becomes excessive immediately reduces profits; if too excessive it may even jeopardize the position of a business. Therefore, a firm's net income should be analyzed in relationship not only to the interest charges but also to other operating expenses.

Ratio of Fixed Assets to Fixed Debts

The ratio of fixed assets to fixed debts should be at least 1 to 1, assuming the assets to be shown as depreciated, so that payment of the fixed liabilities can come from the liquidation of the fixed assets. A 2 to 1 or 3 to 1 ratio is not as important in this particular ratio, because there is no need for immediate conversion; consequently, the probability of the deterioration of the asset below the amount of the liability is not as great.

Ratio of Fixed Assets to Capital

The ratio of noncurrent assets to owned capital introduces an important question: Should not all fixed assets that are essential in the fabrication process of an organization and on which the success of the enterprise depends be owned free and clear of any debt pressure? If a mortgagee could foreclose such an asset when through economic failure the asset might temporarily be idle, the organization would be in jeopardy of losing control of that asset and possibly even being put out of business entirely. Therefore, most analysts feel that such assets should be on a retirement basis so that the eventual ownership of the assets will rest completely with the company. The analysis of the ratio of fixed debt to capital is therefore vital to be sure that the assets are not in jeopardy.

Ratio of Capital to Total Liability

Probably the second most-used ratio in the analysis of financial statements is that of capital to total liability, sometimes called the net worth to total liability. As the name indicates, this ratio measures the relationship of the net worth to the total debt of the organization.

In the comparison of net worth to total liabilities, a ratio that shows a normal increase in net worth indicates control of the operating capital by the owners and an increase in the strength of the organization. It is most important that this ratio also be at least 1 to 1, so that should it be necessary to liquidate the organization no loss would be suffered by the creditors. Of course, not all organizations can show this desirable position; however, there must be adequate strength in other areas before such an organization could be considered a satisfactory risk for an unsecured loan.

It should be emphasized that most real estate financing would not require such a detailed scrutiny of the financial statement and the operation statement.

Ratio of Net Profits to Net Worth

This ratio is sometimes referred to as the ratio of net income to equity. It is used to determine the success of an investment. The investment of funds in an organization (such funds constitute capital) indicates that a return is anticipated by the investor. An investment in any business entails a risk greater than an investment in government bonds, bank interests, or first deeds of trust. Therefore, the yield must be such as to entice capital into the investment.

For proper analysis other ratios should be used in connection with this one to determine whether management is doing a proper job. One of these others is the ratio of profits to sales. If this ratio is compared with the averages and found to be unfavorable, the analyst's interpretation of the net income to equity ratio will be affected.

Ratio of Sales to Operating Capital

This ratio is based on an economic theory that capital should be transformed into the production of additional wealth. If sales are too low for the proper use of capital as represented by the total assets, then either sales proficiency is not up to par or the company may have invested too much in fixed assets. Such a condition is usually one in which the total debt is high as measured by the ratio of net worth to debt.

Ratio of Net Profits to Sales

One of the main incentives for an individual to go into business is the possibility that profits will accrue to the owners of the business. Profits represent the margin between the total cost of producing and selling an article and the sales price. Consequently, the profits are a measure of the success of a business, and that success is indicated by the ratio of net profits to sales. Since this ratio is considered an indicator of the margin of profit, it is significant because it measures the amount by which costs can rise before losses appear. A slight decline in the margin between the selling price and the cost could

easily wipe out the profits. This ratio is therefore an important tool in the analyst's consideration of a financial statement.

Ratio of Dividends to Net Income

In the case of a small corporation closely held, this is probably one of the more important ratios to consider. It is by dividends that profits are removed from the business and diverted to the pockets of stockholders or owners. It is by dividends that the nominal wage the owner takes from the business is supplemented, and it is by dividends that profits are withdrawn from potential capital, thereby reducing the firm's ability to weather a financial storm.

From the financial statement the analyst should determine that the owners are not bleeding the corporation to its detriment. Where such a program is in force, the major ratios will very often reflect the withdrawal of earnings. When such a ratio reflects an adverse condition, it is desirable to discuss with the owners of the business the danger that could lie ahead.

OTHER IMPORTANT ITEMS ON THE FINANCIAL STATEMENT

A financial statement analyst should consider other items as well as ratios.

Adequacy of Depreciation

All assets deteriorate: some assets become obsolete; other assets experience economic depreciation caused by influences outside the asset itself. To offset these losses, organizations are allowed to establish regular depreciation schedules for all capital assets. The Internal Revenue Service has established maximum depreciation periods for almost all types of buildings and equipment. An analyst should see that adequate depreciation is being charged against the asset so that the organization will benefit from the allowable expense each year and will have the asset charged off when it no longer has any value, thus saving an unusually heavy charge for liquidation at the time of the sale, should the depreciation not have been adequate.

Adequacy of Repairs and Maintenance

It is difficult to determine from the financial statement whether adequate repairs and maintenance are being made. However, converting the expense of repairs and maintenance to a percentage of the gross profits and comparing this percentage with the national averages would indicate whether this particular business is extending itself beyond the appropriate amount in connection with repairs and maintenance.

Another problem involving repairs and maintenance is failure to make necessary repairs or to maintain equipment properly. Under these circumstances equipment can deteriorate rapidly and replacement can be excessive. If the expense figure converted to a percentage is too far below the average for the nation in that particular line of business, some consideration should be given to a change in policy.

Evaluation of Intangibles

Intangibles such as good will are often shown on a financial statement. In some cases, it is easy to see that there is a credit for good will far in excess of the amount actually enjoyed by the organization. In many instances the financial analyst will ignore such intangibles completely. In other instances, he or she may feel that, although the statement contains no indication of good will, such provision should be made because the individual is the business and is solely responsible for its success. His or her name on the business has value.

When such a business is sold, although the seller has created good will and will charge for it, that good will is often impossible to pass on because of the change of personality. Such a change will sometimes result in deterioration of the business and a complete loss of good will.

Inclusion of Managers' or Owners' Wages

The operating statement will often show executive salaries, other salaries, and wages. The question of whether the owner's salary or wages appear in any of these three categories must be considered at this point. It is possible that they may not, in which case they would be indicated as a withdrawal against the capital fund after the profits for the period had been added to the old balance of the capital funds.

A net profit of $5,000 that included the owner's salary of $10,000 would equal a net profit of $15,000 if the owner, after crediting to the capital account, withdrew $10,000. Of course, an analysis of the salary account and of the net profit in comparison to the national average could be inaccurate unless the analyst was certain that he or she was analyzing exactly the same deductions in each case.

Existence of Contingent Liabilities

More losses probably occur simply because the existence of contingent liabilities is not considered than for any other reason. A contingent liability is a liability of an individual to pay another person's debts, although it is not a personal debt nor an obligation that would normally show as such on the financial statement. However, should

the borrower for whom the guarantee was made default, it is a liability and it must be paid. After default, such a liability should appear on the financial statement. An analysis of any financial statement should take into consideration any possible liability of this type that might be assessed against the organization.

Lease Obligations

A *lease obligation,* although not a liability on the financial statement, is a contract expense that occurs monthly for as long as the organization is in operation and is financially able to pay the expense. If a firm has a ten-year lease on a piece of property on which the economic rent is $500, but the firm is paying only $200, this is an asset that, although it does not appear on the asset side of the balance sheet, allows the firm to operate at a lesser expense. It also gives the firm a tangible asset and a source of income, should it decide to sublease. The lease obligation could be reversed, however, with an economic rent of $500 and an actual rent of $700, in which case the firm is obligated to pay a higher rent per month than it would normally pay, should it not be on a lease obligation. Such information, if the profit spread is low, is of use to the analyst in determining the reason for the low ratio of profit to gross sales.

Adequacy of Insurance Coverage

The analyst is very interested in knowing whether the firm carries adequate fire insurance on combustible buildings and material and whether adequate liability insurance protects the organization against claims for damages. In the case of a commercial or industrial building, the analyst must know that there is full coverage on the property, or an 80 or 90 percent coverage clause as designated by the insurance company. If the firm does not have this coverage and suffers a total loss, the payment for the loss will be in a ratio of the insured portion to the total value. For example, let us assume that a $100,000 building is insured for $50,000 and suffers a loss of $50,000. The insurance company would pay a claim of only $25,000; since the insurance against the building was for only 50 percent of its value, they will pay only 50 percent of the loss. The analyst must also know the extent of liability insurance, because of the size of recent damage suits. A judgment against the company could well put it out of business if it did not carry adequate liability insurance.

Certificate of Financial Statement

Finally, the analyst is interested in the certification of the certified public accountant upon the financial statement, and in whether the statement is prepared from figures furnished to the accountant by the organization or prepared by the accountant from audited figures. The statement made by the certified public accountant at the beginning of the financial statement will reveal the type of figures used. If it is an audited statement, the analyst can be sure that all the figures presented are accurate and factual. If the statement is prepared from figures furnished by the individual or the organization, the analyst has no way of knowing that the figures are accurate and must depend upon his or her knowledge of the individual or organization to determine the credibility of the figures composing the financial statement.

QUESTIONS

1. If the cost of replacement is estimated to be $30 a square foot, the approximate cost to build the building in the diagram, rounded to the nearest hundred dollars, would be:
   a. $600,000
   b. $627,600
   c. $537,500
   d. $752,100

2. What is the selling price of a home if the salesperson received $3,350.85 as his or her half of a 6 percent commission charged by the broker?
   a. $111,695
   b. $223,390
   c. $134,035
   d. $ 95,740

3. Mr. Muncie pays 2 percent of total gross sales for rent of his commercial office. There is a minimum base rent of $1,000 per month.

In the past year the sales volume was $400,000. His rent for the year was
   a. $ 8,000
   b. $ 9,000
   c. $11,000
   d. $12,000

4. At what sales volume would Mr. Muncie have to pay on the basis of the 2 percent of gross sales?
   a. $600,001.00
   b. $600,000.01
   c. $600,000.00
   d. $599,999.99

5. Ms. Helen Williams, age fifty-seven, is going to be married. She wants to sell her home so she can take advantage of the one-time capital gains tax break. She advises the real estate broker that she wants the property to sell for a price that will give her $112,500, from which she will pay the usual closing costs. The broker will charge 5 percent. The sales price will be, rounded to the nearest dollar:
   a. $119,680
   b. $119,681
   c. $118,421
   d. $119,048

6. Mr. Layne borrowed $45,000 at 14 percent interest. The loan is amortized over a thirty-year period at $533.25 per month including interest. The principal will be reduced by the first month's payment by:
   a. $525.00
   b. $ 8.25

Diagram for Question 1

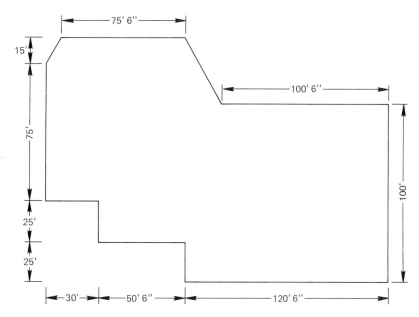

c. $ 33.25
d. $ 48.15

7. One month's interest on a five-year flat note with an annual interest rate of 18.5 percent amounted to $115.63. The face amount of the note was (round to nearest dollar):
a. $ 750
b. $1,387
c. $2,775
d. $7,500

8. Mr. Jones owns a parcel of land that has a frontage of 750 feet on a major road and 850 feet on a minor road. The property is zoned for single-family residences. The county requires fifty-foot improved roads in a subdivision. Mr. Jones plans to put in two fifty-foot hot rolled asphalt roads in his subdivision. One will be across the middle of the width of the area and one across the middle of the length. At $1.02 a square foot, what will be the cost of the two roads.
a. $84,150
b. $81,600
c. $79,050
d. $76,550

9. Mr. Jones' subdivision calls for lots 50 feet × 200 feet. His figures show that his costs, including interest on his loan, ecology report, surveys, roads, various permits, taxes, and selling expenses will be $518,000. He wants to receive a 22.5 percent profit on each lot. What will the sales price of each lot be? Round to the nearest $50.
a. $11,350
b. $11,400
c. $12,350
d. $12,400

10. Over a period of 7 months Ms. Downey paid $485 interest on a flat note of $3,750. The interest rate was:
a. more than 22 percent but less than 23 percent
b. more than 23 percent but less than $23\frac{1}{4}$ percent
c. more than $23\frac{1}{4}$ percent but less than $23\frac{1}{2}$ percent
d. more than $23\frac{1}{2}$ percent but less than $23\frac{3}{4}$ percent

BIBLIOGRAPHY

SALZMAN and MILLER, *Business Math*, 3rd edition, Glenview, IL: Scott-Foresman, 1983.

12

Appraisal for Real Estate Financing Purposes

The appraisal of real estate and real property is an inexact science, and to become adept in this field requires considerable reading and experience. It will be impossible to give all the ramifications of appraising in one chapter. If you are particularly interested in this subject, read one of the many books written since the 1930s, when formal analysis and study were first made with the idea of creating the profession of appraising.[1]

TYPES OF REAL ESTATE APPRAISERS

At the present time there are three types of real estate appraisers. First is the professional appraiser, who has made a thorough study of the profession of appraising and who has a designation such as Member of Appraisers Institute, Senior Residential Appraiser, or Senior Real Estate Appraiser. When a person in this level of appraisal makes an appraisal he or she brings all the professional abilities to bear upon the problem and is able to deliver a very accurate value estimate.

The second type of appraiser spends his or her time working with real estate in some form or another as a real estate salesperson, real estate broker, or possibly as a lending officer of a bank, savings and loan association, or mortgage banking group. This person is not a novice, and in many cases he or she can be fairly accurate in estimating value; however, he or she will be using primarily his or her experience in dealing with various types of properties to arrive at a value.

The last type of appraiser is the novice or the private individual who in his or her daily life has nothing to do with real estate but who from time to time desires to make an investment in real estate, using instinct as to

[1]For example, George H. Miller, H. Glenn Mercer, and Kenneth W. Gilbeau, *California Real Estate Appraisal: Residential Properties*, 2nd ed. (Englewood Cliffs, N.J.: Prentice-Hall, Inc., 1977); and S. McMichael, *McMichael's Appraising Manual*, 4th ed. (Englewood Cliffs, N.J.: Prentice-Hall, Inc., 1951).

good location and good value as the basis of purchase. In effect, every person who has ever bought a home has been an appraiser, for as he or she walked through the house, taking note of items that were appealing and items that were not, he or she was making an appraisal. After studying the house and its location, the potential buyer then decided on his or her own whether the house was worth the asking price. If he or she felt that it was, the house was appraised as having the value of the asking price.

MEANING OF VALUE

For appraisal purposes, three definitions of value have been widely accepted. First, value is the ability of one commodity to command another commodity in exchange, or, in other words, the relationship between a thing that is desired and the individual who desires it. This concept of value can be applied not only to real estate but also to any other property.

Value can also be the present worth of future benefits. With this definition we consider not only the capitalized income to the holder of the property but also the amenities that might develop from ownership of such property.

The third definition has been handed down by the Supreme Court of California (No. 156 Cal. 408): "Market value is the highest price, expressed in terms of money, which the land will bring if exposed for sale in the open market with a reasonable time allowed to find a purchaser buying with full knowledge of all uses and purposes to which it is adapted and for which it is capable of being used."

Factors Affecting Value

Value is created by people, whose activities regarding real estate are governed mainly by social, economic, and political factors. All these forces are complex and somewhat difficult to understand; however, the enumeration of a few examples will help clarify them.

Social factors include items such as changes in the size of families. During the 1930s it was not uncommon to find families with only one child; however, during the 1950s and early 1960s the number of children per family increased—and in the 1970s the number of children in younger families decreased markedly. This social phenomenon resulted in a fluctuating desire for larger houses. Population growth also affects the economic status of an area. If the population is growing in a section of the nation, the economy of that section will generally be flourishing. If population is declining, the area itself is usually declining economically. A third social factor closely aligned to this one is shifts in population density. If the population is moving out of one district in the community and into another, property values will be affected. A social factor that sometimes leads to a shift in population density is the attitude of the population of an area toward education and social activities. If the education is poor and there are no social activities, a shift caused by the lack of these social requirements usually becomes evident. These are only four of the social factors that motivate people to move into or out of an area.

The second factor influencing human interest in real estate is economics. This category includes the employment trends and the wage levels of an area. If unemployment is low and the wage level is high, the individual is usually happy to remain in that area; however, if wage levels should decline and there should be excessive unemployment, population will generally shift away from that area. Social goals are closely tied to such economic factors.

Along with economic trends and wage levels, of course, another item very evident in the economic pattern would be commercial and industrial trends. Without favorable industrial and commercial trends, unemployment and wage levels drop below those of areas in which people are content to work.

Other items we might consider are the quality and quantity of the natural resources available. If there are adequate natural resources that are not near depletion, we can expect the commercial and industrial trends to be up. Good natural resources, therefore, become an economic factor of benefit to an area.

Another economic factor to be considered is the availability of money and credit. Without credit or money to develop the aforementioned items, an area would decline economically and population shifts would probably result.

Still another economic factor is the cost of living in the area, including all commodities and taxes. Tax burdens can sometimes become so heavy that an individual is not willing to remain in an area. These then are some of the economic factors that influence people's decisions in the field of real estate.

Political factors include all things regulated by government or political forces. The government regulations could be countrywide, statewide, or local. National regulations include national rent controls, such as were instituted during World War II; allocation of materials, also in evidence during World War II; and credit controls established by the Federal Reserve Bank.

On a local level political factors include zoning ordinances or building codes, and police and fire protection. An area with favorable social, economic, and political factors will develop, prosper, and have unusual value.

Value has four components: utility, scarcity, demand, and transferability.

The definition of value that considers the present worth of future benefits indicates that a property will be used; however, use alone does not necessarily give value. A valuable item must also be scarce. For instance, the air about us is useful, for without it we would die; however, it is not scarce and consequently no great value is placed upon it. Further, an item may be scarce and it may be useful, but unless there is a demand for the item it still will have no value. For instance, a house might be built in the middle of Death Valley. The house would have utility and it would be scarce; however, there would be very little demand for such a house. Consequently, value would not be attributable to it.

The fourth requirement, transferability, is closely tied to the third. Without transferability there will be no demand, since it is the desires of people that create demand.

DEFINITION OF REAL ESTATE, REAL PROPERTY, PERSONAL PROPERTY, AND APPRAISAL

Real estate refers to the physical land and its appurtenances, including items affixed to it, such as buildings, pipelines, trees, shrubbery, and pumping plants.

Real property refers to the bundle of rights that arises by reason of ownership of the real estate. This bundle of rights is theoretically pyramidal in form, extending from the boundaries of the property at the surface of the earth to the center of the earth and out into space to infinity. The bundle of rights gives the holder of the physical real estate the right to use, lease, sell, give away, and enter, and also the right to refuse to do any of these things. These rights can be limited by the government through taxation, eminent domain, police power, and escheat, or by private agreement through deed restrictions, easements, and the like.

Personal property is all property that is not real property.

The function of an appraisal is to estimate a value for such purposes as loans, taxation, and condemnation and sale. An *appraisal* is an estimate or an opinion, usually in writing, of the value of a described property as of a specific date; it is supported by the presentation and analysis of general and specific data concerning social, economic, and political conditions affecting the particular property.

IMPORTANT ECONOMIC PRINCIPLES

Since economics plays such an important part in the appraisal of property, we shall now review certain economic principles.

The Principle of Supply and Demand

The principle of supply and demand has been recognized for many years. If there is a great demand for a commodity and the supply of it is low or short, its value increases. If supply is great and demand is small, its value declines. This principle applies to real estate and real property as well as to any other commodity. For instance, the amount of land available for use around the shore of Lake Tahoe is rapidly decreasing, whereas the demand for such property is increasing. As a result, very high prices are now being paid for this land. As land of one specific type becomes short in supply while demand remains steady, the value of the land will increase. Land is one of our economic assets that cannot be replaced and as population continues to grow, land use will change, and in certain areas it will become short in supply. Other factors will also affect supply and demand, such as wage rates, taxation, and government controls. The same factors applied to houses will have the same effects upon housing prices and value. Demand for an object is created by desire. The desire, in turn, is created through knowledge of the existence of a certain article, for without such knowledge there could be no desire, and without desire there could be no demand; however, desire may exist but the demand may be restricted if there is no ability, through buying power, to satisfy the desire. In other words, many people would like to live in a better home than they now occupy. If all people who have this desire were able to satisfy it, the demand would be so great that the value of such housing would appreciate considerably in value; however, the inability of many to afford such a move restricts the demand.

The Principle of Conformity

This principle states that maximum value is found when there is a reasonable degree of homogeneity in all factors—social, political, economic, and also physical. Note that we use the term *reasonable* homogeneity: Confor-

mity should not be monotonous uniformity but a reasonable degree of similarity. By conformity we do not mean that one house should be so much like another that a person would have difficulty determining which was his or hers when returning from an evening of entertainment. We do mean, however, that a group of houses should have similar architectural design. There should not be a modernistic home among a group of ranch houses or a two-story colonial among a group of modernistic homes, nor should there be a house costing $60,000 in an area of $25,000 homes. Not only the housing should be similar, but also the incomes of the families. Otherwise, people with higher incomes may create a problem because of ostentatiousness, or people with lower incomes may create a problem through financial inability to maintain their property.

The Principle of Substitution

The principle of substitution requires that property cannot be worth more than the cost of acquiring an equally desirable substitute property, assuming no costly delays. In other words, a less costly product will sell more quickly than a more costly one if the products and their utility are substantially the same.

To apply this principle to housing, from several houses with approximately the same advantages the prospective purchaser will select the one with the lowest cost. The more units available of the type of property being offered, the more easily one can be substituted for another. It might be stated that the market data approach to value is based upon this principle; however, there are several types of property in which it is difficult to find comparable properties that might be substituted, for example, schools, industrial buildings, churches, and other single-purpose buildings.

The principle of substitution created the concept that the cost of producing a new structure equally desirable to an existing structure usually sets the upper limit of value on the existing structure. If a desirable property is found, the upper limit of its value would be the cost of purchasing a lot of like desirability and constructing an identical new building, assuming no costly delay in construction.

The Principle of Competition

This principle states that excess profits in any field of endeavor tend to encourage ruinous competition that, in turn, tends to destroy the profits. A good example of this process is miniature golf, which became popular in the 1930s. In this business a nominal investment brought in fabulous returns. As soon as this became public knowledge, miniature golf courses were constructed on almost every available lot. As a result, profits were spread so thin that before long the courses all went out of business. A few miniature golf courses appeared recently and are doing well. In the Sacramento vicinity, however, the number has been curtailed, and therefore only a few courses are available to the public. As a result, they are making a good profit; however, it is not the excessive profit made during the 1930s.

Shops opened in an area that needs shops generally make very good profits. If the profits are too high, however, an excessive number of other shops will move into the area; before long the area may be overbuilt to the type of shop it originally needed and profits will be reduced to ruinously low levels.

The Principle of Change

This principle declares that no material thing remains static. The phenomenon is evident in almost any item, including human beings. The human being is born, grows, deteriorates, and finally dies. It is the same with individual properties. An area comes into being, buildings are constructed upon the property, they enjoy a period of appreciation, and after reaching a maximum potential, deterioration sets in, the property use changes, and the original structure is destroyed. An appraiser must always consider this theory of change when making an analysis of the area in which a property is located, trying to anticipate through present observable changes the future changes that will affect the property being appraised. The appraiser should always remember that he or she is looking, not at a thing as it will always be, but at an item or object that is changing daily in one respect or another.

The Principle of Highest and Best Use

Basic to the theory of value is the principle of highest and best use, which states that the best use of the property being appraised is the use which will produce at the time of the appraisal the greatest net return, in either cash or amenities, over a given period of time.

The highest and best use of the property is often that use for which it is zoned and for which it is being used at the present time; however, at times the property is in transition, that is, changing from one use to another. Therefore, present use is not necessarily the highest and best use, and this is one reason why, in appraising property, the land value alone is appraised before any consideration is given to the improvements. In the appraisal the land value remains as a separate entity. This will often show whether the property is being used to its highest and best use, since there is a definite relationship between the value of the land and the total value of the real property. If this is out of balance, the property probably is not being used to its highest and best use.

The Principle of Increasing and Decreasing Return

There is a point at which an increase in the application of capital does not produce a greater return, and there is a point beyond which the application of capital will produce a lesser return.

Take as an example a two-bedroom one-bath home valued at $42,500 and located among a group of newer homes that are three-bedroom two-bath homes costing $49,500. The two-bedroom, one-bath house is designed in such a way that a second bath can be added very easily at an approximate cost of $6,500. The application of additional capital to bring the cost to $49,000, making the property conform to those around it, would therefore be justified. However, if a family room and a music room were added at the cost of another $10,000 the house would cost $59,000 but would be located in an area of $49,500 homes. This would violate the principle of conformity and would result in a lesser return on the capital of $10,000 that had been invested in the family room and the music room.

The Principle of Contribution

This principle is somewhat similar to the principle of increasing and decreasing returns. It states that the value of an agent of production is measured by its contribution to the net income over and above its cost when present, or by its detraction from the net income when absent. A good example of this would be a two-story building in which the rooms on the second floor are rented to physicians and surgeons. Because this building is served only by stairs, it is necessary for the patients, some of them almost unable to walk, to climb the stairs to reach the doctors' offices. In appraising this piece of property it would be necessary to determine how much additional rent could be collected from the doctors if there were an elevator in the building. This additional rent would be the contribution the elevator would make to the net income. If the contribution, in the form of additional rent, would exceed the cost of installation and the operation, the net return would justify the elevator installation in this building. If the addition of a second elevator would not contribute sufficiently increased earnings through increased rentals to pay all of its costs, the principle of contribution would be working in reverse, and a second elevator should not be added.

The Principle of Balance

The four agents of production are labor and management, coordination (utilities, supplies, taxes, insurance, and so on), capital, and land.

Under California law, income from a property must go first to pay for labor and management; second, to take care of the utilities, supplies, taxes, insurance, and other items of this nature; third, to pay the interest on the capital investment and the depreciation on the buildings. After paying these three agents of production, whatever is left is said to be attributable to the land and represents the earnings of the land.

The principle of balance affirms that maximum value is achieved when the agents in production are in proper balance with one another. The property would not be considered in proper balance should the building be too small compared to the investment in the land site and therefore constitute an underimprovement to the land. Balance can also become improper when there are too many drugstores or too many grocery stores in one area for all to receive proper earnings from the land.

The Principle of Regression

Good cannot cure the effect of evil. If an area is regressing or deteriorating and one lot in the center of this area is purchased and a very nice structure built upon it, the building of this one structure will not cure the ills of the surrounding neighborhood.

One cannot appraise in a vacuum but must take into consideration all areas that influence a particular parcel. Once a district has started to deteriorate, the only cure is complete reclamation, either in the way of the Sacramento Redevelopment (through federal government aid) or by a group of people joining their individual efforts to destroy the old and to rebuild a new district.

Other principles have an effect on value, but those discussed above are the most important and the most valuable to consider in a short analysis of the appraisal process.

THE NEIGHBORHOOD

Neighborhood is not a word that can easily be defined, nor are the boundaries of a neighborhood easily delineated; however, a neighborhood might be considered as a more or less unified area in which there is a fairly homogeneous population and in which the people have a more or less common interest. Therefore, a neighborhood does not necessarily have to be a residential neighborhood; it can be an industrial, commercial, or farm neighborhood.

A residential neighborhood will very often reveal the characteristics of the people who live in it. If the people are slovenly, the neighborhood is usually slovenly. If the people are neat and show pride in ownership, the properties are usually neat. In analyzing the residential neighborhood, we would use the three factors discussed at first plus a fourth: a physical description of a neighborhood. Our analysis of the neighborhood could therefore be broken into physical, social, economic, and political factors.

Under physical factors we would be interested in (1) street improvements and street patterns; (2) geographical location of the neighborhood in relationship to the city; (3) sanitary and storm sewers; (4) soil and subsoil; (5) natural aspects of the area such as hills, ravines, streams, and other topographical features; (6) hazards such as fog, smog, smoke, industrial noises, vibrations, sonic booms, and testing of rocket motors; (7) approaches to the neighborhood; (8) availability of utilities; (9) convenience and quality of schools, stores, and transportation.

Under social conditions in the neighborhood we would consider (1) prestige of the neighborhood and the social standing of the community; (2) attitude of the inhabitants in the neighborhood toward law and order; (3) homogeneity of the inhabitants of the neighborhood as to social and economic characteristics; (4) size of the family and the ages represented within the average family.

Economic considerations could include (1) rent and income levels; (2) number of vacant living units in the neighborhood; (3) attitude of financial institutions concerning loans in that neighborhood; (4) growth of the neighborhood in recent years; (5) amount of new construction and the number of vacant lots.

Political factors to consider would be (1) special assessments; (2) zoning ordinances; (3) building codes; (4) tax rate; (5) assessment evaluation policies of the area; (6) special districts and their restrictions, such as irrigation districts that supply domestic water.

A neighborhood may be in one of three phases: integration or development; equilibrium, with no development and no deterioration; disintegration. A neighborhood in a period of disintegration may become a blighted area. It does not necessarily have to be an old subdivision or neighborhood to be a blighted area; a poorly planned or poorly financed neighborhood can very rapidly become blighted, in which case the life cycle of the subdivision is very short. It may be in a state of disintegration because it is in a transitional area, which means that other uses for the lands are developing and coming into the district and these uses are encroaching upon the neighborhood. Businesses can be too close together, thus affecting the residential neighborhood that adjoins them. The neighborhood may become blighted by a nonconforming group moving into the area.

The appraisal of a property must start with an inspection of the neighborhood in which the property is located. Although neighborhood boundaries are sometimes difficult to determine, some of the more easily recognized boundaries are natural boundaries such as rivers; wide traffic patterns such as freeways or express routes; a sharp change in property use; and houses or buildings of similar ages.

In analyzing a commercial neighborhood the appraiser must analyze the quality and quantity of the purchasing power available to the commercial neighborhood. Then he or she should try to determine the following: (1) In what direction is the community growing? (2) What land is available for new stores? (3) What is the economic status of the shopping area and in what condition is this shopping area at the present time? (4) How far is it to competition, and how important is this competition? (5) Are the shop owners honorable? (6) Have they invested heavily in inventory? (7) Have they invested heavily in leasehold improvements? (8) What transportation is available to them? (9) How are their goods received from the wholesaler? (10) If customer delivery is necessary, what delivery services are available?

In analyzing an industrial neighborhood, the appraiser should be interested in the availability of raw materials that the plant uses; how the raw materials are received; the possibility of shipping inexpensively to the consumer; the availability of a labor force within easy commuting distance; any necessity for the labor force to come to work through a slum district; and the availability in large quantities of all utilities.

In analyzing a farm neighborhood the appraiser would be interested in the size of the unit farm in the neighberhood; the labor pool available for harvesting crops; the availability of water, power, and transportation for the harvested crop to a center for processing or sale; and the distance of the market from the farm.

THE SITE

After the neighborhood has been analyzed, the site itself should be analyzed. There are eight steps in analyzing a site: (1) Obtain the legal description and the mailing address of the site. After the legal description has been obtained, the restrictions that have been placed on the site should be analyzed. In this way the number of rights of the bundle of rights that are available to the owner may be determined. (2) Obtain the tax valuation and rates plus any outstanding special assessments against the site such as street improvement, sewer, and lighting bonds. (3) Determine the present zoning. Understand what it permits and determine whether any possible changes are pending at the present time or whether any could be caused by developments in the area. (4) Obtain or prepare a plat of the site. On this plat should be checked the frontage, the effective frontage, the effective depth, and the lot shape. Obvious terrain changes such as hills, gullies, and dropoffs should be indicated. Show also any large tree and its size. Indicate the setback of the adjacent property, if improved, and the type of property as well as the topography of the adjacent lots. (5) Determine the nature and location of the utilities. Determine the extent of streets and alleys and who maintains the roads. (6) Check soil type and condition, depth, and so on. This is important because the building must have bearing soil or piles will be necessary to support a foundation. Good

soil is also important for the growth of the site improvements. (7) Check maintenance of homes next door and even beyond if in the neighborhood. (8) Estimate the highest and best use of the lot if it is vacant.

APPROACHES TO VALUE

Now that we have general and specific information concerning the property, we are ready to apply the three approaches to value: market data, cost, and income.

The *market data approach,* as the term implies, is one in which sales prices of similar property are compared. In comparing one property with another the appraiser realizes that no two properties are exactly alike. However, some properties are close enough to each other so that by making simple adjustments as to the time of sale, the location of the property, and the physical aspects of both the site and the improvements, the appraiser can arrive at an estimated value of the subject property. All sales that are used for comparison must be checked to determine that they were normal transactions and were not consummated under duress or pressure of any type, that they were on the market for a reasonable length of time, and that both parties to the transaction were fully cognizant of the uses to which the property could be put.

The market data approach, of course, presupposes a market providing sales with which the subject property can be compared; however, there are times when the market is nonexistent for property, in which case the market data process is not as useful in the final correlation with the appraisal value as the other two approaches. During such times current listings of such property can be used as an indication of the ceiling of value. The market data approach carries much weight in the appraisal of residential real estate, since sales are good barometers of value for this particular type of property. The market data approach is also very valuable in the appraisal of empty land. Since land cannot be manufactured except through reclamation, the market data approach is about the only means of arriving at a value for land.

The second approach to value is the *cost of replacement or reproduction approach.* Although cost is not value, in the principle of substitution we found that cost had a tendency to set the upper limits of value. Therefore, we are interested in the *cost approach* as a possible means of comparison so that a final value estimate can be made. In this method an estimate is made of the cost of reproducing the improvement new at today's prices with materials commonly in use today. From the resulting figures we then deduct the depreciation that has accrued.

There are several methods for determining the cost of reproduction. Probably the most popular today in California is the *square-foot method.* To use the square-foot method, determine the square footage of livable area in the unit. Multiply it by a factor representing the unit cost per square foot for building such a structure in the area in which the structure is located. The unit cost in the area can be determined by the appraiser's working closely with contractors and materialmen. However, the easier method is to subscribe to a service such as Marshall and Swift, which supplies current square-foot costs to its subscribers.

There are both advantages and disadvantages to the square-foot method. For example, it does not take into consideration the height of ceilings. (High ceilings alter the costs.) Second, variation in roof design will also alter the cost estimate. From this it is clear that accuracy is only approximate. However, the square-foot method is faster than some of the other available methods and still gives an acceptable degree of accuracy.

The second method is the *cubic-foot cost analysis*. In this method the outside measurements of the building are cubed by multiplying the width by the depth by the mean height. The mean height is measured from the underside of the basement floor, or floor joist, if there is no basement, to the mean height of the roof. This again has the benefit of being a fast means of computing costs. It has the disadvantage of a third measurement, the mean height, which is difficult to make, as well as the same disadvantages as the square-foot method. However, it is probably a little more accurate in buildings with a variance in ceiling heights.

The third method is the *quantity-survey costs method,* which involves a very detailed estimate of the quantities and costs of labor and materials plus overhead and profits that the contractor would normally expect. This is a method that the contractor uses when he or she prepares the cost estimate from plans and specifications. It has the advantage of being very accurate, but the disadvantage of being slow and tedious.

A fourth method of determining cost is the *unit-in-place cost analysis*. Consideration is given to use of installed prices of various components of the building. These are usually expressed in square-foot cost of wall, the cost of installation of doors and windows, fireplaces, heating units, cooling units, and so on. After all units and components making up the building have been figured, the figures are totaled and an estimate is obtained that is quite accurate but again very detailed and time consuming.

The third approach to value is through *capitalization-of-income approach*. In this approach value is found by the formula $V = NI \div RI$. In our formula V is equal to value, NI is equal to net income, and RI is the rate of return expected on investment.

To obtain the net income required in the formula above, we take the gross annual income of the property owner

and deduct from it all expenses in connection with the production of this income. These would include such items as taxes, insurance, maintenance, repairs, management, various licenses, garbage disposal, heat, light, and water if furnished. The one item not deducted would be depreciation, because depreciation as an expense presupposes a knowledge of value. At this point we do not have a knowledge of value; therefore, depreciation cannot be included as a deductible expense.

The most popular method of figuring depreciation is probably the straight-line concept, in which a certain percentage is deducted each year. For instance, if it were determined that the property had an economic life expectancy of twenty years, there would be a 5 percent depreciation each year. The straight-line depreciation has been borrowed from the accounting profession and is acceptable although it does not take into consideration individual variations of the property. Therefore, an effective-age concept of depreciation has been developed that has a straight-line depreciation behavior but compares the property with other typical property of equivalent usefulness and condition and sets up a life expectancy on this basis. In this method the chronological age may be higher or lower than the actual age of the property. When we know the remaining economic life, the rate of depreciation and the percentage that is to be expected can then be determined.

The next problem is to develop a rate that would represent the return an individual would expect to receive on his or her capital investment. There are various ways to determine this interest rate. One device is the rate selection by summation. This method builds an interest rate by setting up various components, which, when added together, constitute the total interest rate. In this method of selecting a rate, the components consist of, first, the safe rate or nonrisk rate. This is a rate you might receive from government bonds or investment in savings accounts in banks. Added to this rate would be the rate for lack of safety. Depending upon the property and the individual, this rate would be high or low. The third rate to be added would be the rate for nonliquidity, for it is recognized that investment in real estate, although a secure investment, is not a liquid investment; there are periods when quite some time must pass before a sale can be consummated. The fourth component is the rate for the burden of management. Regardless of how little, a certain amount of management is nevertheless necessary in any real estate investment.

If we were to build up such a rate, using the above, we would probably use the following figures: safe rate or nonrisk rate—12 percent, since it is possible to obtain ten-year government notes that yield a 12 percent rate; rate for lack of safety—1.5 percent—a fairly safe investment; rate for nonliquidity—1 percent; rate for burden of management—1 percent. The total summation rate is 15.5 percent. If the risk were higher, the risk rate might have been 2.5 percent instead of 1.5 percent, making the rate for capital interest 16.5 percent.

Capitalization, using the formula above, has come under fire in the days of extremely high interest rates, rapid appreciation, and the more complex methods of computing depreciation. The formula was good for use with straight-line depreciation. Some appraisers are using value equals net income divided by rate of return expected on the investment. Here, the depreciation is included in the expenses. Other appraisers, who specialize in income property appraising, use a complicated formula in which one year of appreciation is included in the net income in order to show a realistic capitalization for appraisal purposes in the current market.

It is also possible to use what is known as band-of-investment theory, by which a rate is determined by compiling the figures of mortgage and equity rate that the market would disclose.

Another rate selection would be by comparison of quality attributes. Still another would be a rate selection by direct comparison. This would supply the last figure in our equation needed to arrive at a value using the income approach.

To illustrate, suppose that the net income from a piece of property is $25,000. Using the following figures, a capitalization rate of 15.5 percent, as above, we would obtain the equation V equals 15.5 percent, which would equal $25,000 divided by 15.5 percent. Value, then, would be $161,300. This value has been found by the property residual method of capitalization of income, which assumes the income comes from the land and any improvements as a unit or whole entity.

There is also a land residual method that can be used when the cost of worth of the building is known and the value of the land is unknown. In this case the capitalization rate of 15.5 percent plus the depreciation rate of 2.5 percent, assuming an economic life of forty years for the improvements, would be applied to the building's value to determine the amount of income attributable to the building alone. The building's income would then be subtracted from the total income in order to find the income earned by the land. This income is then divided by the capitalization rate only, as land is theoretically not depreciable. This method is accurate only when the improvements are relatively new or their value is clearly known.

Assume the building has a known value of $121,000. The depreciation at 2.5 percent would be $3,025 a year on the straight-line depreciation method. This amount plus the capitalization rate of 15.5 percent equals 18 percent and the total income would be $28,025, including the depreciation on the building.

$$\$121,000 \ \times \ \ \ \ 0.18 \ = \ \ \ \$21,780$$

(value of building) (interest) (income earned

by building)

This amount is subtracted from the total earnings.

$$\$28,025 \ - \ \$21,780 \ = \ \$6,245$$

Thus, $6,245 is the income attributable to the land alone. This is capitalized by dividing the $6,245 by the capitalization rate only—15.5 percent—which equals $40,300, the value of the land. To summarize, using the previous example

$$\$121,000 \ + \ \ \ \ \$40,300 \ = \ \ \ \$161,300$$

(building's value) (land's value) (property's value)

There is a third method—the building residual method. In this case the value of the land is known as well as the capitalization rate. This rate times the value of the land gives the amount of income that is attributable to the land. The balance is earned by the building. This amount can then be used to obtain the building's value. As an example, using the figures from the previous example, we find that the value of the land, $40,300, multiplied by the capitalization rate, 0.155 (15.5%), will give us the earnings for the land.

$$\$40,300 \ \times \ 0.155 \ = \ \$6,247$$

When this amount is subtracted from the total income, we find that $21,778 is the income that the building earned. This amount divided by 18 percent (includes the 2.5 percent depreciation) gives the value of the building.

$$\$21,778 \ \div \ \ \ \ 0.18 \ = \ \ \ \$121,000$$
$$\$121,000 \ + \ \ \ \ \$40,300 \ = \ \ \ \$161,300$$

(building's value) (land's value) (property's value)

Rules of thumb are useful only if people realize that they are not absolute, but only approximations. The use of a *gross rent multipler* on income property is used by people so often that it should be considered here. The gross rent multiplier is obtained by going to the marketplace to find comparable property that has sold recently. The sales price and the monthly gross rent must be determined. Only one comparable is needed. The monthly gross multiplier is found by dividing the sales price of the known property by its monthly gross rent income.

Consider the following example. A ten-unit apartment sold recently for $200,000. The gross monthly rent was $1,750.

Monthly gross rent
multiplier (MGRM) = $200,000 ÷ $1,750

= $114.29

There is a comparable apartment that has a monthly gross rent of $2,250 a month. It has one more unit in the complex than the unit that was recently sold. Using the MGRM, what would its value be?

V = $114.29 × $2,250

= $257,152

An annual multiplier can also be used, in which case the annual gross income is divided by the sales price as above.

We now have three values of the property we have been appraising: through the market data approach, through the cost approach, and through the capitalization-of-income approach. Should any of these three values equal each other, it would be a remarkable coincidence.

The final appraisal is not found by adding the three values and dividing the total by three. Instead, we analyze the information that has been collected, determine which approach has the most bearing on this particular problem, and, using a correlation of the three, arrive at a final estimate of value.

QUESTIONS

1. Social factors can affect the value of real estate. Which of the following is not a social factor?
   a. change in the size of families
   b. employment trends
   c. shifts in population density
   d. attitude toward education and social activities

2. Economic factors also affect the value of real estate. Which of the following are considered economic factors?
   a. wage levels of an area
   b. employment opportunities
   c. commercial and industrial development
   d. all of the above

3. There are several principles that must be considered in appraising. One of these is the principle of conformity. This means that
   a. a house costing $100,000 would be appraised for more if it is built among houses costing $50,000
   b. a house costing $50,000 has a tendency to be valued for less if built among houses costing $100,000
   c. maximum value is found when there is a reasonable amount of homogeneity in all factors
   d. all of the above

4. The principle of substitution is based on the fact that
   a. property cannot be worth more than the cost of acquiring an equally desirable property, assuming no costly delays
   b. competition comes when excess profits are made
   c. value decreases when excess improvements are made
   d. value is based on the use to which property can be put

5. The neighborhood can influence the appraisal value of property by
   a. having a nice approach to the area
   b. having a slovenly appearance
   c. availability of most utilities
   d. all of the above

6. An approach to value is
   a. cost
   b. market data (comparison)
   c. capitalization
   d. all of the above

7. To arrive at an appraised value, first, values must be obtained by all methods, then
   a. each is analyzed and evaluated, and from this evaluation an appraisal value is reached
   b. the three methods should produce the same value
   c. the three values are totaled, then divided by three. This is the appraisal value
   d. none of the above

8. A commercial building is being appraised by James Lawrence. The building is fully rented. He has used the three approaches to value. They did not all produce equal values. Which approach will carry the most weight even though it might be adjusted?
   a. the cost approach
   b. the comparison or market data approach
   c. the capitalization approach
   d. none of the above

9. In determining a current rate of return for capitalizing income, all the following should be considered except
   a. cost of the property
   b. safe interest rate, such as interest on government bonds
   c. lack of liquidity
   d. management costs

10. Cost valuation is obtained by using a factor times
    a. the square footage in a building
    b. the cubic footage in a building
    c. actual material used in construction
    d. all of the above

BIBLIOGRAPHY

American Institute of Real Estate Appraisers, "The Appraisal of Real Estate." Published by the American Institute of Real Estate Appraisers, 1978.

McMICHAEL, S, *McMichael's Appraisal Manual*, 4th ed. Englewood Cliffs, NJ: Prentice-Hall, 1951.

MILLER, GEORGE H., H. GLENN MERCER, and KENNETH W. BILBEAU, *California Real Estate Appraisal: Residential Properties*, 2nd ed. 1977.

13

Government Real Estate Finance Programs

GENERAL LENDING PRACTICES PRIOR TO 1934

Before 1934 it was the practice of lending institutions to make real estate loans on a nonamortized basis for a short period of time. At maturity, the loans could be rewritten with new title insurance obtained, or extension agreements could be drawn, in which case continuation policies could be received from the title insurance companies. Both methods of handling the short-term note were expensive and time-consuming as far as the lending officers were concerned. But since they required new appraisals or inspections, they did keep the lending institution informed of the condition of the property on which they were taking mortgages.

Because of the short term of a note and the expense of handling it, the interest rates had to be high. The laws required that there be a low ratio of the loan to value, and therefore it took time for an individual to accumulate enough money to make a down payment and buy a home, or it became necessary to obtain junior financing at an even higher interest rate.

Prior to 1934 it was very difficult for a lending agency located outside the county seat to check the tax records to determine that the ad valorem taxes had been paid against the property used for security. The resulting great number of tax delinquencies sometimes resulted in the sale to the state of the property that was used as security. Up to 1934 inadequate credit analyses were made of the borrowers, since the lenders felt secure because of the high investment the borrower supposedly had in the property. Also, it was not unusual to find a poorly constructed home next to a home that was very well constructed with more than the usual necessary building requirements. This situation existed because up to that time few counties had a minimum construction code.

These were some of the situations the Federal Housing Administration attempted to correct. It established low down payments, low interest rates, monthly amortization over a long term, collection of prorated portions of taxes and hazard insurance, and standard means of making credit analyses. It also established minimum property standards.

HISTORY OF THE FEDERAL HOUSING ADMINISTRATION (FHA)

In 1934 the economy of the United States, including California, was seriously depressed. It was felt that if work could be provided for such artisans as carpenters, electricians, plumbers, and laborers the economy would improve. With this thought in mind, Congress passed the Federal Housing Administration Act, which became law on June 27, 1934. At the time of its passage, it had two sections: Title I and Title II. Title I, for modernization of existing homes, also provided for the conversion, repair, and alteration of existing structures and for the building of small, nonresidential structures. At first the maximum amount that could be insured under Title I was $2,500. The FHA insured the lender against loss up to 80 percent of the loan and up to 20 percent of all such loans made by the institution. This was later changed to 90 percent of the loan and 10 percent of all such loans made by the lending institution. The cost of this insurance was 0.5 percent of the amount of the loan. Title II was to make it possible for a person to buy a home with a small down payment. It also made it possible, under Section 203, for him or her to construct a new home under rigid inspection for a small down payment. Actually, this has been the most popular section of the Federal Housing Administration Act through the years and has accounted for more loans than any other section of the act.

Title III was established as a means of providing a secondary market for mortgages. It was hoped that, through the use of Title III, mortgagees would be able to discount their mortgages to purchasers, thus freeing their capital for additional loans.

From time to time during the life of the Federal Housing Administration, Congress has found it desirable to add new sections to provide insurance for various types of loans that are in demand and badly needed in the country. Title VI was added in 1941 as a means of providing housing for workers employed in defense industries during World War II. This provision was for low-cost housing. Thus, as costs increased and the need for lower down payments arose, Congress adjusted the Act to meet the demands and needs of the country.

More recently problems have developed in connection with the provision of housing for the elderly, of homes for those displaced by slum clearance, of nursing homes, and of larger home improvement loans. In the late 1960s additions were made to the Act to help those in the lower income bracket find housing. The assistance varied from partial government assistance to outright subsidy. The programs administered by the Federal Housing Administration increased from two in 1934 to sixty-six in 1982. The vast majority of the new programs were added between 1960 and 1968. Most of these benefit people in the low- and the middle-income brackets. The Act has been amended as these needs have arisen; in this manner the Federal Housing Administration has helped solve some of the more pressing problems of housing in the United States. Title II, as it was originally set up, was an emergency measure that received many modifications by Congress, and each year the life of the supposedly temporary agency was extended by Congress with additional mortgage limits established. In 1946 Congress recognized that insured mortgage loans were a firm part of our economy and gave permanent life to the Federal Housing Administration.

BASIC PURPOSES OF THE FEDERAL HOUSING ADMINISTRATION

As expressed in the Act, the basic purpose of the FHA is to encourage improvement in housing standards and conditions, to facilitate sound home financing on reasonable terms, and to exert a stabilizing influence in the mortgage market. The Federal Housing Administration was not established as and never has been a lending agency, nor does it plan or build homes. It is an insurer of loans, for which service it receives a fee of 0.5 percent, amortized monthly, of the loan balance on each anniversary of the date of the note. This insurance, called mutual mortgage insurance, insures the lender against loss by default of the borrower, rather than insuring the life of the individual purchasing the home. Not only does this 0.5 percent insure the mortgagee against loss, but it also provides funds for the full operation of the Federal

Housing Administration. In establishing this coverage, the FHA has affected the design of homes, the standard to which the homes are constructed, the sites upon which homes are built, and the lending practices of lending institutions, but it does not loan money to the borrower.

Since FHA-insured loans are insured through a government agency, they are termed nonrisk loans by examining authorities for life insurance companies, savings and loan associations, and banks. Therefore, lending agencies need not consider them in their computation of ratios to deposits, thus freeing additional funds for loaning and other uses in our economy.

As a result of the requirements established by the FHA's insurance program, there has been greater conformity in building standards, desirable planning, and reliable borrowers. FHA-insured loans have found a ready secondary market, and funds that under previous conditions would have remained in the vault have found their way into communities far distant from the purchaser of the FHA-insured loan. Insurance companies in Florida and on the East Coast have bought many millions of dollars' worth of FHA-insured loans made on the West Coast. They feel that they can make this investment safely, because they know that the house must conform to a minimum property requirement, that the borrower has been analyzed, and that the loan is insured.

TYPES OF LOANS NOW AVAILABLE FOR INSURANCE UNDER FHA

Title I, Section 2: Modernization or Improvement Loan

There are several different classes of modernization home loans, called Title I, Class 1(a), Class 1(b), Class 2(a), Class 2(b), and Title I mobile home loans. There are enough differences in each type of loan that they should be considered separately.

Class 1(a) loans. The purpose of the Class 1(a) loan is to finance alterations, repairs, or improvements upon or in connection with existing structures. The improvements are to protect or substantially improve the basic livability of the structure. All types of structures are eligible for this type of loan; however, if the loan exclusive of financing charges exceeds $600 and is to finance improvements on a home, the structure must have been completed and occupied for at least ninety days. This particular restriction does not apply if the loan is for the construction of a civil defense shelter or for a repair in connection with major disaster damage. Maximum loan under a Class 1(a) note is $15,000, and the maximum term is for fifteen years and thirty-two days.

It is possible for such a loan to be rewritten should a

person desire to refinance the loan, but in no case may the total maturity exceed fifteen years from the original date on the note. In other words, an individual might pay for three years on a home improvement loan, get into financial difficulties, and request that the loan be rewritten for another twelve years and thirty-two days. Since the loan has run for only three years, it would be possible for the individual to make such an adjustment and reduce the payments due on the obligation, since the total time would be only twelve years and thirty-two days, thus qualifying under the refinancing restrictions.

The lender may require a mortgage or deed of trust to secure the note under this Section. In this case, the borrower may be required to pay title fees and recording fees, but the fees may not be deducted from the amount of the note.

The interest rate (annual percentage rate) is set by the Secretary of Housing and Urban Development. And to insure such a loan, the FHA charges 0.5 percent, or fifty cents per $100 per year on the amount advanced.

Class 1(b) loans.

The purpose of the Class 1(b) loan is to finance alterations, repairs, and improvements to existing structures used as apartment houses or dwellings for two or more families. Such improvements are to protect or substantially improve the livability or utility of the structure. The maximum net loan amount under the Class 1(b) improvement loan is an average of $7,500 per unit, not to exceed $37,500 per structure. The maturity of the note cannot exceed fifteen years and thirty-two days. Like Class 1(a), the Class 1(b) loan may be refinanced at a later date; however, the same rule applies that the maximum maturity may not be more than fifteen years from the date of the original note.

If title insurance is taken on this loan, the recording fees and cost of the title search may not be paid on the proceeds of the loan or included in the face amount of the loan but must be paid in cash by the borrower. The charge that the FHA makes for insuring this type of loan is 50 cents per $100, or 0.5 percent per year on the amount advanced.

Class 2(a) loans.

The purpose of the Class 2(a) loan is to finance construction of proposed nonresidential or nonfarm structures. They can be commercial structures, such as service stations or small real estate offices. The maximum net loan available for this type of construction is $10,000, with a maturity of fifteen years. The loan can be refinanced as long as the total maturity does not exceed fifteen years from the date of the original note. If the lender decides to take security using a trust deed on the property, then the borrower may be required to pay recording fees and title insurance costs; however, these may not be taken out of the proceeds of the loan

or included in the face amount of the loan and must be paid in cash by the borrower. The insurance charge by the Federal Housing Administration is again 50 cents per $100 per year, or 0.5 percent per year on the amount advanced.

Class 2(b) loans.

The purpose of the Class 2(b) loan is to finance the construction of proposed nonresidential farm structures such as a barn, chicken house, or tool shed. The maximum loan available to an individual borrowing under Class 2(b) is $15,000 exclusive of financing charges. The maximum maturity of such a loan is fifteen years. If the note is secured and is written for fifteen years, it can be refinanced for a maximum period of twenty-five years from the date of the original note. The refinanced note must still be secured by the first trust deed or first lien against the property.

If the lender requires a first lien on the property, the recording fees and cost of title searches shall be paid by the borrower; however, they may not be deducted from the proceeds of the loan or added to the face amount of the loan. The insurance charged by the Federal Housing Administration is again 50 cents per $100 per year of the amount advanced, or 0.5 percent per year.

Section 2, Title 1, mobile home loans.

Mobile homes have become increasingly important in the home sales market. A few years ago every sixth home sold for under $20,000 was a mobile home. In 1975 every third such home sold was a mobile home, and in 1976 every second home sold under $20,000 was a mobile home. The purpose of the mobile home FHA Title I loan is to finance the purchase of a mobile home that will be used by the buyer as his or her principal residence. To qualify, the mobile home must meet the FHA minimum standards, which are the same as those required by banks and savings and loan associations. The maximum amount of the loan is $18,000 for what is termed a single wide and the maximum maturity is fifteen years and thirty-two days; the maximum loan is $27,000 on a double wide, with a maximum maturity of twenty-three years. Both loans may be refinanced so long as the total period of time does not exceed twenty-three years from the date of the original note. The maximum annual percentage rate is set by the Secretary of HUD and a 54 cents per $100 per year is charged for insurance on the original amount advanced. A security agreement is required if the mobile home is to be placed on a rented lot. The lot must be approved by the FHA if it is outside a mobile home park, and the park must be approved by the FHA if the mobile home is to be placed in a mobile home park. If the mobile home is to be placed on property owned in fee, a deed of trust must be taken on the land.

Most loans insured under Title I are unsecured loans,

similar to personal loans in their credit approach. Responsibility for the credit approval rests upon the lending institution unless the loan is in excess of the amount of $7,500, in which case prior approval must be obtained from the FHA. The credit application must always be taken in connection with the Title I loan, but there is no need under Title I to verify bank deposits, employment, or ownership of the land. (The land must be owned by the borrower unless he or she has a lease on the property that extends at least six months beyond the maturity of the note.) If the property to be improved is owned by the borrower under a lease, it is not unusual for the lending agency to request the person owning the property to co-sign the note. The note must be valid and enforceable against the borrower or borrowers and all signatures must be genuine. Title I insurance does not cover losses resulting from forgery or any other cause of making the note unenforceable. Claims in case of default are paid in cash after all rights to the note are assigned to the FHA.

A claim in case of default must be filed no later than six months after the due date of the final instalment unless an extension is allowed by the FHA. The insurance protection on an individual loan is 90 percent of the amount of the lender's loss.

The Federal Housing Administration has set certain guidelines in connection with the Title I mobile home loan. To qualify, the applicant must have sufficient funds to make the required down payment and must have an income adequate to make payments on the loan as they become due. The applicant must intend to use the mobile home as his or her major residence and have a site acceptable to the Federal Housing Administration on which the mobile home is to be placed. The site may be rented space in a mobile home park that has been approved by the FHA, or it may be land owned by the applicant that has met the standard set by the commissioner. The buyer and the seller both must certify that there will be no violation of zoning requirements or other regulations applicable to mobile homes. An FHA Title I mobile home loan is secured by a financing statement and a security agreement properly recorded under the Uniform Commercial Code.

Title II

Section 202. Section 202 is a section that provides for financing new construction of housing for the elderly or handicapped. The funds are allocated on a basis of so many units to a metropolitan area and so many to nonmetropolitan areas. Areas are designated from which applications will be accepted for evaluation and approval. Applications for nondesignated areas will not be considered unless insufficient applications are received from designated areas in order to fill allocations. Applications will be evaluated for approval in any area if the housing is designed exclusively or primarily for nonelderly handicapped.

Section 203 loans. Section 203 has subsections 203(b), 203(b)$_2$, 203(h), 203(i) and 203(k). Section 203(b) is the subsection under which most of the FHA loans have been qualified in the past forty-eight years.

Section 203(b) loans. The purpose of the 203(b) loan is to insure the financing of proposed or existing dwellings for one to four families.

The year 1980 found a shortage of housing in areas of great demand for housing. This resulted in an uneven appreciation in California, with home prices in areas of concentration and close to industries outpacing the prices of homes in areas of less concentration. For the first time it became necessary for HUD to treat the various market areas separately as far as maximum loans are concerned. The loan to value ratio is 97 percent of the first $25,000 and 95 percent of the balance of the estimated value to the maximum loan allowed for the market area in which the property is located. See Table 13-1 for the maximum loans available in the various California market areas. In computing the amount of loan the FHA will insure, the estimated closing costs to the borrower are included in the total acquisition costs (appraised value plus estimated closing costs) of the property. On July 13, 1979, FHA issued its Circular Letter 79–7 specifying the estimated closing costs that would be allowed. The amounts are based on the appraised value, and vary from $250 for an appraised property value of $00 to $11,999, to $950 for a property appraised at or above $75,000, for all property under Schedule I, which includes all California Counties except: Calaveras, Colusa, Plumas, San Joaquin, Shasta, Tuolumne, Trinity, Butte, El Dorado, and Placer. Schedule II covers the counties excepted above and the amounts allowed under Schedule II vary from $350 for an appraised property value of $00 to $15,999, to $1,150 for a property appraised at or above $79,000.

The fact that FHA includes the closing costs in the total acquisition cost means that the buyer can borrow 95 percent of the closing costs when the costs are included in the amount FHA will insure. Closing costs may include the loan origination fee, the ALTA policy fee (for the lender), FHA application fee, recording fee, and, where it is the custom for the buyer to pay, the escrow fee and the title insurance policy. Closing costs will not include the costs of impound account payments, credit report, or pest control inspection. However, if the seller pays any of the costs that are normally included in the estimated closing costs, the FHA will not allow them to be included in the total cost of acquisition.

TABLE 13-1 Maximum loans by market areas under Section 203(b)

MARKET AREA	LOCALITIES	SECTION 203(b) MORTGAGE LIMITS				SECTION 234(c) CONDO MORTGAGE LIMIT
		1-FAMILY	2-FAMILY	3-FAMILY	4-FAMILY	
Fresno Service Office	Fresno County Kern County Kings County Madera County Mariposa County Merced County Stanislaus County Tulare County	$71,500	$80,500	$98,000	$113,000	$71,500
Los Angeles Area Office Metropolitan and Nonmetropolitan Areas	Los Angeles County San Luis Obispo County Santa Barbara County Ventura County	90,000	101,300	122,600	142,600	74,900
Sacramento Service Office Metropolitan and Nonmetropolitan Areas	Alpine County Amador County Butte County Calaveras County Colusa County El Dorado County Glenn County Lassen County Modoc County Nevada County Placer County Plumas County Sacramento County San Joaquin County Shasta County Sierra County Siskiyou County Sutter County Tehama County Trinity County Tuolumne County Yolo County Yuba County	84,000	95,000	115,000	133,500	74,900
San Francisco Area Office Metropolitan and Nonmetropolitan Areas	Alameda County Contra Costa County Del Norte County Humboldt County Lake County Marin County Mendocino County Monterey County Napa County San Benito County San Francisco County San Mateo County Santa Clara County Santa Cruz County Solano County Sonoma County	90,000	101,300	122,600	142,600	74,900

continued

TABLE 13-1   Maximum loans by market areas under Section 203(b) (*Continued*)

MARKET AREA	LOCALITIES	SECTION 203(b) MORTGAGE LIMITS				SECTION 234(c) CONDO MORTGAGE LIMIT
Santa Ana Service Office Metropolitan Area	Orange County Riverside County San Bernardino County	$90,000	$101,300	$122,600	$142,600	$74,900
Santa Ana Service Office Nonmetropolitan Area	Inyo County Mono County	71,500	80,500	98,000	113,000	71,500
San Diego Service Office Metropolitan and Nonmetropolitan Areas	Imperial County	90,000	101,300	122,600	142,600	74,900

Courtesy of HUD-FHA

Assume an estimated value of property in San Luis Obispo is $80,000 and the allowable estimated costs (by Circular Letter 79–7) of $950. What would be the insurable loan? Use the San Luis Obispo loan limits.

$$\begin{array}{lll} \$80,000 + & \$950 = & \$80,950 \\ \text{(Value)} & \text{(Costs)} & \text{(Estimated acquisition cost)} \end{array}$$

$$\$25,000 \times 0.97 = \$24,250$$

$$\$55,950 \times 0.95 = \$53,152$$

$$24,250 + \$53,152 = \$77,402$$

Reducing to the nearest multiple of $50, the insurable loan would be $77,400. Now assume the same single-family home was located in Fresno instead of San Luis Obispo.

$$\begin{array}{lll} \$80,000 + & \$950 = & \$80,950 \\ \text{(Value)} & \text{(Costs)} & \text{(Total acquisition costs)} \end{array}$$

$$\$25,000 \times 0.97 = \$24,250$$

$$\$55,950 \times 0.95 = \$53,152$$

$$\$24,250 + \$53,152 = \$77,402$$

The total insurable loan would be $71,500, since that is the maximum insurable loan in the Fresno Service Office. Refer to Table 13-1.

Section 203(b) mobile homes loan.   July 1, 1981 marked a change in the use of mobile homes (manufac-

tured homes) in California. They can now be placed on any residential lot as long as they have a pitched roof and an eve overhang and do not detract from other homes in the area. They must be on a permanent foundation with a proper crawl hole. The home must be connected to permanently installed utilities and must be protected from freezing. The utilities should include water, which could be an individual well or a public utility; electricity; and sewer or septic tank. The Act states that the mobile home will no longer be considered personal property for tax purposes, but it will be taxed as real property. The FHA has felt that it was necessary to make another plan available to lenders than that provided under Title I, Class 2 loans. It issued its Circular Letter 81–4 on February 12, 1981, setting forth the criteria for qualifying a mobile home (manufactured home) under Section 203(b). It includes the requirements cited above plus the following. The mobile home must be double wide or wider and bear the HUD label. Expandos, tip-outs, or tag-alongs do not qualify as double wides. The home must be anchored to and supported by a permanent foundation acceptable to FHA. FHA will review the foundation plans before construction upon request to ensure that the foundation will be acceptable. The site and location of the property must meet the criteria set out in HUD-FHA Handbook, 4150.1, *Valuation Analysis for Home Mortgage Insurance.* The mobile home site must be a single residence lot.

The processing of an application for conditional commitment for an existing permanently sited mobile home is the same as processing an application for a single-family residence under Section 203(b). The application must show the manufacturer's name, model name and number, and date of manufacture. The fact that it is a mobile home should also be shown on the application.

The following exhibits are required to accompany the application for commitment.

1. Two copies of plans and specifications for any new improvements to be installed, including plot plan with lot dimensions, location of foundation, and other improvements.
2. Preliminary title report
3. County health approval of sewage disposal and water source
4. Plans and specifications of all on-site improvements permanently affixed to the property, such as garage, shed, and slabs
5. Map of the location of the property
6. Evidence of ownership or option to buy the property and name and location of dealer of the purchased mobile home if not already on the site
7. A copy of the purchase agreement of the mobile home (The serial number for each unit must be clearly legible.)
8. A copy of the recorded tract restrictions

When the mobile is new and it is included with the land and the improvements, the following additional exhibits are needed.

1. Evidence of land ownership, purchase date, purchase price, amount owing, and lender's statement of payment record
2. Foundation cost estimate from contractor
3. Utility hookup costs (If bonds or other indebtedness are owed, the balance must be included.)
4. Transportation and setup costs for the mobile home
5. Sales contract for the mobile home units
6. Closing costs including discount points. All of the above costs need to be set out and documented, so the buyer's actual costs can be determined.

The Federal Housing Administration will accept applications for insurance on a mobile home (on a permanent foundation) loan under almost any section in Title II.

Section 203(b)2. If the borrower is a veteran and is purchasing a single-family dwelling, he or she may borrow 100 percent of the first $25,000 of the FHA estimate of the property's value and closing costs, plus 95 percent of the balance of the FHA estimate of value plus closing costs. The veteran must pay at least $200 either as down payment or part of the closing costs or prepaid expenses. Let us assume an estimated value on a home is $40,000, with closing costs of $550. Adding these, the estimated cost of acquisition is $40,550.

$$\$25,000 \times 1.00 = \$25,000$$

$$\$25,000 - \$200 = \$24,800$$

$$\$15,500 \times 0.95 = \$14,772$$

$$\$14,772 + 24,800 = \$39,572$$

Reducing this to the nearest $50 gives us $39,550. Thus, the total cash investment would be $450 ($40,000 − $39,550) plus the deposit for recurring expenses.

This is an FHA veteran's program and has nothing to do with the Veterans Administration or the Cal-Vet loans. It is available to all veterans holding an honorable discharge who have served ninety days, or less if the service was in a hazardous theater. A copy of separation papers must accompany the application. The ratio of loan to value changes if the home was started or completed less than one year from the date of purchase. The veteran's loan is then based on 90 percent of the first $35,000 of the FHA estimate of value plus 85 percent of the amount of the FHA estimate of value over $35,000, plus estimated closing costs.

The regular Section 203(b) loan for a home started or completed with one year of the purchase would be subject to a loan-to-value ratio of 90 percent of the first $35,000 of the FHA estimate of value plus 80 percent of that amount over $35,000. Closing costs would be added to the estimated value and would be included either in the 90 percent computation or the above $35,000, as the case might be.

A person who buys property and does not intend to live in it would be eligible for a loan amounting to 85 percent of that available to an owner-occupant (nonveteran).

The term of the Section 203(b) and Section 203(b)2 loans is thirty years or three-quarters of the economic life of the dwelling, whichever is less. For instance, if the economic life is thirty-two years, the maximum term would be twenty-four years. The loan can be extended to thirty-five years if the loan is unacceptable for the thirty-year term and the home was built under, and inspected by, the FHA or VA. An operative builder will be allowed a term of only twenty years or three-quarters of the economic life of the home, whichever is less.

The maximum loan available under Section 203(b) and Section 203(b)2 is dependent upon where the property is located. Refer back to Table 13-1.

For the first time since FHA inception there were interest rate reductions in 1971. During 1970 the maximum interest rate allowable had climbed to 8.5 percent, plus an insurance premium of 0.5 percent. This premium, of course, is for mortgage insurance, not life insurance. In 1971 the rate was reduced to 8 percent and finally to 7 percent plus 0.5 percent. 1973, 1974, and 1975 saw increases in the interest rate until it reached 9.5 percent in 1975. It dropped to 8.5 percent as of March 1, 1976, but by 1981, the interest rate reached an all-time high of 17.5 percent. This made the interest rate on loans comparable to the rates charged by lending institutions for their conventional loan. Under these conditions there should be no points to the seller as long as the interest charged on the two types of loans remains comparable. Interest rates change so rapidly that current rates should be obtained from a lending institution for all Title II loan applications before quoting rates. The Secretary of Housing and Urban Development will determine and set the maximum rate that can be charged on HUD-FHA loans. This will change from time to time as necessary.

There are some special factors to be considered in connection with an application for FHA loans. First, the mortgagor must receive the FHA's statement of appraised value and must certify that he or she has received such a statement. Second, in connection with a proposed construction, the application must be accompanied by the builder's warranty. Third, all notes must be drawn to allow for open-end advances where the local law permits. Fourth, a mortgagor who is sixty years of age or older may borrow the down payments, settlement costs, and prepaid expenses from an approved corporation or from an individual. This is the only time such borrowings may be allowed by the FHA. Fifth, a VA certificate of reasonable value may be presented to establish value of the property upon which an application is being presented.

Negotiated Interest Rate.

A new program available for loans under Section 203(b) and only Section 203(b) was made available on May 20, 1982. This is a program that has been established for a limited number of loans and is to be closely monitored. It is known as the negotiated interest rate mortgage.

The main requirements and provisions of the program are as follows: (a) The interest rate must be freely negotiated between the borrower and the lender. The HUD-FHA maximum interest limitations do not apply. (b) The borrower or any other party may pay all or a part of the discount points. The usual 1 percent origination fee will still be collected from the borrower. (c) A commitment fee may be charged by the lender. This fee is in repayment for the lender agreeing to make a loan at the agreed interest rate for an agreed number of discount points, any time within thirty days or more. If the loan cannot be closed within the stated time, the commitment may be renewed for an extended period of time upon the agreement of all parties. If the loan cannot be made through no fault of the borrower, the commitment fee must be refunded. However, if the borrower does not want to close, the lender may retain the commitment fee. Upon closing, the commitment fee is credited to the closing costs. If the commitment fee is more than the closing costs, the excess must be refunded to the borrower. (d) The lender and the borrower must enter into a formal commitment agreement on Form HUD-FHA 9722, (Commitment), to make a HUD-FHA mortgage loan at a negotiated interest rate.

The borrower and the lender must both sign form HUD-FHA 9722. It is sent to the HUD-FHA office with the application for an FHA firm commitment (Form HUD 92900). Form HUD-FHA 9722 provides for (a) the agreed interest rate, discount points payable by the borrower and the seller of the property (and/or the real estate broker), and the amount of the commitment fee that is payable by the borrower, if any; (b) the length of time (minimum thirty days from the date the form is received at the HUD-FHA field office) for which the commitment is binding on the lender; (c) the maximum interest rate for the standard Section 203(b) loan in effect at the time of signing, and an estimate of the prevailing number of discount points for that rate of interest.

After the loan has been insured, or if it is rejected, HUD Form 9723, Statistical Supplement for Negotiated Interest Rate Program, is completed as required by Congress and sent to the field office of HUD, so that proper monitoring can be accomplished.

Section 203(h) loans.

Section 203(h) provides home mortgage insurance for financing homes for victims of disasters such as floods, earthquakes, and wind storms. Under this section it is possible to finance the purchase or construction of a one-family dwelling that is to be owner-occupied by the victim of a disaster. The maximum loan available under this Section is $14,400, and 100 percent of the FHA estimate of value plus closing costs can be borrowed. The maximum term of the loan is thirty years or three-quarters of the remaining economic life, whichever is less. The thirty years may be extended to thirty-five years if the borrower does not meet the standards for a thirty-year loan but would qualify for a thirty-five-year loan. Under these conditions, the house must have been constructed subject to FHA or VA inspection.

Section 203(i) loans.

The purpose of Section 203(i) is to provide for the purchase of proposed or existing single family nonfarm or farm dwellings on five or more acres adjacent to a highway. The maximum loan insurable to an occupant mortgagor is $16,200. If the loan is to an operative builder or a nonoccupant mortgagor, then the maximum loan is $14,150. The maximum loan-to-value ratio is 97 percent of the FHA's estimate of property value and closing costs if the loan is for the purchase of an existing property that has been completed more than one year on the date of application, or in the case of a proposed construction if the construction was approved by the FHA prior to the start of the construction. If the construction was begun and completed less than one year from the date of the application, then the maximum loan-to-value ratio would only be 90 percent plus closing costs.

If an operative builder is concerned with the construction of this type of property, the maximum loan to him or her would be 85 percent of the sum of the FHA estimated value of the property plus closing costs. The maximum term would be thirty years or three-quarters of the remaining economic life, whichever is less. Once again the term may be extended to thirty-five years if the mortgagor would be unacceptable at thirty years and the property was constructed subject to FHA and VA inspection. An operative builder would be able to borrow only for twenty years or three-quarters of the remaining economic life, whichever is less.

Once again it would be necessary for the mortgagor to certify that he or she had received a copy of the FHA statement of appraised value. Second, the builder's warranty would again be required on proposed construction. Third, the ability to make open-end advances where the law permits would be required. Fourth, the VA certificate of reasonable value would be acceptable to establish value of the property. Fifth, an unusual situation would be allowed in that the down payment, settlement costs, and prepaid expenses could be borrowed from an approved individual or corporation.

Section 203(k) loans. This section was added to make it possible for loans to be insured in connection with major home improvements to existing structures outside urban renewal areas. On June 20, 1980, the scope of Section 203(k) was increased to include provisions for the refinance, purchase, or rehabilitation of a one- to four-family dwelling. The maximum amount that may be borrowed under Section 203(k) depends on the number of family units in the dwelling that is to be improved. However, under Section 203(k), the maximum is $16,875 per unit; thus, for a four-family dwelling the maximum loan would be $67,500. The total of the improvement loan plus the existing debt may not exceed the loan-to-value ratio specified under Section 203(b). The maximum term of the loan is twenty years or three-quarters of the remaining economic life, whichever is less.

To qualify for a loan under Section 203(k), the dwelling must be at least ten years old unless the loan is to make major structural improvements to correct faults that were not recognized at the time of completion or to correct damage caused by fire, flood, or other casualties. Section 203(k) can also be used to construct civil defense shelters. The loan proceeds may be used to pay city or county assessments or charges for water, sewer, or other bonded indebtedness. It is not necessary for the occupant to hold the title to the property under fee simple. It may be under a lease if the lease runs more than ten years beyond the maturity of the loan. A deed of trust is taken to secure a loan under Section 203(k), but it may be a second trust deed.

Section 207 loans. Section 207 has two purposes. The first is to finance construction or rehabilitation of detached, semi-detached, row, walkup, or elevator-type rental housing for eight or more family units. The maximum loan depends on the size of the units and whether there are elevators for the convenience of the tenants. The loan-to-value ratio is 90 percent.

The second purpose of Section 207 is to finance construction or rehabilitation of mobile home parks. The maximum loan is $3,250 per space or 90 percent of the loan-to-value ratio. In high-cost construction areas, the maximum per space may be increased as much as 45 percent.

Section 213 loans. Section 213 is unusual. A group of living units is often constructed as a cooperative housing unit. In some instances such a cooperative has not been a success, and it has become necessary for the units to be sold as individual living units. Section 213 was designed for the financing of such units.

The maximum loan available under Section 213 is the amount of indebtedness existing on that one unit that can be allocated from the master note. The maximum term is thirty years except that, should the purchaser be unacceptable on a thirty-year basis but acceptable on a thirty-five-year basis, a thirty-five-year term may be extended. There is a 0.5 percent charge for the mortgage insurance premium. There is no application fee for Section 213 loans.

This type of loan is eligible for open-end advances if the local law permits such advances. The builder must issue a warranty on the construction.

Section 220 loans. Under Section 220 one- to eleven-family housing units in an approved urban renewal area are purchased or improved. This Section would also apply to areas in which code enforcement requires radical rehabilitation. The properties must be improved pursuant to an approved urban renewal plan.

The maximum loan to an owner-occupant is $45,000 if the unit is for one family. If it is to house two or three families, the maximum loan is $48,750. If the unit is to house four families, then the maximum loan is $56,000 with an allowance of $7,000 per unit over four units to a maximum of eleven units.

If the property is to be held for an investment or for rental purposes, and the owner is not to occupy any of the units, the maximum loan would be 93 percent of the amount available to the occupant-mortgagor.

If the property is purchased and improved with the idea that it is to be held for sale to an owner-occupant, then the maximum loan to the person purchasing the property would be 85 percent of the amount available to the owner-occupant-mortgagor. The maximum loan-to-value ratio to an owner-occupant who received approval by the FHA before the beginning of construction of a unit that was completed more than one year before the date of the application would be 97 percent of the first $25,000 of estimated value, plus 95 percent of the balance to the maximum allowed, plus closing costs.

If the applicant is a veteran who has been honorably discharged after serving ninety days or more in active military service, whether or not he or she has used his or her GI loan entitlement, the veteran is entitled to borrow 100 percent of the first $25,000 of value plus closing costs, or $25,000 plus prepaid expenses less $200, whichever is less, plus 95 percent to the maximum allowed.

If the construction was begun or completed within less than one year and not under FHA supervision on the date of the application, then the maximum loan would be 95 percent of the first $35,000 of appraised value, plus closing costs, plus 80 percent of all estimated appraised value, plus closing costs over $35,000.

All this information has to do with purchase of property under Section 220. If the property is to be improved, then the ratios referred to would apply to the value before rehabilitation; the estimated cost of rehabilitation, or the estimated cost plus the amount required to refinance the existing indebtedness on the property, whichever is less, would be the maximum allowed for rehabilitation as an improvement.

If the property is not to be owner-occupied but is to be held for rental purposes, then the maximum amount available would be 93 percent of the amount shown for owner-occupant. The deed of trust or mortgage may not exceed the estimated cost of improvement plus an amount equal to the amount necessary to refinance the existing indebtedness. The maximum term would be thirty years or three-quarters of the remaining economic life, whichever is less. Once again the thirty-year period may be extended to thirty-five years if the mortgagor would be unacceptable for a thirty-year term and the property was constructed subject to FHA and VA inspections.

In the case of an operative builder, the maximum term of loan would be twenty years to three-quarters of the economic life, whichever is less.

Some special factors must be considered. The note and deed of trust must be eligible for open-end advancements wherever the local law permits. Second, the mortgagor must sign a certificate indicating that the FHA estimated value had been received prior to closing if the unit is for one- or two-family housing. Third, a builder's warranty is required on proposed construction of one- to four-family units.

Section 220(h) loans.   Section 220(h) is the Section under which major alterations, repairs, and improvements to existing one- to eleven-family units in approved

urban renewal areas are financed. To qualify, the property must be in an approved urban renewal redevelopment or code enforcement area or in an area receiving rehabilitation assistance due to a disaster. The proceeds of the loan may be used to pay sewer, water, sidewalk, curb, or municipal assessments or other public improvement assessments as well as for structural improvements. To qualify for the 220(h) improvement loan, a structure must be at least ten years old unless that loan is for the purpose of making major structural improvements to correct faults not known when the house was completed or caused by fire, flood, or other casualty. It is possible to use Section 220(h) for the construction of a civil defense shelter.

The maximum loan available under this type of financing is $12,000 per family unit with a maximum of $40,000. In high-cost areas, it is possible for the family unit limit to be increased up to 45 percent. The ratio of loan to value is the same as for Section 220, and the loan plus existing debts may not exceed the amounts insurable under that Section.

The maximum term of the loan is twenty years or three-quarters of the remaining economic life of the unit, whichever is less. The lessee of a qualifying property can obtain an insured loan if the term of the lease is longer than ten years beyond the maturity of the loan. If there are five or more family units to be improved, a cost certificate is required.

Section 221 (home) loans.   Sections 220 and 221 of Title II were added to the program of the Federal Housing Administration to aid in elimination of slums and blighted areas and to prevent the deterioration of residential property. Section 221(d)(2) is used to finance proposed or existing low-cost one- to four-family dwellings or rehabilitation of such dwellings for families displaced by urban renewal or other government action as well as for other low- and moderate-income families. The amount of loan insurable under Section 221(d)(2) for an existing property in good condition or for the construction of a new housing unit or units to an owner-occupant-mortgagor is from $31,000 to $36,000 for a one-family unit or from $36,000 to $42,000 if the family has five or more children and if the house has four or more bedrooms. For a two-family unit the maximum loan is from $35,000 to $45,000. For a three-family unit the maximum loan is from $48,600 to $57,600. For a four-family unit the maximum loan is from $59,400 to $68,400. The maximum amount available to a displaced person would be the sum of the FHA appraisal and closing costs, or the sum of the FHA appraisal of value, plus closing costs, plus prepaid expenses, minus $200 per unit, whichever is less. This formula would apply only if the units were constructed under FHA approval and inspection or had been completed more than one year earlier.

If the construction had been completed less than one year and not under FHA inspection and approval, then the maximum amount available for a displaced person would be 90 percent of the sum of the FHA appraised value and closing costs.

If the property purchased is to be rehabilitated, then the maximum loan would be based on the FHA appraised value before rehabilitation, plus closing costs, plus the estimated cost of the rehabilitation, or the FHA's appraised value as a completed project, plus prepaid expenses, plus closing costs, minus $200 per unit, whichever is less.

If the person purchasing the units, instead of being a displaced person, belongs to a low- or moderate-income family, then the maximum loan would be the sum of the FHA's appraisal value of the property and closing costs, or 97 percent of the sum of the FHA estimate of value and closing costs, plus prepaid expenses, whichever is less. This formula would apply only if the units had been constructed under FHA approval and inspection or completed more than one year before the application. If the property had been completed less than one year and not under the approval and inspection of the FHA, then the maximum loan would be 90 percent of the sum of the FHA's appraised value and closing costs.

It is possible for an operative builder to participate in the Section 221(d)(2) program. In the case of proposed construction, the maximum loan for such a builder would be 85 percent of the sum of the FHA appraised value, plus closing costs. However, if it were a case of rehabilitation, then the following formula would apply: whichever is less of (1) 85 percent of the FHA appraised value after rehabilitation plus closing costs, or (2) five times the estimated cost of improvements, or (3) 85 percent of purchase price of the property, or (4) FHA's appraised value of property before rehabilitation, plus the estimated rehabilitation costs, plus closing costs.

The maximum maturity of a Section 221(d)(2) loan is thirty years, except thirty-five or forty years may be approved if the mortgagor is unacceptable under a thirty-year term but would be acceptable under the longer term.

If the purchaser is other than occupant-mortgagor, then the maximum term would be thirty years. However, if the mortgagor is unacceptable under the thirty-year term and housing has been built under FHA and VA inspections, then it may be extended to thirty-five or forty years if the lender desires. All the maturity, of course, is subject to the usual three-quarters of the remaining economic life. If this should be shorter than the thirty years, then that period of time would apply.

Section 221(h) loans.   Section 221(h), a companion Section to Section 221(d)(2), provides for the acquisition by low-income families of individual units that might be released from the Section 221(h) project mortgage. The amount that is insurable and the loan-to-value ratio is 100 percent of the unpaid balance of the project mortgage allocated to the unit being sold. The term of the mortgage is limited to the remaining term of the project mortgage. The interest rate is 1, 2, or 3 percent, depending upon the mortgagor's income. The minimum down payment under Section 221(h) is $200 in cash or its equivalent, for example, what is termed sweat equity—work done on the property such as installing fences, planting lawns, or painting the exterior and interior of the house. When this is done the contractor makes a dollar allowance for the amount of work accomplished, and this applies as down payment or toward closing costs or both. Under Section 221(h) there are no insurance premiums for mortgage insurance, nor are there any application fees.

Section 221(i) loans.   Section 221(i) was established to allow low-income and moderate-income families to purchase properties built or improved under Section 221(d) as condominium family units. The maximum amount of loan to be insured and the loan-to-value ratio is 100 percent of the appraised value of the family unit, including the mortgagor's interest in the common areas and facilities. Under no circumstances may the purchase price of the individual family units exceed the appraised value. There is a required 3 percent down payment, but this amount may be applied to closing costs so that the total cost of the units may be insured. The maximum term of the mortgage must meet with the approval of the FHA commissioner, but it may not exceed the lesser of forty years or three-quarters of the remaining economic life. The interest rate is established at the time of the insurance endorsement at 3, 4, 5, or 6 percent, depending upon the mortgagor's income. As the mortgagor's income increases, the interest rate may increase. It is not necessary under Section 221(i) to provide for an insurance premium for mortgage insurance. The application fee is $40 for each dwelling unit. There is no application fee in connection with the initial conversion from a 221(d) to a condominium unit.

Section 222 loans.   Section 222 was designed to provide a benefit to members of the military service, the Coast Guard, and servicepersons of the National Oceanic and Atmospheric Administration. Loans in this Section are based on the regular single-family Section 203(b) loan. The payment schedule and the ratio of loan to value are the same; so are the amounts of maximum loans. The only difference is that the military member did not pay the 0.5 percent mutual mortgage insurance. It was paid by either the Department of Defense, Department of Transportation, or Department of Commerce.

After March 31, 1980, no applications for Section 222 loans were accepted, unless it was from a member of the Coast Guard or the National Oceanic and Atmospheric Administration. The Department of Defense will continue to pay the 0.5 percent mutual mortgage insurance on those loans that were outstanding on March 31, 1980.

Any loan on a single-family home that is owned by a member of the military and that was purchased under some other Section of the National Housing Act is eligible for transfer to Section 222 if the military member is eligible.

Section 223(f) loans.   Section 223(f) is a rescue program for distressed apartment projects. It insures FHA take-out loans or permanent loans for financing and refinancing existing buildings now saddled with construction loans. Approximately 20,000 units qualify for help under this Section, most of which are held by real estate investment trusts. The buildings need not have been constructed under FHA supervision to qualify for a loan under Section 223(f). The Section also provides for the rehabilitation of existing buildings into a viable and economically sound investment, thus acting as a counterforce in areas of decline and blight.

The loan-to-value ratio is 80 percent of the value of the property based on the cash flow on existing property or the projected cash flow on new or rehabilitated property. For evaluation of the property on the basis of income, the capitalization rate is established at 8.5 percent. There is a second method of determining the maximum loan amount: 85 percent of the acquisition cost.

Section 233 loans.   Section 233 concerns experimental housing or experimental neighborhood design and has not had much acceptance. The purpose of this particular Section is to insure the financing of proposed construction or rehabilitation of existing structures using advance housing technology in an effort to reduce costs and improve quality.

Section 234(c) loans.   This Section is used to finance ownership of individual units in multifamily housing projects. HUD-FHA will insure mortgages or trust deeds made by private lenders for the purchase of individual condominium units in a multifamily complex of four or more units. It will also insure sponsors for the construction of or rehabilitation of housing projects which will be sold as individual condominium units under Section 234(d). The units may be attached, semi-detached, row, walkup, or elevator units.

Table 13-1 in the beginning of the chapter lists the maximum insured loans for California. The loans can be as high as 97 percent of the first $25,000 plus 95 percent of the balance of the sales price plus closing costs to the maximum shown. These figures are for owner-occupied

units. The insured loan can only be 85 percent of the amount cited above if the owner is not to occupy the unit. The maximum term for the loan is thirty years or three-quarters of the remaining economic life, whichever is less. However, if the thirty-year limit would not qualify the purchaser, then at the option of the lender the term may be extended to thirty-five years.

The FHA has decreed that no mortgagor may own more than four condominium units under Section 234(c). Also, if the mortgagor is sixty years of age or older, he or she may borrow the down payment, settlment costs, or prepaid expenses. Of course, this is contrary to the usual FHA procedures and requirements.

Section 235 loans.   Section 235 has probably been the most controversial of all FHA loan programs. The Act was written to provide that only 15 percent of the loans made under Section 235 could be made against existing homes, and many people felt the program should have applied to all housing. As it turned out, the real problems arose with the loans made on existing homes that were supposedly rehabilitated. Other problems concerned Section 235 houses located in areas where the average cost per house was much higher than the cost of the Section 235 houses. In 1973 the program was suspended.

On January 8, 1976, the program was reactivated but on a more conservative basis. The FHA is still interested in insuring loans so that those whose incomes are 80 percent or less of the median income in their area will be able to benefit from lower monthly payments. The lower monthly payment is possible because the FHA will pay interest charges over 6.75 percent; however, the owner must use at least 20 percent of his or her monthly income in payments to the loan. (See Table 13-2.)

The maximum loan that can be insured is $38,000 (with a maximum sales price of $41,600) if there are three or fewer bedrooms in the home and $44,000 (with a maximum sales price of $52,800) if there are four or more bedrooms and five or more people in the family. The emphasis is still on new homes, but substantially rehabilitated single-family homes may qualify. Substantially rehabilitated means that the cost of such rehabilitation must be at least 25 percent of the value of the property after completion of the rehabilitation. Under no circumstance can the cost of the property exceed 120 percent of the loan amount. The minimum down payment is 3 percent, plus estimated allowed closing costs. The down payment will exceed 3 percent if the cost of the home exceeds the amount of the allowable maximum loan. For example, the maximum insured loan on a two-bedroom home is $38,000, and the maximum purchase price allowed is $45,600; for a four-bedroom house for five or more people, the maximum loan would be $44,000

TABLE 13-2   Sample of income limits for Section 235: metropolitan counties and nonmetropolitan counties

	PERSONS IN FAMILY							
	1[a]	2	3	4	5	6	7	8
Metropolitan counties[b]	$14,250	$16,250	$18,300	$20,350	$21,600	$22,850	$24,150	$25,400
Nonmetropolitan counties[c]	12,350	14,150	15,900	17,650	18,750	19,900	21,000	22,100

[a]Elderly or handicapped persons only.

[b]Metropolitan counties would include Los Angeles County, Sacramento County, and San Joaquin County. For a complete list, check with the local HUD-FHA office.

[c]Nonmetropolitan counties would include Alpine County, Tuolumne County, and Modoc County. For a complete list, check with the local HUD-FHA office.

on a $52,800 house. Assume that a person buys a home costing $41,500 under Section 235. The down payment would be $3,500 ($41,500–$38,000).

Section 235 has had two new section numbers assigned to it for accounting purposes—Section 265 and Section 255. These sections are the same as Section 235 and have the same restrictions and limitations.

On May 27, 1981, a new provision was added to Section 235, which has been designated as Section 235(i) for accounting purposes. This provides for the recapture of all or a portion of the assistance payments made by the Secretary of Housing and Urban Development. The buyers, in cases involving firm commitments after May 27, 1981, will be required to sign, at closing, a secondary note and deed of trust in favor of the Secretary of HUD to assure repayment of the assistance. The property is thus pledged as security for the repayment of the note and deed of trust as well as the assistance. The recapture will be made under the following conditions: When (1) the property is sold to a homeowner who is not eligible for assistance payments; (2) the borrower has not made a payment on the insured trust deed for 90 continuous days; (3) the borrower has rented the property for more than one year; and (4) the borrower requests that the Secretary's lien be satisfied. The amount to be repaid by the borrower will be the lesser of the amount of the assistance, or 50 percent of the net appreciation of the property, *as determined by the Secretary of HUD*. Any of these will require the recapture.

The lender, before obtaining insurance, must furnish a copy of "Notice to Buy," a HUD form, to the buyer and he or she must sign and date the original, which will accompany the other exhibits with the application to the HUD field office. This form outlines the provisions under which the recapture of assistance is required. It also provides spaces for improvements and maintenance expenses the buyer may have in connection with the property. These must be fully documented and are considered when the appreciation is computed.

There is a prepurchase counseling session required of all applicants before a firm application can be reviewed by the HUD-FHA Mortgage Credit staff for financial capacity and credit worthiness. There is a homebuyer's information kit, which will suffice if counseling is not available. The application must show that the kit was received.

The maximum amount of subsidy cannot exceed the amount necessary to reduce the mortagage interest to 6.75 percent. The homeowner must contribute at least 20 percent of his or her monthly income to the monthly mortgage payment. The maximum term allowed is thirty years. There is a charge for mortgage insurance of 0.7 percent.

Each year the borrower must recertify the amount of the family income, the family size, and the fact that he or she still occupies the property. The recertification must also list the amount of annual gross income reported on the latest federal income tax return for each adult family member. If the amount shown on the tax return is more than 25 percent greater than that shown on the recertification, the lender must obtain a new recertification or a written explanation. In addition, the lender will request a new recertification from any borrower if it is learned that any adult member of the family residing on the property has received a $50 or more per month increase in income above that shown on the application for assistance at the last recertification. Payments for assistance will cease when the borrower sells the property. Assumption of the payment with subsidy will not be allowed.

The new Section 235 program includes a restriction on the number of units permitted in a subdivision: Not more than 40 percent of the units, or twenty-five units, whichever is greater, can be insured under Section 235. Those units previously insured under Section 235 will be counted toward the total. Second, a builder applying for reservation of Section 235 commitments must either own the sites or have a valid option on the sites. Third, the marketability of the completed homes will be very carefully examined. Marginal sites will not be considered acceptable. Fourth, subdivisions and condominiums must be well located with acceptance from a proven market. Fifth, the FHA will not insure loans on properties that lack certain amenities, adversely affecting the long-term marketability of the home. Sixth, housing without frills but that meets basic living needs will be encouraged by the FHA. Seventh, any subdivision of more than thirteen Section 235 homes must clear the local government, which has thirty days to reply.

There are four steps to consider in determining whether a family is eligible for a Section 235 loan:

1. The adjusted gross income must be determined, that is, the gross annual income of the family less 5 percent of the adults' earnings, less $300 for each minor child in the family, less any unusual or non-reoccurring income, less any earnings of a minor child included in the gross family income.
2. The initial investment of the buyer must be determined. If the adjusted gross income of the purchaser is lower than the maximum allowed for the area in which the property is located, payment of $200 will be required from the borrower. If the adjusted gross income is more than the scheduled amount, the purchaser does not qualify and should try to qualify under Section 203(b).
3. The normal monthly payment must be determined. The monthly payment will include payment to principal, interest, taxes, hazard insurance, and FHA mortgage insurance (0.5 percent of the principal balance on the loan existing on the anniversary date of the loan; the amount is then divided into twelve equal payments).
4. The government's subsidy payment must be computed. This is accomplished by finding the average monthly income for the family, using the adjusted gross family income, and taking 20 percent of this amount to find the monthly payment the purchaser will be required to make. The difference between the normal payment and the 20 percent of income payment is the amount the government is subsidizing. However, the FHA requires the purchaser to pay at least 1 percent interest on the debt and enough to pay off the debt in full within the allocated time. The factor to compute this monthly payment is $3.22 a month per thousand for thirty years.

As of October 1978, over 892,861 homes insured for a total of $12 billion had been financed under Section 235 financing. For a long time the houses were spotted indiscriminately among houses of greater value, regardless of the protests of other area residents and of area planners. Finally, in February 1971, Secretary of Housing and Urban Development George Romney admitted that the plan was wrong in this regard and suggested that in the future the homes be built in areas of comparable value.

There was another reversal of policy in connection with all applications, regardless of the section under which the application is made. This reversal, made on January 25, 1971, stated that in the future, to gather data on minority group mortgagors, the mortgagee shall enter on all applications a group identification code number, as follows:

1. White (nonminority)
2. Negro/Black
3. American Indian
4. Oriental
5. Spanish-American
6. Other

In the past it had been illegal to indicate in any manner the race of an applicant.

Section 23 loans.   This Section has been superceded by Section 8 loans. Those which are outstanding may be converted to Section 8 Existing Housing program.

Section 245(a) loans.   The rapidly increasing cost of homes was pricing home buyers out of the housing market in 1976. As an experiment, the HUD-FHA, on November 1, 1976, authorized a new type of financing designated as Section 245(a) of the National Housing Act. Under Section 245(a) the HUD-FHA was to insure 3,000 single-family home loans. Each HUD-FHA district office was allocated a certain number of Section 245(a) loans it could insure. The experiment was so successful that it became a permanent program with no restrictions on funding in November 1977.

The plan calls for five different programs of repayment, each based on the idea that a person's income will increase each year and therefore the monthly payments could be increased as well. Each person's potential is different, which is the reason for the five repayment programs.

Plan 1 requires an increase in monthly payments of 2.5 percent each year for five years.

Plan 2 requires an increase in monthly payments of 5 percent each year for five years.

Plan 3 requires an increase in monthly payments of 7.5 percent each year for five years.

Plan 4 requires an increase in monthly payments of 2 percent each year for ten years.

Plan 5 requires an increase in monthly payments of 3 percent each year for ten years.

Starting with the sixth year in Plans 1, 2, and 3 and in the eleventh year in Plans 4 and 5, the monthly payments will remain constant. The minimum down payment will be somewhat larger than that required under Section 203(b), because there will be a negative amortization (principal will increase) during the early part of the loan. This is because the interest charged will be greater than the payment received, and at no time can the principal amount

TABLE 13-3   Highest principal balance factors by which the 203(b) gross loan amount is divided

INTEREST RATE	PLAN 1	PLAN 2	PLAN 3	PLAN 4	PLAN 5
12.00%	1,015.4743	1,046.7169	1,078.7082	1,038.6198	1,076.6526
12.50	1,018.1930	1,050.8562	1,084.3752	1,043.9734	1,084.1449
13.00	1,020.7547	1,055.1576	1,089.8422	1,049.0358	1,091.2753
13.50	1,023.1694	1,059.2707	1,095.1195	1,053.8076	1,098.0588
14.00	1,025.4470	1,063.2066	1,100.2169	1,058.8317	1,104.5107
14.50	1,027.5968	1,066.9759	1,105.1441	1,063.7745	1,111.4367
15.00	1,029.6745	1,077.5886	1,109.9105	1,068.4884	1,118.0528
16.00	1,034.2312	1,077.3825	1,118.9957	1,077.0624	1,234.1255

Table from FHA

be greater than the maximum insurable loan under Section 203(b). Assumptions of Section 245(a) loans will be allowed if the assumer agrees to the terms of the plan.

To compute the maximum loan allowed under Section 245(a), the first step is to compute the maximum insurable loan under 203(b). Assume a home has an appraised value of $65,000, and closing costs are estimated by the HUD-FHA to be $900. Total acquisition is $65,900.

$$97\% \text{ of } \$25,000 = \$24,250$$
$$95\% \text{ of } \$40,900 = \$38,855$$
$$\$24,250 + \$38,855 = \$63,105$$

The maximum loan under Section 203(b) would be $63,100; but for Section 245(a), use the gross figure of $63,105.

The second step is to divide $63,105 by the factor shown in Table 13-3 under Plan 3 for 16 percent. Plan 3 is the most frequently used.

$$\$63,105 \div 1118.9957 = 56.3943$$
$$56.3943 \times 1,000 = \$56,394.31$$

Reduce $56,394.31 to the nearest $50 increment, $56,350. The maximum loan would be $56,350.

The monthly payment is determined by using Table 13-4.

$$56.350 \times 10.5918 = \$596.84$$

This is the principal and interest payment for the first year. The following five years of Plan 3 would be as follows:

Year 2	$596.84 \times 1.075 = \$641.60$
Year 3	$641.60 \times 1.075 = \$689.72$
Year 4	$689.72 \times 1.075 = \$741.45$
Year 5	$741.45 \times 1.075 = \$797.06$
Year 6	$797.06 \times 1.075 = \$856.83$

All future payments of principal and interest to maturity will be $856.83. The mutual mortgage insurance (MMI) is computed each year on the anniversary date of the loan on the reduced amount of the principal. The MMI would be on the original balance for the first year at 0.5 percent per year. The first year's monthly MMI could be approximated by:

$$\$56,350 \times 0.005 = 281.75$$
$$281.75 \div 12 = \$23.48$$

The total payment for interest, principal, and MMI would be $620.32 for the first year. Other graduated payment mortgage plans would be computed in the same way. Section 245(a) loans may be made to credit worthy applicants who have reasonable expectations of increasing income.

Growing Equity Mortgages.   Loans secured by a Growing Equity Mortgages (GEMs) are made under Section 245(a) since this Section authorizes insurance of mortgages that provide for varying rates of amortization.

Unlike the typical Section 245(a) loan there is no negative amortization or deferral of interest connected

TABLE 13-4   Principal and interest factors[a]

INTEREST RATE	PLAN 1	PLAN 2	PLAN 3	PLAN 4	PLAN 5
12.00%	9.4238	8.6348	7.9138	9.2237	8.7238
12.50	9.7882	8.9777	8.2358	9.5905	9.0802
13.00	10.1560	9.3243	8.5618	9.9611	9.4409
13.50	10.5269	9.6745	8.8917	10.3353	9.8055
14.00	10.9008	10.0279	9.2252	10.7128	10.1737
14.50	11.2775	10.3845	9.5621	11.0934	10.5455
15.00	11.6566	10.7444	9.9023	11.4768	10.9204
16.00	12.4217	11.4712	10.5918	12.2513	11.6792

Table from FHA

[a]All figures are in dollars per thousand per month for the first year.

with a GEM, so the down payment is computed as if it were for a 203(b) loan. The payments then increase by 2 or 3 percent, as desired by the borrower and/or the lender, each year for ten years. The payments then stabilize to maturity. As a result GEMs have a much shorter maturity than a standard graduated payment loan or level payment loan. This reduces the expense to the borrower. In order to identify these loans, they bear the code number 70. A special GEM certificate must be completed and submitted with the application for firm commitment—HUD Form 92900.

As an example of the savings to a borrower, consider the following example. Ms. Janes buys a home on which she obtains a $40,000 Section 203(b) loan at 12 percent for thirty years. The payment to principal and interest is $10.29 per thousand per month, or $411.60 for 360 months. The total amount she would pay over the life of the loan is $148,176.00.

Now consider what would have happened if she had taken the same loan amount at the same interest rate under a GEM with only a 2 percent increase each year in the monthly payments for ten years. The payments from the eleventh year through maturity would be level. The first year's monthly payments to principal and interest would be $411.60, and the next year's monthly payments would be $419.67. The payments would then continue to increase 2 percent each year for eight more years. At the start of the eleventh year, the payments would be $501.55 monthly and continue in this amount through payment 214. The loan would be paid off with the completion of the payment of payment 214, instead of 360—a difference of 146 months, or 12.17 years. The total amount that would be paid on this 2 percent GEM loan would be $101,219.52—a savings of $46,956.48.

Section 245(b) loans. This program was established to enable home buyers to have an alternative to Section 245(a) that would allow a smaller down payment. There are much greater restrictions on the Section 245(b) loans than on the Section 245(a) loans. In order for applicants to be eligible for a 245(b) loan, they cannot have owned a home during the last three years; they cannot reasonably qualify for a Section 245(a) loan, nor for any other HUD-FHA insured loan; they cannot hold an interest in other real estate; if two or more borrowers are requesting a loan under Section 245(b), one may have owned an interest in real estate within the last three years, but none can have an interest at the time of application.

Financial ability is an important factor in determining whether applicants are eligible for a Section 245(b) loan. The following criteria are used to determine if the applicants are eligible for a Section 245(b) loan. First, the maximum loan under Section 203(b) is determined and the total housing expenses are computed, including level payments of interest and principal at the rate of interest and term and loan amount shown on the application. The application may be processed for a Section 245(b) loan if the total housing expense exceeds 35 percent of the effective income. Second, the amount of a maximum loan is determined under Section 245(a), Plan 3, and then the application is reviewed to see if the applicants have sufficient cash or quickly convertible assets, such as stocks or bonds, to pay the necessary closing cost for the regular program. The applicants will not qualify for a Section 245(b) loan if they can close under Section 245(a) with assets on hand. If they cannot, then they might qualify for a Section 245(b) loan.

There are only two graduated payment loan payment plans available under Section 245(b). They are based on loan-to-value tables and cash percentages. These apply to veterans and nonveterans alike. The maximum loan shall not exceed the lesser of (1) the loan amount insurable under Section 203(b) or a percentage of the appraised value as shown in Table 13-5 according to the interest rate; (2) the appraisal may not exceed 110 percent of the median prototype housing cost. That figure is to be determined by the HUD-FHA Commissioner for that particular region. (3) The amount owed by the borrower may not exceed 113 percent of the initial appraised value when the accrued, unpaid interest is added to the original loan.

Borrowers under Section 245(b) must have reasonable expectations for income increases to service the additional payments as they become due. A letter from their respective employers stating this fact is required. Two full years of financial statements, balance sheets, and income statements are required if the applicants are self-employed. All cash assets must be verified, and if some of the cash represents money from close friends or relatives, a letter of gift is required.

The application is processed the same as an application for a Section 203(b) or Section 234(c) loan, except loans originating under the Section 203(b) program will show Section 245(b)–261, and those under Section 234(c) will show 245(b)–262 on the application.

Plan 1 for Section 245(b) loans calls for a loan on which the monthly payments increase 7.5 percent each year for five years. Plan 2 calls for annual increases in the monthly payments of 4.9 percent for ten years. This is the program that is being used most often.

Remember, the maximum insurable loan under Section 245(b) is the lesser of two amounts—the amount insurable under Section 203(b) or a percentage of the value. The percentage is determined by the interest authorized at the time of purchase (see Table 13-5). The amount applies to both veterans and nonveterans; however, there is a minimum investment required by the interest on the loan.

TABLE 13-5
Maximum loan for veteran or nonveteran, Plan 1, 7½% for five years

12%	13%	14%	14½%	15%	16%
98.86% of Value	96.63% of Value	96.29% of Value	95.90% of Value	95.90% of Value	95.53% of Value

Minimum investment for nonveteran only, Plan 1, 7½% for five years[a]

3.14% of Acquisition Cost	3.37% of Acquisition Cost	3.71% of Acquisition Cost	4.10% of Acquisition Cost	4.10% of Acquisition Cost	4.47% of Acquisition Cost

Maximum loan for veteran or nonveteran, Plan 2, 4.9% for ten years

96.76% of Value	96.08% of Value	94.43% of Value	92.95% of Value		91.56% of Value

Minimum investment for nonveteran only, Plan 2, 4.9% for ten years[a]

3.24% of Acquisition Cost	3.92% of Acquisition Cost	5.57% of Acquisition Cost	7.05% of Acquisition Cost		8.44% of Acquisition Cost

[a]Again, there are two amounts to consider in computing the minimum investment the buyer must make. They are the amount required under Section 203(b) and the cost of acquisition multiplied by the factor shown in Table 13-5 for the plan and interest rate that is applicable. The larger amount will be the investment required of the buyer.

Tables from FHA

EXAMPLE PLAN 2, SECTION 245(b), 16 PERCENT

House appraised value = $65,000

Closing costs = $ 900

Acquisition Costs = $65,000 + $900

= $65,900

$0.97 \times 25,000 = $24,250$

$0.95 \times 40,000 = $38,000$

Maximum loan

under Section 203(b) = $24,250 + $38,000

= $62,250

$65,000 \times 0.9156 = $59,514$

Reduced to nearest $50 increment, $59,500

The maximum loan using Table 13-5 rounds to $59,500. The maximum loan would be $62,250, since the maximum loan under Section 203(b) exceeds the value times the percentage from Table 13-5. Since the buyer in our example is not a veteran, it becomes necessary to compute the minimum investment the buyer must make.

$65,900 - $62,250 = $3,650

Under Section 203(b), the investment would be $3,650. The acquisition cost ($65,900) × 0.0844 (from Table 13-5) = $5,561.95. Since the figure obtained by using the table is larger than that required under Section 203(b),

the required investment for the nonveteran buyer would be $5,561.95.

The monthly payment for the veteran buyer would be computed by using the factor shown in Table 13-6, as follows:

$62.25 \times 10.6417 = 662.45 (principal and interest)

$0.005 \times $66,250 = $311.25

$311.25 \div 12 = 25.94 (mutual mortgage insurance)

$25.94 + $662.45 = $688.39

The monthly payment for the first year would be $688.39 including interest, principal, and mutual mortage insurance. For the next ten years, the interest and principal payments would increase 4.9 percent each year and the mutual mortgage insurance would decrease. The new amount would be based on the principal balance re-

TABLE 13-6   Alternate graduated payment factor table

	PLAN 1 7.5% YEARLY INCREASE 5 YEARS	PLAN 2 4.9% YEARLY INCREASE 10 YEARS
14½%	9.5621	9.5572
15%	9.9023	9.9151
16%	10.5918	10.6417

Table from FHA

maining on the anniversary of the note times 0.5 percent. The interest and principal payment would be $1,068.82 beginning with the eleventh year and continuing to maturity.

Nonveterans would have a minimum investment of $5,561.95 (round to $5,600), so their maximum loan would be cost of acquisition less $5,600, or $60,300.

$$60.3 \times 10.6417 \text{ (from Table 13-6)} = \$641.69$$

This would be the monthly interest and principal payment the first year.

Other sections of Title II deal with the financing of multifamily units. However, the sections we have covered at this time are those used most under the FHA program.

Application for FHA Appraisals and Fees

On June 1, 1980, a new procedure was established in connection with fees and appraisals. The reason for the change was to increase the efficiency in handling the application. After that date HUD-FHA made no fee or application charges. The inspections and appraisals will all be done by fee appraisers. After the inspection or appraisal has been done, a voucher will be sent to the lender and it will make payment directly to the appraiser. HUD-FHA will no longer act as an intermediary. See Table 13-7 for maximum fees that can be charged by the lender for payment to the appraiser on receipt of a voucher.

Applying for a Title II Section 203(b) home loan. Now that we have reviewed the more popular sections of Title II, we should consider the procedures for obtaining loan insurance for the most popular sections: Section 203(b), Section 235(i), 245(a), and 245(b). Many real estate offices in California have on hand the forms necessary for applying for a real estate loan that is to be insured by the Federal Housing Administration. It is not unusual for these offices to help the applicant complete the application and provide some of the other documentation necessary, such as verification of employment and verification of deposit. At one time the agent was allowed to have the two latter forms completed and to present them to the lending institution; however, the FHA now requires that the individual applying for the loan obtain the two forms, have them completed by his or her employer and by the bank or savings and loan association, and deliver them personally to the lending institution. The real estate agent may, however, complete an application for credit investigation and an FHA application, and present these papers as a package deal to the institution that he or she wishes to have make the

TABLE 13-7 Maximum fee schedule

APPRAISAL FEES	
Individual existing property appraisals	
One-family	$ 75.00[a]
More than one family, per additional unit	15.00
Individual proposed property	
One-family	80.00
More than one family, per additional unit	15.00
Committee appraisals per plan	
Including PUDs, for each committee member	80.00
First 50 units	7.00 each
Additional units	5.00 each
Additional per unit for PUD	5.00 each
Condominium appraisals	
Individual units in a project	130.00
Committee Appraisals per plan (each member)	110.00
Each unit appraised	5.00
Mobile home site appraisal	45.00
Mobile home park approval	45.00
Foreclosure appraisals	75.00
Sections 203(k) and 235 Rehabilitation	120.00
Inspection fees (compliance)	20.00
Repair inspections	20.00

[a]Depending on the locations of the property, there may be a mileage charge of 20 cents a mile for the distance that is more than ten miles from the city limits of the appraiser's office.

Table from FHA

loan. Under these circumstances the lender may often process the loan up to the point of the borrower's signature on the legal documents without ever having seen the applicant.

It is not necessary for the loan application to originate in this manner; the applicant can go directly to the lending institution to make his or her application. Almost all savings and loan associations, life insurance companies, and commercial banks accept applications for FHA insured loans. Mortgage companies and mortgage banks can accept real estate applications for FHA loans if they have a capitalization of at least $100,000 and have been approved as an agency by the FHA commissioner. Often the application will be accepted in two parts. The first part is brought to the lending institution by the homeowner who desires to sell his or her home and wishes to have an available FHA document indicating the maximum amount that can be loaned on the property for FHA insurance. In this case he or she comes to the bank and makes an application for property appraisal and commitment.

In 1965 a great many changes were made in FHA procedures. To overcome the tremendous backlog of applications for commitment, the FHA developed what was known as the *Hartford Plan* to speed the processing of commitments and appraisals. This resulted in FHA Form 2800, a snap-out form that, when completed by the bank, provided much more information for the Federal Housing Administration office than was provided by old FHA Form 2004. It also facilitated direct routing of completed forms to different departments in the office for that department's analysis. The present snap-out form has eight pages. To prepare the application for commitment, it is desirable to have a copy of the preliminary report or title insurance that the owner received when he or she purchased the property. You will notice that the application in Figure 13-1 requires the legal description of the property. It requests that all known easements, restrictions, and encroachments be shown and also asks whether there are mineral reservations. All this information is obtainable from a title policy, and having one available facilitates completion of the application. You will also notice that there is a request for a plat of the lot in relation to the street upon which it is located and in relation to the closest intersection. Should the property be a vacant lot, it is desirable to show the actual footage from the intersection to the closest point of the lot. Of course, all dimensions of the lots should be included in the plat and it should be compass-oriented. The title insurance policy often has a plat attached to it, which will also help in completing this section of the application. Notice that in the upper left corner of the form there are two blocks. One shows Section 203(b) and the other is for a section than can be filled in. No application for commitment will be entertained for property unless one of the sections is indicated. In the case of Section 203(b), it is now desirable not only to check Section 203(b) but also to insert Section 235(i), 245(a), or 245(b), since this form is used for these applications, and in many instances if the property is being placed for sale it could qualify for either section. No application for commitment will be entertained by the FHA on property that does not have frontage upon a county road. The commitment application is signed by the owner of the property and submitted to the FHA for its approval. The FHA will not authorize any appraisal on any property unless someone of responsible age is present in the house when the appraisal is made and accompanies the appraiser at all times. The same form is used for an application for proposed construction.

The FHA will return the second page (see Figure 13-2) of the application to the lending institution after having assigned an FHA number to it. It will also show the number to use when referring to the application in future correspondence. Page 3 of the snap-out form of the application (Figure 13-3) is filed in the FHA's file case binder and contains information noted by the appraiser. Page 4 of the application form is sent to the research and statistical department of the FHA after the insurance has

been issued to the lending agency (see Figure 13-4). It contains the original information typed on it by the bank, plus a portion of the appraiser's report. Page 5 of the commitment application form is the actual commitment (see Figure 13-5), which is returned to the lending institution. It indicates the estimated FHA value and gives the commitment terms such as the maximum mortgage amount it will insure and the maximum interest rate as well as the maximum number of months for which the loan may run to maturity. A duplicate of page 5 will find its way into the FHA case binder of this specific property. Page 6 of the form (see Figure 13-6), the third copy of the commitment, must be delivered to the home purchasers before they sign the note and deed of trust or the mortgage and other loan papers. Page 7 is the same as the original and is retained by the lending agency.

After the appraisal has been made and the maximum amount of insurable loan determined, the commitment copy will be returned to the agency requesting the appraisal and commitment. If any corrections must be made to the physical improvements before the loan will be accepted, the commitment will be issued subject to the corrections shown. Termite inspection will usually be requested; if some structural change must be made, the appraiser will make a future compliance inspection to be sure that the change has been made as requested. In the case of a termite inspection, an authorized termite inspector's certificate that any required work has been done will satisfy the FHA. When the seller has received the evaluation of the property and knows the amount of the loan the lender will make, he or she is ready to place the property on the market and accept bids on it.

When a purchaser is found, the second part of the transaction is started. A deposit receipt is issued specifying the amount of the down payment, the sales price, the date, the description of the property (either can be the legal description or the street number), and the conditions under which the seller will sell and the buyer will buy. Bearing a certified copy of the sales agreeement and the deposit receipt, the buyer comes to the lending institution and completes FHA Form No. 92900, application for credit approval (see Figures 13-7 through 9). FHA Form No. 92900 is a new form used by the lending agencies to obtain credit approval and a firm commitment in the name of an applicant. It is a snap-out form consisting of eight pages. When the purchaser is known at the time the application for appraisal and commitment is made, both Forms 2800 and 92900 may be completed at the same time and forwarded to the Federal Housing Administration. The cover sheet of Form 92900 is also an instruction sheet and a worksheet on the reverse side. The remaining eight snap-out copies are inserted and typed from the worksheet. By varying the number of carbon copies, various sections of the Federal Housing

FIGURE 13-1 FHA Form 2800, First Page[a]

Form Approved
OMB No 63-R1366

FHA MORTGAGEE NO. *(Please Verify)*	U.S. DEPARTMENT OF HOUSING AND URBAN DEVELOPMENT FEDERAL HOUSING ADMINISTRATION	FHA CASE NO.

MORTGAGEE'S APPLICATION FOR PROPERTY APPRAISAL AND COMMITMENT FOR MORTGAGE INSURANCE UNDER THE NATIONAL HOUSING ACT

PROPERTY ADDRESS

☐ SEC. 203(b)   ☐ SEC. _____

MORTGAGEE Name and Address including ZIP Code *(Please Type)*
(Please locate address within corner marks)

This form is a request for an appraisal and a commitment to insure a loan on an individual property.

We cannot process incomplete applications.
Rejecting them is costly.
Please help by giving us well prepared applications.
Keep all entries within alloted spaces.

Telephone No.

EXISTING HOUSE ☐ | Name of Occupant *(or person to call if unoccupied)* | Tel. No | Key Encl. ☐ *(If unfurnished)*

Mon. & Yr. Completed | ☐ Never Occup | ☐ Vacant | Occupied by ☐ Owner ☐ Tenant at $ | Per Mo ☐ Furn ☐ Unfurn

PROPOSED ☐
SUBSTAN. REHAB. ☐
UNDER CONSTR. ☐ | Builder's Name & Address Including ZIP Code | Tel. No | Model Identification

☐ Plans | ☐ First Subm. | Prob. Repeat Cases ☐ Yes ☐ No | Prev. Proc. as FHA Case No.

Mineral Rights Reserved ☐ No ☐ Yes *(Explain)*

Utilities	Public	Comm.	Individual
Water	☐	☐	☐
Gas	☐	☐	☐
Elect	☐	☐	☐

☐ Underground Wiring

Sanitary Sewer			Sept Tank	Cess Pool
	☐	☐	☐	☐

Living Units

SPEC. ASSESS. Prepayable. $ _____ Non-Prepay. $ _____
Int _____ % Ann. Pay. $ _____ Unpd. Bal. $ _____ Rem. Term _____ Yrs

ANN. R. EST. TAXES $ | **ANN. FIRE INS. $**

LOT _____ x _____ ☐ Irr ☐ Acres _____ Sq. Ft
GENERAL LOCATION:
SALE PRICE $

EQUAL OPPORTUNITY IN HOUSING

Federal laws and regulations prohibit discrimination because of race, color, religion, sex, or national origin in the sale or rental of residential property. Numerous state statutes and local ordinances also prohibit such discrimination. In addition, section 805 of the Civil Rights Act of 1968 prohibits discriminatory practices in connection with the financing of housing.

If FHA finds there is noncompliance with any applicable antidiscrimination laws or regulations, it may discontinue FHA business with the violator.

LEGAL DESCRIPTION *(Attach one page if necessary)*

SHOW BELOW: Shape, location, distance from nearest intersection and street names. Mark N at NORTH point

Please consider the following TITLE EXCEPTIONS in value:

Please consider the following Equipment in value:

LEASEHOLD | **Ground Rent** *(Per Yr) $* | Lease is: ☐ 99 years | ☐ Renewable | ☐ FHA Approved | Expires

In submitting this application for a conditional commitment for mortgage insurance, it is agreed and understood by the parties involved in the transaction, that if, at the time of application for a Firm Commitment, the identity of the seller has changed, the application for a Firm Commitment will be rejected and the application for a Conditional Commitment will be reprocessed upon request by the mortgagee.
It is further agreed and understood that in submitting the request for a Firm Commitment for mortgage insurance, the seller, the purchaser and the broker involved in the transaction shall each certify that the terms of the contract for purchase are true to his best knowledge and belief, and that any other agreement entered into by any of these parties in connection with this transaction is attached to the sales agreement.

BUILDER/SELLER'S AGREEMENT: All Houses: The undersigned agrees to deliver to the purchaser FHA's statement of appraised value. Proposed Construction: The undersigned agrees, upon sale or conveyance of title within one year from date of initial occupancy, to deliver to the purchaser FHA Form 2544, warranting that the house is constructed in substantial conformity with the plans and specifications on which FHA based its value and to furnish FHA a conformed copy with the purchaser's receipt thereon that the original warranty was delivered to him. All Houses: In consideration of the issuance of the commitment requested by this application, I (we) hereby agree that any deposit or down payment made in connection with the purchase of the property described above, whether received by the undersigned or an agent of the undersigned, shall upon receipt be deposited in escrow or in trust or in a special account which is not subject to the claims of my creditors and where it will be maintained until it has been disbursed for the benefit of the purchaser or otherwise disposed of in accordance with the terms of the contract of sale.

Signature: ☐ Mortgagee ☐ Builder ☐ Seller ☐ Other   19

MORTGAGEE'S CERTIFICATE: The undersigned mortgagee certifies that to the best of its knowledge all statements made in this application and the supporting documents are true, correct and complete.

Signature/Title of Mortgagee Officer   19

WARNING: Section 1010 of Title 18, U.S.C., provides: "Whoever, for the purpose of . . . influencing such Administration . . . makes, passes, utters, or publishes any statement, knowing the same to be false . . . shall be fined not more than $5,000 or imprisoned not more than two years, or both."

FHA FORM NO. 2800 1 Rev. 7/76   FHA COPY — FILE IN CASE BINDER

[a]Form 2800, presented in Figures 13-1–13-6, is reprinted courtesy of FHA.

FIGURE 13-2   FHA Form 2800, Second Page

Administration obtain the information pertinent to their particular section. The original copy (Figure 13-7), which will be inserted into the FHA case binder concerning the particular property, is the application. The second copy differs somewhat from the first on the lower part of the form (see Figure 13-8). It provides a space for the use of the FHA in analyzing the mortgage pattern features such as ratio of loan to value, ratio of term of mortgage to remaining economic life of the property, ratio of total payment to rental value, and an analysis of the mortgagor's credit characteristics, motivating interest in ownership, importance of monetary interest, adequacy of available assets, stability of effective income, and adequacy of the effective income. To facilitate these analyses, FHA Form 92900 should be completed carefully. This is an easy form to follow, but one point should be emphasized: If the commitment shows a value of $35,000 and insurable loan of $33,750 but the sales price is $33,500, the insurable loan is not $33,500 but the amount allowed under the Act in proportion to the sales price—in this case, 97% of $25,000 + 95% of $8500 or $32,325. (However, this figure would be rounded to the lower $50 amount; therefore, the conversion commitment would be for $32,300.) The lending officer will be able to help the applicant complete the form; however, certain items, concerning previous fixed monthly charges, will require the applicant to do some researching either before or after coming to the lending officer. The third page of Form 92900 is just the same as page 2; however, it is routed to the research and statistics division after the insurance endorsement has been placed on the loan. The fourth page of Form 92900, the firm commitment (see Figure 13-9), indicates that a note, trust deed, or mortgage as applied for or modified will be insured under the National Housing Act, provided one of the mortgagors will be owner-occupant and all conditions appearing in the outstanding commitment issued under the relevant case number are fulfilled. Page 4 provides space for additional

conditions, should any exist. It also contains the mortgagor's certificate and the mortgagee's certificate, both of which must be completed and understood before they are signed. After the loan has been closed and the firm commitment signed by both mortgagor and mortgagee, this commitment copy is returned to the FHA together with a copy of the note, a copy of the trust deed, a copy of the loan closing statement, a settlement sheet or a statement signed by the mortgagee that itemizes all charges and fees collected by the mortgagee from the mortgagor, and the mortgagee certificate completed with a case number, section of the National Housing Act under which the loan is made, the deed of trust or mortgage amount, the property address, the mortgagor's name, and mortgagee's name and address. The fifth, sixth, and seventh pages are duplicates of page 4. Page 5 is to be given to the borrower. Page 6 is completed and forwarded to the HUD-FHA with other documents at the time application for insurance is made by the lender. Page 7 is retained by HUD-FHA for its case file. Page 8 is retained by the lender for its files and is the same as page 2.

After the proposed borrower has completed Form 92900 and it appears that there will be sufficient money in his or her statement to cover the costs that will be incurred and that are reflected on Form 92900, the lending officer completes an application for an FHA credit report. This report must come from an agency approved to complete the type of credit report required by the Federal Housing Administration. The Retailers' Credit Association is one such approved organization. An FHA credit report is a detailed statement requiring much of the same information that appears on Form 92900, plus additional information concerning previous credit references.

The lending officer gives the applicant a verification of employment form (FHA Form 2004g) and a verification of deposit form (FHA Form 2004f) for each account located in a separate depositary. When completed, these are returned to the lender by the applicant—(they

FIGURE 13-3 FHA Form 2800, Third Page

Form Approved
OMB No 63-R1366

1 FHA MORTGAGEE NO.	FHA UNDERWRITING REPORT	2 FHA CASE ▲ NO.

3 NEIGHBORHOOD CODE

▲1 ☐ 2 ☐ 4 ☐ ▲1 ☐ 2 ☐ 4 ☐ ▲1 ☐ 2 ☐ 4 ☐ ▲1 ☐ 2 ☐ 4 ☐
Core City / Other City / Sub-urban / Model City / Peri of MC / Rural / URA / Code Enf / Bligh-ted

4 ▲ PROPERTY ADDRESS ▲ CENSUS TRACT

MORTGAGE TO BE INSURED UNDER

☐ SEC. 203(b) ☐ SEC. _____

3

LEGAL-LOT BLK. TR./SUBD.

5 MORTGAGEE

6 ESTIMATED VALUE OF PROPERTY . . . . $_____

8 COMMITTED FOR INSURANCE

COMMITMENT

Issued _____ 19
Expires _____ 19

7 MONTHLY EXPENSE ESTIMATE

Fire Ins . . . . . . $_____
Taxes . . . . $_____
Condo. Com. Exp $_____
Maint & Repairs $_____
Heat & Utilities $_____

9 ESTIMATED CLOSING COST . . . . $_____

10 COMMITMENT TERMS MAX MORT AMT $_____ NO MOS _____ MAX INTEREST _____ %

11 ☐ EXISTING ☐ PROPOSED

12 ▲ EXISTING HOUSE 4 ☐ Name of Occupant *(or person to call if unoccupied)* Tel No Key Encl ☐ *(If unfurnished)*

Mon & Yr Completed ▲ ☐ Never Occup ☐ Vacant Occupied by ☐ Owner ☐ Tenant at $ _____ Per Mo ☐ Furn ☐ Unfurn

13 ▲ PROPOSED 1. ☐
SUBSTAN. REHAB. 2. ☐
UNDER CONSTR. 3. ☐

Builder's Name & Address Including ZIP Code Tel No Model Identification

☐ Plans ☐ First Subm Prob. Repeat Cases ☐ Yes ☐ No ☐ Prev Proc as FHA Case No

14 DESCRIPTION

▲1 ☐ Wood siding
2 ☐ Wood shingle
3 ☐ Asb shingle
4 ☐ Fiber board
5 ☐ Brick or stone
6 ☐ Stuc or c. blk
7 ☐ Aluminum
8 ☐ Asph siding
9 ☐

▲1 ☐ Detached
2 ☐ Semi-det
3 ☐ Row

▲1 ☐ Frame
2 ☐ Masonry
3 ☐ Concrete

Factory Fabricated
▲1 ☐ Yes 2 ☐ No

▲ ___ Stories
7 ☐ Split Foyer
8 ☐ Bi-Level
9 ☐ Split Level

▲1 ☐ Full Basement
2 ☐ __% Basement
3 ☐ Slab on Gr
4 ☐ Crawl Space

▲ ___ Living Units

▲ ___ Bedrooms
___ Liv Room
___ Din Room
___ Kitchen
___ No rms

▲ ___ Baths
▲ ___ ½ Baths

% Non-Res

☐ Store Rm
☐ Util Rm

▲1 ☐ Garage
9 ☐ Carport
___ No of cars

▲1 ☐ Built-in
▲2 ☐ Attached
▲3 ☐ Detached

Mineral Rights Reserved
☐ No ☐ Yes *(Explain)*

Utilities Public Comm Individual
Water ▲1 ☐ 2 ☐ 3 ☐
Gas ☐ ☐ ☐
Elect ☐ ☐ ☐
▲1 ☐ Underground Wiring

Sanitary Sept Cess Tank Pool
Sewer ▲1 ☐ 2 ☐ 3 ☐ 4 ☐

▲ Type of Heating

▲1 ☐ Cent. Air Cond
2 ☐ Wall Air Cond

Type of Paving (Str)
☐ None

☐ Curb & Gutter
☐ Sidewalk
☐ Storm Sewer

EXTRA FEATURES

▲1 ☐ Fireplace 2 ☐ Rec Room 4 ☐ Sw Pool ▲1 ☐ Enclosed Porch 2 ☐ Breezeway 4 ☐ Fence
▲1 ☐ Extra Fire Pl 2 ☐ Expand Attic 4 ☐ Fin Attic ▲1 ☐ 2 ☐ 4 ☐

15 SPEC. ASSESS. Prepayable. $_____ Non-Prepay. $_____
Int ___% Ann. Pay. $_____ Unpd Bal $_____ Rem Term ___ Yrs

16 ▲ LOT _____ x _____ 1 ☐ Irr 2 ☐ Acres _____ Sq Ft
17 GENERAL LOCATION:

18 ANN. R. EST. TAXES $ **19 ANN. FIRE INS. $** **20 ▲ SALE PRICE $** $ Mo Yr

21 EQUIPMENT IN VALUE: ▲1 ☐ Range or Counter cook unit & oven 2 ☐ Refrig 4 ☐ Dishwasher
▲1 ☐ Auto. washer 2 ☐ Dryer 4 ☐ ▲1 ☐ Garb Disp 2 ☐ Vent Fan 4 ☐ Carpet

| Net variations . . . . $_____ |
| Basic cost . . . . $_____ |

22 ▲ LOC. CODE

30 COST DATA: 2800-3 for _____ ☐ Integ
2014-d ☐ 2014
Cost @ $ _____ Per Sq Ft = $ _____

Main Bldg *Sub totals* . . . $_____

23 BASIC CASE Gar Carport . . . . $_____
24 SUB FILE NO Porches Terraces . . . . . $_____
25 REM. LIFE ☐ ECON. ☐ PHYS. ___ YRS

31 BLDG. DESC/VARS. ___ +

Walks Drives . . . . $_____

26 CONDITION AS APPRAISED
▲1 ☐ Excellent 2 ☐ Good 3 ☐ Fair 4 ☐ Poor

Fdns _____ Frpl _____

Ldsp Pltg Fin Gr . . . . . $_____

27 NEIGHBORHOOD DATA
Pres. Land Use _____

Ext Wall _____

Other on-site imp . . . . . $_____

Anticip. Land Use _____

Shtg _____

On-site imp unadj *Totals* $_____

Owner Occp. Appeal _____
Demand for Amenity Inc. Prop _____
___ % Blt. up ___ % own. ___ % Ten ___ % Vac
Age Typ. Bldg _____ to _____
Typ. Mo. Rent to $ _____
▲ Price Range $ ___ to $ ___

Sub Fl _____ Fin Fl _____
Rfg _____ Int Wall _____
Plg _____
Htg _____ Insul _____

2511 Comb . . . $ x wkmp ___ % = ___ %
On-site imp adj . . . . . . $_____
Arch services . . . . $_____
Water sewer tap charges . . $_____
EST. REPL. COST IMP. . $

32 REPL. COST Review
▲ Repl cost imp . . . . $_____
▲ Mkt Price Eq site . . $_____
Misc Allow Costs . . . $_____
Mktg Expense . . . . $_____
▲ Repl Cost . . . . . . $_____

28 ▲ Location ☐ Acceptable ☐ Reject ☐ 223e
Property ☐ Acceptable ☐ Reject

29 IMPROVED ▲ LIVING AREA _____ Sq Ft

Equip _____
Total Variations $ _____

33 COST OF REPAIRS/IMPROVEMENTS
Prop $ Req $

34 COMPARABLE PROPERTIES

	Sq Ft Imp Area	Sto-ries	Rms	Bed Rms	Bath	Const	Gar	Yr /cond	Price	Date	S /L	Date Inspec	+ /=	Variations
SUBJECT PROPERTY														
(1)														
(2)														
(3)														

35 CAP. INC: (Mon Rent $ ___ $ ___ $ ___) — Exc exp $ ___ = $ ___ x Rent mult of ___ = **CAP. INC. $**

36 APPRAISAL SUMMARY: Capitalized Income $_____ Cost $_____ Market ▲ $_____
VALUE: Val *(Excl. Cl. Costs)* $_____ Closing Costs $_____ Total ▲ $_____

37 LEASE: ANN. GRD. RENT $_____ CAP AT ___ % = ▲ $_____ Val of Leased Fee _____ Val of Leasehold Est $_____

38 (1) Remarks (2) Spec. Cond (3) Rej Reasons (4) Neigh Charac (5) Land excl From Val (6) Items Excl From Repl Cost

39 INSPECTIONS:
☐ Proposed Construction ☐ Repair
☐ Mortgagee's Certificate

☐ Appr Arch Proc Date
☐ Reject
Review

☐ Commit Staff Val ☐ Other
☐ Reject
Review Date

WARNING: All persons by signing this report certify that they have no interest present or future, in the property, application or mortgage.

FHA FORM NO. 2800-3 Rev 7-76 NOTE TO PROCESSOR: INSERT CARBON BEFORE COMPLETION OF ITEMS 24 THRU 39 FHA COPY - FILE IN CASE BINDER

216

FIGURE 13-4   FHA Form 2800, Fourth Page

FHA Form 2800, Fourth Page — Data Page

Form Approved
OMB No 63-R1366

| 1 FHA MORTGAGEE NO. | DATA PAGE | 2 FHA CASE NO. |

3 NEIGHBORHOOD CODE
▲1 ☐ Core City   2 ☐ Other City   4 ☐ Sub urban   ▲1 ☐ Model City   2 ☐ Peri of MC   4 ☐ Rural   ▲1 ☐ URA   2 ☐ Code Enf   4 ☐ Bligh ted   ▲1 ☐   2 ☐   4 ☐

4 ▲ PROPERTY ADDRESS   ▲ CENSUS TRACT

MORTGAGE TO BE INSURED UNDER
☐ SEC 203(b)   ☐ SEC _____

3

LEGAL LOT _____   BLK. _____   TR./SUBD. _____

5 MORTGAGEE

6 ESTIMATED VALUE OF PROPERTY .... $_____

8 COMMITTED FOR INSURANCE

COMMITMENT
Issued _____ 19
Expires _____ 19

7 MONTHLY EXPENSE ESTIMATE
Fire Ins .... $_____
Taxes .... $_____
Condo Com Exp $_____
Maint & Repairs $_____
Heat & Utilities $_____

9 ESTIMATED CLOSING COST .... $_____

10 COMMITMENT TERMS   MAX MORT AMT $_____   NO MOS _____   MAX INTEREST _____ %

11 ☐ EXISTING ☐ PROPOSED

12 ▲ EXISTING HOUSE 4 ☐   Name of Occupant _____   Tel No _____   Key Encl _____   ☐ (if unfurnished)
Mon & Yr Completed ▲ _____   ☐ Never Occup   ☐ Vacant   Occupied by ☐ Owner ☐ Tenant at $_____ Per Mo ☐ Furn ☐ Unfurn

13 ▲ PROPOSED 1 ☐   SUBSTAN REHAB 2 ☐   UNDER CONSTR 3 ☐   Builder's Name & Address Including ZIP Code _____   Tel No _____   Model Identification _____
☐ Plans   ☐ First Subm   Prob Repeat Cases ☐ Yes ☐ No   Prev Proc as FHA Case No _____

14 DESCRIPTION
▲1 ☐ Detached   2 ☐ Semi det   3 ☐ Row
▲1 ☐ Frame   2 ☐ Masonry   3 ☐ Concrete
Factory Fabricated
▲1 ☐ Yes 2 ☐ No

▲1 ☐ Wood siding   2 ☐ Wood shingle   3 ☐ Asb shingle   4 ☐ Fiber board   5 ☐ Brick or stone   6 ☐ Stuc or c blk   7 ☐ Aluminum   8 ☐ Asph siding   9 ☐

▲ _____ Stories   7 ☐ Split Foyer   8 ☐ Bi Level   9 ☐ Split Level
▲1 ☐ Full Basement   2 ☐ % Basement   3 ☐ Slab on Gr   4 ☐ Crawl Space
▲ Living Units

▲ _____ Bedrooms   _____ Liv Room   _____ Din Room   _____ Kitchen
▲ _____ No rms
▲ _____ Baths   _____ ½ Baths
_____ % Non Res

☐ Store Rm   ☐ Util Rm
▲1 ☐ Garage   9 ☐ Carport   No of cars _____
▲1 ☐ Built in   ▲2 ☐ Attached   ▲3 ☐ Detached

Mineral Rights Reserved ☐ No ☐ Yes (Explain)
Util ities   Public   Comm   Individual
Water ▲1 ☐   2 ☐   3 ☐
Gas ☐ ☐ ☐
Elect ▲1 ☐ ☐ ☐   Underground Wiring
Sanitary Sewer ▲1 ☐ 2 ☐ 3 ☐ 4 ☐

▲ Type of Heating
▲1 ☐ Cent Air Cond   2 ☐ Wall Air Cond
Type of Paving (Str) ☐ None
Sept Cess Tank Pool ☐ Curb & Gutter ☐ Sidewalk ☐ Storm Sewer

EXTRA FEATURES
▲1 ☐ Fireplace   2 ☐ Rec Room   4 ☐ Sw Pool   ▲1 ☐ Enclosed Porch   2 ☐ Breezeway   4 ☐ Fence
▲1 ☐ Extra Fire Pl   2 ☐ Expand Attic   4 ☐ Fin Attic   ▲1 ☐   2 ☐   4 ☐

15   SPEC ASSESS Prepayable $_____   Non Prepay $_____
Int _____ % Ann Pay $_____   Unpd Bal $_____   Rem Term _____ Yrs

16 ▲ LOT _____ x _____   1 ☐ Irr   2 ☐ Acres _____ Sq Ft
17 GENERAL LOCATION _____

18 ANN R EST TAXES $ **19 ANN FIRE INS $**   **20 ▲ SALE PRICE $** $ _____   Mo _____   Yr _____

21 EQUIPMENT IN VALUE ▲1 ☐ Range or Counter cook unit & oven   2 ☐ Refrig   4 ☐ Dishwasher
▲1 ☐ Auto washer   2 ☐ Dryer   4 ☐   ▲1 ☐ Garb Disp   2 ☐ Vent Fan   4 ☐ Carpet

| Net variations .... $_____ |
| Basic cost .... $_____ |
| Main Bldg (Subtotal) ... $_____ |

22 ▲ LOC CODE

30 COST DATA: 2800 3 for _____   ☐ Integ   ☐ 2014
2014 d _____
Cost @ $_____ Per Sq Ft = $_____

| Gar /Carport .... $_____ |
| Porches/Terraces ..... $_____ |

23 BASIC CASE

24 SUB FILE NO

| Walks/Drives .... $_____ |

25 REM LIFE ☐ ECON ☐ PHYS ☐ YRS

31 BLDG DESC/VARS _____ — _____ + _____

| Ldsp /Pltg /Fin Gr .... $_____ |

26 CONDITION AS APPRAISED
▲1 ☐ Excellent 2 ☐ Good 3 ☐ Fair 4 ☐ Poor

Fdns _____ Frpl _____
Ext Wall _____

| Other on-site imp ..... $_____ |
| On-site imp unadj (Subtotal) $_____ |

27 NEIGHBORHOOD DATA
Pres Land Use _____
Anticip Land Use _____
Owner Occp Appeal _____
Demand for Amenity Inc Prop _____
_____ % Blt up _____ % own _____ % Ten _____ % Vac
Age Typ Bldg _____ to _____
Typ Mo Rent $_____ to $_____
▲ Price Range $_____ to $_____

Shtg _____
Sub Fl _____ Fin Fl _____
Rfg _____ Int Wall _____
Plg _____
Htg _____ Insul _____

| 2511 Comb _____ % x wkmp _____ % = _____ % |
| On-site imp adj ...... $_____ |
| Arch services .... $_____ |
| Water/sewer tap charges $_____ |
| **EST REPL COST IMP** $_____ |

32 REPL COST   Review
▲ Repl cost imp ...... $_____
▲ Mkt Price Eq site ... $_____
Misc Allow Costs ... $_____
Mktg Expense ..... $_____
▲ Repl Cost .... $_____

28 ▲ Location ☐ Acceptable ☐ Reject ☐ 223e
Property ☐ Acceptable ☐ Reject

29 IMPROVED ▲ LIVING AREA _____ Sq Ft

Equip _____
Total Variations _____ $_____

33 COST OF REPAIRS/IMPROVEMENTS
Prop $_____   Req $_____

34 COMPARABLE PROPERTIES

	Sq Ft Imp Area	Sto ries	Rms	Bed Rms	Bath	Const	Gar	Yr /cond	Price	Date	S /L	Date Inspec	+ =	Variations
SUBJECT PROPERTY														
(1)														
(2)														
(3)														

35 CAP INC (Mon Rent $ _____ $_____ $_____) — Exc exp $_____ = $_____ x Rent mult of _____ = CAP INC $_____

36 APPRAISAL SUMMARY: Capitalized Income $_____   Cost $_____   Market ▲ $_____
VALUE: Val (Excl Cl Costs) $_____   Closing Costs $_____   Total ▲ $_____

37 LEASE: ANN GRD RENT $_____   CAP AT _____ % = ▲ $_____   Val of Leased Fee _____   Val of Leasehold Est $_____

38 (1) Remarks (2) Spec Cond (3) Rej Reasons (4) Neigh Charac (5) Land excl From Val (6) Items Excl From Repl Cost

39 INSPECTIONS
☐ Proposed Construction   ☐ Repair
☐ Mortgagee's Certificate
☐ Appr Arch Proc   Date _____
☐ Reject
Review
☐ Commit Staff Val   ☐ Other
☐ Reject
Review   Date _____

WARNING All persons by signing this report certify that they have no interest present or future in the property application or mortgage

FHA FORM NO 2800 4 Rev 7 76

FHA COPY — SEND TO MANAGEMENT INFORMATION SYSTEMS DIVISION AFTER INSURANCE ENDORSEMENT

FIGURE 13-5 FHA Form 2800, Fifth Page

| FHA MORTGAGEE NO. | U.S. DEPARTMENT OF HOUSING AND URBAN DEVELOPMENT FEDERAL HOUSING ADMINISTRATION | FHA CASE NO. | Form Approved OMB No 63-R1 366 |

CONDITIONAL COMMITMENT FOR MORTGAGE INSURANCE UNDER THE NATIONAL HOUSING ACT

☐ SEC. 203(b)   ☐ SEC.

PROPERTY ADDRESS

MORTGAGEE	ESTIMATED VALUE OF PROPERTY .... $ _____	7. MONTHLY EXPENSE ESTIMATE
	COMMITTED FOR INSURANCE	Fire Ins .... $ ———
		Taxes .... $ ———
		Condo Com Exp $ ———
		Maint & Repairs $ ———
	COMMITMENT	Heat & Utilities $ ———
	Issued 19	ESTIMATED CLOSING
	Expires 19	COST .... $ ———

☐ EXISTING ☐ PROPOSED *(See Gen. Cond. 3)*

COMMITMENT TERMS MAX MORT AMT $ _____ NO MOS _____ MAX INTEREST _____%

| Improved Living Area | Sq Ft |

INFORMATION

The estimates of fire insurance, taxes, maintenance/repairs, heat/utilities and closing costs are furnished for mortgagee's and mortgagor's information. They may be used to prepare FHA Form 2900, Application for Credit Approval, when a firm commitment is desired.

GENERAL COMMITMENT CONDITIONS

1. **MAXIMUM MORTGAGE AMOUNT AND TERMS** -

    (a) **OCCUPANT MORTGAGORS**: - the mortgage amount and term set forth in the heading are the maximum approved for this property assuming a satisfactory owner-occupant mortgagor. The maximum amount and term in the heading may be changed depending upon FHA's rating of the borrower, his income and credit.

    (b) **NONOCCUPANT MORTGAGORS**: - If the mortgagor does not occupy the house, the law limits the maximum mortgage amount to not exceed 85% of the maximum amount available to an eligible mortgagor who will occupy the house (85% of value if Sec. 203(i) or 221). In the case of nonoccupant mortgagors, the firm commitment when issued will reduce the mortgage amount and terms below that stated in the heading.

    (c) **COMMITMENT CHANGES**: - The Commissioner may, upon request of the approved mortgagee, change the mortgage amount and term set forth in the heading. If the application is accompanied by a VA CRV, changes will be made only if VA issues an amendment.

    (d) **FLOOD INSURANCE COMMITMENT CONDITIONS**: - This commitment is issued on the condition that if the property is located in a flood hazard area as identified on the latest FIA Flood Hazard

Boundary Map in effect for the community prior to the date of closing, the property will be covered by flood insurance in accordance with FHA Regulation 203.16a.

2. **FIRM COMMITMENT**: - A firm commitment to insure a loan will be issued upon receipt of an Application for Credit Approval, FHA Form 2900, executed by an approved mortgagee and a borrower satisfactory to the Commissioner.

3. **COMMITMENT TERM**: - This commitment shall expire **SIX MONTHS** from the issue date in the case of an **EXISTING HOUSE** or **ONE YEAR** from its date in the case of PROPOSED CONSTRUCTION. *(FHA classifies all cases as either "EXISTING" or "PROPOSED" for the purpose of determining when a commitment expires. Accordingly, a house, even though still under construction, may be classified as an existing house if it was not approved by FHA or VA prior to the beginning of construction.)*

4. **CANCELLATION**: - This commitment may be cancelled after 60 days from the date of issuance if construction has not started, unless the mortgagee has disbursed loan proceeds.

5. **PROPERTY STANDARDS**: All construction, repairs, or alterations proposed in the application or on the drawings and specifications returned herewith, shall equal or exceed the FHA Minimum Property Standards.

SPECIFIC COMMITMENT CONDITIONS *(Applicable when checked)*

1. **HEALTH AUTHORITY APPROVAL**: - Execution of Form 2573 ☐ by the Health Authority indicating approval of the water supply and/or sewage disposal installation is required. (Approval by letter or Health Authority Form may be used.)

2. **TERMITE CONTROL**: - (a) EXISTING HOUSE - Furnish certi- ☐ ficate from a recognized termite control operator that the house and other structures within the legal boundaries of the property shows no evidence of active termite infestation. (b) PROPOSED CONSTRUCTION - Furnish one copy of Termite Soil Treatment Guarantee FHA Form 2052.

3. **PREFABRICATOR'S CERTIFICATE**: - Provide Prefabrication ☐ Certificate required by related Engineering Bulletin.

4. **CARPET UNDERFLOORING**: - Notice of subflooring or finish ☐ flooring installed under carpet shall be posted at a conspicuous location within the dwelling.

5. **SUBDIVISION REQUIREMENTS**: - Comply with Requirements No. ☐ _____

    from Report dated _____ for _____
    _____ Subdivision.

6. **BUILDER'S WARRANTY**: - The builder shall execute FHA Form ☐ 2544, Builder's Warranty.

7. **PROPERTY INSPECTIONS**: - A notice of construction status shall ☐ be given by Form 2289X, letter or telephone at the time indicated below:
    a. Proposed Construction Cases:
        (1) ☐ Notification shall be given for all Proposed Construction Cases at least two work days before "beginning of construction" and as may be instructed below.
        (2) ☐ When the building is enclosed, structural framing completely exposed and roughing-in of plumbing, heating and electrical work installed and visible.
        (3) ☐ When construction completed and property ready for occupancy.
    ☐ b. REPAIRS: Notify FHA upon completion of required repairs.
    ☐ c. CERTIFICATE OF COMPLETION: A certificate stating that the mortgagee has examined the proposed or required repairs and that they have been satisfactorily completed will be accepted.

8. **VA INSPECTIONS**: - Furnish a copy of a clear VA final report. ☐

9. **ASSURANCE OF COMPLETION**: - If the required repairs cannot ☐ be completed prior to submission of closing papers, a Form 2300 escrow in the amount of $ _____ (or such additional amount as the lender desires) may be established as the means to assure completion.

10. **SELLER'S AGREEMENT AND ESCROW FOR EXISTING** ☐ **PROPERTIES FINANCED UNDER SECTION 235**-Section 518.

    This commitment is issued on the condition that if the mortgage is to be insured under Section 235, the seller will execute an agreement to reimburse HUD for expenses incurred in repairing structual or other defects with respect to the property being sold. The form of agreement shall be prescribed by the Secretary and a seller who is not the occupant of the property will deposit 5 percent of the sales price in escrow with the mortgage in accordance with the terms of the agreement.

11. **SECTION 223** ☐ This Commitment is issued under Section _____ Pursuant to Section 223e.

12. **SECTION 221(d)(2)** ☐ The Maximum Insurable mortgage for a mortgagor other than a displaced family presenting a Certificate of Eligibility, FHA Form 3476, is $ _____.

13. **CODE ENFORCEMENT** ☐ Submit a statement from Public Authority that the subject property meets Code Requirements. If the mortgage encumbering the property is to be insured under Section 221(d)(2) a code compliance inspection is required.

14. **REQUIRED CERTIFICATIONS**. ☐ ☐ Electrical ☐ Heating ☐ Roofing ☐ Plumbing

15. **EXPIRATION DATE**: - The Total Value stated above is based ☐ on Veterans Administration Certification of Reasonable Value, case number _____, dated _____. Regardless of General Commitment Condition Number 3, above, this commitment expires on

16. See special conditions No. ☐ _____ below or on attached sheet.

FHA FORM NO. 2800-5 Rev. 7/76

SEND TO MORTGAGEE AFTER AUTHORIZED AGENT SIGNS

FIGURE 13-6 FHA Form 2800, Sixth Page

Form Approved
OMB No 63-R1 366

FHA MORTGAGEE NO.	U S DEPARTMENT OF HOUSING AND URBAN DEVELOPMENT FEDERAL HOUSING ADMINISTRATION	FHA CASE NO.

STATEMENT OF APPRAISED VALUE FOR
A MORTGAGE TO BE INSURED UNDER
THE NATIONAL HOUSING ACT

☐ SEC. 203(b) ☐ SEC. _____

PROPERTY ADDRESS

MORTGAGEE

ESTIMATED VALUE OF PROPERTY . . . . $ _____

Fire Ins . . . . $ _____
Taxes . . . . $ _____
Condo Com Exp $ _____
Maint & Repairs $ _____
Heat & Utilities $ _____

COMMITTED FOR INSURANCE

COMMITMENT

Issued _____ 19
Expires _____ 19

ESTIMATED CLOSING COST . . . . $ _____

DEFINITION OF VALUE

The Federal Housing Commissioner has valued the above identified property for mortgage insurance purposes in the amount equal to the sum of the estimated value of property plus the estimated closing cost.

FHA'S estimate of "Value" ("Replacement Cost" in Section 213 or 220) does not fix a sales price, except when the mortgage is to be insured under section 235(i); does not indicate FHA approval of a purchaser of the property; nor does it indicate the amount of an insured mortgage that would be approved.

"VALUE OF PROPERTY" IS FHA'S ESTIMATE OF THE VALUE OF THE PROPERTY.
"Closing Costs" is the FHA estimate of the cost of closing a mortgage loan on the property. These costs may be paid by either the buyer or the seller.

The maximum mortgage which FHA can insure is based on the sum of the value of the property plus the estimate of closing costs. Under those sections of the National Housing Act (such as 213 or 220) where the maximum mortgage amount must be based on estimated replacement cost, the "Value of Property shall be deemed to mean replacement cost for mortgage insurance purposes."

"Replacement Cost" is an estimate of the current cost to reproduce the property including land, labor, site survey and marketing expense but excluding payments for prepaid expenses such as taxes and insurance and closing costs.

If the contract price of the property is equal to or less than "Value of Property", and the buyer pays closing costs, a part of the closing costs can be included in the mortgage. IF THE CONTRACT PRICE OF THE PROPERTY IS MORE THAN "VALUE OF PROPERTY" AND THE BUYER PAYS THE CLOSING COSTS, THE BUYER IS PAYING MORE FOR THE PROPERTY THAN FHA'S ESTIMATE OF ITS VALUE.

The law requires that FHA mortgagors receive a statement of "appraised value" prior to the sale of the property. If the sales contract has been signed before the mortgagor receives such a statement, the contract must contain, or must be amended to include the following language:

"It is . . . agreed that, ... the purchaser shall not be obligated to complete the purchase...or to incur any penalty...unless the seller has delivered to the purchaser a written statement setting forth...the value of the property (excluding closing costs) not less than $ _____ The purchaser shall have the privilege...of preceeding with...this contract without regard to the amount of the...valuation."

ADVICE TO HOME BUYERS

EXISTING PROPERTIES- WHERE THE APPLICATION INVOLVES AN EXISTING PROPERTY, FHA MAKES AN APPRAISAL ONLY TO DETERMINE THE PROPERTY'S VALUE. AN APPRAISAL DOES NOT IN ANY WAY WARRANT THE CONDITION OF THE PROPERTY. POTENTIAL BUYERS SHOULD EXAMINE THE PROPERTY CAREFULLY AND TAKE ALL NECESSARY PRECAUTIONS BEFORE SIGNING A PURCHASE CONTRACT. THE FHA DOES NOT HAVE AUTHORITY TO PROVIDE FINANCIAL ASSISTANCE IN CONNECTION WITH MAKING NEEDED REPAIRS.

ADVANCE PAYMENTS - Make extra payments when able. You pay less interest and have your home paid for sooner. Notify the lender in writing at least 30 days before the regular payment date on which you intend to make an advance payment.

DELINQUENT PAYMENTS - Monthly payments are due the first day of each month and should be made on or before that date. The lender may make a late charge up to 2 cents for each dollar of any payment more than 15 days late. If you fail for 30 days to make a payment, or to perform any other agreement in the mortgage, your lender may foreclose. You could lose your home, damage your credit, and prevent your obtaining further mortgage loans. If extraordinary circumstances prevent your making payments on time, see your lender at once. If you are temporarily unable to make your payments because of illness, loss of job, etc., your lender may be able to help you. Ask your lender to explain FHA's forbearance policy. **YOUR CREDIT IS AN IMPORTANT ASSET; DON'T LOSE IT THROUGH NEGLECT.**

MORTGAGE INSURANCE PREMIUM - The FHA charges a mortgage insurance premium-in the amount of $\frac{1}{2}$ of 1% a year on the average outstanding principal obligation for the preceding 12 months without taking into account delinquent payments or prepayments. 1/12 of the mortgage insurance premium due each year is collected in the borrower's monthly mortgage payment to allow the lender to accumulate, one month prior to the premium due date, sufficient funds to pay the mortgage insurance premium.

TAXES, ASSESSMENTS, AND INSURANCE- Send your lender bills for taxes, special assessments, or fire insurance that come to you. The fire insurance the lender requires you to carry usually covers only the balance of the loan. Check this with your lender. You may wish to take out additional insurance so that if the house is damaged your loss will be covered as well as the lender's. If your home is damaged by fire, windstorm, or other cause, write your lender at once. Taxes for the coming year can't be known until the bills are received. If they exceed the amount accumulated from your payments, you will be asked to pay the difference. If they are less, the difference will be credited to your account. The same is true of fire insurance. Some States allow homestead or veteran's tax exemptions. Apply for any exemption to which you may be entitled. When it is approved, notify your lender.

CLOSING COSTS - In the heading is FHA's estimate of anticipated closing costs, such as fees for preparation of mortgage instruments, attorney's fees, title insurance, origination fees and documentary stamp taxes. The estimate does not include charges for such prepayable items as taxes, fire insurance.

NEW CONSTRUCTION - When FHA approves plans and specifications before construction, the builder is required to warrant that the house conforms to approved plans. This warranty is for 1 year following the date on which title is conveyed to the original buyer or the date on which the house was first occupied whichever occurs first. If during the warranty period you notice defects for which you believe the builder is responsible, ask him in writing to correct them. If he fails to do so, notify the HUD/FHA Field Office in writing. Mention the FHA case number shown above. If inspection shows the builder to be at fault, the FHA will try to persuade him to make correction. If he does not, you may be able to obtain legal relief under the builder's warranty and where a structual defect is involved the FHA has authority to provide financial assistance in connection with making corrections. Most builders take pride in their work and will make justifiable corrections. They cannot be expected to correct damage caused by ordinary wear and tear or by poor maintenance. Keeping the house in good condition is the owner's responsibility.

IF YOU SELL - If you sell while the mortgage exists, the buyer may finance several ways. Understand how these arrangements may affect you. Consult your lender.
  1. You may sell for all cash and pay off your mortgage. This ends your liability
  2. The buyer can assume the mortgage and pay the difference between the unpaid balance and the selling price in cash. If the FHA and the lender are willing to accept the buyer as a mortgagor, you can be released from further liability. This requires the specific approval of the lender and the FHA.
  3. The buyer can pay the difference in cash and purchase subject to the unpaid mortgage balance. FHA or lender approval is not necessary **BUT YOU REMAIN LIABLE FOR THE DEBT. IF THE BUYER DEFAULTS, IT COULD RESULT IN A DEFICIENCY JUDGMENT AND IMPAIR YOUR CREDIT STANDING.**

(METHODS 1 AND 2 ARE PREFERABLE TO METHOD NUMBER 3)

OPERATING EXPENSES - In the heading are FHA estimates of monthly costs of taxes, heat and utilities, fire insurance, maintenance and repairs. The estimated figures will probably have to be adjusted when you receive the actual bills. **BEAR IN MIND THAT IN MOST COMMUNITIES TAXES AND OTHER OPERATING COSTS ARE INCREASING.** The estimates should give some idea of what you can expect the costs to be at the beginning. In some areas FHA's estimate of taxes may also include charges such as sewer charges, garbage collection fee, water rates, etc.

☐ "THIS HOUSING WAS CONSTRUCTED BEFORE 1950. THERE IS A POSSIBILITY THAT IT MAY CONTAIN SOME LEAD PAINT THAT WAS IN USE BEFORE THAT TIME". THE LENDING INSTITUTION IS REQUIRED TO PROVIDE YOU WITH A COPY OF THE BROCHURE ENTITLED "WATCH OUT FOR LEAD PAINT POISONING".

AMOUNT TO BE BORROWED

When you borrow to buy a home, you pay interest and other charges which add to your cost. A larger down-payment will result in a smaller mortgage. Borrow as little as you need and repay in the shortest time.

FHA FORM NO. 2800-6 Rev. 7/76   SEND TO MORTGAGEE FOR DELIVERY TO HOME BUYER

FIGURE 13-7 FHA Form 92900, Page One[a]

Form Approved
OMB No. 63-R1062

1. U.S. DEPARTMENT OF HOUSING AND URBAN DEVELOPMENT HOUSING · FEDERAL HOUSING COMMISSIONER	2. FHA CASE NUMBER

MORTGAGEE'S APPLICATION FOR MORTGAGOR APPROVAL AND COMMITMENT FOR MORTGAGE INSURANCE UNDER THE NATIONAL HOUSING ACT

☐ SEC. 203(b)   ☐ SEC.
(Note: See Reverse for Privacy Act Statement)

3. PROPERTY ADDRESS

4. MORTGAGORS/BORROWERS

Mtgor. _____ Age ____

5. MORTGAGEE (Name, Address, Zip Code) (Please Type)

Co-Mtgor. _____ Age ____
Address _____

Married ____ Yrs. No. of Dependents ____ Ages ____
Co-Mortgagor(s) _____ Age(s) ____

(Please locate address within corner marks)

6. MORTGAGE APPLIED FOR →

	Mortgage Amount	*Interest Rate	No. of Months	Monthly Payment
	$	%		$

7. PURPOSE OF LOAN MORTGAGOR WILL BE

☐ Finance Constr. on Own Land ☐ Finance Purchase ☐ Refinance Exist. Loan ☐ Finance Impr. to Exist Prop. ☐ Other
☐ Occupant ☐ Landlord ☐ Builder ☐ Escrow Commit. Mortgagor

8. ASSETS

Cash accounts _____ $ _____

Marketable securities _____
Other (Explain) _____ _____
OTHER ASSETS   (A) ASSETS TO CLOSE _____
Cash deposit on purchase . . . . _____
Other (Explain) _____ _____

(B) TOTAL ASSETS $ _____

9. LIABILITIES

	Monthly Payment	Unpaid Bal.
Automobile	$	$
Debts, other Real Estate		
Life Insurance Loans		
Notes payable		
Credit Union		
Retail accounts		
NAME ACCOUNT NO.		
TOTAL	$	$

(If more space is needed, attach schedule)

10. EMPLOYMENT

Mortgagor's occupation _____
Employer's name & address _____

_____ years employed _____

Co-Mtgor. occupation _____
Employer's name & address _____

_____ years employed _____

11. MONTHLY INCOME

Mortgagor's base pay . . . . $ _____
Other Earnings (Explain) . . . . _____
Co-Mortagor base pay . . . . _____
Other Earnings (Explain) . . . . _____
Gross Income, Real Estate . . . . . . _____
Other (Explain) . . . . _____

TOTAL $ _____

Alimony, child support or separate maintenance income need not be revealed if you do not wish to have it considered as a basis for repaying this obligation.

12. SETTLEMENT REQUIREMENTS

(a) Existing debt (Refinancing only) . . . . $ _____
(b) Sale price (Realty only) . . . . _____
(c) Repairs and Improvements. . . . . _____
(d) Closing Costs . . . . _____
(e) TOTAL (a + b + c + d) Acquisition cost . . . . . . _____
(f) Mortgage amount . . . . _____
(g) Mortgagor's required Invest. (e−f) . . . . _____
(h) Prepayable expenses . . . . _____
(i) Non-realty and other items. . . . . _____
(j) TOTAL REQUIREMENTS (g + h + j) . . . . _____
(k) Amt. pd. ☐ Cash ☐ Other (Explain) . . . . _____
(l) Amt. to be pd. ☐ Cash ☐ Other (Explain) . . . . _____
(m) Amount to Close . . . . $ _____

13. FUTURE MONTHLY PAYMENTS

(a) Principal and Interest . . . . $ _____
(b) FHA Mortgage Insurance Premium . . . . _____
(c) Ground rent (Leasehold only) . . . . _____
(d) TOTAL DEBT SERVICE (a + b + c) . . . . _____
(e) Hazard Insurance . . . . _____
(f) Taxes, special assessments . . . . _____
(g) TOTAL MTGE. PAYT. (d + e + f) . . . . _____
(h) Maintenance & Common Expense . . . . _____
(i) Heat and Utilities . . . . _____
(j) TOTAL HSG. EXPENSE (g + h + i) . . . . _____
(k) Other recurring charges (Explain) . . . . _____
(l) TOTAL FIXED PAYMENTS (j + k) . . . . $ _____

14. PREVIOUS MO. HOUSING EXP.

Mortgage payment or rent . . . . $ _____
Hazard Insurance . . . . _____
Taxes, special assessments . . . . _____
Maintenance . . . . _____
Heat and Utilities . . . . _____
Other (Explain) . . . . _____

TOTAL $ _____

15. PREVIOUS MO. FIXED CHARGES

Federal, State & Local income taxes . . . . $ _____
Prem. for $ _____   Life insurance. . . _____
Social Security and Retirement Payments . . . . . . _____
Installment account payments . . . . _____
Operating Expenses, other Real Estate . . . . _____
Other (Explain) . . . . _____

TOTAL $ _____

16. Do you own other Real Estate? ☐Yes ☐No Unpaid Bal. $ ____ Is it to be sold? ☐Yes ☐No FHA Mortgage? ☐Yes ☐No Sales Price $ ____
Address _____ Lender _____ Orig.Mtge.Amt. $ ____

17. MORTGAGOR'S CERTIFICATE: I ☐ have ☐ have not received a copy of the HUD/FHA Statement of Value (Form FHA-2800-6) or Veteran Administration Certificate of Reasonable Value (VA Form 26-1843) showing the estimated value of the property described in the application. Within the past 12 months, have you sold real estate which was subject to a HUD- FHA insured mortgage? ☐ Yes ☐ No. If mortgage was assumed, give Sales Price $_____ and Present Balance $ _____ . Have you ever been obligated on a home loan, home improvement loan or a mobile home loan which resulted in foreclosure, transfer of title in lieu of foreclosure or judgement? ☐ Yes ☐ No. If "Yes" give details including date, property address, name and address of lender, FHA or VA Case Number, if any, and reasons for the action. If dwelling to be covered by this mortgage is to be rented, is it a part of adjacent or contiguous to any project subdivision or group rental properties involving eight or more dwelling units in which you have any financial interest? ☐Yes ☐ No ☐ Not to be rented. If "Yes" give details. Do you own four or more dwelling units with mortgage insured under any title of the National Housing Act? ☐ Yes ☐ No. If "Yes" submit form FHA-2561/HUD-92561. By signing this form you are certifying that all the information given in this application is given for the purpose of obtaining a loan to be insured under the National Housing Act and is true and complete to the best of your knowledge and belief. You also agree that we may check on the information provided by contacting any source which you have named. *NOTE: The interest rate shown in Item 6 is the FHA-Va maximum rate in effect on the date of this commitment and may increase prior to closing unless buyer and lender agree otherwise. (For properties constructed prior to 1950), I have received the brochure "Watchout for Lead Paint Poisoning."

18. MORTGAGEE'S CERTIFICATE: A. The mortgagee certifies that all information in this application is true and complete to the best of its knowledge and belief. B. The mortgagee certifies that the Financial Privacy Act Notice has been delivered to the applicant.

Signature _____   Date _____   19 ____

WARNING: Section 1010 of Title 18, U.S.C. "Department of Housing and Urban Development Transactions," provides, "Whoever, for the purpose of. . .influencing in any way the action of such Department. . .makes, passes, utters, or publishes any statement, knowing the same to be false. . .shall be fined not more than $5,000 or imprisoned not more than two years, or both."

FHA COPY · FILE IN CASE BINDER   HUD-92900-1 (3-79)

[a]Form 92900, presented in Figure 13-7–13-9, is reprinted courtesy of FHA.

FIGURE 13-8 FHA Form 92900, Page Two

Form Approved
OMB No. 63-R1062

1. SPECIAL PROCESSING ▲
  1☐ Veteran   2☐ Assistance Payment   4☐

CREDIT ANALYSIS PAGE
MORTGAGE TO BE INSURED UNDER

☐ SEC. 203(b)   ☐ SEC.   **3**

2. FHA CASE NUMBER ▲

3. PROPERTY ADDRESS

4. MORTGAGORS/BORROWERS

Mtgor. _____ Age ____

Co-Mtgor. _____ Age ____
Address _____

Married▲ Yrs. No. of Dependents▲ Ages

Co-Mortgagor(s)   Age(s)

5. MORTGAGEE (Name, Address, Zip Code) (Please Type)

(Please locate address within corner marks)

6. MORTGAGE APPLIED FOR →

	Mortgage Amount	*Interest Rate	No. of Months	Monthly Payment
	$	%		$

7. PURPOSE OF LOAN ▲ ☐ Finance Constr on Own Land ☐ Finance Purchase ☐ Refinance Exist. Loan ☐ Finance Impr. to Exist Prop. ☐ Other
   MORTGAGOR WILL BE ▲ ☐ Occupant ☐ Landlord ☐ Builder ☐ Escrow Commit. Mortgagor

ASSETS

8.
Cash accounts _____ $ _____
Marketable securities _____
Other (Explain) _____
OTHER ASSETS   (A) ASSETS TO CLOSE ▲ $ _____
Cash deposit on purchase _____
Other (Explain) _____
(B) TOTAL ASSETS $ _____

LIABILITIES

9.   Monthly Payment   Unpaid Bal.
Automobile .... $ _____ $ _____
Debts, other Real Estate ....
Life Insurance Loans ....
Notes payable ....
Credit Union ....
Retail accounts ....
NAME   ACCOUNT NO.
TOTAL $ _____ ▲ $ _____
(If more space is needed, attach schedule)

EMPLOYMENT

10.
Mortgagor's occupation _____
Employer's name & address _____
_____ years employed ____
Co-Mtgor. occupation _____
Employer's name & address _____
_____ years employed

MONTHLY INCOME

11. EFFECTIVE INCOME   MONTHLY INCOME
▲ $ _____ .... Mortgagor's base pay ..... ▲ $ ____
_____ ...... Other Earnings ....
▲ _____ .. Co-Mortgagor's base pay .... ▲ ____
_____ ...... Other Earnings ....
_____ ... Income, other Real Estate ....
_____ .... Other ....
▲ _____ .... TOTAL ...... ▲ $ ____
_____ .. Less Federal Income Tax ....
▲ $ ____ NET EFFECTIVE INCOME

SETTLEMENT REQUIREMENTS

12. (a) Existing debt (Refinancing only) ... $ _____ $ _____
(b) Sale price (Realty only) .... ▲
(c) Repairs and Improvements. . . . . . .
(d) Closing Costs . . . . ▲
(e) TOTAL (a+b+c+d) Acquisition cost ____ ▲
(f) Mortgage amount . . . .
(g) Mortgagor's required Invest. (e−f) . . .
(h) Prepayable expenses . . . .
(i) Non-realty and other items. . . . . . .
(j) TOTAL REQUIREMENTS (g+h+j) ____
(k) Amt. pd. ☐ Cash ☐ Other (Explain) ____
(l) Amt. to be pd. ☐Cash ☐Other (Explain) ____
(m) Amount to Close . . . . $ ____ $ ____

FUTURE MONTHLY PAYMENTS

13. (a) Principal and Interest. . . . . $ ____ $ ____
(b) FHA Mortgage Insurance Premium . . .
(c) Ground rent (Leasehold only) . . . .
(d) TOTAL DEBT SERVICE (a+b+c) ____
(e) Hazard Insurance . . . .
(f) Taxes, special assessments . . . . . . ▲
(g) TOTAL MTGE. PAYT. (d+e+f) ____ ▲
(h) Maintenance & Common Expense . . . ▲
(i) Heat and Utilities . . . .
(j) TOTAL HSG. EXPENSE (g+h+i) ____ ▲
(k) Other recurring charges (Explain) . . .
(l) TOTAL FIXED PAYMENTS (j+k) .. $ ____ ▲ $

PREVIOUS MO. HOUSING EXP.

14.
Mortgage payment or rent . . . . $ ____
Hazard Insurance . . . .
Taxes, special assessments . . . .
Maintenance . . . .
Heat and Utilities . . . .
Other (Explain) . . . .
TOTAL ▲ $ ____

PREVIOUS MO. FIXED CHARGES

15.
Federal, State & Local income taxes . . . . $ ____
Prem. for $ _____ Life insurance. . .
Social Security and Retirement Payments . . . .
Installment account payments. . . . .
Operating Expenses, other Real Estate . . . .
Other (Explain)
TOTAL $ ____

16. Do you own other Real Estate? ☐Yes ☐No Unpaid Bal. $ ____ Is it to be sold? ☐Yes ☐No FHA Mortgage? ☐Yes ☐No Sales Price $ ____
Address _____ Lender _____ Orig.Mtge.Amt. $ ____

17. RATIOS:
Loan to Value ____ % Term to Remain Econ. Life ____ % Total Payt. to Rental Value ____ % Debt. Serv. to Rent Inc. ____ %

18. MORTGAGOR RATING _____
Credit Characteristics _____ Motivating Interest in Ownership _____ Importance of Monetary Interest _____
Adequacy of Available Assets _____ Stability of Effective Income _____ Adequacy of Effective Income _____

Remarks

Ratio of net effective income to:

Housing Expense _____ %

Total Fixed Payment _____ %

Examiner: _____ Reviewer: _____ Date _____ 19__

FHA COPY - FILE IN CASE BINDER

HUD-92900-2 (3-79)

221

FIGURE 13-9   FHA Form 92900, Page Four

Form Approved
OMB No. 63-R1062

| U.S. DEPARTMENT OF HOUSING AND URBAN DEVELOPMENT
HOUSING - FEDERAL HOUSING COMMISSIONER | 2. FHA CASE NUMBER ▲ |
| | 3. PROPERTY ADDRESS |

FIRM COMMITMENT FOR MORTGAGE INSURANCE UNDER THE NATIONAL HOUSING ACT

☐ SEC. 203(b)   ☐ SEC.

4. MORTGAGORS/BORROWERS

Mtgor. _____ Age ____

5. MORTGAGEE *(Name, Address, Zip Code) (Please Type)*

Co-Mtgor. _____ Age ____

Address _____

Married ▲   Yrs.   No. of Dependents: ▲   Ages

Co-Mortgagor(s)   Age(s)

(Please locate address within corner marks)

| 6. MORTGAGE APPLIED FOR → | Mortgage Amount $ | *Interest Rate % | No. of Months | Monthly Payment $ |

☐ **ACCEPTED:** A note and mortgage described above or as modified below will be insured under the National Housing Act provided one of the mortgagors will be an owner-occupant and all conditions appearing in any outstanding commitment issued under the above case number and those set forth below are fulfilled.

| ☐ Modified and Accepted as follows:........... | Mortgage Amount $ | Interest Rate % | No. of Months | Monthly Payment $ |

ESTIMATE OF VALUE AND CLOSING COSTS

VALUE OF PROPERTY $ _____
Closing Costs .... $ _____
TOTAL *(For Mortgage Insurance Purposes)* $ _____

ADDITIONAL CONDITIONS

☐ 2544 - Builders warranty required.   ☐ Owner-occupancy NOT required. *(Delete (c) - Mortgagor's Certificate)*

☐ The property is to be insured under Section 221(d)(2); a code compliance inspection is required.

This is to certify, in compliance with the Right to Financial Privacy Act of 1978, that, in connection with any subsequent request for access to financial records for the purpose of considering or administering assistance to this applicant, the Department of Housing and Urban Development is in compliance with the applicable provisions of said Act.

THIS COMMITMENT EXPIRES:

DATE OF THIS COMMITMENT

_____ , 19 ____

_____ , 19 ____
(Expiration Date)   *(Authorized Agent for the Federal Housing Commissioner)*   *(Field Office)*

INSTRUCTIONS TO MORTGAGEE - *Forward to the insuring office: (1) this commitment signed by the mortgagee and mortgagor; (2) a copy of the note, bond or other credit instrument; (3) a copy of the mortgage or other security instrument; (4) a copy of the settlement statement, (Form HUD-1) signed by the mortgagee which itemizes all charges and fees collected by the mortgagee from the mortgagor and seller; and (5) FHA Mortgage Insurance Certificate completed with case number, Section of the National Housing Act, mortgage amount, property address, mortgagors' names and mortgagee's name and address. Attach Form 2900 Supplement.*

MORTGAGOR'S CERTIFICATE - I certify that:
(a) The mortgaged property, including removable equipment items shown on any outstanding commitment issued under the above case number and those set forth above, will be owned by me free and clear of all liens other than that of this mortgage.
(b) I will not have outstanding any other unpaid obligations contracted in connection with the mortgage transaction or the purchase of the property except obligations which are secured by property or collateral owned by me independently of the said mortgaged property, or obligations approved by the Commissioner.
(c) One of the undersigned will live in the property. *(NOTE: Delete Item (c) if owner occupancy not required by commitment.)*
(d) All charges and fees collected from me as shown in the settlement statement have been paid from my own funds, and no other charges have been or will be paid by me in respect to this transaction.
(e) *(Check Applicable Box)*

☐ The FHA Statement of Appraised Value or VA Certificate of Reasonable Value was not received by me prior to my signing the contract to purchase, but the contract to purchase contained the following language: "It is expressly agreed that, notwithstanding any other provisions of this contract, the purchaser shall not be obligated to complete the purchase of the property described herein or to incur any penalty by forfeiture of earnest money deposits or otherwise unless the seller has delivered to the purchaser a written statement issued by the Federal Housing Commissioner setting forth the appraised value of the property *(excluding closing costs)* of not less than $ _____ which statement the seller hereby agrees to deliver to the purchaser promptly after such appraised value statement is made available to the seller. The purchaser shall, however, have the privilege and option of proceeding with the consummation of the contract without regard to the amount of the appraised valuation made by the Federal Housing Commissioner. The appraised valuation is arrived at to determine the maximum mortgage the Department of Housing and Urban Development will insure. HUD does not warrant the value or the condition of the property. The purchaser should satisfy himself/herself that the price and condition of the property are acceptable."
(IF THE AMENDMENT PROCEDURE WAS NECESSARY, THE DOLLAR AMOUNT USED IN THE AMENDATORY CLAUSE IS INSERTED IN THE ABOVE BLANK.)
(f) Neither I, nor anyone authorized to act for me, will refuse to sell or rent, after the making of a bona fide offer, or refuse to negotiate for the sale or rental of, or otherwise make unavailable or deny the dwelling or property covered by this loan to any person because of race, color, religion, sex, marital status or national origin. I recognize that any restrictive covenant on this property relating to race, color, religion, sex, marital status or national origin is illegal and void and any such covenant is hereby specifically disclaimed. I understand that civil action for preventative relief may be brought by the Attorney General of the United States in any appropriate U.S. District Court against any person responsible for a violation of this certification. *NOTE: The interest rate shown is the FHA-VA maximum rate in effect on the date of this commitment and may increase prior to closing unless buyer and lender agree otherwise.

Signature(s)   Date _____ , 19

MORTGAGEE'S CERTIFICATE - The undersigned certifies that to the best of its knowledge: Date_____ , 19 ____
(a) None of the statements made in its application for insurance nor in the Mortgagor's Certificate are untrue or incorrect.
(b) The conditions listed above or appearing in any outstanding commitment issued under the above case number have been fulfilled.
(c) Complete disbursement of the loan has been made to the Mortgagor, or to his creditors for his account and with his consent.
(d) The security instrument has been recorded and is a good and valid first lien on the property described.
(e) No charge has been made to or paid by the Mortgagor except as permitted under HUD Regulations.
(f) The copies of the credit and security instruments which are submitted herewith are true and exact copies as executed and filed for record.
(g) It has not paid any kickbacks, fees or consideration of any type, directly or indirectly, on or after May 1, 1972, to any party in connection with this transaction except as permitted under Section 203.7(a)(6) of the HUD Regulations and administrative instructions issued pursuant thereto.

| NOTE: If commitment is executed by an agent in name of the mortgagee, the agent must enter the mortgagee's code number and type code number in blocks below:

Code   Type | MORTGAGEE *(Please use FHA imprint stamp, or other approved device)*

(Signature and Title of Officer) |

MORTGAGEE COPY

HUD-92900-4 (3-79)

222

should never be given to an agent for delivery to the lending organization)—and the lender submits the conditional commitment together with Forms 92900, 2004f, and 2004g, the credit report, the deposit receipt, and the sales agreement to the Federal Housing Administration. If the application is approved, that is, if the applicant's income is adequate according to the credit requirements of the FHA and his or her credit history is good, the firm commitment is issued by the FHA in the name of the borrower for the amount requested but not to exceed the amount shown on the commitment for insurance that was received as a result of the application for appraisal and commitment. This commitment will be in multiples of $50.

If a person operates a business or is self-employed, a balance sheet of the business, a profit-and-loss statement, and his or her personal financial statement must accompany Form 92900.

The sales agreement must be supplemented with a statement that it

is expressly agreed that notwithstanding any other provisions of this contract the purchaser shall not be obligated to complete the purchase of the property described herein or to encourage any penalty or forfeiture of earnest money deposited or otherwise unless the seller has delivered to the purchaser a written statement issued by the Federal Housing Administration setting forth the appraisal value of the property for mortgage insurance purposes of not less than _____dollars which statement the seller hereby agrees to deliver to the purchaser promptly upon such appraised value settlement is made available to the seller.

(The purchaser shall, however, have the privilege and option of proceeding with the consummation of this contract without regard to the amount of the appraised value made by the Federal Housing Commissioner.) If there is a statement similar to this in the sales agreement, the supplement is not necessary. The purpose of this statement is to prohibit a sale being made in excess of the FHA evaluation without the purchaser being explicitly advised of the discrepancy.

After the firm commitment has been received, the lending agency carries out its normal procedures for making a real estate loan. At the time the note and deed of trust are signed, the mortgagee also completes the mortgagee statement on page 4 of Form 92900 and the mortgagor signs his or her statement on the same form. After the loan has been disbursed, this form together with application for insurance is sent to the Federal Housing Administration, which insures the loan and returns the certificate to the lending agency or mortgagee.

We stated previously that to qualify for a Title II, Section 203(b) loan the borrower must show that he or she has the ability to make the payments when they fall

due and must have sufficient funds available to pay all closing costs and down payments. Age does not enter into the consideration. A person may be sixty-five years old and still qualify for a thirty-year FHA Title II, Section 203(b) loan. It is the assumption of Federal Housing Administration that there will be an estate and that the beneficiaries will want to continue with the loan payments and take advantage of the home either by retaining it for their personal use or by selling it and realizing the equity involved.

In February 1983, at a meeting with representatives of the California Association of Realtors (CAR), HUD under secretary Donald I. Hovde announced that the FHA, in an effort to reduce the backlog of applications for loan insurance, is trying a new procedure. In nineteen area offices, a direct endorsement program has been authorized. Under the program, authorized lenders are to review the information on FHA Form 92900 and close the loan, if it is one that would be made normally by that lender. After the loan has been closed, the FHA Form 92900 package is sent to the FHA for insurance. If the program is successful in these nineteen areas, it will be completely implemented in late 1983 or 1984.

The under secretary announced that FHA is considering allowing secondary mortgages on property covered by a first FHA mortgage. The total indebtedness would have to conform to the FHA loan to value ratio requirements. In addition, he indicated that the FHA might be less stringent in its requirements for home repairs before a commitment for insurance could be issued. And he also said that the FHA is considering revising its condominium policies to include units that are presently undergoing conversion. These are changes to which we can look forward.

Applying for a Title II Section 235 home loan. Now let us consider the requirements for Section 235(i), insuring a loan under Section 235 of Title II. Section 235 loans are intended to help people with lower incomes to qualify for a home of their own. One of the requirements is that the applicant not have any equity in other real estate or be a homeowner. He or she cannot sell or otherwise dispose of a home he or she owns to qualify under a Section 235 loan program. Exceptions can be made to this rule if the home was taken through condemnation or if it was destroyed by natural causes.

Only the income of the adults in the family is considered for qualifying an individual for Section 235 housing. There can be children making $200 or $300 a month, but as long as they are not adults, even though they live in the same dwelling, their income is exempt from consideration. Each area in the state has its own limitation as to the maximum income allowed for the family to qualify for a Section 235 loan. (See Table 13-2 for comparison.) The reason for the difference is that living and building costs in certain areas are higher than in others.

The monthly payment against the loan is computed on the basis of one-fifth of the buyer's income. The maximum interest subsidy that can be paid by the government is $780 per year, or $65 per month, and the borrower must recertify his or her income every two years. Upon recertification his or her payment is adjusted if there has been a change in annual income, so that his or her monthly payments will again be one-fifth of his or her income.

FHA Form 3100 is used to make application for a Section 235 commitment. The form is a snap-out form with six copies, all of which are the same as the original. The application contains a record of all income received by the applicant and a section for computing the certified adjusted monthly income. Another section computes the assistance for which the applicant is eligible. The first page of the application is sent to the FHA and is returned to the mortgagee after it has been reviewed. The second page is filed in the FHA case binder. The third page is forwarded to the statistics division in Washington, D.C. The fourth page is the copy that the mortgagee retains in its file, and the fifth copy is sent to the Farmers Home Administration if the case is to be processed by that agency. The sixth copy is retained by the mortgagee.

Under this program it is not necessary for the lender to foreclose on any of the properties. If a property becomes delinquent for sixty days the mortgagee assigns the mortgage to the FHA and receives cash payment. At that time the FHA determines what it is going to do with the property and whether it will allow the purchaser to remain in it.

For the loan to be insured the house must be occupied by the borrower at the time of the issuance of the insurance if he or she indicated on the application that it was to be owner-occupied. Otherwise, the loan to be insured would be 85 percent of the amount previously specified. It is most important that the applicant, at the time he or she makes the application and indicates that he or she is going to occupy the house, be advised that he or she must occupy it *at all times* until the insurance has been issued by the FHA. There have been instances when an individual purchased a home with the intent to obtain the property as a rental, live in it for a short time, and then rent it. The buyer occupied the house for one week or less, and when the FHA inspected to see that the owner was the occupant and found a renter, it declined to insure the loan for the amount that had been disbursed. Under these circumstances the lending agency finds itself with an illegal loan and has no alternative but to call the loan and force collection.

The basic application described above contains all the documentation required in connection with a loan on existing property. However, there are other ways in which the loan application can be made.

The application for conditional commitment can be requested from a lender and obtained by a real estate broker who is trying to sell a piece of property for a client. After the conditional commitment is received the broker knows the maximum amount that can be loaned against the property, and he or she also knows what the FHA considers to be a fair market valuation. If the real estate broker's client is asking more than the FHA feels is a fair market valuation, the broker then has a document for support, should he or she receive an offer for a smaller amount. If the real estate broker obtains an offer on the property that is accepted by the seller, a mortgagee's application and mortgagor's statement for conversion commitment, FHA Form 92900, and the accompanying documents will have to be prepared. They can be prepared by the broker and taken to his or her lending agency as a package or the broker can take the applicant to the lending agency, where the lending officer will obtain the necessary additional information, depending upon the desires of the lending agency and upon the broker's understanding with it.

In the case of an application for construction of a home under FHA commitment, if the home is to be owner-occupied and owner-built, the following documents must be submitted to the FHA: the application for firm commitment; FHA Form 92900-1; the verification of employment; the verification of deposits; the credit report, accompanied by two sets of plans and specifications; the firm bid by the contractor who will construct the improvements; two copies of the FHA form for list of materials; and a signed purchase agreement for the lot if purchased within one year. If the loan application is approved, the FHA retains one set of plans and specifications and the contract and returns the second set of plans and specifications, together with a commitment that after the house is satisfactorily constructed according to the plans and specifications and under the usual compliance and inspections, the FHA will insure a loan up to the amount indicated. The plans and specifications returned are the property of the FHA and must be kept at all times at the construction site. Plans and specifications should contain a detailed floor plan with electrical and heating plans (either as separate units, if a comprehensive complex plan is needed, or included in the usual floor plan, if a simple plan can be used), a typical cross section, the four elevations of the house or improvement, and cabinet details. The plans must carry a county-approved plan for septic tank or sewage disposal, where there is no public sewage disposal. Also required is a plat plan showing the dimensions of the lot and the exact location in profile of the home on that lot. When the property is to be owner-occupied and built under contract for the owner, the maximum loan is the same as under purchase, 97 percent of the first $25,000 of appraised value, 95 percent of the remaining balance up to a maximum loan (see Figure 13-7). The loan period shall not be for less than ten years or more than thirty years from the date of the beginning of the amortization, if existing construction, and not less than ten years or more than thirty-five years from the date of the beginning of amortization, if proposed construction.

In the case of proposed construction the builder or the mortgagee must request compliance inspections when suitable stages have been completed. The first compliance inspection is usually made either when the excavation is completed and ready for footings and foundations or when the foundation walls are completed and ready for back-fill. The second compliance inspection is made when the building is enclosed but the structural members are still exposed, and all rough-in plumbing, heating, and electrical work is in place, but visible. The third compliance inspection is made when all the work has been completed and the buildings are ready to be occupied.

Other compliance inspections may be required in cases where the inspector has found fault with some of the construction. The inspector will request that corrections be made and will request a second compliance inspection for that particular stage.

PARTIAL RECONVEYANCES

The FHA prefers to insure houses constructed on normal-sized lots rather than on acreage or on lots large enough to be divided. It feels that within the life of the loan, if the lot is larger than required for one home, an occasion might arise when the owner of the property will want to sell the extra portion. This causes a great deal of paper work to amend the FHA's insurance and records. The FHA would therefore prefer that the insurance cover only a house and a single lot. However, if insurance should be issued on a parcel that is larger than normally required and if there is a later request for a partial reconveyance, the partial reconveyance can be issued. In such instances, the lender submits to the FHA insuring office a request for a partial release of security. This request must contain the following information in letter form (there is no FHA form for such a request): (1) a statement of whether the mortgage or loan is in good standing; (2) a statement of the amount of the outstanding principal balance; (3) the date on which the last payment was made by the borrower and, if there is a delinquency, the number of monthly payments past due; (4) a statement of any unpaid special assessments and the total amount due; (5) a complete legal description of the parcel to be released; (6) the

mortgagor's reason for desiring the lender to make a partial reconveyance; (7) a statement of the contemplated use of the land that is to be reconveyed; (8) the payment, if any, that the mortgagor will receive for the property; (9) the amount of prepayment that will be required; (10) a statement of any restrictions to be imposed upon the land involved in the release; (11) a survey or plat of the property, showing the dimensions of the portion to be released, the location of the present improvements in relation to the surrounding properties and any proposed improvements (the proposed portion for reconveyance should be outlined in red and the total parcel in black); (12) specifications and an estimate of the cost of improvements that will be made on the property after reconveyance. If such a reconveyance is approved by the FHA, it will notify the lender in writing and completion of the partial reconveyance is then his or her responsibility; however, the FHA must be advised by the lender after the partial reconveyance has been completed. If any conditions, set forth by the FHA, attended the partial reconveyance, the lender must also indicate that the conditions have been met.

SALE OF AN FHA-INSURED HOME

In California, an individual may sell his or her home and allow the purchaser to assume the obligation that is in existence on that home, the seller taking cash or second trust deed for his or her equity. Most lending associations have incorporated in their deeds of trust an agreement allowing them to call the note, should there be a sale in which the individual purchasing the property does not meet their qualifications. Under the FHA, however, there is no such agreement in the trust deed and it is possible for a homeowner to sell his or her equity and allow the purchaser to assume the obligation in existence upon the property. The seller can take cash for all the equity or cash for a portion of the equity and a second trust deed for the balance. This is one of the few cases in which a second trust deed is allowed on a property insured by the FHA. If the seller allows the purchaser to buy the home subject to or by assuming the existing trust deed and note, the lender will usually have the two parties to the sale complete an assumption agreement whereby the purchaser agrees to assume the obligations and the seller agrees that, should the purchaser be unable to make the payments and foreclosure steps be considered, the seller will again assume responsibility for the payments on the note. Under such an assumption agreement, the seller remains liable upon the obligation as long as that obligation exists.

There is a second way in which a seller may dispose of an FHA-insured home, receive cash for the equity, and be immediately removed from liability of the original instrument. In this case the sale is made and the FHA agrees to a substitution of mortgagor. For the sale to be consumated in this fashion, the mortgagee (lender) must file FHA Form 2210, request for credit approval of substitute mortgagor (see Figure 13-10). This form must be accompanied by a credit report from an acceptable credit reporting agency, a verification of deposit, a verification of employment, and a certified copy of the signed purchase agreement.

After the FHA has notified the mortgagee that the substitution is acceptable, the buyer and the seller have ninety days to complete their transaction. As soon as title to the property has passed to the new owner, the mortgagee must complete FHA Form 2080, mortgage record change, advising the FHA of the title change. At the same time the mortgagee must send FHA Form 2210-1, approval of purchaser and release of seller, to the seller of the property. The seller keeps a copy of this to present to the FHA together with other exhibits, should he or she ever decide to buy a home under FHA at a later date. This commitment is good for ninety days.

REPORTING DEFAULT

For a lending institution to maintain its insured position, an initial default report must be made within sixty days of the date of default, allowing a thirty-day grace period beginning thirty days after the due date of the default in payment. In other words, if a payment due on January 1 is not made in January or February, then on the sixtieth day a notice of default status, FHA Form 2068, should be filed with the local Federal Housing Administration office.

On the initial report must be shown the monthly payments that have not been made, the mortgage status, the date of the first payment, whether any payments have been made on the trust deed, the term of the mortgage in years, and the reason for nonpayment. The FHA form provides for twelve different reasons for nonpayment: death of principal mortgagor; illness of principal mortgagor; illness or death of mortgagor's family; marital difficulties; curtailment of income; excessive obligations; improper regard for obligations; distant employment transfer; unsatisfactory property; inability to sell or rent property; military service; and miscellaneous, with space for an explanation of the miscellaneous reason. FHA Form 2068 also requires information as to whether there has been a change of mortgagor, and if so, the date on which the change occurred. If the default is cured after consulting with the mortgagor, it is still necessary to file FHA Form 2068. If it is not cured and six monthly installments become delinquent, another notice of default must be filed indicating that six months' payments are delinquent. After this form has been filed with the FHA,

the FHA must be advised every sixty days of the condition of default. If a forbearance (see below) is placed into effect by the lender, then notice of default indicating forbearance must be filed with the FHA. If it becomes necessary for the lender to assign the mortgage and note to the FHA in exchange for insurance benefits, then a notice of default status form must be filed with the local FHA office. If foreclosure proceedings become imminent, regardless of the number of monthly installments delinquent, the notice of default status must be filed with the FHA immediately and again at the time that the foreclosure is started. Should this default be cured between the time of filing of foreclosure proceedings and the completion of the foreclosure, the notice of the cure must be forwarded to the FHA in the notice of default status form. If it is not cured and foreclosure is completed, the FHA is advised of the foreclosure again by use of notice of default status form.

Foreclosure under the FHA can start any time after the initial report of default has been made. Most lending organizations will start foreclosure procedures at least by the sixth month of delinquency.

FORBEARANCE

In 1961 the FHA made provisions for the forbearance of foreclosure in situations in which default on a loan occurred through no fault of the borrower. It was felt that under these circumstances it was desirable to find some relief for the mortgagor so that he or she might work out the problems and bring the loan, over a period of time, back into a current position. Such assistance is temporary and must have the prior approval of the director of the insuring office in whose territory the property is located before it can be extended. The director will withold forbearance approval should the mortgagor be a builder or a dealer in real estate. For forbearance to be approved by the FHA director, the default must be of circumstances beyond the control of the mortgagor who has a sincere desire to retain his or her home and in the foreseeable future will be able to resume regular payments after the immediate cause of default is overcome.

Forbearance should not be requested when it is evident that there is little likelihood of the mortgage being reinstated. The following conditions would probably be considered beyond the control of the mortgagor: loss of employment, with probable return to the same or equivalent employment; illness or death in the family; and damage to the property from flood or other catastrophic causes not covered by insurance. Forbearance is requested by letter and should be accompanied by FHA Form 2068, notice of default status. Such a letter should include the following information: the conditions that caused the default, which conditions were beyond the mortgagor's

FIGURE 13-10 Request for Credit Approval of Substitute Mortgagor[a]

FHA FORM NO. 2210
Rev. 9/67

Form Approved
Budget Bureau No. 63-R0804

U. S. DEPARTMENT OF HOUSING AND URBAN DEVELOPMENT
FEDERAL HOUSING ADMINISTRATION

REQUEST FOR CREDIT APPROVAL OF SUBSTITUTE MORTGAGOR

FHA Case Number

INSTRUCTIONS: This form is for use in cases involving the release of a Mortgagor from liability for a deficiency occurring as a result of foreclosure. Submit original only to FHA.

SECTION OF THE NATIONAL HOUSING ACT

☐ 203   ☐ _____

MORTGAGEE (Name, Address & Zip Code)

Property Address (Street, City & State)

SELLER (Name, Address & Zip Code)

PURCHASER (Name, Address & Zip Code)

A. MORTGAGEE'S REQUEST FOR SUBSTITUTION:

It is requested that the above named purchaser be accepted as Mortgagor and the Seller released from financial responsibility for a deficiency occurring as a result of foreclosure.

An FHA Form 2900, Mortgagor's Application for Credit Approval, with required exhibits is submitted herewith and the statements contained therein are true and complete to the best knowledge and belief of the undersigned.

Title Of The Above Property:	Monthly Mortgage Payment (Total Principal, Interest, M.I.P., Ins., Taxes, and any ground Rent or Special Assessments)	Remaining Term of Mortgage	Face Amount of Original Mortgage
☐ Has been Transferred ☐ Will be Transferred	⟶ $	Months	$
MORTGAGE - ☐ IS ☐ IS NOT CURRENT	Date of First Payment (Original)	Purchaser is or will be Owner-Occupant ☐ Yes ☐ No	Insured under Escrow ☐ Commitment Procedure

Date _____ By _____
Name and Title of Officer

B. CONSENT BY THE FEDERAL HOUSING COMMISSIONER

The above named Purchaser is acceptable as a Mortgagor and, subject to compliance with the following conditions, if any, and the issuance of Form 2210-1 to the Seller, consent is given to the release of the Seller from Financial liability for a deficiency occurring as a result of foreclosure in connection with the above numbered loan. Form 2210-1 shall not be executed by the Mortgagee until the sale to the above named Purchaser is concluded and conditions specified below are met.

SPECIFIC CONDITIONS

☐ The principal balance of the mortgage be reduced to $_____ or less.

☐ The purchaser deposit with you in escrow, trust or special account $_____ under an agreement whereby; (1) the funds will not be disbursed until the property is sold to an owner-occupant purchaser acceptable to FHA; and (2) if the property is not sold within 18 months from the date of transfer to the above named purchaser, the funds shall be applied as a mandatory prepayment to the mortgage principal.

ASSISTANT SECRETARY-COMMISSIONER

Date _____ By _____
Authorized Agent

NOTE TO MORTGAGEE

A copy of this form has not been retained by FHA in its files. Within 30 days of change, you are required to submit to FHA, Form 2080, Mortgage Record Change, to the Assistant Commissioner-Comptroller, Federal Housing Administration, Department of Housing and Urban Development, Att: Receipts and Deposits, Washington, D. C. 20412.

53975-P Rev. 9/67   HUD-Wash., D. C.   FHA FORM NO. 2210 Rev. 9/67

*Form 2210 is reprinted courtesy of FHA.

control and created a hardship case; the proposed number of months, not to exceed eighteen, for which payments shall be reduced or suspended; an outline of the proposed payment arrangements, including the amount of any payment to be made on a reduced basis during the forbearance period, the arrangements of the resumption of the regular monthly payments, and the manner in which the mortgagor expects to be able to bring the note into current condition.

The director of the FHA expects the mortgagee and the mortgagor to work out an appropriate payment arrangement and will probably accept such an arrangement, provided that the arrangement contains both a provision requiring the mortgagor to resume the regular monthly payments at a date no later than at the end of the forbearance period and a program for restoring the loan to good condition within a reasonable period of time. If the director determines that forbearance should be allowed, he or she will advise the mortgagee by letter. Upon approval of the proposed forbearance agreement, the mortgagee will forward to the director of the insuring office a signed copy of the forbearance agreement with the mortgagor. No additional default notices will be required during the period of forbearance provided that the mortgagor complies with the forbearance agreement. If the mortgagor does not comply with the forbearance agreement, the mortgagee should file default notice with the FHA, and if foreclosure becomes necessary, such steps should be taken.

If the lender is not interested in working out a forbearance program, and if the borrower is about to lose his or her home because of one of the conditions listed above that are beyond control, he or she may apply for an assignment of the note and trust deed to HUD-FHA. It will then determine whether to accept the assignment. If it takes over the obligation, HUD-FHA will adjust the payments for a period of time until the owner can resume his or her financial obligations.

REFINANCING

Often an individual who has purchased a home will find that, because of unforeseen expenses, he or she will be unable to maintain the payments now being made. His or her loan may already be an FHA-insured loan or it may be a loan carried by another organization for a shorter term, resulting in higher payments. At any rate, he or she finds it desirable to try to lower the payments by refinancing through the FHA. If the home was purchased more than six months before the date of application, his or her application is considered to be for refinancing. If the application is made within six months of the purchase, then it is considered to be for a new home purchase rather than for home refinancing.

Under refinancing, the same documentation is obtained as for a purchase, including the application for commitment, the mortgagor's and mortgagee's statements, verification of deposits, verification of employment, verification of present balance, and status of the existing loan. These documents are submitted to the FHA and a commitment for an insurable loan is made. The amount is limited to the amount of the existing indebtedness against the property, plus the cost of the proposed repairs, alterations, or additions to the property, plus the nonrecurring closing costs, or to 85 percent of the maximum amount available to an occupant mortgagor under a purchase transaction, whichever is greater. If the application for refinancing is on a property recently purchased on a thirty-year note in which there is little equity, the applicant will experience little relief; however, if the application for refinancing is on a short-term note, such as ten or fifteen years, on which one or two years have expired and the application is for a thirty-year loan, the applicant will receive considerable benefit. Unless there is a sizable amount of equity in the property, the possibility of obtaining cash from a refinancing program is slight, since under a refinancing program only 85 percent of the normal amount loanable will be guaranteed by the FHA. Therefore, the benefit under refinancing is to the applicant with an equity in his or her property and to the applicant who needs relief on monthly payments because of a short-term note.

SALE OF FHA-OWNED PROPERTY

In April 1963, the FHA, having acquired numerous properties through foreclosure by insured lenders, undertook a program of private financing for the sale of these properties. To do this they contacted all their approved mortgagees, inquiring whether the mortgagees might be interested in furnishing purchase money mortgages for the acquisition of such properties. The response encouraged the FHA to proceed with this type of sale, and it supplied to brokers listings of properties together with lists of approved mortgagees who would accept such applications for commitments.

Under this program the FHA has agreed to pay reasonable costs: the usual closing costs, including service charges (origination fee), not to exceed 1 percent of the principal amount of the mortgage; title insurance costs, including the American Title Association Policy; credit reports; state and federal revenue tax stamps; transfer taxes, if any; recording fees; tax agency service fees; and such other customary charges and fees as may be approved. In addition, the FHA has agreed to pay a reasonable discount, not to exceed 2 percent, for arranging financing. All these fees must be shown by the mortgagee on FHA Form 2004W, for financing and closing costs.

This form, together with Form 2384, the FHA sales contract, will be submitted to the FHA along with the other forms usually required in connection with the application for firm commitment. The sales contract is obtained by the broker presenting to the Federal Housing Administration a contract of purchase and a deposit for the purchase of FHA-owned property. If the contract is in order, it will be accepted by the FHA and the purchaser-signed copy will be returned to the broker. He or she will then contact the approved mortgagee for the additional processing and gathering of information. The necessary forms, the same as those required for a firm commitment, are application for commitment, Form 2900; mortgagor's and mortgagee's statements, Form 2900-1; credit report; verification of deposits; verification of employment; and if the applicant is self-employed, a copy of the recent operating statement and balance sheet. When the applications are completed and the accompanying documents are ready for transmittal, they should be submitted to the FHA insuring office with the notation "sale of FHA-acquired property" indicated in the upper left corner of the application. On such an application, no FHA application fee is charged. Upon receipt of the commitment for insurance, closing of the loan should be arranged in the usual manner. So that the deed and closing instructions can be forwarded to the title company, FHA Form 755A—the notice of closing—can be prepared and forwarded to the FHA, which will then provide the title insuring company with the necessary deed and closing instructions. After closing, the usual endorsement of the creditor instruments by the FHA should be obtained.

PLANNED UNIT DEVELOPMENT WITH A HOMES ASSOCIATION

In 1960 the FHA helped to develop a new type of housing, called the *townhouse* concept, in the Hartshorn Homes Development in Richmond, Virginia. This experiment was successful, and in May 1963 the FHA began an intensive study into the need for and means of development of the townhouse concept. The purposes of this exploration were to achieve a development that would create a neighborhood of lasting credit to the community, to keep the value of the property high, and to stimulate home sales and maintain continued marketability of the property. The townhouse concept involves an effort to divorce the homeowner from the continuing maintenance of yard and property so that he or she may have more time available for recreation.

Some of the planned unit developments provide for recreational facilities such as swimming pools, hobby areas, and, in some of the more elaborate, even golf courses. The FHA appraises not only the home but also the common property available for use by the home-owner. The development may take several forms: detached homes; multiple dwellings on one level, such as duplexes or quadruplexes; or multistoried, multifamily dwellings. In instances in which only two walls are open to the air, a great deal of skill has been required to bring into the concept designs that provide entry, light, and ventilation as well as the functional and esthetic accommodations usually found where all four walls are open to the air. The problem has been a challenge to designers. *Land Planning Bulletin No. 6,* published by the Federal Housing Administration, gives some of the solutions to these problems.

Because the area is planned as a unit, the building structures need not follow the usual patterns or streets take the usual designs. New plans for better use are encouraged and such concepts as the patio house, court house, and atrium house are all considered. The FHA, in its analysis of the townhouse concept proposal, is very conscious of land-use intensity, and in this light it will consider the square-foot amount of total floor area, all stories included, for each square foot of land area of the property. The land intensity rating can be considered in three major categories, from the low intensity rating of 1.0 for rural land use, with one modest 1,000-square-foot home on one acre of land, through an intensity rating of 3.0 for suburban land use, with three or four modest homes per acre, to a land-use intensity rating of 8.0 for very intensive land use in the most desirable locations with up to approximately 160 living units per gross acre or approximately 200 units per net acre. For additional information concerning land use and its intensity, see FHA *Planning Bulletin No. 7.*

To obtain an agency approval of a planned unit development certain conditions must be met. These conditions deal with the proper organization of the homes association, with its financing, and with the rights and responsibilities of the homeowner as they pertain to the use, management, and ownership of the common property.

The subdivision plat, dedication, covenants, and other recorded legal agreements must (1) legally create an automatic-membership, nonprofit homes association; (2) give title to the common property to the homes association or indicate that it will automatically be given to the homes association within a reasonable definite time; (3) limit the uses of the common property; (4) give the owner of each lot the right to use and enjoy the common property; (5) indicate that responsibility for the maintenance and operation of the common property is under the direction of the homes association; and (6) establish an association charge on each lot that will (a) assure adequate association funds; (b) provide sufficient safeguards for the lot owners against undesirably high charges; and (c) give each lot owner a vote in the running of the association.

When a builder decides to construct a planned unit development he or she must, before the first lot is sold, incorporate a nonprofit organization that will be a homes association and record the land's subdivision plat and protective covenants for all the land in the planned unit. The land agreements will establish the land-use patterns and make it possible for the plan to continue into the future. The plat and covenants identify the property to be established as common property, the streets, the individual residential lots, and any other parcels that are to be set aside such as shopping centers, church sites, and school sites. The common property areas are set aside by being included in the subdivision plat and are thus established upon their recording. They can also be established through the recording of a separate document that records the property in the name of the homes association and is probably more desirable, since it does not imply that the land is available for public use as might be implied by the information being set on recorded plat of subdivision.

Because the common land is given into the title of the homes association, the association can borrow for the improvement of the common property. The function of the covenants is to make the homes association responsible for maintenance and operation of the common property, for the supervision and maintenance of architectural controls, for enforcement of other rules and regulations, and for the maintenance of all or part of the exterior improvements of the individual property. The function of the covenants is also to provide an adequate assessment flexibility so that future adjustments may be made to any changes in the association's activities or operation costs.

The covenants also make membership in the homes association automatic for each and every owner of a lot and give each owner a voting right in the association and use privileges in the common properties. When there are multifamily units in the development, they are usually included in the homes association with the assessment based on the number of living units and voted by the property owners.

Most of the townhouse units are insured by the FHA under Section 213, project sales, which allows a maximum loan of 97 percent of replacement cost and a maximum term of thirty-five years. However, a project can also be financed under Section 231 if it is a project for the aged, with a high proportion of the owners aged 62 and over, and a lower age limit of 52. Under Section 231, the inclusion of hospital and drug facilities is also possible in the cooperative townhouse unit.

When the foundation for each individual unit is on the ground and it is possible to provide for each unit a deed to a piece of land, the townhouse concept can be used under Section 203(b), but in this case a district must be established for the construction and maintenance of the common property and common property improvements.

It is important to remember that under FHA insurance one pays not only interest and principal each month, but also the mutual mortgage insurance premium of 0.5 percent each month. Also included is $^1/_{12}$ of the annual cost of insurance and of the annual ad valorem taxes. If there are assessments against the property, $^1/_{12}$ of the annual charge of these assessments must also be collected. Such collection is mandatory under the Federal Housing Administration Act and cannot be waived by the lending agency.

LOANS TO VETERANS

In California two types of loans are available to war veterans. One loan, set up under the Federal Veterans Administration Act, is administered by the Department of Veterans Benefits; the second, established by the California Veterans Act, is administered by the California Department of Veterans Affairs.

California Home and Farm Purchase Program

The California Home and Farm Purchase Program (Cal-Vet) was created by the state legislature in 1921 to help California veterans of World War I purchase a home or farm property at a low financing cost. The funds to provide these loans are obtained through the issuance of state bonds periodically voted by the people of California to replenish the loan fund as money is needed. The cost of both the bonds and the administration of the Department of Veterans Affairs is paid by the veterans through their monthly payments of interest and principal on their loans; therefore, this particular program costs the taxpayer nothing.

Eligibility. The eligibility of a veteran is determined by his or her filing an application for certificate of eligibility (Form DVA 1). This form may be obtained through any veterans affairs office or at any county veterans service office. At the time it is submitted to the Department of Veterans Affairs, the form must be accompanied by a clear photocopy of the veteran's discharge or discharges, notices of separation, or certificates of service. (These documents will be returned to the veteran; however, if he or she sends the originals rather than a photocopy, they should be sent by registered mail with a return mail receipt requested.)

The Veterans Farm and Home Act of 1974 set the date of May 7, 1975, as the termination date for veterans to qualify for a Cal-Vet loan and other benefits. Members of the military whose service began after May 7, 1975, do not qualify for benefits under the Cal-Vet program.

This loan is available only to California veterans who have served in the Armed Forces of the United States and whose enlistment began on or before May 7, 1975. Such veterans must be natives of California or must have been bona fide residents of the state at the time of entry into active service. Veterans of Japanese ancestry who were born to bona fide California residents and born in another state during World War II may be eligible also. They must have served ninety days on active duty, a portion of which must have been in one of the following war periods or in a campaign or expedition for which a medal was awarded by the United States Government: War periods were World War I—April 5, 1917, to November 11, 1918; World War II—September 16, 1940, to December 31, 1946; Korean Conflict—June 27, 1950, to January 31, 1955; Army of Occupation of Berlin— May 9, 1945, still open; Army of Occupation of Austria—May 9, 1945, to July 27, 1955; Navy Occupation of Austria—May 9, 1945, to October 25, 1955; Units of the Naval Sixth Fleet—May 9, 1945, to October 25, 1955; China Service Medal (extended)—September 2, 1945, to April 1, 1957; Vietnam Service Medal—July 4, 1965, to April 30, 1975. Armed Forces Expeditionary Medals were Lebanon—July 1, 1958, to November 1, 1958; Vietnam—July 1, 1958, to July 3, 1965; Quemoy and Matsu Islands—August 23, 1958, to June 1, 1963; Taiwan Straits, August 23, 1958, to January 1, 1959; Congo—July 14, 1960, to September 1, 1962; Laos— April 19, 1961, to October 7, 1962; Berlin—September 14, 1961, to June 1, 1963; Cuba—October 24, 1962, to June 1, 1963; Dominican Republic—April 27, 1965, to September 21, 1966; Service in Korea—October 1, 1966, to June 30, 1974.

In the 1974 session of the California legislature, the code was changed again, this time to require all eligible veterans to apply for their Cal-Vet loans within twenty-five years of their discharge date. This requirement does not apply to those who were wounded or disabled as a result of wartime service or who were prisoners of war.

California veterans discharged with fewer than ninety days of service because of service-connected disability are eligible if they otherwise qualify.

Minors who lived in California for six months immediately preceding entry into service from California may also qualify. The veteran must have been released under honorable conditions or still be in service. If the veteran was in service simply for processing, physical examination, or training, he or she is not eligible for a California Veterans loan.

Veterans who were wounded during their service period are given preference in the benefits of this program. After establishing eligibility, the veteran should make arrangements for an interview with a representative of the department, at which time he or she will be asked for information concerning his or her financial condition and employment status and for other information usually requested in a normal application for a real estate loan. If the veteran is determined to be eligible, he or she can submit suitable property for appraisal.

Terms of the California Veterans loan. Most California Veterans loans are based on a maximum repayment period of twenty-five years; however, the repayment period may be less in some individual cases, such as the economic life of the home being less than the twenty-five years. Loans secured by mobile homes have a repayment period from fifteen years to twenty years in length. The length of the loan is determined by the department according to the amount of the loan, the age of the property, the condition of the property, and the financial ability of the borrower. The interest rate is variable and is determined by cost of the interest paid on the State of California revenue bonds which fund the Cal-Vet program without cost to the taxpayer. The original Act called for a minimum interest rate of 2.5 percent and maximum rate of 5 percent. The Act was amended in 1974 because of the increased interest rate on the bonds. This increase was necessary in order to obtain buyers for the revenue bonds. As a result of the change, the minimum rate, as of June 1, 1974, is 6.25 percent, and there is no maximum set. It is still a variable rate which can be changed anytime it is necessary. There are two ways the extra cost can be set up for the veteran: (1) The monthly payment can be increased. (2) The monthly payment can remain the same, but the maturity can be extended. The interest charged to the veteran borrower as of June 15, 1981, was 6.85 percent and 7.85 percent for mobile homes. This, in all probability, will have to be increased as the legislature passed a bill authorizing an 11 percent interest ceiling on Cal-Vet bonds. The State Treasurer sold $150 million in new bonds at the new rate on June 23, 1981. The old ceiling was 9 percent.

There is one very important thing to remember. The application for a California Veterans loan must be in the Department of Veteran Affairs Office *before* the purchase or acquisition of an interest in a property that is being financed. This does not apply, however, if (1) the dwelling has not been finished, (2) the veteran has an interest of record in the building site, and (3) a certificate of occupancy has not been issued. There are no loan fees, points, or appraisal fees collected for Cal-Vet financing. However, there is a $75 inspection fee for mobile homes. Also, all loan applicants for a Cal-Vet loan must apply for the Home Protection Plan Insurance.

Life insurance. Life insurance is available to all applicants who are under sixty-five at the time of the effective date of the loan and can show their insurability.

After the physical examination, applicants are classified as standard, substandard, or uninsurable; however, the applicant will not be classified as substandard or uninsurable solely because of a military-connected disability. If the applicant is classified as a standard risk, he or she must take out insurance through the program for an amount equal to the amount of the loan. The substandard risk does not have to take out insurance, but may do so, only at a higher rate. For instance, at age thirty-five to forty, the cost is 17 cents per thousand borrowed for the standard risk, while it is 43 cents per thousand for the substandard risk. The insurance will pay off the unpaid balance on the loan at the time of the insured's death. It will not pay in case of suicide within the two years from the effective date of the loan. The policy will terminate at age seventy. It will also terminate when the contract is paid in full, is cancelled, or when the insured's interest in the property has come to an end, voluntarily or involuntarily, by operation of the law or otherwise. Also, it will terminate when the Department of Veterans Affairs' master contract with the insurance company expires.

Permanent total disability.   Any individual who has a Cal-Vet loan is eligible for this insurance provided he or she (1) is actively and gainfully employed for at least thirty hours a week at the time of application; (2) gives satisfactory evidence of insurability; (3) is under sixty years of age; (4) is not a member of the armed forces on active duty; (5) is insured under the life insurance coverage. If the applicant is not employed at the time of application, he or she may apply after having been employed continuously for six months and still being under sixty years old. This policy will pay to the division of Home and Farm Purchases an amount equal to the amount of the monthly loan installment for credit to the loan of the insured if the insured has been totally disabled for more than three months. Payments begin on the first day of the month after the three months of total disability and continue monthly thereafter until the contract is paid off, or is otherwise terminated, or until the insured is sixty-eight years of age. The cost per hundred for a person thirty-five to forty years is $4.37. The rate increases as the age at time of the application increases. For instance, a person between fifty-five and sixty would pay $9.61 a hundred, whereas one younger than twenty-five would only pay $1.11.

Fire insurance.   Low-cost fire insurance on the improvements is provided through an agreement between the Veterans Affairs Department and a large group of fire insurance companies. This agreement covers all Cal-Vet properties except certain condominium units. Insurance is in an amount equal to the cost of replacing the buildings. Broad coverage, including earthquake and flood in certain areas, is provided on dwellings and appurtenant structures. Farm buildings and other buildings are insured against lightning, fire, and extended coverage. The premium is paid by the department and then included in the owner's monthly payment.

Single-family home and mobile home loans. California Veterans loans can be used to buy single-family homes and mobile homes on land owned by the borrower or in approved mobile parks. The maximum loan on a single-family residence is $75,000. When the purchase price is $35,000 or less, the down payment required is 3 percent of the appraised value. When the purchase exceeds $35,000, the down payment required is 5 percent of the appraised value. Homes that have solar heating devices may be approved for an additional $5,000 in loan amount. This means that a home with solar heating could qualify for a $80,000 loan. The maximum loan for a mobile home on property owned by the borrower is $75,000; but for a mobile home on a lot in a mobile park the maximum loan would be only $55,000. If the sales price is to be more than the maximum loan allowed, the borrower may still buy the home, but he or she must make up the difference. There is no longer a ceiling on the amount the veteran can pay for a home. If additional financing is needed, junior financing may be approved by the Department. When such additional financing is obtained, the total indebtedness cannot exceed 90 percent of the appraised value.

A California Veterans loan may be prepaid at any time. The only time a prepayment service charge is made is when the loan is paid off within the first two years of the loan. The service charge under this condition is 2 percent of the original loan amount.

In the case of a home that is to be constructed, the department will issue a firm commitment indicating that, when the house has been completed according to plans and specifications approved by the Department, the Department will take title and pay off the interim financing. Sometimes a construction loan can be obtained from the Department, but the Department usually prefers the individual to find interim financing for construction. Such construction is done under a progressive payment plan with inspections being made by the Veterans Affairs Department during its construction to determine that it does meet with the approved plans and specifications. Not only the plans and specifications but also the lot upon which the house is to be built must be approved prior to the issuance of the letter of commitment. In the case of a home loan the veteran must certify that he or she will move into the property within sixty days from the date of purchase by the Department and that he or she will maintain and keep this home as his or her residence until such time as it is paid off. He or she may not transfer, sign, encumber, or rent the property without the prior written consent of the Department.

It is possible for a veteran to own a home and acquire a second home under the Cal-Vet loan; however, he or she must live in the house that is financed by the Cal-Vet loan. He or she may not purchase under a Cal-Vet loan a home that has a rental upon it, nor may a portion of the property after he or she has acquired be rented unless the state has been paid off, or unless such an arrangement is approved by the Department. Any changes in or additions to the structure or to the property must be approved by the California Veterans Affairs Department before such additions or alterations can be made.

The intent of the Act was to help veterans acquire a home at a low-financing cost, not to help them acquire income property. The one exception to this principle is in connection with a farm upon which a veteran may obtain a Cal-Vet Loan.

Farm loans.   It is possible for a California veteran to obtain a Cal-Vet loan for purchase of a working farm. As of July 1, 1983, the maximum amount for this type of loan was $200,000. The term of the loan is determined by the Department at the time of application, which takes into consideration the productivity of the farm, the amount of the loan, and the individual obtaining the loan. The maximum loan is based on 95 percent of the appraised value (based on productivity) of the farm with a ceiling of $200,000. The veteran must have cash or the Department's approval for a junior lien for the difference between the acquisition cost and the loan available. The borrower of a Cal-Vet farm loan does not have to live on the farm, but he or she must work the farm. It cannot be rented out. The farm must have sufficient records to show that it will be able to provide an adequate living for the veteran and his or her family and to repay the amount of the loan.

There are certain minimum standards for suitability. A veteran should consult with the Department of Veterans Affairs before he or she is obligated to a property.

Veterans Affairs construction loans.   Should the Veterans Affairs Department decide to make a loan to a veteran for the construction of a home, it will require that the veteran own a lot acceptable to the Department and that he or she agree to deed this lot to the Department of Veterans Affairs and the state of California without cost. His or her contractor must be licensed in the state of California, must agree to erect improvements on the property in accordance with accepted plans and specifications, and must provide an acceptable performance bond. Before the loan will be approved, the veteran must deposit in escrow the difference between the amount

authorized for a loan by the Department and the total cost of the improvement. If the veteran pays off the contract within two years of the original date of the contract, a 2 percent penalty is assessed on the basis of the original amount of the loan.

Occasionally the demand for veterans loans becomes so great that the funds available for making such loans are exhausted. Whenever this situation occurs, each veteran applying for a loan must file a priority application to establish his or her place on the waiting list. When the application can be considered, a loan application will be sent to him or her and he or she will then be allowed fifteen days in which to submit the property he or she wishes to purchase. If the veteran has already purchased a home and holds an equity in it, he or she may not use a Cal-Vet loan to refinance that particular home unless he or she is paying over 6 percent.

A Cal-Vet loan is a very desirable type of loan. It has low interest rates and a low insurance cost, and it provides low-cost life insurance for the balance of the amount of the contract plus 20 percent in cash to the widow or beneficiary should the veteran die. The term is adequate to provide a low monthly payment. If a buyer can qualify, this is one of the better types of loans to try to obtain.

Improvement loans.   Cal-Vet improvement loans are available to veterans for improvements and maintenance of homes and farms held under contract purchase loans. These loans are available for repairs or replacement work for usual maintenance and for replacement of material to improve the utility and livability of the home, garage, or carport. Such things as energy-conserving installations, porches, patios, walks, driveways, fences, domestic water and sewage systems, and modernizing kitchens would be considered under a Cal-Vet improvement loan. Structural additions to the main dwelling, the veteran's share of new improvement assessments for community projects, and permanent improvements to farm property that would improve the farm's productivity would also qualify for a Cal-Vet improvement loan. There are some things that would not qualify such as swimming pools, sprinkler systems, landscaping, hot tubs, pool house/cabanas/dressing rooms, and so forth.

The interest rate for these loans is the same as that for Cal-Vet acquisition loans. On June 1, 1981, for instance, the rate was 6.85 percent, a very low rate when compared with the 16 to 18 percent interest charged by other lenders at that time.

The minimum improvement loan is $500, and the maximum is $10,000. The term is based on the amount of the loan and the borrower's ability to repay. The maximum term is ten years, but it cannot extend beyond forty years of the date of the original loan contract. There can be no improvement loan made during the first two years of the contract, nor if there is less than twelve months to the maturity of the original loan contract. The veteran is eligible for only one improvement loan in each five-year period or when the first improvement loan is paid in full. The combined balance of the original loan and the improvement loan cannot exceed 90 percent of increased appraisal value.

Loan transfers. A Cal-Vet loan balance can be transferred by the veteran owner-purchaser from one eligible property to another property of adequate security. The transfer is accomplished by the simultaneous exchange of deeds. There is no requirement for a change in the contractual provisions or life and disability insurance in such a transfer.

Second loan eligibility. A veteran may apply for a second Cal-Vet loan if he or she served in two separate qualifying war periods or, if the spouse is also a qualified veteran, an application may be filed for a second loan. However, the first loan must be paid in full and the occupancy provision must be met. An eligible, retiring serviceperson or a retired eligible veteran may apply for a second Cal-Vet loan if the first loan was made during active military service, the loan has been paid in full, and more than one period for which eligibility is given has been served. In such cases there is no requirement for separate periods of service. A veteran purchaser may be given a second loan for the purchase of another home or farm property if the purchaser pays off the existing loan in full, applies for the second loan within six months from the date the loan is paid in full, and reinvests the net equity received. He or she must qualify as an eligible veteran at that time. To qualify for a second loan, the home or farm must have been sold because of (1) change of employment, (2) health problem, (3) condemnation of the property, (4) increase in real estate taxes to the point the veteran can no longer afford the property, (5) increase or decrease in family obligations which makes the property too small or too large for the family.

The Servicemen's Readjustment Act of 1944

The Servicemen's Readjustment Act of 1944, commonly known as the GI Bill of Rights, established a broad program of benefits for the veterans of World War II. It was hoped that this program would help them readjust to civilian life.

The Act is divided into six parts, or titles. Under Title III, the one concerned with real estate finance, a lender is entitled to obtain the Veterans Administration's guarantee *or* insurance on a loan to a veteran. Title III is specifically for loans to veterans for the purpose of constructing or purchasing a home or farm. It was designed to help the veteran obtain a loan for these purposes and still provide protection against loss to the lender.

The GI loan can be obtained on any real property located in the United States, its territories, or its possessions. As the Act was amended, veterans of World War II had until July 25, 1967, to apply for a loan, and veterans of the Korean conflict had until January 31, 1975, to make their applications for a GI loan. On October 23, 1970, President Richard Nixon signed an amendment to the Act that revived the expired loan guarantee entitlement of World War II and Korean conflict veterans and made all loan guarantee entitlements available until used, whether such entitlement is derived from World War II, the Korean conflict, or post–Korean conflict service. Two classes of lenders—supervised and nonsupervised—may make loans to veterans and receive insurance or guarantees. Under the Servicemen's Readjustment Act a lender is the payee, assignee, or transferee of any note or obligation at the time it is guaranteed or insured. Under the Act any person, firm, association, or government agency (state, federal, or corporate) may be a lender.

Supervised lenders. A *supervised lender* is any federal land bank, national bank, state bank, private bank, savings and loan association, building and loan association, insurance company, credit union, or mortgage and loan company that is subject to examination and supervision by an agency of the United States or any state or territory, including the District of Columbia. A supervised lender is also any state or any mortgagee approved as a certified agent of the Federal Housing Administration and acceptable to the Veterans Administration.

One of the major benefits that accrues to the supervised lender is its ability to make a GI loan and receive automatic guarantee or automatic insurance without prior approval from the Veterans Administration. There are, however, some exceptions to this automatic approval. For instance, a supervised lender may not receive automatic guarantee or insurance when a loan is made to two or more borrowers who have become jointly or jointly and severally liable, or when a loan is upon a multiple unit or a cooperative housing project in which more than ten individuals will participate; nor shall a supervised lender make a supplemental loan for the alteration, repair, improvement, extension, replacement, or expansion of a home, business, farm, or farming operation without obtaining prior approval for guarantee or insurance. Although all supervised agencies, as indicated, are eligible to make automatically guaranteed or insured loans, the Veterans Administration may at any time, after thirty days' notice, require all loans being made by any lender or class of lenders to be submitted for prior approval, and no guarantee or insurance shall be in existence unless such prior approval has been obtained.

When a loan is made and application for automatic insurance or guarantee is filed, the Veterans Administration will not require submission of a credit report on the borrower but will accept the judgment of the lender as to the desirability of the credit standing of the borrower. In the absence of fraud, the Veterans Administration will not question the credit analysis of the lender. However, should problems in the credit investigation and lending practices of one particular lender become evident, the Veterans Administration may advise that organization that changes must be made in its analysis of credit or its automatic insurance and guarantee rights will be withdrawn. The previous records will be reviewed with the lender by the Veterans Administration, and should the practice continue, the Veterans Administration may then require that all loans receive prior approval to qualify for insurance or guarantee.

Whenever approval is obtained from the Veterans Administration before a loan is made, a credit report on the applicant must accompany the application for loan. Under certain circumstances the Veterans Administration might feel that the credit report is not adequate, in which case it may request that the lender submit additional data for analysis.

Nonsupervised lenders. A *nonsupervised lender* is any lender not in the category of a supervised lender. A nonsupervised lender may make loans eligible for insurance or guarantee only upon prior approval by the Veterans Administration.

In the case of an assignment of a note and deed of trust by a lender to another holder, the Veterans Administration does not require that it be notified of the assignment provided that the loan is on a guaranteed basis. Should the loan be on an insured basis, notice of the assignment is required by the Veterans Administration; this notification is necessary so that the insurance credits available to the holders may be adjusted to reflect their new positions.

Eligible veterans. Veterans of World War II with discharges other than dishonorable who served ninety days or more on active duty with at least one day of service between September 16, 1940, and July 25, 1947, are eligible for a GI loan. Those who have service-connected disabilities are exempt from the ninety-day service requirement. Veterans who served 180 days of active service in the armed forces from July 25, 1947, to June 27, 1950, are also eligible if they were discharged with a rating other than dishonorable. This was known as the postwar era. Veterans who served at least ninety days active service during the Korean conflict (June 27, 1950,

to January 31, 1955) are eligible for a GI loan if they have discharges other than dishonorable. If they received a service-connected disability during that time, the ninety-day requirement is waived. Veterans who served in the post–Korean conflict era (January 31, 1955, to August 5, 1964) and who had at least 180 days active duty during that period are eligible for a GI loan if they have other than a dishonorable discharge. A veteran is eligible for a GI loan if he or she served at least ninety days active duty during the Vietnam conflict (August 5, 1964, to May 7, 1975) and received other than a dishonorable discharge, unless there is a service-connected disability, in which case the ninety-day period is waived. The Vietnam veteran was brought under the Serviceman's Readjustment Act in the Housing Act of 1978.

Veterans of the post–Vietnam era (subsequent to May 7, 1975) with 180 days of active duty are eligible for a GI loan provided they were not dishonorably discharged. A serviceperson who is still on active duty and has served at least two years may be eligible for an entitlement. Service in the National Guard or the Reserves does not qualify a person for a GI loan.

Also eligible for a GI loan is the unremarried surviving spouse of a veteran who qualified under the service requirements for a loan benefit and who died either in service or after separation from the service as a result of an injury or disease incurred or aggravated by such service in the line of duty. To be eligible, an unremarried widow cannot have received an entitlement as a result of her own service in the armed forces. However, should her husband have taken advantage of his entitlement, her rights as an unremarried widow of an eligible veteran are not affected and she is eligible for a loan provided for in the Servicemen's Readjustment Act of 1944 without her entitlement being decreased by the amount of use attributable to the husband.

Any veteran who fulfills all the other qualifications but who is in the hospital waiting for his or her honorable discharge is eligible and entitled to the rights provided under the Servicemen's Readjustment Act. An honorable discharge certificate is usually enough to qualify the veteran as eligible if one day of that service from which he or she was discharged occurred during one of the designated periods and if he or she served for 180 days; that is, only one day of the 180 days needs to have fallen within the time periods. However, the fact that a veteran has an unendorsed honorable discharge certificate does not necessarily mean that any entitlement is available to him or her, since many veterans have more than one honorable discharge. A veteran may have taken an honorable discharge to accept an appointment as an officer, or he or she may have taken an honorable discharge and later have been recalled to service, or he or she may have taken an honorable discharge and then at a later date have voluntarily reenlisted and have received another honorable discharge. So the fact that an unendorsed honorable discharge is presented does not necessarily mean that an entitlement is available to the individual, since he or she may have used it previously.

If the lender relies upon an unendorsed discharge certificate, he or she assumes the risk that a prior loan exists and that the guarantee benefits of the veteran are no longer available. Under such circumstances it is better for the lender to have the veteran apply for a certificate of eligibility or to submit the application to the Veterans Administration for prior approval.

Veteran's entitlement.   The veteran's entitlement is that amount of benefit available to the veteran as a result of his or her service in the armed forces during World War II, the Korean conflict, or subsequent conflicts.

Originally the Act was drawn so that it would terminate ten years after the officially designated termination date of World War II; however, the Emergency Housing Act of 1958 advanced the termination date for the entitlement to the veteran, and it was extended again in 1970 to read that the entitlements would be good until used by the veteran. The Housing Act of 1980 increased the maximum entitlement to $27,500. This is the fifth time that the entitlement has been increased. The original Act called for an entitlement of $4,000 with a loan guarantee of 50 percent. The loan guarantee was increased to 60 percent of the loan or the amount of the entitlement at a later date. The guarantee of 60 percent of the loan or the amount of the entitlement, whichever is less, was not changed in the 1980 Act. However, the Federal National Mortgage Association indicated it would purchase GI loans on which there was no down payment to a maximum of $110,000 or four times the amount of the entitlement, whichever was less. The maximum loan it would buy without a down payment made to a veteran who had previously used $8,500 of his or her entitlement would be $76,000 ($27,500 − $8,500 × 4 = $76,000). FNMA will buy GI loans over $110,000 to a maximum of $135,000, but the veteran must make a down payment of at least 25 percent. If the full entitlement is available, the loan would be $110,000 ($27,500 × 4 = $110,000) with no down payment.

It may be possible to increase the loan amount to more than four times the remaining entitlement if the purchase price and the certificate of reasonable value (CRV) is more than four times the remaining entitlement. In the example above, assuming the sales price and CRV is $80,000, it would seem a down payment of $4,000 would be required. The amount of loan could be computed in the following way:

Sales price	$80,000
Times allowable percentage	0.75
Allowed portion of sales price	$60,000
Plus remaining entitlement	$19,000
Maximum loan	$79,000
Down payment	$ 1,000

This would allow a loan of $79,000 instead of $76,000.

Consider the way a property selling for $125,000 on which the CRV is in a like amount and full entitlement is available could be financed.

Sales price	$125,000
Times allowable percentage	0.75
Allowed portion sales price	$ 93,750
Plus entitlement	$ 27,500
Maximum loan	$121,250
Down payment	$ 3,750

GI loans computed in this way are acceptable to FNMA. Not all organizations will make loans in this way. An organization that intends to retain the GI loans it makes will probably use the other formula—four times the entitlement, or the entitlement is 60 percent of the loan.

Veterans who have used their full entitlement under previous limits are eligible for the difference between the current amount and the amount used when they obtained their previous loan. This means that a veteran who used his or her full entitlement in January 1968 when the entitlement was $7,500 would have an additional entitlement of $20,000 ($27,500 − $7,500 = $20,000) today. This could be used toward an additional loan of $33,300 ($20,000 ÷ 0.60 = $33,333) or, in certain instances shown above, $80,000 ($20,000 × 4 = $80,000).

The history of the changes in entitlements are as follows:

September 16, 1940, to September 1, 1951	$ 4,000
September 1, 1951, to May 7, 1968	$ 7,500
May 7, 1968, to December 31, 1974	$12,500
December 31, 1974, to October 1, 1978	$17,500
October 1, 1978, to October 1, 1980	$25,000
October 1, 1980, to date	$27,500

The Veterans Housing Act of 1970 made it possible for the first time for a veteran to use his or her entitlement for the refinancing of an existing debt on his or her home or farm residence. The purpose of this Act was to allow those whose entitlement had expired unused (but been revived in October 1970) to use their entitlement to better their position. Such refinancing could result in lower payments because of extended term and reduction of equity, thus giving the veteran cash for personal use or to make improvements to the property. Refinancing loans are subject to the same restrictions as a loan for purchase.

If a veteran has World War II service as well as Korean

conflict service, he or she has only one entitlement, since the Korean conflict cancels out the entitlement for World War II. If the veteran has used a portion of his or her World War II entitlement, that amount is deducted from the amount available from the Korean conflict entitlement. In other words, if the veteran had used $5,000 of the $27,500 World War II entitlement and was called back into service for the required length of time during the Korean conflict, the $5,000 that he or she had used under the World War II entitlement would be deducted from the $27,500 that would have been his or her Korean conflict entitlement, leaving a balance of $22,500 available for use in the purchase of a new home. This would be true only if he or she still owned the property which was on the original loan or if the Veterans Administration had not incurred a liability or suffered a loss as the result of the previous indebtedness of the veteran to the government. In the latter situation, the veteran may make complete restitution for the loss or the liability to the government, in which case his or her entitlement would be restored.

Under certain circumstances a veteran may obtain additional entitlement even though he or she may previously have used all the entitlement. If the property for which the entitlement was previously used is taken by condemnation or for some other public use by the local, county, state, or federal government, he or she may apply for a review of his or her entitlement and will probably be issued a new entitlement. He or she may also file for new entitlement if the property is destroyed by fire or by natural phenomena such as earthquake, flood, tornado, or any other act that is not a result of his or her omission or destructive act, or if indebtedness is paid.

A veteran may also apply for an additional entitlement should he or she be required to move from the area either by a necessary job transfer, for health, or for other compelling reasons caused by no fault of the veteran. In such instances the application would have to be reviewed by the Veterans Administration, but it would probably be favorably received. However, for the Veterans Administration to issue a new entitlement, it would have to be released from guarantee or insurance on the loan and on the security of the property being disposed of by the veteran to make the required move. Of course, this release would also be necessary on property being taken by condemnation.

Guarantee of loan. When the Veterans Administration refers to a loan as guaranteed, it is indicating to the lender that it will repay a specific percentage of the loan upon the default of the borrower. The maximum guarantee issued by the Veterans Administration on a loan made to an eligible veteran is 60 percent of a loan

(but not more than $27,500) used to buy a home for the eligible veteran. In case of default after several years of payment, the liability of the Veterans Administration will be in the same proportion to the present indebtedness as existed when the loan was first made. In other words, if the purpose of the loan was for home purchase and the home cost $45,800 under the 60 percent maximum, the guarantee by the Veterans Administration would be $27,480. Assuming that there is a balance on the property of $30,000 at the time of default, the Veterans Administration guarantee would cover $18,000. The liability of the guarantee decreases or increases, therefore, in proportion to any change in the amount of the indebtedness outstanding; however, under no circumstances will the amount exceed that established when the loan was first made and guaranteed.

For example, let us assume that the loan to the veteran is $45,800 with a $27,480 guarantee. The veteran pays the loan down to $30,000 and decides to make an addition that costs $20,000. This will bring the total indebtedness to $50,000, but since the guarantee cannot exceed the amount originally guaranteed, the guarantee will still be $27,480 and in this case 55 percent of the total indebtedness. However, this maximum would not decrease until the loan again fell below $45,800, at which time the ratio of 60 percent of the loan being guaranteed would once again come into effect, and as the loan balance decreased the guarantee would proportionately decrease.

The note—evidence of the veteran's debt—has been written so that it will mature in thirty years and thirty-two days from the date of the note or the economic life of the property, with reasonably equal monthly payments. On January 1, 1982, the Veterans Administration indicated it would allow the notes to be drawn with a graduated payment. The graduated payment would be the same as that offered by HUD-FHA under its Plan 3 of Section 245(a)—an annual increase of 7.5 percent in the monthly payments for five years, after which the payments would remain the same over the life of the loan.

The maximum loan allowed under the VA (GI) guarantee is four times the veterans existing entitlement. If the entitlement has never been used, the maximum loan would be $110,000 (4 × $27,500).

Insurance. Under the insurance provision of the Veterans Administration Act, the United States Government agreed to pay the lender or holder of an obligation for any loss incurred as a result of a default on an insured loan. Any loan that at its inception could be guaranteed under the Veterans Administration Act may be insured instead of guaranteed. Whether the loan is to be insured or guaranteed is left to the desire of the lender and the borrower, who must state to the Veterans Administration under which program the loan is being made at the time the loan is reported. If the lender does not indicate that a loan is to be insured at the time it is reported, it will automatically be placed as a guaranteed loan by the Veterans Administration and it cannot be changed from this category.

Under the Veterans Administration loan insurance program the Veterans Administration creates an account for each supervised or nonsupervised lender either making or buying insured loans. Whenever an insured loan is made, the lender's account is credited with 15 percent of the loan; however, the credit to the lender cannot exceed $4,000 on a real estate loan.

The amount for which the Veterans Administration is liable under an insured loan is the net loss, established after the security for the loan has been liquidated. This liability is, of course, subject to the insured lender's having the amount of the loss available to his or her credit in his or her insurance account. However, should the insured lender not have sufficient funds in the insurance account to cover the loss when it occurs, he or she may file a supplemental claim at any time within five years after filing the original claim. In this way the lender can build up his or her insurance account and at a later date offset the loss that he or she has been forced to take. It is possible for the Veterans Administration to terminate any lender's insurance account with six months' notice, which means that after the notice has been given, the insurance account can be used only for loans made before the termination of the insurance account.

Certificate of eligibility.

When the Servicemen's Readjustment Act was established in 1944, the entitlements or benefits that accrued to veterans were intended to phase out over a period of time. The expiration of the entitlements would not be the same for all veterans, since it depended upon the veteran's length of service and the period from which the entitlement stemmed. For instance, a World War II veteran's entitlement would expire ten years from the date of his or her discharge or release from active duty (any part of which occurred during World War II), plus an additional period computed on the basis of one year for each three months of service unless he or she used his or her full entitlement before July 25, 1962. However, under no conditions, regardless of time in active service, would the entitlement remain in effect beyond July 25, 1967, for World War II veterans.

The expiration of the entitlement for a Korean conflict veteran was to be computed by the same formula, and unless all entitlements were used before January 31, 1965, the entitlement would expire by January 31, 1975, regardless of term of duty.

Some World War II entitlements were allowed to lapse, as were some entitlements of Korean conflict veterans who did not have long terms of service. However, under the Veterans Housing Act of 1970, the lapsed entitlements were restored to the veterans of all conflicts and cold wars since World War I. The entitlements now have an open end and there is no set time for expiration of the entitlements except as they are used in full by the veteran.

Additional changes in the use of the entitlements were made in 1975. An entitlement that shows an original balance of $7,500 can be used for a guarantee of up to $27,500. A veteran who has used $12,500 of the entitlement has $15,000 remaining that can be used on another loan. If he or she has used his or her whole entitlement and sells his or her home, paying off the VA loan, the full amount of the entitlement ($27,500) can be reinstated. The veteran can reinstate the total amount of the entitlement if he or she sells a home with a VA loan after receiving the VA's consent to transfer, or the entitlement can be reinstated if he or she pays off the home in the due course of the loan.

Home loans.

A lender may obtain Veterans Administration insurance or guarantee on a loan made to an eligible veteran for the purchase or construction of a dwelling that is to be owned and occupied by the veteran as his or her home. Under the home loan classification, the Veterans Administration may also guarantee or insure a loan for the purchase of a farm on which there is a farm residence that the veteran will occupy as his or her home, or for the construction on land owned by a veteran of a farm residence that the veteran will occupy as his or her home. The lender may also make and receive insurance or guarantee on loans for the repair, alterations, or improvements of a farm residence or other dwelling owned by the veteran and occupied as his or her home.

If the veteran is purchasing a farm residence or other dwelling for investment purposes, the loan is not eligible for guarantee or insurance as a home loan. Construction loans or purchase loans to an eligible veteran for residential property consisting of not more than four family units are eligible for insurance or guarantee. If the property is to be owned by two or more eligible veterans, the property may consist of four-family units plus one additional unit for each veteran involved in the ownership of the property. Thus a husband and wife, both of whom are veterans, can purchase up to five family units. Such loans may also be processed as home loans. The total guarantee could be $35,000 or 60 percent.

No guarantee or insurance can be issued on a loan for the purchase or construction of residential property unless the veteran certifies when he or she applies for the loan and also when the loan is closed that he or she intends to occupy the property as his or her home. Neither may any loan for alterations, repairs, or improvements of a home owned by a veteran be insured or guaranteed unless he or she certifies at the time of application and at the time of disbursement that he or she is occupying the property.

The Veterans Administration will guarantee or insure loans the total of which includes items such as dishwashers, built-in refrigerators, garbage disposals, built-in ranges, and ovens, if the equipment installed is compatible with the type of property in which it is installed and if the equipment is considered necessary under present living standards. In some areas these items are considered not as part of the real estate but as personal property. Under these circumstances a security agreement must be taken by the lender, whose responsibility it is to see that a proper and binding security agreement is placed against the property.

Some convenience items found in many homes today are not eligible for insurance or guarantee, and no portion of the money obtained from the loan against the property may be used for the purchase of these items. These items include blenders, mixers, intercommunication systems, hi-fi systems, warning systems for fire overheating, rotary and fixed television antennas, automatic roasting and barbecue equipment for indoor fireplaces, and central vacuum-cleaning systems. These items are not included in the Veterans Administration appraisal of value but are listed as separate items along with their approximate cost. Under no circumstances can proceeds of the loan be used for the purchase of these items; therefore, it is not necessary that the lender take a security agreement on them. The maximum term is thirty years and thirty-two days.

Farm loans. A lender may make to an eligible veteran a loan for purchasing land, livestock, buildings, equipment, machinery, supplies, or tools to be used in a farming operation. He or she may also make a loan for the repairing, constructing, altering, or improving of any land, buildings, or equipment to be used in the farming operations. He or she may make a loan for purchasing stock in a cooperative association when the purchase of stock is necessary for the operation of the farm. This could include stock in irrigation companies. In all cases in which the loan is to be guaranteed or insured by the Veterans Administration, the veteran must have a reasonable amount of experience in farming. The proceeds of the loan must be used in a manner necessary to conduct an efficient farming operation, and there must be reasonable likelihood that the veteran will succeed on the farm.

In the case of a full-time farm operation the income must be such that it may be expected to pay the operating expenses including taxes and insurance, to provide a

living for the veteran, to retire the principal indebtedness, and to make the interest instalments on the loan.

In the case of a part-time farming operation, the proceeds from the sale of the produce, in excess of the veteran's needs, supplemented by other income upon which the veteran can rely, must provide the veteran with sufficient income to pay operating and living expenses and to repay the loan in accordance with its terms. The supplementary income that the farmer-veteran must have may not be such that the farm operation will suffer through his or her producing the supplementary income.

The farming operation should also justify the capital expenditure for the production and the marketing of crops. Whether part-time or full-time, the farming operation should supply the farmer's sustenance needs.

In all cases in which the farmer-veteran hires labor, he or she must be responsible for the supervision of the work. A farm purchased through a Veterans Administration guaranteed or insured loan may not be operated by a tenant farmer or by an unsupervised employee.

Loans for the installation of equipment that becomes a fixture on the land, or for repairs, alterations, or improvements to property occupied by the veteran under a lease with an unexpired term of not less than the length of the loan, are eligible for insurance or guarantee if the property is used in connection with the veteran's farming operation and if it is possible for the income of the operation to repay the obligation within the term of the loan.

Mobile home loans. A veteran may use his or her entitlement for the purchase of a mobile home. Under the Housing Act of 1978, the maximum guarantee was established as the lesser amount of 50 percent of the loan, or the amount of the entitlement available, but not to exceed $27,500. The maximum term for a single wide mobile home is fifteen years and thirty-two days, whereas for double wide mobile homes the term is twenty-five years and thirty-two days. Use and restoration of entitlements for mobile home loans is the same as for other loans except a restored entitlement cannot be used for the purchase of another mobile home. As in all GI loans, the value of the unit is based on an appraisal of the unit and lot or the cost of the new unit.

Since January 1975 the Veterans Administration has had the authority to guarantee loans for used mobile homes. At the same time, federal credit unions were authorized to make VA-guaranteed mobile home loans.

Loans to handicapped veterans. One aspect of the Servicemen's Readjustment Act of 1944 that has not received the publicity it deserves deals with certain rights of paraplegics. The Act provides for a grant of $30,000 for the purpose of buying a home that is suitable to, or can be remodeled to be suitable to, a paraplegic's needs, such as wide doors, wide halls, ramps instead of steps, low counters, and special bathroom fixtures.

If the cost of the home is more than $30,000, the grant (which does not have to be paid back) can serve as a down payment and any type of financing can be used. This program is known as Section 702 housing. To qualify the veteran must have a doctor's certification that he or she is a paraplegic. The disability must be service-connected. The loan must be for a single-family home, and the veteran must be able to use the home.

Loans to refinance delinquent indebtedness.

Other types of loans can qualify for Veterans Administration insurance or guarantee. One such loan is for the refinancing of delinquent indebtedness. The delinquent indebtedness must be secured by property used or occupied by the veteran as a home or for farming purposes. To qualify for such a loan, the veteran must show that such financing will aid him or her in economic readjustment. No loan for an eligible veteran will be insured in connection with indebtedness that is less than sixty days delinquent. The holder of the obligation must write a letter to the Veterans Administration proving that the obligation is delinquent. Any delinquent loan or obligation that was made to buy property or that occurred within one year of the application must be referred to the Veterans Administration for prior approval with a report of the veteran's income and expenses and his or her affidavit concerning the price of the property purchased with the proceeds of the delinquent loan. If the delinquent loan is a Veterans Administration loan, the veteran cannot obtain a VA loan for refinancing the obligation.

When two loans are outstanding, one secured by a first trust deed and the second by a second trust deed, and either of the trust deeds is delinquent, an eligible veteran may obtain a loan on which the Veterans Administration will issue a guarantee or insurance for the full amount of the combined loan, assuming proper appraisal. The loans will be treated for insurance or guarantee purposes as though they were both delinquent.

Junior lien financing is now allowed for obtaining a new GI loan if the combined first and second liens do not exceed the amount of the certificate of reasonable value. The interest rate on the second cannot exceed the maximum interest allowed by the Veterans Administration. The second trust deed and note must be on the VA forms and must run concurrently with the first. The second must be fully amortized with no balloon payment. The term of the note can be for a shorter maturity than the first but not longer. The veteran must be able to qualify for both loans. Copies of the proposed note and deed of trust must be included in the credit package when

it is submitted to the Veterans Administration. It is still permissible to place a second lien on the property once the GI loan has been made. This is usually done at a later date in an effort to pay indebtedness or to take advantage of accumulated equity.

Loan details.

A guarantee may be placed on a home purchase loan of any amount; however, the maximum guarantee will cover only 60 percent of the loan or $27,500, whichever is less. Loans of $25,000 or more for the purchase of farm property, to be eligible for guarantee or insurance, must have the prior approval of the Veterans Administration.

The interest rate on Veterans Administration loans has been as low as 4 percent, and although many loans were written at this rate, the interest rate on those loans has not been increased by the Veterans Administration to equal its current rate of 16.5 percent, since by statute the rate at which the loan is written must be in effect during the life of the loan.

Veteran buyers, under a GI loan, usually cannot be charged points, escrow fees, termite and dry rot inspection fees, or photography fees. However, under certain conditions they may pay points. The conditions which would allow the buyer to pay points are as follows: (1) there is no seller, such as a veteran building a home on a lot he or she owns; (2) if the seller is legally unable to pay points; (3) or if the seller is someone legally stopped from paying points under any conditions. Of course, if a veteran is allowed to pay the necessary points, his or her best interests must be served by paying the points.

The lender may charge a late charge on his loans, but such late charges may not exceed 4 percent of the instalment amount and may not be assessed until fifteen days after the due date. Late charges may not be deducted from the regular payments but must be collected separately and in addition to the normal payments.

The maximum maturity of the loan is five years for a nonamortized loan and thirty years and 32 days for amortized home loans. In cases of loans for the purchase of farms and farm real estate, the maximum maturity is forty years; however, the maturity of any loan may under no circumstances exceed the maximum economic life of the property that secures the loan.

Unlike the Federal Housing Administration note maturity, the Veterans Administration maturity is figured from the date of the note, so that if a veteran purchases a home and the note is dated July 1974, the note must mature on July 1, 2004, or sooner, regardless of when the first payment is made.

All loans having a maturity more than five years from the date of the loan must be amortized. The payments under the amortization schedule must be approximately the same and must include a principal reduction at least once a year during the life of the loan, except that on a farm real estate loan the principal payment may be postponed for not more than two years from the date of the note.

Balloon payments are not permitted under the Veterans Administration program, and the final payment may never exceed twice the normal payment except in connection with a construction loan, in which case the final instalment shall not be more than 5 percent of the original amount of the loan. If the loan is less than five years in maturing from the date of the note or from the date of assumption by the eligible veteran, the note need not be amortized. The terms of the loan may be extended by a written agreement between the holder and the borrower in the event of default, to forestall imminent foreclosure, where there is a justification for the action. Prior approval of the Veterans Administration is not required in such a case; however, the extension must be such that at least 80 percent of the extended loan balance must be amortized within the maximum maturity for loans of the same class. If at least 80 percent of the loan will not be amortized within the maximum limit, it is possible to submit the program to the Veterans Administration for prior approval. Submission does not necessarily mean automatic approval, for the maturity date of the extended note cannot exceed the maximum allowed by law for the type of loan involved.

Loan processing.   As with the FHA loan application, it is possible through agreement with the lending agency for the documentation of the application to be prepared by a realtor or by an agent of the lending agency before it is presented to the lending agency. When a veteran has found a parcel that he or she wishes to buy, whether it be a home, other real estate, or a farm, he or she must determine his or her entitlement and the valuation of the property. Both requests may be filed simultaneously. The lending agency may forward these documents to the Veterans Administration office before it takes any further action on the application.

Veterans Administration Form 26–1880 request for determination of eligibility and available loan entitlement, is used to determine the eligibility of the veteran and his or her entitlement. A copy of this form is shown in Figure 13-11. This form is forwarded to the Veterans Administration regional office together with any previously issued certficates of elgibility and all discharge or separation papers from the wartime period of active service. If proper discharge and separation papers are not available, they should be procured from a representative of the Veterans Administration. Form 26-1880 should be completed in full wherever the information is applicable. It is not necessary that the request for determination of reasonable value accompany the request for determina-

tion of eligibility; however, time will be saved if these two operations can be performed simultaneously by the Veterans Administration.

Veterans Administration Form 26-1805 (Figure 13-12), request for determination of reasonable value, must be completed in detail. To expedite the processing of applications and appraisals, Form 26-1805 is a snap-out form. The first, seventh, and eighth copies are the same. The first is for the Veterans Administration, the seventh for the appraiser, and the eighth for the mortgagee (see Figure 13-12). The second, third, and fourth copies are the same and are copies of the certificate of reasonable value (see Figure 13-13). The upper part of the certificate is the same as that shown on the request. The lower part, completed by the Veterans Administration, shows the reasonable value, inspections that may be required, and repairs that must be made before the VA will guarantee the loan. The first copy of the certificate goes to the mortgagee or lender, the second to the VA file, and the third to the veteran borrower. The fifth and sixth copies are the same; the lower part is the appraiser's report of valuation. The original goes to the VA files and the second copy is for the appraiser's records (see Figure 13-14). When the applicant applies for a certificate of reasonable value, he or she will need a legal description of the property. If the applicant has a copy of the preliminary title report he or she should have the report at the time of application. The report will not only give the legal description but will also show the outstanding easements against the property, which are also required on Form 26-1805. The applicant should also bring a recent tax bill to the lending officer so that the assessed value and the current ad valorem tax can be shown on the application.

On the reverse of Form 26-1805 are (1) a certification that must be used in connection with proposed construction or existing housing not previously occupied, and (2) a request for master certificates of reasonable value on proposed or existing construction. The certificate is not necessary in connection with a request for the appraisal of an existing, previously occupied property.

If the application is for a home that is to be constructed on a lot owned by the veteran that was not previously purchased from the contractor, the certificate must be completed. The certification states that the applicant will not refuse to sell the property being appraised to a prospective purchaser because of his or her race, color, creed, or national origin.

The request for determination of reasonable value should be accompanied by the purchase agreement or contract when a sale is involved. The appraisal fee of $90 for an existing house or $95 for a proposed house is paid to the lending agency at the time of application.

If the lending agency intends to request prior approval

FIGURE 13-11   VA Form 26–1880ᵃ

FIGURE 13-11   VA Form 26–1880ᵃ

		Form Approved Budget Bureau No. 76-R371.7

VETERANS ADMINISTRATION
REQUEST FOR DETERMINATION OF ELIGIBILITY AND AVAILABLE LOAN GUARANTY ENTITLEMENT

TO   VETERANS ADMINISTRATION
ATTN: Loan Guaranty Division

NOTE: Please read instructions on reverse before completing this form.

1. LAST - FIRST - MIDDLE NAME OF VETERAN

2. ADDRESS OF VETERAN (No., street or rural route, city or P.O., State and Zip Code)

3A. DATE OF BIRTH

3B. SOCIAL SECURITY NUMBER

4. MILITARY SERVICE DATA.--I request the Veterans Administration to determine my eligibility and the amount of entitlement based on the following period(s) of active military duty: (Start with latest period of service and list all periods of active duty since September 16, 1940.)

PERIOD OF ACTIVE SERVICE		NAME (Show your name exactly as it appears on your discharge papers for each period of service)	SERVICE NUMBER	BRANCH OF SERV.
DATE FROM	DATE TO			
4A.				
4B.				
4C.				
4D.				
4E.				
4F.				

5A. WERE YOU DISCHARGED, RETIRED, OR SEPARATED FROM SERVICE BECAUSE OF DISABILITY, OR DO YOU NOW HAVE ANY SERVICE-CONNECTED DISABILITIES?
☐ YES ☐ NO (If "Yes," complete Item 5B)

5B. VA CLAIM NUMBER
C-

6A. ARE YOU NOW ON ACTIVE MILITARY DUTY?
☐ YES ☐ NO

6B. WERE YOU ON ACTIVE MILITARY DUTY ON THE DAY FOLLOWING THE DATE OF SEPARATION INDICATED IN THE PAPERS SUBMITTED?
☐ YES ☐ NO

6C. HAVE YOU BEEN ON ACTIVE DUTY SINCE JANUARY 31, 1955?
☐ YES ☐ NO

7A. IS THERE A CERTIFICATE OF ELIGIBILITY FOR LOAN GUARANTY OR DIRECT LOAN PURPOSE ENCLOSED?
☐ YES ☐ NO (If "No," complete Items 7b and 7c)

7B. HAVE YOU PREVIOUSLY APPLIED FOR A CERTIFICATE OF ELIGIBILITY FOR LOAN GUARANTY OR DIRECT LOAN PURPOSES?
☐ YES ☐ NO (If "Yes," give location of VA office involved) ▶

ADDRESS OF VA OFFICE

7C. HAVE YOU PREVIOUSLY RECEIVED SUCH A CERTIFICATE OF ELIGIBILITY?
☐ YES ☐ NO (If "Yes," give location of VA office involved) ▶

8A. HAVE YOU PREVIOUSLY SECURED A VA DIRECT HOME LOAN?
☐ YES ☐ NO (If "Yes," give location of VA office involved) ▶

8B. HAVE YOU PREVIOUSLY OBTAINED HOME, FARM, OR BUSINESS LOAN(S) WHICH WERE GUARANTEED OR INSURED BY VA?
☐ YES ☐ NO (If "Yes," give location of VA office involved) ▶

9 Check only if this is a request for a DUPLICATE Certificate of Eligibility ▶
☐ PLEASE ISSUE A DUPLICATE CERTIFICATE OF ELIGIBILITY IN MY NAME. THE CERTIFICATE PREVIOUSLY ISSUED TO ME IS NOT AVAILABLE BECAUSE IT HAS BEEN LOST, DESTROYED OR STOLEN. IF IT IS RECOVERED, IT WILL BE RETURNED TO THE VA FOR CANCELLATION.

I certify that the statements herein are true to the best of my knowledge and belief.

10. SIGNATURE OF VETERAN

11. DATE

FEDERAL STATUTES PROVIDE SEVERE PENALTIES FOR FRAUD, INTENTIONAL MISREPRESENTATION, CRIMINAL CONNIVANCE, OR CONSPIRACY PURPOSED TO INFLUENCE THE ISSUANCE OF ANY GUARANTY OR INSURANCE BY THE ADMINISTRATOR.

THIS SECTION FOR VA USE ONLY

DATE CERTIFICATE ISSUED AND DISCHARGE OR SEPARATION PAPERS AND VA PAMPHLETS MAILED	TYPE OF DISCHARGE OR SEPARATION PAPERS RETURNED	CERTIFICATION OF ELIGIBILITY VALID THROUGH:	
		TERMINAL DATE	INTERIM DATE

IMPORTANT INSTRUCTIONS: If the Certificate of Eligibility is to be sent to the veteran, his complete mailing address should be shown in Item 12. If it is desired that the certificate be sent to other than the veteran, the name and address of such person or firm should be shown in Item 12.

VA FORM 26-1880, MAY 1969

DO NOT DETACH

The amount of loan guaranty entitlement available for use is endorsed on the reverse of the enclosed Certificate of Eligibility. This certificate must be returned to the VA at the time a loan application or loan report is submitted.

12. RETURN TO:

[Please deliver the enclosed pamphlets and discharge or separation papers to the veteran promptly. Thank you.]

VA FORM MAY 1969 **26-1880**

EXISTING STOCKS OF VA FORM 26-1880, AUG 1968 WILL BE USED.

*The forms shown in Figures 13-11 through 13-17 are reprinted courtesy of the Veterans Administration

FIGURE 13-12   VA Form 26–1805, Page One

Form Approved
OMB No. 76-R0231

VETERANS ADMINISTRATION

REQUEST FOR DETERMINATION OF REASONABLE VALUE (Real Estate)

CASE NUMBER

On receipt of "Certificate of Reasonable Value" or advice from the Veterans Administration that a "Certificate of Reasonable Value" will not be issued, we agree to forward to the appraiser the approved fee which we are holding for this purpose.

1. STATUS OF PROPERTY	2. CONSTRUCTION COMPLETED BEFORE DATE HEREOF

☐ A. PROPOSED   ☐ B. EXISTING, NOT PREVIOUSLY OCCUPIED   ☐ C. EXISTING, PREVIOUSLY OCCUPIED   ☐ D. ALTERATIONS, IMPROVEM'TS OR REPAIRS   ☐ E. REFINANCING-VETERAN APPLICANT OWNS AND OCCUPIES RESIDENCE AS HOME

☐ A. WITHIN 12 CALENDAR MOS.   ☐ B. MORE THAN 12 CALENDAR MOS

3. NAME AND ADDRESS OF FIRM OR PERSON MAKING REQUEST (Complete mailing address. Include ZIP Code.)

4. PROPERTY ADDRESS (Include ZIP Code)

5. TYPE OF PROPERTY	6. MANDATORY HOME ASSOCIATION MEMBERSHIP?	7A. NO. BLDGS.
☐ HOME		7B. NO. LIVING UNITS
☐ MOBILE HOME LOT	☐ YES ☐ NO	
8. LOT DIMENSIONS		

9. DESCRIPTION	WOOD SIDING	CINDER BLOCK	SPLIT LEVEL	NO. ROOMS	DINING ROOM	CAR GARAGE	GAS	CEN. AIR COND.
DETACHED	WOOD SHINGLE	STONE	% BASEMENT	BEDROOMS	KITCHEN	CAR CARPORT	UNDERGRD.WIRE	TYPE HEAT. & FUEL
SEMI-DET.	ALUM. SIDING	BRICK & BLOCK	SLAB	BATHS	FAMILY RM.	WATER (Public)	SEWER (Public)	
ROW	ASB. SHINGLE	STUCCO	CRAWL SPACE	½ BATHS	UTILITY RM.	WATER (Comm.)	SEWER (Comm.)	ROOFING DESCRIP.
CONDOMINIUM	BRICK VENEER	STORIES	YRS. EST. AGE	LIVING RMS.	FIREPLACE	WATER (Ind.)	SEPTIC TANK	

10. LEGAL DESCRIPTION	11. TITLE LIMITATIONS, INCLUDING EASEMENTS, RESTRICTIONS, ENCROACHMENTS, HOMEOWNERS ASSOCIATION AND SPECIAL ASSESSMENTS, ETC.	12. OFFSITE IMPROVEMENTS

12. OFFSITE IMPROVEMENTS
A. STREET SURFACE.
B. STREET ACCESS   ☐ PRIV.   ☐ PUB.
C. STREET MAINT.   ☐ PRIV.   ☐ PUB.
D. ADD'L. IMPROVEMENTS   ☐ STORM SEWER   ☐ SIDEWALK   ☐ CURB/GUTTER

13. VETERAN PURCHASER'S NAME AND ADDRESS (Complete mailing address. Include ZIP Code)	14. REMOVABLE EQUIPMENT INCLUDED IN PURCHASE PRICE OR COST

14. REMOVABLE EQUIPMENT
☐ RANGE OR COUNTER TOP UNIT   ☐ DISHWASHER   ☐ REFRIGERATOR
☐ AUTOMATIC WASHER   ☐ DRYER   ☐ WALL-TO-WALL CARPETING
☐ OTHER(S) (Specify)

15A. OCCUPANT'S NAME	15B. TELEPHONE NO.	16A. BROKER'S NAME	16B. TELEPHONE NO.

17. DATE AND TIME AVAILABLE FOR INSPECTION AM PM	18. KEYS AT (Address)	19. NAME OF OWNER

20. COMPLIANCE INSPECTIONS WILL BE OR WERE MADE BY	21. NUMBER OF MASTER CERTIFICATE OF REASONABLE VALUE (If any)	22. PROPOSED SALES CONTRACT ATTACHED	23. CONTRACT NO. PREVIOUSLY APPROVED BY VA THAT WILL BE USED
☐ FHA ☐ VA ☐ NONE MADE		☐ YES ☐ NO	

24A. NAME AND ADDRESS OF BUILDER (Include ZIP Code)	24B. TELEPHONE NO.	25A. NAME AND ADDRESS OF WARRANTOR (Include ZIP Code)	25B. TELEPHONE NO.

26. PLANS (Check one)	27. PLANS PREVIOUSLY PROCESSED UNDER VA CASE NO.	28. ANNUAL REAL EST. TAXES (If exist, construction)
☐ FIRST SUBMISSION ☐ REPEAT CASE (If repeat case, complete Item 27)		$

29. COMMENTS ON SPECIAL ASSESSMENTS AND/OR HOMEOWNER ASSOCIATION CHARGES	30. SHOW BELOW: Shape, location, distance from nearest intersection, and street names. Mark N. at north point.

EQUAL OPPORTUNITY IN HOUSING - NOTICE

Federal laws and regulations prohibit discrimination because of race, color, religion, national origin, or sex in the sale or rental or financing of residential property. Numerous state statutes and local ordinances also prohibit such discrimination.

Non-compliance with applicable antidiscrimination laws and regulations in respect to any property included in this request shall be a proper basis for refusal by the VA to do business with the violator and for refusal to appraise properties with which the violator is identified. Denial of participation in any program administered by the Federal Housing Administration because of such violation shall constitute basis for similar action by the VA.

CERTIFICATION REQUIRED ON CONSTRUCTION UNDER FHA SUPERVISION (Strike out inappropriate phrases in parentheses)

I hereby certify that plans and specifications and related exhibits, including acceptable FHA Change Orders, if any, supplied to VA in this case, are identical to those (submitted to) (to be submitted to) (approved by) FHA, and that FHA inspections (have been) (will be) made pursuant to FHA approval for mortgage insurance on the basis of proposed construction under Sec.

31A. NAME AND ADDRESS OF PROSPECTIVE LENDER (Include ZIP Code)	31B. TELEPHONE NO. OF LENDER REQUESTER	32. SALE PRICE OF PROPERTY	33. REFINANCING AMT. OF PROPOSED LOAN
		$	$

34. SIGNATURE OF PERSON AUTHORIZING THIS REQUEST	35. TITLE	36. DATE

Federal statutes provide severe penalties for any fraud, intentional misrepresentation, or criminal connivance or conspiracy purposed to influence the issuance of any guaranty or insurance or the granting of any loan by the Administrator.

37. DATE OF ASSIGNMENT	38. NAME OF APPRAISER

VA FORM AUG 1977 26-1805

EXISTING STOCKS OF VA FORM 26-1805, NOV 1972, WILL BE USED.

VA FILE COPY 1

FIGURE 13-13   VA Form 26–1803, Page Four

1. ESTIMATED REASONABLE VALUE	VETERANS ADMINISTRATION	2. CASE NUMBER
	NOTIFICATION OF REASONABLE VALUE	3. EXPIRATION OF VALIDITY PERIOD
$	*(VA GUARANTEED LOAN)*	

NOTE: Read carefully the information below. Show the above case number on all correspondence.

IDENTITY OF PROPERTY APPRAISED ▶	4. PROPERTY ADDRESS (Include ZIP Code)

IMPORTANT INFORMATION

THE PROPERTY DESCRIBED IN ITEM 4 HAS BEEN APPRAISED AND THE VETERANS ADMINISTRATION HAS DETERMINED THAT ITS REASONABLE VALUE IS THE AMOUNT SHOWN IN ITEM 1. WE CONSIDER REASONABLE VALUE TO BE THE SAME, AS A PRACTICAL MATTER, AS CURRENT MARKET VALUE.

THE MAXIMUM VA GUARANTEED LOAN A PRIVATE LENDER CAN MAKE TO YOU IS THE AMOUNT IN ITEM 1 ABOVE.

IT IS IMPORTANT TO NOTE THAT IF THE PURCHASE PRICE OR COST OF THE PROPERTY EXCEEDS THE AMOUNT IN ITEM 1, YOU MUST PAY IN CASH FROM YOUR OWN RESOURCES AT OR PRIOR TO LOAN CLOSING AN AMOUNT EQUAL TO THE DIFFERENCE BETWEEN THE PURCHASE PRICE OR COST OF THE PROPERTY AND THE REASONABLE VALUE IN ITEM 1.

YOU MUST BE ABLE TO FUND THE CLOSING COSTS WHICH YOU ARE TO PAY AND ANY DIFFERENCE THERE MAY BE BETWEEN THE PURCHASE PRICE OR COST OF THE PROPERTY AND THE LOAN AMOUNT.

5. VETERAN PURCHASER'S NAME AND ADDRESS (Complete mailing address. Include ZIP Code)	*THE REASONABLE VALUE AS SET FORTH HEREIN IS PREDICATED UPON CONDITIONS RECITED BELOW.*
	THIS IS ONLY A NOTICE ABOUT THE APPRAISAL. IT DOES NOT MEAN VA HAS APPROVED YOUR LOAN. RETAIN THIS NOTICE FOR FUTURE REFERENCE.

GENERAL CONDITIONS

(NOTE: THE VETERANS ADMINISTRATION DOES NOT ASSUME ANY RESPONSIBILITY FOR THE CONDITION OF THE PROPERTY. THE CORRECTION OF ANY DEFECTS NOW EXISTING OR THAT MAY DEVELOP WILL BE THE RESPONSIBILITY OF THE PURCHASER.)

1. This certificate will remain effective as to any written contract of sale entered into by an eligible veteran within the validity period indicated.
2. This dwelling conforms with the Minimum Property Requirements prescribed by the Administrator of Veterans Affairs.
3. The aggregate of any loan secured by this property plus the amount of any assessment consequent on any special improvements as to which a lien or right to a lien shall exist against the property, except as provided in Item 16 below, may not exceed the reasonable value in Item 1 above.
4. Proposed construction shall be completed in accordance with the plans and specifications identified below, relating to both on-site and off-site improvements upon which this valuation is based and shall otherwise conform fully to the VA Minimum Property Requirements. Satisfactory completion must be evidenced by either
   A. VA Final Compliance Inspection Report (VA Form 26-1839), or
   B. VA Acceptance of FHA Compliance Inspection Reports (FHA Forms 2051) or other evidence of completion under FHA supervision applicable to proposed construction.
5. By contracting to sell property, as proposed construction or existing construction not previously occupied, to a veteran purchaser who is to be assisted in the purchase by a loan made, guaranteed, or insured by VA, the builder or other seller agrees to place any down payment received by the seller or agent of the seller in a special trust account as required by section 1806 of Title 38, U. S. Code.
6. The VA guaranty is subject to and conditioned upon the lending institution's compliance, at the time of the making, increasing, extending or renewing of the proposed loan, with section 102 of P.L. 93-234, "Flood Disaster Protection Act of 1973."

SPECIFIC CONDITIONS *(Applicable when checked or completed)*

6. THE REASONABLE VALUE ESTABLISHED HEREIN FOR THE RELATED PROPERTY IS	7. PROPOSED CONSTRUCTION TO BE COMPLETED (Identify plans, specifications and exhibits)
☐ BASED UPON OBSERVATION OF THE PROPERTY IN ITS "AS IS" CONDITION ☐ PREDICATED UPON COMPLETION OF PROPOSED CONSTRUCTION (If checked complete item 7) ☐ PREDICATED UPON COMPLETION OF REPAIRS LISTED IN ITEM 9	

8. INSPECTIONS REQUIRED	9. REPAIRS TO BE COMPLETED
☐ FHA COMPLIANCE INSPECTIONS FOR PROPOSED CONSTRUCTION ☐ VA COMPLIANCE INSPECTIONS ☐ LENDER TO CERTIFY	
10. NAME OF COMPLIANCE INSPECTOR	

11. HEALTH AUTHORITY APPROVAL – Execution of VA Form 26-6395 by the Health Authority indicating approval of the water supply and/or sewage disposal installation is required. (Approval by letter ☐ or Health Authority Form may be used.)	12. This document is subject to the provisions of Executive Orders 11246 and 11375, and the Rules and Regulations of the Secretary of Labor in effect this date, and VA Regulations 4390 through 4393, and also the provision of the certification executed by the builder, sponsor ☐ or developer named herein which is on file in this office.

13. TERMITE CERTIFICATE – The seller shall furnish the veteran-purchaser at no cost to the veteran prior to settlement a written statement (or certification) from a recognized exterminator that based on careful visual inspection of accessible areas and on sounding of accessible structural members, there is no evidence of termite or other wood-destroying insect infestation in the subject property, and, if such infestation previously existed, it has been corrected and any damage due to such infestation has also been corrected or alternatively been fully disclosed as follows . . .

14. WARRANTY	15. NAME OF WARRANTOR	16. SEE GENERAL CONDITIONS ABOVE
☐ (If checked, complete item 15)		

17. OTHER REQUIREMENTS

18. DATE	19. ADMINISTRATOR OF VETERANS AFFAIRS, BY (Signature of authorized agent)	20. VA OFFICE

VA FORM
AUG 1977 **26-1843g**

VETERAN'S COPY 4

FIGURE 13-14 VA Form 26–1803, Page Six

Form Approved
OMB No. 76-R0240

VETERANS ADMINISTRATION
RESIDENTIAL APPRAISAL REPORT

CASE NUMBER

1. MAJOR STRUCTURES	A. TYPICAL COND.	B. BUILT-UP	C. AGE TYPE BLDG.	D. OWN OCCUP.	E. VACANCY	F. ZONING	G. LAND USE CHGS.	2. PROPER-TY IS	3. BLDG. WARRANTY IN FORCE?
NEIGHBORHOOD	%			%	%			☐ OCCU-PIED	☐ YES ☐ NO
BLOCK	%			%	%			☐ VACANT	☐ UNKNOWN

4. STATUS OF PROPERTY

☐ A. PROPOSED ☐ B. EXISTING, NOT PREVIOUSLY OCCUPIED ☐ C. EXISTING, PREVIOUSLY OCCUPIED ☐ D. ALTERATIONS, IMPROVEMTS. OR REPAIRS ☐ E. REFINANCING - VETERAN AP-PLICANT OWNS AND OCCUPIES RESIDENCE AS HOME

5. CONSTRUCTION COMPLETED BEFORE DATE HEREOF.
☐ A. WITHIN 12 CALENDAR MOS. ☐ B. MORE THAN 12 CALENDAR MOS.

6. NAME AND ADDRESS OF FIRM OR PERSON MAKING REQUEST (*Complete mailing address. Include ZIP Code*)

7. PROPERTY ADDRESS (*Include ZIP Code*)

8. TYPE OF PROPERTY	9. MANDATORY HOME ASSOCIA-TION MEMBER-SHIP?	10A. NO. BLDGS.
☐ HOME		
☐ MOBILE HOME LOT	☐ YES ☐ NO	10B. NO. LIVING UNITS

11. LOT DIMENSIONS

12. DESCRIPTION	WOOD SIDING	CINDER BLOCK	SPLIT LEVEL	NO. ROOMS	DINING ROOM	CAR GARAGE	GAS	CEN. AIR COND.
DETACHED	WOOD SHINGLE	STONE	% BASEMENT	BEDROOMS	KITCHEN	CAR CARPORT	UNDERGRD. WIRE	TYPE HEAT. & FUEL.
SEMI-DET.	ALUM. SIDING	BRICK & BLOCK	SLAB	BATHS	FAMILY. RM.	WATER (Public)	SEWER (Public)	
ROW	ASB. SHINGLE	STUCCO	CRAWL SPACE	1/2 BATHS	UTILITY RM.	WATER (Comm.)	SEWER (Comm.)	ROOFING DESCRIP.
CONDOMINIUM	BRICK VENEER	STORIES	YRS. EST. AGE	LIVING RM.	FIREPLACE	WATER (Ind.)	SEPTIC TANK	

13. LEGAL DESCRIPTION	14. TITLE LIMITATIONS, INCLUDING EASEMENTS, RESTRIC-TIONS, ENCROACHMENTS, HOMEOWNERS ASSOCIATION AND SPECIAL ASSESSMENTS, ETC.	15. OFFSITE IMPROVEMENTS
		A. STREET SURFACE
		B. STREET ACCESS ☐ PRIV. ☐ PUB. D. ADD'L. IMPROVEMENTS ☐ STORM SEWER
		C. STREET MAINT. ☐ SIDEWALK
		☐ PRIV. ☐ PUB. ☐ CURB/GUTTER

16. REPAIRS NECESSARY TO MAKE PROPERTY CONFORM TO APPLIC. MPR'S	17. REMARKS (*Complete A through F. Use supplemental sheet or reverse, if necessary.*)
	A. DETRIMENTAL INFLUENCES
$	B. REAL ESTATE MARKET IN COMMUNITY
	C. HIGHEST AND BEST USE
	D. FEDERAL FLOOD HAZARD MAP ISSUED? ☐ YES ☐ NO (*If "Yes," complete Item 17E*) E. PROP. IN SPECIAL FLOOD HAZARD AREA? ☐ YES ☐ NO
	F. EXPLAIN DEPRECIATION
TOTAL ESTIMATED COST OF REPAIRS $	

18. MARKET DATA

ITEM	SUBJECT PROPERTY	COMPARABLE NO. 1		COMPARABLE NO. 2		COMPARABLE NO. 3	
ADDRESS							
SALE PRICE		$		$		$	
TYPE OF FINANCING							
	DESCRIPTION	DESCRIPTION	ADJ.	DESCRIPTION	ADJ.	DESCRIPTION	ADJ.
DATE OF SALE			$		$		$
LOCATION							
SITE/IMPROVEMENT							
AGE/CONDITION							
GARAGE/CARPORT							
CONSTRUCTION							
PORCHES, POOL, ETC.							
ROOM COUNT/SIZE	ROOMS BDRMS BATH S.F. AREA	ROOMS BDRMS BATH S.F. AREA		ROOMS BDRMS BATH S.F. AREA		ROOMS BDRMS BATH S.F. AREA	
NET ADJUSTMENT (*Show (+) or (−) adjustment*)		$		$		$	
INDICATED VALUE OF SUBJECT PROPERTY		$		$		$	

19. PROPERTY SHOWS EVIDENCE OF (*Check*)	20. ESTATE (*Check*)	21. REMAINING ECONOMIC LIFE (*Years*)	22. COST APPROACH
☐ TERMITE ☐ DRY ROT ☐ DAMP-NESS ☐ SETTLE-MENT ☐ NO EVIDENCE	☐ A. FEE SIMPLE ☐ B. LEASE-HOLD	MAIN OTHER	MAIN CU SQ OTHER

23. DATA	DESCRIPTION	CONDITION	24. EQUIP.	DESCRIPTION	DEPR. VALUE	25. OTHER IMPROVEMENTS	DEPR. VALUE		
ROOF					$		$	RATE PER FT. $	
FOUND.							$	REPLMT. COST $	
BSMT.							$	PHYSICAL DEP. $	
FLOORS							$	FUNCTIONAL $	
INT. WALLS							$	ECONOMIC $	
BATH FINISH							$	TOTAL DEP. $	
GUTTERS							$	DEPR. COST $	
26. ANNUAL TAXES								TOTAL DEPR. COST OF IMPR. $	
GENERAL	SPECIAL	OTHER						OTHER IMPR. AND EQUIP. $	
								LAND VALUE $	
$	$	$		TOTAL $		TOTAL $		TOTAL DEPR COST OF PROP. $	

27. DOES PROPERTY CONFORM TO APPLICABLE MINIMUM PROPERTY REQUIREMENTS?	28. ESTIMATE FAIR MONTHLY RENT TIMES RENT MULTIPLIER (*If applicable*)	29. RECONCILIATION		
☐ YES ☐ NO (*If "No" explain on reverse*)	$ × $	A. MARKET APPROACH $	B. COST APPROACH $	C. INCOME APPROACH (*If applicable*) $

NOTE: No determination of reasonable value may be made unless a completed appraisal report is received (38 U.S.C. 1810).
I HEREBY CERTIFY that (a) I have carefully viewed the property described in this report, INSIDE AND OUTSIDE, so far as it has been completed; that (b) it is the same property that is identified by description in my appraisal assignment; that (c) I HAVE NOT RECEIVED, HAVE NO AGREEMENT TO RECEIVE, NOR WILL I ACCEPT FROM ANY PARTY ANY GRATUITY OR EMOLUMENT OTHER THAN MY APPRAISAL FEE FOR MAKING THIS APPRAISAL; that (d) I have no interest, present or prospective, in the applicant, seller, property, or mortgage; that (e) in arriving at the estimated reasonable value I have not been influenced in any manner whatsoever by the race, color, religion, national origin, or sex of any person residing in the property or in the neighborhood wherein it is located. I understand that violation of this certification can result in removal from the fee appraiser's roster.

30. I ESTIMATE "REASONABLE VALUE" ☐ "AS IS" ☐ "AS REPAIRED" ☐ "AS COMPLETED"	31. ESTIMATED REASONABLE VALUE $	32. SIGNATURE OF APPRAISER	33. DATE SIGNED

VA FORM
AUG 1977 **26-1803**

APPRAISER'S COPY 6

245

of the loan from the Veterans Administration, Form 26-1802a should be completed in duplicate (see Figure 13-15). The original is sent to the Veterans Administration and a duplicate is retained by the lender. Attached to this form, application for home loan guarantee or insurance, should be a credit report on the veteran from a credit-gathering agency. The front of the application for home loan guarantee or insurance involves the purposes and terms of the proposed loan and the financial status of the veteran; the reverse concerns the estimation of the total cost of the property, including purchase, construction, and prepaid items such as taxes, insurance, and special assessments.

Because the Veterans Administration is not able to interview the applicant, it relies largely upon the full completion of the required documents.

The next form that the veteran must complete is 26-1820a, veteran's certification of intent to occupy the residence. This form (Figure 13-16) must be signed at the time of application and again when the loan is disbursed so that the Veterans Administration knows for sure that the loan is being used for the purposes for which the Act was passed.

All these documents are forwarded to the Veterans Administration simultaneously if the lender is asking for prior approval of the contemplated loan. However, if it is to be an automatically guaranteed or insured loan, it is not necessary that the lender file any forms with the Veterans Administration at the loan's inception other than the request for determination of eligibility, the available loan guarantee entitlement, and the request for determination of reasonable value, together with the sales agreement or contract. After the certificate of eligibility has been returned to the lender and the appraised value has been determined, under the automatic procedures the lender can disburse the loan and then file with the Veterans Administration the report of home loan processed on an automatic basis. Veterans Administration Form 26-1820 (Figure 13-17) is completed in duplicate. The original is forwarded to the Veterans Administration and the duplicate is retained in the files of the lender. Accompanying the report of home loan processed on an automatic basis are the application for home loan guarantee or insurance that was completed at the time of the original application, a copy of the employer's verification of employment and income, and a copy of the credit report on the borrower. The lender will also include the Veterans Administration certification of eligibility so that it may be endorsed as to the amount used.

The report of home loan processed on automatic basis is a form similar in many respects to the original application, but it includes additional necessary information.

In the case of a construction loan the same forms are used except that two copies of the plans and specifications and a signed contract for the construction must be submitted with the other forms. The plans should show the four elevations of the building, a typical section of the building, a detailed floor plan with electrical and heating detail, a sewage disposal system if public facilities are not available, details of cabinets, exterior walks, concrete patios, and so forth. After the plans and specifications have been approved by the Veterans Administration, one copy is retained by it and the other copy is maintained at the site. A third copy will be required by the lending agency. However, this copy will not have the approval of the Veterans Administration stamped on it.

After the property has been completed and the compliance inspections have been made, a warranty of completion of construction will be completed by the builder and the purchaser and filed with the Veterans Administration.

There are several advantages to Veterans Administration loans. No down payments are required by the Veterans Administration; the only down payment is that required by the lender. Maximum loans are available under the GI loan since no limit has been placed on the Veterans Administration loans by the government, except that the veteran's entitlement shall not be more than 15 percent of the total loan. The amortization plan is somewhat more lenient than in the case of other loans, since it can be any of the generally recognized plans used by established lending institutions.

Prepayment under the GI loan can be made without penalty, in full, in $100 additional payments, or in additional even monthly payments.

Soldiers and Sailors Civil Relief Act of 1942

The two different types of loans available to veterans in California have been discussed to show what the state of California and the United State Government have done to help discharged members of the armed forces readjust to civilian life. Although the main sections discussed above involve the financing of homes, other sections provide many other benefits to all service personnel. The United States Government and many states have passed additional legislation to give some protection to male and female soldiers, sailors, marines, and other members of the armed forces during the time that they are in the service.

The Soldiers and Sailors Civil Relief Act of 1942 applies to obligations contracted before entry into the armed forces and provides protection to the individual during the time that he or she is in the armed forces insofar as those obligations are concerned.

Two sections are of particular interest in a discussion of relief to members of the armed forces. Section 301 of

FIGURE 13-15 VA Form 26–1802a

VETERANS ADMINISTRATION **APPLICATION FOR HOME LOAN GUARANTY**	1A. VA LOAN NUMBER	1B. LENDER'S LOAN NO.

2A. NAME AND PRESENT ADDRESS OF VETERAN (Include ZIP Code)	2B. RACE OR ETHNIC ORIGIN OF VETERAN
	☐ WHITE (Non Minority) ☐ NEGRO BLACK
	☐ SPANISH AMERICAN ☐ AMERICAN INDIAN
	☐ ORIENTAL ☐ OTHER

3. NAME AND ADDRESS OF LENDER (Include number, street or rural route, city or P.O., State and ZIP Code)	2C. SOCIAL SECURITY NUMBER
	4. PROPERTY ADDRESS INCLUDING NAME OF SUBDIVISION LOT AND BLOCK NO. AND ZIP CODE

5. AMOUNT OF LOAN	6A. INTEREST RATE	6B. PROPOSED MATURITY
	%	YRS MOS

The undersigned veteran and lender hereby apply to the Administrator of Veterans' Affairs for Guaranty of the loan described herein under Section 1810, Chapter 37, Title 38, United States Code to the full extent permitted by the veteran's available entitlement and severally agree that the Regulations promulgated pursuant to Chapter 37 and in effect on the date of the loan shall govern the rights, duties, and liabilities of the parties.

SECTION I — PURPOSE, AMOUNT, TERMS OF AND SECURITY FOR PROPOSED LOAN

7. PURPOSE OF LOAN — TO			7a. PURCHASE CONDOMINIUM UNIT
☐ PURCHASE EXISTING HOME — PREVIOUSLY OCCUPIED	☐ CONSTRUCT A HOME-PROCEEDS TO BE PAID OUT DURING CONSTRUCTION	☐ PURCHASE EXISTING HOME — NOT PREVIOUSLY OCCUPIED	☐ NEW ☐ EXISTING

8. TITLE WILL BE VESTED IN	9. LIEN	10. ESTATE WILL BE
☐ VETERAN ☐ VETERAN AND SPOUSE ☐ OTHER (Specify)	☐ 1st MORTGAGE	☐ FEE SIMPLE ☐ LEASEHOLD (Show expiration date)

11. ESTIMATED TAXES, INSURANCE AND ASSESSMENTS		12. ESTIMATED MONTHLY PAYMENT	
A. ANNUAL TAXES	$	A. PRINCIPAL AND INTEREST	$
B. AMOUNT OF HAZARD INSURANCE ON SECURITY		B. TAXES AND INSURANCE DEPOSITS	
C. ANNUAL HAZARD INSURANCE PREMIUMS		C. OTHER	
D. ANNUAL SPECIAL ASSESSMENT PAYMENT			
E. UNPAID SPECIAL ASSESSMENT BALANCE			
F. ANNUAL MAINTENANCE ASSESSMENT		D. TOTAL	$

SECTION II — PERSONAL AND FINANCIAL STATUS OF VETERAN

13. MARITAL STATUS	14. AGE OF SPOUSE	15. AGE(S) OF DEPENDENT(S)
☐ MARRIED ☐ WIDOWED ☐ DIVORCED ☐ SEPARATED ☐ NEVER MARRIED		

16. ASSETS		17. LIABILITIES (Itemize all debts)		
		NAME OF CREDITOR	MO. PAYMENT	BALANCE
A. CASH (Including deposit on purchase)	$		$	$
B. SAVINGS BONDS, OTHER SECURITIES				
C. REAL ESTATE OWNED				
D. AUTO				
E. FURNITURE AND HOUSEHOLD GOODS				
F. OTHER (Use separate sheet, if necessary)				
G. TOTAL	$			

18. Monthly Payment on Rented Premises Vet. Now Occupies				
A. RENT	B. UTILITIES INCLUDED ☐ YES ☐ NO		TOTAL $	$

19. INCOME AND OCCUPATIONAL STATUS			20. ESTIMATED TOTAL COST	
ITEM	VETERAN	SPOUSE	ITEM	AMOUNT
A. OCCUPATION			A. PURCHASE EXISTING HOME	$
			B. ALTERATIONS, IMPRV., REPAIRS	
B. NAME OF EMPLOYER			C. CONSTRUCTION	
			D. LAND (If acquired separately)	
			E. PURCHASE OF CONDOMINIUM UNIT	
C. NUMBER OF YRS. EMPLOYED			F. PREPAID ITEMS	
			G. ESTIMATED CLOSING COST	
D. GROSS PAY	MONTHLY $ HOURLY $	MONTHLY $ HOURLY $	H. TOTAL COST (Add items 20A through 20G)	$
			I. LESS CASH FROM VETERAN	
E. OTHER INCOME	$	$	J. LESS OTHER CREDITS	
			K. AMOUNT OF LOAN	$

NOTE — IF LAND ACQUIRED BY SEPARATE TRANSACTION, COMPLETE ITEMS 21A AND 21B	21A. DATE ACQUIRED	21B. UNPAID BALANCE $

SECTION III — CERTIFICATION (Must be signed by veteran and lender)

THE UNDERSIGNED VETERAN CERTIFIES THAT: (Complete Item 22A and Check Items 22B and 22F in all cases.) (Check Items 22C, 22D and 22E, whenever the contract price or cost exceeds the VA reasonable value determination.)

22A. ☐ I have been informed that $ _____ is the reasonable value of the property as determined by the VA.

22B. ☐ I now actually occupy the property identified herein as my home or intend to move into and occupy it as my home within a reasonable period of time after completion of the loan.

22C. ☐ I was ☐ was not ☐ aware of the VA reasonable value determination when I signed my contract.

22D. ☐ Having been informed of the VA reasonable value determination, I do hereby represent that I desire to complete the transaction at the contract price or cost.

22E. ☐ I have paid or will pay in cash from my own resources at or prior to loan closing the difference between the contract price or cost and the VA reasonable value, and I do not now have and will not have outstanding after loan closing any unpaid contractual obligation on account of such cash payment.

22F. ☐ The foregoing information contained in these certifications and in Section II of this application are true and complete to the best of my knowledge and belief.

READ CERTIFICATION CAREFULLY — DO NOT SIGN APPLICATION UNLESS IT IS FULLY COMPLETED

23. DATE	24. SIGNATURE OF VETERAN (Read certification carefully before signing)

THE UNDERSIGNED LENDER CERTIFIES THAT ALL INFORMATION REFLECTED IN THIS APPLICATION IS TRUE TO THE BEST OF MY KNOWLEDGE AND BELIEF

25. DATE	26. NAME OF LENDER	27. TELEPHONE NO.	28. SIGNATURE AND TITLE OF OFFICER OF LENDER

FEDERAL STATUTES PROVIDE SEVERE PENALTIES FOR ANY FRAUD, INTENTIONAL MISREPRESENTATION, OR CRIMINAL CONNIVANCE OR CONSPIRACY PURPOSED TO INFLUENCE THE ISSUANCE OF ANY GUARANTY OR INSURANCE BY THE ADMINISTRATOR.

VA FORM FEB 1971 **26-1802a**   SUPERSEDES VA FORM 26-1802a, MAR 1969 WHICH WILL NOT BE USED   **VA 2**

FIGURE 13-16   VA Form 26–1820a

Form approved.
Budget Bureau No. 76–R159.10

VETERANS ADMINISTRATION

VETERAN'S CERTIFICATION OF INTENTION TO OCCUPY RESIDENTIAL PROPERTY
TO BE ACQUIRED WITH ASSISTANCE OF GI LOAN

INSTRUCTIONS: This certification is to be made by Veteran when applying to a supervised lender for a loan for any of the purposes specified in Section 1810, Title 38, U.S. Code, which loan the lender closes and reports under the automatic procedure.

TO

1 ADDRESS *(complete)*

Veterans Administration Regional Office
ATTN: Loan Guaranty Division

2 ADDRESS OF PROPERTY TO WHICH CERTIFICATION RELATES

3 PURPOSE OF LOAN FOR WHICH UNDERSIGNED HAS APPLIED *(Check appropriate box)*

☐ a. To finance the purchase of a home for the undersigned,

☐ b. To finance the construction of a home for the undersigned,

☐ c. To finance repairs, alterations, or improvements to a home now owned by the undersigned,

☐ d. To refund indebtedness incurred by the undersigned in connection with the purchase or construction of the home now owned by the undersigned, or which was incurred in connection with the repair, alteration, or improvement of the home now owned by the undersigned.   (Section 36.4306, VA Loan Guaranty Regulations.)

4 THE UNDERSIGNED VETERAN CERTIFIES THAT *(Check box corresponding to box checked in item 3)*

☐ a. I now actually occupy as my home the property to be purchased with the proceeds of the loan applied for or I intend to move into and occupy that property as my home within a reasonable period of time after completion of the loan.

☐ b. I actually intend to occupy as my home the property to be constructed with the proceeds of the loan applied for and upon completion of the dwelling to move into the property personally within a reasonable time and utilize such property as my home.

☐ c. I am the owner of the property to be repaired, altered, or improved with the proceeds of the loan applied for, and actually live in the property personally as my home.

☐ d. I am the owner of and personally occupy as my home the subject property in respect to which the undersigned has applied for a loan to refund indebtedness incurred in connection with the purchase, construction, repair, alteration, or improvement thereof.   (Section 36.4306, VA Loan Guaranty Regulations.)

5 DATE

6 SIGNATURE OF VETERAN

FEDERAL STATUTES PROVIDE SEVERE PENALTIES FOR ANY FRAUD, INTENTIONAL MISREPRESENTATION, CRIMINAL CONNIVANCE, OR CONSPIRACY PURPOSED TO INFLUENCE THE ISSUANCE OF ANY GUARANTY OR INSURANCE BY THE ADMINISTRATOR.

VA FORM
NOV 1959   26–1820a   EXISTING STOCK OF VA FORM VB4–1820a, FEB 1957, WILL BE USED

---

the Soldiers and Sailors Civil Relief Act of 1942 involves instalment contracts for the purchase of personal and real property. It states that no person or assignor who has received, under contract for the purchase of real or personal property, an instalment of the purchase price, or a deposit or instalment under contract from a person or assignor of a person who after having made such an instalment payment has been caused to enter or has entered military service, shall be able to rescind or terminate the contract or retake possession of the property for non-payment of any instalment called for under the terms of the contract or for any other breach of the terms provided in the contract during such period of military service except by action in a court of competent jurisdiction, or

FIGURE 13-17   VA Form 26–1820

Form Approved.
Budget Bureau No 76–R159.11

VETERANS ADMINISTRATION
REPORT OF HOME LOAN PROCESSED ON AUTOMATIC BASIS

NOTE.—For use by lenders of a class specified in Section 1802(d).   ORIGINAL to be forwarded to Veterans Administration; DUPLICATE to be retained by lender.   The lender is required to submit with this report a copy of the loan application (showing income, assets, and obligations) executed by the borrower when applying to the lender for the loan, a copy of the employer's verification of employment and income, and a copy of the credit report on the borrower.   The lender will also submit as attachments either the veteran's discharge OR the VA Certificate of Eligibility, if any, issued to the veteran.   In special cases, such as loans to refinance delinquent indebtedness, loans wherein some of the proceeds are to be escrowed to cover the completion of postponed exterior improvements, etc., other attachments to the report may be necessary.   Lenders should consult with the VA regional office in this regard.

VA LOAN NO
LH
DATE OF REPORT
PROCESSED UNDER SECTION *(Check)*
☐ 1810   ☐ 1814

LAST NAME—FIRST NAME—MIDDLE NAME OF VETERAN *(Print or type)*	ADDRESS OF VETERAN

This report of the undersigned lender is made pursuant to Section 1802(c), Title 38, United States Code. The lender and borrower severally agree that the Regulations issued under Title 38, U.S.C. and in effect on the date the loan is accepted or approved for ☐ GUARANTY ☐ INSURANCE shall govern the rights, duties, and liabilities of the parties to such loan and any provisions of the loan instruments inconsistent with such Regulations are hereby amended and supplemented to conform thereto *(Section 36:4334 of the Regulations.)*

SECTION I.—PURPOSE, AMOUNT, TERMS OF AND SECURITY FOR LOAN

1. PURPOSE OF LOAN—TO

☐ PURCHASE EXISTING HOME—PREVIOUSLY OCCUPIED   ☐ CONSTRUCT A HOME—PROCEEDS TO BE PAID OUT DURING CONSTRUCTION   ☐ PURCHASE EXISTING HOME—NOT PREVIOUSLY OCCUPIED   ☐ REPAIR, ALTER, OR IMPROVE HOME

☐ OTHER *(Specify)*

2. ADDRESS OF PROPERTY *(Include lot and block numbers and subdivision name)*

3. AMOUNT OF LOAN	TERMS OF LOAN		
$	4A PAYMENTS TO BE MADE *(Check)* ☐ MONTHLY ☐ QUARTERLY ☐ SEMIANNUALLY ☐ ANNUALLY	4B AMOUNT OF PAYMENT *(Including interest)* $ 4D DATE OF NOTE 4E TERM OF LOAN YRS MOS	4C RATE OF INTEREST PER ANNUM PERCENT 4F DATE LOAN WAS CLOSED

5. OTHERS, IF ANY, LIABLE ON INDEBTEDNESS *(Cosigners, guarantors, etc.)*

6. TYPE OF LIEN *(Reg. 36.4351)*

☐ FIRST REALTY MORTGAGE   ☐ SECOND REALTY MORTGAGE   ☐ FIRST CHATTEL MORTGAGE   ☐ UNSECURED   ☐ OTHER *(Specify)*

7. TITLE TO PROPERTY IS VESTED IN THE FOLLOWING PERSON(S)

☐ VETERAN   ☐ VETERAN AND SPOUSE   ☐ OTHER *(Identify and state interest of each person)*

8. ESTATE IN PROPERTY IS *(Reg. 36.4350)*

☐ FEE SIMPLE   ☐ LEASEHOLD *(Give expiration date)*   ☐ OTHER *(Specify)*

9. DESCRIBE NONREALTY, IF ANY, ACQUIRED WITH PROCEEDS OF LOAN

10. DESCRIBE ADDITIONAL SECURITY TAKEN, IF ANY

11 APPROXIMATE ANNUAL REAL ESTATE TAXES	12 APPROXIMATE ANNUAL HAZARD INSURANCE PREMIUM	13A APPROXIMATE ANNUAL SPECIAL ASSESSMENT PAYMENT	13B TOTAL UNPAID SPECIAL ASSESSMENTS
$	$	$	$

SECTION II.—DESCRIPTION OF PRIMARY LIEN
(Fill in items 1 through 8 only if the loan being reported is secured by other than a first lien)

1 NAME OF HOLDER	8 MORTGAGE LOAN ACCOUNT *(Check)* ☐ DELINQUENT *(If "delinquent," fill in items A through F)* ☐ CURRENT IN ALL RESPECTS	
	A PRINCIPAL	$
2 ADDRESS OF HOLDER	B INTEREST	
	C REAL ESTATE TAXES *(Specify period)*	
3 DATE OF LIEN 4 TERMS OF REPAYMENT $ PER	D INSURANCE PREMIUMS	
	E OTHER *(Specify)*	
5 MATURITY DATE 6 UNPAID PRINCIPAL $ AS OF *(Date)*		
		TOTAL $
7 PRIMARY LIEN *(Check)* ☐ GUARANTEED OR INSURED BY VA ☐ INSURED BY FHA ☐ NOT GUARANTEED OR INSURED BY FEDERAL AGENCY	F CREDIT BALANCE IN REAL ESTATE TAX AND INSURANCE FUND IF ON DEPOSIT WITH LENDER ▶	$

VA FORM
SEP 1962   **26–1820**   EXISTING STOCKS OF VA FORM 26–1820, FEB 1961, WILL BE USED

FIGURE 13-17, *continued*

SECTION III.—STATEMENT OF TOTAL COST			COL. A	COL. B
1. PURCHASE OF IMPROVED REALTY				$
2. CONSTRUC- TION	COST OF IMPROVEMENTS		$	
	UNPAID BALANCE ON LAND			
	TOTAL			$
3. REPAIRS, ALTERATIONS, OR IMPROVEMENTS *(Existing dwelling unit)*				
4. REFINANCE DELINQUENT INDEBTEDNESS *(Sec. 1814; attach VA Form 4-1868)*				
5. REFINANCE UNPAID BALANCE OF LAND SALE CONTRACT *(Sec. 36.4354)*	DATE OF CONTRACT	ORIGINAL CONTRACT PRICE $		
6. TOTAL *(Items 1 through 5, Col. B)*				
7. CLOSING COSTS	CREDIT REPORT		$	
	RECORDING FEES			
	VA APPRAISAL FEE			
	VA COMPLIANCE INSPECTION FEES			
	SURVEY			
	TITLE EXAMINATION			
	TITLE INSURANCE			
	ATTORNEY FEES			
	ORIGINATION CHARGE *(See VA Fee Schedule)*			
	OTHER *(Specify)*			
		TOTAL CLOSING COSTS		$
8. PREPAID ITEMS	TAXES		$	
	INSURANCE			
	SPECIAL ASSESSMENTS			
	OTHER *(Specify)*			
		TOTAL PREPAID ITEMS		$
9. TOTAL COST TO VETERAN *(Add items 6 through 8, Col. B)*				
10. LESS	CASH FROM VETERAN		$	
	OTHER CREDITS *(Include any obligations incurred, e.g. junior liens, unsecured loans, etc., and describe terms of repayment.)*			
		TOTAL CREDITS		$
11. AMOUNT OF LOAN *(Item 9 less item 10, Col. B)*				

12 IF LAND ACQUIRED BY SEPARATE TRANSACTION, COMPLETE ITEMS 12A AND 12B ▶	12A DATE ACQUIRED	12B PURCHASE PRICE *(If acquired other than by purchase, state "None")* $	13 AMOUNT WITHHELD FROM LOAN PROCEEDS *(Item 11)* AND DEPOSITED IN ☐ ESCROW ☐ EARMARKED ACCOUNT $

SECTION IV.—CERTIFICATIONS (NOTE.—Must be signed by Veteran and Lender. READ CAREFULLY BEFORE SIGNING.)

The following certification MUST be executed by the veteran on the date loan is closed.

I, THE UNDERSIGNED VETERAN, CERTIFY THAT: *(Check appropriate box(es))*

☐ The purpose of this loan is to finance the ☐ purchase ☐ construction of the residential property to which the loan identified herein relates and which (a) I now do actually occupy as my home and intend to occupy as my home, or (b) I intend to move into and occupy as my home within a reasonable time after the actual ultimate payout of the full proceeds of the loan.

☐ The purpose of this loan is to finance the repair, alteration, or improvement of residential property owned and occupied by me personally as my home.

☐ The purpose of this loan is to refund indebtedness incurred by me in connection with the purchase, construction, repair, alteration or improvement of residential property now owned and occupied by me personally as my home (Reference Section 36:4306 VA Loan Guaranty Regulations.)

I ☐ DO ☐ DO NOT have an application pending for guaranty or insurance of any other loan under Chapter 37, Title 38, United States Code,

I ☐ HAVE ☐ HAVE NOT used my guaranty or insurance entitlement for other loans;

I hereby authorize a charge against my entitlement of $ _____ and such additional sum as may be available and necessary to allow the maximum amount of guaranty or insurance credit on this loan.

DATE	SIGNATURE OF VETERAN

I, THE UNDERSIGNED LENDER, CERTIFY THAT:

1. Ultimate payment of the full proceeds of the loan was completed *(Date)*

2. No default exists on the loan reported herein which has continued for more than 30 days.

3. It has not imposed and will not impose any charges or fees against the veteran borrower in excess of those permissible under the schedule set forth in paragraph (d) of section 36:4312 of the VA Loan Guaranty and Insurance Regulations.

4. Any construction, repairs, alterations, or improvements upon which the reasonable value of the property is predicated and which were not inspected and approved subsequent to completion by a compliance inspector designated by the Administrator have been completed properly. (Attach FHA Form 2051, if any.)

5. The loan conforms otherwise with the applicable provisions of Title 38, U.S.C. and of the Regulations concerning guaranty or insurance of loans to veterans.

6. All information reflected in this report is true to the best of the lender's knowledge and belief.

SIGNATURE AND TITLE OF OFFICER OF LENDER	DATE	NAME AND ADDRESS OF LENDER

FEDERAL STATUTES PROVIDE SEVERE PENALTIES FOR ANY FRAUD, INTENTIONAL MISREPRESENTATION, OR CRIMINAL CONNIVANCE OR CONSPIRACY PURPOSED TO INFLUENCE THE ISSUANCE OF ANY GUARANTY OR INSURANCE BY THE ADMINISTRATOR.

GPO 1962 O—658659

upon agreement in writing signed by all parties and dated during or after the period of service. It need not be a formal form but it must show that the individual is now in the military service of the United States and is unable to fulfill the provisions of his or her contract. The contract should then be described and the agreement should state that he or she conveys all his or her rights to the property described in the contract. The statement should also show that in consideration of his or her release of the property all further payments are to be waived and the contract canceled. The agreement must then be signed by the member of the service and his or her spouse, if any, and approved by the lending institution. It must, of course, be dated.

If a spouse of a member of the armed forces purchases something in his or her name, including real estate, before his or her spouse goes into service, the item may be repossessed unless the spouse goes to court and asks that he or she be allowed to act under the Soldiers and Sailors Civil Relief Act. After the court deliberates, it may give the spouse that right. Section 301 also provides that any person who knowingly repossesses or tries to repossess property that is the subject of Section 1 (real property or personal property) is guilty of a misdemeanor and subject to a year in prison or $100 fine or both, except as provided above. Upon a request for court action and upon the court's hearing request for foreclosure action, the court may order repayment of prior instalments or any part thereof as a condition to the termination of the instalment contract in the repossession of the property by the seller. However, if the court finds that the member of the armed forces is perfectly capable with his or her income from military service of continuing to make the payments on the property, the court may instruct the individual to continue making such payments or face foreclosure and reposssession.

Section 302 of the Act considers only actions that might arise out of default of mortgages, deeds of trust, or other documents of security. It does not consider in any way items other than mortgages or trust deeds. Section 302 considers the foreclosure under the power of sale in the mortgage or trust deed; although it does not expressly forbid foreclosure, it does forbid foreclosure without a court order. However, there have been rulings in which a foreclosure without a court order has been held valid when the person in military service had definite knowledge of the foreclosure and had taken no steps to indicate his or her objections to the foreclosure. Notice of foreclosure in this instance would have to be made directly to the member of the armed forces and not to a local agent, since the rights under the Act are personal and may not be waived by any person other than the individual.

Section 302 is not limited in its coverage to mortgages or trust deeds on property used for the business or home of the mortgagor, nor is it necessarily limited to the owner of record when the mortgagee knows the owners of the property.

The protection under Section 302 is available not only to the equitable owners of the property but also to the legal owners of the property. For foreclosure to be suspended, the individual must be in the armed services and the foreclosure must have started during his or her time in service. If the foreclosure is started before his or her entry into the service, the subsequent entry into service will not cause the foreclosure action to be suspended. In any actions commenced in any court during the period of military service to enforce an obligation arising out of default of any sum or other breach of terms of trust deed or mortgage, the court, after hearing the conditions that exist in the case, unless the defendant is able to comply with the terms of the obligation since his or her income, although in military service, has not been materially affected, may (1) stop the foreclosure proceedings; (2) make other arrangements for parties as may be fair to preserve the interests of all parties; and (3) invoke the rule that no sale, foreclosure, or seizure of property for nonpayment of any payment due under the obligation or for other breach of terms thereof, whether under power of sale or under a judgment entered under warranty of attorney, shall be valid if made after the date of the enactment of the Soldiers and Sailors Civil Relief Act amendment of October 6, 1942, or during the periods of military service or within three months thereafter except as by agreement unless on bond order previously granted by the court and a return thereto made and approved by the court. In other words, the veteran has three months after his or her discharge from service to make arrangements with the lender to catch up on the back payments and to bring the loan into a current position. It does not necessarily mean that the lender will hold him or her to bringing all payments current by the end of the three months, but the veteran will have three months in which to reach an agreement with the lender or possibly to refinance the property.

Section 302 also provides that any person who knowingly makes or causes to be made a sale, foreclosure, or seizure of the property shall be guilty of misdemeanor and subject to not more than one year's imprisonment or $1,000 fine or both. Contrary to many beliefs, this does not completely free an individual from responsibility during his or her stay in the service. If the individual and the lender cannot reach an understanding as to how he or she will maintain his or her account while in service, the lender has the right to go to court. Upon hearing the evidence, the court will instruct the defendant as to the manner in which he or she will make payments. In some instances monthly payments of interest will be required. In other instances the court may instruct the individual to rent the property and pay the lender the proceeds of the rental, which will apply to interest, taxes, and, if any is left, to principal. The court may also instruct him or her to make a reduced monthly payment, or the court may appoint three persons to appraise the property and, based upon the report of these appraisers, the court may order the lender to pay the member of the armed service or his or her dependents such sums, if any, as may be just as a conditon of taking possession of the property. The duty of the appraisers is to establish a fair value of the property involved.

In October 1962, when President John F. Kennedy began calling up reserves during the Cuban crisis, the Soldiers and Sailors Civil Relief Act of 1942 was still available to those people being called back into service. After 1947 not much thought was given to the Soldiers and Sailors Civil Relief Act, because lenders were experiencing few problems as a result of the modified draft that was in effect. However, the Act was available and it still provides protection to any who are called into service or who volunteer. It will continue to be available until the Act is removed by Congress. Under the Act, the statutes of limitations do not continue to run during the period of a person's military service, if a debt was contracted before entering military service. The Act is still available, if needed in 1983.

QUESTIONS

1. A junior lien may be placed on a HUD-FHA loan if
   a. it is a part of the acquisition payment
   b. HUD-FHA determines that the purchaser's income is adequate to service both loans
   c. the first lien has been insured by HUD-FHA and the junior lien is given at a later date
   d. all of the above

2. HUD-FHA's function is to
   a. insure qualified loans made by approved lenders
   b. make loans to qualified borrowers
   c. make loans for low-cost housing
   d. none of the above

3. The maximum loan HUD-FHA will accept is uniform throughout
   a. the state of California
   b. the West Coast
   c. the Midwest
   d. none of the above

4. HUD-FHA will insure the following Section 203(b):
   a. 97 percent of the first $25,000 of the appraised value plus 95 percent of the balance of the purchase price
   b. 97 percent of the first $25,000 of the appraised value plus 95 percent of the balance of the purchase price plus the estimated costs
   c. 97 percent of the first $25,000 of the appriased value plus 95 percent of the balance of the purchase price plus the estimated costs to a maximum allowed for that area
   d. 97 percent of the first $25,000 of the appraised value plus 95 percent of the next $25,000 plus 85 percent of the balance of the appraised value

5. Mobile home loans may be insured under Section 203(b) if
   a. the home is either a double wide or wider and bears the HUD label
   b. the home is anchored and supported by a permanent foundation acceptable to HUD-FHA
   c. the site and location are acceptable to HUD-FHA and the home complies with the California Act of July 1, 1981.
   d. all of the above

6. The maximum term for a HUD-FHA insured Section 203(b) loan is
   a. three-quarters of the economic life or thirty years
   b. three-quarters of the economic life or forty years
   c. three-quarters of the economic life or twenty-five years
   d. three-quarters of the economic life or twenty years

7. Section 222 of HUD-FHA was designed to help service personnel purchase a home. Under this section, the Department of Defense paid the 0.05 percent MMI fee. As of March 31, 1980, no further applications for Section 222 loans will be accepted except for
   a. those in the Army
   b. those in the Air Corp
   c. those in the Navy
   d. those in the Coast Guard or National Oceanic and Atmospheric Administration

8. Section 245(a) loans provide for
   a. negative amortization
   b. five programs under which the monthly payments increase each year
   c. the interest rate to remain constant
   d. all of the above

9. Section 245(b) loans provide for all of the following except:
   a. negative amortization
   b. loans to individuals who do not qualify under other HUD-FHA programs
   c. loan approval for those whose payments would approximate 40 percent of their monthly income
   d. for two programs under which monthly payments could be increased annually

10. Title I of the HUD-FHA program provides for
    a. home improvement loans
    b. construction of small nonresidential structures
    c. purchase of mobile homes
    d. all of the above

11. An eligible California veteran makes an application for a Cal-Vet loan to
    a. any California bank
    b. the Department of Veterans Affairs
    c. any savings and loan association
    d. any mortgage banker

12. The money to make Cal-Vet loans comes from
    a. taxes assessed by the state of California on income
    b. revenue bonds issued and sold by the state of California upon the approval of the voters
    c. funds provided by the United States Government
    d. general obligation bonds issued by the state of California

13. Cal-Vet loans provide funds to eligible California veterans for the purchase of the following, except for
    a. a home
    b. a farm
    c. a ranch
    d. an apartment

14. The maximum loan for a home under the Cal-Vet program is
    a. $35,000
    b. $45,000
    c. $55,000
    d. $60,000

15. The maximum loan for purchase of a farm or ranch under the Cal-Vet program is
    a. 180,000
    b. 170,000
    c. 160,000
    d. 150,000

16. The minimum down payment for the purchase of a home or farm or ranch financed by Cal-Vet costing over $35,000 is

    a. 3 percent
    b. 5 percent
    c. 7.5 percent
    d. 10 percent

17. The entitlement to a veteran under the Servicemen's Readjustment Act of 1944 was increased in 1980 to
    a. $ 4,000
    b. $ 7,500
    c. $17,500
    d. $27,500

18. An eligible veteran used $5,000 of his or her $7,500 entitlement in 1965. He or she found another home he or she wanted to buy in 1981. The amount of the entitlement at that time was
    a. $ 2,500
    b. $12,500
    c. $15,000
    d. none of the above

19. The Federal National Mortgage Association will buy GI loans up to a maximum of
    a. $110,000
    b. $107,000
    c. $ 70,000
    d. all of the above

20. GI loan applications may be made at
    a. all banks
    b. all savings and loan associations
    c. mortgage banks
    d. all of the above

BIBLIOGRAPHY

American Bankers Association, "Analysis of the Soldiers and Sailors Act." Published by American Bankers Association, 1942.

United States Department of Housing and Urban Development, "Departmental Programs." Published by U. S. Government Printing Office.

United States Department of Housing and Urban Development, "Digest of Insurable Loans, 1975." Published by U. S. Government Printing Office.

United States Department of Housing and Urban Development, "Valuation Analysis for Home Mortgage Insurance." Published by the U. S. Government Printing Office.

California Real Estate. A magazine published monthly except July/August and November/December, which are combined into one issue. Published by California Association of Realtors.

Real Estate Today. A magazine published monthly except for the March/April, July/August, and November/December issues. Published by National Association of Realtors.

Veterans' Administration, "Lenders Handbook," Washington, D.C.

14

Secondary Mortgage Market, Investors, and Organizations

FEDERAL NATIONAL MORTGAGE ASSOCIATION (FNMA)

History

The Federal National Mortgage Association is nicknamed Fanny Mae, from the initials FNMA. It began in 1935, when the Reconstruction Finance Mortgage Company, a subsidiary of the Reconstruction Finance Corporation, was organized to bring into the mortgage field funds for the refinancing of existing delinquent debts (secured by real estate bonds). The Reconstruction Finance Mortgage Company was also authorized to make loans for the refinancing of income-producing properties such as apartment houses, hotels, and office buildings that could not be financed or refinanced through the usual sources. It could also provide loan funds for the construction of income-producing properties. Another function was the purchase of FHA-insured mortgages on properties of more than four family units to provide a secondary market for these mortgages and consequently to encourage individuals to loan against such properties.

The Reconstruction Finance Mortgage Company was not a great success, and in 1938 the Federal National Mortgage Association was formed as a subsidiary of the Reconstruction Finance Corporation to provide a secondary mortgage market for insured mortgages. It continued to operate as a subsidiary of the RFC until 1950, when it was reorganized and placed under the Housing and Home Financing Agency Mortgage Association Charter Act of that year. This Act gave FNMA the right to manage and liquidate its mortgage loan portfolio. The Act also gave FNMA the right to make direct special assistance loans to certain segments of the housing market, such as housing for the elderly, military housing, urban renewal, and other segments that might not obtain financing through normal channels. The old program of providing a secondary market for FHA-insured real estate

loans was still in existence and in 1948 had been extended to include VA-guaranteed loans. In 1970 the right to use conventional real estate loans in the FNMA secondary market was approved. There were some problems in connection with allowing conventional loans to be sold to FNMA; indeed, there was and still is no uniform real estate loan law in the United States. Therefore, it was determined that this portion of the Act would not go into effect until there was such a law, or until 1972, at which time the Federal National Mortgage Association would have developed forms to be used in all states by lenders planning to sell their loans to FNMA. The 1954 Charter Act also provided for the conversion of FNMA from a self-supporting corporate entity in the United States Department of Housing and Urban Development to a government-sponsored private corporation. This conversion occurred as a result of the passage of the Housing and Urban Development Act of 1968, which established the new Government National Mortgage Association. The special assistance loans were removed from the jurisdiction of FNMA and transferred to GNMA, as were the management and collection (liquidation) functions. The transfer of these functions was effected 120 days after the signing of the Act, leaving FNMA with only its secondary financing work.

Current Functions

The Federal National Mortgage Association has been established in its present form to provide a secondary market for trust deeds and mortgage financing. It was hoped that organizations holding Federal Housing Administration, Veterans Administration, and conventional loans would decide to sell loans to FNMA. This in turn would make more money available to the organizations, which would enter the open market, finance additional loans for housing and commerce, and thereby stimulate the economy. As loans aged and were proven, FNMA would make them available to investors who needed real estate loans to round out their investment portfolios.

FNMA and the Secondary Market Operation

For many years the Federal National Mortgage Association was a government-owned subsidiary of the RFC. The Charter Act of 1954 was passed because people felt that the government-owned agency was not able to do as complete a job as was necessary and that it should be replaced gradually by a private organization wholly owned by private capital and managed by private individuals.

The Charter Act of 1954 also provided that government participation would be slowly replaced by private enterprise. To accomplish this, it proposed the issuance of $100 per share preferred stock to be bought by the secretary of the Treasury. The first offering was made November 1, 1954, in the amount of $92,800,000.

The Charter Act also provided for the issuance of common stock with a $100 par value. By June 30, 1970, there were about 6,500 shareholders who owned 1,967,841 shares. On July 1, 1970, the stock split four for one, resulting in almost 8,000,000 shares outstanding. This expanded the stock base but reduced the value per share to approximately $25. On August 8, 1970, Federal National Mortgage Association stock was listed on the New York Stock Exchange. Since then the price has fluctuated between $8 and $25. To increase its cash position FNMA may sell additional shares to sellers of mortgages.

As a privately owned, federally chartered corporation, FNMA may also issue bonds against blocks of mortgages owned by it and guaranteed by the Government National Mortgage Association. These bonds may then be sold in the private sector or to banks and savings and loan associations. It can issue short-term (30- to 270-day) discount notes. It may issue debentures, and it may establish lines of credit at banks. Its credit reputation is bolstered by the fact that the United States Treasury has been authorized to buy up to $2,250,000,000 in FNMA securities if FNMA is unable to sell an issue. The total debt of FNMA may not exceed twenty-five times the sum of its capital surplus, general surplus, reserves, and undistributed profits. Money raised by the above methods is used to purchase loans from authorized sellers.

Because the Federal National Mortgage Association was intended to become a private enterprise, it has always been subject to corporate income taxes on its earnings.

FNMA is allowed to pay dividends, which cannot exceed the amount paid on the preferred stock and under no circumstances can exceed 5 percent. FNMA will purchase trust deeds and mortgages from all lenders includ-

ing banks, savings and loan associations, mortgage bankers, and other organizations that can qualify as eligible sellers and that will execute a selling agreement providing for servicing of the loans bought by FNMA, unless the loan is on a multifamily dwelling. FNMA will service the multifamily dwelling loan. When FNMA in turn sells a loan to another mortgagee, the new mortgagee must decide whether it wishes to have the old mortgagee continue servicing the note.

Administration

The management of the Federal National Mortgage Association through 1967 was in the hands of a president appointed by the President of the United States and a nine-member board of directors appointed by the secretary of Housing and Urban Development. In May 1968 the first stockholders' meeting was held and the procedure for the conversion of the Federal National Mortgage Association to a private enterprise was initiated. Two of the nine directors were elected by the stockholders and the other seven were appointed by the secretary of Housing and Urban Development. Provisions were made for the election of four directors at the following two annual stockholders' meetings.

At the annual stockholders' meeting held in May 1970, George Romney, then Secretary of Housing and Urban Development, certified that one-third of the Federal National Mortgage Association's stock was held by private sources. In accordance with the original concept, he declared the Federal National Mortgage Association to be a private corporation. At the meeting of the stockholders the board of directors was expanded to a total membership of fifteen, ten elected and five appointed by the President. The five appointees are to be from the following fields: mortgage banking, homebuilding, real estate, housing and urban development, and the United States Treasury. The chairman of the board was elected by the board of directors. The first chairman was retired Army General Lucius D. Clay.

Purchasing Procedures

Before May 1968 the Federal National Mortgage Association was set up so that it could purchase mortgages at a discount figure set by the FNMA in two ways, either by immediate purchase or by making advance commitments for future purchases. In the case of immediate purchases, the seller had existing trust deeds or mortgages that were acceptable to FNMA. On completion of the agreement with FNMA, the seller presented the trust deeds and mortgages he or she wished to sell and received funds after assigning the notes and trust deeds to FNMA.

In the case of advance commitments, the seller determined that a certain number of loans could be made in the area under the FHA or VA program, decided that he or she had the facilities to service the loans, and felt that to serve the community he or she should make funds available for such housing. Such an individual could go to the Federal National Mortgage Association and obtain a commitment from it for the future purchase of a certain dollar volume of notes and deeds of trust. The contract that the seller signed with FNMA allowed financing for construction and provided commitments for take-out of the loans. As of March 1, 1976, FHA, VA, and conventional loans on single-family and multifamily dwellings qualify for secondary financing under FNMA. The advance commitments require a fee to hold the funds for the seller. If the advance period is 120 days or less, the fee is 0.5 percent of the loan balances; if it is longer than 120 days, the fee is 1 percent of the loan balances.

In May 1968 sweeping changes were proposed by Raymond Lapin, then president of the Federal National Mortgage Association. The changes were approved by Congress and the board of directors of FNMA. The proposal was made because FNMA had been receiving offerings of about $50 million a week. In the face of such activity, Mr. Lapin felt that FNMA should not have to buy at the artificially high prices set by the administration, but by an auction at which a certain amount would be made available for the purchase of notes and deeds of trust. Each seller would then bid on the funds available.

It was thought that an auction would free the prices through competitive bidding. The initial anticipated effect would be to lower prices and raise discounts for home builders, but it was thought that the industry would benefit in the long run from a steadier flow of money.

Under the auction plan the Federal National Mortgage Association offers a reasonably consistent amount for forward-commitment purchases, usually in the neighborhood of $50 million. Approved Federal National Mortgage Association dealers bid for the money with HUD-FHA, VA loans, or conventional loans of the type eligible for purchase. The maximum loan HUD-FHA or VA will insure or guarantee establishes the ratio of loan to value the FNMA will allow. The conventional loan-to-value ratio allowed is 95 percent if the home is owner-occupied and 80 percent if not owner-occupied. For such high loan-to-value ratios, private insurance is required on at least the upper 20 percent. The loans that are bid on now include notes and trust deeds on single-family dwellings, duplexes, apartment houses, condominiums, and hospitals. The auction is posted to be held every other Monday. The dealer also bids on the servicing fee, usually 0.5 percent or 0.38 percent.

Separate bids are taken on trust deeds or mortgages on used homes, to be delivered in four months; on loans secured by new homes, to be delivered in eight months; and on loans on new construction, to be delivered in one year. In all cases the homes must be occupied at the time of the transfer of the note and deed of trust or mortgage to FNMA. Bids are offered on FNMA forms and delivered under seal to the office of the Federal National Mortgage Association. A fee is charged for each bid received. If the bid is for funds to be committed for four months, the fee is 0.5 percent. If the bid is for delivery of funds in eight months, the fee is 0.5 percent on commitment and 0.5 percent on delivery of the documents.

Purchase volume is controlled by the agency, which may reject any and all bids. Losing bidders may adjust their offers and submit the new bid on the following Monday. Any bidder may submit up to three bids each week for each of the commitment periods. Purchase volume can be controlled by placing a ceiling on the amount of each loan. The maximum loan FNMA will buy, as of January 11, 1982, is $107,000 on a single-family dwelling, $136,800 on a duplex, $165,100 on a triplex, and $205,300 on a quadruplex.

FNMA will pay to the seller a servicing fee of 0.5 to 0.38 percent per year on the unpaid balance, the fee to be computed in the same way that the interest is computed. For this fee FNMA will expect the seller to collect the monthly instalments, including taxes and insurance premiums, to pay the taxes and insurance premiums as they fall due, to pay any special assessments against the property, to make periodic inspections of the property to see that it is being maintained properly, to make personal efforts to collect delinquent accounts, to keep adequate records to assure proper bookkeeping, to make a proper accounting of all funds collected, and, when all efforts at collection have failed, to turn the account over to the Federal National Mortgage Association for foreclosure.

The FNMA will purchase conventional mortgages now that are subject to buydown interest plans. The purchase price will be determined by the interest rate of the note, not the rate as specified in the buydown plan.

There are certain requirements the conventional loan must fulfill before FNMA will consider buying the loan. The loan must be a conventional loan, and there is no special loan-to-value ratio limitation. The term of the plan can be as long as five years, but not shorter than one year. The plan can reduce the interest rate no more than 3 percent in any one year. If the buydown plan provides for graduated payments during the life of the plan, the change must occur at the end of each twelve-month period. The buydown payment is to be held by FNMA and it will apply the necessary payment each month as it comes due. There must be a written statement that indicates the borrower has no interest in the buydown funds except as they are applied each month to the monthly payments, and that in case the loan is paid off before the whole of the buydown payment has been used, the borrower will have no interest in the remainder.

On February 15, 1982, FNMA increased the maximum for which a buydown can be made from five years to ten years. The 12 percent limit for a buydown was removed, and it was ruled that the monthly payments cannot be increased over 7.5 percent with a limit of change restricted to 15 percent from one year to the next. Another important change was that anyone, including the buyer, can make the buydown without any limitations.

As of February 15, 1982, FNMA will also permit buydowns to be used in conjunction with adjustable rate mortgages as well as fixed rate mortgages and graduated payment mortgages. The purpose is to lower the monthly payments so that more buyers can qualify for loans.

On November 30, 1981, the FNMA was authorized to buy loans secured by second liens. These loans may be against property on which FNMA holds the first lien or they can be held by another lender. The total of both loans, the first and second, may not exceed 80 percent of the fair market value of the home if it is owner-occupied and 70 percent if it is not owner-occupied. There will be two types of loans purchased—one that with reasonably equal monthly payments will completely amortize the interest and principal over a period of three to fifteen years and one that provides for partial payments with the balance due when the term of the loan expires. The term for this type of loan may be five to fifteen years. When FNMA owns the first trust deed, the total of the first and second lien notes may not exceed $107,000. If FNMA does not own the first lien, the second mortgage alone may be $107,000 on a single-family home. Another aspect of this change is that FNMA can now buy second mortgages, as well as firsts, that are taken by individuals in order to sell their home.

Resale Mortgage Program and Refinance Program

On November 10, 1980, FNMA started a program in which they would purchase new conventional trust deed notes at an interest rate below the market rate on those properties on which they already held the present loan, which could be an FHA, VA, or conventional loan. The new loans are available only to purchasers who will occupy the homes and are restricted to single-family detached homes and to condominiums or townhouses in projects approved by FNMA. Two things are accomplished by these loans. First, the low interest rate loan on the FNMA's books is replaced by a higher interest rate loan; and second, the buyer obtains a loan that has a lower rate of interest than would otherwise be available. These loans also obviate the need for a junior lien with high payments or a balloon payment. Of course, the loan would depend on the current appraisal of the dwelling and on the individual, who must be able to make the monthly payments and who must have a good credit reputation.

Refinancing is also available to the present owner of the property. Originally the refinance program was intended to be used by the purchaser or owner to make improvements to the property. The program was available to purchaser or owners of property housing one to four families. There was a requirement that such improvements would increase the value of the property by 15 percent and the improvements should be finished within one year. It is now possible for a property to be refinanced with the funds obtained by the owner being used for any purpose. Again the interest rate is below the going market rate. However, it removes a low-yield, unprofitable loan from the books and replaces it with a loan that is at or above FNMA's cost of money. The refinancing loan is made through the agency that is presently servicing the loan. After the loan has been disbursed, it is sold to FNMA and the old loan paid off. When the FNMA buys the loan, the lender signs a repurchase agreement that states the lender will buy back the loan in case of default.

Program for Home Sellers

FNMA developed a program in November 1980 that allows an owner of a house to sell that home, take a first lien against the property, and sell the note and deed of trust to FNMA at a later date, thus converting the loan to cash for the seller. There had been no mechanism by which individuals could make such loans (purchase money mortgages or deeds of trust) and sell them to FNMA up to this time.

There are certain procedures that have to be followed in order for the sellers to be able to sell the note and deed of trust to FNMA. The note and deed of trust must be drawn on standard documents in conformity to FNMA's credit and appraisal requirements. Such documentation is done by the seller using the services of a professional mortgage lender who has been approved by FNMA to originate loans and collect monthly payments. When and if the sellers decide to cash out the note and deed of trust, they make arrangements with a lender approved by FNMA to sell the loan to FNMA. They will receive the face amount of the loan if the prevailing interest rate is equal to or below the rate of interest on the note being sold. However, if the note's interest rate is less, the note will be discounted to compensate for the difference. The seller pays a fee to the professional mortgage lender for drawing up the documents in connection with the loan, a service charge for collecting the monthly payments and for the general servicing of the loan, and a fee when the loan is sold to FNMA at a later date.

The Seven-Year Conventional Mortgage or Deed of Trust

There are a few states in which the courts have ruled that the due-on-sale clause cannot be exercised. California is one of those. Since November 10, 1980, FNMA will not buy any conventional note and deed of trust or mortgage from those states that have a maturity of more than seven years, unless it is an adjustable rate mortgage, the terms of which are acceptable to FNMA. As a result, many banks, savings and loan associations, and other institutional lenders are writing their notes with five- to seven-year maturities. The reason this term was chosen is that most property changes hands every four and a half to seven years. This way if the prevailing rate is higher than the interest rate on the note, it can be called and rewritten. The seven-year note is written so that the monthly payments will fully amortize the loan in thirty years. FNMA has thirty days from the maturity of the seven-year note to call it. If FNMA does not take advantage of the call period, then the note will continue undisturbed for the remaining twenty-three years. FHA and GI loans are not affected by this provision.

Financing

A review of how FNMA obtains its funds to carry on its secondary market operation is in order. Eight million shares of capital stock with a par value of $25 were issued. FNMA may issue bonds against blocks of notes and trust deeds or mortgages owned by it and guaranteed by the Government National Mortgage Association. These bonds may then be sold to the private sector or to banks and savings and loan associations. FNMA may also issue short-term (30- to 270-day) discount notes. It may issue debentures and establish lines of credit at banks. Its credit reputation is bolstered by the fact that the United States Treasury has been authorized to buy up to $2,250 million in FNMA stock if the Association is unable to sell an issue. The lenders who sell loans to FNMA are required to hold shares of FNMAs in a certain ratio to the loans being serviced.

GOVERNMENT NATIONAL MORTGAGE ASSOCIATION (GNMA)

The Housing and Urban Development Act of 1968, signed into law by President Lyndon Johnson on August 1, 1968, provided for the manner in which the Federal National Mortgage Association would attain private status. It established the new Government National Mortgage Association, also known as GNMA or Ginny Mae. The Act provided for the Government National Mortgage Association to take over the handling of the special assistance loans and the management and liquidation functions of the Federal National Mortgage Association. The Act was to become effective 120 days after signing. The Federal National Mortgage Association is now a private corporation interested only in being a source of secondary financing for real estate loans, as we stated earlier.

The Government National Mortgage Association is a wholly owned corporate instrumentality of the United States operating under the supervision of the Department of Housing and Urban Development. The Act allows the Government National Mortgage Association to function in any state of the United States, the District of Columbia, the Commonwealth of Puerto Rico, and possessions of the United States. GNMA operates from its principal office at 451 Seventh Street, S.W., Washington, D.C. 20410.

The main function of the Government National Mortgage Association is to guarantee securities issued and secured by mortgages (or deeds of trust). The other two functions were taken over from FNMA.

Eligible Issuers

To be eligible to issue securities that can be guaranteed by GNMA, the issuer must be an approved mortgagee in good standing. This does not mean that an authorized loan correspondent of an approved mortgagee would be eligible to issue securities; however, his or her principal would be eligible.

A state or local government instrumentality that has been approved as a mortgagee by the Federal Housing Administration and that has adequate experience and facilities to issue mortgage-backed securities may be approved for a guarantee by GNMA; however, no guarantee will be made of any security that is tax-exempt.

Securities

The securities to be issued may be one of three types, but only one type may be issued against any single pool of mortgages. The types of securities are known as (1) straight pass-through securities, (2) modified pass-through securities, also known as partially modified pass-through securities, and (3) fully modified pass-through securities.

The terms of a *straight pass-through security* provide for a payment to each registered holder by the fifteenth day after the close of the month in which collections on the pooled mortgages have been received. The payment by the issuer is to be in the amount of each registered owner's proportionate share of the principal and interest, including all prepayments and all mortgage liquidation proceeds, when such are collected by the issuer under reasonable and accepted procedures of mortgage servicing, less servicing fees, foreclosure costs, and other specified costs approved by GNMA.

The terms of a *partially modified pass-through se-*

curity are much the same as the straight pass-through security, except that an interest payment must be made to the registered security holder at a given rate each month, even though the issuer has not been able to collect it.

The *fully modified pass-through security* provides for a payment to each registered holder by the fifteenth day after the close of the month in which collections on the pooled mortgages have been received by the issuer. In this case the payment is in a specified amount of principal, whether or not collected from the mortgagor, plus interest on the unpaid principal balance of each security, at a fixed rate, whether or not collected by the issuer, plus the mortgagor's principal prepayments when such are collected by the issuer (such amounts reduce the amount of subsequent specified principal payments on a proportionate basis).

The modified pass-through program is the one most used for GNMA mortgage-backed securities. In 1974 $4.5 billion in mortgage-backed securities were issued; in 1975 there was a sharp rise to $7.4 billion.

For securities to be issued, there must be a pool of at least $1 million in mortgages. The mortgages must cover residential property, although part of the residential building may be used for commercial purposes. If any mortgage is found unacceptable to GNMA, it must be replaced by the issuer. The Government National Mortgage Association reserves the right to require that any or all of the mortgaged property be insured for unusual hazards such as fire, flood, or earthquake. The maturity dates on the mortgages must all be reasonably close, and the interest rates must be the same. If it is not possible for one lender to make a pool of mortgages amounting to $1 million, other lenders may participate. The pool can consist of any combination of HUD-FHA–, VA-, or GI-insured or guaranteed loans and conventional loans on which the loan-to-value ratio or sales price does not exceed 95 percent if there is approved private insurance to 75 percent. The mortgages may be on owner-occupied, single-family residences, fee-simple condominiums, planned unit developments, and townhouses. The mortgages cannot be over one year old, and they must all bear the same interest rate. The maximum loan amount is $98,500 except in Hawaii and Alaska where the maximum loan is $123,100. The minimum term of the loan is twenty-five years and the maximum term is thirty years.

GNMA will designate one of the lenders as the principal for dealing with GNMA and will hold that lender responsible for the actions of the others.

The securities are registered and the issuer must maintain a register by name, address, and denomination of the securities issued to each purchaser. The securities must be dated and issued no later than twelve months from the date of the commitment to guarantee if the mortgages in the pool cover single-family residences, or twenty-four months if the mortgages are on multiple-family dwellings.

Application for the Approval to Issue Securities

The application and all exhibits are forwarded to the office of the secretary-treasurer of the Government National Mortgage Association.

If it is decided that the proposed issue of securities is eligible for guarantee, GNMA will issue a commitment to guarantee mortgage-backed securities, Form HUD 1704. Upon the issuer's compliance with the specific and general conditions stated in the commitment, GNMA will endorse the securities for guarantee. If it is decided that the issue of securities, as proposed, is not eligible for guarantee, the applicant is so advised and the reasons for the rejection are given. Once the commitment has been given, the applicant is under no obligation to issue the securities; however, the Government National Mortgage Association should be advised of the decision not to issue not later than thirty days prior to the date of expiration of the commitment.

Delivery and Examination of Documents

After the commitment has been received, the issuer compiles a list of the mortgages and a prospectus for the use of possible purchasers of the securities. From the list, the issuer prepares a folder on each mortgage that is to be included in the pool. Each folder will contain the original note and deed of trust or mortgage note and mortgage; the evidence of insurance or guarantee; an assignment to GNMA, duly executed but not recorded; title insurance policy; and such other exhibits as GNMA may require. These are then delivered to the custodian, a federal- or state-regulated financial institution satisfactory to GNMA, with a schedule of pooled mortgages submitted in triplicate. The custodian will review each folder to make sure that all required documents have been received and that the documents relate to the mortgages identified in the schedule of pooled mortgages.

After the custodian has completed his or her verification and is satisfied that the documents in the folders are in order, he or she will certify that by signing the certification form on the back of the form HUD 1706, schedule of pooled mortgages, which is then forwarded directly to the GNMA Washington office. The second copy will also be signed and given to the issuer as a receipt for the mortgages. After GNMA has received the certification from the custodian and all other documents conform to the proposal as submitted, it will issue the security instruments in minimum denominations of $5,000 and $10,000 thereafter, bearing GNMA's guarantee, and it will deliver them to the issuer, who will in turn deliver the securities to the purchasers and receive payment for them. The Government National Mortgage Association charges a fee for its guarantee. The annual fee is calculated on the principal balance of guaranteed securities outstanding on the last day of the month being reported and is computed and paid monthly based on the following schedule for each type of security instrument: straight pass-through—0.04 percent; partially modified pass-through—0.05 percent; fully modified pass-through—0.06 percent. The issuer is allowed a servicing fee of 0.5 percent of the outstanding principal balances of mortgages comprising the pool. Now the issuer has additional funds that can be used for more real estate loans.

The guarantee given by the Government National Mortgage Association on mortgage-backed securities is backed by the full faith and credit of the United States. In case of a default on the securities for forty-five days, the GNMA should be notified. It will investigate the reason for the default, and if it cannot be cleared up, GNMA will notify the custodian to forward all mortgages remaining at that particular pool to GNMA. The assignments will be recorded and payments will be resumed as set up in the security instrument.

It is anticipated that pension funds will take the opportunity to use GNMA to increase their income through use of increased funds made available to them by the GNMA program. So far, the principal users of the program have been the savings and loan associations and the Federal National Mortgage Association. The use of GNMA by FNMA is natural when you consider that FNMA is in the business of buying mortgages and has a large portfolio of almost all kinds of maturity and interest rate mortgages.

Managing Functions

The Federal National Mortgage Association Charter Act of 1954 made it the second duty of the Federal National Mortgage Association to manage and liquidate through collection and sale those mortgages that were taken when the agency was operating as part of the Reconstruction Finance Corporation and the Reconstruction Finance Mortgage Company. At the time of the reorganization, outstanding mortgages amounted to $2,368 million, with commitments for the purchase of an additional $603 million. The total of loans assigned to the new Federal National Mortgage Association under the Charter Act of 1954 amounted to $3,013 million. The Charter Act indicated that these loans were to be reduced through amortization until they were completely paid off. The Federal National Mortgage Association has been successful in carrying out this phase of its operation, sizably re-

ducing the debt that it assumed for liquidation and management. Although the Act states that this procedure shall be carried on in an orderly manner and at a minimum loss to the government, up to August 1, 1968, the operation was actually handled on a profit basis; at that time the operation was turned over to the Government National Mortgage Association.

Special Assistance

The special assistance functions of FNMA were added to its obligations by the Charter Act of 1954 and were removed from FNMA and given to the Government National Mortgage Association in August 1968. Special assistance loans can be bought in areas where the President of the United States has deemed it necessary that special assistance be given to residential construction because of need and public interest. This portion of the Act is designed to meet needs in two general fields: first, housing in undeveloped areas when such housing cannot be financed under established home loan programs; second, loans in areas where mortgage lending and building have declined and the lack of building threatens the stability of the high level of the national economy.

Such loans secured by deeds of trust and mortgages are supposed to meet, as far as possible, the prevailing standards for such loans, had they been made by private enterprise. This is the type of loan that has been used for disaster areas, for the construction of homes in Guam, for urban renewal loans for home construction in Alaska, and for disaster construction in Alaska.

Homes for the aged have also come under this particular classification. In the past, so has military and defense housing as well as low-cost housing. In addition to the special programs allotted to presidential edict, Congress has authorized FNMA to take three additional types of housing into its portfolio: (1) cooperative housing; (2) housing for the armed forces; and (3) low- and moderate-priced housing ($13,500 or less) under FHA and VA. Like the other operations of FNMA, the special assistance functions are considered to be self-supporting, with the initial funds being voted by Congress and provided by the United States Treasury. As indicated previously, not only does FNMA buy notes, deeds of trust, and mortgages, but it also sells notes and deeds of trust through published lists available to prospective buyers. These notes and deeds of trust are offered at the prevailing prices in the open market at the time of the offering. At no time are notes made for special assistance sold at less than cost. Not only may the purchaser buy notes and deeds of trust on single-family dwellings, but he or she may also buy through the Federal National Mortgage Association notes secured by deeds of trust on multifamily properties. Although the Association publishes a list of notes and deeds of trust and quotes prices on them, the actual price paid is that required at the time of the actual transfer of the note.

After a reasonable time if the loans are not sold they can be sold to GNMA to be carried in their special assistance section. Funds for this section are allocated by Congress and are usually in rather short supply so they are allocated where needed most. In 1981 and 1982 the special assistance programs were curtailed, but they can be reactivated on request of the President.

When there is an agency agreement for the collection and servicing of the note, the purchaser of the note and deed of trust may cancel such agreement on thirty days' notice to the servicing agency.

Tandem financing. The tandem financing program, set up in late 1974, became an important factor in financing in 1975, a year of great money shortage for real estate loans and other purposes. As a result of the shortage, interest rates climbed high: The prime rate climbed to 12 percent and the discount rate to 8 percent. Loans secured by trust deeds from banks and savings and loan associations brought 10 to 12 percent, depending on the property and the borrower. Loans made by mortgage banks and others were limited to 10 percent because of the usury laws.

The tandem plan enabled a certain number of loans ($6.8 billion in the first allocation) to be made at a lower rate of interest, so that people who could not qualify for loans at the higher interest rate might qualify to buy new homes that had been finished but never occupied. It was hoped that the plan would not only use up the large inventory of existing new homes, but also encourage new construction. Completed homes could be no older than fifteen months and no one but a caretaker could have lived in the home. The maximum loan under the tandem plan is $38,000 for a three-bedroom home and $40,500 for a home with four bedrooms. The interest rate on the first blocks of loans was 7.75 percent. (A loan of $30,000 for thirty years would require a payment of $214.93 per month at 7.75 percent; the same loan at 10 percent would require payments of $263.27.) The second block of loans was written to draw 8.25 percent.

The FHA is a part of the tandem plan only to approve the plans and specifications, issue a valuation, oversee the construction, and insure the loan. First, the builder submits plans and specifications to a lender, who submits them to the FHA for a commitment. Second, the FHA issues the commitment. Next the builder applies to FNMA for an advance commitment for the reduced interest rate and agrees to pay four points for the purchase of the loan and a 0.5 percent commitment fee. After FNMA issues its commitment, the builder obtains interim financing from the lender that obtained the FHA commitment. Then

the home is sold under the tandem financing plan. (The plan need not be used if the builder can sell the home under regular financing.)

The lending agency draws the loan documents, processes the loan, and has the FHA insure the loan. The lending agency immediately sells the loan to FNMA under the builder's advance commitment from FNMA. Finally, FNMA tries to sell the note on the open market for six months. If FNMA is unable to sell the note and deed of trust on the open market, it then sells it to GNMA.

On April 1, 1980, GNMA held $3,919 million in notes secured by real estate, approximately 81 percent of which were on multifamily dwellings and the balance on single-family homes. FNMA held $53,990 million in notes, 90 percent of which were against single-family dwellings and the balance on multifamily dwellings. FHLMC held $4,235 million in notes, 76 percent of which were against single-family dwellings.

FEDERAL HOME LOAN MORTGAGE CORPORATION (FHLMC)

The Emergency Home Finance Act of 1970 authorized the Federal Home Loan Bank Board to set up its own secondary market. The Federal Home Loan Mortgage Corporation (also called Freddie Mac), a result of that authority, purchases mortgages and trust deeds from savings and loan associations and banks. Congress allocates funds to the Federal Home Loan Bank Board which in turn makes them available to the FHLMC. FHLMC may buy HUD-FHA, VA, or conventional loans. This procedure was to make it possible for savings and loan associations and banks to process more loans from the proceeds of the mortgages sold.

FHLMC obtains additional funds by pooling mortgages it has bought and by issuing participation certificates, which are sold to investors. These certificates have a ready market since they are secured by loans on real estate and are backed by the FHLMC. It may also sell loans that it has purchased from lending institutions.

The lending institutions may sell their loans outright or they may sell only a portion of a loan. If the total loan is sold, it is called a sale on the *whole loan program*. If only a portion of the loan is sold, it is called a *participation program*. Under this program the selling institution may sell as little as 15 percent but no more than 50 percent of a loan.

Conventional Loans Requirements

The maximum original loan-to-value ratio or sales price, whichever was the smaller, was 95 percent if owner-occupied or 80 percent if not owner-occupied. The maximum original loan amount as of January 1, 1982, for an owner-occupied, single-family home was $107,000.

FHLMC will also buy loans on one- to four-unit property if one unit is owner-occupied. The maximum original loan on a duplex is $136,800; on a triplex, $165,100; and on a quadruplex, $205,300.

If a loan is secured by a loan on a unit in a planned unit development or on a condominium, the owners' association dues must be considered in the monthly payments, which also include interest, principal, taxes, and insurance. The total of the payments should not exceed 36 percent of the borrower's stable income. A higher ratio may be approved under various circumstances.

In late 1980, FHLMC started purchasing second trust deeds and notes made for the purpose of home improvements from qualified lenders. The maximum original loan amount could be for $30,000 for a single-family dwelling; $60,000 for a loan on a two- to four-family dwelling; and $15,000 on a condominium. In all cases, the owner must be the occupant of one unit. The total of all financing could not exceed 90 percent of the value. The value of the improvements could be included in the evaluation. Eligible loans are amortized over five, ten, or fifteen years, as the borrower and lender agree. Loans over $30,000 may be amortized over twenty years. A junior lien that was made for other than home improvements cannot be sold to FHLMC.

Banks, savings and loan associations, mortgage bankers, and credit unions are eligible to participate in this program if they meet certain standards concerning their experience, volume, and loss record.

The Federal Home Loan Mortgage Corporation has established a policy of allowing assumptions even though there is a due-on-sale clause in the note or deed of trust. The seller of the note and trust deed, or mortgage, continues to service the note the same as for loans sold to FNMA.

On December 18, 1981, the Federal Home Loan Mortgage Corporation let it be known that it would purchase loans in which there was shared equity. For example, a person could make all or a portion of the down payment in return for a share in the future appreciation of the property. This condition can come into being when a buyer does not have adequate funds for the down payment. A second person provides for a part of the down payment or in some cases all of the down payment. When the property is sold or a certain amount of time passes, the individual who made it possible for the owner to buy the property shares in the equity at that time. The manner in which the equity is to be shared does not make any difference to FHLMC.

FHLMC treats these notes and trust deeds as comparable to regular notes and trust deeds. It will purchase shared-equity loans in amounts up to $107,000 on single-family dwellings if both the home buyer and the person putting up the money have a good credit reputation; if both the home buyer and the investor sign the note and trust deed; if the investor is not a corporation, a trust, or a limited partner; and if the arrangement between the buyer and the investor does not require the sale or a division of the equity earlier than seven years from the date of the note.

FHLMC will also purchase adjustable rate mortgages. The adjustments must be based on the Federal Home Loan Bank Board's cost of money schedule.

Mortgage brokers were unhappy to see the FHLMC enter the secondary finance field, because it made more money available to savings and loans, thus reducing demand for their service and reducing the need for outsiders to service loans sold.

The advent of the Federal Home Loan Mortgage Corporation into the secondary mortgage market provided FNMA and GNMA with competition that, on occasion, can become confusing because of the different attitudes in purchasing.

QUESTIONS

1. The Federal National Mortgage Association is
   a. a subsidiary of the Reconstruction Finance Corporation
   b. a government-owned agency
   c. a privately owned, federally chartered corporation
   d. none of the above
2. The FNMA is active in the secondary mortgage market. Which of the following is incorrect?
   a. FNMA buys HUD-FHA and VA loans
   b. FNMA buys conventional loans if FNMA forms are used
   c. FNMA buys loans from banks, mortgage companies, and individuals
   d. FNMA buys only notes secured by first liens
3. Which of the following is incorrect? The FNMA is financed by
   a. sale of stock
   b. sale of its loans to investors
   c. funds from the sale of short-term bonds to the United States Treasury
   d. none of the above
4. Loans are sold to FNMA
   a. on a first-come, first-served basis
   b. at an interest rate set by the United States government
   c. at an auction where lenders bid for commitments to purchase any amount of loans the lenders expect to have for sale

d. at an auction where lenders bid for forward commitments, the amounts limited to a minimum and maximum bid any one lender can offer

5. The Government National Mortgage Association took over some of FNMA's activities when it was set up in 1968. These included all of the following except
   a. handling special assistance loans
   b. collection and management of RFC loans still on the books
   c. collecting service fees on all loans
   d. none of the above

6. The Government National Mortgage Association is a
   a. privately owned corporation
   b. privately owned, federally chartered corporation
   c. wholly owned corporate instrumentality of the United States Government
   d. unincorporated agency of the United States Government

7. At times the GNMA buys loans from
   a. the Federal National Mortgage Association
   b. banks
   c. savings and loan associations
   d. individuals

8. The GNMA will guarantee securities issued against a block of acceptable notes and deeds of trust by the following, except:
   a. tax-free securities issued by a state or local government that has been approved as a mortgagee by the HUD-FHA
   b. issued by a bank
   c. issued by a savings and loan association
   d. issued by a mortgage bank

9. The Federal Home Loan Mortgage Corporation is
   a. an instrumentality of the Federal Home Loan Bank
   b. a privately owned corporation
   c. a secondary market for only savings and loan associations
   d. a secondary market for only HUD-FHA loans

10. The FHLMC gets money for purchasing loans
    a. directly from the United States Treasury
    b. from the sale of its stock
    c. from the Federal Home Loan Bank, which receives the funds from the United States Treasury
    d. from the sale of its bonds

11. The FHLMC will purchase loans
    a. if they are on the FHLMC forms
    b. but only a part of the loan (the maximum amount of participation is 75 percent, the minimum is 40 percent.)
    c. the maximum loan-to-value ratio of which is 85 percent for owner-occupied and 75 percent for nonowner-occupied
    d. if the payment of interest and principal does not exceed 30 percent

12. The Federal Home Loan Mortgage Company
    a. can make a pool of mortgages and offer an interest in the pool to investors
    b. can treat each application for a loan purchase separately
    c. does not issue commitments
    d. does all of the above

BIBLIOGRAPHY

Federal Reserve Bank Board of Governors, "Federal Reserve Bank Bulletin." Published monthly by the Federal Reserve Bank.

15

Construction and Off-Site Improvements Financing

CONSTRUCTION FINANCING

A construction loan is made for the purpose of building improvements on real property, the proceeds of the loan being disbursed as the construction of the improvement reaches certain stages previously agreed upon by the lending agency, the builder, and the owner.

In the past forty years home construction has made great advances. Before the Depression from 1929–35, an owner usually contracted an architect, who would draw up plans and specifications and then, through several means, formalize them. The plans would be submitted to bidding and awarded to the low bidder by the owner of the property. The payments would be made by the owner in instalments after approval by the architect. However, in order to build, the owner needed cash in hand or the contractor needed enough capital to carry the project until the building was completed, at which time a loan could be placed on the property and payment made to the contractor.

This practice has changed. Today it is not uncommon for an institutional lender to enter into a construction loan, taking a note, deed of trust, or mortgage for the full amount of the final loan and seeing that payments are made to the contractor as satisfactory progress is made through certain stages in the construction.

Characteristics of a Construction Loan

In the case of construction loans, the lending agency agrees to make the loan before there are any improvements upon the real estate, subject to plans and specifications that have been submitted. Since there are no improvements, this type of loan is probably one of the most hazardous that can be made. (However, if certain precautions are taken and rigid controls exerted, the con-

struction loan can be a source of good income to the lender.) Of course, the major hazard is the inability of the contractor to complete the building because of possible lack of capital, delays caused by bad weather, material shortages, labor strikes, excessive losses through poor estimations of other jobs, or other such reasons. Whatever the cause for the failure, under such circumstances the lender is liable to end up in a position of having to complete the building to protect his or her loan. Of course, under these circumstances, it would be unusual for the lender to have a conforming loan upon completion of the building or to dispose of the property for the amount he or she had invested in the improvements.

Another hazard is that of mechanic's and material liens. Under the lien laws of California, it is the right of materialmen and mechanics to record a lien against property upon which materials have been used and labor expended for its improvement. These liens shall have priority in relation to the time at which the work is done. In other words, if a lender decides to make a construction loan on property upon which construction has already started, the workers and materialmen, in case of nonpayment, would have the privilege of filing a lien against the property, and since the work had been done before the lender's lien had been filed, their lien would come ahead of the lender's. To protect his or her loan, it would be necessary for the lender to pay off the material or mechanic's liens before his or her lien would take precedent. Of course, this could lead to an excessive nonconforming loan.

In the case of the construction loan, two separate lenders are frequently involved. The first lender is the one making the loan for the construction of the improvements and the second is the final lender, who would advance the money for the purchase of the property to the owner after the construction is completed.

Interim Financing

The construction loan is usually referred to as an *interim-finance loan* and the final loan as a *take-out* or *final loan*. It is not necessary in all cases for two lending agencies to be involved, since several agencies in California make both interim-finance loans and take-out loans. National banks are allowed to make interim loans, and if the purchaser of the property meets their standards, they may also make the final loan. In the case of an owner-builder, the construction loan may become the final and only loan required by the bank.

The state banks of California are allowed to make the same type of loan, but under a slightly different ratio of loan to value and period of time as far as the construction term is concerned. State and national banks are limited to a maximum maturity of thirty years on a construction loan unless the loan is insured by an agency of the federal government, such as the FHA or the VA. The maturity date of such a loan is thirty years from the date of the loan, not from the date of the first payment, as in the case of Federal Housing Administration loans. Under these circumstances, a note dated May 16, 1964, with a first payment falling due on July 1, 1964, with an amortization of thirty years and the maturity date of July 1, 1994, would be an illegal loan by fifteen days even though the maturity was thirty years from the first payment. Under these circumstances the final payment would have to be on a date preceding May 16, 1994. The last payment would be somewhat larger than the others, since two payments would be due at that time.

Savings and loan associations in California may also make construction loans on an interim basis or on a final basis, whether they are state- or federally chartered.

The interim-finance program is particularly beneficial to organizations located outside California or outside the lending area of the institution that will contract to make the final loan. Such interim loans benefit them because they know that the building they have approved from plans and specifications will be constructed on the proper lot under proper supervision, and will be available for their loan upon completion. In this way areas with money to loan have been able to aid areas in which there has been a shortage of permanent real estate loan money; for example, life insurance companies on the East Coast have been able to make satisfactory loans on property located on the West Coast. This practice has also been beneficial to California veterans who applied and received commitments from the Cal-Vet program.

In California, mortgage companies also make construction loans. The purpose for which the loan is made—that is, whether it is to be held in the company's portfolio or sold to some insurance company for whom the mortgage company is acting as correspondent—will determine the amount it will loan toward the construction. If the mortgage company knows that it will sell the loan to an insurance company after construction is completed, then the maximum loan it will make will be 75 percent on homes and commercial buildings. On the other hand, should a company make a loan that it desires to keep in its own portfolio, there are no restrictions; the amount of the loan will depend upon the individual and the property.

The mortgage company and the mortgage banker provide their organizations with a certain amount of capital and then make loans against these funds until the funds are exhausted. The mortgage company will then either request from a bank a line of credit secured by the existing loans or sell its existing loans to an organization that wants to obtain loans in the area covered by the mortgage company. With funds obtained in either of these ways, the mortgage company will again process loans.

Construction Interim-Finance Loan Terms

State-chartered savings and loan associations may make home construction loans with the same security and term as loans made on existing property. However, no loan for the purchase of land and construction of improvements may exceed 85 percent of the fair market value. The same is true for federally chartered savings and loan associations.

National banks may loan under home construction financing 80 percent of either the total appraised value or the acquisition costs, whichever is smaller, for thirty-six months. State banks may lend 85 percent of the appraised value of land and proposed improvements for thirty-six months. The mortgage company, as previously indicated, is unrestricted regarding such loans.

Much legislation has been passed to put state and national banks more in competition with savings and loan associations. Under the old program, which had a maximum of nine months' maturity for the national bank on a construction loan, it was impossible for the bank to make loans on the construction of large commercial buildings or, in some instances, large apartment units. State banks also were restricted to the extent that they were unable to compete with savings and loan associations. Today, however, with the eighteen-month and thirty-six-month construction loan allowed, both state and national banks can compete fairly well with savings and loan associations for the larger long-term construction financing.

As a rule, the interest rates are comparable to the take-out loan. From 1979 to 1982, because of money conditions, interim-finance loans have been written with interest rates of 16.5 to 21 percent. Because of the additional hazards and the extra work connected with the construction loan, it has become customary to make a service charge for these loans. This service charge has varied from 2 to 5 points or more in some instances. These charges, of course, increase the effective gross interest, and if it is possible to use the same funds for two or three interim-financing loans during the year, the lender's effective income can be increased considerably.

Therefore, almost all financial institutions capable of handling construction loans look with favor upon this type of financing as a means of increasing their average net interest yield. The maximum legal maturity for construction loans has been made fairly uniform; however, depending upon the area in which the lending institution is located and upon the type of property being constructed, the maturity will vary somewhat.

Most national banks feel that it should not take more than 120 days to complete a residence and therefore usually write their construction loans for home financing for a period not to exceed nine months, which is supposed to give adequate time for the home to be constructed and a buyer to be found. If the property is to be a duplex, much the same schedule will hold; however, if it involves large-scale construction such as apartment houses or commercial buildings, the note will usually be written for the maximum term. This practice also applies to state-chartered banks.

Savings and loan associations write their construction loans for the maximum period regardless of the type of building being constructed.

The loan-to-value ratios of various lending agencies have also been approaching equality.

Application Procedures
for Construction Loans

In the case of construction loans, the applicant is usually the builder or the owner of the property. Sometimes the builder is also the owner, in which case the owner-builder almost always makes the application to the lender. If it is to be an FHA-insured loan, the application is for a conditional or a firm commitment depending upon whether the owner is to be the final occupant of the completed building or whether the property is to be available for purchase by an unknown individual at the time the commitment is made. The commitment might also be a firm commitment including a dual commitment; under these circumstances a firm commitment is made with the additional provision that if the builder is unable to find a purchaser within a reasonable length of time, he or she may take over the loan at the lower loan figure provided when the builder is building on speculation.

If the take-out loan is to be used, the applicant should

also make provisions with the final lender to issue the take-out letter in the form of a commitment binding the lending institution to make the final loan after the building has been completed according to the plans and specifications submitted to the lender.

Documentation

The applicant for a construction loan should always have available for the lending officer a complete and detailed set of plans and specifications bearing the owner's and contractor's signatures, whether the loan is to be Federal Housing Administration, Veterans Administration, or conventional. Plans should be complete in all details, and specifications should also be complete so that when the inspectors examine the property for conformity to plans and specifications there will be no difficulty in determining whether the plans and specifications are being followed.

Accompanying the plans and specifications should be a builder's contract, indicating that the builder will furnish all materials and labor and complete the building according to the plans and specifications submitted or attached for a certain definite amount. This contract must be signed by the contractor, and it is desirable that his or her license number appear so that it will be easy for the lending agency to determine that he or she has the right to contract as a general contractor and that the license is valid and unrestricted. It will make the appraiser's job somewhat easier if the contract is accompanied by a cost breakdown sheet. When the applicant has all these documents, he or she is ready to approach the lending officer to make his or her formal application. The application will contain the amount of loan desired, the length of time for which the loan is requested, and the schedule proposed for the repayment of the obligation. The application will, as usual, contain a financial statement of the applicant. If the contractor is unknown to the lending institution, the lending officer will probably request that the applicant obtain for the lending institution a recent financial statement and operation statement of the contractor.

It will facilitate matters if the application is accompanied by a description and photographs of the property and by an indication of its location. In the case of large projects, the lending agency will probably request an economic survey so that it may determine that a need actually exists for the construction being proposed. The lending officer will ask whether the property is free and clear. If it is not free and clear, the applicant must have some indication that the people holding the deed of trust on the property are willing to subordinate their first lien to the first lien that will be put on the property by the lending agency for their construction loan. There should also be some indication of how the subordinated lien will be paid off. The lending institution particularly desires to know whether the applicant plans to pay off the subordinated lien on the property from the proceeds of the loan at some stage during the construction of the building. Subordination agreements were very popular during the late 1950s and early 1960s. However, since then the subordination agreement has fallen into disrepute and is not being used as extensively as before. The decline in its popularity is due to the numerous cases in which it has been necessary for the seller of the property under the first deed of trust, later subordinated, to take back the property that he or she previously sold. In these instances the seller often found that there was a building under construction that needed several thousand dollars' more work before it would be completed, that street bonds had been placed on the property, and that to take back the property he or she had to assume the construction deed of trust, pay off the street bonds, and then complete the building. Should the building have been completed, it would still be necessary for him or her to assume the deed of trust to which his or her own deed of trust had been subordinated. In many instances it was financially impossible for the seller to take back his or her property under these circumstances. As a result of such occurrences, the subordination agreement received a great deal of bad publicity.

In some areas with no sewage facilities, counties require that before a building permit will be issued, a test hole be dug to determine whether adequate sewage disposal is available through a septic tank and leaching field or a septic tank and deep well system. In cases such as this, the lending agency would naturally want to see the results of the test to make sure that the loan it is proposing to make to the builder will be used to construct a building that will be occupied after it has been completed.

Loan Processing

After the application has been received, the next step is the appraisal of the project. In connection with the appraisal, the site must be analyzed to make sure that it complies with all local regulations. Some communities, for example, require that a lot contain 10,000 square feet for a single-family home to be built on it. Lots have been submitted measuring 100 feet by 100 feet, which appear to conform with this regulation; however, upon investigation it has been found that the lot measures to the center of a road 40 feet wide, making the usable lot area only 80 feet by 100 feet (8,000 square feet), and therefore disqualifying the lot under the local ordinance. Therefore, it is important to be sure that the lot does comply with local regulations before the lending agency proceeds much further with a loan.

The lending agency is next interested in the off-site improvements. In some instances in which there are no

sidewalks, curbs, or gutters, a recorded provision states that the owner of the property shall, under county requirement, install curbs and gutters at his or her own cost. Should the owner fail to install the curbs and gutters, the country has the authority to install the curbs and gutters itself and to bill the property owner for the expense incurred. If the road is only graveled, a problem arises in connection with its maintenance and with possible future macadamizing of it.

The lender is interested in the feasibility of the project and in whether there will be a demand for the type of property that the completed project will provide. The lender will therefore appraise the plans and specifications on a cost of construction basis. While the lender is doing this, he or she will also analyze the practicality of the plans, taking into consideration the location of the rooms, the size of the rooms, and the presence or absence of built-in features. If there is a large discrepancy in the cost of the improvements, whether an overcharge or an undercharge, the lending officer might require the builder to come in and justify the contract that has been submitted. In their discussions they may make comparisons of similar units and their costs. If a discrepancy still exists, the lender might ask to examine the subcontracts to see whether some error has been made in their preparation. If the cost is too low, the lender realizes the possibility of the contractor's going bankrupt before the building is completed; if the cost is too high, he or she wants to see that there is justification for the extra charge.

If the loan is to be interim financing and no take-out commitment has been issued, the lender will probably request that the final lender be provided with the documents necessary to their making a fair analysis and determining whether a take-out loan will be available; otherwise, they sometimes find it necessary to lower their standards to help a builder dispose of a subdivision or building that does not sell quickly.

Analysis of the Contractor

In some instances the builder may be the contractor, but in all instances the lender is interested in the contractor who is doing the construction of the building. In the analysis of the contractor the lender realizes that several methods of operation are possible for a contractor. He or she may be operating as a corporation, in which case the liability of the contractor is limited to the assets of the corporation. He or she may be operating as an individual or as a partnership, in which case liability extends to both the assets of the business and the assets of each partner.

In conducting an investigation of a contractor whom he or she does not know, the lending officer will obtain a list of previous projects upon which this contractor has worked. The lending officer should visit enough of these projects to determine what type of builder the contractor is. The inspection of these properties will reveal the type of finished work produced, and a few questions will reveal the reputation of the contractor for that particular project. If he or she is a good contractor, there will be no complaints; however, if the contractor has not done a satisfactory job, many complaints can be brought to light by questioning the occupants of the contractor's previously completed projects.

Trade journals will often reveal both favorable and unfavorable information concerning the contractor. Organizations such as the Builders' Exchange can supply information concerning various contractors in the area, as can the local chapter of the National Association of Home Builders. A sure source of information as to the payment practices and the dependability of the contractor is his or her subcontractors and suppliers. As a rule these people will also be able to tell the lender about the contractor's reputation. The subcontractors and suppliers often work through collection agencies such as the Retail Credit Association in cases of difficult collections and in cases in which it has become necessary to file liens against the property. The Retail Credit Association will usually have information concerning these liens; therefore, another source available to the lending officer for investigation of the contractor is the various credit agencies.

Whether or not the lending agency is satisfied with the information that it has developed concerning the contractor, it will usually require a financial statement. This financial statement will be analyzed as to whether the amount of working capital that is available to the contractor is sufficient to pay the bills and accounts payable that are shown. The contractor's net worth will be computed to see that there is sufficient worth available to meet any contingency that might occur in connection with the proposed project.

Disbursement of the Construction Loan

There are three usual methods of disbursement for construction loans. First is the *voucher system,* a method in which the contractor is reimbursed for receipted bills. Reimbursement is made upon presentation of the bills to the lending agency. With this method it is important for the lending agency to verify that the material and labor have been used on the job covered by the loan being disbursed.

The second system is the *warrant system,* under which the bills, as they occur, are presented to the lender and are in turn paid by the lender directly to the supplier of material or labor. Once again, it is important that the lender make sure that the bills being paid are for the project covered under the construction loan.

The third system of disbursement of the construction loan is by the *fixed disbursement schedule.* Under this program the lender, the builder, and the contractor agree on the number of payments that will be made during the construction of the property and on the stages at which these payments will be made. The number of payments varies from three to six. The most popular payment schedule, probably because more FHA loans are made than others, is the schedule established for the payment of construction loans under FHA inspection and construction. This program provides for three inspections, and after satisfactory completion of each of these three stages the contractor is entitled to payment. The fourth payment is made after the notice of completion is filed and the lien rights period has expired.

Another popular schedule calls for five payments. The schedule usually calls for one-fifth of the contract price to be paid when the foundation is in and has been backfilled; some schedules call for the subflooring to be on also. One-fifth is paid when the framing is completed and the roof is on; one-fifth when it is enclosed and ready for painting; one-fifth when the notice of completion is filed; and the final one-fifth after the lien right period has expired.

Another means of disbursement popular for a while was the use of a builders' control organization. This was an organization entirely separate from the lending agency, established to analyze plans and specifications to determine that they could be built for the amount of the contract. The builders' control then made supervised and controlled payments to the contractor of funds received from the lender or the borrower as satisfactory progress was made. These organizations were very successful, and they controlled payments of the loans satisfactorily provided that they were actually separate from the lender and the contractor. However, some of the contracting corporations established builders' controls that had the same personnel as the corporate contracting entity. Under these circumstances the builders' control was of no particular value because the loan was being paid directly to the builder's control, which was, in effect, the contractor. As a result of the bad publicity obtained by the builders' control organizations as a whole, they have lost popularity. A charge was made for this type of service, usually from 1 to 1.5 percent of the amount of the contract, and there was usually a minimum charge that varied from $50 to $150, depending upon the agency.

For all these methods of disbursement one axiom must be remembered: At no time should the amount disbursed be more than the cost of the improvements constructed to that point. A second important rule is always to hold funds back until the lien period has expired so that funds will be available to satisfy any liens that might be filed as a result of the construction. This lien period is an important factor in construction financing, since it gives the contractors, subcontractors, and materialmen an opportunity to file a lien against the property for work that was done but for which no payment was received. Such liens may be filed for a period from thirty to sixty days after the notice of completion on the property has been filed. All materialmen and subcontractors who have worked on or supplied material for the construction of a building under a general contractor have thirty days in which to file a lien against that property for any payment not received. The general contractor, in turn, has sixty days in which to file a lien against the property for work and material for which he or she has received no pay. Both the subcontractors and the general contractor have ninety days in which to file a mechanic's and labor lien if a valid notice of completion was not recorded.

To be able to file a lien against property on which he or she has worked or to which he or she has delivered material, a subcontractor or materialman must give preliminary notice that he or she intends to record a lien against the property if not paid for labor and material. The notice must be given to the owner of the property, the general contractor, and the construction lender. If the subcontractor or materialman feels that it may be necessary to file a lien against any particular job, the preliminary notice must be given within twenty days after material is delivered to the job or work is done on the job. If the twenty-day period should expire, the subcontractor or materialman can still file a preliminary notice, but it will be effective only against work done on the job and material delivered to the job after the date of the preliminary notice. The notice is served either by hand or by registered, certified, or first class mail. If the mailing is by registered or certified mail, the notice is considered to have been served on the date of mailing. It is considered served on the date received if it is sent by first class mail. See Chapter 10 for additional information on this type of lien.

If construction is handled by an individual without a contractor's license (in other words, an owner builder who has subcontracted construction of the building), all subcontractors in this case become general contractors and have sixty days in which to file a lien against the property for amounts of money owed to them.

Any general contractor may waive his or her lien rights upon written notification to the lending agency. Under these circumstances, if the building was constructed under general contract, the general contractor at the end of thirty days could waive his or her lien rights for the additional thirty days and, after allowing a few days to see that no liens had been filed that had not been previously caught, he or she could be paid the final payment due under the disbursement schedule. Subcontractors working as general contractors would be able to waive their lien rights after thirty days.

Normally a payment is not made until thirty-five days after the filing of the notice of completion; the additional five days is a precautionary measure allowing additional time for items to be found that might have been filed with the county recorder's office and not listed.

The term *notice of completion* has been used several times in connection with lien rights. The notice of completion is an indication that the property has been completely finished and that all work has been terminated on the construction of this particular building. The notice of completion, recorded by the owner of the property, states the name of the contractor, the date and amount of the contract, and the location of the property upon which the building has been constructed. It is signed by the owner of the property and recorded within ten days of actual completion. This notice of completion puts all materialmen, subcontractors, and contractors on notice that their lien right period has started; it says, in effect, that if they do not receive payment wthin a short period they should file a lien against the property unless they are otherwise protected. A notice of completion may be a valid notice of completion, in which case the time limits discussed above prevail. However, the notice of completion may be invalid, in which case liens may be filed beyond the stated periods. A notice of completion may be invalid because of failure to file it within ten days of the actual completion of the building, or because of errors in description or date, or because of any other error that might appear in the document itself. A title company will not usually issue a title certificate until ninety days after filing of an invalid notice of completion.

At the time the application is made, the applicant should be informed of the importance of having a valid first lien in the name of the lender against the property. In connection with this the applicant should be advised that under no circumstances should he or she or the contractor outline upon the lot the foundation of the improvements, not even with temporary stakes, nor should any excavation whatsoever be made upon the property, including the removal of weeds or shrubs. The applicant should further inform the contractor that he or she should not have any material delivered to the lot or allow any of his or her equipment to be sent to the lot. None of the old fences, buildings, or retaining walls should be removed, nor should a start be made toward their removal. Items such as water meters, power poles, and gas lines should not be allowed to be installed, since any such work that might be done on the property before the lending agency records its deed of trust would destroy the valid first lien it must have to provide a construction loan.

The Completed Construction Loan

Before disbursing any funds from the construction loan, the lending agency should be sure that the following documents are in its file. First, an application for a loan and an agreement for repayment, completely filled in as discussed in the chapter on loan applications. Second, if a take-out loan is to be required, the file should contain a firm take-out commitment from the lending agency that will make the final loan. Third, almost all lending agencies now require a completion bond from the contractor. This bond, issued by an insurance company and paid for by the builder, states in effect that if the contractor does not complete the building according to plans and specifications and deliver it to the owner free of liens, the insurance company will step in, finish the building, and deliver it to the owner lien-free. Fourth, the file should contain a copy of the loan agreement, which will establish for the lending agency the individual to whom the payments are to be made upon certain stages of completion being reached; the number of inspections that will be made; the number of payments that will be made, and the agreement to deposit with the lending agency the funds over and above the loan up to the amount of the contract plus the costs involved in the construction loan. Fifth, there should be a title insurance policy showing that the lending agency has a first lien subject only to the usual rights of way and taxes due but not yet payable. Sixth, the proper fire insurance and other risk insurance policies should be in the file, showing a lender's loss-payable endorsement to the lending agency. The insurance policy should be for at least the amount of the loan to be disbursed. When there is potential earthquake or flood damage, the lending agency may request that the borrower obtain coverage for these risks . Seventh, before the first payment is disbursed, there should be an endorsement to the title insurance policy from the title insurance company indicating that no work was done prior to the recording of the deed of trust and that the building is on the property described within the deed of trust and insured under the title insurance policy. Eighth, there should be an authorization from the borrower to disburse funds according to the loan agreement. Ninth, before the final disbursement is made, there should be in the file an endorsement from the title insurance company indicating that it has searched the records, that the lien period has expired, and that no liens have been filed against the property. If the lien period has been shortened by the general contractor's waiving his or her lien rights, the title insurance company should indicate that it has such a waiver or the waiver should be in the file of the lending company.

Review

Construction financing involves (1) a detailed analysis of the plans, specifications, and cost estimate; (2) an inspection and analysis of the lot size, shape, location, topography, accessibility, and use; (3) a careful projec-

tion of the estimated costs or contracted costs to determine that the costs are comparable to other projects or published costs; (4) a thorough investigation of the abilities and financial condition of the contractor; (5) disbursement of the funds only after determining that the job has properly reached the point of completion called for in the schedule and that the funds invested are always in excess of the funds paid; (6) a careful inspection of the property from time to time to make sure that the work is being done according to plans and specifications; (7) the retention of a sufficient part of the loan to provide payment for items that may not be finished or paid for by the contractor, after the lien period has expired; (8) the proper recording of a valid notice of completion when the project is completed so that the lien period may be properly terminated.

FINANCING OFF-SITE IMPROVEMENTS

California's growth in the last three decades caused a great demand for new housing and new subdivisions. The demand for housing became so great that a way had to be found of financing off-site improvements to the subdivisions such as curbs, sidewalks, and streets.

The first subdivisions were established by individuals having sufficient capital to finance the off-site improvements and to include them in the cost of the lot, each lot taking its prorated share of the total cost. As more people entered the subdivision business a means of 100 percent financing of the off-site improvements became necessary.

There are many ways to build such improvements. General obligation bonds may be supported by large communities to build the public improvements to serve the area. There are revenue bonds, which are income bonds retired by revenue of the district and not by tax against the property. Special assessment bonds and also a lease purchase agreement may be used for such financing. Finally, of course, there is the type of financing that consists of short-term borrowing by the subdivider or, as indicated at first, a project may be financed with cash the subdivider gets back from the subdivision when the lots are sold. The system most extensively used today for the financing of off-site improvement is probably the establishment of assessment districts. The two basic assessment procedures in California are commonly referred to as the 1911 Procedures Act and the 1913 Procedures Act.

The 1911 Assessment Act

The 1911 Assessment Act establishes the procedures for forming a district to do work, call for bids, levy assessments, create liens, and issue the bonds that are the result of the liens' being created. Assessment procedures are normally initiated by property owners, who want streets, curbs, gutters, and other public improvements for health measures, such as sewers and drainage. It is also common for a public body to initiate procedures for forming an assessment district, particularly for health measures. In most cases, however, a group of property owners who desire the improvements will initiate the request for an assessment district.

To bring the desires of the people to the attention of the board of supervisors, a petition is circulated. After 60 percent of the property owners have signed the petition it is taken to the board of supervisors, which will declare that an assessment district has been formed. At this point the board of supervisors or the public agency to which the petition has been presented acts as an agency between the contractors and the underwriters of the bond issue.

The public agency hires an engineer to draw plans and specifications for the improvements that are to be installed, accepts sealed construction bids from the contractors, and awards a contract to the lowest responsible bidder. The successful bidder must provide a surety bond and a completion bond. After the contract is awarded, the contractor proceeds with the work.

Under the 1911 Assessment Act, the contractor does not receive any money for the job until it is completed, which means, of course, that the contractor will need interim financing. This is obtained by using his or her contract with the agency. The contractor needs a firm take-out on the assessment warrant[1] that he or she will get after completing the job. He or she will normally arrange for a firm take-out from a bond underwriter who is willing to accept the job of the sale and distribution of the bonds, which can be issued to pay the contractor for his or her work.

For interim financing the contractor will usually approach a bank. If his or her own bank does not wish to carry the interim financing, the contractor will often ask the bond underwriter for the name of a bank willing to provide the interim financing. The contractor then proceeds with the work. When it is completed, he or she files a notice of completion with the public agency, which then levies an assessment against each property in accordance with the assessment that is based on the value of the benefits received by the property. In the case of street improvements, the assessment is usually a footage basis. On sewers it is usually a combination of footage and area. In California there is a great deal of flexibility as to how assessments can be levied. The lien against each property is created and confirmed by the public agency. The sum total of all the liens is given to the contractor who has performed the work. Technically he or she has a map that indicates the lien against each property and an assessment warrant, which gives him or

her the right to collect the money indicated on the map or to receive bonds for all the assessments that remain unpaid after his or her cash collection efforts. This method of financing is the 1911 procedure, and its most important feature is that the contractor does not receive any payment until the work is completed, so that all the work that is done prior to completion must be financed by the contractor through means other than public funds.

The 1913 Assessment Act

The second financing procedure is set forth by the 1913 Act. Under this Act the job is a cash job to the contractor. The city or public agency makes arrangements for the bond issues and sells them, thus creating cash to pay the contractor.

Under the construction procedure of the 1913 Act (although it is similar to the 1911 Act in that the assessments are spread over the various properties), the assessments are spread on the basis of estimates rather than by contract figures. The estimates of the work are drawn by the engineer of the public agency at the beginning stages of the project. The engineer presents estimates and maps to the public agency, which approves them, files a report, calls for a public hearing, and then calls for bids on the project. The construction bids come in, the report and the assessments are altered to match the bid that is accepted, and the work progresses.

The public agency then begins trying to collect from property owners the amount assessed against each property. After it has made its cash collections it must sell the bonds for unpaid assessments. With the money from the cash collections and from the sale of the bonds the public agency pays the contractor for the work as it is done.

One other phase of the 1913 procedure has come into use, called the acquisition procedure. In this case the work is done ahead of time by the developer on his or her own. When the work is completed the developer goes to the public agency, states that the work has been completed according to the required plans and specifications, and requests that the public agency issue bonds in the amount of the cost of the development so that the developer can be paid. The public agency will then contact an underwriter and sell the bonds.

The major difference between the two acts is the manner in which the contractor receives payment . Under the 1911 Act the money is not received until after the work is completed. The contractor must arrange for interim financing and take-out and also for the sale of the bonds. Under the 1913 Act the public agency collects the money from the property owners, issues bonds through an underwriter for the unpaid assessments, and through the underwriter makes arrangements for the sale of the bonds

[1] A list of the lots in the district indicating the charge against each lot.

and pays the contractor as the work is progressing and when it is completed. Each of these acts makes provisions for the levying of assessments and states that bonds may be issued for the assessments that might remain unpaid.

Bond Acts

There are two bond acts—the 1911 Act and the 1915 Act—under which the bonds can be issued. Both acts create liens against property. The lien, a first, can be second only to a previous assessment bond lien. Deeds of trust, rights of way, and homesteads are all liens that are subordinate to a lien established for an assessment bond.

There have been instances in which as many as five assessment bond liens for improvements have been put in steps rather than all at once. For instance, a first assessment bond might be for streets, a second for sidewalks and gutters, a third for sewers, a fourth for drainage, a fifth for water, and so forth. However, these are only types of liens that can be ahead of an assessment lien, which is not unlike taxes and will often appear in the tax figure on the preliminary report as a total of taxes and assessment liens which are due. As a rule, the assessment will be broken out of the figure at the foot of the preliminary report.

At a special session of the legislature in 1963, the acts were modified to require that the lien be recorded with the county recorder so that the knowledge of such lien was readily available.

The 1911 Bond Act. Under the 1911 Act the only lien security is a specific property. The treasurer of the public agency acts as an agent between the property owner and the bondholder, bills the property owner for the amount due under the assessment, and, upon surrender of the coupon of the bond owner, pays the bond owner the interest due.

The body of the bonds issued provides for the rate of interest, the frequency of payment of the interest, the face value of the bond, and the bond's maturity. It also states what property is acting as security for the bond, including the legal description of the parcel. If the payments are not made in the normal course of maturity of the bond, or if the interest is not paid when it falls due, the bond is in default. This does not necessarily mean that the bond is not good, but that the people owning the property have not paid their assessment. The lien that has been created is against one property only, and although the payment may not have been made, the bond may be adequately secured by the property. Since the lien is against only the property, it cannot be against the owner of the property and continues as a lien on the

property from owner to owner until paid in full. It does not matter whether the property contains a commercial building, a garage, a $40,000 dwelling, or is simply vacant. The lien is against the land; therefore the bondholder's security is the land and the improvements thereon. In the case of a delinquency the bondholder has the right to foreclose the lien. This is not usually done unless there is a long delinquency, but the bondholder has the right to foreclose the lien ahead of all other liens that might be shown on the property.

There is no liability for any public agency in connection with these bonds other than to bill the property owner for the amount due, collect this amount, and pay the bondholder. Penalties on delinquent instalments accrue at the rate of 1 percent per month. The bonds normally run for a term of fifteen years, although in southern California the majority of assessment bonds are for ten years. The interest rate is usually 6 percent. However, the interest on some of these bonds reached 12% in 1983 and there are provisions for a prior redemption penalty of 5 percent of the amount of the bond outstanding at the time the bond is paid off.

It is not unusual when property changes hands through a sale for the new financing agency to request that the bonds be paid off. The bonds may be paid off by going to the public agency treasurer, obtaining the amount still outstanding, adding the 5 percent premium to this amount, and clearing the records.

The 1915 Bond Act. The 1915 Bond Act is completely different. Rather than the basic security's being a lien against each individual property whose owner did not pay the assessment levied, it is against the collective unpaid assessments for the cost of the improvements, and thus a lien against the whole public agency. The public agency takes this collective unpaid assessment, for example, $150,000, and puts it into a serial bond issue with $10,000 due each year, much like the serial bonds with a certain group maturing each year, and general obligation bonds. Therefore, under the 1915 Bond Act the holder of the bond does not have a lien against any specific piece of property. The bondholder cannot identify the piece of property against which his or her particular bond is issued, as could be done under the 1911 Act. He or she is able to identify only the district against which the bond was issued. Under these circumstances, the bondholder has no direct access to the property in case of delinquency. This is the major difference between the 1915 and the 1911 Bond Acts.

As soon as a delinquency occurs, it is the mandatory duty of the issuing agency, whether it is city, state, or county, to levy a tax, not to exceed 10 cents per $100 of the assessed valuation of the county, city, or district, not only of the local neighborhood in which the delinquency occurs, to create the funds necessary to clear the delinquency or the default. The public agency, in turn, verifies the defaults and can move against the property whose owner has not paid the assessment after the usual grace period. In the meantime the agency has paid the bondholders from the additional tax.

There is a great deal of security behind this type of bond because of the 10-cent levy that can be assessed by the supervising agency to take care of any delinquency. In effect, the people of the entire county, city, or district are permitting their property to be used as additional collateral for the bonds issued under the 1915 Act.

Although this procedure sounds radical, it is not, because the cost of these improvements does not nearly equal the assessed valuation of the properties. Normally these assessment bonds, whether for curbs, sewers, gutters, sidewalks, streets, electricity, or other purpose, represent only 5 to 15 percent of the total value of the property. Therefore, when a community uses the 1915 Act, it is in no danger and it can actually achieve a better interest rate because of the more secure position of the bond and the smaller likelihood of trouble for the bondholder.

The 1915 Act *can* be dangerous if used indiscriminately by public districts in areas in which the development is sparse, the means for prepayment by the residents are limited, and the improvements to property will exceed 40 to 50 percent of the valuation of the property.

The 1915 Act provides for a much more desirable type of bond than the 1911 Act. It is a cleaner operation in every way. A bond is issued to a certain maturity; there is no need to compute the principal payment for the bondholder, no need to do any more than clip the coupon during the life of the bond. The bond is drawn with a definite maturity and upon that date the bond will be paid. The market for 1915 bonds is therefore better and also the interest rates are not as high. The current rate is between 3.5 and 4 percent, and very seldom does one exceed 5 percent. A good quality 1911 bond in today's market will yield about 5.5 percent, which shows that the 1915 Act bond is better accepted by the people who are investing their money in bonds.

The 1911 Assessment Act and 1913 Assessment Act and the 1911 and 1915 Bond Acts have been discussed. The 1911 Assessment Act may have either a 1911 or a 1915 Bond Act bond. The 1913 Assessments Act may also be supported by a 1911 or 1915 Act bond. The 1913 Assessment Act is a procedural act only and contains no bonds or bond provisions. At the time it was first enacted, the 1911 bond was the type required to be supplied with the 1913 procedures. Of course, when the 1915 Bond Act was approved, it became possible for either type of bond to be used in connection with the 1913 procedures. Using either procedure with a 1915 bond is one way in which a group of people at one end of town may, through a public agency, put in improvements and have the people at the other end of town lend their support to the improvement; and, of course, the reverse is also possible.

Assessment financing of off-site improvements is a means of providing long-term financing for improvements desired by the people in an area. This really is desirable, since each person does not have savings adequate to pay the assessments. Since all the people in a district have the opportunity either of paying cash for the improvements or of having assessment bonds issued against the value of their property to be combined with the others, this provides flexible means for several neighbors getting together and having desirable improvements made.

One of the limitations of the assessment acts is that they provide machinery for making only public improvements. Although this broad area includes landing strips, marinas, and other facilities, the improvements must be public to qualify. One of the main uses for these procedures and bond issues is subdivisions.

Use of Assessment Acts by Subdividers

The subdivider has found the assessment acts to be a ready source of money. He or she can go into a district and install curbs, gutters, streets, sidewalks, and other improvements; take back fifteen-year bonds that will draw up to 6 percent; obtain cash by selling them at a slight discount; and then go into another district and do the same thing over again. This method appears to be a fine way of financing off-site improvements, and it is, provided that the security, the value of the property, and the know-how are present. In some counties this method is used almost exclusively for subdivision work, which includes public work. The subdivider with, for example, 1,000 acres must install the sewage treatment plant, streets, curbs, and gutters, and he or she does not want to put the total cost against only one unit. He or she also wants to spread the cost over a long period. As a result, the assessment method is used. It is normally less expensive to subdivide this way than to use equity money or short-term loans. Although a discount is normally involved in the 1911 Assessment Act provisions, it is at least on a par with the expense of some commitment fees or loan fees charged by other lending institutions. Certainly the term is much more desirable.

The assessment procedure to be used would be decided by the builder on the basis of what is best for him or her and the development. The use of these procedures has advantages in connection with subdivisions, one of which is that the person putting in the improvements knows that he or she will receive all the money at least by the time the job is completed. If the work is being done with equity money, the subdivider may have to construct additional streets as the on-site improvements are constructed, and this means more expense to him or her. It also means that the accounts receivable will be tied up, possibly for a considerable time. The assessment procedure means that he or she will have cash available at a date no later than the time at which the work is completed. If the work is done under the 1913 Act, the money will be paid in progressions.

The public agency likes to see this type of financing because it can exercise more control over the work being done. It can control the money and the plans and specifications of the work being installed, and it can make inspections of the work as it progresses. Also, higher quality work is usually done because there is no particular squeeze such as could be assessed against the equity financing.

The method has some limitations, primarily limitations of time, since it takes time to set up the assessment proceedings. Time-consuming legal proceedings are necessary, in terms of both hearings and drawing of papers. Another limitation is that some work cannot be done under the assessment acts. Lots can be neither excavated nor filled under these acts, since this is private work. For example, a great deal of costly excavation and filling done in connection with the construction of the roads to a hillside lot is considered private work and is not eligible to be financed under an assessment act.

Another limitation arises when the builder is borrowing his or her financing to build the houses in the subdivision on which there are assessments, and there may or may not be a provision for a take-out loan. The lender, whether interim or take-out, does not like to see the prior liens upon the title report and sometimes will require that they be paid off before the construction loan is granted or at least before the take-out loan is consummated. If the lender does not require that the assessment bond be paid off, he or she will often penalize the property by this amount, thus affecting the amount of funds available to the builder and the purchaser through the loan.

The law has been changed so that assessment bonds can be allowed to go out for as long as twenty-five years. Lenders may look upon this type of lien with more approval if the relationship of the bond to the improvement is sound and if the purchaser of the property is sound.

When the lender requires the bond to be paid off, it is paid off in its full amount. Of course, the prepayment fee is 5 percent, which makes the financing cost high.

Role of the Bond Underwriter

The role of the bond underwriter is fairly simple: He or she is in business to buy and sell bonds to and from clients who want tax exemptions. The interest income from these bonds is exempt from both federal and California state income taxes.

These bonds are strong; therefore, even in the case of general obligation bonds, to underwrite and distribute these bonds the underwriter must go where the bonds are available. As a result, the underwriter deals with the contractor, the public agencies, the developers, and the real estate people. A good underwriter must be aware of all bond issues or potential bond issues that will be available, and it is desirable that the underwriter bid on all bond issues as they become available. The bids that the underwriters submit reflect primarily the investigation that has been made on the district, the property, the values of the property, the work to be done, the proposed lien, the subdivision, who is doing the subdivision, the ability of the subdivider, his or her ability to pay, and also his or her willingness to pay. In some instances the subdivider has used a corporate structure, has hidden behind the structure in case of difficulty, and had deliberately allowed the corporate structure to become bankrupt.

The location of the property, the probable success of the subdivision, and many other basic factors are normally considered at the time the loan is granted. After the information has been obtained it is analyzed in connection with the bond market and the possible future of the district, since in buying or underwriting a bond the future (up to fifteen years) is being supported by the bond. Often, rather than bidding on bonds when a district is known to be developing, the bond underwriter may negotiate for the bonds. When handled in this way, the bond issue is developed as agreed in the negotiations and never is bid by any underwriter. A bond underwriter may also work with an individual who is planning a development by meeting with the individual, the attorney, and the public agency to work out a plan or program for the development of the property and the subsequent sale of the bonds.

Public agencies often prefer to have the matter handled in this way, since they know that when the work has been completed the reputable investment broker will take over the bonds and pay off the indebtedness under a firm contract. This saves the public agency a great deal of difficulty, work, and concern about the final disposition of the bonds. Such a contract among the builder, the public agency, and the investment broker is a firm contract and can be used at the subdivider's bank as security for the interim financing of the off-site improvements.

Under this contract the investment broker is not a

broker, but a party to the contract. Upon delivery of the bonds by the contractor, the investment broker is bound under the terms of the contract to pay the contractor the agreed amount. This means of payment is under the 1911 Assessment Act. If it is under the 1915 Assessment Act, when the agency delivers the bonds to the investment broker, to fulfill the term of the contract the investment broker is obligated to pay to the public agency the agreed sums.

The assessment procedure is gaining favor in California, where growth and the need for funds have both been enormous, making it very challenging to find ways of financing this growth. The laws are constantly being changed to provide the machinery for such financing.

The FHA and Off-Site Improvements

The Housing and Urban Development Act of 1965 authorized the FHA to insure mortgages for land development. This authorization, enacted as Title X of the National Housing Act, is designed to help private enterprise to serve the needs of a rapidly expanding urban population by enabling private developers to purchase raw land and develop it, thus providing a steadier supply of improved building sites in an orderly and more economical manner.

The types of improvements that may be financed through the use of Title X include streets, water lines, water sources, sewer lines and sewage systems, curbs and gutters, sidewalks, storm drainage facilities, and other common public facilities such as clubhouses, swimming pools and facilities, and parking garages to be owned and maintained jointly by the property owners.

Title X is especially attractive to developers of more than 100 lots since smaller developments are more easily financed through conventional loans. The maximum loan that HUD-FHA will insure under Title X is 85 percent of the estimated value of the completed development; or the sum of 80 percent of the estimated value of the property as is, plus 90 percent of the cost of improvements, whichever is the smaller amount.

Title X has not been used too much for three reasons. First, very little is known about Title X. Second, it can take from one to three years from the time an application is made to the time the loan is made. Third, there is a very short payout time, two years.

QUESTIONS

1. Construction loans can become a problem if
   a. mechanics and materialmen are not paid
   b. the contractor does not have enough capital
   c. there is a material shortage
   d. all of the above

2. A notice of completion is a valid notice if
   a. the contractor signs the notice
   b. the notice is recorded before all work is completed
   c. the notice, when properly completed, is filed within ten days of completion
   d. all of the above

3. How long does the general contractor have to file a lien against the property in case of an invalid notice of completion?
   a. ninety days
   b. sixty days
   c. forty-five days
   d. thirty days

4. If there is a valid notice of completion, the general contractor has
   a. ninety days in which to file a lien against the property
   b. sixty days in which to file a lien against the property
   c. forty-five days in which to file a lien against the property
   d. thirty days in which to file a lien against the property

5. In order to have a first lien against the property in favor of the lender for a construction loan, the contractor may
   a. place survey stakes
   b. clear the lot
   c. have material delivered to the site
   d. none of the above

6. Funds for a construction loan are usually disbursed under several conditions. Which provides the least protection for the lender?
   a. payments made as each stage of completion is reached, usually four or five
   b. presentation of bills for labor and material with payment being made by the lender
   c. disbursement made by a builder's control where the control is owned by the contractor with his or her employees doing the disbursing
   d. voucher system

7. The lender can be sure that the improvements are constructed on the right property if
   a. the lot is checked by the owner
   b. the title company issues an endorsement to its policy to that effect
   c. the site is verified by the contractor
   d. the lender inspects the lot before construction starts

8. A lender should disburse funds for a construction loan only
   a. when the cost of improvements is more than the amount disbursed
   b. when the owner of the property okays the payment
   c. when a subcontractor requests payment
   d. none of the above

9. After a labor or material lien has been filed against a property on which a construction loan was made, the lien may be removed
   a. by payment of the debt by the owner and by recording a notice of satisfaction
   b. by payment of the debt by the bank and by recording a notice of satisfaction
   c. after a time if no sale or further action is taken by those filing the lien
   d. by all of the above

10. How long does a subcontractor have to file a lien if an invalid notice of completion, or no notice at all, is filed?
    a. ninety days from completion
    b. sixty days from completion
    c. forty-five days from completion
    d. thirty days from completion

11. The 1911 Assessment Act for bonded improvements provides for
    a. payment to the contractor as the work progresses
    b. payment when 50 percent of the work has been completed
    c. payment when 60 percent of the work has been completed
    d. payment in full when the work has been completed with no interim payment

12. Under the 1911 Assessment Act each parcel in the assessment district is
    a. assessed an equal amount
    b. assessed according to the benefit received from the improvement
    c. assessments are computed in the same way for all types of improvements
    d. all of the above

13. Under the Assessment Act of 1911 the financing is arranged by the
    a. contractor
    b. the county recorder
    c. the county administrator
    d. none of the above

14. Interest on the bonds secured by liens on the assessment district is
    a. billed by the treasurer of the public agency
    b. collected by the treasurer
    c. paid by the treasurer on surrender of the interest coupon by the bondholder
    d. all of the above

15. Under the 1911 Assessment Act
    a. there is a lien against each parcel for the amount of benefit it received
    b. the bond is not worthless just because an interest or principal payment is missed
    c. the property can be sold if the delinquency continues for a period of time.
    d. all of the above

16. Under the 1913 Assessment Act for bonded improvements
    a. as soon as the contract is let, the public agency starts trying to collect the amount assessed to each parcel from the owner
    b. the owners must pay cash when they are billed
    c. the owners must pay cash before the work is completed
    d. none of the above

17. Under the 1915 Bond Act, the security is
    a. each individual parcel
    b. the whole public agency
    c. certain areas within the public agency
    d. half of each individual parcel

18. Under the 1915 Bond Act
    a. the bondholder does not have recourse against any particular parcel of land
    b. the bondholder can identify the district against which the lien was created
    c. in case of delinquency, the treasurers of the issuing agency, whether it be city, county, or state, must levy a tax not to exceed 10 cents per $100 of assessed value against every parcel in the city, county, district, or state, not only in just the neighborhood in which the delinquency occurs
    d. all of the above

19. Under Title X of the National Housing Act, the following are some of the things that can be financed, except
    a. streets, water lines, water sources
    b. sewers, sewer lines
    c. storm drainage, club houses, swimming pools
    d. model homes

BIBLIOGRAPHY

Assessment Act of 1911, California State Printing Office.
Assessment Act of 1913, California State Printing Office.
United States Department of Housing and Urban Development, "Digest of Insurable Loans." Published by United States Department of Housing and Urban Development.

16

Income Tax Aspects of Real Estate Financing and Ownership

For many years investors have used real estate transactions and expenses incurred in connection with real estate operation as a source of tax shelter. In this chapter we shall consider some of the tax shelters available to an investor, along with some of the common pitfalls in the sale and purchase of real estate.

DEALER VERSUS INVESTOR

Real estate has always been considered a capital investment. Under proper circumstances it has been subject to the capital gains law as far as payment of income tax is concerned. In other words, under certain conditions it is necessary to pay income tax on only 40 percent of the profit enjoyed from the sale of real estate. However, when the investment in real estate ceases to be capital investment and becomes a stock in trade, the profit becomes subject to ordinary income tax.

The problem seems to be the determination of the point at which the purchase and subsequent sale of real estate cease to be an investment and become a stock in trade.

If a retired person's major source of income came from the purchase and sale of real estate, he or she might have difficulty convincing the Internal Revenue Service that one sale a year was a capital gains sale. On the other hand, a person receiving the major portion of his or her annual income from a source other than profit from sale of real estate might be able to sell two or three parcels a year and still benefit from the capital gains portion of the Internal Revenue Code. However, if such a person continues to succeed in this manner over a period of years, even this might be enough to deprive the individual of the benefits of the capital gains portion. The indefinite interpretation of the Code by the Internal Revenue Service can be a pitfall to the unwary real estate investor. It would be helpful if the law were as explicit regarding

real estate capital gains as it is regarding the purchase and sale of stocks and bonds.

An individual who does not list his or her vocation as stockbroker or bondbroker has the benefit of the capital gains provision, no matter how many stocks or bonds he or she buys in one year. Regardless of the amount of profit the individual makes from the sale and purchase of the stock and bonds, provided that he or she holds them for a certain minimum period before selling them, the interpretation is that he or she has made a capital investment and any gain he or she enjoys from the sale of this capital investment is subject to the capital gains portion of the Internal Revenue Code. The minimum period for which a capital asset must be owned to qualify for capital gains treatment is twelve months, increased from nine months for the year 1977 and from six months before that.

In general, real estate such as subdivided land, improved or unimproved, held for sale to the general public would not be eligible for capital gains treatment since the holder of such property would be considered a dealer. Such property may be qualified for capital gains treatment if the owners can show that (1) they are not dealers in real estate and do not hold any other land primarily for sale to others in the normal course of their business—the taint of dealership cannot be removed by selling or giving the property to a relative—and that they have not previously held subdivided land for sale to customers in the normal course of their business; (2) that they did not make major improvements to the real estate that increased the value of the lots sold; and (3) that they have held the land for five years or inherited it.

Property held as a person's residence, including a mobile home, a yacht, a single-family residence, or a condominium, would be eligible for capital gains treatment.

Unimproved real estate bought as an investment and held for longer than twelve months or longer for capital growth, producing no income, would be eligible for capital gains treatment.

Real estate held for the production of an income, such as an apartment house, a commercial building, or a ranch, would be considered eligible for capital gains treatment if held for the required period.

Real estate held and used in producing an income in the owner's trade, such as a factory building, a motel, an apartment building, or a commercial building in which the owner has his or her business, would be eligible for the capital gains tax approach.

It is important to understand which property is eligible for capital gains treatment and which is not, because the two are treated differently by the Internal Revenue Service. Ordinary income (wages, commissions, interest, business profit) is taxed on a sliding scale depending on the amount of income. The rate varies from 0 percent to 50 percent for an individual. If an asset is held for less than the required period (one year or less) before its sale at a profit, this is considered a short-term capital gain and treated as ordinary income. A capital asset held at least the required time (over one year) before its sale at a profit or loss is said to have produced a long-term capital gain or loss. Long-term capital gains or losses are treated differently from ordinary income. A long-term capital gain is offset against any long-term capital loss. If there is a net long-term capital loss, this loss can be deducted from ordinary income on a ratio of 1 for 2 up to a maximum of $3,000 in any one year. For example, a long-term capital gain loss of $7,500 is suffered in 1982. Using the ratio of $1 for every $2 loss, the amount deducted from ordinary income would be $3,000, assuming a normal income in excess of $3,000. There would be a carry-over of $750 ($7,500 − 6,000 = $1,500; $1,500 × 0.05 = $750). The carry-over can be deducted from ensuing returns until paid, but never more than $3,000 in any one year. In the case of a net long-term capital gain, 40 percent of the capital gain is included in the other taxable income. In this way the amount of tax on the long-term capital gain depends on the tax rate of the total income. Suppose the total income is such that the taxpayers find themselves in a 30 percent tax bracket. They would then be paying only a 12 percent tax on the long-term capital gain (0.40 × 0.30 = 0.12). The maximum that can be assessed is 20 percent. This would be the case if the taxpayers find themselves in a 50 percent or higher bracket. There is a second way of computing the tax on the long-term capital gain. The taxpayers can use the one that causes them to pay the least tax. The alternative method is to compute the amount of tax that is to be paid on the ordinary income less the long-term capital gain. Then multiply the 40 percent of the net long-term capital gain by 20 percent. The total tax is then computed by adding the two types of taxes together.

DEPRECIATION

Depreciation is one of the expenses of owning income-producing property that can be deducted from income for the purpose of income tax reporting. As far as the Internal Revenue Service is concerned, land does not depreciate; only the improvements on the land can be depreciated. (A person's residence may not be depreciated, however.)

If there is a second home that is rented part of the time and used by the owner part of the time, expenses and depreciation must be prorated to comply with the rules of the Internal Revenue Service. The IRS will not allow deductions in excess of the gross rental income if the owner personally uses the property more than fourteen days a year or 10 percent of the rental days, whichever is more.

For example, assume that a cabin is accessible only during June, July, August, and September. It is rented for two months and the owner uses it for the other two months. Since the cabin was not available for rent full time, it cannot be considered a business and cannot receive the tax exemptions available to a business. The exemptions allowed are prorated and limited to the amount taken as rental income. Let us say that the amount received for the two months' rental was $2,000. Property taxes amounted to $1,000; interest on the property loan was $600; and maintenance and utility costs were $1,000. Depreciation was computed at $900. The taxes and the interest would total $1,600. The Internal Revenue Service holds that this would have been an expense whether or not the cabin was rented; as such, it must come off the top of the $2,000 rental income. This leaves $400 to be allocated to the prorated expense shares. Because the property was rented only 50 percent of the time, only 50 percent of the expenses could be claimed. The allowable deduction for utilities and maintenance would be $500 and for depreciation $450. But the IRS does not allow deductions in excess of the allowed allocation of income. So the maximum deduction would be $400, the difference between $2,000 income and $1,600 taxes and interest expense. The additional $100 of the 50 percent of the total maintenance and utility expense would not be allowed, and none of the depreciation would be allowed.

The story would be different if the cabin had been bought as an income venture, available for rent during the four months and never used by the owners in excess of the fourteen days or 10 percent (in this case twelve days). Under these circumstances all expenses would be allowed because the cabin would be considered a business regardless of the vacancy ratio (50 percent). Time spent by the owner does not count toward the fourteen days if the majority of the time is spent in maintenance or repairs.

It is not necessary to report the deductions and rental income if the property is rented fewer than fifteen days a year.

Depreciable Property

Any property except land, or any improvement to property, that was bought for income is depreciable property. This would include structures on the land, orchards, vineyards, fruit and nut trees, sidewalks, curbs and gutters, swimming pools, additions to a building, and so forth.

Calculating Depreciation

The 1981 Tax Act rewrote the way in which depreciation on all personal and real property could be computed. There are three sections of the Act that make it easier for all those who have items that can be depreciated for tax purposes. First, the useful life of all property has been clearly stated and grouped into one of four classifications; three years, five years, ten years, and fifteen years. Under certain conditions it might be advantageous to extend the asset recovery cost over a longer term. Second, it is no longer necessary to estimate the salvage value of an asset. Third, the method of depreciation is automatically set by law according to the type of asset, although straight-line depreciation may be used instead of the fixed-acceleration method. These conditions all apply to property in 1981 and through 1984. It is possible that the Act will be extended beyond 1984.

The extra first-year depreciation will no longer be allowed for business equipment bought in 1981; however, in 1982, an immediate deduction up to $5,000 for purchase of business equipment by a direct charge to expense is allowed.

Up to the time of the enactment of the 1981 Tax Act, it was possible to use the component method of depreciation. Under this method each component of a building such as the roof, the furnace, the air conditioner, and so forth, could be depreciated at the rate allocated to its useful life. The component system can no longer be used; the depreciation must be on the whole building. However, if a substantial improvement is made to a building, it is possible to use either the straight-line depreciation or the accelerated cost recovery system, regardless of the system used on the original building. What constitutes substantial improvement? There are two guidelines: First, the improvements are made at least three years after the building was placed in service; second, the improvements that were made over the two-year period added to the capital account for the building, contributed at least 25 percent to the adjusted basis of the building (disregarding adjustments made for depreciation) as of the first day of that period. When the property is sold, the recapture of the depreciation taken under the accelerated cost recovery system is treated as ordinary income and that portion of recaptured depreciation that is attributed to straight-line depreciation is treated as a capital gain.

Reference has been made to accelerated cost recovery system and the straight-line depreciation system. Taxpayers may elect to use either one, depending on their situation. The straight-line system may be of benefit if they are just starting a business and do not want to show a loss. In the case of the straight-line system, the depreciation schedule may be made for thirty-five to forty-five years. The deductions remain constant over the life of the asset. Assume an asset is purchased at a cost of $10,000 and it is to be depreciated over ten years, the amount charged to depreciation would be $1,000 each year ($1/_{10} \times \$10,000 = \$1,000$). The same theory applies to a $200,000 duplex which is to be depreciated over thirty-five years. Under these circumstances the amount that would be charged to depreciation would be $5,714.29 ($1/_{35} \times \$200,000 = \$5,714.29$) each year.

The accelerated cost recovery system (ACRS) (see Table 16-1) is a combination of 175 percent declining balance system for the early years the asset is owned and the straight-line system in the later fifteen years of ownership, during which depreciation deductions are allowed. Any recapture of depreciation under the ACRS is treated as ordinary income.

Table 16-1 is used in the following way. Assume an apartment complex is purchased and put into the new owners' service in January 1982. The cost was $950,000. Assume that the new owners report on a calendar basis. The table shows that for the first year a depreciation (recapture) of 12 percent is allowed, and that for the fourth year the amount would be 8 percent ($950,000 \times 0.12 = \$114,000$ and $\$950,000 \times 0.08 = \$76,000$), and so on. If the owners should decide to use the straight-line method of recapture, the amount would be 1/15th of $950,000 or $63,333 each year for 15 years. However, if the property had been put into service in September, the amount of recapture for the first year would be only 4 percent and for the fourth year it would be 9 percent.

Depreciation recapture on the sale of an asset placed in service prior to July 1, 1981, is treated as ordinary income for tax purposes, whereas any recapture of depreciation on an asset placed in service after July 1, 1981, and depreciated by the straight-line system is treated as a capital gain.

When an asset is sold before a full year has expired, the total amount for that year is computed and one-twelfth of the amount is deducted for each month of the year the asset was not used.

TABLE 16-1   Real estate cost recovery rate. All real property qualifies for the fifteen-year write-off except for mobile homes and theme parks (ten-year write-off) and agricultural, horticultural, and petroleum storage structures (five-year write-off).

IF THE RECOVERY YEAR IS	PERCENTAGE RATE IS LISTED UNDER THE MONTH IN FIRST YEAR THE PROPERTY IS PLACED IN SERVICE											
	1ST	2ND	3RD	4TH	5TH	6TH	7TH	8TH	9TH	10TH	11TH	12TH
1	12	11	10	9	8	7	6	5	4	3	2	1
2	10	10	11	11	11	11	11	11	11	11	11	12
3	9	9	9	9	10	10	10	10	10	10	10	10
4	8	8	8	8	8	8	9	9	9	9	9	9
5	7	7	7	7	7	7	8	8	8	8	8	8
6	6	6	6	6	7	7	7	7	7	7	7	7
7	6	6	6	6	6	6	6	6	6	6	6	6
8	6	6	6	6	6	6	5	6	6	6	6	6
9	6	6	6	6	5	5	5	5	5	6	6	6
10	5	6	5	6	5	5	5	5	5	5	6	5
11	5	5	5	5	5	5	5	5	5	5	5	5
12	5	5	5	5	5	5	5	5	5	5	5	5
13	5	5	5	5	5	5	5	5	5	5	5	5
14	5	5	5	5	5	5	5	5	5	5	5	5
15	5	5	5	5	5	5	5	5	5	5	5	5
16	—	—	1	1	2	2	3	3	4	4	4	5

PERSONAL RESIDENCE

A personal residence does not provide as many tax shelters as income property, but there are a few that should not be overlooked. The first of these is the interest the owner pays on the note and deed of trust against his or her residence. The second is any uninsured casualty loss in excess of $100, and the third is ad valorem taxes paid. All of these expenses may be deducted from ordinary income.

Certain expenses that may be incurred against a personal residence cannot be deducted from ordinary income. These include the cost of electrical repairs, plumbing repairs, painting, and other normal repairs and maintenance. No deduction for depreciation is allowed.

Certain expenditures may be added to the base (acquisition) price of the residence, including the cost of building a patio, installing a swimming pool, fencing the property, landscaping the property, and making an addition to the home. A few repairs to the property may be added to the base price. Putting on a new roof is one of these expenses, as is any repair or maintenance such as painting and installing new fixtures in connection with preparing the property for sale, if it is done within ninety days of the sale of the property.

Losses that result from the sale of a personal residence are not deductible from ordinary income. If there is a long-term capital loss, it must be offset by being applied against long-term capital gains.

The income tax on a long-term capital gain from the sale of a personal residence may be deferred if another home is bought costing as much or more than the one sold. The new home must be bought or built and occupied within two years before or after the old house is sold. Although the tax on the profit is deferred, a complete record of the adjusted cost and the adjusted sales price must be kept during the time that no other home is bought after the final sale, and it is necessary to report the net capital gain enjoyed over the years. It will be necessary to report the net capital gain if more than twenty-four months pass between the sale of a personal home and the occupation of a new home.

The discussion above applies only to a principal residence. If two homes are owned, only one may be considered the principal residence. A home that is used for recreational purposes is sold for a capital gain, and the gain must be reported in the period the gain is made. If there is a loss it must be offset by a capital gain. Mobile homes and factory-built homes now qualify for the same treatment as stick-built homes.

Tax on Sale of Homes by Those over Fifty-five Years of Age

Capital gains tax may be avoided, if desired, by people fifty-five years old or older who sell their personal, principal residence if the gain is up to $125,000 and if the home is sold after July 20, 1981. Homes sold before that date have a forgiveness of only $100,000. Those who are under fifty-five years of age must defer paying tax if they buy or build another principal residence within the two-year period set forth by the regulations. There is no choice under these conditions, and it is mandatory that the tax be deferred; however, if no new home is bought or built and occupied within the two-year period, the gain must be declared and a tax paid. The same rules apply when the property is a duplex or an apartment building and one of the units is the owner's principal residence. That part of the profit attributable to the owner's residence is deferrable, and the balance must be paid in the tax return for the year of the sale.

In order to qualify for this preferential treatment, besides one of the sellers being fifty-five years of age or older, they must have owned the property for at least five years; they must have lived in the home for at least three of the last five years; and they must elect to avoid the tax. The three-year residency requirement need not be consecutive. For instance, the owners could have lived in the home for two years, lived elsewhere for two, and then lived in the home for one additional year. They would have owned the property for five years and would have lived in it for three years, thus qualifying for the special tax treatment. If the capital gain is $125,000 or less, there will be no capital gains tax. For example, assume that Mr. and Mrs. B were married for three years in 1934 and were able to buy a home for which they paid $3,500. They have owned the home and lived in it since that time. On August 28, 1981, they sold the home for $90,000. They have maintained the home very well; the bathroom was modernized in 1970, and the kitchen in 1971; central heat and air conditioning were installed in 1965. The adjusted cost basis because of the improvements was $11,500. The long-term capital gain was $78,500. Since this is less than $125,000, the capital gain tax was forgiven. This is a one time exemption. Any home purchased in the future will be subject to a deferred tax when sold.

If a widow and a widower who plan to marry each own a home, are both over fifty-five, and they plan to sell their homes and buy a new home, they should each sell their home before they are married so that both can qualify for the $125,000 exemption. If they sell the homes after they are married they are a new entity and are eligible for only one exemption.

Remember, a principal residence may be a house, a mobile or factory-built home, a boat, a trailer, a house boat, a cooperative apartment, or a condominium.

The exclusion may be combined with the deferred tax benefit. This can be helpful to those who want to get away from a large home and into a smaller home. The senior citizens are the ones who will find this section beneficial. As an example, consider Mr. and Mrs. John Hughes. He is sixty-seven and she is sixty-two. They bought a nice home when Ben, their son, was seven in 1955. The basis for their home is $25,000. In August of 1981, they decided to sell the home and buy a mobile home. In preparation for placing the home on the market, they had the exterior painted. They also had the kitchen, the master bathroom, and the master bedroom painted. All of this work was finished on September 15, 1981. The cost was $3,500. The home was sold on October 10, 1981, for $175,000, well within the ninety days allowed for deductions in preparing a house for sale. The taxable long-term capital gain would be computed as follows:

Selling price	$175,000
Less selling expenses	−$2,000
Amount realized	$173,000
Less basis of the home	−$25,000
Actual gain	$148,000
Amount realized	$173,000
Less fix-up costs	−$3,500
Net Profit	$144,500

Mr. and Mrs. Hughes elected to take the $125,000 exclusion in order not to pay capital gains on such a large amount, so computation would be done as follows:

Selling price	$175,000
Less selling expense	−$2,000
Adjusted selling price	$173,000
Less excluded gain	$125,000
Taxable income	$48,000

Now this amount may be deferred if, within two years, the Hughes family buys a home costing $48,000 or more. On November 11, 1981, Mr. and Mrs. Hughes purchased a mobile home at a cost of $64,500. At this point, the taxable income was deferred but, by adjusting the basis by the amount of the deferred capital gain, the cost basis became $16,500 ($64,500 − $48,000).

RENTING TO FAMILY

Since December 1981 the Internal Revenue Service has had to change its treatment for deductions made by owners of property rented to members of their family. Under the tax code of 1976, anyone who rented any type of real property to a relative, regardless of the amount charged, was considered to have made personal use of the property.

This made it impossible to make deductions normally available to owners of rental property. These would include repairs, maintenance, depreciation, and other legitimate costs. The 1981 family rental tax amendment has taken care of such problems as long as the property is rented at a fair market rate—the same rent or higher than that paid in the market for similar accommodations. There can be no substantial gift passed between the owner and the renter. If these conditions are met, then the property qualifies for all normal deductions. These regulations are retroactive to December 1975.

CASUAL RENTING

The pitfall in connection with casual renting is created by the following type of situation. A person—let us call him Mr. A—leaves an area and moves to another area without being able to sell his home before he leaves. Few people can afford to carry two homes or the expense of two homes at one time, so it is only natural that as soon as possible, Mr. A will rent the home he is not using, since he is unable to sell.

At the time of the move Mr. A fully intended to sell the home so that he could take the payment for his equity in that home and purchase a new home in the area to which he moved; however, not being able to sell the home, he in turn rented a home in the new location.

After a period of time he decides that he wishes to terminate his status as a renter; therefore, he raises enough money to purchase another home. This purchase becomes a completely new purchase. As soon as the new home is purchased the old house will be removed from the home classification and will be considered no longer a casual rental but a full-time rental subject to the usual deductions, such as repairs, insurance, commissions, and depreciation. There are certain items that must be considered as income in the year received such as, first and last month rent paid in advance, security deposit if there is no intent to refund it, payment for canceling a lease, and expenses (insurance and taxes) paid for the owner by the rentor. Assume next that a year and a half passes and Mr. A finally decides that it is too much effort to maintain the rental and that he had better sell the old house. When he sells the property he finds that his income from the sale cannot be used in connection with the purchase of his new home; instead, he must report the sale of this property as a completed transaction and must pay a capital gains tax upon it.

Since the Internal Revenue Service now considers the old home a rental property, he might have been able to exchange it for a rental property in the area more convenient to his supervision. This exchange, tax-deferred under Section 1031, would not be subject to income tax. (Exchanges are discussed later in the chapter.)

INSTALMENT SALE

If real property is sold in 1981 and one or more payments are made in later years, the sale *must* be reported as an *instalment sale,* unless an election is made not to use the benefits of the instalment sale. There must be a timely notice of such an election, usually before filing the current return (plus extensions) for the current year. This notice is recorded on Schedule D. Such an election is usually made when the taxpayers have a large long-term capital loss against which the long-term capital gain on the sale of the real property can be offset.

There are no longer any restrictions involving the amount that can be received in the year of the sale. Prior to 1981, payments in excess of 30 percent of the sale price invalidated the instalment contract as far as the IRS was concerned, and the tax on the profit of the sale became due in the year of the sale. Now any percentage of sales price can be taken in the year of the sale, and it will be treated as an instalment sale.

Three terms should be understood in connection with the proration of taxable gain each year: selling price, gross profit, and contract price. *Selling price* includes cash received from the buyer, the face value of the note, the note and deed of trust on the property being sold, and any existing note and deed of trust on the property, whether assumed by the buyer or not. *Gross profit* is the selling price less the adjusted basis of the property sold, less selling expenses such as broker's commission and legal expenses. *Contract price* is the selling price if the property is clear. If there is an existing note and deed of trust against the property, then the contract price is the selling price less the outstanding obligation.

EXCHANGES

Certain types of property, when exchanged, enable one party to the exchange to defer payment of the tax on the gain. If neither party realizes a gain there would be no tax. To be eligible for exchange treatment, like property must be exchanged for like property. The IRS has been liberal with its interpretation of like for like. Some examples might be (1) farm or ranch property for city property; (2) unimproved land for improved real estate; (3) store building for a rental house; (4) business property for a thirty-year or more leasehold in the same type of property. The property exchanged must have been for productive use or investment for property for productive use or investment. It cannot be for personal use, such as a family residence for rentals.

A tax-free exchange is not recommended if the exchange will result in a loss since it is not possible to deduct a loss in a tax-free exchange. If a loss is to result from a tax-free exchange, it is better to sell the property and buy the other property with the proceeds.

Since each party usually has a different equity in a property, something extra has to be given by one of the parties to the exchange. The Internal Revenue Service refers to this extra as *boot.* Boot may be given in the form of cash; a note and trust deed executed in favor of the other party; or personal property such as an automobile, a boat, stock, or anything else of value. Boot might also include the assumption of a larger note and deed of trust on the property.

The party trading up (the one who has to pay the boot) is not subject to tax at that time: the tax can be deferred if he or she so desires. The one who receives boot in any form must pay a tax on his or her capital gain.

To compute equities it is necessary to determine the market value and subtract the loan against the property from the market value. Let us consider Ms. A and Mr. B: A has a property valued at $35,000, with a loan of $25,000 against the property. Her equity is $35,000 − $25,000, or $10,000. B has a property valued at $55,000, but he has a loan against it for $30,000. His equity is $55,000 − $30,000, or $25,000. In an exchange A would have to give B boot in the amount of $15,000 ($25,000 − $10,000 = $15,000).

Since A had to pay B boot, any gain that she had from the exchange can be deferred. However, assume that B's book value on his property is $50,000. The exchange was based on a market value of $55,000. Under these conditions there would be a potential gain of $5,000, which he would have to report. For boot, B would have received cash in the amount of $15,000 and a note deed of trust relief in the amount of $5,000 ($30,000 − $25,000 = $5,000), or a total boot of $20,000. Since the potential gain was only $5,000, the balance would be returned to capital.

MULTIPARTY EXCHANGE

Exchanges between more than two parties can be quite involved, but under certain conditions can qualify for the partially tax-free exchange. Just as in the two-way exchange, anyone receiving boot is subject to tax on any gain. In many cases there is a mortgage on the property being exchanged. In this case the mortgage released is treated as boot, whether the other party takes the property subject to the mortgage or assumes the mortgage. Consider the following example. Mr. A has a small commercial building, which is valued at $150,000 and on which there is a $130,000 mortgage. He wants to exchange it for Ms. B's building, which is valued at $155,000 and which has a mortgage of $120,000, for $5,000 in cash. B wants cash for her equity, though, and is not interested in a trade. Thus the broker finds Mr. C, who is interested in A's property. C agrees to buy B's property by paying B cash for her equity—$35,000—and by assuming the mortgage. This is one part of the transaction and should be treated separately. Now that the sale is complete, C can exchange his new property for A's property under the original exchange terms proposed.

For what Mr. A received see the table below. However, the actual gain is taxed only up to the amount of the boot, which, in this example is $130,000 (amount of the mortgage on the property traded) − $120,000 (amount of the mortgage assumed on Mr. C's property) + $5,000 cash = $15,000.

A slight variation would be for Mr. A and Mr. C to exchange under the following arrangement: B buys A's old property from C. An additional variation would be A owns a lot that B wants to buy. A refuses to sell but would agree to an exchange on another lot if B would buy that lot and make certain improvements on the lot. B buys the lot, makes the improvements, and the exchange is made. Remember each leg of the transaction must be a separate and complete transaction.

RETENTION OF USE OF PROPERTY

There are times when the tax shelter to be found in the sale of property and leaseback of that property can be of benefit to a taxpayer. The amount of rental that can be charged for the use of property under lease is often greater than the amount allowed as depreciation. Of course, this would reduce the amount of normal income and consequently the tax that the taxpayer would have to pay. Another benefit that accrues under these circumstances is that the taxpayer is able to replace capital that has been in fixed asset with cash or a current asset that can benefit the business. This allows him or her to increase inventory, discount accounts payable, and invest in leasehold improvements necessary to carry on his or her operation properly.

An understanding of leases is necessary in connection with real estate financing of property on which there is a lease.

CHARACTERISTICS OF LEASES AND LEASEHOLDS

A lease is a contract between a *lessor* (owner) and a *lessee* (tenant) whereby the lessor agrees to turn over to the lessee the right to use land, improvements, or both in return for rent or other considerations. The lease will

| $155,000 (Present value of Mr. C's property) | + | $5,000 (Cash) | + | $130,000 (Mortgage on property traded) | = | $290,000 |
| $290,000 (Amount Mr. A received) | − | $150,000 (Adjusted base of building traded) | − | $120,000 (Mortgage assumed by Mr. A on Mr. C's property) | = | $20,000 |

also stipulate the term of the occupancy and the conditions under which the occupancy may be enjoyed by the lessee. It creates an estate for years for the lessee and is personal property of the lessee. Any improvements made to the property by the lessee become his or her personal property.

The leasehold is the lessee's interest in the real estate arising from his or her right to use the property under the terms of the lease. Any improvement made under the terms of the leasehold are called leasehold improvements and do not accrue to the real property unless the terms of the lease specify that the leasehold improvements are to become part of the real property at the termination of the lease.

Leases are usually classified as either *short-term* or *long-term*. The short-term lease is usually one in which the agreement is entered into for a period of five years or less and whose terms may be set forth in either little or great detail. A long-term lease is usually one in which the agreement runs for a period of six years or more. The terms of such a lease are usually set forth in great detail in legally correct and complete form. Under a long-term lease the tenant usually desires or is required to spend considerable money for maintenance, remodeling, and, in some cases, construction.

Leases can be further classified by the responsibility that the lessee assumes in maintaining the property. A *net* lease is one in which the lessor pays for maintenance and taxes. In a *net net* lease the lessee agrees to pay some, but not all, of the maintenance, taxes, and insurance; when the terms are *net net net,* the lessee agrees to pay all maintenance, all taxes, all insurance, and so forth. The rent received under a net net net lease becomes net income to the lessor; however, such payment made by the lessee must be reported as income by the lessor to the IRS.

Leases are also classified by the manner in which payment is to be made to the lessor. A *fixed rate* lease provides for the same periodic payment throughout the term of the lease. The *percentage* lease provides that a certain percentage of the lessee's gross sales will be the amount required for the periodic rent payment. This lease will usually provide that there shall be a minimum monthly rate, although sometimes the lease will call for a straight percentage of the gross sales, without a minimum. In either event, this type of lease serves the purpose of making the landlord or lessor a partner in the business, and as the business improves the landlord's income automatically increases.

The *graduated* lease provides for a flat rent that will be stepped up or stepped down after an initial period of occupancy by the lessee. This type of lease, particularly when the lease includes a step-up clause, is beneficial to the tenant who is just getting a start in business; it provides a low rate of rent during the initial period and, as business improves, the lease can call for additional payment.

A good example of a step-up lease would be one that provided for a rent of $250 per month for the first year, $350 for the second year, $450 for the third through fifth years, and $500 after the fifth year. It is possible for a percentage of the gross sales to be attached to such a step-up lease, using the designated base as a minimum from which to work.

The step-down graduated lease, the opposite of the step-up lease, can be used when it is evident that the shopping district is moving away from the area in which the property is located; therefore, the lessee can expect to do decreasing business and can demand when the lease is drawn that it provide for a stepdown in the rent as business deteriorates.

The *revaluation* lease is another effort on the part of the lessor to be sure that he or she receives maximum rent from his or her property over the term of the lease. It provides for a periodic review of the rent based on the revaluation of the property, with the rent to be a certain percentage of that valuation. The percentage of income is previously designated in the lease. The revaluation lease usually provides that the lessor and the lessee will each appoint an appraiser to appraise the property. After the appraisals have been made, the lessee and lessor confer, and if they are unable to come to a friendly understanding of value from the two figures, an umpire is appointed by the two appraisers and the lessee and lessor agree to stand by his or her decision.

Another type of lease, the *index* lease, is also an attempt by the lessor to protect himself or herself against the future. The rent of the property is tied to an index, possibly the cost of living index. The index is reviewed periodically and any increase or decrease is reflected in the rent that the lessee must pay.

Every type of lease should contain several provisions. It should identify the property and also the parties to the lease. If the parties so desire, it should provide for a renewal of the lease. There should be specific information concerning maintenance, the improvements, and replacement of the improvements in case of destruction. It should provide for the disposition of any improvements made to the property by the lessee and should specify the ownership of the improvements at the termination of the lease. It should designate the rents, payments, time of payment, insurances that are to be carried, the rights of the parties in case of forfeitures, the right to sublease if so desired, the rights of the lessee in case of condemnation proceedings, and many other items upon which disagreement could possibly occur. Such a document is very complex and should be drawn by competent attorneys.

In California, a lease should be recorded if it is for a term longer than one year. It must provide specific dates for the commencement and for the termination of the lease.

Leases may not run for longer than ninety-nine years on city or town lots in California, or for longer than fifty-one years on agricultural lands. Leases drawn for the maximum term may provide for options to renew.

When there are a deed of trust and lease on the same property, the document recorded first takes precedence. For instance, if there is a lease on a piece of property and a loan is obtained at a later date that is secured by a deed of trust recorded subsequent to the lease, the lease has prior rights over the deed of trust. Should it later become necessary for the beneficiary of the deed of trust to foreclose the deed of trust, he or she may do so. However, since the lease was recorded first, it will be necessary for him or her to observe the dictates of the lease after the title has been obtained through foreclosure. Should the deed of trust be recorded first and the lease be recorded subsequently, the deed of trust has prior rights and at the time of foreclosure the property is vested in the name of the beneficiary under the deed of trust, the rights of the lessee are terminated, and it will be necessary for him or her to establish a new lease with the beneficiary or to vacate the premises.

In some instances, when the lease has been recorded first and it is desirable for the lessee to allow the owner to borrow against the property, the lessee may subordinate his or her rights under the lease and upon recording of the subordination agreement, the trust deed will take precedence over the lease. Should it become necessary for the beneficiary to foreclose, the lessee will lose rights under the terms of the lease. The situation could occur with a construction loan, should the lessee desire improvements to the property that the lessor is willing to furnish but cannot finance because of the prior recording of the lease.

SIGNIFICANCE OF LEASING IN REAL ESTATE FINANCE

A strong lease is of great importance to the lender who contemplates making a loan on income property or on proposed income property. If the applicant has leases from very strong organizations such as F. W. Woolworth, Montgomery Ward, J. C. Penney Company, Pacific Telephone and Telegraph, and others of this caliber, his or her flow of income is of the highest quality and can be safely used by the lender in determining a capitalized value of the property. On the other hand, if the lease is from a small local organization that is just starting, it does not lend any particular value to the property because there is no assurance that the organization will remain in business during the period and term of the lease.

It is doubtful whether the lending organization would be willing to make a real estate loan where the leases are of the latter class. It is easy to see, therefore, that a strong lease adds to the valuation of the property and consequently helps to influence the lender toward making a loan that will benefit the owner. Of course, the lender will want to see the lease and have his or her legal department check all aspects of it to be sure that it gives the desired protection.

In some instances, leasing can be an alternative to financing. Often a benefit accrues to the lessee who is able to lease rather than finance. In financing the construction or purchase of property, it is always necessary to have a certain amount of equity, which immediately ties up capital into a term asset. Although it is possible to borrow on short term from banks for inventory purchases and to discount accounts receivable, these funds always have to be repaid within a short period of time, which leaves the assets fairly well frozen in term assets over a period of time. With earnings that can accrue from guidance line financing, it is possible to build up the current asset portion of the statement;[1] however, this process is lengthy and expensive, in that interest must be paid on the funds used.

By leasing rather than investing in capital term assets, the businessperson has all the money used in the investment immediately available as cash, thus allowing him or her to carry out the mechandising program. The lessee whose only right in the real estate property is the leasehold may decide that he or she wants to do additional building or improving. Sometimes this is done by obtaining a mortgage secured loan with the leasehold and buildings as security if the buildings are leasehold improvements. The mortgagee will have a junior position on the leasehold mortgage and will insist on certain protections, since the construction of any additional building on the property adds to the interest of the lessor. The mortgagee will look to the lessor for protection. In turn, the lessor will request that he or she receive notice before any action is taken to cancel the lease on account of breach of lease, so that the mortgagee can assume the position of lessee should he or she so desire.

It is very difficult to obtain financing for improvements on reappraisal leaseholds, since most mortgagees feel that any appreciation in land value should be to the benefit of the lessor instead of the lessee. The shorter the term of the lease, the harder it is for the lessee to obtain financing for improvements. Most mortgagees, in making a loan on a leasehold, prefer that the lessee have an

---

[1] A guidance line is the amount a person can borrow. It is an amount that a lender sets, after analyzing a statement, as a top unsecured loan.

option for purchase at a price not too much in excess of the value of the land. The lessee might also choose to issue first mortgage leasehold bonds against interest in the leasehold and in the improvements that are his or hers. Although these bonds are termed first mortgage, they are actually not on the real property but on the leasehold, as indicated, and should it become necessary for the underlying deed of trust or mortgage to be foreclosed, the bonds could become valueless.

In some instances, particularly when there is a straight lease at a nominal figure and the property has become very valuable, the lease itself could have acquired considerable value that, if the lease has adequate time to run, might provide sufficient value against which the lessee could borrow. For instance, assume that in 1933 a commercial building was leased for ninety-nine years at a flat rate of $6,000 per year. Today, because of the economic growth of the area in which this property is located, the building should be bringing rent (economic rent) of $50,000 a year. This means that the lease has a value of $44,000 per year, and since the lease has until 2032 to run, it would probably have sufficient value so that a loan could be obtained against the lease and leasehold alone.

Most institutional lenders do not like to make loans on leaseholds with less than fifty years to run. Banks in California are not allowed to make a loan unless the lease runs at least ten years beyond the loan maturity.

Just as there can be an advantage to leasing rather than financing, there can also be an advantage to selling the property but retaining the use of the property. This practice, commonly called *sale and leaseback,* provides working capital as well as the same benefits provided by ownership.

VALUATION OF LEASES AND LEASEHOLDS

Before any loan can be made against any right, the value of that right must be known so that the loan will not exceed the value of that right, and normally the loan will be a certain percentage of the value. Both the lessor and the lessee have an interest in a lease, and both interests have a value, and it is possible for them to sell that value as well as to borrow against it. The lessor's interest is valued by computing the present value (present worth) of a series of payments over a period of time and adding to it the present value of the reversionary interest in the improvements at the termination of the lease. (See Table 16-2.)

As an example, assume that the lessor has a lease with ten years to run on which annual payments are $10,000, and that the present normal interest is 6 percent. From a "table for present value of $1 per year" we find that at

TABLE 16-2   Present value of one dollar

| | FUTURE RETURN | |
| | SINGLE | ANNUITY |
Year	Sum	
1.	0.943397	0.9434
2.	0.889997	1.8334
3.	0.893620	2.6730
4.	0.792095	3.4651
5.	0.747260	4.2123
6.	0.704963	4.9173
7.	0.665059	5.5823
8.	0.627415	6.2098
9.	0.591901	6.8016
10.	0.558398	7.3600
11.	0.526790	7.8868

6 percent for ten years the factor is 7.360, which means that the present value of an annually recurring $1 per year payment with a yield of 6 percent is $7.36. Therefore, with an annual payment of $10,000 the present value of the rent for ten years at $10,000 per year would be $73,600; or, to put it another way, $73,600 placed on deposit today at 6 percent will equal $100,000 ten years from now.

In the above example, assume a building which will have a depreciated value of $20,000 at the time the property reverts to the lessor. This means that the lessor has a reversionary interest in this building of $20,000 ten years from now. By locating in the table the present value of the single payment of $1 at a future date, again using the 6 percent interest for ten years, we find that the factor is .558395. This factor is the present value of $1 ten years from now. Multiplying it by the $20,000 value we find that the present worth of the reversionary interest of $20,000 is $11,167.90. Therefore, the lessor's interest at the present time is $73,600 plus $11,167.90, or $84,767.90.

The lessee's interest also has a value, which consists of the present value of the excess of the economic rent (or rent to sublessee) over the contract rent, plus the present value of the improvements made for the period of the lease, plus the present value of any settlement with the lessor at the lease termination concerning the usable improvements, if any. To use the previous example, add one ingredient, the present economic rent. Assume that the present economic rent is $40,000, which means that the lessee has the difference between $10,000 contract rent and $40,000 economic rent, or $30,000, as a valid asset.

From the same table of the present worth of $1 per year for ten years at 6 percent, we find the factor is still 7.360. Multiplying 7.360 by $30,000 gives the present worth of the $30,000 a year for ten years as $220,800. Assume that the $40,000 improvement has been depreciated to $20,000, which therefore is the present value of the leasehold improvements that have been made and depreciated. If there is no agreement for a reimbursement for the leasehold improvements that revert to the owner, the lessee's interest would be valued at $240,800. However, assume that the lessor has agreed to pay $5,000 for the improvements when they revert to him or her, which causes the lessee's interest to be valued at $245,800.

When the values of the interests are known and the lending organization has determined that it will make a loan against these interests, it will ask for the lease and will check to see what percentage of the property is covered by the lease. The lessor may lease any portion of the fee; he or she does not have to lease the total fee to any one individual.

Under certain circumstances five or six leases could cover the same property, but different fees. For instance, an owner could make a lease to the Weyerhauser Lumber Company for the timber and thereby create a timber lease. At the same time the owner could make a lease to the Natomas Gold Mining Company for the mineral rights to the property. He might even lease grazing rights to the H. Moffat Meat Company, and a commercial building site to John Doe for construction. Therefore, it is important to know what percentage of the property is covered by leases.

The next important item for the lender to know is the financial responsibility of the lessee and the credit reputation that he or she enjoys. The lender will then inspect the lease to see what type of lease is involved, whether a fixed rental, a percentage rental with a minimum or a flat rent, or a rent tied to an index. Unless there are minimums, it is difficult to appraise and evaluate percentage leases or leases tied to indexes, since it is impossible to be 100 percent accurate in predicting what will happen in the future.

The lender will then be sure that there is an understanding concerning the arrangements for repairs, taxes, and other expenses. Then he or she will check various items that contribute to the safety of the lessor, who is, of course, the loan applicant in this case. Some of these items follow:

1. There must be a clear and specific term to the lease and a clear and specific description of the property.
2. The right to assign, subject to the landlord's approval, should be included.
3. There should be a percentage rental with a minimum specified, as a hedge for inflation.
4. The lease should provide for proper use of advertising signs, observance of restrictions, and so on.
5. The lease should contain covenants against liens.

6. There should be a specific understanding established regarding liabilities for damage and destruction.
7. The lease should provide for proper insurance and maintenance on a net net basis, or in some instances on a net net net basis.
8. The lease should provide for a sublet of the property upon default, insolvency, or bankruptcy of the tenant.
9. There should be guarantees for payments, insurance, and taxes.
10. The profits from subletting in case of default, insolvency, or bankruptcy of the tenant should go to the owner.

SALE AND LEASEBACK TRANSACTIONS

Sale and leaseback transactions have already been mentioned in connection with financing and taxes. This type of transaction is a sale in which, for consideration, title passes from a company or individual making use of an asset to an investor, who thereupon leases the asset back to the original owner, who continues to use the property as before.

The principal sources of purchase funds for such transactions normally come from large insurance companies, or from tax-free institutions such as universities, pension funds, union funds, or churches.

The type of person looking for such a transaction is usually an owner, the depreciated base value of whose property is considerably lower than the market value. By selling his or her property and leasing it back, he or she can take advantage of the capital gain over the difference between the depreciated value and the market value. Other cases might involve owners who need to raise working capital for their business, or a new purchaser or an old owner who is improving the property, finds no way to obtain the additional financing necessary to complete the improvements, and therefore sells a portion of the land to obtain funds to complete the buildings. Leases given on a sale and leaseback are usually long-term leases with options for renewal. The leases are usually on a net net basis. Typical users are industrial firms, retail establishments, and office building owners.

The sale and leaseback can be an advantage to the seller-lessee if it is the only source of working capital available. In any instance it is probably the cheapest source, since it is not borrowed money and the rent paid provides an additional deduction from the earnings of the company, which in turn means a lower income tax payment. Certainly the balance sheet position will be improved, since leases are not considered a liability and in the transaction a fixed asset becomes a current asset. Other advantages to the seller are that if the book value of the asset was low, the gain on the sale is subject only to capital gains tax, and that the rent expenditures are partly offset by the usually small annual depreciation deductions before the sale.

One of the principal advantages to the purchaser-lessor is that such a transaction will yield a higher rate than a first trust deed. The yield will usually be between 1 and 1.5 percent higher; of course, if there is any appreciation in the property through inflation or location becoming more desirable, the owner of the property benefits. Another advantage for the purchaser-lessor is that there are often substantial reversionary interests. The improvements as they revert to the owner-lessor at the termination of the lease may be more valuable than the depreciated value indicates, since the lessee must depreciate his or her leasehold improvements within the term of the lease. Finally, such a transaction is usually a long-term investment that is not subject to prepayment or refinancing with any other institution. Under these conditions the advantages to all parties concerned under the sale and leaseback program are clear.

QUESTIONS

1. Individuals selling their home may claim a capital gains exemption up to $125,000 if
    a. they are fifty-five years of age or over
    b. they have lived in the home 3 of the past five years
    c. one of the owners claimed the deduction before he or she married his or her present spouse
    d. all of the above
2. The depreciation of an apartment building may be computed if placed in service after July 1, 1981, by the
    a. 200 percent declining-balance method
    b. the sum-of-the-digits method
    c. 150 percent declining-balance method
    d. straight-line method
3. An apartment building may be depreciated, if placed in service after July 1, 1981, over a period of
    a. ten years
    b. fifteen years
    c. twenty years
    d. twenty-five years
4. If a capital gains tax is to be deferred when a home is sold, another must be bought or constructed of equal or more value within
    a. one year from the sale of the old home
    b. eighteen months from the sale of the old home
    c. two years from the sale of the old home, and it must be lived in within that time

d. two years where a contract must be let for construction of a new home which must be reasonably close to completion
5. In order to benefit from an instalment sale of property,
    a. the Internal Revenue Service must be informed of the election to treat the sale as an instalment sale
    b. no more than 30 percent of the sale price can be received in one year
    c. there must be one or more payments made in a later year or years
    d. the property cannot be a farm
6. If it is desired to use the benefit of deferring capital gain tax from the sale of a personal residence,
    a. the sale must be reported to the IRS
    b. all records of basis price and improvements must be kept and used to determine a basis for the new home
    c. and if a loss is suffered on the sale of the home, the loss cannot be deducted but it can be deducted from the next basis
    d. all of the above
7. A second home can be a source of deduction against reportable income if
    a. it is rented at least two weeks each year
    b. it is used for one month by the owners and rented for two months of a four-month potential rental period
    c. the owner uses it for two weeks and it has a three-month rental period
    d. it is available for rent for sixty days, if the owner uses it for two weeks, and if the owner's father and mother use it for two weeks
8. The maximum the IRS can collect on a capital gain when the long-term capital is treated separately from ordinary income is
    a. 60 percent
    b. 50 percent
    c. 40 percent
    d. 30 percent
9. Net operating loss can now be carried over for
    a. seven years
    b. nine years
    c. ten years
    d. fifteen years

BIBLIOGRAPHY

LASSER, J. K., *"J. K. Lasser's Your Income Tax,"* 1982 edition, New York: Simon and Schuster, 1982.

17

Financing Shopping Centers and Office, Special-Purpose, Industrial, and Apartment Buildings

Income properties such as shopping centers and office buildings have been developed to their present income-producing potential only during the twentieth century. Unlike longer-established properties such as farms and small commercial buildings, shopping centers and office buildings are products of modern technology. Therefore, the development and the financing of these properties must consider the changing technology of our society. Trends in business and shopping practices will have a significant effect, either advantageous or disadvantageous, upon the investment value of such properties.

The modern office building has been made possible by technological advancements in the building arts and by the practice of business and professional people of carrying on their vocations from offices located in a central area of the city. The shopping center has also enjoyed the beneficial effects of new industrial and construction techniques that make economically possible large centralized shopping districts that offer shoppers increased protection from the elements. The urban sprawl has created the need for shopping facilities away from the established centers of cities. There is no reason to believe that technological changes and population movement will cease and thereby create a static environment for these types of real estate development. If anything, the degree and rate of change in these areas (which directly affect the utility derived from a developed parcel of land and hence its value) will increase.

ATTRACTIVE INVESTMENTS

Shopping centers and office buildings have been attractive outlets for investment capital over a considerable period. There have also been periods of general investor disenchantment with office buildings, as the 1930s. Occasionally the incorrect location of an office building, resulting in a pitifully small return or in a loss, has caused limited distress with the investment among a small group

of investors directly interested in the property. Generally, however, when a reasonably favorable economic climate exists, investments in such properties by investors exercising knowledgeable discretion prove to be as attractive as other investment opportunities. In some cases real estate investments have greater potential and desirability for investors because of a higher return on capital and a greater safety factor than corporation equity and debt security.

A greater yield is often obtainable from real estate because of the opportunity for creating a leveraged investment, a concept perfected in the field of business corporations. In the corporate situation a relatively small investment in common stock represented the ownership equity in the entire business, and also the voting control. The size of the investment controlled was considerable, mainly because of the devices of issuing nonvoting classes of common stock or preferred stock and various classes of debt instruments known as bonds. Control was maintained for as long as there was sufficient income to pay the dividends due on the preferred stock and interest to the bondholders. Default upon these obligations—especially in the form of failing to pay interest due—could lead to loss of control of the enterprise by conditional voting power (held by these other security interests) coming into existence or by foreclosure upon the physical assets of the firm to satisfy the debt owed to the bondholders.

Actually with the increasing degree of regulation of corporate enterprises and restraints on the credit available for individual margin purchasers of stock, real estate has been the highest-leveraged investment possible in this country. This situation is due to the absence of the restrictive government controls that apply to corporate security acquisitions and to the willingness of mortgage lenders to lend a relatively high proportion of the appraised value of improved real estate such as shopping centers and office buildings. In the 1950s there was a return to substantial junior financing to provide the financial structure for properties such as hotels, some office buildings, and shopping centers. With this increase in the proportion of debt to equity in such properties a more precarious position has developed for the equity interest, since the interest charges that must be met on the increased debt are greater. The sale of properties financed in such a manner has often been necessary when property could not provide the operational profits needed to meet the interest obligations. There have also been a few formal foreclosures of such properties. These experiences are a reminder that a highly leveraged instrument will produce a higher yield on the equity investment—but that the great dangers of falling property income are very real.

In addition to the advantage of high yield through leverage, equity investments in these properties have benefited from (1) steadily appreciating value as the utility of well-located properties increases due to increased use; (2) a hedge against the steady inflation that has continued since 1946; and (3) protection for income derived from the investment because of provisions of the federal income tax law providing for certain deductions and favorable tax treatment of the profit produced upon the sale of the property. Of course, there may be a greater risk potential in the case of a specific property so that the higher return on the investment is necessary. Nevertheless, these particular aspects of real estate investments are very attractive to many investors.

ATTRACTIONS FOR CREDITORS

Financing investments in such properties is a two-way street. The owners usually need and want loans that are large in terms of their relationship to the appraised value of the property. Such lending also holds certain advantages for the institution making the loans. The most obvious advantages are (1) reduced cost of establishing and servicing the loans, since the lender is dealing with a relatively small number of separate borrowers; (2) the debtors may be more dependable on the whole than in the typical residential loan situation; (3) the loans are amply secured by valuable property that will usually increase in value; (4) the loans are established for relatively long terms, thus minimizing the problem of having loans prepaid and creating the necessity of finding a suitable outlet for the funds a short time after placing them; (5) there is no particular public relations problem in foreclosing on a property owned by a corporate borrower; (6) the loans may produce a higher than average yield over their term because of less favorable application of the usury laws to corporate borrowers, reduced costs of loan servicing, and comparatively few defaults; and (7) with these types of investment properties, the lender, in negotiating for a loan, can arrange for participative financing—for example, in addition to a relatively high interest rate or possibly a variable interest rate, the lender may obtain a percentage of the developer-borrower's ownership interest in the property, which entitles the lender to a proportionate share in any profits when the property is sold and possibly to a percentage of annual gross or net rents received from tenants.

DANGERS TO CREDITORS

Although creditors have many reasons for considering such loans to be comparatively attractive, some dangers are peculiar to them. One is the placement of a substantial amount of money in one location in a specific economic environment. This all-or-nothing aspect of the loan can be disturbing because the success of the loan is to a marked degree connected with the economic conditions of the city or region. If the general economic climate deteriorates, the volume of business activity can be reduced and circumstances can be created leading to diminishing property values and ultimately to default. Also, there is the problem of competition from other shopping centers and office buildings, which can reduce the profitability of a property. The lender is peculiarly dependent upon the ability of the business people leasing space to compete and to earn a reasonable profit from their enterprises. The management of an office building or shopping center is crucial, for if it is poor, the shopping center as a unit loses business and the office building has increased vacancies because of the undesirability of the property as a business address. Both these managerial failings can imperil, to a certain degree, the security and profitability of such a loan.

To some extent large corporate lenders apparently feel that they have offset the perils inherent in such loans by requiring extensive research into the feasibility of a shopping center or office building before they undertake such a financial commitment. Opinions vary on the real worth of these studies made by real estate consultants, but no evidence indicates that they are falling from disfavor with large institutional lenders. If anything, the incidence of requiring such a study as a condition precedent to obtaining such a loan is increasing.

CATEGORIES OF INCOME PROPERTY

So-called income property is usually valuable because it provides a site for the conduct of business or professional activities. These are activities distinguished from endeavors connected directly with the land or its products, such as farming, mining, and lumbering. Income properties (in a broad sense) include (1) commercial buildings, for example, office buildings, stores, and hotels; (2) industrial buildings (essentially structures in which processing or assembly of material is carried on); (3) residential buildings, including single-family houses and apartments; and (4) special-purpose properties that, although usually connected with the business of buying and selling something, may be used for professional or industrial undertakings.

SOURCES ON FINANCING FOR SHOPPING CENTERS AND OFFICE BUILDINGS

Two types of capital will typically be found in shopping center and office building properties: the ownership (or equity) interest and the creditor (or debt) interest. The equity interest will control the property (except as its use and disposition are limited by the police power of the state and by the interests of the creditor established by the terms of the debt contract and the trust deed or mortgage), in the sense that the owners of such an interest will manage the property. The debt interest plays a passive role in the management of the property until those events occur that will allow and usually compel the creditors to participate in the operation of the property to protect the capital lent to the owners of the property. Institutional lenders such as commercial banks and life insurance companies have furnished most of the long-term mortgage funds for shopping centers. Such loans have also been available from mutual savings banks and real estate investment trusts.

The actual arrangement between the equity and debt interests in any one property is based upon the contracts that create the relationship. These contracts are usually negotiated and therefore the rights and duties of creditor and debtor often vary in different properties. There are some legal limitations upon these contracts. Most of these limitations apply to the lender, because loans for these types of property are made by institutional lenders. Therefore, when we later consider the terms of such loans we will have to consider the limitations imposed upon the lending capacities of these institutions by the government that chartered them and that may regulate their activities as well. The old adversity of the interests of the negotiating parties in the contract situation exists in this loan situation. In addition to the legal limitations that exist for institutional lenders, there are economic limitations that will govern the terms of most prudent loans. These economic facts of life concern the income derived from such properties, the value of the security, and the ratio of equity and debt interests to the estimated value of the improved property in its completed and most profitable state.

Clearly, the type of lending discussed here is based upon an examination, analysis, and prediction of the future for a specific property development. As with all predictions, there is a large possibility of error. The present state of the art of making predictions based upon the methodology employed in most economic feasibility studies should be described as empirical; that is, such analyses involve a considerable exercise of judgment to determine the probability of success for a proposed development. No truly scientific method exists for exact determination of the effect of future developments upon the financial success of a particular investment. However, since this empirical method is the only one available, the individuals who make the decisions on such loans must be cognizant of the present state of economic analysis for such investments.

THE NATURE AND CHARACTERISTICS OF SHOPPING CENTERS

A shopping center is a community of about ten or more retail stores, usually contiguous, with free parking provided on the premises, and with the entire property controlled by one owner. There are small neighborhood shopping centers, medium-sized "community" centers, and large (often fifty or more stores) regional developments.

Why were there no suburban shopping centers in 1900? These types of retail outlets were not needed because not enough people lived far enough from established stores or had the economic ability or personal inclination to patronize shopping centers and make them economically feasible. If a shopping center had been opened up ten miles south of the San Francisco city limits in 1900, it probably would have been a commercial ghost town.

What has happened as the twentieth century has progressed to make the shopping center virtually a necessity for a substantial number of Americans? The reasons for the successful development of shopping centers in growth areas such as California are (1) virtual elimination of family economic self-sufficiency; (2) the movement of large numbers of people to the suburbs, resulting in their being inclined to shop at retail outlets established between their homes and the central section of the city; (3) greater mobility of all citizens (especially housewives) due to the ready availability of the automobile; (4) a substantial increase in disposable income for most families; (5) extreme congestion in many downtown areas; (6) increasing expense of parking cars downtown; (7) stricter enforcement of parking laws; (8) increasing cost of public transportation service that seems continually to decline in quality; (9) an increase in population; (10) greater ability of merchants to create a desire for goods, resulting in more purchases being made; (11) the evolution of shopping into a type of family recreation in the pleasant surroundings of modern stores; and (12) the managerial and marketing backwardness of many down-town merchants who did not adapt to the trends toward modern stores, liberal credit arrangements, improved customer relations, and a self-service approach to retail sales (especially in grocery stores).

The chain stores were often in the forefront of the retailing revolution that started in the 1940s. Thus, the chain store outlet has often been a major element in shopping centers because of the corporation's financial strength, type of merchandise sold, and customer loyalty. In fact, in some situations the virtual necessity of having a chain store tenant in a shopping center has put such concerns in a formidable bargaining position with the owners of such centers.

The neighborhood shopping center is small (ten to fifteen stores), usually providing essential goods and ser-vices to the residents of the immediate area. Because such a collection of shops does not constitute a complete array of stores and services for family needs, it is not truly a shopping center. Nevertheless, this term is used to designate those commercial operations that draw their clientele from residents living within a mile or from peo-ple who pass through the area on some other business.

This type of center will usually have a key tenant (not necessarily a highly rated national concern) such as a supermarket, accompanied by such establishments as shoe repair and dry cleaning shops, beauty and barber shops, a drugstore, a hardware store, and possibly a small res-taurant. The adjoining trade area for such a development should contain anywhere from 5,000 to 10,000 people able and inclined to make purchases from center mer-chants.

If the market research study for such a shopping center looks favorable in terms of the present market, its growth potential, and absence of present or future competition, loans are often available from institutional sources. Be-cause of the comparative ease of constructing a com-peting neighborhood shopping center, only loans in com-paratively small ratio to appraised value may be obtained for this type of enterprise.

The community shopping center will be larger in area (twenty to thirty-five acres), have a greater variety of tenants, and have from three to six major tenants. There should be a minimum of 30,000 people within a four-mile radius who will be inclined to patronize the mer-chants located here. This center should be located on two major traffic arteries and near a freeway if at all possible. The major tenants are important because they bring to the center the benefit of previous advertising plus an appealing selection of merchandise, which will add to the competitive capability of this center. It is usually desirable to have each of these key tenants operate one of the following establishments: (1) junior department store; (2) drugstore; (3) supermarket; and (4) variety store. Banks and savings and loan associations are not typical sources of loans for this type of commercial undertaking. Most loans for this class of shopping centers are made by insurance companies.

The regional center is the largest, most complex type of shopping center. It is therefore costlier and possibly riskier to develop than others, but it also promises the likelihood of a greater return on invested capital. Ideally there should be at least 300,000 people within a six-mile radius of the center, no comparable competition within six to fifteen miles, and no immediate prospect for such competition to be developed before the merchants in the center are established and have a substantial following. It is desirable for a center to be located where the number of economically viable families is increasing, to maxi-mize the possibility of increasing business volume in the future. It is vital to such an extensive retail development that there be at least one major department store as a tenant. (There will typically be at least four major tenants operating compatible businesses.) In addition to this es-sential major tenant, such a center will usually have com-plementary stores such as a supermarket, drugstore, men's clothing store, ladies' apparel shop, miscellaneous spe-cialty shops (bookstores, jewelry stores), restaurants, hardware stores, a bank, and possibly a new car outlet. This type of shopping center should be located on major traffic arteries (freeways if possible) and should be de-signed and situated to provide a maximum of inviting exposure to passers-by. To the extent that these trans-portation and design factors are missing, a regional shop-ping center will be operating under a handicap that causes a loss of revenue.

During the last several years some new, more spe-cialized types of shopping centers have been developed and built at appropriate locations in various sections of the United States. These innovative shopping centers are called (1) discount centers, (2) high fashion centers, (3) automotive centers, (4) town and country centers, (5) small shopping center malls, and (6) specialty shopping centers. The significant aspects of financing these shop-ping centers are basically comparable to the essentials involved in making prudent mortgage loans on neigh-borhood, community, and regional shopping centers. The particular distinctive characteristics of these more spe-cialized shopping centers are discussed below.

Discount centers.   Discount centers offer a com-plete line of merchandise and approximate a building area of 100,000 square feet. Of this total space a chain drug store will be a typical tenant, along with a 20,000-to 30,000-square-foot supermarket. Much of the remain-ing space is devoted to a chain merchandising retail operation such as K Mart, Zayre, Korvette, Gemco, or Woolco. The discount center caters mainly to lower-middle-income families.

High fashion centers.   National name stores such as Saks Fifth Avenue, Lord and Taylor, and Nieman Marcus have located major department stores in high-income suburban locations outside cities such as Atlanta, Georgia; the District of Columbia; and San Francisco.

Automotive centers.   A collection of new car dealers, typically located just off a major highway in a suburban location, establishes this type of specialized shopping center. The merchants in such a center are really competing against each other, but they collaborate to the extent that they are willing to become associated in such a common enterprise on the basis of the principle of cumulative attraction, which maximizes the number of potential purchasers drawn to such a location and thereby enables the individual car dealers to sell more merchandise than they would if they were located in distinctly separate locations. Besides new car dealers, such shopping centers can successfully include merchants who sell goods related to automobiles such as accessories, tires, and batteries, and also finance companies, banks, and restaurants.

Town and country centers.   Depending upon their size, these suburban shopping centers are either neighborhood or community centers, with the distinctive characteristic of being rustic open malls in design, construction, and building configuration. They are typically located in affluent suburbs.

Small shopping center malls.   Mini-malls are centers of 150,000 to 300,000 square feet of retail space, enclosed to protect customers from rain or snow and extreme cold or heat. These shopping centers are most successful in suburban areas ten to fifteen miles from regional shopping centers. Independent merchants are attracted to these shopping centers by reduced competition from large department stores, lower rents due to reduced common area maintenance expenses, and a reduced period for construction of the center before tenants can occupy it.

Specialty shopping centers.   The specialty shopping center is decidedly smaller than a regional center and made up exclusively of shops that deal in one type of merchandise. The specialization of the individual tenant is typically limited to one type of food, fashion, or goods. The successful shopping center of this type will entertain the shoppers, be smaller than a regional center, and consist mainly of a series of small restaurants and shops.

Determining Investment Feasibility

The determination of the economic potential of a site for a shopping center can be done at various times by a developer. Exactly when this vital task is accomplished will depend upon the method used to acquire the land. Land can be obtained by direct purchase, option-to-purchase agreement, or ground lease.

The ground lease (usually for a term of fifty to ninety-nine years) is not often used in California because land suitable for shopping centers is not so scarce as to put land owners in a position in which it seems advisable or possible to enter into such an arrangement. (In Hawaii ground leases are common due to the shortage of usable land, which allows the owners to require use on their own terms; the value potential of the land for the next 100 years seems to be great because of the forces of supply and demand operating on land in the area.) The option agreement has been used often since shopping centers began to be developed in quantity after World War II. This arrangement has the distinct advantage to the developer of giving him or her, for a certain period (usually six months to a year), the exclusive right to purchase a given parcel of land while he or she proceeds to plan, analyze, and locate the necessary tenants for the proposed project. As land owners have become sophisticated and as land suitable for this type of development has become more scarce, the chances of a developer's negotiating an option contract have lessened considerably.

Starting in the 1960s most land for shopping centers was purchased outright by the developer, usually in a typical land purchase transaction with the seller financing a portion of the sale price by taking back a promissory note secured by a trust deed. For a number of years it was almost standard procedure for the contract of sale to provide for a maximum down payment of 29 percent of the purchase price and for the deed of trust to be subordinated to any subsequent financing necessary to improve the property. The result was that the seller did not receive the entire sale price until two to ten years after the date of sale and had to hold a junior trust deed securing the debt for a substantial portion of this period. This very convenient buyer's financing arrangement was replaced in many sections of California by stricter terms. The down payment may now be larger, the term of the loan shorter, and a blanket trust deed arrangement may replace the subordination clause, thus requiring the payment of substantial sums of money by the developer if the land title is to be cleared so that a first lien can be obtained upon it by interim or permanent lenders. The effect of the evolution in land sales contracts in California has been to increase the amount of equity capital needed to bring the plans for a shopping center to fruition.

A complete economic survey for a regional shopping center will usually determine (1) the present and probable future size of the trading area; (2) present and probable future population of the area; (3) composition of the population as to sex, marital status, family size, and age; (4) purchasing power of family units; (5) consumer purchasing habits and patterns; (6) capacity of existing retail facilities to meet present and future demand; (7) number of customers not now shopping in the area who could be attracted to the planned shopping center; (8) present and future competition; (9) accessibility of the center; (10) existing zoning laws (to determine the feasibility of obtaining the usual necessary rezoning and the "zoning out" of future competition); and (11) future plans for public road development to make sure that the possibilities of condemnation or of roadways splitting the developed shopping center are minimal.

The suitability of a location for shopping center development will be affected by: (1) ease of accessibility from freeways and lesser roads; (2) service furnished by public transportation; (3) amount and convenience of parking space; (4) visibility of the shopping center from adjoining traffic arteries; (5) location in relation to residential areas, and to commercial, industrial, and government buildings; and (6) the quantity of relatively nearby land available for development of competing regional centers.

The design and layout of the buildings composing the center, which is vital to maximizing the degree of success enjoyed by the development, is the function of the architect commissioned to design and plan the center. This specialist should be knowledgeable and experienced in such a task so as to require no supervision. Basic to a good shopping center is minimization of the walking distance from cars to the stores. Thus, most successful shopping centers are II-, L-, or U-shaped. The U and II shapes are commonly used for regional centers, whereas the L shape has particular utility in the community development.

The buildings and surrounding grounds should be esthetically pleasing. The most suitable type of architecture depends upon the cultural background of the people. The design of a shopping center pleasing to residents of Lake Forest, Illinois, might not appeal to many residents of the San Fernando Valley, California. To maximize potential, the center should be designed to produce a unified effect, but should nevertheless be expandable in a logical, esthetic fashion if such a need arises.

Crucial to the layout of a sizable shopping center is engineering the parking area so as to maximize the ease of traffic flow, thereby keeping congestion to a minimum. Ease of parking and efficient traffic flow are two outstanding reasons why shopping centers appeal to increasing numbers of Americans. Therefore, any mistakes creating unnecessary inconvenience and delay detract from the desirability of the development.

The creation of the proper tenant mix is one of the most important decisions to be made by the developer. This aspect of a shopping center is the financial heart of the enterprise because to the extent that the tenants are financially strong and skilled merchandisers a volume business will be done at the location. An additional reason for obtaining leases with at least some nationally known and established retailers is that lenders usually require some tenants of this caliber before they will even begin to consider lending funds for such a project.

The tenant mix should therefore be established with due regard to (1) the requirements of the major permanent lender as to reputation for retailing skill and financial resources; (2) a logical combination of stores that complement each other by providing different and needed merchandise; (3) customer loyalty already held by both local and national retailers; and (4) nonmerchandising businesses that will attract people to the center, such as motion picture theaters and bowling alleys.

The acceptability of tenants (especially major ones) to the permanent lender is of crucial importance. These tenants must be able and willing to sign relatively long-term leases, twenty to twenty-five years, for example, possibly with renewal options. This type of arrangement with major tenants is essential because most lenders will not make loans for a term in excess of the lease terms of major tenants. If these lease terms are shorter than the term of the loan, the financial burden assumed by the borrower may become overwhelming because the periodic loan payments due toward the end of the loan period may be in excess of the profit derived from the retailing operations of the center. Therefore, the feasibility of many large shopping centers is dependent upon the developer's ability to negotiate a suitable lease with a major retailing concern.

The estimation of the value of a shopping center can be accomplished in various ways. Determining value according to the replacement cost of the developed property is an accepted appraisal approach. In practice, this approach has limited utility in that it will establish only the upper limit of value for the property. (Here the assumption is made that a parcel of land with comparable utility can be acquired and improved within a reasonable time so that the income derived from the present location can also be obtained from this other site.) The comparative approach to value (also known as the market approach) can sometimes be used in determining the value of a shopping center. For this approach to result in a useful value estimate, two or more such establishments would have to be located in similar places, have essentially the same advantages and disadvantages, be of the same age, and have comparable gross receipts and expenses incident to their operations. Although such comparable properties may be found when the property being appraised is a neighborhood or community shopping center, the likelihood of this occurring in the regional shopping center situation is remote. Because of the problems connected with the use of these two approaches to appraising a shopping center, they are often of little use. The value of an existing shopping center (especially a regional one) is usually determined by capitalizing the net income derived from the investment in the property. A capitalization rate (which for a successful center should be between 10 and 17 percent of the owner's equity investment) is applied to the net income returned from the operation of the property. The capitalization rate is derived from the market (assuming that there are comparable shopping centers from which this figure can be developed) or by "building" a capitalization rate from economic elements that bear upon the value of the kind of property being analyzed.

Terms of lending.   In developing a shopping center the owner must usually obtain a loan to cover the cost of constructing the improvements and a long-term loan that will be placed after the improvements have been built. Ordinarily a commercial bank will make the construction loan, which is later replaced by a long-term loan—typically from an insurance company. The construction loan is the interim loan; the long-term financing is the take-out loan.

Before a long term loan commitment will be made (often by a national insurance company), the lender will have to be satisfied that (1) a reasonable need exists for such a shopping center; (2) good plans and specifications have been developed; (3) no significant changes in construction will be made without its consent; (4) appropriate leases have been entered into with dependable tenants for the required term of years; (5) experienced people are planning, designing, constructing, and managing the property; and (6) the developer (whether a general partnership, limited partnership, trust, corporation, or joint venture) has adequate capital (equity) to bring the venture to fruition. These loans, when made, usually contain a prepayment penalty clause to assure their remaining in effect for the agreed term.

Certain requirements have been established, either by law or by business practice, governing the terms and specific requirements for such loans. Some of the guidelines are based upon economic standards for measuring such factors as earning capacity, potential, and value in terms of the highest possible value that can be achieved in the property.

In the mid-1970s $50,000 per acre was not an excessive price for land to be developed into a shopping center of at least average profit potential. The Urban Land Institute determined that the sales volume of the three classes of shopping centers was $50 per square foot for regional centers, $60 per square foot for neighborhood centers, and $49 per square foot for community centers. Thus, shopping centers presumably produced an acceptable, "successful" return for their owners.

Statutes enacted by various state legislatures control to a considerable extent the loans and the terms of such commitments as can be made by various financial institutions. These statutory regulations typically regulate the percentage of the lender's assets that can be lent in any one category, where the loans can be made, the period of the loan, interest charged, and whether it is to be a term or amortized loan.

There is a slight possibility that various types of trust or pension plans could be a source of borrowed capital for a shopping center. Limitations on the size of the loan compared with the appraised value of the property and on what type of security is required would be established by relevant state legislation and charter documents establishing the fund. If no such formal legal limitations are created, the fiduciary responsibility of trustees or directors will probably limit the loan ratio to 60 to 70 percent of the appraised value.

Savings and loan associations can make some commercial loans. Because of restrictions relating to the percentage of total assets that can be loaned on any one property, only the largest such associations would be of any use to the regional shopping center developer. In these types of loans the usual conservative ratio of loan to appraised value will prevail.

A corporation may be formed for the purpose of developing a shopping center, selling bonds to make up the difference between the equity capital raised through the sale of stock and the total cost of developing the property. This source of financing is unusual today because the shopping center corporation would seldom be widely known and a substantial number of prospective bond purchasers still have memories of the real estate bond debacles of the 1920s and 1930s.

There is a direct relationship between the financing of shopping centers and the terms of the leases employed in renting the available space. The lease will establish the long-term value of the security by providing for its successful development as an integrated center, and will also provide for the payment of a minimal rental by all tenants that will cover the cost of the debt service incurred under the loan. These leases are negotiated between the parties. Chain stores usually pay the lowest rent for space, whereas the smaller, more specialized establishments pay the highest rates. It is not uncommon for smaller merchants to occupy about one-third of the space in a shopping center while paying one-half of the total rent collected. On a volume-of-space basis, therefore, the larger tenants apparently get more for their money.

The provisions of shopping center leases that protect the integrity of the property and that are nonfinancial cover such items as (1) renewal options; (2) parking privileges (ordinarily there should be three square feet of parking space for every square foot of store space); (3) responsibility for maintenance of parking space; (4) lease cancellation by tenants in case of condemnation or building destruction; (5) landlord's responsibility to the tenant in case of destruction of the building; (6) restrictive covenants limiting the number of competing businesses (very important to both the tenants and the developer as a means of increasing business volume and profits); (7) the obligation of tenants to pay increases in property taxes levied against the owner; (8) responsibility of the lessor to maintain the center; (9) creation, financial support, and operation of a merchants' association to promote the center; (10) artificial lighting of the center; (11) accounting procedures to be followed by tenants; (12) business hours to be observed by the merchants; and (13) terms of tenancy. Any particular lease could possibly contain more provisions, but this list includes most of the vital ones.

After a little more than ten years of shopping center construction proceeding apace, the competition suddenly became greater than ever before. Not only was there competition from other shopping centers but also from rejuvenated downtown areas and other business communities. By the middle of the 1980s there were approximately 13,000 shopping centers of all classes in the United States. The cost of deluxe regional centers had increased to more than $15,000,000. This type of commercial enterprise has become, in large part, reserved for the large, experienced, dependable concerns with the necessary equity capital and with influence that facilitated the acquisition and development of land, the leasing of space to essential tenants, and the borrowing from the big institutional lenders of the millions of dollars necessary.

OFFICE BUILDINGS

Nature and Characteristics

The office building is a phenomenon peculiar to a highly industrialized society. This type of building is needed because managers and professional people need conve-niently located space in which to carry on activities that do not involve the manufacturing, warehousing, or selling of goods with the buyer taking immediate delivery from an inventory maintained on the premises.

Development and Operation

The industrial and economic growth of this country was reflected in the urbanization of most of the population. Accompanying this trend toward population concentration was the location of office space from which were conducted the high-level financial, managerial, marketing, and professional activities necessary for the operation of the increasing number of private concerns engaged in productive activities. The functions of top-level corporate management came to be carried on in office buildings located in a few cities. New York City is unquestionably the "corporate headquarters" of the nation. Plants and other operational facilities of American corporations may be located thousands of miles from New York, but their higher echelons of managerial personnel conduct the firms' businesses from New York headquarters. The same pattern of moving the offices of corporate managers from the plant location has resulted in office space being needed for such personnel in cities such as San Francisco, Los Angeles, Seattle, Chicago, Dallas, and Houston.

The space needs of American business constitute a prime source of the demand for office buildings. The demand from this section of the economy is obviously connected with the general economic climate of the nation and with what business leaders think it will be in the future. The Great Depression was responsible to a substantial degree for the high vacancy factor in office buildings in major commercial centers of the country. When office buildings are located in cities that do not have any national or regional headquarter characteristics, tenants renting office space are usually from the local area. This means that any faltering of the prime basic industries whose personnel have offices in the community can cause vacancy problems in existing structures and magnify the effect of overbuilding if that condition exists or is about to occur in the city.

The future of the office building as a reasonably profitable investment is dependent upon many factors and conditions over which a building manager can exercise little control. Those elements that can mean the life or death of office buildings are very diverse and in some cases completely unforeseeable. Some of the factors affecting the value of office buildings are (1) technological developments that render existing buildings obsolete; (2) increase in traffic congestion; (3) decisions by branches of government to relocate buildings such as courthouses, city halls, and general office buildings; (4) a federal urban renewal program's increasing or decreasing the supply of space; (5) the structural quality of other office buildings; (6) personal idiosyncracies such as where a corporation president's spouse wants to live or whether the president wants to walk to work; (7) whether the architectural design of a building is "forward looking" so that it does not suffer from obvious obsolescence; and (8) the ability of a firm to automate so that activities formerly performed by large numbers of people are now done by machines.

There have been essentially four eras in the American experience with the office building. The first started in the closing years of the nineteenth century and continued until the end of World War I. The second ran from 1920 through 1945. The third commenced in 1946, developed into a boom in cities such as New York, and continued on into the 1960s. The fourth commenced at the beginning of the 1980s.

Buildings constructed in the 1880s, 1890s, and early 1900s were usually ornate masonary structures. The use of structural steel and elevators gradually increased in office building construction, making technologically possible giants such as the Empire State and Pan-American buildings. Rapid improvement in building materials and their uses has created a very real danger of building value loss due to declining income as strikingly different, more attractive competing space makes the structures obsolete. Such obsolescence is found in the architecture and facility aspects of office buildings. The obsolescence of structures built before 1919 could not be readily cured; therefore, most of these structures have been razed, or if still in existence, they are not really competitive in today's market. The buildings constructed during the following eras either are already modern in design and equipment or the effect of obsolescence can be substantially reduced by modernization of facilities and architectural design. This more hopeful situation is true for most buildings built during and after the 1920s because they have a basically modern structure, that is, steel frame construction, standard room spacing, and space for modern heating, air conditioning, lighting, and elevator facilities. Therefore, while it is economically feasible to wreck structures put up during the first era of office construction, buildings erected in the 1920s and subsequent periods will continue to be competitive and economically useful until the year 2000 if periodically modernized.

Today in the United States, office buildings can be classified in one of three ways according to ownership and rental program. These categories are (1) the corporate occupancy—occupied by corporations as tenants; (2) the single occupancy—occupied primarily by one major firm that owns or controls the structure; and (3) the multiple occupancy—occupied by a relatively wide range of tenants.

Theoretically, any of these types of buildings can exist in any location. However, since the great increase in office building construction in many cities has now continued for a decade or more, there has been, because of the great risk attached to additional construction, a distinct narrowing of the possibilities as to the type of building that will be built. In the 1950s and 1960s, most office buildings were built by and for one major firm, which occupies a substantial portion of the space in the building. This occupant usually has an attractive business reputation—therefore proximity to it certainly is not unfavorable to tenants—and in addition possesses the financial strength and credit rating necessary to obtain the loans for the construction of the building. Thus, most of the recently built major office buildings have been sponsored by insurance companies, banks, or other major corporations. Examples of such building sponsorship are the Chase Manhattan Bank Building and the Seagram Building in New York City; the Crocker National Bank Building in San Diego, California; the Alcoa Building in Pittsburgh, Pennsylvania; and the First National Bank Building in Dallas, Texas.

The multiple occupancy building is most often a speculative undertaking, erected by a concern that is primarily in the office building construction and rental business. Since this firm does not carry on any other business, it does not occupy much space in the building. In terms of financing, leasing, and managing, such a structure may pose more and greater problems than the corporate or single occupancy structure.

Only a very small margin of error need occur in locating, designing, financing, leasing, or managing an office building for very serious adverse consequences to result. This is because the investment is large and immovable, and because the operating expenses in even the most valuable properties take up a substantial portion of gross income. Many of these expenses also have the aggravating characteristic of continuing at substantially the same high level whether or not the space is all rented at a price high enough to produce a satisfactory return. This very real and great danger connected with the promotion or ownership of such buildings explains why lenders typically require extensive study of all aspects bearing upon the probable success of such a venture.

Categories of Funds Needed

Two broad classes of investment capital are needed in the office building situation: equity funds and creditor funds. The equity capital is often provided by a corporation that will be the major occupant in the structure, and that will own and be responsible for its management. Obtaining the necessary money usually poses no problem in this situation. Equity funds may also be raised by the sale of common stock in a corporation established primarily for the purpose of owning and operating one or more buildings.

A single building may be financed as to the necessary equity interest through a syndicate (usually organized as a limited partnership or business trust) whereby ownership interests in the equity are sold in varying amounts to prospective owners.

Creditor's funds. Three identifiable phases of financing office buildings have occurred in the United States.

The first such buildings that had to be financed were owned largely by the major occupant who, because of the large equity in the property, was able to obtain a single first mortgage loan for the balance of the needed funds. Many concerns that needed a considerable amount of office space erected their own buildings. These structures were often deliberately built so as to provide, at the time of erection, space in excess of the owner's immediate needs. The excess space was rented out to reduce the cost to the owner of occupying the building. This type of financial arrangement for office building ownership is still common today.

During the 1920s office buildings began to be built by firms whose only business was building ownership and management. The basic financial structure for such buildings was relatively simple. A corporation would be established (for example the 10004 South La Salle Street Corporation), which would sell common stock in an amount sufficient to cover a minor part of the investment in the property. It would then proceed to sell corporate bonds that were secured by a first mortgage on the improved property and supervised by a corporate trustee for the benefit of the bondholders. The amount of money raised through the sale of bonds was sufficient to cover most of the cost of the property. This arrangement usually resulted in a highly leveraged real estate investment, and the great dangers typically connected with leverage investments existed in this incorporated approach to office building ownership. During the early 1930s the gross income of many of these properties declined drastically and the net income did likewise—disappearing altogether in many cases. The result of this situation was default by the building corporations on the property taxes due, and, of course, on the interest payments owed to the bondholders. These properties had often been overcapitalized. Even without a major depression these investments may not have had the income-earning potential necessary to carry the heavy debt structure that had been built up. These corporations typically went through bankruptcy and reorganization of their financial structures. The result of such procedures was that the original common stock interest was eliminated and the bondholders' securities were replaced with equity securities, thereby eliminating the fixed obligations originally created to fi-

nance the enterprise. After many of these building corporations had been reorganized, they still did not earn enough profit to pay dividends to the shareholders. The ultimate result was that many investors holding these bonds received no return on their investment, in addition to having their bonds replaced with shares of stock having little or no immediate value.

Most multiple occupancy office buildings erected in major business centers such as New York City have followed a third identifiable pattern of financing. In this financial scheme, (1) an amount of capital is raised sufficient to purchase outright a parcel of land convenient for an office building; (2) an architect is engaged to develop several designs and plans that can be tested as to economic feasibility for actual construction; (3) a substantial amount of space is tentatively leased to one or more triple A (financially rated) tenants; (4) banks are approached, with these tenant commitments, for the necessary construction loans; (5) attempts are made, meanwhile, to lease space in the building to more tenants acceptable to the insurance companies with which negotiations are being conducted for the permanent loan on the property. This final loan is actually made on the basis of the property value established and assured by the relatively long-term leases to prime tenants. Commercial banks did not actually commit themselves to making construction loans until the long-term take-out loan commitment had been obtained by the developer-borrower from another lender such as a life insurance company. (Briefly, from 1968 through 1970 some office building developers borrowed construction funds from banks before leasing 70 percent of the building space to triple A–rated tenants and before obtaining take-out loans. They were not able to obtain the take-out loans before the construction loans were repaid. They could not achieve a large enough tenant occupancy rate in the building to justify a long-term take-out loan. As a result, the construction loan went into default—setting the stage for the ultimate foreclosure on the land and office building by the construction lender.)

After 1945 syndicated ownership of office buildings and other properties became common. In this plan limited partners or trust beneficiaries purchased ownership interests in these business organizations, thereby providing the equity capital. The firm would then arrange for the large loan necessary to acquire the property on a permanent basis. The result was a highly leveraged operation with all the dangers incident to this method of creating an opportunity for possible high yield on the owner's investment. In the early 1960s a number of these syndicates were incorporated and began to raise equity money through public offerings of securities. In time a number of the real estate corporations resulting from this incorporation movement experienced considerable financial difficulty and embarrassment because of the deaths of key managers, excessive valuation of property for financing purposes, a decline in net profits due to management mistakes, and a more competitive real estate market.

Investment Worth

The investment worth of an office building is a relevant consideration when planning to build such a structure and certainly when appraising an existing property for loan or sale purposes. The approach to these difficult problems is still basically an empirical one involving considerable use of judgment. A cursory exploration of the unknowns relevant to office building value will explode any myths of the exactness and correctness of decision making in this area. For example, no one knows for sure (1) how large the potential market for space is in any community; (2) how much competing space will be erected after it is decided to commence construction; (3) whether the location of the building will represent the highest and best use of the land for the estimated economic life of the improvement; (4) exactly when to build an office building; (5) what architectural design will be superior in the sense of remaining current for the longest possible time, thus postponing obsolescence; and (6) whether the market will enable the owners of a building to rent space at the minimal price they must have if the investment is to earn a reasonable return. (Many office building managers feel that a net return of 8 percent on the owner's equity is minimal, and, considering the possible risks incident to such an investment, probably still too small.)

The terms of lending for office buildings can vary with the results of negotiation between the two parties. The financial strength of the borrower, the condition of the money market, and the probable success of the venture will all affect the terms of a specific loan. Disregarding special circumstances, the basic provisions of such a loan are usually (1) a maximum term of up to twenty-five years (with ten to twenty years common); (2) loans up to 75 percent of property value; (3) amortization of principal over the life of the loan; (4) payments made quarterly; (5) when the building is well located, being

ing because tenants will pay for its enhancement of their business or professional standing and their income; (8) parking and auxiliary facilities needed by building occupants that are either in the building or close by; (9) lack of available nearby space upon which competing buildings could be built;[2] (10) an attractive, mechanically efficient, well-managed structure.[3]

The investment worth of an office building is dependent primarily upon the net income stream derived from the property during its economic life. This investment life-blood is obtained and assured by the leases negotiated with tenants. To the extent that the lease does its job effectively in providing this income, the value of the building is secured and possibly enhanced. Such leases are in writing and all contain certain basic elements. Clauses in these leases that are peculiar to office building space rental pertain to (1) lessor paying utilities and maintaining the space; (2) relatively long terms desired, that is, at least five to ten years; (3) rental adjustment, so that when basic operational costs increase during the lease term the tenant bears this burden and thus protects the net income derived from the lease; and (4) fees to be paid for extras furnished by the lessor, such as dividing spaces, interior decorating, and special floor coverings.

The manager usually attempts to lease to tenants who will be personally and professionally compatible and who will enhance rather than detract from the general reputation of a building. This requirement also means that the manager will make every attempt to lease to firms of some prestige and of known financial strength.

The management of a major office building must be carefully selected so that only competent managers handle the property. This is vital because managers' mistakes can be legally locked into a long-term lease or can destroy the reputation of the building in the eyes of potential lessees, resulting in a leasing handicap that may last for years, all the while reducing gross and net incomes. Some of the most important functions of the property manager are his or her responsibilities to (1) analyze the space market so that the vacancy rate is kept as low as possible while at the same time charging a reasonable rental—neither too high nor too low; (2) see that tenants are reasonably satisfied with the property, receiving sub-

---

[1]A parcel of land is suitable for a major office building if it is within or adjacent to the financial or retail trade sections of a large city. This type of location usually provides the necessary "nearness factor," that is, business and professional people like to and need to be near enough to each other to conduct business, if necessary, on a face-to-face basis. Also, if clients want to see all the people in a certain business or profession in a particular city, they appreciate having to go to only one section of the community to see them. Buildings remote from the downtown area of a city typically represent an overimprovement of the land and are notoriously unsuccessful in the sense that they do not produce enough income to service the financial obligations incurred to acquire them.

[2]This desired benefit from a location is seldom achieved because of the considerable amount of commercially zoned space usually available at a price in most cities. For example, before the Pam-American Building in New York City was completed, two office buildings one block south on Park Avenue were being torn down so that new office buildings could be constructed. All that can be done after the decision is made to proceed with the construction of a major office building is to hope that other parties will analyze the market, take your space supply into consideration, and refrain from glutting the market with additional buildings and thereby making an unprofitable investment.

[3]An office building is considered to be reasonably efficient in design if approximately 75 percent of the total square footage produces rental revenue.

stantially what they bargained for; and (3) continually study building operations to see that every truly worthwhile cost-cutting approach is employed in running the property.

A primary responsibility of the office building manager is the establishment of a proper rent schedule, which is more often an art than a science because factors that may justify raising or lowering rents are not always definitely measurable.

Judgment and hard economic facts are very important in determining rent schedules. Before a building is constructed assurance must be gained from an analysis of the market that the space can be rented at a price that will at least amortize the investment over the period of its estimated economic life, pay operational expenses, and result in the investor's obtaining a reasonable return on his or her investment.

All space in an office building will not rent for the same price because of varying elements that affect amenities, prestige, and convenience of different offices. Factors reflecting such differences that are implemented into a rent schedule include (1) height above ground level (usually the higher a space the more rent that must and can be charged); (2) pleasantness of the view from the office; (3) convenience of location; (4) nearness to a major prestigious tenant (creating considerable traffic valuable to lesser firms); and (5) presence of corner space. The property manager can never consider the rent schedule to be settled. He or she must always be researching and analyzing the market to be aware of any developing trends.

To assure the continuance of the building's income stream to the greatest extent possible, managers should usually negotiate term leases with tenants. Thus, even if the tenant is enticed away from the property before the expiration of the lease term, the building owner is still entitled to the payment of rent from the original tenant if the property cannot be readily rented at the contract rent rate after the vacation of the space.

In the case of the long-term office building loan the borrower is usually a corporation. Thus, the subject property and the net worth of the corporation constitute the major existing assets that assure the repayment of the loan according to its terms. The lender will also be concerned with the personnel of the borrowing company—particularly with whether any of the senior executives have had experience in developing or managing such properties. Whether the firm has a reputation as an investor or as a speculator, and the reason for its wanting a particular building, are all-important factors in determining the wisdom of making the loan at any given time.

The actual development of a dollar figure representing the present value of a certain building is usually accomplished by using the three approaches to the valuation problem. The replacement cost approach sets the upper limit of possible property value. The market (or comparative) approach can be a good indicator of probable value if a property similar to the one being appraised can be found. This basic requirement—similar properties that can be compared in value with the subject property—usually cannot be fulfilled because of the uniqueness of most major office buildings. The most often used method of estimating the value of an office building is to capitalize the net income derived annually from the building over its economic life and to add the result to the land value to obtain the present value of the property.

The terms of lending for office buildings can vary with the results of negotiation between the two parties. The financial strength of the borrower, the condition of the money market, and the probable success of the venture will all affect the terms of a specific loan. Disregarding special circumstances, the basic provisions of such a loan are usually (1) a maximum term of up to twenty-five years (with ten to twenty years common); (2) loans up to 75 percent of property value; (3) amortization of principal over the life of the loan; (4) payments made quarterly; (5) when the building is well located, being built in times of a favorable real estate market, and leased to triple-A tenants, the interest paid will be the going rate for prime real estate loans; and (6) payment of a percentage of either gross or net rental income.

INDUSTRIAL PROPERTIES

Nature and Characteristics

The construction, financing, and use of industrial property is so intertwined with the needs, future prospects, and financial strength of manufacturing corporations that financing such property is probably more in the realm of corporation finance than real estate finance. However, since the occasion may arise for financing the construction of a new plant, the renovation or expansion of an existing one, or the acquisition of an industrial facility, we shall review some considerations bearing upon this type of financing.

As usual there will be two classes of financial interest in the property—equity and debt. Because of the substantial additional risk connected with such property that arises from the great volatility of its value, the ratio of loan to value is traditionally much lower than in other types of loans. If you doubt this "roller coaster" aspect of the value of industrial plant property, reflect a minute upon the ghost towns of the West and upon the miles of old, vacant, obsolete industrial plants alongside railroad tracks between Chicago and New England. It is because of the relatively large supply of land suitable for industrial use and because of buildings already in existence that loans on such property are made primarily on the basis of the financial strength of the industrial user—not the estimated value of the land and improvements. This situation explains the requirement of large ownership interest in the property and of financial considerations in addition to the value of the property accepted as security for the loan.

Determining the value of industrial property usually involves consideration of the income-producing potential of the facility if it is used by one specific manufacturer producing certain products on the premises. This in turn involves analyzing the economic aspects of a certain industry, such as its raw material, water, power, labor, transportation, and marketing requirements. Therefore, it is virtually impossible to determine with any accuracy the value of a particular industrial plant without knowing what product will be manufactured by what corporation at that location.

The financial condition of the debtor and his other credit standing, therefore, are usually more important that the value of the property in deciding the feasibility of making a loan for the acquisition or improvement of industrial property. In the financial analysis of a prospective borrower, since we are considering a corporate structure, the most practical method is to apply to the problem at hand the principles set forth in texts on corporation finance and financial analysis.

If funds can be borrowed for the acquisition or improvement of an industrial property, the usual available sources (except for a corporation selling securities or having a seller finance a sale) are commercial banks and insurance companies. If a bank were to lend the money the term would typically be short (five years), the interest rather high, and the loan an amortizing one. This cautious attitude is typical of banks, because of their liquidity requirements. An insurance company (since it is not under the liquidity pressures that might exist for commercial banks) might make a loan on industrial property for ten years, with a higher loan-to-value ratio, at a lower rate of interest, and with less amortization of the loan over its term. Such secured loans in California would be based upon the promissory note and trust deed typically found in all real estate loans.

While many loans for the development or purchase of industrial property are credit loans (made on the basis of the borrower's financial strength) rather than primarily real estate loans (made on the basis of the market value of the collateral real estate and the annual net income it will produce to pay mortgage principal and interest), institutional lenders do make real estate loans on industrial properties. In making an industrial real estate loan, institutional lenders require favorable answers to the following questions: (1) Is the site desirable; that is, does it have good transportation service (highways or rail-

road), is it free from nearby adverse influences, is its size adequate for storage and loading docks, are water and utility service available now and in the foreseeable future, is there an adequate labor pool, is it suitably located in relation to markets for industrial goods? (2) Is there now or is there likely to be in the future an oversupply of competitive space that will reduce rents or sales prices? (3) Is the property being developed in the form of an industrial park with appropriate building material, design, and land use restrictions? (4) Is there now a verified adequate level of effective demand for the type of industrial property to be developed? (5) If the property is a building or a series of buildings to be rented, will the gross rent schedule produce enough income to pay expenses of operation and produce a net profit sufficient to cover mortgage debt service charges by at least a ratio of 1.5 or 2 to 1? Are the tenant or tenants financially responsible? Is the net income from the tenants assured by lease clauses providing rent increases to cover general inflation and real property tax increases? Does the period of the lease exceed the repayment term of the mortgage loan?

APARTMENT PROPERTIES

General Characteristics

During the twentieth century, apartments have constituted an investment outlet of vast size and great economic importance. The economic significance of this type of shelter directly affects real estate lending institutions and investors seeking advantageous investments. Real estate is certainly an acceptable investment for many people and institutions. Apartments have long been high on the preference list for those persons controlling the investment of substantial sums of money. As with every investment in which the return sought will presumably be more than the "safe rate" on United States Government securities, an additional degree of risk is assumed when funds are committed to this type of property. This risk factor must be considered by both owners and creditors if the advisability of making a loan or investment in a particular property is to be properly evaluated.

In recent years, the increasing housing shortage and inflation in many urban areas have resulted in increased rents being charged apartment tenants. As a result of this situation, tenants in various cities in California have complained to local officials about this. Using police power, many of these cities have enacted rent-control ordinances that limit the legal ability of apartment owners to raise rents. A result of this rent control, new rental apartment developers and investors have been discouraged from contructing or from buying existing rental apartment complexes. Also, the high cost of construction and the shortage of land zoned for apartments in California cities—resulting in the necessity of higher rents to cover operational expenses and to amortize the investment in structures—make it more difficult and risky to build rental apartments, largely because many households do not have incomes adequate to pay the rent required if such developments are to be financially sound.

Analysis and Classification

Individual apartments are customarily classified according to the number of rooms that they contain. Typical classifications are (1) efficiency, or studio (for one person); and (2) one-,two-,or three-bedroom. The entire apartment building may be classified according to the number of living units it contains, for example, duplex, fourplex, and so forth, or according to its design, for example, high-rise, walk-up, or garden.

Experience indicates that apartments are not ordinarily occupied by relatively large families, nor are they economically successful in sparsely populated areas of the country. Apartments are the homes of single persons, couples, and couples with one or two children. This means that such residential space is most attractive to young married couples, persons who have never married, divorced or separated people, older people who have raised their families and who now do not need or want much excess living space, and people who have retired. Demographic studies indicate that family units with these characteristics exist in the greatest number in large, long-established cities such as New York and Chicago.

The inclination of large numbers of people to live in apartments depends upon the economic and social forces operating in an area and upon the personal circumstances that determine the most practical type of housing for any given family. Apartment living is widespread in the "city belt," which covers the area from Washington, D.C., to Boston. Because of the desirability or practicality of such housing, most of the residential space available in New York City is in this form. Except for cities such as Chicago and San Francisco, it cannot be said that there is a tradition of apartment living in other urban areas of the nation; therefore the competition provided by the single-family dwelling increases the risk connected with such investments in these regions. The competition provided by the single-family residence is certainly very real in the San Francisco Bay area outside San Francisco, in the Los Angeles area, and in San Diego County.

The basic inclination of people in certain areas of the country to live in or not to live in apartments indicates the fluctuation of the desire for apartment living. Difficulty in measuring the propensity of people to live in apartments is a real problem for owners and lenders alike. In the decade of the 1980s, very high housing prices and mortgage loan interest rates prevented millions of households from achieving the "American dream" of home-ownership. As a result of this situation, effective demand for rental apartments increased, with vacancy factors in many cities less than 5 percent of the total inventory of such units. It is likely that this "forced effective demand" for rental apartments in cities will continue as long as mortgage interest rates and housing prices remain so high that few households can financially afford to buy their own home.

Cooperative and condominium apartments have been discussed in detail in a separate chapter. Many of the economic, social, design, construction, and psychological aspects of apartments in general apply also to these two special types of multiunit dwellings.

Types of Financing Available

In the financial structure developed for the typical privately owned apartment house will be found equity and creditor capital. In discussing the financing of such properties one is usually primarily interested in the debt aspects of raising the funds necessary to acquire such a property.

The equity interest in apartment houses may be (1) generated out of "thin air," in that the appraisal of the property results in loans being made for the full cost of development (a situation usually achieved by questionable appraisal of the property); (2) derived from one person's investment in a property; (3) derived from institutional ownership of such property, for example, apartments owned by insurance companies in New York; (4) based upon shareholders' investments in a corporation owning and managing the building; or (5) derived from investments in limited partnerships, trusts, or joint ventures that are the organizational bases for investment groups commonly known as syndicates.

The necessary credit for the creation or acquisition of an apartment property can be obtained from (1) the seller; (2) savings and loan associations; (3) insurance companies; (4) commercial banks; (5) mortgage companies; and (6) agencies of the federal government if the apartment property is to be used by special groups such as retired persons or members of religious denominations.

Determination of Investment Worth

The determination of the value of a given apartment property is essentially based upon the exercise of expert judgment upon a given set of facts. This is an empirical operation, not a scientific approach to the problem resulting in a mathematically certain answer.

Determining the value of a given apartment building requires general information relating to the economy of the nation, the region, and the city, in addition to the social and psychological factors of living that seem to affect large numbers of people. Specific detailed information should be gathered to accomplish this valuation task. The required information relates to the present and to the foreseeable future. This emphasis upon conditions affecting the income-earning capabilities of a specific property one to three years hence is of critical importance because in the case of constructing new apartments the space will not actually be available for some time. If this aspect of new construction is not considered, the result can be a disaster if much more such space comes on the market than can possibly be rented at an adequate price.

The number of factors that affect apartment property value favorably or unfavorably is very large. Articles are continually being written on the subjects of enhancing, maintaining, or creating value for this type of property. In few areas of real estate is constant perceptive research as necessary as in the areas of purchasing, operating, and financing apartment buildings, primarily because of the volatility of the market for such space.

The following factors are generally thought to affect the value of apartment buildings in the sense of increasing or at least maintaining the value of a given property:

1. Upward trends in apartment house demand that are firmly based upon continuing long-term growth are favorable. These trends can be national or local.

2. The business and real estate cycles are favorable factors just after a depression phase or in the early part of a prosperity phase. At these times the demand for residential space and the price levels will usually improve to the benefit of owners and lenders.

3. Increased burdens of commuting upon the suburban resident benefit apartments. There is evidence in some large cities, such as New York, Chicago, and Los Angeles, that the increased expense, time, and effort involved in commuting were inclining an increasing number of suburban residents to move back to the city and to live in apartments. This is a local matter that would have to be researched in every city to determine its existence and force as a favorable factor for apartment housing.

4. Except for specialized situations such as retirement quarters and recreational areas, apartments will have a sound long-term value only where an urban population of reasonably prosperous citizens is increasing in size. The economic reasons for the increase in population should be sound, in that the jobs held by the new residents are in legitimate long-term growth industries. This should rule out great reliance upon industries that are quickly depressed in times of economic stress (recreational or luxury industries). Unstable industrial economic activity is sometimes carried on by companies contracting with the federal government. The instability is primarily due to the short-term aspects of some contracts and to the fact that they are usually subject to cancellation on short notice.

5. Changes in patterns of urban growth can affect apartments favorably by increasing the amenities of an area. For example, parks, theaters, libraries, museums, and the like are expanded or built in these areas.

6. Demographic data are important and favorable to apartment properties when they show an increase in those age groups that have typically been receptive to the concept of apartment living. (This demographic trend has continued well into the 1980s. The number of people between the ages of twenty and thirty and over fifty-five is expanding rapidly. This bodes well for apartments, since people in these ages categories either cannot afford single-family houses or they have no inclination toward such a residence because of the bother of caring for more space than they really need.

7. An apartment property is obviously favored if the supply-and-demand ratio is in its favor, that is, if there are more people seeking space than there is space available of the quality desired.

8. The location of an apartment is important, although not as significant as in the case of a major office building. A favorable location for an apartment house typically will provide the following advantages: (1) location will be convenient for people of the economic and social classes most likely to rent space; (2) amenities will be provided to the maximum degree compatible with an efficient location; (3) the surrounding neighborhood will be favorable to the city dweller, having recreational, commercial, and cultural facilities nearby; (4) there will be a minimum of nuisance-type land uses in the immediate vicinity; and (5) public utilities and parking will be adequate to service the property.

9. The building should be of quality construction and designed in an architectural style appealing to a relatively large number of people. To assure maximum long-term net-income-producing capability, an apartment building will have (1) attractive architectural design; (2) efficient heating and air conditioning systems; (3) attractive recreational facilities; (4) adequate, well-planned living space (the trend in many communities is toward larger apartments); (5) soundproofing (very important). The square-foot area in an apartment, along with other features, depends upon what is in demand in the market and upon the price that will be charged for the space. This price will vary from the $100 or more room rate charged for large, soundproofed, professionally decorated units with built-in appliances and air conditioning, to small, "space only," apartments that rent for less per room.

10. Materials in apartments should be long-lasting and as free from periodic maintenance requirements as possible. Building an apartment house with this objective will increase net income through cutting down on labor and material costs necessary to maintain the property during its economic life. This is a significant factor in the investment value of a property, one that is all too often overlooked because many such structures are built for immediate sale to an undetermined buyer, and consequently the builder does not often spend any more money to erect the building than is absolutely necessary. The result of this situation is a building costly to maintain and commonly not as attractive as it might be. If space in this type of building must be marketed in a highly competitive market, the dismal net income situation that may well arise can be very disadvantageous to both owner and lender.

11. An apartment property should have at least an average expense-to-income ratio. This ratio is determined for

various categories of property (elevator serviced, walk-up, and garden apartments) located in various sections of the country. (For example, the Institute of Real Estate Management in its annual, *Apartment Building Experience Exchange,* has determined that in the operation of garden apartments in Los Angeles all operational expenses consumed 39.1 percent gross rental income.) Any substantial departure from this ratio could constitute a forewarning of possible financial failure of the property.

The importance of this ratio highlights the importance of having not merely an average manager in charge of rental property but a really good one who can obtain the maximum gross income for the property while constantly striving to reduce the cost of property operation.

Factors adversely affecting the value of apartments are virtually the opposite of the items favorable to increasing or maintaining property worth. For example, an apartment house upon which many adverse characteristics are operating to depress its value would be (1) built at the height of a real estate boom; (2) located on land remote (in terms of both travel time and distance) from the centers of business, industry, education, culture, and recreation; (3) dismal and uninspiring in design; (4) too large or too small for the family size most often found in the local apartment market; (5) furnished when it should be unfurnished, or vice versa; (6) situated on low-lying land with no view or breeze; (7) lacking air conditioning although located in a town with a hot climate; (8) designed to force tenants to mingle with each other (virtually no privacy with maximum traffic past most of the units); (9) located very near a noisy, dustry, smoky, or malodorous nuisance such as a freeway, gas station, industrial plant, or establishment catering to nighttime revelers; (10) lacking any degree of effective soundproofing in common walls; (11) providing virtually no storage space; (12) built by incompetent or careless workers; and (13) built during a period of high costs so that the rentals obtainable when the space does come on the market are too low to amortize the cost of the building over its economic life. Although our imaginary building does not include all possible factors of failure, it points out many common errors that create fatal investment traps for the unwary owner and lending institution.

The question any lender must answer satisfactorily before lending money on an apartment house is whether this particular apartment house possesses characteristics that, over the term of the loan, will enable it to earn the income necessary to pay the costs of operation, amortize the loan, return the cost of improvements, and pay a reasonable return to the investor owning the property. Consideration of the presence or absence of the factors discussed above will facilitate the intelligent answering of this all-important question.

Quantitative Evaluation

The estimation of the value of an apartment property is accomplished by using the three approaches (cost, market, income) that have been established as integral parts of the appraisal process. Thus, the principles applying to this type of value problem are those ordinarily considered relevant in valuing all but very unusual properties. In addition to the three conventional methods used in determining value, considerable use is made of what is called the gross income multiplier. Although this last technique is a rather offhand approach to the value problem, it is used often and thus has a measurable effect upon the real estate market and upon valuation estimates derived through use of the established appraisal methodology.

The cost approach to determining the value of apartment properties serves (as it usually does in the appraisal process) to determine the upper limit of value for the income-producing unit. In this approach the value of the land is determined (usually by the market approach), and to this is added the present cost of reproducing the building less loss of value due to depreciation, resulting in the present value of the entire property. If the building is the highest and best use for a site and is virtually brand new, and if the rental market is strong, the cost approach will often give an accurate estimate of property value.

The comparative (or market) approach to value compares the property to be appraised (subject property) with similar apartments in the area. It is usually possible to find enough comparable properties (three to five) to assure sufficient data for a reasonably accurate result through this approach.

The income approach is traditionally based upon capitalizing the net income derived from a certain property. In this approach (as with the other appraisal techniques) certain assumptions are made. If substantial errors flaw these assumptions, the accuracy of the ultimate estimate of value will suffer. In the income approach the economic life of the improvement is estimated, probable gross income from the property is determined, all operational expenses are subtracted from gross income to obtain the probable annual net income from the property, and an appropriate capitalization rate is determined, either from the market (that is, from what the investor in comparable properties is receiving as a return on his or her investment) or by "building a rate" (determining the risk factors that should be accounted for over and above the interest paid on United States government securities) that is applied to the net income expected to be produced by the improvement, resulting in the estimated value of the structure. The capitalization rate also allows for amortization of the investment in the improvements. The value of the land is often derived from the market. Finally, to arrive at the value estimate for the complete property (land and buildings), the value of the land is added to the value of the building.

When apartment property is purchased by an investor, what is really being acquired is the legal right to receive a flow of income from a specific property. Because of this emphasis upon the net income returned from the property, the income approach is the main determinant of the estimated value of a given apartment house. The other two approaches (especially the cost technique) are merely checks upon the income approach to see that the value estimate is not excessive in the sense that more is paid for an existing property than would have to be paid for the construction of virtually the same physical facilities in a similar location.

The gross income multiplier is a relatively simple method from which an estimate of value is derived. First, a determination is made of what multiple of the gross annual income received from comparable properties is being paid by investors to acquire such apartment houses. For example, if $480,000 is the total selling price for a property producing $60,000 per year gross income, the gross income multiplier is 8. If the property that is to be bought is similar to this $480,000 property (which sold readily in the market) as to location, age, type of construction, design, room plan, operating expense ratio, and size, the multiplier of 8 can be considered reasonable and can be used to arrive at a value estimate. Should the gross annual income from the subject property be $50,000 and the seller's asking price be $480,000, one would conclude that this price is too high because the multiplier of 8 indicates a value of $400,000 for this property.

The big problem with the gross income multiplier is the comparative lack of analysis of the property from the standpoints of operational efficiency and the economic life of the improvements. However, despite the theoretical objections to this approach to the determination of property value, there is one important factor in favor of this valuation technique:—its successful operation for many investors. It is very difficult to argue with success.

Sources and Terms of Mortgage Lending

A substantial number of possible sources exists for loans on apartment properties. In fact, during the early 1960s and 1970s, prospective borrowers often found considerable competition among institutional lenders to make such loans. The most active lenders in this loan field have been (1) savings and loan associations; (2) commercial banks; (3) mutual savings banks; (4) insurance companies; (5) mortgage companies; (6) the sellers of apartment properties; (7) various branches of the federal government that are authorized to make loans for apartments rented by special groups, such as the aged and infirm; and (8) special private sources, such as pension funds and foundations.

In determining the terms and provisions of possible credit arrangements we are again dealing with legally established limitations upon such loans as well as those established by past experience and by the economic factors that seem to operate on the debt arrangement. Within these limitations the lender and the borrower can negotiate the terms of specific loan agreement. However, as with the terms of loans for other purposes, loans on apartment properties will be governed primarily by statute and by administrative regulation.

If a government agency or private corporation insures the repayment of a loan, the loan-to-value ratio for certain institutional loans may exceed 90 percent. If there is no such insurance of the debt, the maximum for such loans is usually 75 percent of appraised value. For institutions such as banks, in which liquidity is particularly important to financial soundness, the ratio may sometimes drop to between 50 and 66.6 percent. Private sources of credit such as the seller, mortgage companies, and pension funds have greater latitude in making loans; therefore, they may well exceed the two-thirds loan-to-value ratio.

If there is a possibility that a loan will be made on an apartment property, the usual procedure is for the lender to invite an application from the prospective borrower. Such application forms typically ask for (1) name of borrower; (2) location of property; (3) amount of money desired to be borrowed; (4) length of repayment period; (5) size of building; (6) type of construction; (7) gross rental income; (8) expenses of operation; (9) total number of apartments; (10) size of apartments; (11) borrower's experience in property management; (12) financial condition of the borrower; (13) whether apartments are rented furnished or unfurnished; and (14) type of building (elevator, walk-up, garden). Many more items can be included in an application form, but they are usually the result of a more fractionalized approach to the information gathering problem.

The property will usually be appraised by a qualified person. This valuation estimate and additional factual data produced by the appraisal will also be considered in making the loan, as well as by financial institutions and government agencies such as the Federal Housing Administration. In making a decision on a loan, therefore, the lender will have information relating to the request for credit based upon the financial statement of the borrower, the loan application, the appraiser's report, and any current market studies. However, after all this information is made available to the decision makers, the final approval or disapproval of the request is a matter of personal judgment.

In most areas of the country financial institutions are in a particularly sensitive position relative to the existing supply of apartment space. If they do not furnish the necessary credit in times of a space shortage, the community suffers, and if they continue to make funds available when there is already an adequate supply of space for the foreseeable future, they contribute to a detrimental situation regarding real estate investments and loans. If the institutional lenders do not use their power to control the supply of residential space in the community so as to prevent the creation of an injurious oversupply, the only force that will accomplish this is the final operation of the "lemming phenomenon." (Like the hordes of Scandinavian rodents that periodically rush to their demise in the sea, many builders will continue to build at capacity rates for as long as the funds necessary to finance construction can be obtained. Apparently paying no attention to market supply and demand, they rush toward financial ruin and bankruptcy.) The negative effects upon apartment complexes caused by city rent controls coupled with the lack of positive economic feasibility projections for proposed new rental apartment complexes have caused many financial institutions to limit the amount of money loaned for the construction and long-term financing of large new rental apartment complexes. While there is always the possibility of the "lemming phenomenon" recurring, this is less likely during the next decade.

In considering applications for residential loans, officers in financial institutions should have the knowledge and the courage to discharge properly their significant responsibilities to the public, to the owners of the funds they control, and to the debtors borrowing from the lending establishment.

SPECIAL-PURPOSE PROPERTIES

Special-purpose properties characteristically have specialized uses. Such properties are essentially commercial with regard to the nature of the activities conducted on the premises; thus, industrial and residential land uses are not within this category. There are no firm limits, however, upon the specific categories of commercial activities that can be included with the term *special-purpose property*.

Definition

Special-purpose properties are those wherein the improvements constructed on the land are suited for basically one commercial purpose rather than for industrial or residential use. This is not to say that a special-purpose property cannot successfully be used for any but its orig-

inal purpose; however, such different use is uncommon because of the rigid limitations imposed upon a building's usefulness by its structural design and because of the considerable expense necessary to modify such a structure so that it is practical to employ it for a commercial enterprise different from the one it was originally built to accommodate.

Types of Properties

In this section, we discuss hotels, motels, medical buildings, bowling alleys, gasoline stations, churches, and mini-warehouses. To facilitate the conduct of these enterprises by making appropriate loans, the lender must have adequate knowledge of the economics of the particular activity. For example, he or she must be generally familiar with the managerial aspects of hotel operation, in addition to the local situation relative to the present and future profitability of such a business.

Because of the primary importance of a business operation to the value of such real property, the managerial ability of a prospective borrower in the theater business, for example, may be of more significance than the present value of the physical property. Thus, we are dealing with a more uncertain situation with special-purpose properties than with residential loans.

Common Characteristics of Special-Purpose Properties

Virtually all special-purpose properties have the following characteristics: They are the site for the conduct of an income-producing business. The value of the real property is greatly dependent upon the skill and competence of the people managing the business enterprise. Such properties should never be created unless studies indicate that at least a reasonable opportunity exists for the business to succeed. When a determination has been made that a reasonable chance of success does exist, the enterprise should be soundly and vigorously promoted by an adequately financed management. A great danger connected with special-purpose properties, and consequently shared by any lender on such property, is the utter uselessness of most of these properties for any purpose other than that for which they were designed. To appreciate fully the magnitude of this problem, consider the number of abandoned gas stations, theaters, churches, motels, and small-town hotels. In virtually all cases in which the commercial activity intended to be carried on has been unsuccessful, the property is useless. Therefore, the improvement on the land may actually constitute a detriment to the value of the land in the sense that land value will be reduced by the cost of removing the improvement from the premises.

This complex and bleak picture is not completely adverse to the owner or lender involved in such properties. Bowling alleys have been turned into fraternal lodge meeting rooms, and theater buildings into grocery stores, offices, and dance halls; however, considering the number of such conversions, the percentage of successful efforts is extremely small. Despite the remote possibility of effecting such conversions of special-purpose properties, it is generally true that if the management of a business using such a building fails, most of the investment in the building is also lost, because of its limited utility.

Competition

A problem that may adversely affect all commercial enterprises, but especially firms using special-purpose properties, is the operation of the principle of competition upon successful business enterprises. Large numbers of firms establish businesses that are competitive with already operating and successful enterprises. The classic example of this development was the miniature golf business during the 1920s. During the late 1950s and early 1960s the same thing happened to bowling alleys. (In one California community with a population of 20,000, two separate corporations surveyed the market and determined that the town could support forty lanes; each proceeded to construct that number of lanes. The result, after two competitive years, was the bankruptcy of both corporations.)

How can devastating competition be minimized? It is difficult to eliminate this possiblity completely. Zoning may provide some protection if the required commercially zoned land is not available. A situation in which it is obvious that only those enterprises now operating can be financially successful will effectively discourage new competition.

The extraordinary risks connected with special-purpose business properties usually lead to conservatism in financing the real property necessary for such enterprises. Such conservatism is typically manifested by higher interest rates, shorter terms, amortization of the loan, and a relatively low loan-to-value ratio (all of which result in the owner's having a comparatively large equity in the property.)

Because of the many uncertainties connected with such properties, often no credit at all will be available for the acquisition or development of special-purpose facilities. Many such loans are made only because they offer the possibility of providing the lender with a preferred lien on property other than the specially developed real estate. For example, a loan for the expansion of a bowling alley might be made only because the borrower is able to pledge 1,000 shares of blue-chip corporate securities as collateral. The participation of institutional lenders in this type of lending is limited—in fact, some of these lenders may not seek this kind of business at all.

Hotels

Hotel financing does not account for much of the total volume of loans made on commercial property, mainly because such structures are rarely built in any but the largest cities. Even in these centers of population, a decade or so may pass before a major hotel is constructed. The infrequency of building hotels is due in part to the existing supply of such space, to time-saving jet travel, to the decline in the volume of train traffic (which originally provided the big downtown hotel with most of its business), and to the tremendous increase in automobile travel, a boon to motels typically built on the outskirts of cities along the major traffic arteries leading into the city center. The big hotel (and hotels in small towns, also, where the necessity of travelers' stopping has diminished because of faster cars, superhighways, and the contruction of more attractive motels) has been squeezed from several sides, with general decline in the level of business. In major cities the occupancy rate of many hotels declined steadily after 1946, falling to 55 to 65 percent by the 1970s. Such occupancy rates spell nothing but financial trouble for hotels and for creditors who have lent money for such buildings. In the 1970s there was no indication of a solution to the hotels' occupancy problem. For many older hotels the dilemma had grown worse because of construction of new major hotels in some cities and because of the continued construction of motels, including deluxe motels in the downtown areas. As this struggle continues, there is every indication that in most cases the older hotels will not be able to survive and therefore will constitute failures in the sense that they simply cannot pay their way. The plight of many hotels is merely one indication of how technological changes coupled with public fads or attitudes can substantially affect a business carried on in a specialized property.

Fortunately for the prospective lender, more is known about the hotel business than about any other business conducted in specially constructed buildings. There are schools of hotel management in various American universities, and accounting practices and the management of such enterprises have been standardized so that a fairly perceptive comparative analysis of the effectiveness of hotel operation can be made.

In considering an application for a hotel loan, the lender will (1) examine the financial records of its last ten years of operation; (2) compare the operation of this hotel with averages for the operation of such properties; (3) consider the value of the real property from the standpoints of location and of functional and architectural obsolescence; (4) analyze the future of the hotel business in that city and region; (5) determine what competing hotels exist or may be built in the near future.

Sources of funds for hotel loans. For obvious reasons, a hotel loan is not overly attractive to most institutional lenders. If they do participate in such lending, it is on a limited scale. Much of the money for the financing of hotels has come from large insurance companies. Usually, they have lent money to well-known, established corporations that operate their own and leased hotels. These lenders might be persuaded to make a loan on a small, independently owned hotel property, but if such a loan were made, it would be a relatively high-interest loan, for a comparatively short term, at a low loan-to-value ratio, and with the real property appraised conservatively.

Banks might be persuaded to make such loans, but only if the management had demonstrated its competence over a considerable period, the earning capability of the property was definitely established, the hotel enjoyed a virtual monopoly on such business in the city, and the property was definitely competitive with other hotels in the region. Even under these favorable circumstances, the loan may well be less than 50 percent of appraised value.

The equity captial for such ventures usually comes from hotel corporations; however, some small-town properties are owned by individuals. In larger cities syndicates have been established for the purpose of raising equity capital in amounts large enough to acquire hotels.

Motels

Except for some temporary sanctuaries, the motel business is highly competitive. This situation is due in part to the nationwide or regional motel corporations that have been established. These operations usually facilitate advance room reservations for travelers from one city to another, thus reducing the opportunity for purely local motels to obtain business from every traveler driving through a community. Competition is also enhanced by the almost unlimited supply of land on which to erect such establishments. In addition to these factors favoring intense competition, financing motels (as opposed to hotels) is comparatively easy because institutional lenders commonly seek out motel lending business.

Lenders should be knowledgeable about good management practices, competitive techniques, economical and efficient design, and the problems or dangers incident to motel property. Thus, in considering an application for such a loan, specific consideration will be given to

(1) possiblities for an increase in business due to a growing local economy or to new road construction increasing the number of travelers in the area who will need overnight accommodations; (2) the management record of the borrower; (3) locational avantages or disadvantages affecting the prospects for continued property value; (4) whether the motel accommodations and prices will produce the necessary volume of business; (5) whether the motel is approved by national accommodation rating organizations; (6) the financial condition of the borrower; and (7) the value of the improved property. During the 1974–75 recession, motels and hotels experienced serious financial problems because of the following: (1) excessive number of rooms in relation to effective demand in a market area; (2) bad location; (3) higher costs and shortage of energy due primarily to the Arab oil embargo; and (4) fewer travelers willing and able to pay increased room fees necessary to cover higher operating costs of these types of properties.

Sources of equity and creditor funds. Equity money is usually provided by corporations operating a chain of motels on a regional or nationwide basis, by syndicates formed through the business trust or limited partnership organization, or by individual proprietorships or small firms operating one motel. The amount of equity capital that must usually be provided for a motel is large, because it is often difficult to obtain a loan for more than 50 percent of the appraised value of the property.

The requirement for a sizable equity interest in motels can be met when an established motel concern acquires the land for a motel and leases it to a franchised operator who is buying the building. This practice, especially when the land is relatively expensive, will provide a sound economic basis for the required loan by providing an ownership interest that may equal 25 percent or more of the total investment. A motel corporation may also own the complete property (and therefore borrow part of the necessary capital itself) and lease the complete operable motel to a manager.

If a properly drawn long-term lease of land to a motel corporation is negotiated, it can (assuming it provides the necessary security for a first lien) eliminate to a considerable degree the problem of raising the needed amount of equity capital. This approach to the problem may well become more common as the cost of land suitable for motels increases.

Loans for motels may be made by private parties, insurance companies, or local financial institutions. Local savings institutions have shown increasing interest in this type of loan business.

The loans made on motels are usually more expensive and less desirable from the borrower's standpoint than loans for office buildings and apartments. A motel loan will often carry a 0.5 to 1.5 percent higher interest rate, will rarely exceed a term of ten years, will be amortizing, and will be of an amount less than one-half of the appraised value of the property.

The motel business is probably more risky than some other types of commercial enterprises operated in this country. The higher degree of risk should produce a greater return on capital invested in such properties; for example, a well-located, competently managed motel of thirty to fifty rooms should produce a return of 12 to 20 percent on the owner's equity. The greater degree of financial danger connected with this type of property is caused primarily by motel profits being tied to a prosperous, automobile-oriented economy and by the highly effective competition that exists.

Gasoline Stations

Because of the intense competition in the petroleum industry among giant producing and marketing firms, the majority of gasoline stations are controlled by these firms. The control may be derived from outright ownership by the corporation, which leases the property to an operator; or the corporation may lease the land, erect the station on it, and sublet the complete facility to a tenant-operator. Loans to major oil companies for station construction are usually arranged primarily on the basis of the credit standing and financial strength of the corporation. Conceivably a very profitable, integrated oil company might own a substantial portion of its retail outlets and have them operated under a lease arrangement.

Lending for the construction or purchase of a gasoline station is not common among institutional lenders because most gasoline stations are financed by the oil company whose products are sold from the site. Thus, the necessary funds for such facilities are usually provided as a part of the financing of a corporate enterprise, not by the placing of one individual loan on a specific property. Although the volume of these loans is small, we shall consider the process of making such loans and their typical provisions.

Usually, the party seeking a loan for the construction or purchase of a gasoline station must already have tentatively arranged for a fairly long-term lease of the property to a strong, successful oil company. This is a primary requirement because the value of such a commercial property is based primarily on the net income derived from the use of the premises. If the gasoline station is not successful, the land and improvements may be of questionable worth in terms of market value. (Actually, a gasoline station with a great deal of pavement and with large tanks sunk in the ground may reduce the value of the land to a level below that of adjoining undeveloped property, because this material would have to be removed from the premises to make it useable for some other purpose.)

In evaluating an application for a loan on a gasoline station (apart from the major oil company lease requirement), a lender would consider (1) the location, particularly with regard to its long-term potential as an attractive site for marketing petroleum products; (2) the possiblities for neighborhood business; (3) present and future gallonage sold; (4) existing and possible future competition; (5) the opportunity for sale of specialized services and items related to automobile operation; (6) evaluation of the managerial ability of the operator and his personality; and (7) the size of the owner's equity in the property, in addition to his general financial condition.

A successful gasoline station will usually possess the following characteristics: (1) it will be leased to a highly regarded, active national oil company or a reduced-price independent distributor acceptable to the public; (2) it will have no effective competition or possibility of such competition in the immediate area; (3) it will be located on a corner; (4) it will be on the side of the street with a substantial amount of traffic turning right (thus passing the station twice and maximizing the traffic count); (5) the traffic past the corner will consist primarily of large cars using high-test gasoline (thus maximizing the chance to sell services and a more profitable grade of gasoline); (6) it will be situated so as to maximize the inclination of people to go in and do business; and (7) it will sell more than 10,000 gallons of gasoline a month.

In the winter of 1973–74 the United States was subjected to an oil shipment embargo by overseas producers of petroleum. The result of this development was twofold; (1) a shortage of all products made from oil, causing a shortage of gasoline for motorists and long lines of cars at any station that had gasoline to sell; and (2) a substantial increase in the price of oil-related products, virtually doubling the price of gasoline. A retail merchant cannot stay in business if there is no merchandise to sell. Reduced supplies of gasoline and much higher prices reduced effective demand, and many retail gasoline stations closed because they were no longer sufficiently profitable. The oil embargo started a trend that continues in the 1980s: only the established, volume-sales station will remain in business, and relatively few new stations will be built. The potential for future oil embargoes, coupled with the domestic energy shortage resulting in much higher prices for gasoline, makes the ownership and financing of retail gasoline stations more hazardous than ever. As a result, lenders who consider loans on gasoline stations will have to be surer than ever that the prerequisites for a successful station exist. If the loan is made, it will probably be more conservative than in the past in terms of loan-to-value ratio (lower), length of repayment terms (shorter), and higher interest rate, because of the increased risk to the lender.

In financing the acquisition or development of the typical gasoline station, the promissory note and trust deed arrangement will be used. It is important that the lender definitely establish in this lien the legal status of all improvements, preferably as fixtures rather than as personal property.

Loans have been made on filling stations by insurance companies and commercial banks. Their loans are often for a relatively small percentage of appraised value, carry a rate of interst above the prime rate, are amortizing, and will seldom run for more than fifteen years (the generally agreed maximum estimate for the economic life of a new gasoline station).

Medical Buildings

Since the end of World War II there has been a new development in the special property field—the advent of the medical office building located away from the major commercial areas of cities. This development has occurred because of (1) inadequate parking space downtown; (2) an increase in the proportion of a physician's practice carried on in his or her office; (3) the movement of increasingly large numbers of people to the suburbs; (4) the advantages of being located closer to the homes of patients and to hospitals; (5) the economic advantages that may be obtained by a physician's owning or leasing space in these new properties.

The financial structure of such a property will usually consist of both equity and creditor interests. The equity may be created by (1) one person buying the land and otherwise providing the necessary owner investment; (2) a syndicate (limited partnership or trust) being established with member purchases providing capital; (3) a mutually owned medical center being established, with a corporation acquiring land, selling shares of stock to physician-tenants in proportion to the value of the space occupied, and then leasing space to them at a price sufficient to pay for maintenance, operation, and debt amortization costs.

As with any other special-purpose properties, definite dangers accompany investment in a medical center that are not found with office buildings or apartment properties. The most significant are (1) competition from better-located office facilities; (2) the additional investment ordinarily necessitated by the special power and plumbing requirements of many physicians; (3) difficulty and expense of converting such property to other use if the

medical center does not prove economically feasible; (4) the unwillingness of some physicians, such as psychiatrists, to take offices in relatively small buildings because of the nature of their practice; (5) the professional reputation of particular physicians as a force attracting or repelling the best practitioners to or from a medical center; and (6) competition from the development of hospital medical center complexes that have proven very attractive to many physicians whose practice is particularly dependent upon the use of hospital facilities.

In considering a loan application for a medical building, the lender would be primarily interested in determining (1) that the location is suitable; (2) that the financial resources of the developing concern are satisfactory (equity captial must be available in a satisfactory amount); (3) that the plan of the building is functional and the design reasonably attractive; (4) that there is an adequate amount of free parking; (5) that a sufficient amount of space has been leased to known, respected, and dependable physicians; (6) that no present or immediate future competition will effectively reduce the income of the property; (7) that the center is reasonably large, maximizing opportunities for construction economies and minimizing the effect of vacancies; and (8) that there is a reasonable need for such a structure in the proposed area. Of course, when the medical center is yet to be built, the lender would have to determine that the income estimated to be derived from leasing space will be adequate and the management competent, so that the center will be able to pay all costs connected with its operation and return a satisfactory yield to the owner.

As more institutional lenders have become familiar with medical centers and as the medical profession has come to accept them readily, it has become easier to finance these properties through institutional loan sources. If a center has most of the major requirements for success and if more than 50 percent of the space is leased, institutional loans for one-half to two-thirds of the appraised value can be obtained with some ease. These loans are usually for a period of ten to fifteen years (depending to some extent upon the lease terms), at the existing rate of interest, and established on an amortizing basis.

The loan documents will be a promissory note secured by a first trust deed on the property. The usual requirements for the protection of the rights of the lender on the debt and for preservation of the first lien priority and the value of the security will be established in these documents.

In a community needing additional modern medical office space, properly located, designed, and operated medical buildings may well turn out to be prime investments.

Bowling Alleys

A bowling alley is very dependent upon general regional prosperity, because bowling is a recreational activity and therefore can be substantially reduced or eliminated as a family expense if sufficient financial stress is encountered. Thus, an investment in a bowling alley is subject to a greater risk than investments in many other types of commerical enterprises.

In addition to this fundamental economic disadvantage, the nature of the structure greatly increases the risk of loss should there be a decrease in revenues derived from bowling and its ancillary activities. The buildings housing modern bowling alleys with automatic pinsetting equipment are large, substantial structures, often built of brick, concrete, or conrete block with structural steel supporting the large roof over the vast open areas typical of such structures. The lanes are constructed of expensive hardwood installed by a time-consuming handcraft method. All these construction features add to the cost of such a building. Because of their size and parking requirements the newer alleys are often located on the urban fringe or in less desirable commercial neighborhoods; thus, if a bowling alley enterprise fails, the opportunity for converting the building to some other financially successful use may well be limited.

However, if one is fortunate enough to construct a large, appropriately located bowling alley in a community experiencing a resurgence of bowling among an increasingly prosperous population, the net profit will be large. With automatic pinsetting equipment, bowling can earn substantial profits when use of the plant is maximized because there is little proportionate increase in the expense connected with such an operation when the incidence of facility use by customers increases. It is very important, therefore, that any lender accurately weigh the prospects for the bowling business in a community before lending money for the purchase or construction of a bowling alley.

In considering the feasibility of this kind of a loan a lender would want to check on (1) the status of present or future competition (hoping that there is very little); (2) demographic data revealing the size of the bowling population; (3) the adequacy of location and parking space; (4) provisions in the plans for the most efficient combination of size and arrangement of alleys, bar, restaurant, conference rooms, and babysitting and spectator space; and (5) the equipment, which should be fully automatic. The lender would also be very interested in the competence and experience of the alley management. It is also important to be informed of the general financial condition of the borrower so that an adequate determination of financial capacity can be made.

Bowling alleys are usually considered to be so risky or unorthodox that institutional lending on such property is virtually nonexistent in many sections of the United States. Consequently, most lending on this type of property is from private sources.

The financing of a bowling alley will usually be composed of a large (50 percent or more) equity interest derived from an individual proprietor, general partnership, small corporation, or syndicate of the limited partnership or trust form. Any creditor capital will be obtained though a relatively short-term (five to ten years at most) amortizing loan with a comparatively high interest rate. Since the heart of the modern bowling alley is the pinsetting equipment, it is common to make the commitment for the real estate loan conditional upon the borrower's also being able to finance the installation of such equipment. This all-important machinery is either financed by the manufacturer and seller, in the case of outright purchase, or leased to the alley owner.

Despite the substantial dangers in loans on bowling alleys, some especially good properties, along with other financial resources of the borrower, may afford a satisfactory lending opportunity.

Churches

Although churches are obviously not properties constructed for commercial use, the demand for church loans may increase; therefore we shall consider the financing of such special-purpose buildings. On a national basis, loans to churches by institutional lenders are usually small in proportion to the total amount of money lent.

Church buildings seldom have much value for other than the originally intended purposes. A church might be converted into a successful restaurant, store, office building, or theater, but experience has shown that this is not often done. The conversion possibilities depend to a great extent upon architectural design and floor plan. Traditional church architecture leaves little chance for truly effective conversion. Some churches constructed since 1946 are difficult to distinguish from schools, restaurants, theaters, or warehouses; therefore, the opportunity for using them in some other fashion is probably greater than in the case of older churches. This problem of limited building utility is one of the really great limitations on church loans from the lender's standpoint of having an adequately secured loan.

Another major drawback to church loans for the lender is the public relations problem if the property is actually disposed of by a foreclosure proceeding. For all practical purposes this problem renders such loans unsecured, because the lien on real property as security for the debt is almost useless.

In weighing the pros and cons of a loan to a congregation for church building purposes, a lender will be concerned with (1) the size and growth trend of the congregation; (2) per capita financial support of the church; (3) the financial history of the church; (4) the present financial status of the body and operating statement for the previous year; (5) the wealth of individual members of the congregation; (6) the degree of enthusiasm in the congregation's support of the church building plans; (7) financial support or guarantee by a regional or national office of the church; (8) the quality of financial management demonstrated in church affairs; and (9) the budget for the current year.

A secured real estate loan to a congregation for church building purposes will be made by using a promissory note and first trust deed. The usual provisions found in such instruments will be contained in these documents.

The sources of church loans are limited. Some insurance companies and banks have made such loans in the past. The loans are usually very conservative, with the maximum loan being computed on the basis of a factor times the number of members in the church. If a church has 200 members and the factor the lending agency uses is $200, the maximum loan will be $40,000. Another way of computing the maximum loan is on the basis of the annual budget times a factor such as 2. If the same church has a budget of $20,000 and the factor used is 2, the maximum loan will be $40,000. Of course, the appraised value would have to accommodate the legal limits for the lending agency.

A considerable volume of church lending is conducted on the basis of the sale of bonds secured by a first trust deed on the property improved. The bonds pay from 0.5 to 1 percent more than the prevailing rate of interest on savings deposits and are heavily secured; that is, they are issued only in the amount of 20 to 40 percent of the property's appraised value.

Although not bulking large in the total lending by financial institutions, the post–World War II church building boom should continue to provide opportunities for the making of loans advantageous to both lender and borrower.

Mini-Warehouses

During the last several years a unique type of real estate development called the *mini-warehouse* has appeared in numerous communities. The mini-warehouse complex consists of a multitude of dry storage areas ranging in size from that of a typical single-car garage down to that of a large clothes closet. These structures are usually concrete-block, single-story, flat-roof structures 20 to 50 feet in width and 200 to 500 feet long, with four or five such buildings on a three- to five-acre site. The simple nature of mini-warehouse buildings makes them relatively inexpensive to build; virtually no plumbing is involved, electrical wiring is minimal, and the only other elements are driveways and a small office space. Mini-warehouses can also be created out of existing older warehouses or other structures that can be economically converted into numerous small storage areas.

The effective demand for this type of space is created by business firms that lack adequate storage space and by residents of small houses and apartments who do not have enough space to store all their belongings in their residences. It is not unusual for 30 to 40 percent of the rentable space in a mini-warehouse complex to be rented by occupants of nearby apartments. Obviously, the continuation of effective demand for mini-warehouse units depends primarily upon an adequate population of apartment dwellers whose incomes are large enough to enable them to accumulate more storable goods than their residential units will hold.

A suitable location for mini-warehouses is within five miles of 1,000 to 3,000 rental apartments or small residences, very visible from a main traffic artery, and readily accessible by automobile. The absence of present or future competition increases the economic feasibility of a specific mini-warehouse complex.

Some institutional lenders such as commercial banks and savings and loan associations may be convinced to make mortgage loans on this type of property. In the absence of making a credit loan to a financially strong borrower, they would want to extend real estate mortgage credit on the basis of net income to cover annual mortgage loan servicing costs 1.5 to 2.0 times, a conservative loan-to-value ratio (50 to 60 percent of market value), and a relatively short repayment period of ten to fifteen years or less. In some locales it may be possible to obtain real estate mortgage financing only from noninstitutional sources. Properly located and marketed mini-warehouse complexes in California cities and suburbs have often produced square-foot gross rent schedules of 75 to 80 percent of rents obtained for typical apartments. Since the costs of operating them (electricity, water, real property taxes, insurance, security, management, and advertising) amount to only 15 to 25 percent of gross rent (with almost no vacancy or bad debt losses), the return on investment in such properties to the first investors in them has been very attractive. As there is more competition to rent such space in urban locations, the gross rent schedules will probably decline. Like most other special-purpose properties, mini-warehouse buildings are typically unfit for use for many other purposes.

QUESTIONS

1. Shopping centers have increased in number during the past thirty years. This is due mainly to
   a. the private automobile becoming the major means of transportation
   b. the continuing trend toward concentrating population in urban areas
   c. the continuing trend of households to move to the suburbs
   d. shopping has, over the past years, tended to become a form of family recreation
   e. all of the above

2. An advantage to the lender of financing a successful shopping center is
   a. the relatively little risk of funds and a possible chance for the lender to receive an extraordinary yield on the funds provided through participatory financing arrangements
   b. deductibility of operational expenses from gross taxable income
   c. capital gains income tax rates apply to any profit made by selling the center at a later date at a higher price than the cost of acquiring it
   d. improvements can be depreciated under federal income tax laws, thereby constituting a form of tax shelter
   e. none of the above

3. For a shopping center to stand a reasonable chance of financial success, the developer must make sure that
   a. some people live within five miles of the center
   b. the merchant-tenant mix in the center is favorable, relative to the economic and social characteristics of most of the population in the center's primary trading area
   c. the structure of the shopping center is a two-level one
   d. there are no other shopping centers in the city
   e. all of the above

4. The total financing plan for raising mortgage money to finance the construction of a new, major office building on a lot in a city will typically involve
   a. an economic feasibility study
   b. an appraisal by the income approach to determine the potential value of the planned building
   c. estimating the annual net income to be derived from the property over its economic life

d. arranging a take-out loan commitment from an institutional-type lender and then using this loan commitment to arrange for a construction loan
   e. all of the above

5. Some unique problems in financing industrial properties are
   a. that, if privately owned, they are subject to local real property taxes
   b. since they are often single-purpose properties, the value of such improved industrial properties is relatively unstable, and is subject to great fluctuations
   c. the financial condition of a manufacturer-owner has little to do with the financial feasibility of such a loan
   d. only commercial banks typically finance such properties
   e. all of the above

6. Of particular relevance and importance to the economic feasibility of rental apartment complexes are
   a. that the size of the various apartments is a reasonable match for the number of people in the typical households that can be expected to be tenants
   b. that the complex is located in what is, as a practical matter, logically a rental unit neighborhood
   c. that there is little practical possibility of rent control being imposed in the community
   d. that the complex is conveniently situated to provide access to the community's transportation system and is not too close to or too far from places that most working people frequent
   e. all of the above

7. Some unique characteristics of special-purpose properties are
   a. the structural improvements constructed on the land are mainly suited for one commercial-type purpose
   b. the improvements on the land are never, in an economically practical sense, convertible to another profitable use
   c. owners of such properties expect to make a profit by conducting a commercial-type operation at such a site
   d. there is nothing particularly difficult about appraising such properties
   e. all of the above

8. An example of a special-purpose property is
   a. a rental apartment complex
   b. an office building
   c. a church

d. a manufacturing plant
e. all of the above

BIBLIOGRAPHY

CASE, FREDERICK, E., JOHN M. CLAPP, *Real Estate Financing,* New York: John Wiley, 1978, Chapters 12–14.

HINES, MARY ALICE, *Real Estate Finance,* Englewood Cliffs, NJ: Prentice-Hall, 1978.

HOAGLAND, HENRY E., LEO D. STONE, and WILLIAM B. BRUEGGEMAN, *Real Estate Finance* (6th ed.), Chapter 11. Homewood, IL: Richard D. Irwin, 1977.

KRATOVIL, ROBERT, and RAYMOND J. WERNER, *Real Estate Law* (7th ed.), Englewood Cliffs, NJ: Prentice-Hall, 1979, Chapters 35–37.

Appendix: Compendium of Laws Dealing with Equal Access to Residential Accommodations and Credit

The problem with which laws concerned with equal access to residential accommodations and credit deal is that of people discriminating against minority group members in the leasing or sale of real property and the granting of credit. The result of such discrimination is to relegate, through a system of segregation, minority people to certain sections of urban areas in the United States. The sections of communities where the minority population is concentrated are typically substandard in comparison to many residential neighborhoods occupied by members of the majority.

Legal action designed to eliminate discrimination on the basis of race, creed, color, religion, or place of national origin in the leasing or sale of residential property and in the granting of credit usually defines such conduct as a crime and establishes penalties to be imposed by a court of law upon persons convicted of committing such crimes. Sophisticated open-housing statutes provide for (1) efforts at conciliation to settle the dispute between the party accused of discrimination and the accuser, (2) courts or administrative agencies issuing orders restraining the accused party from leasing or selling the residential property in question, and finally, (3) the trial of the party accused of such illegal discrimination in a criminal court, possibly resulting in a guilty verdict and the imposition of various punishments.

This compendium of laws dealing with legal methods of providing equal access for all people to residential accommodations and credit consists mainly of reference material that speaks for itself. Excerpts from recognized studies of racial discrimination, statutes, and appellate court decisions present an overview of the development of this body of law. Of course, there will continue to be changes in this field of law, but as of the enactment of the Civil Rights Act of 1968 by Congress and the handing down of the decision *Jones* v. *Alfred H. Mayer Company* (88 Sup Ct. 2186) by the United States Supreme Court, the basic legal framework designed to prevent racial discrimination in the leasing or sale of residential property had been established.

A vast body of reference material pertains to the development of open housing. Periodical articles, books, appellate court decisions, statutes, and executive orders constitute thousands of pages of printed material. In this book we shall reprint material that is historically significant to understanding various aspects of the subject or that presents a comprehensive view of the usual legal methods of preventing this type of discrimination.

An American Dilemma, by Gunnar Myrdal, describes various aspects of discrimination against minority people in this country. With regard to discrimination in the leasing and sale of residential property, Myrdal made various observations pertinent to the topic of the legal aspects of open housing.

Housing is much more than just shelter.[1] It provides the setting for the whole life of the family. Indeed, whether or not any organized family life will be at all possible depends very much on the character of the house or dwelling unit. Children cannot be reared in a satisfactory manner if there is no place for them at home where they can play without constantly irritating the adults or being irritated by them. Over-crowding may keep them out of their homes more than is good for them—in fact so much that family controls become weak. The result is that some of the children become juvenile delinquents. This danger may become even more pronounced if there are insufficient recreational facilities in the neighborhood, something which is often characteristic of Negro areas. Children in crowded homes usually have great difficulties in doing their homework; their achievements in school may suffer in consequence. The presence of boarders in the homes, or the "doubling up" of families in a single residence unit, which is much more frequent in Negro than in white families, usually means that there cannot be much privacy; often it means a constant

---

[1]The following extract is abridged from pp. 375, 376, 377, 379, 619, 622–624 in *An American Dilemma,* 20th Anniversary Edition by Gunnar Myrdal. Copyright © 1944, 1962 by Harper & Row, Publishers, Inc. By permission of the publisher.

threat to family morals. Crowding in general has similar effects. In addition to the moral and mental health risks, there are all the obvious physical health hazards. . . . Nothing is so obvious about the Negroes' level of living as the fact that most of them suffer from poor housing conditions. It is a matter of such common knowledge that it does not need much emphasis. . . .

. . . Urban Negro housing is poorer than even the low income status of the Negroes would enable them to buy. This may be due to the fact that, at least in Southern cities and villages, Negroes, even at a given income level, spend less money on housing than do whites. It seems, however, that there is another and even more fundamental cause: the artificial limitation in the choice of housing for Negroes brought about by residental segregation. . . .

We have found that Negro families in Southern cities and villages use a somewhat smaller part of their total expenditure for housing than do white families in the same income class. This appears also when rent-paying families are studied separately. The situation seems to be different in New York, however, where Negro families in most income groups pay higher rentals than do whites. When all income groups are combined, urban Negroes are usually found to use a greater portion of their total expenditures for housing than is usual in the white population. The reason, of course, is the fact that poor families generally have to use a larger part of their income for housing than do the more well-to-do families. The housing item in the budget seems to be particularly cumbersome in New York, where, according to the Consumer Purchases Study, nonrelief Negro families used as much as 27 percent of their total expenditure for this purpose, whereas the corresponding figure for white families was 22 percent. There is a general complaint among Negroes that they have to pay higher rents than do whites for equal housing accommodations. It is difficult to get any unequivocal statistical evidence on this problem, and it seems that this is one of the main aspects of Negro housing on which additional research work is needed. Nevertheless, we feel inclined to believe that rents are higher, on the average, in Negro- than in white-occupied dwelling units even when size and quality are equal. Most housing experts and real estate people who have had experience with Negro housing have made statements to this effect. Not only does there seem to be consensus on the matter among those who have studied the Negro housing problem, but there is also a good logical reason for it: housing segregation. (Some white real estate dealers attribute the higher rent for Negroes to their carelessness and destructiveness. From our point of view, the important thing is that they observe the fact of higher rents.) Particularly when the Negro population is increasing in a city, it is hard to see how this factor can fail to make Negro rents increase to an even greater extent than would have been the case if the Negroes had been free to seek accommodations wherever in the city they could afford to pay the rent. The fact that they are not wanted where they have not already been accepted must put them in an extremely disadvantaged position in any question of renting or of buying a house. . . .

Residential concentration tends to be determined by three main factors: poverty preventing individuals from paying for anything more than the cheapest housng accommodation; ethnic attachment; segregation enforced by white people. Even in the absence of enforced segregation, Negroes would not be evenly distributed in every city because as a group, they are much poorer than urban whites. This applies with particular strength to the masses of Northern Negroes who are newly arrived from the South. Negroes would also be likely to cluster together for convenience and mutual protection. . . .

Probably the chief force maintaining residential segregation of Negroes has been informal social pressure from the whites. Few white property owners in white neighborhoods would ever consider selling or renting to Negroes; and even if a few Negro families did succeed in getting a foothold, they would be made to feel the spontaneous hatred of the whites both socially and physically. The main reason why informal social pressure has not always been effective in preventing Negroes from moving into a white neighborhood has been the tremendous need of Negroes to move out of their intensely overcrowded ghettos and their willingness to bear a great deal of physical and mental punishment to satisfy that need.

The clash of interests is particularly dramatic in the big cities of the North to which Negro immigrants from the South have been streaming since the First World War. When white residents of a neighborhood see that they cannot remove the few Negro intruders and also see more Negro families moving in, they conjure up certain stereotypes of how bad Negro neighbors are and move out of the neighborhood with almost panic speed. For this reason, Negroes are dangerous for property values, as well as for neighborhood business, and all whites are aware of this fact. (If white property owners in a neighborhood rush to sell their property all at once, property values are naturally hurt. After the transition to Negro occupancy is made, however, property values rise again at least to the level justified by the aging and lack of improvement of the buildings.) In describing the succession of Negroes down the South Side in Chicago, an informant said, "This was not an incoming of the Negroes, so much as an outgoing of the whites. If one colored person moved into the neighborhood, the rest of the white people immediately moved out."

Such a situation creates a vicious circle, in which race prejudice, economic interests, and residential segregation mutually reinforce one another. When a few Negro families do come into a white neighborhood, some more white families move away. Other Negroes hasten to take their places, because the existing Negro neighborhoods are overcrowded due to segregation. This constant movement of Negroes into white neighborhoods makes the bulk of the white residents feel that their neighborhood is doomed to be predominantly Negro, and they move out—with their attitudes against the Negro reinforced. Yet, if there were no segregation, this wholesale invasion would not have occurred; but because it does occur, segregational attitudes are increased, and the vigil and pressure to stall the Negroes at the borderline is kept up.

Various organized techniques have been used to reinforce the spontaneous segregational attitudes and practices of whites in keeping Negro residences restricted to certain areas in a city. These include local zoning ordinances, restrictive covenants, and terrorism.

The earliest important legal step to enforce segregation was taken in 1910 when an ordinance was passed in Baltimore, Maryland, after a Negro family had moved into what had previously been an all-white block. Many Southern and border cities followed suit, after state courts upheld zoning ordinances. Even after the Louisville ordinance was declared unconstitutional by the Supreme Court of the United States in 1917, certain cities put into effect other segregative laws designed to get around the decision. A more comprehensive and severe denunciation of segregation by law was made in the 1927 decision of the Supreme Court in the New Orleans case, but even as recently as 1940, the North Carolina State Supreme Court had to invalidate a residential segregation ordinance passed in Winston-Salem. When the courts' opposition to segregation laws passed by public bodies became manifest, and there was more migration of Negroes to cities, organized activities on the part of the interested whites became more widespread. The restrictive covenant—an agreement by property owners in a neighborhood not to sell or rent their property to colored people for a definite period—has been popular, especially in the North. The exact extent of the use of the restrictive covenant has not been ascertained, but: "In Chicago, it has been estimated that 80 percent of the city is covered by such agreements." This technique has come up several times for court review, but, because of technicalities, the Supreme Court has as yet avoided the principal issue of the general legal status of the covenants. If the court should follow up its action of declaring illegal also the private restrictive covenants, segregation in the North would be nearly doomed, and segregation in the South would be set back slightly.

In the summer of 1967 racial riots shook several large urban areas of the United States to their very foundations. After these events, President Lyndon Johnson appointed a National Advisory Commission on Civil Disorders. Early in 1968 this commission produced its report, entitled *Report of the National Advisory Commission on Civil Disorders*. This study, completed and published twenty-four years after *An American Dilemma*, contains various observations on housing conditions for minority people in various American urban areas.

The early pattern of Negro settlement within each metropolitan area followed that of immigrant groups. Migrants converged on the older sections of the central city because the lowest cost housing was there, friends and relatives were likely to be there, and the older neighborhoods then often had good public transportation.

But the later phases of Negro settlement and expansion in metropolitan areas diverge sharply from those typical of white immigrants. As the whites were absorbed by the larger society, many left their predominantly ethnic neighborhoods and moved to outlying areas to obtain newer housing and better schools. Some scattered randomly over the suburban area. Others established new ethnic clusters in the suburbs, but even these rarely contained solely members of a single ethnic group. As a result, most middle-class neighborhoods—both in the suburbs and within central cities—have no distinctive ethnic character, except that they are white.

Nowhere has the expansion of America's urban Negro population followed this pattern of dispersal. Thousands of Negro families have attained incomes, living standards, and

cultural levels matching or surpassing those of whites who have upgraded themselves from distinctly ethnic neighborhoods. Yet most Negro families have remained within predominantly Negro neighborhoods, primarily because they have been effectively excluded from white residential areas.

Their exclusion has been accomplished through various discriminatory practices, some obvious and overt, others subtle and hidden. Deliberate efforts are sometimes made to discourage Negro families from purchasing or renting homes in all-white neighborhoods. Intimidation and threats of violence have ranged from throwing garbage on lawns and making threatening phone calls to burning crosses in yards and even dynamiting property. More often, real estate agents simply refuse to show homes to Negro buyers.

Many middle-class Negro families, therefore, cease looking for homes beyond all-Negro areas or nearby "changing" neighborhoods. For them, trying to move into all-white neighborhoods is not worth the psychological efforts and costs required.

Another form of discrimination just as significant is "white-flight"—withdrawal from or refusal to enter neighborhoods where large numbers of Negroes are moving or already residing. Normal population turnover causes about 20 percent of the residents of average United States neighborhoods to move out every year because of income changes, job transfers, shifts in life-cycle position, or deaths. This normal turnover rate is even higher in apartment areas. The refusal of whites to move into "changing" areas when vacancies occur there from normal turnover means that most vacancies are eventually occupied by Negroes. An inexorable shift toward heavy Negro occupancy results.

Once this happens, the remaining whites seek to leave, and this seems to confirm the existing belief among whites that complete transformation of a neighborhood is inevitable once Negroes begin to enter. Since the belief itself is one of the major causes of the transformation, it becomes a self-fulfilling prophecy, which inhibits the development of racially integrated neighborhoods.

Thus, Negro settlements expand almost entirely through "massive racial transition" at the edges of existing all-Negro neighborhoods, rather than by a gradual dispersion of population throughout the metropolitan area. Two important points to note about this phenomenon are that:

"Massive transition" requires no panic or flight by the original white residents of a neighborhood into which Negroes begin moving. All it requires is the failure or refusal of other whites to fill the vacancies resulting from normal turnover.

Thus, efforts to stop massive transition by persuading present white residents to remain will ultimately fail unless whites outside the neighborhood can be persuaded to move in.

Some residential separation of whites and Negroes would occur even without discriminatory practices by whites. Separation would result from the desires of some Negroes to live in predominantly Negro neighborhoods like many other groups, and from differences in meaningful social variables, such as income and educational levels, between many

Negroes and many whites. But these factors would not lead to the almost complete segregation of whites and Negroes, which has developed in our metropolitan areas.

The process of racial transition in central-city neighborhoods has been only one factor among many others causing millions of whites to move out of central cities as the Negro populations there expanded. More basic perhaps have been the rising mobility and affluence of middle-class families and the more attractive living conditions—particularly better schools—in the suburbs.[2]

THE GENERAL RIGHT OF THE OWNER OF REAL PROPERTY TO USE AND CONTROL THE USE MADE OF THAT PROPERTY

From the material excerpted above, it is seen that the discrimination against minorities in the sale and leasing of real property is closely connected to the power of an owner to deal with his or her property in a manner that effects this discrimination. To lessen this discrimination certain legal limitations have been placed upon the property owner's power to determine who will buy or lease his or her property. To appreciate more fully the nature of limitations placed upon the owner's rights in his or her real property so as to minimize this discriminatory disposition of it, we need to understand the nature of property, real property, and the limitations that may be placed upon its use and disposition. The power of the owner of land to dispose, use, or lease it may be limited through private agreements or action of the state. If such restrictions upon this property right are to be enforceable in the courts, they must meet legal tests of being constitutional and in accordance with public policy.

Property has been defined in numerous ways, some of which are set forth below:

Property is that which is peculiar or proper to any person; that which belongs exclusively to one: in the strict legal sense, an aggregate of rights which are guaranteed and protected by the government.

The term *property* is said to extend to every species of valuable right and interest.

Property means more specifically ownership; the unrestricted and exclusive right to a thing; the right to dispose of a thing in every legal way, to possess it, to use it, and to exclude everyone else from interfering with it. That dominion or indefinite right of use or disposition which one may lawfully exercise over particular things or subjects.

The right of property is that sole and despotic dominion which one man claims and exercises over the external things of the world, in total exclusion of the right of any other individual in the universe. It consists in the free use, enjoyment, and disposal of all a person's acquisitions,

without any control or diminution save only by the laws of the land.[3]

The interest (estate) that the purchaser of a typical single-family house on a lot in an urban area of the United States receives from the seller is known as *fee simple*. This estate (interest) in land should be understood in terms of the legal position of its owner if one is to comprehend the effect of legal steps taken to lessen or eliminate racial discrimination in the sale or leasing of residential property.

The fee-simple estate in real property has been defined in various ways, some of which are set forth below:

A fee-simple absolute is an estate limited absolutely to a man and his heirs and assigns forever without limitation or condition.

An absolute or fee-simple estate is one in which the owner is entitled to the entire property, with unconditional power of disposition during his life, and descending to his heirs and legal representatives upon his death intestate.

Fee-simple signifies a pure fee; an absolute estate of inheritance clear of any condition or restriction to particular heirs, being descendible to the heirs general, whether male or female, linear or collateral. It is the largest estate and most extensive interest that can be enjoyed in land.[4]

Keeping in mind the "absoluteness" of the fee-simple owner's interst in real property, we shall direct our attention to limitations and restrictions that can and do exist upon such a property right. A fee-simple estate is subject to (1) the state's power to tax, (2) the state's power of eminent domain, (3) the police power of the state, (4) legal principles prohibiting use to be made of property that constitutes a public or private nuisance, and (5) any enforceable private restrictive covenants that limit the use of land in ways compatible with established public policy. This list of limitations upon the absolute uncontrolled use and disposition of land held in fee simple indicates that most owners of real property in the United States are not complete, absolute, unfettered rulers of their property.

For the purpose of lessening or eliminating discrimination against minorities in the sale and leasing of real property, the police power of the state is probably the most important government power that may be exercised over land. This power is exercised by the state to protect the health, safety, welfare, and morals of the community. It must be reasonably exercised in that there is a direct relationship between the public interests cited above and the enforcement of such power against a certain class of

---

[2]*Report of the National Advisory Commission on Civil Disorders* (New York: Bantam Books, Inc., 1968), pp. 243, 244, 245.

[3]*Black's Law Dictionary,* 4th ed. (St. Paul, Minn.: West Publishing Company, 1951), p. 1382.
[4]Ibid., p. 742.

citizens and/or their property. The power must be implemented in a constitutional manner; that is, due process of law and all other constitutional protections for the rights of the individual and his or her property are complied with. The exercise of such power, which typically restricts the freedom of the individual and the use made of the property, must result in a direct, recognizable, legitimate benefit to the public. Historical examples of the correct use of this power of government are (1) traffic laws regulating the speed of automobiles on streets, (2) laws regulating the sale of alcoholic beverages, (3) building codes establishing minimum standards for safety in the construction of buildings, (4) zoning ordinances regulating the use made of land by its owner, (5) laws regulating the practice of learned professions such as law and medicine, and (6) laws controlling activities that cause air pollution. Typically, public recognition of a threat to the public health, safety, welfare, and morals causes the appropriate legislative body to enact legislation authorizing the exercise of this power by the state under the police power.

The term *police power* has been defined in various ways, some of which are set forth below:

The power vested in the legislature to make, ordain, and establish all manner of wholesome and reasonable laws, statutes, and ordinances, either with penalties or without, not repugnant to the constitution, as they shall judge to be for the good and welfare of the commonwealth, and of the subjects of the same.

That inherent and plenary power in a state over persons and property which enables the people to prohibit all things inimical to comfort, safety, health, and welfare of society.

It is true that the legislation which secures to all protection in their rights, and the equal use and enjoyment of their property, embraces an almost infinite variety of subjects. Whatever affects the peace, good order, morals, and health of the community comes within its scope; and everyone must use and enjoy his property subject to the restrictions which such legislation imposes. What is termed the "police power" of the state, which, from the language often used respecting it, one would suppose to be an undefined and irresponsible element in government, can only interfere with the conduct of individuals, in their intercourse with each other, and in the use of their property, so far as may be required to secure these objects.[5]

What the state's police power is and how it may be legitimately employed has been discussed by appellate courts:

The police power of a state today embraces regulations designed to promote the public convenience or the general prosperity as well as those to promote public safety, health, morals, and is not confined to the suppression of what is

offensive, disorderly, or unsanitary, but extends to what is for the greatest welfare of the State.[6]

Because the police power of a State is the least limitable of the exercises of government, such limitations as are applicable thereto are not readily definable. Being neither susceptible of circumstantial precision, nor discoverable by any formula, these limitations can be determined only through appropriate regard to the subject matter of the exercise of that power.[7]

It is settled that neither the "contract" clause nor the "due process" clause has the effect of overriding the power of the State to establish all regulations that are reasonably necessary to secure the health, safety, good order, comfort, or general welfare of the community; that this power can neither be abdicated nor bargained away, and is inalienable even by express grant; and that all contract and property (or other vested) rights are held subject to its fair exercise.[8]

Insofar as the police power is utilized by a state, the means employed to effect its exercise can be neither arbitrary nor oppressive, but must bear a real and substantial relation to an end which is public, specifically, the public health, public safety, or public morals, or some other phase of the general welfare.[9]

The general rule is that if a police power regulation goes too far, it will be recognized as a taking of property for which compensation must be paid.[10]

Statutes enacted by state and local legislative bodies limiting the owner's exercise of dominion over real property in that selling or leasing it is carried on for the purpose and effect of discriminating against persons of certain races are usually based upon the police power. Federal legislation designed to prevent such discrimination by owners of real property can be based upon the United States Constitution as amended. (Specifically, the constitutional basis for federal statutes could be any of the following: Section 8, "The Congress shall have power to regulate commerce with foreign nations, and among the several states, and with the Indian tribes"; the Thirteenth Amendment, Section 1, "Neither slavery nor involuntary servitude, except as punishment for crime whereof the party shall have been duly convicted, shall exist within the United States, or any place subject to their jurisdiction"; Section 2, "Congress shall have power to enforce this article by appropriate legislation"; and the Fourteenth Amendment, Section 1, "All persons born or naturalized in the United States and subject to the jurisdiction thereof, are citizens of the United States and the State wherein they reside. No State shall make or enforce any law which shall abridge the privileges and immun-

---

[5]Ibid., p. 1317.

[6]*Reduction Company* v. *Sanitary Works*, 199 US 306, 318 (1905).

[7]*Hudson Water Company* v. *McCarter*, 209 U.S. 349 (1908).

[8]*Atlantic Coast Line* v. *Goldsboro*, 232 U.S. 548, 558 (1914).

[9]*Liggett and Company* v. *Baldridge*, 278 U.S. 105, 111–112 (1928).

[10]*Pennsylvania Coal Company* v. *Mahon*, 260 U.S. 393 (1922).

ities of citizens of the United States; nor shall any State deprive any person of life, liberty, or property, without due process of law; nor deny to any person within its jurisdiction the equal protection of the laws.")

Let us now consider specific appellate court decisions, statutes, and executive orders that indicate the state of the law with regard to this type of discrimination and the means whereby various legislative bodies and the federal executive sought to eliminate it.

The United States Supreme Court decision of *Shelley* v. *Kraemer,* 334 U.S. 1 (1948), is a landmark in the history of the evolution of the law relating to discrimination in the sale or rental of real property based upon the race, religion, color, or national origin of the prospective purchaser or lessee.

In this case the United States Supreme Court outlawed the enforcement by state courts of racial restrictions as to the ownership or use of real property. The following language in the opinion by Chief Justice Vinson sets forth the rationale of the decision.

"In the case from Missouri the property was restricted as to use and occupancy in that no part of said property shall for a term of 50 years be occupied by any person not of the caucasian race, it being intended hereby to restrict the use of said property for said period of time against occupancy as owners or tenants of any portion of said property for resident or other purpose by people of the Negro or Mongolian race. The restriction seeks to proscribe use and occupancy of the affected properties by members of the excluded class and in addition—as construed by the Missouri courts, the agreement required that title of any person who uses his property in violation of the restriction shall be divested. The restriction of the covenant in the Michigan case seeks to bar occupancy by persons of the excluded class. We hold that in granting judicial enforcement of the restrictive agreements in these cases, the states have denied petitioner (Shelley) the equal protection of the laws and that, therefore the action of the state courts cannot stand."

After *Shelley* v. *Kraemer,* racially restrictive land-use covenants were no longer enforceable in the state or federal courts of this country. If they were voluntarily complied with by owners of property subject to them, such a restriction use plan could be effectively maintained.

After the decision of *Shelley* v. *Kraemer,* racial discrimination affecting the sale and leasing of real property could legally be carried out by (1) owners who did not have to go to court to enforce a private contractual agreement, (2) lending institutions, and (3) real estate brokers. Legal steps to eliminate discrimination against minorities in the sale or leasing of real property were now specifically directed to these aspects of real property control and the marketing of it. The action that was taken to limit the legal prerogative to discriminate on a racial basis in selling or leasing real property, financing it, or mar-

keting it through a brokerage operation took place in the legislative, executive, and judicial branches of government.

The following material, from California Government Code Sections 12955, 12980–12988, constitutes a summary of the effect of the statutes enacted by the California legislature to deal with the problem of discrimination on the basis of race, creed, religion, color, or national origin in the sale and leasing of real property.

California prohibits discrimination in all public housing and urban renewal housing, in other publicly assisted housing except two-family houses, and in private housing except for houses with four or fewer units. Real estate brokers and financial institutions are covered by the provisions of the law. Enforcement is by the Fair Employment Practice Commission. An aggrieved person may file a complaint with the commission, but the commission itself may not initiate a complaint. If the commission determines by investigation that probable cause exists for believing the allegations of the complaint, it may attempt to eliminate the violation by conciliation. Also, a temporary restraining order may be obtained (for not more than twenty days) enjoining the owner of the housing from selling or leasing it until the commission has made a final determination. If attempts at conciliation fail, a hearing is held before a hearing officer sitting alone; he prepares a proposed decision, copies of which are served on the parties. The commission may adopt the decision as drafted or adopt the decision and reduce the penalty. Alternately, the commission may decide the case on the record, with or without taking additional evidence, but in such a case the parties must be provided with an opportunity for oral or written argument. If the commission finds that an unlawful practice has been engaged in, it issues a cease and desist order and requires the transfer of the housing accommodation in question, the transfer of a like accommodation, or the payment to the complainant of damages not to exceed $500, if the remedy of transfer is not available. Willful violation of such orders is punishable by a fine not to exceed $500, imprisonment not to exceed six months, or both. Judicial review of commission orders is available. If the commission believes that its orders are being violated it may obtain a court injunction against further violation.

California also has a statute that provides that all persons, regardless of their race, color, religion, or national origin, are entitled to the full and equal accommodations, facilities, and services of all business establishments. This law has been construed by the courts to apply to real estate brokers and developers. Persons aggrieved by violations may bring civil suits for the actual damages suffered plus $250. Another statute voids racial and religious restrictive convenants in written instruments relating to real property.

Citations to California statutes dealing with the prohibition and punishment of discrimination in the sale or leasing of housing on the basis of race, creed, color, religion, or national origin are set forth below:

California Health and Safety Code Sections 33050, 33436, 35700–35744.

California Labor Code Sections 1414–1430.
California Government Code Sections 11500–11528.
California Code of Civil Procedure Section 1094.5.
California Civil Code Sections 51–53.

In 1964 the voters of California enacted a ballot initiative identified as Proposition 14. This proposition amended the California Constitution in a manner so as to nullify Sections 35700—35744 of the California Health and Safety Code (known as the Rumford Act). Proposition 14 consisted of the following language:

Neither the State nor any subdivision or agency thereof shall deny, limit, or abridge, directly or indirectly, the right of any person, who is willing or desires to sell, lease or rent any part or all of his real property, to decline to sell, lease or rent such property to such person or persons as he, in his absolute discretion, chooses. "Person" includes individuals, partnerships, corporations and other legal entities and their agents or representatives but does not include the State or any subdivision thereof with respect to the sale, lease or rental of property owned by it.

"Real property" consists of any interest in real property of any kind or quality, present or future, irrespective of how obtained or financed, which is used, designed, constructed, zoned or otherwise devoted to or limited for residential purposes whether as a single family dwelling or as a dwelling for two or more persons or families living together or independently of each other. This article shall not apply to the obtaining of property by eminent domain pursuant to Article I, Section 14 and 14½ of this Constitution, nor to the renting or providing of any accommodations for lodging purposes by a hotel, motel, or other similar public place engaged in furnishing lodging to transient guests. If any part or provision of this Article, or the application thereof to any person or circumstance, is held invalid, the remainder of the Article including the application of such part or provision to other persons or circumstances, shall not be affected thereby and shall continue in full force and effect. To this end the provisions of this Article are severable.

This amendment is to be added as Section 26 of Article I of the Constitution of the State of California.

Proposition 14 became Section 26 of Article I of the California Constitution. The constitutionality of this amendment was challenged in the state courts. Ultimately, there was an appeal from the decision of the California Supreme Court to the United States Supreme Court. An abbreviated version of this appellate court decision follows:

REITMAN v. MULKEY
87 Sup. Ct. 1627, May 29, 1967

Mr. Justice WHITE delivered the opinion of the court.

The question here is whether ART. I, para. 26 of the California Constitution denies "to any person . . . the equal protection of the laws" within the meaning of the Fourteenth Amendment of the Constitution of the United States. Section 26 of Art. I, an initiated measure submitted to the people as Proposition 14 in a statewide ballot in 1964, provides in part as follows:

"Neither the State nor any subdivision or agency thereof shall deny, limit or abridge, directly or indirectly, the right of any person, who is willing or desires to sell, lease or rent any part or all of his real property, to decline to sell, lease or rent such property to such person or persons as he, in his absolute discretion, chooses."

The real property covered by para. 26 is limited to residential property and contains an exception for state-owned real estate.

The issue arose in two separate actions in the California courts, *Reitman* v. *Mulkey* and *Prendergast* v. *Snyder*. In *Reitman*, the Mulkeys who are husband and wife and respondents here, sued under para. 51 and para. 52 of the California Civil Code alleging that petitioners had refused to rent them an apartment solely on account of their race. An injunction and damages were demanded. Petitioners moved for summary judgment on the ground that paragraphs 51 and 52, insofar as they were the basis for the Mulkey's action, had been rendered null and void by the adoption of Proposition 14 after the filing of the complaint. The trial court granted the motion and respondents took the case to the California Supreme Court.

In the *Prendergast* case, respondents, husband and wife, filed suit in December 1964 seeking to enjoin eviction from their apartment; respondents alleged that the eviction was motivated by racial prejudice and therefore would violate paragraphs 51 and 52 of the Civil Code. Petitioner Snyder cross-complained for a judicial declaration that he was entitled to terminate the month-to-month tenancy even if his action was based on racial considerations. In denying petitioner's motion for summary judgment, the trial court found it unnecessary to consider the validity of Proposition 14 because it concluded that judicial enforcement of an eviction based on racial grounds would in any event violate the Equal Protection Clause of the United States Constitution. The cross-complaint was dismissed with prejudice and petitioner Snyder appealed to the California Supreme Court which considered the case along with *Reitman* v. *Mulkey*. That court, in reversing the *Reitman* case, held that Art. I, para. 26, was invalid as denying the equal protection of the laws guaranteed by the Fourteenth Amendment. 64 Cal. 2d 529, 50 Cal. Rptr. 881, 413 P.2d 825. For similar reasons, the court affirmed the judgment in the *Prendergast* case. 64 Cal. 2d 877, 50 Cal. Rptr. 903, 413 P.2d 847. We granted certiorari because the cases involve an important issue arising under the Fourteenth Amendment. 385 U.S. 967, 87 S.Ct. 500, 17 L.Ed.2d 431.

[1, 2] We affirm the judgment of the California Supreme Court. We first turn to the opinion of that court, which quite properly undertook to examine the constitutionality of para. 26 in terms of its "immediate objective," its "ultimate impact" and its "historical context and the conditions existing prior to its enactment." Judgments such as these we have frequently undertaken ourselves. . . .

But here the California Supreme Court has addressed itself to these matters and we should give careful consideration to its views because they concern the purpose, scope, and operative effect of a provision of the California Constitution.

First, the court considered whether para. 26 was concerned at all with private discriminations in residential housing. This involved a review of past efforts by the California Legislature to regulate such discriminations. . . .

Second, the court conceded that the State was permitted a neutral position with respect to private racial discrimination and that the state was not bound by the Federal Constitution to forbid them. But, because a significant state involvement in private discriminations could amount to unconstituional state action, *Burton* v. *Wilmington Parking Authority*, 365 U.S. 715, 81 S.Ct. 856, 6 L.Ed.2d 45, the court deemed it necessary to determine whether Propositon 14 invalidly involved the State in racial discimintations in the housing market. Its conclusion was that it did. . . .

Also of particular interest to the court was Mr. Justice Stewart's concurrence in *Burton* v. *Wilmington Parking Authority*, 365 U.S. 715, 81 S.Ct. 856, 6 L.Ed.2d 45, where it was said that the Delaware courts had construed an existing Delaware statute as "authorizing" racial discrimination in restaurants and that the statute was therefore invalid. To the California Court "[t]he instant case presents an undeniably analogous situation" wherein the State had taken affirmative action designed to make private discriminations legally possible. Section 26 was said to have changed the situation from one in which discriminatory practices were restricted "to one wherein it is encouraged, within the meaning of the cited decisions"; para. 26 was legislative action "which authorized private discrimination" and made the State "at least a partner in the instant act of discrimination. . . ." The judgment of the California court was that para. 26 unconstitutionally involves the State in racial discriminations and is therefore invalid under the Fourteenth Amendment.

There is no sound reason for rejecting this judgment. Petitioners contend that the California court has misconstrued the Fourteenth Amendment since the repeal of any statute prohibiting racial discrimination, which is constitutionally permissible, may be said to "authorize" and "encourage" discrimination because it makes legally permissible that which was formerly proscribed. But as we understand the California court, it did not posit a constitutional violation on the mere repeal of the Unruh and Rumford Acts. It did not read either our cases or the Fourteenth Amendment as establishing an automatic constitutional barrier to the repeal of an existing law prohibiting racial discriminations in housing; nor did the court rule that a State may never put in statutory form an existing policy of neutrality with respect to private discriminations. What the court below did was first to reflect the notion that the State was required to have a statute prohibiting racial discriminations in housing. Second, it held the purpose and intent of para. 26 was to authorize private racial discriminations in the housing market, to repeal the Unruh and Rumford Acts and to create a constitutional right to discriminate on racial grounds in the sale and leasing of real property. Hence, the court dealt with para. 26 as though it expressly authorized and constitutionalized the private right to discriminate. Third, the court assessed the ultimate impact of para. 26 in the California environment and concluded that the section would encourage and significantly involve the

State in private racial discrimination contrary to the Fourteenth Amendment.

The California court could very reasonably conclude that para. 26 would and did have wider impact than a mere repeal of existing statutes. Section 26 mentioned neither the Unruh nor Rumford Acts in so many words. Instead, it announced the constitutional right of any person to decline to sell or lease his real property to anyone to whom he did not desire to sell or lease. Unruh and Rumford were thereby *pro tanto* repealed. But the section struck more deeply and more widely. Private discriminations in housing were now not only free from Rumford and Unruh but they also enjoyed a far different status than was true before the passage of those statutes. The right to discriminate, including the right to discriminate on racial grounds, was now embodied in the State's basic charter, immune from legislative, executive, or judicial regulation at any level of the state government. Those practicing racial discriminations need no longer rely solely on their personal choice. They could now invoke express constitutional authority, free from censure or interference of any kind from official sources. All individuals, partnerships, corporations and other legal entitites, as well as their agents and representatives, could now discriminate with respect to their residential real property, which is defined as any interest in real property of any kind or quality, "irrespective of how obtained or financed," and seemingly irrespective of the relationship of the State to such interests in real property. Only the State is excluded with respect to property owned by it.

[3, 4] This Court has never attempted the "impossible task" of formulating an infallible test for determining whether the State "in any of its manifestations" has become significantly involved in private discriminations. "Only by sifting the facts and weighing the circumstances" on a case-to-case basis can a "nonobvious involvement of the State in private conduct be attributed its true significance." *Burton* v. *Wilmington Parking Authority*, 365 U.S. 715, 722, 81 S.Ct. 856, 869. Here the California court, armed as it was with the knowledge of the facts and circumstances concerning the passage and potential impact of para. 26, and familiar with the milieu in which that provision would operate, has determined that the provision would involve the State in private racial discriminations to an unconstitutional degree. We accept this holding of the California court. . . .

In *Burton* v. *Wilmington Parking Authority*, 365 U.S. 715, 81 S.Ct. 856, the operator-lessee of a restaurant located in a building owned by the State and otherwise operated for public purposes, refused service to Negroes. Although the State neither commanded nor expressly authorized or encouraged the discriminations, the State had "elected to place its power, property and prestige behind the admitted discrimination" and by "its inaction . . . has . . . made itself a party to the refusal of service . . ." which therefore could not be considered the purely private choice of the restaurant operator. . . .

[5] None of these cases squarely controls the case we now have before us. But they do illustrate the range of situations in which discriminatory state action has been identified. They do exemplify the necessity for a court to assess the potential impact of official action in determining whether the State has significantly involved itself with invidious

discriminations. Here we are dealing with a provision which does not just repeal an existing law forbidding private racial discriminations. Section 26 was intended to authorize, and does authorize, racial discrimination in the housing market. The right to discriminate is now one of the basic policies of the State. The California Supreme Court believes that the section will significantly encourage and involve the State in private discriminations. We have been presented with no persuasive considerations indicating that this judgment should be overturned.

Affirmed. . . .

On June 17, 1968, the United States Supreme Court handed down its opinion in the case of *Joseph Lee Jones et ux., Petitioners* v. *Alfred H. Mayer Co., et al.,* 88 S.Ct. 2186. An abbreviated version of this landmark decision is set forth below.

JONES v. ALFRED H. MAYER COMPANY
88 S. Ct. 2186 (1968)

Mr. Justice STEWART delivered the opinion of the Court.

In this case we are called upon to determinee the scope and constitutionality of an Act of Congress, 42 U.S.C. para. 1982, which provides that:

"All citizens of the United States shall have the same right, in every State and Territory, as is enjoyed by white citizens thereof to inherit, purchase, lease, sell, hold, and convey real and personal property."

[1–3] On September 2, 1965, the petitioners filed a complaint in the District Court for the Eastern District of Missouri, alleging that the respondents had refused to sell them a home in the Paddock Woods community of St. Louis County for the sole reason that petitioner Joseph Lee Jones is a Negro. Relying in part upon para. 1982, the petitioners sought injunctive and other relief. The District Court sustained the respondents' motion to dismiss the complaint, and the Court of Appeals for the Eighth Circuit affirmed, concluding that para. 1982 applies only to state action and does not reach private refusals to sell. We granted certiorari to consider the questions thus presented. For the reasons that follow, we reverse the judgment of the Court of Appeals. We hold that para. 1982 bars *all* racial discrimination, private as well as public, in the sale or rental of property, and that the statute thus construed, is a valid exercise of the power of Congress to enforce the Thirteenth Amendment.

I.

[4, 5] At the outset, it is important to make clear precisely what this case does *not* involve. Whatever else it may be, 42 U.S.C. para 1982 is not a comprehensive open housing law. In sharp contrast to the Fair Housing Title (Title VIII) of the Civil Rights Act of 1968, Pub.L 90-284, 82 Stat. 73, the statute in this case deals only with racial discrimination and does not address itself to discrimination on grounds of religion or national origin. It does not deal specifically with discrimination in the provision of services or facilities in connection with the sale or rental of a dwelling. It does not

prohibit advertising or other representations that indicate discriminatory preferences. It does not refer explicitly to discrimination in financing arrangements or in the provision of brokerage services. It does not empower a federal administrative agency to assist aggrieved parties. It makes no provision for intervention by the Attorney General. And, although it can be enforced by injunction, it contains no provision expressly authorizing a federal court to order the payment of damages.

Thus, although para. 1982 contains none of the exemptions that Congress included in the Civil Rights Act of 1968, it would be a serious mistake to suppose that para. 1982 in any way diminished the significance of the law recently enacted by Congress. Indeed, the Senate Subcommittee on Housing and Urban Affairs was informed in hearings held after the Court of Appeals had rendered its decision in this case that para. 1982 might well be "a presently valid federal statutory ban against discrimination by private persons in the sale or lease of real property." The Subcommittee was told, however, that even if this Court should so construe para. 1982, the existence of that statute would not "eliminate the need for congressional action" to spell out "responsibility on the part of the Federal Government to enforce the rights it protects." The point was made that, in light of the many difficulties confronted by private litigants seeking to enforce such rights on their own, "legislation is needed to establish federal machinery for enforcement of the rights guaranteed under Section 1982 of Title 42 even if the plaintiffs in *Jones* v. *Alfred H. Mayer Company* should prevail in the United States Supreme Court.". . .

III.

[9, 10] We begin with the language of the statute itself. In plain and unambiguous terms, para. 1982 grants to all citizens, without regard to race or color "the same right" to purchase and lease property "as is enjoyed by white citizens." As the Court of Appeals in this case evidently recognized, that right can be impaired as effectively by "those who place property on the market" as by the State itself. For, even if the State and its agents lend no support to those who wish to exclude persons from their communities on racial grounds, the fact remains that, whenever property "is placed on the market for whites only, whites have a right denied to Negroes." So long as a Negro citizen who wants to buy or rent a home can be turned away simply because he is not white, he cannot be said to enjoy "the *same* right . . . as is enjoyed by white citizens . . . to . . . purchase [and] lease . . . real and personal property." 42 U.S.C. para. 1982. (Emphasis added.)

On its face, therefore, para. 1982 appears to prohibit *all* discrimination against Negroes in the sale or rental of property—discrimination by private owners as well as discrimination by public authorities. Indeed, even the respondents seem to concede that, if para. 1982 "means what it says"—to use the words of the respondents' brief—then it must encompass every racially motivated refusal to sell or rent and cannot be confined to officially sanctioned segregation in housing. Stressing what they consider to be the revolutionary implications of so literal a reading of para. 1982, the respondents argue that Congress cannot possibly have intended any such result. Our examination of the relevant history, however, persuades us that Congress meant exactly what it said.

IV.

[ii] In its original form, 42 U.S.C. para. 1982 was part of para. 1 of the Civil Rights Act of 1866. That section was cast in sweeping terms:

"Be it enacted by the Senate and House of Representatives of the United States of America in Congress assembled, That all persons born in the United States and not subject to any foreign power, . . . are hereby declared to be citizens of the United States; and such citizens, of every race and color, without regard to any previous condition of slavery or involuntary servitude . . . shall have the same right, in every State and Territory in the United States, to make and enforce contracts, to sue, to be parties, and give evidence, to inherit, purchase, lease, sell, hold, and convey real and personal property, and to full and equal benefit of all laws and proceedings for the security of person and property, as is enjoyed by white citizens, and shall be subject to like punishment, pains, and penalties, and to none other, any law, statute, ordinance, regulation, or custom, to the contrary notwithstanding."

The crucial language for our purposes was that which guaranteed all citizens "the same right, in every State and Territory in the United States, . . . to inherit, purchase, lease, sell, hold, and convey real and personal property . . . as is enjoyed by white citizens. . . ." To the Congress that passed the Civil Rights Act of 1866, it was clear that the right to do these things might be infringed not only by "State or local law" but also by "custom, or prejudice." Thus, when Congress provided in para. 1 of the Civil Rights Act that the right to purchase and lease property was to be enjoyed equally throughout the United States by Negro and white citizens alike, it plainly meant to secure that right against interference from any source whatever, whether governmental or private.

Indeed, if para. 1 had been intended to grant nothing more than an immunity from *governmental* interference, then much of para. 2 would have made no sense at all. For that section, which provided fines and prison terms for certain individuals who deprived others of rights "secured or protected" by para. 1, was carefully drafted to exempt private violations of para. 1 from criminal sanctions it imposed. There would, of course, have been no private violations to exempt if the only "right" granted by para. 1 had been a right to be free of discrimination by public officials. Hence the structure of the 1866 Act, as well as its language, points to the conclusion urged by the petitioners in this case—that para. 1 was meant to prohibit *all* racially motivated deprivations of the rights enumerated in the statute, although only those deprivations perpetrated "under color of law" were to be criminally punishable under para. 2. . . .

It thus appears that, when the House passed the Civil Rights Act on March 13, 1866, it did so on the same assumption that had prevailed in the Senate: It too believed that it was approving a comprehensive statute forbidding *all* racial discrimination affecting the basic civil rights enumerated in the Act. . . .

[15] As we said in a somewhat different setting two Terms ago, "We think that history leaves no doubt that, if we are to give [the law] the scope that its origins dictate, we must accord it a sweep as broad as its language." *United States* v. *Price,* 383 U.S. 787, 801, 86 S.Ct. 1152, 1160. "We are not at liberty to seek ingenious analytical instruments," ibid., to carve from para. 1982 any exception for private conduct—even though its application to such conduct in the present context is without established precedent. And, as the Attorney General of the United States said at the oral argument of this case, "The fact that the statute lay partially dormant for many years cannot be held to diminish its force today."

V.

The remaining question is whether Congress has power under the Constitution to do what para. 1982 purports to do: to prohibit all racial discrimination, private and public, in the sale and rental of property. Our starting point is the Thirteenth Amendment, for it was pursuant to that constitutional provision that Congress originally enacted what is now para. 1982. The Amendment consists of two parts. Section 1 states:

"Neither slavery nor involuntary servitude, except as a punishment for a crime whereby the party shall have been duly convicted, shall exist within the United States, or any place subject to their jurisdiction."

Section 2 provides:

"Congress shall have power to enforce this article by appropriate legislation."

[16, 17] As its text reveals, the Thirteenth Amendment "is not a mere prohibition of state laws establishing or upholding slavery, but an absolute declaration that slavery or involuntary servitude shall not exist in any part of the United States." *Civil Rights Cases* 109 U.S. 3, 3 S.Ct. 18, 28, 27 L.Ed. 835. It has never been doubted therefore, "that the power vested in Congress to enforce the article by appropriate legislation," ibid., includes the power to enact laws "direct and primarily operating upon the acts of individuals, whether sanctioned by state legislation or not." Id., at 23, 3 S.Ct., at 30.

[18, 19] Thus, the fact that para. 1982 operates upon the unofficial acts of private individuals, whether or not sanctioned by state law, presents no constitutional problem. If Congress has power under the Thirteenth Amendment to eradicate conditions that prevent Negroes from buying and renting property because of their race or color, then no federal statute calculated to achieve that objective can be thought to exceed the constitutional power of Congress simply because it reaches beyond state individuals. The constitutional question in this case, therefore, comes to this: Does the authority of Congress to enforce the Thirteenth Amendment "by appropriate legislation" include the power to eliminate all racial barriers to the acquisition of real and personal property? We think the answer to that question is plainly yes.

[20] "By its own unaided force and effect," the Thirteenth Amendment "abolished slavery, and established universal freedom." *Civil Rights Cases,* 109 U.S. 3, 20, 3 S.Ct. 18,

28. Whether or not the Amendment *itself* did any more than that—a question not involved in this case—it is at least clear that the Enabling Clause of that Amendment empowered Congress to do much more. For that clause clothed "Congress with power to pass *all laws necessary and proper for abolishing all badges and incidents of slavery in the United States.*" (Emphasis added.) . . .

[21] Surely Senator Trumbull was right. Surely Congress has the power under the Thirteenth Amendment rationally to determine what are the badges and the incidents of slavery, and the authority to translate that determination into effective legislation. Nor can we say that the determination Congress has made is an irrational one. For this Court recognized long ago that, whatever else they may have encompassed, the badges and incidents of slavery—its "burdens and disabilities"—included restraints upon "those fundamental rights which are the essence of civil freedom, namely, the same right . . . to inherit, purchase, lease, sell and convey property, as is enjoyed by white citizens." *Civil Rights Cases,* 109 U.S. 3, 22, 3 S.Ct. 18, 29. Just as the Black Codes, enacted after the Civil War to restrict the free exercise of those rights, were substitutes for the slave system, so the exclusion of Negroes from white communities became a substitute for the Black Codes. And when racial discrimination herds men into ghettos and makes their ability to buy property turn on the color of their skin, then it too is a relic of slavery.

[22] Negro citizens North and South, who saw in the Thirteenth Amendment a promise of freedom—freedom to "go and come at pleasure" and to "buy and sell when they please"—would be left with "a mere paper guarantee" if Congress were powerless to assure that a dollar in the hands of a Negro will purchase the same thing as a dollar in the hands of a white man. At the very least, the freedom that Congress is empowered to secure under the Thirteenth Amendment includes the freedom to buy whatever a white man can buy, the right to live wherever a white man can live. If Congress cannot say that being a free man means at least this much, then the Thirteenth Amendment made a promise the Nation cannot keep.

Representative Wilson of Iowa was the floor manager in the House for the Civil Rights Act of 1866. In urging that Congress had ample authority to pass the pending bill, he recalled the celebrated words of Chief Justice Marshall in *McCulloch* v. *State of Maryland,* Wheat. 316, 421, 4 L.Ed. 579:

"Let the end be legitimate, let it be within the scope of the constitution, and all means which are appropriate, which are plainly adapted to that end, which are not prohibited, but consist with the letter and spirit of the constitution, are constitutional."

"The end is legitimate," the Congressman said, "because it is defined by the Constitution itself. The end is the maintenance of freedom. . . . A man who enjoys the civil rights mentioned in this bill cannot be reduced to slavery. . . . This settles the appropriateness of this measure, and that settles its constitutionality."

We agree. The judgment is reversed.

Reversed. . . .

With *Jones* v. *Alfred H. Mayer Company* we come to the end of almost a quarter century of legal actions dealing with prohibiting and punishing the action of discriminating against people who seek to buy or lease residential accommodations on the basis of their race, creed, color, religion, or national origin.

The United States Supreme Court decision in *Jones* v. *Alfred H. Mayer Company* left no question that virtually all discrimination based on race, national origin, color, or religion in the sale or rental of housing had been outlawed by statute and judicial decision. There remained the question whether publicly supported housing projects could be located in communities so as to continue racial segregation. The primary financial support for such housing comes from the federal government through the Department of Housing and Urban Development. That this type of housing discrimination based upon the race of occupants could not be continued was determined by the United States Supreme Court in the case of *Hills* v. *Gautreaux et al.* (Supreme Court, 1976) No. 74-1047. The following summary of this decision appears in the May 7, 1976, Prentice-Hall publication *Federal Aids to Financing.*

The U.S. Supreme Court has ruled that the federal courts may order low-income housing to be located in predominantly white suburbs to remedy segregation in a city's public housing. In a unanimous opinion (8–0), the High Court upheld a Court of Appeals decision that required HUD and the Chicago Housing Authority (CHA) to draw up a comprehensive plan for providing public housing throughout Chicago's entire metropolitan area, including the suburbs. The court concluded that a metropolitan remedy is proper here, since both CHA and HUD violated the Constitution, and both have authority to operate outside the city limits of Chicago.

This suit was brought by six black persons who lived in or had applied for units in Chicago's public housing system. It charged CHA with violating the Fourteenth Amendment by locating almost all of the city's public housing in predominantly black areas of the city. In a companion suit, HUD was accused of violating the Fifth Amendment and the Civil Rights Act of 1964 by providing federal funding for the projects operated by CHA. A federal district court concluded that CHA had violated the Constitution by selecting public housing sites and assigning tenants on the basis of race. Later, a federal appeals court found that HUD had knowingly sanctioned and assisted CHA's racially discriminatory public housing program.

In August 1974, the Court of Appeals, Seventh Circuit, ruled that suburban or metropolitan-wide relief would be necessary to correct the policy of segregation in Chicago's public housing. It remanded the case to the District Court for "the adoption of a comprehensive metropolitan area plan that will not only dis-establish the segregated public housing system in the City of Chicago . . . but will increase the supply of dwelling units as rapidly as possible." HUD appealed to the U.S. Supreme Court arguing that there could not be a remedy affecting HUD's conduct beyond the boundaries of Chicago.

Mr. Justice Stewart, writing the opinion for the Court, ruled "that the federal courts do not lack authority to order parties found to have violated the Constitution to undertake remedial efforts beyond the municipal boundaries of the city where the violation occurred." Here, both CHA and HUD committed constitutional violations, and both are authorized to operate outside the boundaries of Chicago. The Court rejected the argument that an order affecting HUD's conduct beyond Chicago's boundaries would interfere with the autonomy of local governments and housing authorities. The approval of local governments is no longer a precondition to the location of Section 8 Lower-Income Housing Assistance under the statute which permits HUD to contract directly with homeowners and developers. However, public housing projects could not be forced on the suburbs. Local governments would still have the right to comment on specific assistance proposals, to reject proposals that are inconsistent with approved housing assistance plans, and to require compliance with zoning and other land use restrictions.

GOVERNMENT ACTION TO ELIMINATE REDLINING

Redlining is the practice among mortgage lenders of refusing to consider making loans in certain sections of communities because of the blight that exists there. The result is that some credit-worthy residential borrowers may be denied credit needed for purchase and construction loans. "Redlined" areas of communities are often inhabited predominantly by members of minority races. The federal and various state governments have been alerted to this situation by residents of these sections of cities, and have taken various actions.

Federal statutes now require various institutional mortgage lenders to collect data and make it available to federal regulatory agencies and the general public. During 1975 and 1976, the Prentice-Hall publication *Federal Aids to Financing* described federal anti-redlining legislative action designated as the Home Mortgage Disclosure Act:

Each house of Congress will consider a major piece of legislation requiring banks and S & L's to disclose lending practices. Neither house is considering any legislation that attempts to inhibit or alter current lending practices. Congress just wants to know where and to whom the banks lend money.

By an 8 to 5 vote the Senate Banking Committee approved a bill that could mean more mortgage money for older neighborhoods and inner-city areas. Sponsors hope to eventually stop or discourage the practice of "redlining." Real estate people and homeowners complained in hearings that this commonly known practice was a "self-fulfilling" prophecy. Banks refuse to make loans in older neighborhoods and then, when these neighborhoods decline

as a result, banks say they were correct to begin with. The Committee-approved bill does not prohibit redlining. All it does is ask lenders in some 227 designated metro areas (more may be added later) to disclose which neighborhoods are receiving loans. Once lending patterns are revealed, backers of the measure hope banks will be more or less forced, or "shamed," into making their mortgage lending practices more equitable.

The Senate passed S. 1281, the Home Mortgage Disclosure Act, on September 4, 1975. The bill would require all makers of "federally related mortgage loans" to keep records as to these mortgages and as to the owners of their savings deposits. A "federally related mortgage loan" is defined as in the Real Estate Settlement Procedures Act and would cover almost all home mortgage lenders and all banks, commerical and savings, and all savings and loan associations.

Under the bill every bank and S & L would have to keep records, open to public inspection, of (a) the number and total dollar amount of mortgages outstanding at the end of its fiscal year, (b) mortgages made during the fiscal year, (c) the number and total dollar amount of savings accounts it held at the close of its fiscal year, and (d) the number of savings accounts it opened during the fiscal year and the amount in them at the end of the fiscal year.

Banks and S & L's would have to further particularize this information by giving the zip code location of the property securing each particular mortgage and zip code address of each savings account holder. Additionally, institutions located in an SMSA (Standard Metropolitan Statistical Area) must disclose the county location of the mortgaged property and account holders not located in the SMSA; institutions not located in an SMSA must give the state location of all out-of-state property mortgaged to them and of their out-of-state account holders. Information on mortgages must also be specific as to the number and dollar amounts of mortgage loans insured by FHA, including home improvement loans, and VA-guaranteed loans.

The bill would authorize the Federal Reserve Board to draw up and issue implementing regulations which would be enforced by an institution's supervisory authority. If enacted, the measure would expire in three years from the date of enactment unless extended by Congress.

With the approach of September 30, 1976, federally regulated lending institutions must be prepared to report on the geographic distribution of their home mortgage loans and home improvement loans. Home loans that must be reported exclude (a) junior liens (such as second mortgages) except for home improvement loans and (b) first mortgages taken as collateral for business purposes. Each lender is required to notify its depositors as to when its mortgage disclosure statement is available and give the name and address of its federal enforcement agency.[11]

Depository institutions that (1) have more than $10 million in assets; (2) have offices in principal metropolitan areas

---

[11]This is now known as the Federal Community Reinvestment Act (CRA), which requires the Federal Deposit Insurance Corporation to evaluate commercial banks' performance in helping to meet the credit needs in their community (by the number of residential mortgage loans made) and to take this evaluation into account when the FDIC decides on certain applications submitted to it by certain banks.

(SMSAs); (3) make first mortgage loans on 1- to 4-family homes; and (4) are federally insured or regulated must comply with the law. "Depository institutions" include commercial banks, S & L's, savings banks, building and loan associations, or homestead associations, and credit unions.

Data on loan reporting must be separated into two main categories: (1) loans originally made by the reporting institution, and (2) loans originated by another institution but bought by the reporter. Each category must be further broken down into loans on property located within the reporter's SMSA and those outside. Each loan on a 1- to 4-family residence must be classified as (1) insured or guaranteed by FHA, VA or the Farmers Home Administration, (2) conventional, or (3) a home improvement loan. Loans on multi-family dwellings must be reported separately. The lender must also specify as to single-family home loans within the SMSA whether or not the borrower intends to live in the home.

Early in 1976 a federal district court refused to conclude that redlining was not a violation of the Civil Rights Act of 1968. An action was brought by individuals under Title VIII of the Civil Rights Act of 1968 alleging redlining lending practices by lending institutions. The court held that redlining is a practice prohibited by the Act, which prohibits discriminatory sales and rental practices and discrimination in housing loans and specifies that such practices are the bases for private and public action.

State of California Prohibition of Redlining

The State of California enacted legislation designed to eliminate redlining. This legislation is known as the Housing Financial Discrimination Act of 1977. The more significant aspects of this statute are as follows:

1. Financial-type institutions that make loans on real estate (savings and loan associations, banks, personal property brokers, industrial loan companies, insurance companies, credit unions, thrift companies, or mortgage bankers) are prohibited from implementing discriminatory loan practices, for example, denying credit altogether or making loans with distinctive discriminatory aspects compared with the "usual loans" made. Discriminatory practices include higher interest rates, shorter repayment terms, and higher down payments. Such discriminatory loan practices are usually based upon, either partially or totally, factors such as conditions, characteristics, or trends in a neighborhood or a geographic area where the property is located; type of collateral property; age, physical condition, income level, race, color, religion, marital status, sex, national origin, or ancestry of loan applicants.
2. The effect of the statute on regulated real estate lenders is to require that such lenders make loans unless the lender can prove to governmental authorities that the loan should not be made to avoid making an unsound, unsafe loan, which is very likely to result in a financial loss.

3. The statute applies in any instance where a person applies for a loan to buy, refinance through an existing loan, build, rehabilitate, renovate, or improve any one- to four-unit, owner-occupied residential property.
4. The statute operates in accordance with a multistep complaint procedure, which involves the following stages: (1) A real estate loan applicant who is refused such a loan (and if it is felt that the rejection of the application is unjustified under the statute) can file a complaint with the Secretary of Business and Transportation of California, who then has thirty days in which to resolve the controversy between the applicant and the financial lender. If the Secretary determines that a violation of this statute has occurred, a legal order can be issued requiring the lender to either make the loan requested by the complainant–loan applicant or order the lender to pay to the complainant–loan applicant actual monetary damages up to a maximum amount of $1,000. (2) The Secretary's order can be appealed by either party to the dispute to the California Office of Administrative Hearings. (3) Either party may appeal the decision of the California Office of Administrative Hearings to the appropriate California Superior Court petitioning for a Writ of Mandate ordering the lender to make the loan or not to make it.
5. Under this statute, the regulated real estate lenders must notify all loan applicants at the time of written application for financial assistance of the prohibitions and right of review provided by law, should the lender turn down the applicant.

Federally chartered savings and loan associations and commercial banks in California have, on occasion, taken the position that they are under the jurisdiction of federal law and therefore must only comply with the Federal Community Reinvestment Act, not with the California Housing Financial Discrimination Act of 1977. This controversy has resulted in litigation, that is as yet unresolved in terms of a final appellate court definitive decision.

PROHIBITING SEX DISCRIMINATION IN REAL ESTATE MORTGAGE LENDING

In addition to public and government concern over denial of housing accommodations and real estate mortgage credit on the basis of race, creed, color, source of national origin, and religion, efforts have also been made to eliminate discrimination based upon sex or marital status in the granting of credit. The federal Equal Credit Opportunity Act took effect on October 28, 1975. The June and September 1975 issues of *Federal Aids to Financing* contain the following comments on federal action to prohibit such discrimination by lending institutions subject to federal regulation or benefiting from federal deposit insurance programs.

The Federal Reserve Board has revised its proposed regulations implementing the Equal Credit Opportunity Act of 1975. The Act prohibits discrimination in extending credit on the grounds of sex or marital status of the loan applicant. The Act covers all lenders who extend credit to individuals including banks, savings and loan associations, finance companies, credit card issuers, and governmental agencies such as the Small Business Administration. The latest regulations provide:

●*Records of a credit application must be kept for one year. . . . As to credit accounts established after November 1, 1976, a creditor, who furnishes information to a consumer reporting agency or others, has to use the name of both spouses, if both use the account.*

●*For the optional use of courtesy titles, for example, Mr., Mrs., Ms., Miss.*

●*For continuing the prohibition on demanding information as to child-bearing capability or birth control practices, but for allowing the creditor to get information on the probable continuity of the applicant's ability to repay.*

●*For requiring the credit application form to carry notice of the right to equal credit opportunity.*

●*For requiring notification of applicant simply as to action on his credit application rather than requiring a statement of reasons for denial.*

●*For defining "discrimination" to mean treatment of one applicant less favorably than others.*

●*That women must not be denied loans just because they are single or divorced.*

It is clear that in the United States of America there can legally be no discrimination against prospective residential buyers or renters on the basis of race, creed, color, national origin, or religion; also, federally regulated or insured financial institutions cannot discriminate in the granting of credit—including real estate credit— on the basis of sex or marital status.

MINOR CHILDREN CANNOT LEGALLY BE EXCLUDED FROM RENTAL UNITS

Another issue related to discrimination that denies certain persons access to renting housing is that of households that contain minor children. A considerable number of owners of rental apartments in California have established "adults only" rental complexes—where no minor child can be a long-term permanent resident.

In February 1982, in the case of *Wolfson* v. *Marina Point Limited,* the California Supreme Court in a 5 to 2 decision (written by Justice Tobriner, who was joined by Chief Justice Bird and Justices Newman, Brousard, and White) ruled as follows:

"An apartment owner's broad, class-based exclusion of minor children violated the anti-discrimination provisions of the Unruh Civil Rights Act. Such exclusion is not permissible—even if children, as a class, are noisier, rowdier, more mischievous and more boistrous than adults.

The Unruh Act was meant to prohibit all arbitrary discrimination by business establishments—including apartment complexes. The Act bars discrimination based on class distinctions—such as race or religion—and families are also entitled to its protection. A society that sanctions wholesale discrimination against its children in obtaining housing engages in suspect activity. Even the most primitive society fosters the protection of its young."

The Court did not require owners of senior citizen housing complexes to admit minor children, stating, "We do not here adjudge such special-purpose housing."

Justice Frank C. Richardson joined by Justice Stanley Mosk dissented from the majority opinion.

"Marina Point's policy was reasonable under the circumstances and not the kind of discrimination that the Unruh Act was designed to combat. It was easy for the majority to oppose wholesale discrimination against children, but what if the question is put a little differently—do our middle-aged or older citizens, having worked long and hard, having raised their own children, having paid both their taxes and their dues to society, retain a right to spend their remaining years in a relatively peaceful and tranquil environment of their own choice? The answer to this question is Why not?"

CALIFORNIA DEPARTMENT OF REAL ESTATE REGULATIONS OF LICENSEES PROHIBITING DISCRIMINATORY CONDUCT IN THE SALE, RENTAL, OR FINANCING OF REAL ESTATE

Article 10, Section 2780 of the Regulations of the Real Estate Commissioner makes discrimination by licensees in financing, selling, and renting real estate against persons based upon their race, color, sex, religion, ancestry, physical handicap, or national origin grounds for the Real Estate Commissioner to take disciplinary action against licensee violaters in the form of license revocation or suspension. (Children can likely be added to the classes of persons protected from licensee discrimination in view of the *Wolfson* v. *Marina Point Limited,* California Supreme Court decision.)

Examples of prohibited conduct under the Real Estate Commissioner's Regulations include

1. Refusing to negotiate for the sale, rental, or financing of the purchase of real property or otherwise making unavailable or denying real property to any person because of such person's race, color, sex, religion, ancestry, physical handicap, or national origin.
2. Refusing or failing to show, rent, sell, or finance the purchase of real property to any person or refusing or failing to provide or volunteer information to any person about real property, or channeling or steering any person away from real property on the basis of race, color, sex, religion, ancestry, physical handicap, or national origin.

(The only exception is if the property is not physically suitable for a physically handicapped person.)

3. Discriminating in the terms, conditions, or privileges of sale, rental, or financing of the purchase of real property. (The only exception is if the premises are not suitable for use by physically handicapped.)

4. Discriminating in providing services or facilities in connection with the sale, rental, or financing of the purchase of real property including processing applications differently or referring prospects to other licensees because of applicants' race, color, sex, religion, ancestry, physical handicap, or national origin.

5. Using, with discriminatory intent or effect, codes or other means of identifying minority prospects.

6. Assigning real estate licensees on the basis of a prospective client's race, color, sex, religion, ancestry, physical handicap, or national origin, or stating that real property is not available for inspection, sale, or rental when such property is in fact available.

7. Processing an application slower than other applications or otherwise acting to delay, hinder, or avoid the sale, rental, or financing of the purchase of real property on account of race, color, sex, religion, ancestry, physical handicap, or national origin.

8. Refusing or failing to cooperate with or assist another real estate licensee in negotiating the sale, rental, or financing of the purchase of real property because of the race, color, sex, religion, ancestry, physical handicap, or national origin of any prospective purchaser or tenant.

9. Making any effort to obstruct, retard, or discourage the purchase, lease, or financing of the purchase of real property by persons whose race, color, sex, religion, ancestry, physical handicap, or national origin differs from that of the majority of persons presently residing in the real property or in the area in which the real property is located.

10. Quoting or charging a price, rent, cleaning, or security deposit for a particular real property to any person which is different from the price, rent, or security deposit quoted or charged to any other person because of differences in the race, color, sex, religion, ancestry, physical handicap, or national origin of such persons.

11. Discrimination because of race, color, sex, religion, ancestry, physical handicap, or national origin in performing any acts in connection with the making of any determination of financing ability or in the processing of any application for the financing or refinancing of real property.

12. Advising a person of the price or value of real property on the basis of factors related to the race, color, sex, religion, ancestry, physical handicap, or national origin of residents of an area or potential residents of an area in which the property is located.

13. Discriminating in the treatment of, or services provided to, occupants of any real property in the course of providing management services for real property because of the race, color, sex, religion, ancestry, physical handicap, or national origin of said occupants.

14. Discriminating against the owners or occupants of real property because of the race, color, sex, religion, ancestry, physical handicap, or national origin of their guests, visitors, or invitees.

15. Making any effort to instruct or encourage—expressly or impliedly, by either words or acts—licensees or their employees or other agents to engage in any discriminatory act in violation of a federal or state fair-housing law.

16. Establishing or implementing rules that have the effect of limiting the opportunity for any person because of his or her race, color, sex, religion, ancestry, physical handicap, or national origin to secure real property through a multiple listing or other real estate service.

17. Assisting or aiding in any way, any person in the sale, rental, or financing of the purchase of real property where there are reasonable grounds to believe that such a person intends to discriminate because of race, color, sex, religion, ancestry, physical handicap, or national origin.

18. Bringing about panic selling of real property by owners is prohibited discriminatory conduct and includes acts such as soliciting sales or rental listings, making written or oral statements creating fear or alarm, transmitting written or oral warnings or threats, or acting in any other manner so as to induce or attempt to induce the sale or lease of rental property through any representation, express or implied, regarding the present or prospective entry of one or more persons of another race, color, sex, religion, ancestry, physical handicap, or national origin into an area or neighborhood.

With this comprehensive set of regulations of California's Real Estate Commissioner pertaining to prohibiting under penalty of disciplinary action real estate sales and broker licensees from discriminating against people on the basis of their race, color, sex, religion, ancestry, physical handicap, or national origin in the sale, renting, and financing of real estate in California, this state is demonstrating its strong commitment to the enforcement of federal and state fair-housing statutes.

Glossary

ACCELERATED DEPRECIATION: A method of accounting acceptable to the Internal Revenue Service, which allows the write-off of an asset in greater amounts during the early years of possession than toward the end of its economic life.

ACCELERATION CLAUSE: A clause in a note, deed of trust, or mortgage that gives a lender the right to demand immediate payment of the balance due if certain things happen, eg., default on payments that are due.

ACQUISITION COST: The cost used by the HUD-FHA in determining the amount of an insured loan. It includes the sales price or the HUD-FHA appraised value plus nonrecurring costs.

ADJUSTABLE RATE MORTGAGE (ARMS): This is a loan on which the interest rate may move up or down according to the needs of the lender. There are no restrictions placed on the movement or number of times a change can be made in a year, except for those restrictions made by the Federal National Mortgage Association on those loans it will buy. It is similar to the *variable rate mortgage*, only without the VRM restrictions.

ADJUSTED COST BASIS: This is the value of a property that is computed by adding the cost of improvements to the sales price of the property, then deducting the amount of depreciation. It is sometimes referred to as the *base value*.

ALIENATION CLAUSE OR DUE-ON-SALE CLAUSE: A clause found in some deeds of trust and notes requiring the note to be paid in full upon the sale of property securing the note.

ALL INCLUSIVE DEED OF TRUST OR WRAPAROUND DEED OF TRUST: This deed of trust includes the amounts of all notes outstanding that are secured by previous deeds of trust plus the new note that is secured by the all-inclusive deed of trust.

ALTA TITLE POLICY: American Land Title Association is a title insurance policy available to both buyers and lenders that is issued by title insurance companies to provide additional coverage not given under a standard policy such as insurance against unrecorded liens, unrecorded easements, rights of individuals in possession of the property, encroachment, and so forth.

AMORTIZATION: The orderly reduction of an obligation by reasonably equal installment payments to interest and principal over a period of time.

AMORTIZED LOAN: One that is paid by amortization.

ANNUAL PERCENTAGE RATE (APR): The interest rate as figured by the formula set forth by the Federal Reserve Bank's Regulation Z covering the federal Truth-in-Lending Act.

APPRAISAL: An estimate or opinion of value given after the qualities of the property have been analyzed.

APPRAISER: An individual who, through education and experience, is qualified to make an appraisal.

ASSIGNMENT OF DEED OF TRUST: An instrument by which the beneficial interest of a deed of trust is transferred.

ASSIGNMENT OF RENTS CLAUSE: A clause found in deeds of trust that assign rents, if any, at the time of signing or at a later date to the beneficiary of the deed in case of default. The collected rents are to be credited toward the loan payments.

ASSUMPTION: The taking of another's obligation as your own.

ASSUMPTION OF A DEED OF TRUST OR MORTGAGE: A person buying a piece of property assumes the responsibility and the liability for making payments on an existing note secured by a deed of trust or mortgage.

BALLOON PAYMENT: A balloon payment is a final payment on an installment note that is considerably larger than those preceding it.

BASIS: Value of property as carried on the owner's books.

BENEFICIARY: One of three parties to a deed of trust. The beneficiary is the lender.

BLANKET DEED OF TRUST OR MORTGAGE: A deed of trust that lists as security more than one parcel of land.

BOOT: In a property exchange transaction, one of the parties to the exchange has to give something of value over and above the value of the property exchanged. The Internal Revenue Service refers to this as *boot*.

BUNDLE OF RIGHTS: The legal rights attached to the ownership of real property including the right of use; the right of possession; the right to sell, give, or rent; and the right to encumber.

CAL-VET LOAN: A loan program administered by the California State Department of Veterans Affairs for the purchase of real estate by qualified California veterans.

CAPITAL GAIN: A gain resulting from the sale of property.

CAPITALIZATION: A method of appraising property whereby the annual net income is divided by the desired capitalization rate.

CERTIFICATE OF ELIGIBILITY: A document issued by the Veterans Administration showing the veteran is eligible for a

Veterans Administration (GI) loan and the amount the VA will guarantee.

CERTIFICATE OF REASONABLE VALUE (CRV): An appraisal report made by the Veterans Administration showing the value of a certain property.

CLOSING COSTS: Recurring and nonrecurring costs paid by the buyer or the seller when property is sold.

CO-MAKER: A person who gives additional security for a loan by joining the borrower in signing the note. Both parties are equally liable for the obligation.

CONDITIONAL COMMITMENT: A commitment for a loan of a definite amount to be made at a future time to someone not known and who has a satisfactory credit reputation.

CONDITIONAL SALES CONTRACT: A contract for the sale of property giving delivery and possession to the buyer, but the title is to remain in the name of the seller until certain conditions have been met.

CONDOMINIUM: A single residence or office owned by an individual or individuals in a multiunit structure with joint ownership of certain common areas such as exterior walls, foundations, roof, swimming pool, recreation areas, building, and so forth, sometimes called a "vertical subdivision."

CONSIDERATION: Anything of value given to encourage another to enter into a contract.

CONSTRUCTION LOAN: A loan made to enable someone to build a home or building with funds being disbursed at certain stages of completion.

CONTRACT OF SALE: An enforceable agreement wherein a seller agrees to sell certain property and a buyer agrees to pay a certain price for it.

CONVENTIONAL LOAN: A loan that is not insured or guaranteed by a government agency such as HUD-FHA or VA.

CORRESPONDENT: An individual or organization that represents another, such as a mortgage bank that represents an insurance company.

CREDIT REPORT: A report issued by an agency whose business is collecting and issuing credit history and background on individuals and organizations.

CYCLICAL MOVEMENT: The recurring changes in economic business cycles from prosperity, to recession, to depression, to recovery, and back to prosperity.

DEBENTURE: A bond issued without security, backed only by the reputation and ability of the organization.

DEED OF RECONVEYANCE: A document issued by the trustee after the obligation secured by the deed of trust has been paid in full. It transfers title back to the trustor (borrower).

DEED OF TRUST: An instrument transferring title to real estate to a third party (the trustee) as security for a real estate loan. It is used in place of a mortgage, almost entirely, in California, and it is sometimes called a *trust deed*.

DEFAULT: Failure to fulfill a promise or duty, failure to make payments on a loan when they become due, or failure to maintain real estate as agreed and as specified in the deed of trust.

DEFICIENCY JUDGMENT: A judgment given when the property securing a loan has been foreclosed and the sale was in an amount less than that owed.

DEFICIT FINANCING: This type of financing occurs when the income from income property does not cover the payments on the loan obtained to finance the purchase.

DEPARTMENT OF HOUSING AND URBAN DEVELOPMENT (HUD): The cabinet level department of the federal government containing the various agencies (FHA, FNMA,

GNMA) that administer and supervise housing, finance, and urban development programs.

DEPOSIT RECEIPT: A form used to acknowledge an earnest money deposit to bind an offer to purchase.

DEPRECIATION: A loss in value owing to either deterioration, functional obsolescence, or economic obsolescence.

DEVELOPMENT LOAN: A loan for the purpose of acquiring a piece of property and making off-site improvements.

DISCOUNT: An amount subtracted from the face amount of a loan whether from the original borrower, or, as in the secondary mortgage market, from the lender when the loan is sold.

DISINTERMEDIATION: The rapid withdrawal of large amounts of money by money savers from financial intermediaries, such as banks, savings and loan associations, insurance companies, and savings banks, to be invested where the return is greater, such as in U.S. Treasury obligations, money market funds, or commercial bonds.

DOWN PAYMENT: The amount remaining of the sales price that the buyer must make up after the real estate loan has been made.

DUE-ON-SALE CLAUSE: See *Alienation Clause*.

EARNEST MONEY: Partial payment of amount due on a purchase as evidence of good faith.

ECONOMIC LIFE: That period of time during which a property will produce enough income or amenities to justify maintaining it.

EFFECTIVE AGE: The apparent age, not necessarily the chronological age.

EFFECTIVE INTEREST RATE: The actual interest rate paid or received, taking into consideration all discounts paid or received, not necessarily the nominal rate.

EQUITY: Difference between the amount owed on a property and the fair market value of that property.

EQUITY PARTICIPATION: In exchange for a high loan-to-value ratio made by the lender, he or she is allowed to participate in the owner's equity.

ESCALATION CLAUSE: A clause found in most deeds of trust that allows the lender to increase payments or interest or demand payment in case the property is sold, payments are not made, the property is not maintained, taxes are not paid, or fire insurance and other needed insurance are not kept on the property.

ESCROW: An agreement whereby a third disinterested party agrees to carry out the instructions of both the buyer and the seller as set forth in the agreement.

EXCHANGE: A means by which ownership of one property is traded for ownership of another.

FAIR MARKET VALUE: The highest price in terms of money a property will bring on the open market when offered for a reasonable period of time with both buyer and seller knowing all the uses to which the property could be put and with neither party being under undue pressure to buy or sell.

FANNIE MAE: See *Federal National Mortgage Association*.

FARMERS HOME ADMINISTRATION (FaHA): An agency of the Department of Agriculture. In recent years it has been active in financing homes for low-income people in areas where other loans have not been available at reasonable cost. It also provides loans for farmers.

FEDERAL DEPOSIT INSURANCE CORPORATION (FDIC): Insures deposits in member banks up to $100,000. The banks pay for this insurance.

FEDERAL HOME LOAN BANK: A regulatory agency for member savings and loan associations, both federal- and state-chartered. Provides similar services for savings and loan associations that the Federal Reserve Bank does for member banks.

FEDERAL HOME LOAN MORTGAGE CORPORATION (FHLMC):   A federal agency that provides a secondary mortgage market for savings and loan associations and others. Also called Freddie Mac.

FEDERAL HOUSING ADMINISTRATION (FHA):   An agency of the federal government under the Department of Housing and Urban Development (HUD) that insures mortgage loans.

FEDERAL NATIONAL MORTGAGE ASSOCIATION (FNMA):   A privately owned corporation that has on its board of directors members appointed by the President of the United States and the Secretary of the Treasury. Its function is to be active in the secondary mortgage market, buying and selling mortgages. Also called Fannie Mae.

FEDERAL RESERVE BANK: A regulatory agency which controls the operation of all member banks and through the Board controls money and credit policies.

FEDERAL SAVINGS AND LOAN INSURANCE CORPORATION (FSLIC):   Insures all member savings and loan associations' deposits up to $100,000.

FEE SIMPLE: The greatest interest one can hold in real property. It is of indefinite duration, freely transferable and inheritable.

FINDER'S FEE: A fee paid by a lender to someone referring a client to the lender when a loan is made.

FIRM COMMITMENT: A commitment made by HUD-FHA indicating that it will insure a loan on a certain property for a certain amount. The commitment has a time limit and is issued for a certain borrower.

FIRST DEED OF TRUST OR MORTGAGE: The first recorded lien against a property subject only to taxes and bonded indebtedness.

FLEXI OR FLEXIBLE LOAN: This loan provides for interest-only payment for the first five years, after which the loan is amortized over the next twenty-five years.

FORECLOSURE: A procedure under which property pledged to secure a loan is sold after the loan is in default in order to pay the debt.

FREDDIE MAC: See *Federal Home Loan Mortgage Corporation*.

GIFT DEED: A deed in which there is no consideration other than love and affection.

GI LOAN: Loans that are guaranteed by the Veterans Administration to qualified veterans, also known as VA loans.

GINNIE MAE: See *Government National Mortgage Association*.

GOVERNMENT NATIONAL MORTGAGE ASSOCIATION (GNMA):   A federal corporation involved in the administration of the mortgage-backed securities program and in the secondary mortgage market.

GRANT DEED: A limited warranty deed that assures the person receiving the property (grantee) that the land has not been deeded to another and that the property is free of any encumbrance placed by the person giving the deed (grantor).

GROSS INCOME: Total income received before any expenses are deducted.

GROSS RATE: A method of collecting interest by adding it to the principal before monthly payments are started.

GROSS RENT MULTIPLIER: The gross rent multiplier is obtained by dividing the sales price by the gross annual income. This gives a figure that, when the annual gross rent of a comparable property is multiplied by it, will give a rule-of-thumb value for the property.

HYPOTHECATE: To pledge something as security for a loan while retaining possession of it.

IMPOUNDS: A trust account set up by a lender to which a portion of the monthly payment on a loan is credited so that funds will be available for payment of bonds, bond interest, taxes, and insurance.

INCOME APPROACH: One of three ways to determine the appraised value of property. It is most pertinent when appraising income property.

INCOME RATIO: The monthly payment on a loan including principal, interest, taxes, and insurance divided by the borrower's monthly gross income.

INSTALMENT LOAN: A loan on which there are two or more payments.

INSTALMENT SALES CONTRACT: Also known as a *land contract*. See *Contract of Sale*.

INSTITUTIONAL LENDER: A financial intermediary such as a bank, savings and loan association, or life insurance company that pools money of its depositors and then invests the funds in various ways including real estate loans.

INTEREST RATE: The charge (rent) for the use (loan) of money expressed as a percentage of the principal.

INTERIM FINANCING: A short-term loan made so that a property can be financed until the permanent loan can be made. Usually a construction loan or a loan made until other funds are available.

INTERMEDIATION: The deposit of funds in financial institutions, or intermediaries. These funds then become available for loans. This is a reversal of disintermediation and can occur when interest rates available to savers at institutions are more comparable with those from other investments.

JOINT NOTE: A note signed by two or more individuals, all of whom are equally liable.

JUDICIAL FORECLOSURE: A sale of property, after a note secured by the property is in default, by court proceedings to satisfy a lien.

JUNIOR MORTGAGE OR DEED OF TRUST: A mortgage or trust deed lien on real property recorded after the recording of another mortgage on the same property or made subordinate by agreement to a later recorded mortgage. The junior lien has a claim on the proceeds of the sale of the collateral property only after prior liens have been paid in full from such sale proceeds.

LAND CONTRACT: See *Conditional Sales Contract*.

LATE PAYMENT: A charge that is made when a scheduled payment is not made within a certain time of the due date, usually ten days.

LEASE: A contract between an owner and a tenant setting forth the conditions and terms, including the length of time the tenant may occupy a property.

LEASEHOLD IMPROVEMENTS: Improvements made by a tenant on leased property.

LEVERAGE: Use of borrowed funds to purchase property in anticipation of gain through appreciation in the value of the property. A high loan-to-value loan is said to give high leverage.

LIEN: A recorded instrument which makes the property security for an obligation (debt). A lien can result from a recorded deed of trust, a mechanic's lien, a judgment, an improvement bond, and so forth.

LIFE ESTATE: An interest in real property held for the duration of the life of some certain person.

LOAN COMMITMENT: An agreement to make a loan when certain conditions have been met.

LOAN FEE: A charge made by the lender for making a loan. It usually covers the cost of processing the loan and often includes the appraisal fee. This is usually included in the closing costs.

LOAN PACKAGE: Includes all papers, documents, forms, and reports used by the lender in reaching a decision on the loan application.

LOAN-TO-VALUE RATIO: The percentage of a property's value a lender can loan. The loan-to-value ratio of any loan may be found by dividing the loan amount by the appraised value, or sales price, whichever is less.

MARGIN OF SECURITY: The difference between the amounts of the note or notes secured by the deeds of trust or mortgages and the appraised value of the property.

MARKET DATA APPROACH TO VALUE: One of three approaches used by appraisers to determine the value of property. It compares known value of comparable properties.

MARKET VALUE: See *Fair Market Value*.

MATURITY: The date on which a note becomes totally due and payable.

MORTGAGE: An instrument by which property is hypothecated to secure an obligation or debt. It is a two-party instrument—the lender (mortgagee) and the borrower (mortgagor).

MORTGAGE-BACKED SECURITIES: Investment securities issued against pooled notes and deeds of trust or mortgages held as security. GNMA issues such securities and guarantees payment.

MORTGAGE BANKING: The accumulation of a pool of notes and deeds of trust or mortgages, using the mortgage banker's own or borrowed money, then selling the whole group to permanent investors but retaining the servicing for which a fee is paid.

MORTGAGE BROKER: An individual or group whose prime purpose is to bring together borrowers and lenders for which they are paid a fee. None of their own or borrowed money is used.

MUTUAL MORTGAGE INSURANCE (MMI): The HUD-FDA insures lenders against loss on HUD-FHA loans. The cost of this insurance is 0.05 percent per year computed on the beginning balance of the loan at the start of each year.

MUTUAL SAVINGS BANK: A savings institution similar to a savings and loan association. Found mostly in Northeastern United States. There are none in California.

NEGOTIABLE INSTRUMENT: A document that meets certain legal requirements, which allows it to circulate freely such as a check or a note.

NET INCOME: Gross income less all expenses, bad debts, and so forth.

NET LEASE: A lease that requires the renter (lessee) to pay charges against the property such as insurance, maintenance costs, and taxes as well as the monthly rent.

NOMINAL INTEREST RATE: The rate of interest that is stated in the note or contract of sale.

NONINSTITUTIONAL LENDER: Any lender other than banks, life insurance companies, and savings and loan associations.

NONRECURRING CLOSING COSTS: Costs that are one-time expenses in connection with the escrow and paid at the time the escrow is closed.

NOTE: A signed instrument, drawn in accordance with the Negotiable Instrument Act, acknowledging a debt and promising payment according to the terms and specifications set forth; a promissory note.

NOTICE OF DEFAULT: A recorded notice that a note, secured by a deed of trust or mortgage, is in default and that the trustee/mortgagee intends to initiate foreclosure procedures.

OBLIGATORY ADVANCES: Disbursements of the proceeds of a construction loan in compliance with the schedule set forth in the construction agreement.

OPEN-END DEED OF TRUST OR MORTGAGE: An instrument containing a clause that allows the borrower to obtain additional money after the loan has been reduced without rewriting the deed of trust.

OPTION: A right given for a consideration to buy or lease a property without obligation to exercise the right.

ORIGINATION FEE: A charge for arranging and processing a loan.

PACKAGE DEED OF TRUST OR MORTGAGE: An instrument securing a note in which the security is personal property as well as real property.

PARTIAL DEED OF RECONVEYANCE: An instrument by which part of the security given by a deed of trust is released.

PARTICIPATION: Where a lender either buys or sells a part of a loan or block of loans to another lender.

PAR VALUE: The nominal value.

PERFORMANCE BOND (COMPLETION BOND): A bond issued by a bonding company that guarantees a building will be completed according to plans and specifications, and that on completion it will be free of mechanic's liens.

PERSONAL PROPERTY: Any property that is not real property.

PLANNED UNIT DEVELOPMENT (PUD): A land-use design that provides for combined private and common areas.

POINTS: A fee paid by borrowers, sometimes sellers, to increase the effective interest on a loan. A point is equal to 1 percent of the loan amount.

PREPAYMENT PENALTY: A charge made by the lender for paying a loan before its maturity.

PRIMARY MORTGAGE MARKET: The market in which loans are made directly to the borrower.

PRINCIPAL: The face amount or balance due on a loan. Interest is calculated on the principal.

PRIVATE MORTGAGE INSURANCE (PMI): Insurance bought from a private insurance company that insures a portion of a real estate loan.

PROMISSORY NOTE: See *Note*.

PURCHASE MONEY DEED OF TRUST OR MORTGAGE: A deed of trust or mortgage given as part or all of the sales price of a piece of real property. In California a loan, secured by a deed of trust, made by a third party, such as a bank, to enable the buyer to purchase real property is considered a purchase money deed of trust.

QUITCLAIM DEED: A deed that transfers any right the grantor might have in a parcel of real property without any warranty of title.

REAL ESTATE INVESTMENT TRUST (REIT): A partnership or corporation formed by a group (100 or more) of investors in order to pool their funds for investment in real estate. There are certain tax benefits under REITs.

REAL ESTATE SETTLEMENT PROCEDURES ACT (RESPA): A federal law that requires a lender to provide borrowers with information on settlement (cost) before the loan is made.

RECURRING CLOSING COSTS: Expenses that are prepaid by the borrower at closing, such as tax reserves, hazard insurance, and prepaid interest.

REFINANCE: To pay off an existing loan and replace it with a new loan on the same property. The loan can be made by the original lender or a different one.

REINSTATE: A loan is reinstated when a default is cured.

RELEASE CLAUSE: A clause that agrees to a release of part of the security, a guarantor of a loan, part of a parcel of land, or personal property, upon the loan being reduced to a certain point.

REPLACEMENT COST: One of three approaches to the appraised value. It is based on what it would cost to build a building in today's market. The most common approach in California is the cost per square foot.

REQUEST FOR NOTICE OF DEFAULT: A recorded notice filed by the holder of a junior lien requesting that he or she be notified in case foreclosure procedures are started by the holder of the first lien.

RISK RATING: A means of measuring the desirability of loan application.

SALE AND LEASEBACK: Land and or buildings can be sold to an investor and then leased back by the occupant. This is a way of raising capital and there are tax advantages.

SAVINGS AND LOAN ASSOCIATION: An institution that specializes in savings accounts and invests the funds in real estate loans.

SECONDARY FINANCING: Using junior liens as sources of secured loans.

SECONDARY MORTGAGE MARKET: The selling and buying of existing notes and deeds of trusts or mortgages.

SERVICING: Supervising and administering a loan after it has been made. This means collecting the payments, distributing the proceeds of the payment as required, keeping records, seeing taxes and insurance premiums are paid, and, in case of default, foreclosing the property.

STANDBY COMMITMENT: An agreement by a lending institution that it will make a loan or loans with certain terms should the borrower need it. FNMA issues standby commitments for a fee that says it will buy so many dollars worth of loans by a certain time at a certain rate of interest. The borrower does not have to deliver the notes and deeds of trust but he or she will lose the commitment fee.

SUBJECT TO: The taking of real property, by individuals, subject to an existing loan, without being personally liable to the existing lender.

SUBORDINATION AGREEMENT: An agreement by which holders of a first lien agree to have their rights set down so that they become holders of a second lien and the junior lien becomes the senior (first) lien.

TAKE-OUT LOAN: The permanent loan that pays off the construction loan.

TAX SERVICE: A service that reviews the county tax records periodically and reports to the lender any loan held in his or her portfolio that is delinquent. There is a small fee for this service that is paid by the borrower at the time the escrow is closed.

TITLE INSURANCE: Insurance that is written by title insurance companies that insures lenders and owners against loss that might occur because of certain title defects.

TRUST DEED: A three-party deed that is given to a trustee by a borrower (trustor) to secure a loan made by the lender (beneficiary). When the loan is paid, the trustee deeds the property back to the borrower.

TRUSTEE'S DEED: A deed given by a trustee to the successful bidder at a trustee's sale resulting from a foreclosure.

TRUTH-IN-LENDING LAW: A federal law designed to show a borrower the total cost of a loan over the duration of the loan and the annual percentage rate (APR) charged by the lender.

UNSECURED LOAN: A loan that is not secured either by real property or personal property.

USURIOUS INTEREST: Unlawful interest. In California the greater amount of the following is allowed—10 percent or 5 percent over the Federal Reserve Bank's discount rate.

VARIABLE INTEREST RATE: An interest rate on a loan that can move up or down with a limit of the total increase over the nominal rate and the number of times a change can be made in one year.

VETERANS ADMINISTRATION (VA): A federal agency that guarantees loans made by approved lenders to qualified borrowers.

WRAPAROUND DEED OF TRUST: See *All-Inclusive Deed of Trust*.

YIELD: The actual interest earned by an investment, whether on real property, personal property, or a loan.

Answers

CHAPTER 1

1. e
2. d
3. e
4. a

CHAPTER 2

1. a
2. c
3. a
4. d
5. a
6. d
7. d
8. d
9. c
10. d

CHAPTER 3

1. e
2. c
3. d
4. c

CHAPTER 4

1. c
2. b
3. a
4. d
5. d
6. b
7. d
8. d
9. d
10. b
11. a
12. d
13. a
14. c
15. c
16. a
17. d
18. c
19. c
20. d
21. a
22. d
23. a
24. c

CHAPTER 5

1. d
2. c
3. d
4. d
5. a
6. d
7. a
8. d
9. a
10. d

CHAPTER 6

1. c
2. d
3. b
4. c
5. a
6. a
7. d
8. c
9. c
10. a

CHAPTER 7

1. d
2. a
3. d
4. b
5. c
6. c
7. a
8. b
9. a
10. c

CHAPTER 8

1. a
2. e
3. b
4. d

CHAPTER 9

1. e
2. d
3. e
4. b
5. a
6. c
7. d
8. c
9. d

CHAPTER 10

1. c
2. d
3. c
4. a
5. d
6. a
7. d
8. c
9. b
10. d

CHAPTER 11

1. b
2. a
3. d
4. b
5. c
6. b
7. d
8. c
9. a
10. a

CHAPTER 12

1. b
2. d
3. c
4. a
5. d
6. d
7. a
8. c
9. a
10. d

CHAPTER 13

1. c
2. a
3. d
4. c
5. d
6. a
7. d
8. d
9. c
10. d
11. b
12. b
13. d
14. c
15. a
16. b
17. d
18. d
19. a
20. d

CHAPTER 14

1. c
2. d
3. d
4. d
5. d
6. c
7. a
8. a
9. a
10. c
11. a
12. d

CHAPTER 15

1. d
2. c
3. a
4. b
5. d
6. c
7. b
8. a
9. d
10. a
11. d
12. c
13. a
14. d
15. d
16. a
17. b
18. d
19. d

CHAPTER 16

1. d
2. d
3. b
4. c
5. c
6. d
7. c
8. c
9. d

CHAPTER 17

1. e
2. a
3. b
4. d
5. b
6. e
7. a
8. c

Index

A

Adjustable rate mortgage (ARM), 45–46
Adverse possession, 110–11
Aerospace industry, 32
Aged persons:
    loans for, 71, 79
    tax advantages for sale of personal
        residences by, 280–81
American Dilemma, An (Gunnar Myrdal),
    315–18
American Institute of Real Estate
    Appraisers, 5
American Land Title Insurance Association
    (ALTA), 85–86
Amortization, 124
    defined, 90
Amortized loan, 8, 71
Amount financed, defined, 21
Annual percentage rate (APR):
    defined, 21
    table, 25, 29
Apartment properties:
    analysis and classification of, 302
    conversion to condominiums, 149
    cooperative, 140–43
    determination of investment worth,
        302–4
    financing of, 302. *See also* Federal
        Housing Administration insured
        loans
    general characteristics, 301–2
    quantitative evaluation, 304–5
    sources and terms for mortgage
        lending, 305–6
    traditional, 140
Apartment survey, 143–44
Appraisal, 185–93
    of apartment properties, 304–5
    appraisers, types of, 185
    approaches to value, 190–93
    definitions, 185–86
    neighborhood analysis, 189–90
    principles of, 187–89
    of shopping centers, 293–94
    site analysis, 190
    supply and demand, 187
    value, meaning of, 185–86
Appraised value, 92
Appraisers Institute, 185

Appreciation participation mortgage
    (APM), 42–43
Assessment procedures for off-site
    improvements, 270–72
ATS accounts, 15
Attachment liens, 126
Automobile industry, 32
Automotive centers, financing for, 293
Avco Financial Services, 64

B

Balance, principle of, 188–89
Balance sheet, 179
Balloon payment, 53, 174–75
Bank of America, 45, 46, 89
Bank of California, 89
Bank of England, 12
Bank of France, 12
Banks:
    deposits, volume of, 4
    California banking system, 89
    before Federal Reserve Act, 11–12
    Federal Reserve Bank controls over,
        14–21
    loan limits, 89
    national, permissive regulations of,
        90–92
    negotiable order of withdrawal (NOW)
        account, 14
    real estate financing by, 89–96
    real estate loan department of, 156–57
    state, permissive regulations of, 92–96
    trust department, 55–56
Blanket trust deed, 122
Bonds:
    as collateral for savings and loan
        associations, 70
    financing through, 59, 60–64
    for off-site improvements, 272–73
    U. S. Government, Federal Reserve
        system purchase of, 15, 17
Boot, defined, 282–83
Bowling alleys, financing of, 311
Bracket creep, 33
Bradler v. *Santa Barbara Savings and
    Loan Association,* 130–31
Bridge loan, 39, 47

Broker, real estate, and loan application,
    162
Builder participation, 41–42
Builders' Exchange, 268
Bureau of Federal Credit Unions, 21
Business cycles, 6, 31
Business and Professions Code of
    California, 150
Business trust, cooperative apartment
    ownership through, 141–43
Buying down rate, 41–42

C

California:
    banking system in, 89
    Department of Real Estate, 3, 50
    Department of Veterans Affairs, 2, 230
    Government Code, 321
    Health and Safety Code, 320
    Housing and Community Development
        (HCD), 47, 73
    Labor Code, 321
    land restrictions, 104
    life insurance companies in, 83–85
    long-term lease, 98
    mortgage companies, 51–52
    Proposition 2, 36
    Proposition 14, 321
    and racial discrimination in housing,
        315–27
    Real Estate Law, 50–51
    Real Property Loan Brokerage Law, 52
    recording statute in, 109
    savings and loan associations, 67
    Statute of Frauds, 135
    stop notices, 128–29
    supply of mortgage funds, 35–36
    Supreme Court, 111
    tax delinquency in, 157
California Bank Law, 92
California Civil Code, 36, 101, 137
California Farm and Home Purchase Plan
    (Cal-Vet loans), 2, 230–34
    construction financing through, 232–33,
        266
    eligibility, 230–31
    farm loans, 233